TABLE 7.11 Checklist of Major Issues to Consider When Designing an Experiment

- Hypothesis about relationship
    - Appropriate population for generalizing
- Operational definitions
    - Construct and content validity
    - Internal and external validity
    - Temporal and ecological validity
- Specify conditions
    - Linear or nonlinear relationship
    - Control groups and a strong manipulation
- Validity and reliability of independent variable
    - Confounding
    - Diffusion of treatment
    - Consistency of procedures: Instructions, automation
    - Pilot study, manipulation check
- Validity and reliability of dependent variable
    - Sensitivity and restriction of range
    - Scoring criteria
    - Automation, instrumentation effects
    - Inter-rater reliability
    - Practice trials and multiple trials per condition
    - Order effects, and counterbalancing or randomizing order
    - Error variance
- Possible confounding by subject variables
    - Counterbalancing and limiting the population
    - Pretesting and matched groups
    - Repeated measures
    - Counterbalancing order effects between conditions
- Demand characteristics
    - Experimental realism, deception
    - Placebos, blind procedures
    - Reactivity, habituation and unobtrusive measures
- Ethical concerns
    - Physical and psychological risks
    - Informed consent and debriefing
- Selection of N and n
    - Variability and power
- Statistical procedures
    - Scale of measurement and type of descriptive statistics
    - Between-subjects or within-subjects design
    - Parametric or nonparametric inferential procedure
    - Number of conditions
    - Power

**Research Methods
in Psychology**

Research Methods in Psychology

Gary W. Heiman
State University of New York, College at Buffalo

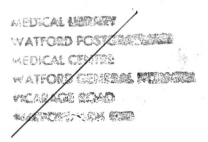

Houghton Mifflin Company   **Boston   Toronto**

Geneva, Illinois   Palo Alto   Princeton, New Jersey

Sponsoring editor: Rebecca Dudley
Senior associate editor: Jane Knetzger
Senior project editor: Rosemary Winfield
Production/design coordinator: Jennifer Waddell
Senior manufacturing coordinator: Marie Barnes
Marketing manager: Pamela Shaffer

Cover design by Harold Burch, Harold Burch Design, New York City; cover illustration
by John Hersey

Printed in the U.S.A.
Library of Congress Catalog Card Number: 94-76507
ISBN: 0-395-64619-7
123456789-DH-97   96   95   94

To Wallace Heiman, my father.

CONTENTS

PREFACE

As is usually the case, the impetus for writing this book was frustration with existing textbooks. After teaching introductory research methods for more years than I care to admit, I could not find a methods book whose style and organization satisfied the demands of the course.

Methods courses tend to have formidable goals. Instructors want students to (1) understand the terminology, logic, and procedures used in research; (2) integrate statistical procedures with research methods; (3) develop critical thinking skills regarding research; and (4) gain the capacity to design and conduct research and write APA-style reports. At the same time, students often have little background in psychological research, have little interest in conducting research, and are usually unsure of the purposes of statistical procedures. Further, students are not proficient in the critical thinking skills needed to evaluate research and are not proficient in the communication skills necessary for clear scientific writing. I have attempted to create a textbook that recognizes students' initial weaknesses, but which brings students within reach of the level of sophisticated understanding of psychological research that most instructors seek.

I recognize that a methods course often requires a laboratory component. Labs, however, pose the following problem: Students must have some knowledge of methods for lab exercises to be meaningful, but the benefits of lab exercises are minimal if students cannot conduct them until late in the semester. Therefore, an instructor often feels pressure to tell students everything they need to know of lab techniques up front, frequently skipping around to different portions of the text. To prevent this, I have written a text that gets students into the lab early in the course. (I envision students completing their first laboratory study in concert with Chapters 3 and 4.)

But the text is written so that it is also appropriate for a course that does not have a lab component. Some texts essentially train future graduate-level researchers, presenting the details of very involved and often esoteric techniques. Others depict methods as an abstract academic discipline, incorporating elaborate histories of methodological developments with copious citations that bury the application of concepts. I have chosen a middle ground, with the goal of leaving both those students who are graduate-school-bound and those who are not with a solid understanding of the basic and common designs found in psychological research. I focus on the decisions and conclusions that a researcher makes in order to engage students.

Students often have difficulty not only understanding the basic concepts, but integrating them, applying them in different contexts, and sometimes simply remembering what a term conveys. I have therefore attempted to write a textbook that teaches the material actively. This book (1) presents the concepts, procedures and evaluation of research in an organized manner, (2) provides an integrated review and discussion of statistics with methods, (3) reviews terminology and concepts frequently, especially as they are reintroduced in new settings, and (4) fosters understanding through application to specific examples. I have tried to anticipate and alleviate students' confusion over terminology, recognizing that an introductory methods course is in part a language course and that achieving literacy requires practice.

Finally, teaching "critical thinking" is not easy. Often, textbook discussions end abruptly, just prior to answering the question "So what?" I have tried to include the "so what" of research methods by pointing out the logical ramifications behind each issue and providing critical analysis. This, together with an eye to integrating the various concepts and providing a researcher's perspective, have led me to focus on the *process* of designing and conducting research.

Organization

The chapter organization of this textbook departs from the typical introductory research methods textbook in three significant ways.

First, the text uses a "top-down" approach that stresses context and the interrelatedness of topics. To give students a background for thinking scientifically and enable them to begin conducting lab exercises, Part I provides an overview of the general, conceptual, design, and statistical issues in the research process. It is a somewhat bare-bones discussion. The goal is to provide a general context for all research designs that is centered on the common goal of demonstrating relationships. Students should understand a few simple sample studies and begin thinking about major design issues. To this end, Chapter 1 introduces the goals of research, the basics of the scientific method, and the logic of research, using simple, everyday examples. Chapter 2 presents the conceptual issues in research, identifying the major design and interpretive concerns by examining one initially unsound sample study of the kind students beginning in research are likely to create. Chapter 3 provides a nonthreatening conceptual review of the role of statistics in research. It describes how the major procedures would be applied to one research example and how design issues influence statistical outcomes through their impact on power. Chapter 4 provides an overview of the major issues within the context of using APA-format as a way to organize one's thinking about research. (A complete sample APA-style report is provided in Appendix C.) Chapters in Parts II and III then revisit these issues, providing more refined and detailed discussions.

A second departure from the typical methods textbook is that such topics as confounding, demand characteristics, and between- and within-subjects designs are not dealt with in separate chapters, and there are no separate ethics or statistics ghettos. In "real" research, these issues arise within the context of the variables, procedures, and subjects to be studied. Part II therefore discusses design, control, statistical, and ethical issues as they arise in each step of designing an experiment. Chapter 5 presents the selecting and designing of independent variables. Chapter 6 discusses the decisions involved when developing the dependent variable, including how a variable leads to parametric and non-parametric statistics. Chapter 7 presents the issues of controlling subject variables and introduces within-subjects designs. Chapter 8 discusses creating studies that investigate multiple independent variables, introducing multifactor statistical analyses and other advanced statistical techniques. (The computational formulas and critical values tables for common statistical procedures are presented in Appendixes A and B.)

A final departure from the norm is that the text focuses on the design of laboratory experiments as early as Part II. By gaining an understanding of the basics of highly controlled experiments, students acquire the background necessary for understanding the strengths and weaknesses of other procedures, described in Part III. Further, since experiments are often complex and difficult to design, investigating them early on leaves much of the semester for students to practice designing and reporting them in their lab exercises. Then, in Part III, Chapter 9 presents correlational designs, including questionnaire development and a brief discussion of advanced correlational statistics. Chapter 10 discusses field experiments, single-subject designs, and animal research. Chapter 11 presents quasi-experiments, survey techniques, and observational/descriptive methods. Relevant design, ethical, and statistical issues are integrated with these chapters as well.

The final chapter, Chapter 12, is unique in that it is a review chapter that allows students to apply and integrate the issues previously discussed. It consists of a series of research problems in which students answer structured questions concerning design, evaluation, and interpretation.

Pedagogical Features

Rather than present a laundry list of the components and characteristics of various research approaches, I have attempted to teach methods (and statistical applications) in an integrated, cohesive manner. I introduce new terms and concepts as they are needed and refer back to previous concepts as they reappear. A conceptual/intuitive discussion of statistical procedures is woven throughout the text, which focuses on how statistics are used by researchers to answer their questions.

Several themes recur throughout the text. Reliability and validity appear repeatedly as the basis for making decisions among various design options. The interaction between statistics and design is present in the recurring concerns of demonstrating relationships and maximizing statistical power. Basic issues such as confounding, demand characteristics, and counterbalancing are also addressed repeatedly. Revisiting these issues in their different contexts allows students to retain and integrate the basic concepts. My intent is that students should understand that the nature of a research question and the goals of the researcher dictate the design. The design has strengths and weaknesses, which in turn dictate the interpretation of results.

All concepts are presented within the context of example studies. When introducing a general technique, I cite a number of different examples so that students gain an appreciation of the variety and scope of the technique. I then present the material in a chapter using one or two detailed example studies. Throughout, I have sought simple, easily understood examples, avoiding unnecessarily sophisticated studies that are beyond the student's psychology background and that might obscure the illustrative purpose of the example. I have also attempted to select interesting examples that convey the elegance and challenge of research that students can easily replicate as class projects.

Each chapter ends with a summary and review. Student review questions, as well as discussion questions for use in class, are also provided. At least one question dealing with ethics is included in each chapter. Answers to review questions and suggested directions for discussion questions are provided in the Instructor's Manual.

The Instructor's Manual also contains a test item file of thirty-five to forty multiple-choice questions and five short-answer questions per chapter as well as several supplementary discussion questions. The complete *Instructor's Manual with Test Items* is available both in print and on disk.

Many people contributed to the production of this text. At Houghton Mifflin Company, I want to thank Karen Donovan and Michael DeRocco who got me started, and all those who saw the project through to completion, including Becky Dudley, Jane Knetzger, Rosemary Winfield, and Chris Arden.

I am also grateful for the support and suggestions of my colleagues in the Psychology Department at the State College at Buffalo: Drs. Christopher Blodgett, Jerry Cataldo, Robert Delprino, Jurgis Karuza, Bradley Lown, John Morganti, Howard Reid, Sunyna Williams, Virginia Wyly, and Michael Zborowski. A special thanks goes to Dr. Karen O'Quin.

Finally, I am grateful to the following reviewers, who in evaluating the manuscript at one stage or another, provided invaluable feedback:

Gordon A. Allen, Miami University

John P. Broida, University of Southern Maine

Robert T. Brown, University of North Carolina–Wilmington

Gail A. Bruder, State University of New York–Buffalo

Margaret M. Gittis, Youngstown State University

Robert L. Hakan, University of North Carolina–Wilmington

Theodore L. Hayes, Wright State University

Daniel W. Leger, University of Nebraska–Lincoln

Neil Lutsky, Carleton College

Beth M. Schwartz-Kenney, Randolph-Macon Woman's College

Alan Searleman, St. Lawrence University

Barry D. Smith, University of Maryland–College Park

Richard Smith, University of Kentucky

John E. Sparrow, University of New Hampshire–Manchester

Ronald Taylor, University of Kentucky

Mark Whisman, Yale University

William Yeaton, University of Michigan–Ann Arbor

Gary W. Heiman

**Research Methods
in Psychology**

PART *I*

Introduction to Psychological Research

OK, so now you're taking a course in research methods. Because you are a student of psychology and psychology is a science, you are in some sense training to be a scientist. Regardless of whether you intend to become an active researcher, if you want to understand, use, and evaluate psychological information, you must understand the methods used in psychological research. This textbook will teach you those methods.

Research methods are the most enjoyable—and the easiest to learn—when you are actively involved, so the approach in this text is to place you in the role of a researcher. As a future researcher, you will learn the goals of science and how scientists operate. You will learn how to phrase questions scientifically, how to design and conduct scientific research, and how to interpret and communicate your results. Along the way, you will also learn about the imperfections and limitations of scientific research. Ultimately, you will not only understand the research of others but be able to conduct and correctly interpret research on your own.

The aim of this course is to discipline your mind so that you can answer questions scientifically. Toward this end, you must deal with three major concerns. First, being a researcher involves a combination of thinking logically, being creative, and, more than anything else, applying a critical eye to all phases of your research. Second, although knowing the rules of science is important, learning to *apply* those rules in the contexts of different research problems is vital. To design and conduct your own studies, you must be able to generalize the rules of research. Third, research has its own language. Psychologists use very specific terms—with very specific meanings—that you must learn. You must strive for a degree of precision that you seldom experience in your day-to-day life, so that you can accurately and concisely communicate the procedures and findings of a study. You should practice using the special vocabulary of research at every opportunity.

Recognize that research methods are inextricably bound to statistical procedures. However, you need not be a "statistician" in order to understand and perform solid psychological research. Statistics are tools used by psychologists, so you need to know how to *use* statistics: to identify which research situation calls for which statistics and to understand what a statistical result indicates about a study. To help you develop skills in using statistics, this book will review statistical procedures throughout.

1

1 Introduction to the Scientific Method

Psychology is often defined as the scientific study of behavior. Accordingly, psychologists want to understand every aspect of behavior—and not just human behavior but the behavior of all organisms. Because the behaviors of organisms constitute a part of the natural world, psychologists study part of "nature," just as biologists and astronomers do. Like all scientists, psychologists are explorers, charting the unknown world of nature. Their exploring is done through research.

On the one hand, research is exciting and challenging, because nature is very secretive and not easily understood. The fun in research comes in devising a way to unlock the mysteries of behavior. On the other hand, creating, conducting, and interpreting research require mental effort, because there are many pitfalls in research that must be steadfastly avoided. (As we will see, the devil is in the details.) This chapter discusses the general characteristics of scientific research and points out the major pitfalls that psychologists and other scientists try to avoid in their search for an understanding of nature.

UNDERSTANDING THE WORLD AROUND US: THE SCIENTIFIC METHOD

If you are at all curious about your own behavior or the behavior of others, you are already part of the way toward becoming a research psychologist. People sometimes think that being curious is not a scientific attitude, but nothing could be further from the truth. All sciences are based on curiosity about nature, and psychology is based on curiosity about behavior. Many people think that psychologists focus only on "abnormal" behavior, but more often psychologists are curious about everyday, normal behavior. As a researcher, your curiosity about any behavior is important, because it is the basis for deciding what you want to learn and how to go about learning it.

REMEMBER   Every decision a researcher makes depends first and foremost on the question the researcher is asking.

But being curious is not enough. The primary difference between scientists and nonscientists lies in the way scientists go about answering the questions they ask about nature: They use the "scientific method." This is a rather broad term, referring to a philosophy and set of rules that have evolved over the past several hundred years. Essentially, the **scientific method** consists of certain assumptions, attitudes, goals, and procedures for creating and answering questions about nature.

Why should psychologists worry about their methods? Because there are many ways of learning about behavior, and some are better than others. Most people think they know a lot about behavior: They have intuitions and personal experiences, they make logical deductions and use common sense, and they refer to the pronouncements of authority figures. But these sources of information are not acceptable to scientists. We do not trust intuitions or personal experience because everyone has different feelings about and experiences of the world. (Whose should we believe?) We do not trust logic because nature does not always conform to our logic. We cannot rely on common sense because it is often contradictory. (Which is true: "Absence makes the heart grow fonder" or "Out of sight, out of mind"?) And, finally, we cannot rely on what authority figures or the so-called 'experts' say, because there is no reason to believe that they correctly understand how nature works either.

The problem with the above sources of knowledge is that they ultimately rely on opinions or beliefs that others may disagree with, or that may be created by someone who is biased or wrong (or downright crazy). After all, anyone can make any kind of statement about the nature of a behavior, but merely because someone says something does not make it true. Implicit in our goals as psychologists, then, is that we will *accurately* understand behavior. In addition, psychology is a source of knowledge used by society in a way that can and does have a serious impact on the lives and well-being of others. At an earlier time, for example, people with a criminal history were thought to have "defective" personalities, which were "remedied" by surgical lobotomy, the removal of portions of their brains! As another example, the educational system in Great Britain was once based on the view that intelligence is genetically determined. From this perspective, it made sense to limit education to those who had the innate intelligence to benefit from it. Therefore, a child's performance on a single intelligence test determined whether he or she could go on to high school and college, or end up virtually relegated to the coal mines (Hearnshaw, 1979).[1] Thus, because we seek a viable understanding of behavior, and because this knowledge can drastically influence the lives of others, psychology's ideal goal is to be perfectly accurate.

Psychology relies on the scientific method because this approach is the best one for eliminating bias and opinion, for reaching a consensus about how a behavior truly operates, and for correcting errors. Using the scientific method means whenever someone makes a statement about behavior, we ask that person, "How do you *know* that?" We do not mean "believe," "feel," or "think"; we mean *know,* with certainty! In the science of psychology, it is the evidence which supports a statement that is most important. The scientific method provides convincing evidence, because the essence of this approach is that, since it is nature we seek to understand, we use the events in nature as the basis for our understanding. Rather than relying on the opinions and beliefs of others, we can look to nature directly; and as nature is available for all of us to see, we all have the same basis for examining it and coming to an agreement about how it works. Thus, as we shall see, the scientific study of psychology is specifically geared toward learning about an organism's behavior by observing and studying that behavior, while minimizing the influences of bias or opinion.

In the remainder of this chapter, we will examine the components of the scientific approach to studying behavior and see how they differ from nonscientific approaches.

---

[1] This parenthetical citation is an example of how psychologists reference someone else's ideas or findings. The name (or names) identify the author(s), and the date specifies when the information was made public. A bibliography provides the complete publication details.

THE SCIENTIFIC APPROACH TO THE STUDY OF BEHAVIOR

Psychology is as much a science as the natural sciences of physics, chemistry, or biology, because they all employ the scientific method (even though psychologists may not always use the fancy apparatus of the other fields). What first distinguishes scientists from nonscientists is the philosophy that scientists adopt toward the entire issue of learning about nature. This philosophy begins with the way scientists conceptualize nature.

The Assumptions of Science

At first glance, any aspect of nature, especially human behavior, seems to be overwhelmingly mysterious and complex, verging on the chaotic. There is a certain audacity to science, in that we would even try to understand such a complicated topic. We make the effort, however, because we do not consider nature to be chaotic and unfathomable. Instead, science makes certain assumptions about nature that allow us to approach it as a regulated and consistent system.

Nature Is Lawful   The basic assumption underlying the scientific method is that nature operates in a lawful manner. We make this explicit assumption because if nature is not lawful, but rather is random, then it can never be understood. Although we speak of the "laws of nature," nobody actually wrote them. Rather, **lawfulness** implies that all of nature is regulated by a complex system of natural causes and that every event can be understood as a sequence of causes and effects. In the same way that we might discuss how the "law of gravity" governs the behavior of planets or how the "laws of aerodynamics" govern the behavior of airplanes, psychologists assume there are laws of nature that govern the behavior of living organisms. Behaviors are regulated by natural laws, so any behavior can be explained in terms of specific causes and effects. Although some natural laws do not describe behaviors for all species (e.g., laws dealing with nest building among birds do not apply to humans), a specific law does apply to all members of a group. Thus, when psychologists study the mating behavior of penguins, or the development of language in humans, they are studying the laws of nature.

Most psychologists, however, would think it grandiose to claim that a research study directly examines a law of nature because of the narrow focus of each study. In fact, the discovery and conclusive definition of these laws are extremely slow and complicated procedures. As we will see, researchers are frequently confronted with contradictory findings and opposing explanations. Thus, a considerable amount of time and research is required to reach a consensus on even a small aspect of a behavior. We do assume, however, that eventually all of the diverse findings will be integrated so that we can truly understand the laws of nature.

Behavior Is Deterministic   Viewing behavior as lawful leads to a second, related assumption: Psychologists assume that the behavior of organisms is "determined." According to the doctrine of **Determinism,** behavior is *solely* influenced by natural causes;

it does not result from "free will" or choice. If we were to assume that organisms can freely decide their behavior, then behavior would truly be chaotic, because the only explanation for every behavior would be "because he or she wanted to." Therefore, we reject the assumtion that free will plays a role, as everyone does when discussing, say, the law of gravity. You cannot walk off the edge of a cliff and "will" yourself not to fall, because gravity will force you to fall. Anyone else in the same situation will also fall because that is how gravity operates. Likewise, the science of psychology assumes that you cannot freely choose to exhibit a particular personality or respond in a particular way in a given situation. The laws of behavior force you to have certain attributes and to behave in a certain way in a certain situation. Anyone else in the same situation will be similarly influenced, because that is how the laws of behavior operate. There are, of course, individual differences, so no two individuals will behave identically. Yet the term *individual differences* is just another way of saying that there are so many influences operating on a behavior at any moment that the situation is unique for each individual. We assume, however, that there are laws of nature that govern even individual differences.

Note that determinism is not the same as "predestination." Predestination suggests that our actions follow some grand scheme or plan that is already laid out for us. But determinism means that, while there is no overall plan, there are predictable, identifiable, and natural causes for every behavior. In a sense, determinism views all living organisms as machinelike: When a specific situation in nature is present, organisms behave in a predictable, lawful way. What keeps psychologists so busy, of course, is the fact that living organisms are the most complex "machines" around.

Nature Is Understandable   As scientists, we must believe in our ability to eventually understand nature, or there is no point in studying it. Our third assumption is that *the laws of nature are* **understandable.** Regardless of how mysterious or complicated nature may appear, we assume that it can be understood. We may not *yet* fully understand some aspect of nature, but we assume that eventually we will.

This assumption affects the way we learn about nature in two important ways. First, we cannot take any statement on faith. Faith is the acceptance of the truth of a statement without questions or proof. But in science it is always appropriate to question and to ask for proof. Second, any scientific statement must logically and rationally fit within the known facts, so that it can be understood. Part of an explanation can never be that we *must* accept an unexplainable mystery or an unresolvable contradiction. If two statements contradict each other at present, it must be logically possible to eventually resolve the debate so that only one statement applies.

The Limited Scope of Science   One implication of the above assumptions is that there are certain topics that cannot be studied scientifically. For example, miracles cannot be studied scientifically because miracles, by definition, do not obey the laws of nature. Likewise, given our assumption of determinism, if there is such a thing as free will, we cannot study it. (We can, however, study people's *perceptions* of miracles or free will, because their perceptions are behaviors that fit our assumptions about nature.)

Because we assume nature is understandable, any topic that requires faith cannot be studied scientifically. Although scientists are entitled to the same religions and beliefs as anyone else, we cannot allow these beliefs to play a part in how we produce and evaluate scientific evidence. For example, according to the Judeo-Christian tradition, God created the universe in six days. Some people refer to the study of this idea as the "science of creationism," but this phrase is a contradiction in terms. Creationism requires belief in the existence of God and science cannot be based on such a belief. If science did allow for faith, whose faith should we use, yours or mine?

> **REMEMBER**   To be studied scientifically, any behavior must be assumed to be *lawful, determined,* and *understandable.*

The Attitudes of Scientists

Scientists also differ from nonscientists in their attitudes toward understanding nature. Despite the formal system of the scientific method, science is a human endeavor and, as such, is not perfect. Science is first and foremost something that scientists do. Therefore, scientists explicitly adopt certain attitudes that guide their activities.

Scientists Are Uncertain   The purpose of science is to learn about nature. Therefore, we recognize that we are engaged in a discovery process and admit that we—all scientists—do not already know how nature works. At any point we may feel we have some degree of understanding of nature, but *no one already knows everything about how nature operates.* There is always a degree of **uncertainty.** For psychologists, this means that no one knows precisely what a behavior entails, no one knows all of the factors that influence a behavior, and no one knows the one correct way to study a behavior. All other steps in scientific research stem from this simple admission.

Scientists Are Open-Minded   If no one knows for certain how nature operates, then any explanation or description of it may be just as appropriate as any other. Therefore, as scientists we are **open-minded.** We must leave our biases and preconceptions behind. An explanation may offend our sensibilities or contradict our beliefs, but that is no reason to dismiss it. As explorers, we look in all directions, at all possible aspects, when trying to understand a behavior.

Scientists Are Fallible   No one is perfect (not even psychologists), and science suffers from human failings. Our attitude must be that *everyone is **fallible.*** We make mistakes because we do not already know how nature works and thus do not know the important factors to consider when figuring it out. The factors we do consider, or the approaches we use, may be the wrong ones! After all, the history of science is littered with descriptions that at first appeared accurate but later turned out to misrepresent nature. (The earth is not flat!) Therefore, we must always question whether the factors proposed as important might actually be irrelevant (or at least not the whole story) and whether the factors proposed as irrelevant might actually be important. (And note: There is nothing miraculous about being called a "scientist" or having the all-mighty Ph.D. As a student, you are as qualified to identify errors as anyone else.)

Scientists Are Skeptical   Because no one knows how nature works and because we are all fallible, any description of nature may be incorrect. Thus, we must be very **skeptical** about accepting the truth of any scientific statement. Remember, the question to ask is "How do you *know* that?" Merely because a person says a statement is true, or has conducted research interpreted in a certain way, does not mean that person is correct. Therefore, we do not fall for the obvious explanation provided, automatically accepting the truth of a statement. Instead, we *critically evaluate* the evidence: using logic and our knowledge of psychological research, we consider whether all and only relevant factors have been included, and determine whether the evidence for any statement is convincing or, conversely, is fraught with problems and contradictions.

Unfortunately, another reason we must be skeptical is that scientists are sometimes guilty of fraud. They may publish research findings when no research was conducted or inaccurately report their findings. Often their motivation is to further support their previous conclusions; at other times they are responding to professional pressures to be productive researchers. As noted previously, the educational system of Great Britain once determined career opportunities using intelligence testing. This system was based largely on the work of Sir Cyril Burt, the first psychologist ever to be knighted. However, using his research turned out to be especially serious because later evidence convincingly showed that Burt had faked his results (Dorfman, 1978).

Because errors arise for one reason or another, a skeptical attitude is an explicit part of the job of being a scientist. Science is a community endeavor in which we share our knowledge through publications and the like. Thus, I can critically evaluate your work, and you can double-check mine. Eventually we will identify and rectify mistakes, so that we have the best, most accurate information.

Scientists Are Cautious   If we assume that critical analysis will eventually produce an error-free understanding of nature, then we must also recognize that, at any moment, we are still in the process of discovering which parts of our information are incorrect. Therefore, our attitude is to be very **cautious** when dealing with scientific findings. Any scientific statement implicitly contains the qualifying statement "given our present knowledge and abilities." Thus, never treat the results of any single study as a "fact" in the usual sense. Instead, a research finding is merely a piece of *evidence* that provides us with some degree of confidence in a statement about nature. For this reason, any researcher—including yourself—should never use the terms *proof* and *proved*.

This attitude often frustrates society because it looks to science to quickly provide solutions to many problems. But scientists must temper the urge to propose definitive solutions with the knowledge that science is imperfect. In a newspaper story, for example, headlines may report the discovery of a new drug for treating AIDS; yet, the researcher quoted actually uses such words as *possibly* or *suggests*—in essence saying, "I don't know, it *appears* that the drug *might* do some good." Implicitly, the researcher is being cautious and skeptical. A single finding is only one small piece of evidence, and it may actually misrepresent nature.

Scientists Are Ethical   Scientists are a part of society, subject to the same ethical responsibilities as anyone else. Although the term *ethics* may conjure up images of moralistic prescriptions, **research ethics** can be summed up as a concern for balancing the goals and desires of researchers with a responsibility to cause no harm to others. First, it is unethical to perpetrate any form of scientific fraud. This includes falsifying results, as well as keeping secret a result that contradicts one's views. As illustrated by the case of Sir Cyril Burt, such fraud not only violates every rule of science but also causes enormous harm. Given the extent to which researchers share and integrate research findings, a fraudulent finding can undermine many areas of psychological knowledge. There is no justification for research fraud.

Second, researchers also have the ethical responsibility to conduct research in a way that does not cause harm to others. In particular, we are concerned with the ethical treatment of the human or nonhuman organisms we study, our **subjects.** The bizarre and inhuman "research" conducted at Nazi concentration camps during World War II was the first impetus for concern about ethical treatment of subjects, though you sometimes hear of more recent cases in which researchers secretly exposed people to high radiation doses or slipped them experimental drugs. Such practices are unethical and therefore unacceptable to the community of scientists: They reflect only the interests of the researcher, without balancing the question of whether subjects are harmed or their rights are violated. In later chapters we will examine the guidelines for ethical research developed by psychologists, but the basic principle throughout is that researchers have certain responsibilities for protecting and caring for their human and nonhuman subjects.

> *REMEMBER* Scientists recognize the *fallibility* of all research, so they are *open-minded, skeptical,* and *cautious.* Scientists are also *ethical,* especially in their treatment of *subjects.*

As scientists, psychologists are led by their assumptions and attitudes to continually evaluate their own research and the research of others. This process of evaluation focuses on certain basic components common to all research studies.

THE COMPONENTS OF SCIENTIFIC RESEARCH

When people think of the difference between scientific and nonscientific research, they usually think of "experiments." Although psychologists often do perform experiments, they also conduct other types of research that are not true experiments. Because any type of research can be conducted in a variety of ways, every specific study we conduct must have a particular "design." A study's **design** is the specific manner in which the study will be conducted. A design includes many components, such as the characteristics of our subjects, the specific situation or sequence of situations under which we will study subjects, the way we will examine their behavior, and the components of the situation and behavior we will consider. The remaining chapters of this book deal with the many details of designing research. As we will see throughout, the scientific method requires every research design to provide evidence that meets certain criteria.

The Criteria for Scientific Evidence

As an example of a behavior we seek to understand, let's begin by discussing one simple behavior we're all familiar with: the perplexing, and often maddening, tendency of people to "channel surf"—that is, to grab the television remote control and change the channel whenever a commercial appears. (Although this behavior may not seem very "psychological," we'll see later why it is.) The design of a study of this behavior should shield us as completely as possible from being clouded by opinion or bias, and from drawing incorrect conclusions. Remember, we seek the best possible evidence for answering the question "How do you *know* that?" Toward this end, scientific evidence must meet the following criteria.

Evidence Must Be Empirical   We learn about nature **empirically**—that is, through our senses, by observation and experience. Psychologists study everything that a subject does, feels, thinks, wants, or remembers, from the microlevel of neurological functioning to the macrolevel of complex, lifelong behaviors. Yet ultimately, all evidence is collected and all debates are resolved by attention to *observable, public* behaviors. Thus, to understand channel changing, we should observe channel changing. Because anyone else can potentially observe this behavior in the same way we do, we all share the same basis for determining how it operates.

Evidence Must Be Objective   We can all experience the same event and still have different personal impressions of it. Therefore, science requires **objective observations** of behaviors and events. We eliminate bias and opinion through objective measurements, using as much *precision* as possible. Counting the number of times a subject changes channels during a specified time period is an objective, precise measurement. Judging whether a subject changes channels "a lot" is subjective, producing possible disagreements and errors. By using objective criteria, we hope to minimize personal interpretation and to base our conclusions as much as possible on precisely what subjects actually do in a given situation.

Evidence Must Be Systematic   Being **systematic** means that we obtain our observations in a methodical, step-by-step fashion. For example, say we think that boring commercials cause channel changing. After we've objectively defined and measured "boring," we would then observe the behavior that occurs when very boring commercials are presented, when less boring commercials are presented, and again when interesting commercials are presented. If we think that the number of people in the room also influences channel changing, we would observe subjects' responses to the various commercials first when alone, then when one other person is present, then when two other people are present, and so on. By being systematic, we determine the role of each factor and combination of factors as they apply to a behavior.

Evidence Must Be Controlled   Because nature is so complex, we must simplify the research situation so that we are not misled. In research design, **control** refers to the elimination of any unintended, extraneous factors that might influence the behaviors we observe. Thus, for example, while observing whether more boring commercials produce more channel changing, we would try to control how boring the television program is, so that this factor, in itself, would not produce more or less channel changing. Likewise, we control the situation by limiting subjects to solely watching television. In short, with control we attempt to create a clearly defined situation in which we observe and measure the specific behavior of interest.

> *REMEMBER*   Scientific research is *empirical, objective, systematic,* and *controlled.*

As we will see, a variety of research designs are available to a researcher for obtaining evidence that meets the above requirements. The specific approach we take depends upon the specific question we are seeking to answer.

The Components of Understanding Behavior

The goal of many areas of human knowledge, including psychology, is to understand a topic. In addition to being skeptical yet open-minded, and seeking empirical, objective evidence, another difference between a scientist and a nonscientist lies in what we mean by "understanding." In the context of the scientific method, a study's design is used to understand behavior through four, interrelated goals.

Describing Behavior   Obviously, we want to know what does and does not occur in nature, so one goal of science is to **describe** nature. Psychologists thus seek to precisely describe a behavior and the conditions under which it occurs. To describe channel changing, we would specify how frequently channels are changed, whether they are changed during all commercials, at all times of the day, and so on. We could also describe channel changing from various perspectives or levels of analysis, in terms of the hand movements necessary to operate the remote control, or the cognitive decision making involved, or the neurological activity occurring in the brain. The same approach is taken when studying other behaviors too, as when we describe the cognitive abilities of children at various stages in development, describe the symptoms of a particular psychological disorder, or describe the behaviors people exhibit when they meet each other for the first time.

Explaining Behavior   Mere description of a behavior is not sufficient for understanding it, because we also want to know why the behavior occurs. A second goal of science, then, is to **explain** events, to specify their causes. Thus, we want to explain what aspect of a commercial, either present or absent, causes channel changing and why. We want to identify the factors—the channel changer's personality, the type of program, the presence of other people in the room—that cause more or less channel changing and determine why. Likewise, in other studies we may seek to explain why a child exhibits certain behaviors at certain stages, what causes certain mental disorders and symptoms, or why a person acts in a particular way when introduced to someone. And again, there are various perspectives we can take, such as explaining these behaviors in terms of neurological, cognitive, motivational, or environmental causes.

In explaining a behavior, we must avoid pseudo-explanations. A **pseudo-explanation** is circular, giving as the reason for an event another name for the same event. For example, a pseudo-explanation of channel changing is that it is caused by the motivation to see what is on other channels—really just another way of saying that people change channels because they want to change channels. Similarly, it is a pseudo-explanation to say that women want to have children because they wish to satisfy their "maternal instinct." What is the maternal instinct if not a desire to have children? We might as well say that women want to have children because they want to have children.

The key to avoiding a pseudo-explanation is to provide an *independent* verification of the supposed cause. If, for example, we could discover a gene that produces the maternal instinct, or a gene that motivates people to change channels, then we would be confident that we were talking about two different things—a cause (the gene) and an effect (wanting a child, or changing channels) —and not merely renaming one thing.

Predicting Behavior   As another aspect of understanding a natural event, we need to know when it will occur or what will bring it about. Thus, an additional goal of psychology is to **predict** behaviors. We want to be able to predict when channel changing will and will not occur, the amount or degree of the behavior to expect from a particular person, or when and how the behavior will change as a person's physiological, cognitive, social, or environmental conditions change. Likewise, we seek to predict the development stage at which a child will have certain capabilities, when and to what degree a psychological disorder will occur, or when people will be friendly when meeting someone and when they will be unfriendly.

Notice that the accuracy with which we can predict a behavior is an indication of how well we have explained it. If we say that a behavior has a particular cause but the presence of the cause does not allow us to accurately predict the occurrence or degree of the behavior, then the explanation is wrong, or at least incomplete.

Controlling Behavior   Nonscientific disciplines may seek to describe, explain, and predict events to varying degrees. A fourth distinguishing aspect of science, however, is the goal of **controlling** events: If we truly understand a behavior, we can create the situation under which it will occur. Thus, in studying channel changing, we want to know how to alter the situation to produce, increase, decrease, or eliminate the behavior. Likewise, we may seek the capability to influence a child's cognitive ability, to ease the symptoms of psychopathology, or to change the behaviors of individuals in social settings.

Being able to control events is another important test of an explanation. If we think we have identified a cause of a behavior, then **manipulating** that cause—turning it on and off or providing more or less of it—should produce changes in the behavior. If it does not, our explanation is either wrong or incomplete.

> *REMEMBER*   To understand behaviors scientifically, we strive to *describe* behaviors, *explain* their causes, and *predict* and *control* their occurrence.

On Meeting the Goals of Science

You can now see how scientific research proceeds: Psychologists attempt to learn about a behavior by obtaining empirical, objective, systematic, and controlled observations that allow us to describe, explain, predict, and control the behavior. Each finding is rigorously evaluated in a skeptical yet open-minded manner, so that an accurate understanding of the laws of behavior can be developed.

You may feel, however, that this approach is massive overkill when studying a behavior as mundane as channel changing. Do we really need to be that fussy? Well yes, if we are to fully understand the behavior; only by examining all of its components can we *know* how nature operates. And what if, instead, our study concerned airplane pilots who turn off their plane's engines in midflight? Understanding this behavior in great detail would truly not be a case of overkill (pardon the pun). For that matter, channel changing is not as mundane an example as you may think. It is a behavior that involves such major psychological processes as decision making, information processing and communication, neural-pathways control, motivation, and social adjustment. Thus, by studying decision making in the context of channel changing, for example, we can learn about decision making in other contexts. Furthermore, research often leads to **serendipitous** findings: In the process of studying one aspect of nature, we may discover another aspect unrelated to the original research. Thus, because we never know where an investigation will lead, we must take every study very seriously and do the best, most complete job we can.

The arguments for obtaining a complete understanding of a behavior may seem more convincing when we're considering something like the errors an airplane pilot makes, because this behavior represents a real-life problem. In fact, most people agree that there's a need for the type of research called applied research. **Applied research** is conducted for the purpose of solving an existing problem. For example, the companies that pay for commercials might conduct applied research into channel changing during their commercials so they can eliminate the resulting problem of wasted advertising money. However, many people often have difficulty seeing the reasons for basic research. **Basic research** is conducted simply for the knowledge it produces. Thus, we might study channel changing simply because it is interesting and adds to our understanding of behavior in general.

Basic research is justified first by the argument that humans seek to understand *all* aspects of nature. A second justification is that basic and applied research overlap. Basic research into channel changing can provide information that advertising companies may apply to solve their problem (and, of course, applied research designed to eliminate channel changing will add to our basic knowledge about the behavior itself). Third, we may later learn that behaviors such as channel changing and turning off airplane engines in midflight share some common factor (perhaps both are caused by boredom). In that event, basic research into channel changing may be useful for the applied topic of preventing airplane pilots from turning off engines in midflight. And, finally, basic research often results in serendipitous applied findings. For example, some of the most common medicinal drugs have been discovered quite by accident. In sum, the terms *basic* and *applied* are general, describing a study only in terms of its obvious, stated purposes. In reality, we never know the ultimate purpose that research will serve (which is another reason for employing very rigorous methods).

> **REMEMBER**   The primary purpose of *basic research* is simply to obtain knowledge; the primary purpose of *applied research* is to solve an existing problem.

Regardless of whether we conduct applied or basic research, however, completely describing, explaining, predicting, and controlling a behavior constitute the ultimate goal of research. Yet no single study can fully meet this goal, given the extreme complexity of behaviors. Consider the variety of perspectives we can take when studying channel changing and the many factors that might influence it. Because we cannot study everything at once, we must simplify nature by examining one factor and taking one perspective at a time. Thus, one study will describe certain aspects of a behavior, another will examine an explanation, other studies will investigate ways to predict the behavior, and still others will focus on controlling the behavior. Any specific study is therefore a momentary "snapshot" of one small portion of a behavior. As a result of this piece-meal approach, the discipline of psychology—and the published research "literature" describing it—may appear to be disjointed and unfocused, seemingly going off in many directions at once. Yet, as these individual pieces of information gradually combine, we eventually do come to understand all aspects of a behavior.

> **REMEMBER**   Any study represents a very limited and simplified view of the complexity found in nature and contributes minutely to the goals of describing, explaining, predicting, and controlling a behavior.

Every decision a researcher makes depends first and foremost on the question the researcher is asking. As we will see, the reason this question determines all other steps in research is that the choice of research design to be employed depends upon whether the primary goal of the study is to describe, explain, predict, or control a behavior. Therefore, the first step in conducting research is to formulate the specific question we wish to answer. That question is called a hypothesis.

CREATING SCIENTIFIC HYPOTHESES

We might ask the question, "What causes channel changing?" This, however, is a very general question, with no direction as to the type of "snapshot" we will obtain in answering it. From which perspective do we mean "what"? Are we seeking the cognitive, social, physiological, or environmental causes? And which aspect of the environment or physiological causes are we talking about? An ambiguous question will result in an ambiguous answer, so it will be very difficult to evaluate whether we have actually and convincingly answered the question. Further, at some point we must go out and seek empirical, objective, and systematic observations of specific subjects in specific situations, so sooner or later we will need to know which behavior needs to be examined and how to examine it. Therefore, researchers translate their general questions into a more specific statement that directs their research and allows them to more clearly determine if they have answered their question.

A **hypothesis** is a formally stated expectation about a behavior that defines the purpose and goals of a study. It is, in essence, a tentative guess about a behavior that usually relates a behavior to some other behavior or influence. Rather than asking a question beginning with "why" or "what," think of a hypothesis as a statement beginning with the phrase "I think that. . . ." Then we learn about the behavior in question by determining if the statement is correct or not.

Because we are always in the process of obtaining and evaluating information, any scientific statement about nature is actually a hypothesis. You might think that we have well-established "facts" in psychology—for example, that positive reinforcement leads to rapid learning (Skinner, 1938), or that a person's behavior reflects stable personality traits (Cattell, 1965). However, because we have not collected all possible evidence and resolved all debates, these are actually only well-supported hypotheses.

There are two general types of hypotheses. In keeping with the goal of explaining and controlling the causes of behavior, we may create a **causal hypothesis,** which tentatively explains a particular influence on, or cause for, a behavior. For example, we might hypothesize that "channel changing is caused by the boring content of commercials." Of course, boring content may not be the only causal influence of the behavior, but it is the cause we are investigating.

On the other hand, in keeping with the goal of describing and predicting behavior, we may create a **descriptive hypothesis,** which tentatively describes a behavior in terms of its characteristics or the situation in which it occurs. A descriptive hypothesis identifies the attributes of the behavior and allows us to predict when it occurs. For example, we might hypothesize that "channel changing occurs more frequently when someone is watching television alone than when other people are present." Notice that even though the number of people present might partially cause channel changing, we have not stated this. A descriptive hypothesis does *not* attempt to identify the causes of a behavior. In fact, sometimes it states simply that certain behaviors occur and can be observed and measured, giving a general goal and direction to our observations. For example, we might hypothesize that "channel changers have certain personality characteristics" and then set about to discover and describe them.

It is extremely important that you always explicitly state whether you are attempting to examine the causes of a behavior, because whether you are is a critical determinant of how you then conduct your research.

> *REMEMBER* A *causal hypothesis* postulates a particular causal influence on a behavior, and a *descriptive hypothesis* postulates particular characteristics of the behavior or provides a goal for our observations.

Once we have explicitly stated our hypothesis, we then proceed to determine whether it is a correct statement. Whereas nonscientists might use logic, personal experiences, or beliefs to support their hypotheses, scientists conduct empirical, objective studies of the behavior to "test" the accuracy of the hypothesis. Scientists therefore have certain rules for creating hypotheses to help protect against faulty reasoning.

The Criteria for Scientific Hypotheses

A hypothesis must reflect our assumptions about the lawfulness and understandability of nature. If it does not, then the hypothesis is not scientific and the description of nature it contains (and the evidence that supports it) is not scientifically admissible. Specifically, a scientific hypothesis must meet the following criteria.

First, a hypothesis must be both *testable* and *falsifiable.* **Testable** means that we can devise a test of a hypothesis. **Falsifiable** means that the test can show that the hypothesis is incorrect. For example, our previous hypotheses about the causes and attributes of channel changing are testable because we can observe channel changing in order to test them. They are falsifiable because we may find evidence that indicates they are incorrect.

It is possible to create hypotheses that are not testable or falsifiable. Alternatively, consider the hypothesis "When people die they see a bright light." This is not a testable hypothesis because we cannot study people's experience after death (they're dead!). Because it is not testable, the hypothesis is also not falsifiable. Alternatively, consider Sigmund Freud's hypothesis that the "id" leads us to express aggression not only directly but also indirectly, through "sublimation" that results in nonaggressive behaviors. This hypothesis is testable, because we can examine people's behavior and determine whether aggression occurs. However, regardless of what we see, we cannot show that the hypothesis is false: If we see aggression, it's because of the id; but if we don't see aggression, it's still because of the id, sublimating aggression into nonaggressive behavior. Given the implicit circular logic here, this hypothesis cannot tell us anything about the id (even Freud was fallible).

> *REMEMBER*   Whenever a hypothesis is not *testable* or *falsifiable,* we cannot determine its accuracy. Instead, we must take the hypothesis on faith, which is not a scientific approach.

A hypothesis must also add to our knowledge in a meaningful way, within our framework of understandable laws of nature. Thus, the hypothesis must be **precise.** Supporting evidence will be provided by a very specific research situation, and the hypothesis cannot go beyond this evidence. For example, to study "after-death" experiences, we can talk to people who have been declared dead and then revived. Our hypothesis in this case is that "people who are declared dead and *then revived* will *claim* to have seen a bright light" (e.g., Ring, 1984). This wording conveys the fact that these people are not truly dead, and also suggests that we cannot verify that they actually experienced the light. Further, the hypothesis is precise in that it contains terms that can be defined and tested. The use of ambiguous terms would have opened the hypothesis to interpretation and opinion, making it less clearly testable and falsifiable.

To be meaningful, a hypothesis must also be rational and parsimonious. By **rational,** we mean that the hypothesis must be possibly true, given what we already know about the laws of behavior. And by **parsimonious,** we mean that, to incorporate the hypothesis in our understanding of behavior, it should require as simple an explanation as possible. For example, our hypothesis about boring commercials causing channel changing fits what we already know about behavior and, if shown to be correct, will mesh easily with existing knowledge. In contrast, consider the *claim* that some people exhibit "telekinesis," the ability to move objects by willing them to move. We cannot formulate a rational hypothesis about this supposed ability, because it contradicts knowledge about the brain and physical energy already developed in psychology, biology, and physics. Given the successes of these sciences, it is unreasonable to dismiss them in favor of telekinesis.

We might propose the existence of new brain components and new energy waves so that telekinesis seems rational, but doing so would not be parsimonious. The assumption of nature as lawful implies that many diverse events can be accounted for by an economical combination of relatively few laws. If we proposed new laws or mechanisms for every situation, we'd merely be renaming nature without explaining it. Instead, we seek a relatively simple hypothesis that applies to broad categories of behaviors and then let the behavioral evidence determine how elaborate our explanations must be. If there were scientific evidence for telekinesis, for example, we would try to explain it using those mechanisms that are already established by previous research. Only if we fail to account for a behavior with accepted explanations and mechanisms are we justified in proposing new ones.

> **REMEMBER**   To be scientific, hypotheses must be *falsifiable, testable,* and *rational;* they must also be stated in a *precise* and *parsimonious* manner.

A hypothesis may have only limited success in meeting these requirements. The degree of success is a way of determining whether a hypothesis is scientifically valuable or "important." Although we should be open-minded about new ideas, an important hypothesis is generally considered to be one that is precisely stated, rationally and parsimoniously adds to our understanding of a broad range of behaviors, and which can be tested and verified in many contexts.

Sources for Hypotheses

Using the above criteria, researchers generate hypotheses from several sources. One obvious source is our opinions, observations, or experiences. It is perfectly acceptable for researchers to base a hypothesis on such sources, as long as they then conduct an empirical, objective study to provide evidence for testing that hypothesis. A second source is the existing research itself: When reading about the results of a study that tested one hypothesis, a researcher is often led to several additional hypotheses. For example, if we find that channel changing increases when someone is alone, we would then want to determine why, identify the factors that modify this influence, and so on. (A study always produces more questions than answers.) A third common source of a hypothesis, as we'll see, is the retesting of a hypothesis previously tested by another researcher.

Theories are another source of hypotheses. A **theory** is a logically organized set of proposals that defines, explains, organizes, and interrelates our knowledge about many behaviors. A theory involves abstract concept so it applies to a broad range of behaviors in a parsimonious way. For example, "Freudian theory" attempted to explain and relate a vast array of normal and abnormal behaviors using such abstract concepts as id, ego, and superego (e.g., Torrey & Fuller, 1992). Likewise, the most common psychological terms are actually theoretical concepts, such as learning, memory, intelligence, creativity, personality, and schizophrenia. These are not real things; you cannot place your personality on a table. They are concepts that help us to organize and explain behaviors, and, as we'll see in the next chapter, we use such concepts to derive specific research hypotheses. For the sake of rational and parsimonious hypotheses, especially when our research begins with personal opinions and experiences, we need to relate our theoretical concepts to the behavior being researched. Thus, for example, we might tie our ideas about boring commercials to existing concepts of "information processing" and "motivation" to explain channel changing, and then design our study using these concepts.

Theoreticians may develop a theory beginning mainly with certain ideas and concepts for which there is little scientific evidence. The theory then provides a direction for the evidence researchers will seek. Or theoreticians may develop a theory after substantial evidence has been collected, providing a way to organize diverse findings. Either way, researchers then derive a specific hypothesis, test it in a research study, and then apply the outcome of the study back to the theoretical concepts, either adding to or correcting the theory. Then, from the modified theory, researchers develop additional hypotheses, which, after testing, are used to further modify the theory. (Note: A study does not test a theory; it tests a hypothesis that may be derived from a theory. Be careful when using the word *theory*.)

A final, related source of hypotheses is a model. A **model** is a generalized, hypothetical description that, by analogy, explains the process underlying a set of common behaviors. Whereas a theory accounts for broad, abstract components of behaviors, a model provides a more concrete analogy for thinking about how these concepts actually operate. This provides a way to discuss and understand the components of a behavior, in the same way that a model airplane provides a way to discuss and understand the components of a real airplane. A psychological model usually involves a flow chart or diagram of certain psychological processes. For example, the "Information Processing Model" describes human memory using a flow chart containing separate boxes that represent the flow of information through short-term and long-term memory (Atkinson & Shiffrin, 1968). Although no one believes the brain contains little boxes labeled short-term and long-term memory, this is a useful analogy for deriving specific hypotheses about how and when information remains in memory only temporarily or more permanently. We then test these hypotheses and use the results of our studies to modify the model, in the same way that theories are modified.

TESTING HYPOTHESES THROUGH RESEARCH

Once we have created a hypothesis, we design a specific study to test it. In doing so, we distinguish between a hypothesis and a prediction. Whereas a hypothesis is a general statement about how a behavior operates, a **prediction** is a specific statement about how we will see the behavior manifested in the research situation, describing the specific results that we expect will be found in our study. Objective measurement of subjects' behavior leads to numbers or scores, and these scores are the **data** in a study. Therefore, we test the accuracy of a hypothesis using the logic that, if the hypothesis is true, we should obtain certain data: The behavior should occur in such a way that the scores measuring the behavior will be high or low, or will change in a predictable manner. For example, let's say we hypothesize that channel changing occurs because of a theoretical cognitive mechanism in humans that is affected by the boring content in commercials. We predict that as more boring commercials occur, the data—subjects' scores—will reflect more frequent, more rapid, or more motivated channel changing. (Notice, by the way, that the word *data* is a plural, like *people.*)

As we will see, there are many procedures for measuring and collecting data. We may use equipment that times subjects' responses or measures their physiological reactions. We may ask subjects questions or have them perform mental or physical tests that we "grade." We also may interview subjects, have them keep diaries, or observe subjects surreptitiously, either directly or indirectly (by examining their school records, their health history, and so on). In all of these approaches, we attempt to obtain as precise and objective a measurement of subject's behaviors as possible, so that we can determine whether the data fit our predictions and hypotheses.

The logical flow that most research follows can be summarized using the model in Figure 1.1. As shown, we first create a scientific hypothesis about a behavior that adds to our ability to describe, explain, predict, and control the behavior. To test our hypothesis,

FIGURE 1.1 The Flow of Scientific Research

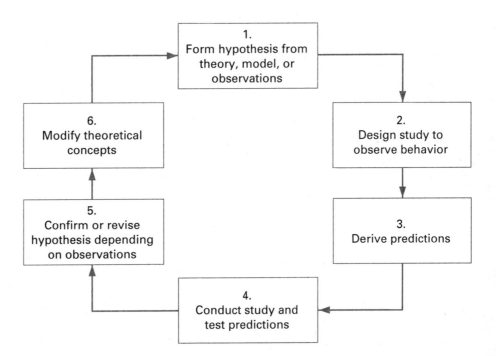

we reason that if our hypothesis is correct, then, in a particular situation, subjects should exhibit the behavior in a certain way. Next we design a study that allows us to examine the situation and observe how the behavior occurs. From our hypothesis about the behavior and the design of our study, we derive a prediction about the data we will see. Then we conduct the study and measure the behavior. If the data confirm our predictions, we have support for our hypothesis. If the data do not confirm our prediction, we do not have support for the hypothesis. From our conclusions about the hypothesis, we add to or modify our general theoretical knowledge. Then we derive additional hypotheses and begin the cycle again. It is through this continual cycle that the science of psychology collates, organizes, and resolves the diverse "snapshots" of behaviors that individual studies provide, so that we can eventually understand the broader laws of nature.

Although research in general follows the above cycle, we employ particular types of designs depending upon whether the primary goal of our study is to describe, explain, predict, or control a behavior. As we shall see, there are many specific types of designs, but these fall into two broad categories: experimental and descriptive methods.

Experimental Methods

As we noted earlier, in a causal hypothesis we propose the causes of and influences on a behavior. To test such a hypothesis, we employ **experimental methods.** The logic behind experimental methods is this: If the hypothesis is correct, then if we *do* this or that to subjects, we should see an influence or change in subjects' behaviors. Thus, if we hypothesize that boring commercials *cause* more channel changing, we would systematically *manipulate* whether subjects view more or less boring commercials to see if we can cause greater channel changing with more boring commercials.

Usually an experiment implies a laboratory setting, but this need not be the case. Though the term *laboratory* might conjure up images of elaborate equipment and mad scientists, a laboratory is simply a location in which the researcher can conduct a study while controlling the situation, the environment, and the behavior of subjects. As we will see in later chapters, the hallmark of experimental methods is that researchers actively control certain aspects of a situation while manipulating or changing other aspects of the situation. Then they examine whether their manipulations cause or influence the behavior being studied.

Descriptive Methods

We also noted that in a descriptive hypothesis we identify the characteristics of the behavior or the situations in which it occurs, so that we can describe or predict the behavior. We test descriptive hypotheses using **descriptive** or **nonexperimental methods.** The logic behind descriptive methods is this: If the hypothesis is accurate, then when we observe the behavior, we should also observe the predicted characteristics of the behavior, subjects, or situation we have hypothesized. Researchers usually conduct descriptive studies in natural "field" settings, not in the laboratory. Thus, to test our hypothesis that channel changing occurs more frequently when a person is alone, we could observe (or obtain records of) subjects as they view television in their homes, measuring how frequently they changed channels when different numbers of people are present. As this example illustrates, the most common approach to nonexperimental methods is a *correlational study* in which we measure two aspects of the situation or behavior and then determine the extent to which the two are associated or "correlated." We will examine descriptive procedures in later chapters, but the hallmark of this approach is that the researcher is a rather passive observer who does not actively control or manipulate the situation or behavior under study.

> **REMEMBER**   In *experimental* designs, the researcher actively controls or manipulates the behavior or situation. In *descriptive* designs, the researcher only observes and measures the behavior or situation.

THE FLAWS IN SCIENTIFIC RESEARCH

Recall that it is difficult to learn about nature because of the possible errors and biases that can cloud our conclusions. Although the rules and criteria we have examined may seem sufficient to eliminate bias and error, they do not guarantee this. There are many ways to design a study, even for such an apparently simple behavior as channel changing. Because so many different designs are possible, and because nature is so complex, there are many opportunities for researchers to make errors, either in the information they collect or in the way they interpret it. Therefore, as scientists, we must always consider that what we know—or *think* we know—depends on (1) the evidence we are attending to and (2) how we are interpreting it.

First, let's consider our evidence.

The Flaws in Scientific Evidence

In an ideal research situation, our observations would be completely empirical, objective, systematic, and controlled, so that we are perfectly accurate in our observations and measurement of the exact behavior we seek, with only the relevant factors coming into play. *However, no study is ideal.* Rather, a study may be more or less empirical, more or less objective, more or less systematic, and more or less controlled. There are four considerations that determine the degree to which a study meets the criteria for scientific evidence.

The Nature of the Behavior Under Study   Some behaviors cannot be studied in a completely empirical, objective, systematic, and controlled manner. For example, we cannot be totally empirical when studying "thinking" because we cannot directly observe thinking. Instead, we must observe some other behavior—such as the number of correct answers to logic problems provided by subjects—from which we draw *inferences* about the unseen behavior. Whenever we focus on unseen theoretical concepts such as learning, emotion, and personality, we *must* draw inferences to some extent, but some designs require greater inferential leaps than others. Likewise, the extent to which we are able to obtain precise and objective measurements depends on the behavior being studied.

There is no physical "yardstick" for objectively measuring such aspects of behavior as aggressiveness or love, and no single observable behavior from which to draw inferences. Instead, we must employ less concrete, more subjective measurement procedures that may include bias and error. Finally, we cannot observe all aspects of all behaviors in a systematic and controlled fashion. For example, let's say we're studying the attitudes of females toward child bearing. We cannot separate the fact that each of our subjects has a female's personality from the fact that each has a female's genes and physiology. Thus, we cannot be sure whether it is a female's personality or her physiology (or both) that influences her attitudes.

Because of such limitations, the studies of some behaviors will not provide us with complete confidence. In these instances, we cannot *know* what our measurements reflect about the behavior or which factors were truly operating.

Characteristics of the Design   The decisions we must make when designing a study may also reduce our confidence in the findings. For example, if we choose to study channel changing as it occurs in the natural environment (someone's living room), we cannot control such factors as when a commercial appears or whether the phone rings in the middle of it (both of which may influence how, why, and when the channel is changed). Conversely, if we study channel changing in a "laboratory" setting, we create an artificial and thus biased picture of the true behavior: People do not normally watch television under laboratory conditions. Likewise, the subjects we study, the way we measure a behavior, and the way we control or manipulate factors may all result in biased evidence.

Technical Limitations   Sometimes we lack the technical capabilities to accurately observe and measure some behavior or factor. In such cases our research may yield limited and potentially misleading information. For example, in the late 1800s, psychology included the study of "phrenology," the idea that various personality traits are reflected by the size of parts of the brain and thus by the bumps on certain parts of the skull. Considering our present techniques for studying personality and brain physiology, however, phrenology now seems silly. We must always consider the inherent limitations arising from our technical abilities.

The Limited Perspective of a Study   Even when the evidence from a particular study is relatively convincing, the results of one study can never tell the whole story. A single study is a "snapshot" that necessarily provides a slanted view, considering certain factors and ignoring others (some of which we do not even know about). This problem is illustrated by an old fable that tells of several blind men trying to describe an elephant (Shah, 1970). One, touching the animal's trunk, describes the elephant as long and narrow, like a pipe. Another, touching the ear, describes the elephant as rough, flat, and wide, like a rug. Another, touching the leg, describes the elephant as resembling a pillar. In studying a behavior, researchers are like the blind men, trying to describe the entire elephant by taking only one limited perspective at a time.

Any study may misrepresent nature, because by taking one approach it automatically excludes others. In our study of channel changing, for example, let's say that we find support for the hypothesis that channel changing is caused by boring commercials. However, this approach does not consider the television program during which the commercials appear. A different study, focusing on the contents of the program, may indicate that channel changing is caused by boring programs. The results of either study alone do not give the complete picture; it's possible, for instance, that channel changing is actually caused by a *combination* of boring commercials and a boring program. Remember, being skeptical means not falling for the obvious explanation provided: The limited perspective of any one study focuses our attention on certain factors, so it is easy to forget other factors. We must always consider whether our attention has been misdirected.

> *REMEMBER* A study's design determines the contents of our "snapshot" of a behavior and thus ultimately our evidence for a particular hypothesis.

Critically Evaluating Scientific Evidence

From the preceding discussion, it is clear that all research is not created equal! Although we will examine techniques for minimizing the above flaws, keep in mind that individual studies can vary greatly in the extent to which they provide "good" data that are based on empirical, objective, systematic, and controlled observations. Thus, we may be limited in our confidence that the data reflect the behavior exactly as it occurs, and that the situation described matches the situation found in nature. In turn, our confidence that the study meets the goals of accurately describing, explaining, controlling, and predicting the behavior as the laws of nature dictate is limited. Therefore, we must examine the evidence provided by any study *very* carefully.

The most important factor in evaluating a scientific finding is evaluation of the design of the study that produced it. First, it is extremely important to recognize that not all designs are equally useful for answering a particular question. Second, within a particular design, there may be many opportunities for misleading bias and error to creep in and influence our interpretations. Thus, as you will see in later chapters, the design and interpretation of a study are completely interrelated. Whether you are evaluating a study you have designed or one designed by someone else, always apply these criteria. Does the study contain flaws that limit the degree to which the design provides empirical, objective, systematic, and controlled observations? The hallmark of a scientist is knowing what can and cannot be confidently concluded from a particular study.

Even when the evidence from a study reflects a minimum of flaws, we still cannot have as much confidence in our conclusions as you might think. We must also be concerned with the way we interpret the results. The first step in this process is to deal with the intrinsic difficulty of "proving" that a hypothesis is true.

The Flaws in Testing Hypotheses

To see how difficult it is to be sure of the truth of a hypothesis, consider the deck of cards shown in Figure 1.2. The card on the left shows a "4." Say our hypothesis is "If there is

FIGURE 1.2 Testing a hypothesis

Shown here is a deck of cards used to test the hypothesis: "If there is an even number on one side of any card, there is a vowel on the other side."

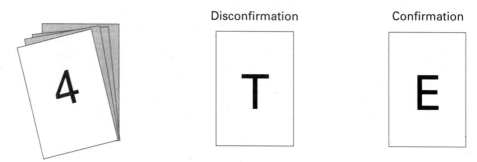

an even number showing on one side of any card, there is a vowel on the other side."[2] The way to test this hypothesis is to turn over the top card showing the "4" and see what is on the reverse side. According to the hypothesis, we predict we will find a vowel. What if, however, we find the consonant "T"? The hypothesis has been **disconfirmed,** so we are confident it is false. Note, however, that although we have disproved the hypothesis as stated, it may contain some element of truth. Maybe the rule does apply, but only if the even number is greater than 4.

What if we turn over the card and the vowel "E" is there? Our observation of a "4" and an "E" is consistent with, or is a **confirming** instance of, our hypothesis that even numbers are paired with vowels. But does this finding prove that the hypothesis is true? Absolutely not! We have not proven that our particular hypothesis is true because the true hypothesis may involve some other mix of vowels and numbers. The card we observe may *coincidentally* fit what is actually an incorrect hypothesis. In other words, there may be a competing or rival *alternative hypothesis* that actually describes the cards. For example, our observation also fits the alternative hypothesis "When there is any kind of number on one side, there is any kind of letter on the other side." Our observation supports both the original hypothesis and the alternative hypothesis. Therefore, we do not *know* for sure which hypothesis is true, so we have not proven our hypothesis.

You might claim that if we examined more cards and they also confirm our hypothesis, we would prove it to be true. However, for as many cards as we examine, a vowel and an even number will confirm both of the above hypotheses, so we can never know which is true. Only if we are able to disconfirm and thus eliminate one hypothesis can we be confident that the other is true. Thus, you must fight the urge to seek only confirming evidence. *The best evidence comes from disconfirming alternative hypotheses while simultaneously confirming your own hypothesis.*

Even then, confirming a hypothesis is not the same as proving it. Confirming a hypothesis is actually a failure on our part to disconfirm it. We may fail to "disprove"

[2]From the four-card problem of Wason (1968).

it for one of two reasons: (1) It is the correct hypothesis, or (2) it is an incorrect hypothesis, but our observations coincidentally fit it. We can never "prove" that our original hypothesis is correct, because for as many cards as are drawn, we can always argue that one more card might be the one to disprove it.

Although this is a serious objection when we have examined only a few cards, it becomes less convincing as we observe more cards. After enough tries we can argue that if a disproving card was out there, we would have found it. If we continually fail to disconfirm the hypothesis as we continue to turn over cards, we come to believe that we have eliminated the coincidence argument and that the hypothesis is not disprovable— that it is correct. Thus, the best we can expect is that if we repeatedly find cards that confirm our hypothesis while disconfirming competing hypotheses, we become *confident* that our hypothesis is true. Eventually, with enough cards, we will come to accept the truth of the hypothesis, even though, technically, we can never "prove" it.

The same rationale applies to our channel-changing experiment. Say we find that with more boring commercials, subjects change channels more frequently. We have not proven that the boring content of commercials causes channel changing, because our observations are merely consistent with what we would expect *if* our hypothesis were true. It may be that our boring commercials coincidentally contain less visual stimulation. Then the correct hypothesis may be that subjects change channels to obtain more visual stimulation, and would do so *regardless* of how boring a commercial is. Given this possibility, we cannot be sure whether the amount of boredom or the amount of visual stimulation in a commercial actually causes channel changing. Only by performing additional experiments in which we confirm our original hypothesis and disconfirm the visual stimulation hypothesis (and any other competing alternative hypotheses) can we confidently conclude that boring commercials cause channel changing.

In the complicated world of psychological hypothesis testing, however, the data are often open to interpretation, so we may find that some data appear to confirm a hypothesis, while other data appear to disconfirm it. Therefore, we must critically evaluate and weigh the evidence and research that produced it. For example, do you accept the hypothesis that dreams predict the future? If you do, it is probably because you have occasionally dreamed of events that ultimately occurred. But consider the quality and quantity of the evidence that supports this hypothesis. First, such a hypothesis is suspect because it is neither rational nor parsimonious. Second, your recall and interpretation of your dreams and your feeling about how they match up with real events lack objectivity and are thus also suspect. Third, all you are relying on is confirmation: Your observation is consistent with the hypothesis that dreams predict the future. But weigh this weak evidence against the amount of disconfirmation that is available. How many times have your dreams *failed* to come true? On balance, the preponderance of evidence heavily disconfirms the hypothesis that dreams predict the future. It makes much more sense to say that those few confirming instances are nothing more than mere coincidence: Some event occurred after you had coincidentally dreamed about it.

In sum, our confidence in any scientific hypothesis is based on the quantity and quality of evidence that confirms *and* disconfirms it. Do we accept the hypothesis that "positive reinforcement" facilitates learning? Yes, there is a tremendous body of convincing evidence that confirms this hypothesis, while disconfirming competing, alternative hypotheses. Do we accept the hypothesis that UFOs exist? Most scientists are not convinced because we have not seen enough confirming, scientifically acceptable evidence, and also because the observations may be explained by alternative hypotheses. (Reports in supermarket tabloids never concern themselves with these criteria.) Of course, some people may feel that there is sufficient evidence to believe in UFOs. As in all scientific debates, additional evidence must be gathered so that, eventually, we will all be convinced one way or the other.

And remember, our statements must be precise so that they accurately reflect the evidence. Above, I said that we are not convinced that UFOs exist; I did not say that UFOs do *not* exist. Scientists are both open-minded and cautious; so when one hypothesis has not been confirmed sufficiently for us to accept it with confidence, our conclusion must be that the jury is still out, not that the opposite of the hypothesis is true.

> *REMEMBER* If we *confirm* a hypothesis, we are merely more confident that it is true than we were before testing it.

Using Replication to Build Confidence in Psychological Facts

As we've seen, the way that we ultimately develop confidence in a hypothesis is by obtaining various types of evidence that repeatedly confirm the hypothesis while disconfirming rival, alternative hypotheses. This final component of the scientific method is called replication. **Replication** is the process of repeatedly conducting studies that test and confirm a hypothesis so that we develop confidence in its truth. The logic behind replication is that because nature is lawful, it is also consistent. Over many studies, therefore, the correct hypotheses and procedures will be consistently supported, while the erroneous, irrelevant ones will not.

Two types of replication are performed by researchers. In a **literal replication** the researcher tries to precisely duplicate the specific design and results of a previous study. Literal replication is performed because there are always chance factors at work—the particular subjects studied, the unique environment of the study, or the particular type of social interplay between the researcher and subjects. These factors may produce findings that mislead us. But because chance factors that may appear in one study are unlikely to consistently appear in others, literal replication demonstrates that the original results are typical. If any researcher can repeatedly obtain the same evidence in the same situation, we have more confidence that the hypothesis accurately depicts nature. Thus, if another researcher literally replicates our study showing that more boring commercials lead to more channel changing, psychologists will have greater confidence in this hypothesis.

In a **conceptual replication** the researcher attempts to provide additional confirmation of a hypothesis, but predictions are tested while measuring the behavior in a different way, examining different types of subjects, or using a different design. Conceptual replication allows us to develop greater confidence in the general applicability of the hypothesis while testing and disconfirming erroneous hypotheses. Thus, for example, conceptual replications of our channel-changing study might include studies of children watching Saturday-morning cartoons and commercials for toys, or adults watching late-night shows. They might also include various types of commercials, such as those for automobiles and those for fast-food restaurants. Then, by combining the findings from different studies, we can see the "big picture" of how the behavior operates and which factors modify it, and further develop our theories and models.

Notice that the scientific method is implicitly a very slow, systematic process. Through replication, scientists build confidence in "facts" in the same way that lawyers build a legal case: We gradually accumulate more and more evidence. Literal replication is analogous to repeatedly questioning the same witnesses to make sure they keep their story straight. Conceptual replication is akin to finding a number of witnesses who, from different vantage points, all report the same event. With enough consistent evidence, we eventually come to believe that we have discovered a fact of nature.

Thus, when a newspaper quotes a researcher saying it will be another five years before a drug for treating AIDS is available to the public, it reflects the recognition that *consistent* convincing evidence of the effectiveness and safety of the drug can be obtained only through time-consuming replication. After all, we accept the "law" of gravity because it always works, in every situation, from every perspective. We use the same logic for making any other scientific claim as well.

PUTTING IT ALL TOGETHER

As should be painfully obvious by now, a study never provides unquestionable "proof." We can never be completely confident that our evidence—our data—reflects the precise behavior we wish to measure, in the precise situation we wish to observe. Further, even with good, convincing data that confirm our hypothesis, the hypothesis may still be incorrect. For that matter, even when a hypothesis is disconfirmed, it may still contain some elements of truth.

Given these problems, you may be wondering why we even bother to conduct research. The issues we have discussed are reasons for being skeptical about any single research finding, not for being negative about the research process. Becoming a researcher means accepting these limitations, not being paralyzed by them. Rather than viewing the difficulties of scientific research as insurmountable problems, researchers view designing a study as a challenge. Therefore, always look for potential flaws in any study. Testing a hypothesis requires you to translate a general, abstract statement about a behavior into a concrete measurable situation, and then to translate the measurements back into conclusions about the general behavior. There is always room for error in the translation, so what seems to correctly describe a behavior from one perspective may be incorrect when viewed from a different perspective. Look for that different perspective.

But do not automatically accept or dismiss any single study. On the one hand, researchers try to design the best study they can, one that provides the clearest evidence for answering the question at hand. Therefore, even with flaws, a study usually allows us to learn *something* about a behavior. On the other hand, keep in mind that a single study will not tell us everything about a behavior. A complete understanding can be gained only by replication, as we repeatedly obtain, through many studies, numerous varied "snapshots" of the behavior.

CHAPTER SUMMARY

1. The *scientific method* includes certain assumptions, attitudes, goals, and procedures for creating and answering questions about nature. The goal is to provide the best evidence for answering the question "How do you know that a statement is true?"

2. The assumptions of psychology are that behaviors are *lawful, determined,* and *understandable.*

3. Scientists are *uncertain, open-minded, skeptical,* and *cautious,* in recognition of the potential *fallibility* of all research. Scientists are also *ethical.*

4. Researchers are concerned with the ethical treatment of the human or nonhuman organisms we study, our *subjects.*

5. The *design* of a study is the specific manner in which the study will be conducted. It should provide for *empirical, objective, systematic,* and *controlled* observations of a behavior.

6. The goals of psychological research are to *describe, explain, predict,* and *control* behavior. *Control* refers to the elimination of any unintended, extraneous factors that might influence the behavior we observe.

7. A *pseudo-explanation* is circular in that it explains the causes of an event merely by renaming the event. To avoid pseudo-explanations, we must obtain independent verification of the supposed cause.

8. The primary purpose of *basic research* is to obtain knowledge. The primary purpose of *applied research* is to solve an existing problem.

9. A *hypothesis* is a formally stated expectation about a behavior that defines the purpose and goals of a study. A *causal hypothesis* postulates a particular causal influence on a behavior. A *descriptive hypothesis* postulates particular characteristics or aspects of the behavior.

10. Scientific hypotheses must be *testable, falsifiable, precise, rational,* and *parsimonious.*

11. A *theory* is a logically organized set of proposals that defines, explains, organizes, and interrelates our knowledge about many behaviors.

12. A *model* is a hypothetical description that, by analogy, explains the process underlying a set of common behaviors.

13. A *prediction* is a statement about the results or *data* that will be found in a specific study.

14. Using *experimental methods,* the researcher actively controls or manipulates the behavior or situation. Using *descriptive* or *nonexperimental methods,* the researcher only observes and measures the behavior or situation.

15. Scientific research should be empirical, objective, systematic, and controlled. The more a study deviates from these criteria, the more likely it is to misrepresent nature, and the less confidence we have in its findings.

16. The fact that the results of a study *confirm* a hypothesis does not prove that the hypothesis is true because the results may only coincidentally fit it. *Disconfirming* a hypothesis provides the greatest confidence in our conclusion about a hypothesis.

17. The fact that a hypothesis has not been sufficiently confirmed for us to have confidence in it does not mean that the opposite of the hypothesis is true.

18. *Replication* is the process of repeatedly conducting studies to build confidence in a hypothesis. *Literal replication* is the precise duplication of a previous study. *Conceptual replication* repeats the test of a hypothesis, but uses a different design.

REVIEW QUESTIONS

1. (a) What are the attitudes that characterize scientists? (b) Why are they necessary?
2. What does it mean for a scientist to behave ethically?
3. What are the four criteria for scientific evidence, and what does each term mean?
4. What is the difference between a theory and a model?
5. What are the five criteria for a scientific hypothesis, and what does each term mean?
6. What is the difference between a causal hypothesis and a descriptive hypothesis?
7. What is the difference between a hypothesis and a prediction?
8. Why must we critically evaluate the design of any study?
9. Why does disconfirmation give us greater confidence than confirmation?
10. What is replication, and why does science rely on it?
11. What is the difference between literal replication and conceptual replication?
12. On a television talk show, a panelist says that listening to rock and roll music causes the listener to become a devil worshiper, a homicidal maniac, or a suicide victim. What questions would you ask this panelist before voting to ban rock and roll?
13. You've read some research in a developmental psychology text that contradicts what you have observed about your younger brother. Whose claim should you believe, your own or the researcher's? Why?
14. A theorist claims that men become homosexual when, as they are growing up, their mother either (a) exhibits too much control over them or (b) provides insufficient control. Scientifically speaking, what is wrong with this hypothesis?
15. The government has announced a very large monetary grant awarded to a scientist to study the sex life of a nearly extinct butterfly. A commentator claims that such research would be a waste of money. Why do you agree or disagree?
16. A researcher explains that the reason people can remember smells is because they have a memory for smells. What is wrong with this explanation?
17. Researchers who accept the existence of extrasensory perception (ESP) argue that the reason others have not found convincing evidence for it is that they do not believe such mental powers exist. What rule of science is violated by this argument?

18. An old tale states that if you dream you are falling off a cliff, you must wake up prior to dreaming that you hit the ground, or you will actually die. This hypothesis appears to be untestable: We would have to find subjects who did not wake up in time and therefore died; but because they are dead, we could not verify the contents of their dreams. (a) Is there a way to test this hypothesis? (b) Even if you collect the appropriate dream information, what problems remain?

DISCUSSION QUESTIONS

1. (a) Is astrology a science? List the reasons why or why not. (b) Explain the problems involved in "proving" that statements from astrology are true.
2. Some students argue that they learn better while listening to the radio when studying. (a) What descriptive and causal hypotheses might you create about this behavior? (b) What predictions do these hypotheses lead to? (c) How would you obtain empirical and objective observations of the behavior? (d) What factors might you manipulate or control to identify the causes of the behavior? (d) Why would the study need to be replicated?
3. Select a behavior and create both a descriptive hypothesis and a causal hypothesis about it. In general terms, how would you design a study to test each hypothesis?
4. Some people argue that the U.S. Food and Drug Administration should not require extensive replication studies before allowing the use of drugs for treating AIDS, so that the drugs can be made available sooner. Identify the two sides of the ethical dilemma here. (Hint: The drug may work, or it may not.)

2 Conceptual Issues in Designing and Interpreting Research

SELECTING A RESEARCH TOPIC

CREATING A HYPOTHESIS

> *Considering the Context of the Behavior*
> *Identifying the Population and the Sample*
> *Identifying the Hypothetical Constructs*
> *Identifying Component Variables of a Construct*
> *Creating Operational Definitions*

TESTING A HYPOTHESIS BY DISCOVERING A RELATIONSHIP

> *Interpreting a Relationship*
> *The Flow of a Study*

CRITICALLY EVALUATING A STUDY

> *Threats to Reliability*
> *Threats to Validity*
> *Drawing Valid Inferences About Our Measurements*
> *Drawing Valid Inferences About the Relationship*

DEALING WITH THREATS TO VALIDITY AND RELIABILITY

> *Identifying Extraneous Variables*
> *Controlling Extraneous Variables*

DESCRIPTIVE RESEARCH METHODS

> *Issues of Validity and Reliability in Descriptive Studies*
> *Problems in Inferring the Causes of a Behavior*
> *Confounding Variables*

EXPERIMENTAL RESEARCH METHODS

> *True Experiments*
> *Quasi-Experiments*

SELECTING A METHOD

> *The Nature of the Research Hypothesis*
> *The Nature of the Behavior Under Study*
> *Issues of Validity*
> *Ethical and Practical Requirements*

PUTTING IT ALL TOGETHER

As we discussed in the previous chapter, research requires us to translate a general, abstract statement about a behavior into a concrete measurable situation, and then translate the measurements back into conclusions about the behavior. More specifically, we create a hypothesis about a behavior and then design a study that provides a situation under which we can objectively, systematically, and ethically measure the behavior of subjects. Depending on whether the data support our predictions, we have evidence that either confirms or disconfirms our hypothesis.

In this chapter, we will expand upon this translation process, filling in some of the details about how we design a study to test a particular hypothesis. As we will see in later chapters, there are many ways to conduct studies; here, however, we will focus on the most common designs that psychologists employ and examine them within the context of one research topic. We will also discover the common types of flaws that occur in research and examine the general ways we deal with them.

SELECTING A RESEARCH TOPIC

The behavior you choose to study is determined first by the topic you find interesting. Animal psychologists find animals interesting, for example, and child psychologists find children interesting. You create a hypothesis about an interesting behavior and design a study to test it. However, as a researcher you would not start from scratch when studying a behavior. An important preliminary step when developing a study is to examine the *psychological literature,* the published research related to a behavior. Although the literature may seem overwhelming, it is more interesting and manageable when you have a specific research question in mind. Each subarea of psychology (e.g., social, cognitive, developmental, or abnormal psychology) provides a large body of established evidence, terminology, hypotheses, and theories. You will also find established research procedures that make designing your study *much* easier. (The specifics of reviewing the literature will be discussed in Chapter 4.)

Your hypothesis may stem from questions raised by previous research, from theories or models, or from literal or conceptual replications of previous studies. Your hypothesis may also develop from your experience with practical problems or your observations of a behavior. The key to developing a hypothesis based on your own experience lies in recognizing the general psychological principles that it reflects, so that your hypothesis rationally and parsimoniously fits previous research and theory. For example, let's say you observe that your friends are more successful at making dates with members of the opposite sex at the student union than you are (aren't they always?). You believe this is so because they are better looking than you (aren't they always!). There is not much psychological research on the subject of making dates at your student union, so you would be starting from scratch in describing and explaining this specific behavior. However, your observation is related to the broader issue of how people form first impressions. Many published studies from the area of social psychology have examined the hypothesis that we form a more positive first impression of members of the opposite sex when we perceive them as more physically attractive (e.g., Eagly, Ashmore, MaKijani & Longo, 1991).

If this hypothesis offends you because it suggests humans are shallow and insensitive, remember that scientists must be open-minded and accept nature as it is, warts and all. Therefore, let's investigate this hypothesis further. Specifically, we will ask whether it applies to the first impressions that females form of males.

CREATING A HYPOTHESIS

Recall from the previous chapter that we may create a causal hypothesis that postulates a cause of a behavior, or a descriptive hypothesis that postulates a characteristic of a behavior. Let's test the descriptive hypothesis that females form more positive first impressions of males who are more physically attractive. Notice that the point here is not that greater attractiveness causes a better first impression, just that we expect more positive impressions and greater physical attraction to occur together. Now we set out to see if this is true. The goal is to design a study that allows us to test our hypothesis without being misled by flaws in our design. Toward this end, our first step is to take a moment and think about the behavior.

Considering the Context of the Behavior

In beginning the design of any study, consider the overall context in which the behavior occurs. Using your knowledge of psychology and some common sense, try to identify all of the factors that may influence the behavior and your observations of it. This approach not only provides numerous ideas for the specific study, but also allows you to foresee potential design problems. So, what might the situation involve when a female forms a first impression and judges a male as attractive ?

First, what might a female consider when determining a male's physical attractiveness? She probably considers his facial attractiveness, the color and style of his hair, his height and weight, his posture, his body's shape, his style of dress, his cleanliness, and so on. She might also consider his behavior when they meet: whether he is silent or talkative, what he says and whether he mumbles, whether he is friendly or condescending. Does he exhibit nervous tics or aggravating mannerisms? Does he make eye contact? Does he smile? Does he make physical contact, and how? (Is his handshake firm or mushy?)

The personal characteristics of the female can also influence her perceptions. Her height and weight determine whether a male is judged tall or short, heavy or thin. Other questions come to mind: Is she different from him in age, style of dress, educational level, culture, or language? Is she actively seeking to meet men, or is she happily married and thus disinterested? Also, how does she form a first impression? It may involve whether she judges him to be intelligent, creative, sexy, likable, interesting, decisive, or some combination of these qualities. How long after she meets him is she beyond first impressions and getting to know him?

We should also consider the environment for our observations. Is she interviewing him for a job or is the meeting social? Is the meeting in a crowded or a deserted room? Does it occur at a shopping mall, a party, or a funeral? Is the environment noisy or quiet, dark or well lit? Remember, too, that we must somehow observe her behavior. Doing so may make her nervous and interfere with her "normal" reactions. Does the sex of the researcher make her more or less self-conscious? How will we measure her impressions? Will she answer honestly?

As the above shows, a female's judgments about her first impression and a male's attractiveness may be defined in numerous ways, influenced by a host of factors, and examined from many perspectives. We cannot study all aspects of this situation at once, so our observations must be systematic and controlled. In other words, when designing a study we must "whittle down" the complexity of the situation so that we can clearly examine one aspect of it. The way we accomplish this is by more precisely defining our hypothesis. We must decide precisely what we mean to study, selecting one specific aspect of "attractiveness," of "first impressions," of a "male meeting a female," and of every other component of the situation. Then we will have a simplified, and we hope, understandable "snapshot" of attractiveness and first impressions.

As we will see, all design decisions are ultimately made in concert, because any one decision has an impact on our other decisions. However, since we must start somewhere, one useful starting point is to identify the population and subjects we will study.

Identifying the Population and the Sample

By speculating that females form more positive first impressions of more attractive males, we have essentially hypothesized a component of a law of nature. A law applies to members of a specific group, which is called the **population**. We must specifically define the target population of our study. Are we talking about young children, college students, senior citizens, or all of the above? Does the hypothesis apply to all cultures, socioeconomic classes, intelligence levels, and personality types? We might hypothesize, for example, that physical appearance is irrelevant to blind people who are forming first impressions, so we may limit our population to sighted individuals only. So, for now, let's define the population for our study as adult sighted females who are citizens of this country.

By defining the population, we also define the subjects we will examine in our study. We now know that we will study the first impressions of a specific type of adult female, and we are most concerned with reading the literature dealing with such subjects. Of course, we cannot study all females, so we will study a sample of females. A **sample** is a relatively small subset of a population that is selected to represent or stand in for the population. The basic technique for selecting a sample is random sampling.

Simple random sampling is the selection of subjects from the population in an unbiased manner, so that all members of the population have an equal chance of being selected. Ideally, we might place the names of everyone in the population in a large hat. After mixing thoroughly, we would randomly draw a certain number of subjects to constitute our sample. More practically, we may use books containing tables of random numbers; by closing our eyes and selecting numbers, we would randomly select subjects having the same identification numbers. Or, we may program a computer to randomly select subjects in this way. Simple random sampling is illustrated in Figure 2.1.

Also illustrated in the figure is **systematic random sampling**. Here, we select every Nth subject from a list of the population. After randomly selecting a starting point in

FIGURE 2.1 Simple and Systematic Sampling Techniques

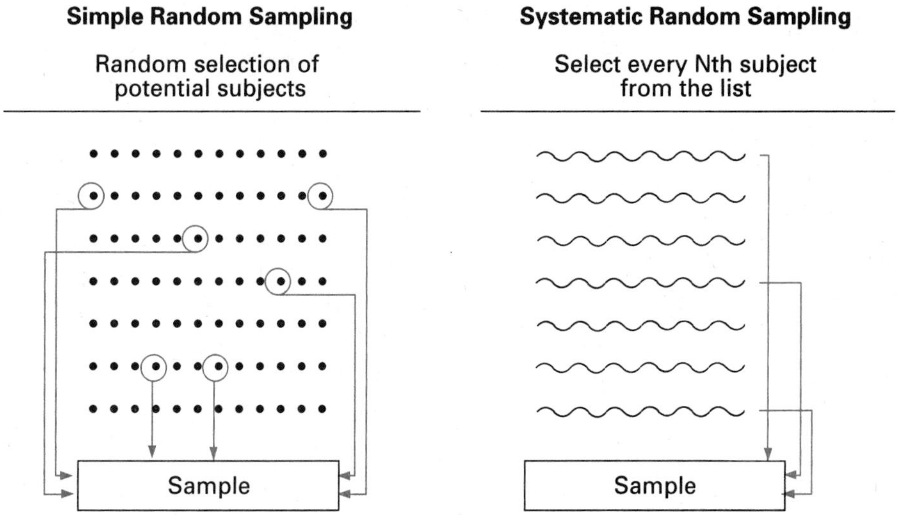

Simple Random Sampling	**Systematic Random Sampling**
Random selection of potential subjects	Select every Nth subject from the list

the list, we might then select every third or every tenth name in the list. This technique is faster than simple random sampling, but we must be careful that all subjects have an equal chance of being selected: If females are listed by age, for example, then we run the risk of filling our sample with young women before we select any older ones further down the list.

By being random and unbiased in our selection, we allow all of the diverse characteristics of females in the population to occur in our sample so that, we hope, it is representative. In a **representative sample,** the characteristics of the subjects and thus their behaviors accurately reflect the characteristics and behaviors of subjects in the population. Likewise, because we will ultimately measure a behavior of the subjects, a representative sample provides scores that are a good example of the scores we would find if we could measure the behavior of the entire population. Conclusions based on a representative sample will also apply to the population, so we will meet our goal of studying a law of behavior as it applies to the larger target group.

Random sampling implies that we have a list of all subjects in the population and that they are available to us. In actual practice, however, researchers can seldom identify or contact *all* members of the population. Instead, they must randomly select from the segment of the population that is at hand. For this reason, there are some members of the population who have *no* chance of being selected. In reality, then, a truly random sample is an ideal that is seldom attained. Therefore, a sample may not be completely representative because we may miss some subjects having important characteristics that are found in the population.

Thus, we must find a way of obtaining our "random" sample of females and determine how this selection process influences their representativeness. In later chapters we'll examine a number of issues regarding representative samples, but for now, given our initial observations at the student union, let's say that we decide to obtain female subjects from among the women attending our local college. Notice that such a decision does have an impact on our study: Our subjects will be most representative of volunteers from the population of females who attend our college or a similar one, because we are excluding those who don't. Nonetheless, we now know that we are interested in those aspects of attractiveness and first impressions that apply to college females.

Identifying the Hypothetical Constructs

In order to begin our investigation into the relationship between attractiveness and first impressions, we must decide what we mean by these concepts. Like other concepts in psychology—learning, perception, memory, thinking, motivation, or intelligence—*attractiveness* and *first impressions* are general terms that refer to a wide variety of reactions, judgments, and behaviors that people exhibit. Because they represent general ideas that we "construct" on the basis of many observations of related behaviors, terms such as *attractiveness, first impressions,* and *intelligence* are called hypothetical constructs. A **hypothetical construct** is an abstract concept used in a particular theoretical manner to relate different behaviors according to their underlying features or causes. It is an idea that allows us to describe, organize, summarize, and communicate our *interpretations* of concrete behaviors. Thus, we interpret the differences among individuals' mental capabilities using the construct of "intelligence." We summarize a person's reactions when first meeting someone else using the construct of a "first impression." And we describe a person's reactions to someone's appearance using the construct of "attractiveness."

Our goal as scientists is to understand the underlying constructs involved in behavior and the processes they entail. We study constructs indirectly, however, by observing components of the physical world that we think reflect them. Then we make inferences about the constructs and the way they operate in nature to determine behavior. Therefore, when conducting research, we must define each hypothetical construct in terms of a specific measurable event that reflects the construct.

Identifying Component Variables of a Construct

The way we learn about hypothetical constructs is by measuring variables. In psychological research, a **variable** is any measurable aspect of a behavior or influence on behavior that may change. By measuring a variable we obtain scores, and the scores then constitute the data of our study. A variable that is a measurable aspect of a subject's behavior may be a physical action or a physiological response. A variable that is a measurable influence on behavior may be a characteristic of the subjects, of the situation, or of a stimulus to which the subjects are responding. By identifying specific variables that reflect a hypothetical construct, we define the construct using more concrete and measurable terms. This allows us to "whittle away" at the complexity of behavior, while simultaneously obtaining empirical evidence that anyone else can also collect and interpret.

When selecting the variables for a study, we first consider the many variables that may reflect our constructs. In our previous consideration of the overall context of first impressions, we saw that the construct of physical attractiveness of males might be reflected by such variables as the attractiveness of his face, his body, or his manner of dress. Each of these can be further reduced into component variables: Facial attractiveness, for instance, includes such variables as the size and shape of the mouth, the nose, and the eyes. Likewise, the hypothetical construct of a first impression may involve such component variables as how intelligent, likable, creative, or honest a female judges a male to be.

Once we've identified the potential component variables of our constructs, we select the specific variables that will be examined in order to answer our original research question. In particular, we must determine what aspects of attractiveness and first impressions we are interested in studying. At the same time, our variables should be a good example of the hypothetical constructs as we conceptualize them, they should allow for objective and precise measurement as much as possible, and, as we will see, they must be compatible with other aspects of the design we create.

Let's say we decide that an important component of a male's physical attractiveness is his facial attractiveness. We will thus measure the variable of "facial attractiveness." Further, let's say we decide that an important component of a first impression is how much a male is initially "liked" by a female subject. We will thus measure the variable of "likability." We have now translated the general hypothesis that first impressions are related to physical attractiveness into the more specific hypothesis that a male's initial likability is related to his facial attractiveness.

> REMEMBER   We examine an aspect of a hypothetical construct in a study by selecting a specific variable that can be measured.

Creating Operational Definitions

Even after selecting a variable, we are still confronted by a variety of ways in which to measure it. Ultimately, we must choose the one way that we will measure the variable. An **operational definition** defines a variable by the operations used to measure it. Researchers use operational definitions to indicate exactly what they mean when discussing any aspect of a behavior or situation. Thus, we might define a male's facial attractiveness as a rating that we have assigned to it ourselves, using some definition based upon symmetry, artistic quality, or even the lack of scars or blemishes. Alternatively, we could ask a panel of judges to rate each male or ask female subjects how attractive a male is. Likewise, we might define the likability of each male by asking each female subject whether she agrees that he meets some definition of likability. We might record the number of times she uses the word *like* when describing a male. Or we could simply ask her how much she likes him.

Notice that the variable we select is essentially an operational definition of our hypothetical construct: We have defined the construct of "first impressions" in terms of the variable we will use to measure it—namely, "likability." Now, say we operationally define the variable of likability as a subject's response to the question "How much do you like this person?" measured on a 6-point rating scale ranging from "Dislike" (1) to "Like" (6). In addition, say we operationally define a male's facial attractiveness as a subject's response to the question "How attractive is this person's face?" which is also measured on a scale ranging from "unattractive" (1) to "attractive" (6). Thus, subjects will answer:

How much do you like this person?

1   2   3   4   5   6

Dislike   Like

How attractive is this person's face?

1   2   3   4   5   6

Unattractive   Attractive

By translating hypothetical constructs into specific operational definitions of variables in this way, we attempt to meet the scientific goal of obtaining empirical, objective, systematic, and controlled observations. By the same token, designing the remainder of our study will essentially involve creating the necessary operational definitions of the variables that characterize the situation in which we are examining the behavior. Thus, we must define the individual components of what we mean by "an initial meeting between a male and our female subjects." Let's say we define our "female subjects" as 12 sighted female volunteers, solicited from a common source of subjects in psychological research—an introductory psychology course. We define the "meeting" as a social, one-on-one introduction, and "initial" as lasting 2 minutes. And we define "meeting males" as bringing each female subject to a student lounge and introducing her to each of 10 of our male friends (call them our male models). After each meeting, the female subject will rate the model on his likability and attractiveness, answering our questions using pencil and paper.

> **REMEMBER**   Each variable in a study must be operationally defined in terms of the procedure that is used to measure it.

You may think that the above design is rather complete. As you will see, it is *not* a good design, because we have not completely thought it through. However, we do now have the most precise translation of our hypothesis: Female subjects who produce higher attractiveness ratings for a male will also produce higher likability scores for him.

TESTING A HYPOTHESIS BY DISCOVERING A RELATIONSHIP

Notice that by operationally defining our variables, we have translated our hypothesis into a *prediction* about the scores that will be observed in the study. If our hypothesis is correct, then when a female subject produces the same attractiveness rating for two models, she should also produce the same likability ratings for them. If a female's attractiveness rating for one model is higher than that for another model, her likability rating should also be higher. In other words, we have predicted a "relationship" between attractiveness and likability. A **relationship** is a pattern in which subjects who have a certain score on one variable tend to have a certain score on another variable as well.

When a relationship exists, as the scores on one variable change, the scores on the other variable tend to change in a consistent manner. A relationship represents an *association* between the scores. In our likability study, for example, lower attractiveness scores should be associated with lower likability scores, and higher attractiveness scores should be associated with higher likability scores. In other words, we predict a "correlation" between the two variables.

Simple relationships may fit this pattern: As X increases, Y increases (as in "the bigger they are, the harder they fall"). Or they may fit this pattern: As X increases, Y decreases (as in "the more beer you drink, the less coordinated you are"). Relationships also form more complex patterns. (As we will see in the next chapter, it is when we are examining the scores and the relationships they form that statistical procedures come into play.) A key goal of research is to demonstrate relationships. As the next section shows, a relationship in the scores provides the basic evidence that a law of nature is at work.

Interpreting a Relationship

We originally hypothesized that the constructs of attractiveness and first impressions are related in nature, such that as attractiveness improves, first impressions also improve. If this is true, then, specifically, as facial attractiveness scores increase, likability scores should also increase. Therefore, after we have collected the data, we will first examine the relationship between the scores in our sample. If we observe the predicted relationship between the scores for at least those females in our sample, we *begin* to have evidence that supports the hypothesis that "the variables of likability and facial attractiveness are related in nature."

Our interpretation does not stop there, however. Researchers are interested in more than just the relationship observed in the sample. Using our sample data, we seek to estimate, or *infer,* that the relationship between our variables would also be found for other subjects in the population, if we could measure them. If we can argue that any sample of similar females would produce a similar relationship, we can argue that all females in the population would behave in this way. "All females in the population" *do* constitute an aspect of nature. Thus, by concluding that this relationship holds for all females, we are describing a law of nature: the laws of nature operate such that greater likability is associated with greater facial attractiveness.

By claiming that our specific observations provide evidence for the general case, we are generalizing. To *generalize* means to apply the conclusions of a study to other subjects or situations. In interpreting research we generalize in two ways. Above, we generalized the relationship in our sample to a relationship between the variables in the population. We also generalize this relationship reflected by the variables to the relationship between the hypothetical constructs we set out to study. That is, our final step is to argue that our results would be found with other variables and operational definitions: As scores on any variable reflecting a male's physical attractiveness increase, scores on any variable reflecting a female's positive first impression will also increase. If we can make this claim, then we have finally confirmed our general hypothesis that nature lawfully operates in such a way that the processes we call first impressions are related to the quality we call physical attractiveness.

REMEMBER   The focus of research is to examine and then generalize relationships.

The Flow of a Study

The previous sections have described the steps involved in a typical research study as we translate from the general to the specific and then back to the general again. We can visualize these translations as the double funnels shown in Figure 2.2.

We begin with hypothetical constructs regarding a behavior. We identify the applicable population and specify our hypothesis as a relationship between variables. We create operational definitions for the variables and then predict the relationship between the scores we seek. Then we select a "random" sample from the population and design a method for obtaining subjects' scores. If we find the relationship between the scores in the sample, we attempt to infer that the variables are related in the population. Finally, on the basis of this inference we seek to generalize to the broader relationship in nature involving the hypothetical constructs we began with.

As we will see, this flow from the general to the specific and back to the general mirrors the sequence and format of most research articles in the psychological literature. In the published report of an actual study, however, each step in the sequence may not

FIGURE 2.2   The Steps in a Typical Research Study

The flow of a study is from a general hypothesis to the specifics of the study, and then back to the general hypothesis.

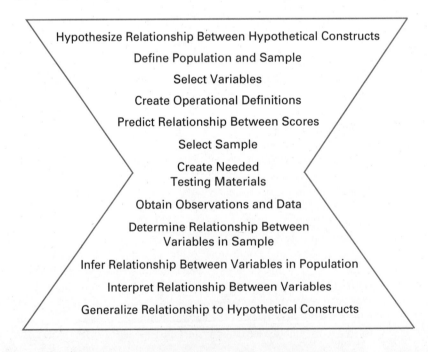

Hypothesize Relationship Between Hypothetical Constructs

Define Population and Sample

Select Variables

Create Operational Definitions

Predict Relationship Between Scores

Select Sample

Create Needed
Testing Materials

Obtain Observations and Data

Determine Relationship Between
Variables in Sample

Infer Relationship Between Variables in Population

Interpret Relationship Between Variables

Generalize Relationship to Hypothetical Constructs

be so clearly delineated. The trick in reading the literature is to identify what the author is saying about each step.

CRITICALLY EVALUATING A STUDY

As we've seen, we constantly draw inferences about what the scores and their relationship in a study indicate. But researchers are fallible, so we must always be concerned with the evidence in our studies and how the evidence is interpreted. Critically evaluating a study means answering the question "How confident are we that the scores *actually* reflect the constructs, variables, and behaviors we think they reflect, and that the observed relationship *actually* reflects the relationship we think it reflects?" Even when we follow all of the right steps in our study to draw conclusions about nature, there is no guarantee that our conclusions will be correct.

At the heart of our concern are the operational definitions we employ, because they are a major source of potential flaws and can produce all kinds of controversy among researchers. Any scientific evidence may be more or less empirical, objective, systematic, and controlled. *How well the evidence meets these requirements depends on our operational definitions.* The problem is that there are many ways to define a construct or variable, and that each definition will provide a very narrow perspective and type of evidence that, in turn, may produce a biased and misleading picture of the behavior.

We can resolve such controversies through conceptual replication. Replications ultimately build our confidence in a construct or explanation because of the process of converging operations. **Converging operations** are two or more procedures that together eliminate alternative hypotheses and bolster our conclusions about a particular behavior. Across studies that employ different operational definitions, we eliminate alternative proposals and obtain different perspectives that "converge" to build a more accurate picture of a behavior.

However, we still want each individual study to be as accurate as possible. Thus, the central concern when critically evaluating a study is to examine each operational definition of the variables, subjects, and situation being observed. At each step, we consider whether the resulting scores indicate what we think they indicate, and whether the relationship reflects what we think it reflects.

> *REMEMBER* Always critically and skeptically examine the perspective provided by the *operational definitions* of a study.

In our likability study, there are many aspects of the design that we have taken for granted. Consequently, there are numerous potential problems that reduce the confidence we'll have in our conclusions about the hypothesis. Here are just some of the things that could go wrong in this study.

1. "Likability" has nothing to do with first impressions, and facial attractiveness cannot be accurately measued by our procedure.

2. Some of our subjects are very weird and atypical, and their data do not reflect the behaviors of females in general.

3. Some male models are wearing a more pleasant aftershave, have more muscular bodies, and dress better than others, and some models talk warmly to subjects while others talk only of car engines and beer-blasts. Some models will be rated as more attractive, but not because of their faces.

4. Some subjects barely speak English. Their answers to our questions are partially a test of their English.

5. Because some meetings last only 30 seconds and others last 2 minutes, we are not always measuring the same kind of first impression.

6. Some subjects cannot decide between a "4" and a "5" on the rating scales we provide. They mentally flip a coin when responding.

7. Some subjects already know our models. Our measurements do not reflect *initial* likability.

8. Some subjects are extremely nearsighted (but vainly do not wear glasses). They can barely see the model and instead just guess at his attractiveness.

9. Sometimes the lounge is hot, noisy, and crowded. This environment prevents some subjects from paying attention to the model.

10. The researcher is a female who introduces the more attractive models in a more positive manner, or the researcher is a male who is jealous of the attractive males and gives negative introductions for them. Either way, scores reflect the tone of the introduction.

11. The lounge is lit by sunlight, but when clouds pass by, some subjects meet the models in a darkened room. Everyone looks more attractive in a dark room.

12. Two subjects are inadvertently given a pencil with a broken point and think that their reaction to this fact is what is being studied. They focus not on attractiveness or likability but on guessing where the hidden camera might be.

Although such problems may strike you as unlikely, they can and do occur. May and Hamilton (1980) found that something as mundane as the type of background music influenced how females rated a male's attractiveness. Because we are skeptical and open-minded, we consider that such things *might* be occurring in our study. This possibility reduces our confidence that scores *actually* reflect the constructs, variables, and behaviors we think they reflect, and that the observed relationship *actually* reflects the relationship we think it reflects. Because there are many parts to these inferences, researchers have a shorthand code for identifying which part they are dealing with. The two overriding issues involved in designing and evaluating any study are reliability and validity.

Threats to Reliability

Our measurements of an event should produce the same score whenever we measure it. **Reliability** is the degree to which a measurement is consistent and reproducible.

Here we ask, "Regardless of what the scores actually measure, do they measure it consistently, without introducing error? For example, if a female indicates that a male is very likable today, we assume her liking of him will not change rapidly. Thus, tomorrow the same subject should indicate that he is likeable to the same degree. If her two scores differ, however, then an error exists in our measurement technique: Either today's score, tomorrow's score, or both contain some error. The problem is that obtaining different scores each time we measure the behavior would lead us to draw different conclusions each time. Thus, unreliable data are "untrustworthy" in the sense that they reflect error and provide a biased perspective.

Any aspect of a procedure that might lead to error or inconsistent measurements is a threat to reliability. We have unreliable scores if our subjects guess when rating attractiveness, because they either cannot clearly see the model or are unable to decide between a "4" and a "5" on the scale we provide. We have unreliable measurements if the stopwatch we use is inaccurate and meetings sometimes last 30 seconds and sometimes 2 minutes. Further, we lack reliability when the scores cannot be reproduced by other researchers. If our stopwatch consistently runs slow, then our measurements will be different from those recorded by another researcher using a different stopwatch, and in describing the actual situation, we have inconsistency and error.

> **REMEMBER** *Reliability* is the degree to which our measurements are consistent and contain a minimum of measurement error.

Threats to Validity

Our measurements should lead to the correct inferences about those constructs, variables, and behaviors we seek to study and reflect how they are actually related. Any time researchers question whether they are correctly drawing inferences about results, they are concerned about validity. **Validity** is the extent to which a procedure measures what it is intended to measure. The greater the validity of a procedure, the greater our confidence that it *actually* and *only* reflects what we think it reflects. An invalid procedure is "untrustworthy" in the sense that it reflects the "wrong" aspects of a situation to some degree, so that we cannot trust our inferences and generalizations about a behavior. We want to make sure that we draw valid conclusions both about our measurements and about the observed relationship between the variables.

Drawing Valid Inferences About Our Measurements

When interpreting a study, we use the scores to draw inferences about each variable and each construct. Whether these inferences are correct is a question of content and construct validity.

Content Validity   **Content validity** is the degree to which our measurements reflect the variable of interest. Here we question whether we have operationally defined the variable so that the "contents" of a measurement *actually* and *only* reflect the behavior we seek to measure. Thus, when subjects are supposedly rating attractiveness, we ask, Is the score that results really measuring the attractiveness of the model. Threats to content validity arise from any unintended component that is also reflected in a score.

If a procedure lacks reliability, it also lacks content validity. For example, if subjects are guessing to some extent when rating a male model's attractiveness, then a score only partly reflects his attractiveness and partly reflects the random error of the subjects' guessing. Likewise, any unintended variables that are also measured by a score reduce content validity. For example, content validity is lacking in the measurement of subjects' perceptions of a male's attractiveness if some subjects barely speak English, because their scores would partially reflect their language ability.

Content validity is also threatened if a subject's rating of a model's facial attractiveness partially reflects her response to his behavior and style of dress. By reflecting these other components, such scores bias our inferences about what is supposedly the single variable of facial attractiveness. In essence, we wouldn't know what we are talking about when it comes to facial attractiveness, because we have not measured facial attractiveness.

Construct Validity   The operational definitions of our variables are also the basis for generalizing to our hypothetical constructs. Therefore, we are concerned with whether our measurement of a variable actually reflects the intended construct. Here we question whether a measurement procedure is an adequate definition of the construct, *actually* and *only* reflecting the construct as it is conceptualized from a particular theoretical viewpoint. **Construct validity** is the extent to which a measurement reflects the hypothetical construct we wish to study.

A classic question of construct validity involves intelligence tests, which determine intelligence by measuring subjects on such variables as vocabulary or problem-solving ability. The question is whether "intelligence" is being measured by these particular variables. Perhaps there are other component variables that are more appropriate for drawing inferences about this construct. Likewise, some females might argue that they are not so shallow as to determine a male's overall physical attractiveness or form a first impression of him based on his facial attractiveness. They are essentially theorizing about what should constitute the construct of physical attractiveness and its relationship to first impressions. For them, our study lacks construct validity because it examines the "wrong" variable—facial attractiveness—and thus will lead to a biased interpretation of behavior.

> *REMEMBER*   *Content validity* refers to whether we actually and only measure the intended variable. *Construct validity* refers to whether measuring the variable actually and only reflects the intended hypothetical construct.

Drawing Valid Inferences About the Relationship

In addition to considering each measurement procedure, researchers must consider the relationship between the variables. In research terminology, our concerns about drawing unbiased inferences about the relationship are referred to as internal and external validity.

Internal Validity   **Internal validity** is the degree to which the observed relationship reflects the relationship between our variables. Internal validity is most important when we think in terms of causes. Are there other variables that cause or are otherwise reflected in the relationship between higher likability and attractiveness? If other variables are operating, our observed relationship may actually reflect other laws of nature and thus mislead us. Essentially, therefore, internal validity is our confidence that the results *actually* and *only* reflect the relationship between the variables that we think is present.

Internal validity is threatened whenever the observed relationship also confirms a rival, alternative hypothesis. For example, let's say that we inadvertently introduce some models to our subjects in a more positive manner. It may be this more positive introduction that the subjects actually react to, rating these models as both more attractive and more likable than others. In this case, the relationship between greater likability and greater attractiveness would also confirm an alternative hypothesis: that "increasingly positive introductions are related to both greater likability and greater attractiveness." Because the observed relationship does not test only our original hypothesis, we have less internal validity for concluding that our hypothesis has been confirmed within our study.

External Validity   If we observe the predicted relationship between likability and facial attractiveness, we will then want to generalize this relationship to the population. **External validity** is the degree to which our results can be found with other subjects and in other situations. Here we question whether the study provides a good example of the relationship that would be observed in situations "external" to our specific study. Essentially, external validity is our confidence that the observed relationship *actually* generalizes well.

External validity is threatened by anything that makes our observations unique and atypical, so that they are unrepresentative of the relationship generally found in nature. The small number of female subjects in our likability study—12—reduces our confidence that our results are representative of the relationship that college women in the population would produce; and by testing only college women, we have reduced our confidence that this relationship generalizes to the population of all females. Likewise, our operational definitions and procedure may result in scores or a relationship that would not be found in other settings. Thus, we cannot automatically infer that researchers would obtain a similar relationship between these variables in another study. If this relationship cannot be found with other subjects and in other settings, then we have a biased and misleading perspective and will incorrectly infer that likability and facial attractiveness—as well as our constructs of first impressions and physical attractiveness—are generally related in this way.

> *REMEMBER*   *Internal validity* is the degree to which we can draw the correct inferences about the relationship within our specific study. *External validity* is the degree to which we can draw the correct inferences when generalizing beyond our study.

These issues of reliability and validity repeatedly occur in research, so they are summarized for you in Table 2.1. In later chapters we will revisit these issues, examine

TABLE 2.1   A Researcher's Terminology for Questioning the Types of Inferences Made in a Study

Inference Made	*Research Term*
Do the scores reflect error?	Reliability
Do the scores reflect the variable?	Content validity
Do the scores reflect the hypothetical construct?	Construct validity
Do the results reflect the variables in our study?	Internal validity
Do the results generalize beyond our study?	External validity

other types of validity referred to by researchers, and look at procedures for determining the degree of reliability and validity a procedure provides.

DEALING WITH THREATS TO VALIDITY AND RELIABILITY

All research suffers from problems of reliability and validity to some extent. The best we can do is minimize the major threats to reliability and validity, so that we are as confident in the results and conclusions of our study as possible. The problem with our likability study is that we did not take the necessary steps to minimize these threats. Note, however, that after a study is completed, there is no way for us to solve such problems. As we've seen, the design and interpretation of a study are completely interrelated, so the appropriate time to worry about our interpretations is when we are designing the study.

To resolve issues of reliability and validity, researchers rely first on the psychological literature. There you will find operational definitions of constructs and variables that, through theoretical debates and replication, are considered to be valid and reliable. You can also devise your own measurement procedures at this point. Remember, however, that you must then critically evaluate them from the various perspectives of reliability and validity as we did above. By using the techniques discussed in later chapters, you can also indicate how you "know" they are valid and reliable.

In addition, you will formulate a hypothesis in a certain way, have certain subjects available, and make arbitrary decisions about how you will test your hypothesis. The sum of these parts makes a study unique in some ways, containing its own unique threats to validity and reliability. The effort to minimize these threats is what makes designing a convincing study such a challenge. As noted in Chapter 1, the devil is in the details. It requires all of a researcher's skill to deal with the important details that threaten reliability and validity.

Identifying Extraneous Variables

Our confidence in the likability study was reduced because of the many unintended influences that *might* have had effect. These influences can be seen as extraneous variables. **Extraneous variables** are variables that can potentially influence our results, but they are not variables we wish to study. Sometimes extraneous variables change *systematically*; that is, they consistently change along with our variables of interest. (For example, the researcher in our study may be consistently more polite when introducing more attractive models.) Such variables may also change *nonsystematically,* with no consistent pattern. (For example, the lounge is sometimes dark, sometimes not.) Because these variables are operating within our study, they reduce internal validity. Conversely, they may not change, thus *biasing* our results because they are present in one particular way. (For example, employing only a male researcher or a female researcher could bias our data.) Then, because we have a rather unique situation, such variables reduce the external validity necessary for generalizing our findings to other settings and subjects.

The greater the potential impact of extraneous variables, the less confidence we have in the validity and reliability of the results. Therefore, you must first try to identify potentially important extraneous variables. To do this, use your knowledge of research and psychology to examine the general context of the behavior, as we did when originally designing our likability study. Organize your approach by considering the four general components of any study: The *researcher* observes *subjects* in a specific *environment* and applies a *measurement* procedure. Then identify the extraneous variables related to each component:

1. *Subject variables,* the personal characteristics and experiences of subjects that may influence their responses.
2. *Researcher variables,* the behaviors and characteristics of the researcher that may influence the reactions of subjects.
3. *Environmental variables,* the aspects of the environment that can influence scores.
4. *Measurement variables,* the aspects of the stimulus presentation and the measurement procedure that may influence scores.

Controlling Extraneous Variables

It is by eliminating the potential influence of extraneous variables that we meet the scientific goal of obtaining controlled observations. By *controlled* we mean that we prevent extraneous variables from influencing or biasing our results. In later chapters, we will examine control techniques in detail. For now, the basic approach is to employ a more precise operational definition of each component of a study: researcher, subjects, environment, and measurement procedure. Employing more precise definitions that take extraneous variables into account would solve some of the problems in our likability study, because we could then control the variables in one of the following ways:

Eliminating Extraneous Variables   We can eliminate many problems simply by eliminating certain variables. For example, we could redefine our models as males from a different school who are all unknown to our subjects; we could eliminate distracting noises and problems with the air-conditioning by moving to a room where they do not occur; we could refuse to admit intruders; and we could avoid the use of broken pencils.

Keeping Extraneous Variables Constant   If we cannot eliminate an extraneous variable, we may keep it at a constant level or amount for all subjects. For example, we could keep the temperature and illumination in the room at constant, normal amounts; we could keep the researcher's behavior constant, precisely defining how all subjects are treated; we could redefine our subjects, selecting females who all speak English well and have corrected vision; and we could select models with the same body type and manner of dress, and provide them with a "script" of what to say and how to behave.

Balancing Extraneous Variables   When an extraneous variable cannot be eliminated and keeping it constant would overly bias our results, we can intentionally change the variable to "balance" its biasing influence. For example, because the use of either a male or a female researcher might seriously bias the subjects, we could test half the subjects with a male researcher and half with a female. Across *all* subjects, the positive or negative effects of the male researcher should balance, or cancel out, the effects of the female researcher. Then we can show the more general relationship between attractiveness and likability that occurs despite the sex of the researcher who is present.

> *REMEMBER*   To control extraneous variables, we eliminate them, keep them constant, or balance their influence.

Deciding on the Controls to Employ   Ideally, of course, we seek the best possible study from all perspectives, so we always correct any flaws that we can. However, reliability and validity are interrelated, so that improving one aspect of a study may have a negative impact on another aspect. (For example, the most reliable procedure available to us may not be the best for studying the hypothetical construct of interest.) In particular, as we will repeatedly see, those procedures we employ to increase internal validity may simultaneously decrease external validity, and vice versa.

There is no set of rules to follow when deciding whether to control an extraneous variable. How we deal with any issue of reliability and validity depends on our particular research hypothesis and how we want to examine a behavior. We may simply accept a threat to reliability or a certain type of validity on the assumption that this particular threat is not important to the purpose of our study. In doing so, however, we must recognize the limitations produced by the threat and refrain from drawing inferences that are invalid because of them.

> *REMEMBER*   Whether you should deal with a threat to reliability or validity depends on whether it seriously threatens the purpose of your study.

DESCRIPTIVE RESEARCH METHODS

In our likability study, our hypothesis described the reactions a female has when first meeting a male, but it does not propose a cause for these reactions. As discussed in chapter 1, we usually test such descriptive hypotheses using descriptive or nonexperimental methods. With a **descriptive design** the researcher does not manipulate or change *the variables of interest*. Rather, descriptive research observes behaviors and relationships so that we may describe them, without attempting to influence behaviors or to "make" a relationship happen. Thus, we did not try to alter the facial attractiveness of our male models or attempt to make them more or less likable.

Our likability study employed the most common descriptive method, called a correlational design. With a **correlational design** we measure subjects' scores on certain variables and determine whether the scores form the predicted relationship. As in our study, we often measure such variables using a questionnaire; but we may also directly measure the subjects' physical actions, interview the subjects, or examine their history by referring to their records. We may perform an in-depth study of the behavior or history of one subject or conduct a survey of many people. Or we may surreptitiously watch people or animals in their natural habitat.

In addition to looking for a predicted relationship, there are two other purposes of descriptive research. Instead of being directed at a very specific hypothesis, the study may involve rather general hypotheses and be directed more toward the goal of *describing* a particular type of behavior or subject and *discovering* relationships. Thus, we might surreptitiously observe people in a social setting simply to describe their meetings. Or we might distribute a survey containing questions reflecting the many variables that might constitute a first impression. From such observations, we can discover variables that are related, develop theoretical constructs, or derive specific hypotheses that we later study in other research.

The second purpose of descriptive procedures is to meet the scientific goal of *predicting* behaviors. We may test the hypothesis that certain variables can be used to predict a behavior, or we may set out to discover variables that are useful for making predictions. Once we have established a relationship between the variables, we can use a subject's score on one variable as the basis for predicting the subject's score (and underlying behaviors) on the other variable. For example, from the relationship obtained in our likability study we will know the typical likability score that a male is given when he is perceived to have a certain facial attractiveness. On the basis of this relationship, we can predict approximately how likable other females will find a particular male, if we know how attractive they find him.

Later in this book we will more closely examine the variety of descriptive designs that researchers use.

> REMEMBER *Descriptive* methods are used to test hypotheses that a predicted relationship exists, describe a behavior or subject, discover relationships, and determine ways to predict a behavior.

Issues of Validity and Reliability in Descriptive Studies

What characterizes descriptive designs is the fact that the researcher does not tinker with the situation and manipulate the variables of interest. Descriptive studies are often conducted outside of the laboratory, where few extraneous variables are controlled, and the full richness and complexity of nature is present. It is for these reasons that descriptive methods are best for describing and predicting behaviors, because our goal is to describe behaviors as they normally occur and to develop our predictions based on their occurrence in natural settings.

In research terminology, descriptive studies tend to produce high *external validity*. That is, our observed results are likely to be repeatable with other subjects and settings. Even with the controls we proposed in our likability study, that research situation has much in common with the way meetings occur in the real world. Our results should generalize to other such meetings in the real world.

Recall, however, that design decisions result in trade-offs. An uncontrolled setting such as a student lounge can reduce the reliability and validity of our measurements. Likewise, the surreptitious observation of an individual or the use of interviews may produce unreliable and invalid measurements of a variable or construct. Most important, the complexity of nature necessarily involves the persence of many extraneous variables that may influence the outcome of our study. Descriptive research, therefore, tends to have weak *internal validity*. As we saw, a more natural setting may present a more confusing situation for the researcher, so that we cannot clearly identify whether other variables might have been operating in our study. Even if we were to conduct a more controlled likability study, numerous extraneous variables could still be operating, because we introduce males and females who may behave in uncontrolled ways, and the meeting takes place in a lounge area that may produce many fluctuating influences.

> **REMEMBER**   The strength of descriptive approaches is that they tend to have greater external validity, but their weakness is that they tend to have less internal validity.

In a descriptive study, we set out to test a description and to learn about natural behaviors. Therefore, we seek observations and relationships having greater external validity that are typical of such behaviors in the real world *in general*. However, we must accept the reduced internal validity that descriptive research provides, accepting that we have less confidence in our understanding of what *specifically* produced the relationship or what it specifically reflects. (We cannot be general and specific at the same time.) In particular, because of the weak internal validity of descriptive approaches, we accept that we cannot make valid inferences about the causes of the behaviors we observe.

Problems in Inferring the Causes of a Behavior

When most people hear of a relationship between X and Y, they automatically conclude that it is a causal relationship, to think that changes in X *cause* changes in Y. This conclusion is a mistake, however, because one variable can be related to another variable without causing it to change. For example, a person's weight is related to his or her height, but the weight does not cause the height. The key to inferring a causal relationship lies not only in the fact that a relationship is demonstrated but also in the *manner* in which it is demonstrated.

To demonstrate a cause of a behavior, we must first produce the correct temporal sequence: To say that X causes Y, we have to show that X occurs *before* Y. In evaluating any finding that claims to show causality, be sure that the supposed cause did in fact occur first. Descriptive methods *cannot* be used to infer a causal relationship between two variables, because these method do not establish positively which variable occurs first. Thus, in our likability study, we cannot say that greater attractiveness causes greater likability, because we are unsure of the order in which subjects' reactions occur. Perhaps it's the subjects' perception of a model as more attractive that causes greater likability. Or, it might be that subjects first decide they like the model, and that greater likability causes them to rate him as more attractive.

To confidently infer a cause we must also be sure that no extraneous variable could actually be the cause. The control of extraneous variables provided by descriptive studies is not sufficient for us to confidently identify the causes of a behavior. For example, let's say we find that models rated as more attractive are also rated as more likable. Coincidentally, however, the models rated as more attractive are also better dressed. The scores may reflect the predicted relationship between facial attractiveness and likability, or they may reflect a relationship in which the subjects inadvertently rated better-dressed models as both more attractive and more likable. The problem is, the data confirm our hypothesis that greater facial attractiveness causes greater likability, while also confirming a rival, alternative hypothesis that fashionable clothes cause greater likability. In this predicament, we do not know which variable causes greater likability, so we do not know which hypothesis to believe. Thus, with a descriptive study, particularly a correlational design, we only describe the relationship between the two variables, without inferring that one causes the other.

> *REMEMBER*   Correlational and other descriptive designs are inappropriate for inferring that changes in variable X cause changes in variable Y, because we cannot be sure that X changes first, or that it is the only changing variable that could cause Y to change.

Confounding Variables

Researchers have an important term for describing a situation in which an extraneous variable systematically changes along with the variables we are measuring. Whenever the study would support both the original hypothesis about a cause, and a competing hypothesis involving an extraneous variable that may be the cause, we are confused or "confounded." A **confounding** occurs when an extraneous variable systematically changes along with the variable we hypothesize is a causal variable. Then we cannot tell which variable is actually causing the behavior to change: Is it the hypothesized causal variable or the extraneous one? In our likability study, for example, if more attractive men were also better dressed, style of dress would be a confounding variable (or we would say it is confounded with attractiveness).

> *REMEMBER*   If two (or more) potential causal variables simultaneously change, then the variables are *confounded*.

Whenever a confounding variable is present, it weakens the study's internal validity: We cannot draw *valid* inferences about what caused the relationship *internal* to our study, let alone in nature. Thus, using research terminology, we say that correlational designs are not used to infer causality because, given their many potential confounding variables, such designs provide little internal validity for such inferences.

The way we increase internal validity is through greater control. If all of our models were dressed the same, then it would make no sense to suggest the alternative hypothesis that differences in dress cause differences in likability. Likewise, if we control *all* other extraneous variables, we can more confidently infer the causal variable. If the *only* variable that systematically differentiates the models is their facial attractiveness, then we can claim that it is the differences in attractiveness that cause differences in likability. To provide this type of control, we conduct an experiment.

EXPERIMENTAL RESEARCH METHODS

To meet our scientific goal of explaining and controlling behaviors, we create and test *causal hypotheses*. In doing so, we follow the same logical flow we did previously, selecting our population and defining our hypothetical constructs in terms of specific variables. Say we propose that a person's physical attractiveness influences the first impression formed of that person. We translate this statement into the hypothesis that greater attractiveness causes better first impressions, and predict a relationship such that, as facial attractiveness increases, likability also increases. Although we may predict the same relationship as that predicted in a correlational study, we go about demonstrating it in a very different way.

As discussed in chapter 1, we test causal hypotheses using *experimental methods*. In such methods, the researcher systematically manipulates or changes a variable and then measures subjects' scores on another variable. Here, we use the logic that "if the hypothesis is correct, then as the researcher changes one variable, there should be a corresponding change in the subjects' behavior as measured by the other variable, so that the predicted relationship is observed."

Experiments are discussed in detail in later chapters, so here we'll briefly review their important features. There are two broad types of experimental methods: true experiments and quasi-experiments.

True Experiments

The research method that best demonstrates a causal relationship is a true experiment. In a **true experiment** the researcher actively changes or manipulates a variable that subjects are exposed to *by the researcher*. This differs from the correlational method, in which the researcher examines whether *naturally* occurring changes in scores from *both* variables form the predicted relationship. To conduct our likability experiment, for example, we would systematically change or manipulate the facial attractiveness of a male model whom our female subjects meet and, for each change, measure subjects' scores on the variable of his likability. Then we look for the predicted relationship in which increasing attractiveness is related to likability scores. In the language of an experiment, we look for the relationship such that, as we change the "independent variable," scores on the "dependent variable" tend to change in a consistent fashion.

The Independent Variable   The **independent variable** is the variable that is systematically changed or manipulated by the experimenter. (An independent variable is also called a *factor*.) In a true experiment, this variable is something that is done *to* subjects, because we think it will cause a change in their behavior. (In our likability experiment, the facial attractiveness of a model is the independent variable.) An independent variable may be *quantitative*, in which case we manipulate the amount of a variable that subjects are exposed to. Or an independent variable may be *qualitative*, in which case we manipulate a quality or attribute of the situation that subjects are exposed to. (If, in a different study, we compare subjects meeting a model in either a lounge or a classroom, we are manipulating a quality of the room.) Either way, we identify a component variable of a construct or of the physical environment that we think causes or influences a behavior. Then we create an operational definition of the variable, stating how we will measure and manipulate it.

Conditions of the Independent Variable   A model's attractiveness can be at any point on the continuum from very attractive to very unattractive. Therefore, we must select specific amounts of the variable for subjects to experience. A **condition** is a specific amount or quality of the independent variable that is applied to subjects. To create our conditions of attractiveness, let's say our operational definition of a model's facial attractiveness is its rating by a panel of judges prior to the study. Then, we might select one model consistently rated as "low," one rated as "medium," and one rated as "high" (specifically defining these terms as well). When female subjects meet the low-rated model, they are in the "low attractiveness condition"; when they meet the medium-rated model they are in the "medium attractiveness condition"; and when they meet the high-rated model they are in the "high attractiveness condition." (Understand that the independent variable is attractiveness, having many different amounts. Our conditions, then, are the specific amounts of attractiveness we present to subjects.) A condition is also known as a *treatment* or a *level*.

A useful way to envision an experimental design is shown in Table 2.2. Note that each column represents a condition under which subjects are tested, and that each X represents a subject's score that we will obtain by measuring the dependent variable.

The Dependent Variable   The **dependent variable** is the variable that is used to measure a subject's response in each condition of the independent variable. You can identify the dependent variable in a study as the one measuring scores that are presumably caused by, or *depend* upon, the condition of the independent variable. In our study, for instance, we propose that a model's likability depends on his facial attractiveness, so likability is the dependent variable (which we must also operationally define). Thus in Table 2.2, we expect to see a relationship in which overall, low likability ratings tend to occur in the low-attractiveness condition, medium ratings are associated with medium

TABLE 2.2   Diagram of an Experiment to Study the Influence of a Model's Attractiveness on His Likability

	Conditions of the independent variable (attractiveness of model)		
	Condition 1: low attractiveness	*Condition 2: medium attractiveness*	*Condition 3: high attractiveness*
Subjects' scores on dependent variable (likability)	X X X ⋮	X X X ⋮	X X X ⋮

attractiveness, and higher ratings are associated with high attractiveness. (Subjects' scores are also called "dependent" scores.)

> *REMEMBER*   In experiments, we look for a relationship such that as we change the specific *conditions* of the *independent variable,* subjects' behavior as measured by scores on the *dependent variable* tends to change in a consistent fashion.

Random Assignment   Not all variables a researcher may study are *true* independent variables producing true experiments. In experiments with a *true independent variable,* subjects are randomly assigned to a particular condition. **Random assignment** means that the condition of the independent variable a subject will experience is determined in a random and unbiased manner. Random assignment is a second step that occurs after we randomly select the subjects for our study. Thus, for example, we might write the names of our three attractiveness conditions (low, medium, high) on slips of paper and mix them in a hat. Then, when a female subject we've randomly selected arrives for the study, we would select a slip from the hat to randomly assign her to one of our conditions.

Random assignment is important because it is a way of "balancing" or canceling out extraneous subject variables. Because our female subjects have been randomly assigned to each condition, a particular condition should contain some subjects who are short and others who are tall, some nervous and others relaxed, some older and others younger, some freshmen and others seniors, and so on. Then, overall, each condition should contain the same types of subjects as the other conditions. This procedure provides greater confidence that the independent variable is not confounded by extraneous subject variables. That is, that differences in likability scores are due to attractiveness and *not* to a difference between the subjects in one condition and the subjects in another condition.

> *REMEMBER*   A true experiment, with a true independent variable, allows random assignment of subjects to each condition.

Issues of Validity and Reliability in True Experiments   We might complete the design of our likability experiment as follows: First, the extraneous variables that constitute a model's behavior and manner of dress can be eliminated by presenting subjects a photograph showing only his face (as in May & Hamilton, 1980.) Second, randomly selected females with corrected eyesight and so on can be randomly assigned to view the photograph of a model rated as low, medium, or high in attractiveness by our judges. Third, we can disguise the purpose of the study, in order to control for the subjects' own biasing attitudes or self-consciousness, by asking subjects to read a paragraph describing a fictitious male that accompanies each photograph. Each subject could then answer several questions about the model, including a rating of his likability. Finally, we can keep the environment constant by conducting the study in a controlled laboratory, keep the researcher's behavior constant, and balance the researcher's gender in each condition.

On the one hand, a true experiment provides us with the greatest confidence that we have demonstrated a causal relationship in our study. First, by presenting the conditions of the independent variable *and then* measuring the dependent variable, we ensure the correct temporal sequence between the supposed cause and its effect. Second, by randomly assigning subjects to conditions, we have tried to avoid confounding subject variables that might actually be the causal variable. And third, by controlling other extraneous variables, we hope to be able to say that the "only" variable that systematically changed was attractiveness—and, therefore, that attractiveness must be the cause of any observed changes in likability.

On the other hand, our controls only build our confidence by default. If the influence of the extraneous variables of a model's behavior and dress are eliminated, then by default we are more confident that the scores and relationship reflect what we think they reflect. But, being skeptical, we recognize that our controls eliminate only some of the many extraneous variables that might simultaneously change with our three levels of attractiveness. Perhaps, for example, the researcher's expectations of how subjects should rate the different models was communicated to subjects. Thus, an alternative, rival hypothesis about a confounding variable may actually describe the true cause of likability. Also, we cannot be positive that our measurements are perfectly reliable and valid: Because beauty is in the eye of the beholder, our judges may not rate a model's attractiveness as our *subjects* see him, so we may not have actually manipulated the models' attractiveness in our subjects' eyes.

Thus, although a well-controlled experiment will give us substantial confidence that we have validly and reliably demonstrated a causal relationship, it will not be "proof." Realistically speaking, we cannot control *every* possible extraneous variable in one study. Only as researchers conduct replication studies that control various confounding variables (at least those we can identify) do we become truly confident of the cause of a behavior. At best, the results of any single experiment allow us to strongly *argue* that we have identified a causal relationship.

> *REMEMBER*   A single experiment gives us only *some* degree of confidence that changes in the independent variable cause changes in the dependent variable.

Recall that there is a trade-off between internal and external validity. It is the hall-mark of experimental methods to seek *high internal validity:* to control extraneous, confounding variables so that we are confident it is actually and only the changes in the independent variable that cause changes in the dependent variable. However, the more controls we add, the more atypical the situation becomes. By creating an unusual and unnatural situation, we reduce external validity, the extent to which the results generalize *beyond* our study and are repeatable with other subjects and situations. Thus, although the controls of our likability experiment greatly reduce our potential confusion about which variables are operating and what subjects are responding to, we are dealing with a rather strange and artificial form of first impressions. In particular, females do not normally form first impressions from photographs! Thus, with experimental methods, we accept that we have greater internal validity for understanding our particular relationship, but at the cost of getting results that are likely to be atypical of, and less generalizable to, other settings.

> *REMEMBER* The strength of experimental methods is that they tend to have greater internal validity, but their weakness is that they tend to have less external validity.

Quasi-Experiments

A true independent variable is something that a researcher exposes subjects to. However, there are many behavior-influencing variables that we cannot control subjects' exposure to, such as their age, race, background, experiences, or personality characteristics. Such variables are called "quasi-independent variables," and studies that employ them are called quasi-experiments. In a **quasi-experiment,** we cannot randomly assign subjects to be exposed to a particular condition. Instead, subjects are assigned to a condition because they already qualify for that condition based upon some *inherent* characteristic. For example, say our hypothesis is that 18-year-old females will like a male of a given attractiveness more than 22-year-old females will. We cannot select females for our study and *make* some of them 18 and others 22. Or, say we want to determine whether male subjects like a model more or less than female subjects do. We cannot randomly assign some subjects to be male and others to be female. Instead, we would create the conditions of 18- and 22-year-olds by randomly selecting one sample of 18-year-old females and another sample of 22-year-old females. Likewise, for the quasi-independent variable of gender, a random sample of males and a random sample of females would create the conditions. Similarly, we create our conditions in this way when studying the influence of accidental events: For example, we might wish to compare people who have and have not experienced a hurricane, or compare the performance of students who happen to have been placed in the classrooms of professors with different teaching styles.

Otherwise, quasi-experiments have the same purpose as true experiments. In conducting them, we seek to demonstrate a relationship in which scores on the dependent variable change as the conditions of the quasi-independent variable change. Thus, we would look to see whether a model's likability changes as the age of subjects changes. Or we would look for a change in his likability as the gender of subjects changes.

Issues of Validity and Reliability in Quasi-Experiments   Along with the problems associated with true experiments, a quasi-experiment has the added problem of lacking random assignment. In the process of assigning subjects to conditions, we may inadvertently create conditions that also differ based on extraneous subject variables such that the independent variable is *confounded*. For example, by selecting female subjects who differ in age, we may end up with subjects who also differ in their amount of dating experience. Thus, we might have the study diagrammed in Table 2.3. As shown, the presence of a confounding variable means that our results may confirm not only our hypothesis that greater age causes greater likability but also the rival, alternative hypothesis that greater dating experience causes greater likability, therefore, we cannot confidently conclude which variable is actually the cause of differences in likability.

Further, the subjects in these two age groups will probably also differ in terms of their year in college, their maturity, and so on. Or, if we create conditions which include both male and female subjects, we may find that these groups also differ in terms of, say, personality, cognitive processes, and sexual stereotypes. Later, we will discuss controls that can be added to rule out some of these rival hypotheses. However, because a quasi-independent variable will never be the only difference between the conditions, *quasi-experiments provide little confidence that our independent variable is truly the cause of the relationship we observe.*

> *REMEMBER*   A quasi-experiment does not involve random assignment of subjects to conditions, so we have greatly reduced internal validity for inferring that the independent variable is the causal variable.

TABLE 2.3   Diagram of Quasi-Experiment Showing a Confounding Variable

	Conditions of study	
	Condition 1	*Condition 2*
Independent variable	*18-year-olds*	*22-year-olds*
Confounding variable	Little dating experience	Much dating experience
Likability scores	X X X ⋮	X X X ⋮

SELECTING A METHOD

Researchers use the terms *descriptive* and *experimental* as a shorthand way of communicating the overall approach of a design. As categories, these terms distinguish the extent to which variables are controlled and, often, the degree to which observations are reliable and have certain types of validity. However, in creating a specific design, researchers have wide latitude in applying controls and mixing experimental and descriptive methods.

In general, there are four major factors that determine the overall approach, the controls we employ, and, of course, the types of inferences we can draw.

The Nature of the Research Hypothesis

First and foremost, the method selected depends upon the question the research is supposed to answer. True experiments are best for testing a causal hypothesis, because they provide the greatest control over potentially confounding variables. Conversely, we should use correlational and other descriptive approaches only when the hypothesis is descriptive or we are seeking to discover a relationship between variables. However, sometimes we may not have a choice.

The Nature of the Behavior Under Study

Some behaviors simply cannot be studied using a particular method. For example, we cannot *make* subjects be Republican or Democrat, have a certain personality or intelligence, be alcoholic, be the victim of sexual abuse, or have a criminal record. Although these variables may influence behavior, they cannot be true independent variables that we expose subjects to. Thus, regardless of the nature of our hypothesis, we are sometimes forced to accept weaker evidence. We may have to study alcoholics using a quasi-experiment, in which the conditions are formed by subjects who already exhibit different degrees of alcoholism. We may be forced to merely describe the relationship between sexual abuse and other variables by asking questions of abuse victims using a correlational design. And to study criminals, we may have to examine their records. Based on such studies, we may propose the causes of such behaviors, but without conducting true experiments, we must recognize that the evidence only *suggests* possible causes.

Issues of Validity

How we decide to conduct our study using a particular method is determined by our concerns with reliability and validity. In particular, we must decide whether our primary concern is for internal or external validity. On the one hand, we can study a highly controlled situation that is easier to understand, but it may also be a rather atypical situation that does not generalize as well. On the other hand, with fewer controls, we may study a situation that is more natural and realistic such that our results generalize better, but we may also experience greater confusion about what specifically influenced the behavior *in* our study. Fortunately, our choice is not completely all-or-nothing. If we added controls to our original likability study in the student lounge, we would have a more internally valid correlational design. If we went further and selected models having low, medium, and high attractiveness, we would have a less controlled but more externally valid experimental design.

For "basic" research in which we seek the underlying causes of behavior or test hypotheses derived from theories, we are usually concerned with internal validity and thus lean toward highly controlled experimental procedures in laboratory settings. These procedures help to develop our conceptual understanding of basic processes, even though they may create a unique or artificial situation that is less externally valid. Conversely, for "applied" research, when we seek to obtain descriptions or to determine whether theoretical explanations are supported in the real world, we lean toward less controlled experiments or toward descriptive designs that are less artificial and thus have greater external validity.

Ethical and Practical Requirements

Recall that researchers must always be ethical: We must not harm subjects, either physically or emotionally, and we must respect their rights. (Another reason we cannot make subjects alcoholic.) In deference to such ethical requirements, we will always accept reduced reliability and validity.

We also must be practical and realistic, accepting that we cannot devise a perfectly reliable and valid study from all perspectives. For example, a vast number of studies have employed subjects drawn from college Introductory Psychology courses, because these courses offer an easily accessible supply of subjects. However, such selection is not random, because people are not randomly selected for college, and students are not randomly assigned to Introductory Psychology courses. We accept that our selection process may decrease our external validity, on the grounds that such subjects do primarily represent the population of Introductory Psychology students and may not represent any broader population. However, unless there is a compelling reason to select a different type of subjects, we are practical and use these students.

We can be practical in such ways because we ultimately rely on replication to determine whether we have made a mistake. Literal replications, studies that duplicate the procedures and subjects of a previous study, increase our confidence that a particular approach is internally valid. And conceptual replications, studies that employ somewhat different procedures and a different type of subjects, increase our confidence that the overall approach is externally valid.

PUTTING IT ALL TOGETHER

Designing a study is a problem-solving task. The problem is to produce the best and clearest evidence we can for testing a particular hypothesis. We solve the problem by designing the study in such a way that it shows the relationship between our variables, minimizes confusion produced by extraneous variables and untrustworthy measurements, and generalizes appropriately.

As a beginning researcher, recognize that you must identify threats to reliability and validity *before* you conduct your study. The key to designing a good, convincing experiment is to anticipate potential threats and build in controls that eliminate them. In particular, the fewer alternative hypotheses your study can support, the more confidence you have that the study provides convincing evidence for your original hypothesis. When designing a study, then, keep these pointers in mind: (1) State the hypothesis clearly, asking a question about one specific behavior. (2) Be a psychologist, using your knowledge of behavior to identify potential flaws in the design. (3) Rely on the research literature, employing solutions that others have already developed. And (4) assume that "Murphy's Law" is constantly operating: anything that can go wrong will go wrong. Design your study accordingly.

At the same time, however, recognize that you cannot control every aspect of a behavior all at once. Deal with the *serious* threats to validity and reliability in your design. You can never create the perfect study, so every decision in research must necessarily be "the lesser of two evils." Any study ultimately involves two major concerns: First, try to eliminate flaws that can be dealt with practically so as to meet your goals. Second, consider any major flaws that remain when interpreting your study. Everything else is left for another day.

CHAPTER SUMMARY

1. A *sample* of subjects is a relatively small subset of a *population,* which consists of all the members of a specific, defined group.

2. *Simple random sampling* is the process of selecting subjects so that all members of the population have an equal chance of being selected. *Systematic random sampling* involves selecting every Nth subject from a list of the members of the population. The goal of both techniques is to generate a *representative sample,* which accurately reflects the characteristics and behaviors of the population from which it is drawn.

3. A *hypothetical construct* is an abstract concept used in a particular theoretical manner to relate different behaviors according to their common underlying features or causes. We study a construct by measuring a variable. A *variable* is any measurable aspect of a behavior or influence on behavior that may change.

4. An *operational definition* defines a construct or variable in terms of the operations used to measure it.

5. Most studies focus on demonstrating a *relationship,* a pattern in which, as the scores on one variable change, scores on another variable also change in a consistent fashion.

6. *Converging operations* are two or more procedures that together eliminate alternative hypotheses and bolster our conclusions about a particular behavior.

7. A relationship between the variables in a sample is used to infer a relationship between the variables in the population, which in turn is used to make inferences about hypothetical constructs.

8. When determining what a measurement reflects, researchers consider (a) *reliability,* the degree to which a measurement is consistent, can be reproduced and avoids error; (b) *content validity,* the degree to which a measurement reflects the variable or behavior of interest; and (c) *construct validity,* the degree to which a measurement reflects the hypothetical construct of interest.

9. When determining what a relationship reflects, researchers consider (a) *internal validity,* the degree to which there are no unintended variables operating that produced the relationship; and (b) *external validity,* the degree to which the relationship generalizes to other subjects and other situations.

10. *Extraneous variables* potentially influence a study's results, but they are not variables we wish to study. They may be subject variables, researcher variables, environmental variables, or measurement variables.

11. We attempt to control extraneous variables by eliminating, keeping constant, or balancing their influence.

12. In *descriptive designs,* we do not manipulate or change the variables of interest. With a *correlational design,* we measure variables to determine whether a predicted relationship occurs.

13. Descriptive methods are best for testing descriptive hypotheses because they tend to have greater external validity. However, they also have less internal validity.

14. To demonstrate that variable X causes variable Y, we must show that X occurs first and is the only changing variable.

15. If two (or more) potential causal variables simultaneously change, then the variables are *confounded.*

16. In a *true experiment,* with a true independent variable, subjects are randomly assigned to a particular condition.

17. In experimental designs, the researcher systematically changes the conditions of the *independent variable* and, for each *condition,* measures subjects' responses on the *dependent variable*.

18. Experimental methods are best for testing causal hypotheses because they tend to have greater internal validity. However, they also have less external validity.

19. *Random assignment* means that the condition a subject experiences is determined in an random and unbiased manner.

20. In a *quasi-experiment,* with a quasi-independent variable, subjects cannot be randomly assigned to any condition but, instead, are assigned to a condition based upon some inherent characteristic. Because the independent variable may be confounded by other extraneous subject variables, quasi-experiments have much less internal validity than true experiments.

21. When designing a study, researchers consider (a) the nature of the research hypothesis, (b) the nature of the behavior under study, (c) their concern for reliability and particular types of validity, and (d) ethical and practical requirements.

REVIEW QUESTIONS

1. Explain what researchers mean when they express concern about (a) reliability, (b) content validity, (c) construct validity, (d) internal validity, and (e) external validity.
2. (a) What is the difference between descriptive and experimental research methods? (b) What primary purpose of your study directs you to select one approach over the other?
3. (a) What are the advantages and disadvantages of descriptive research methods? (b) How do they influence a researcher's conclusions?
4. (a) What are the advantages and disadvantages of experimental research methods? (b) How do they influence a researcher's conclusions?
5. How can you identify the independent variable, the conditions, and the dependent variable in an experiment?
6. What do we mean by the term "confounding variable"?
7. (a) What is the difference between a true independent variable and a quasi-independent variable? (b) What is the problem with using the latter to draw causal inferences?
8. After taking a test, you express the following conclusions. Identify the issue that arises in terms of reliability and the various types of validity. (a) You complain that the test is unfair because it does not reflect your "knowledge" of the material. (b) The questions were "tricky" and required that you be good at solving riddles. (c) Your essay makes the same points as your friend's, but you obtained a lower grade. (d) Based on your grade in this course, you believe that your study techniques will also allow you to do well in other courses. (e) The instructor concludes that the reason some students performed poorly on the test was that they did not study sufficiently.
9. Drinking red wine daily may help prevent heart disease. To test this hypothesis, we select elderly subjects who have typically drunk zero, one, or two glasses of red wine daily during their lives and determine the health of their hearts. (a) What type of design is this? (b) What term do we use to refer to the amount of wine a subject drinks? (c) What do we call the amounts we examine? (d) What do we call the healthiness of subjects' hearts? (e) How confident can we be in our conclusion that drinking more wine causes reduced heart disease? Why?
10. How would we conduct the above study using a correlational design?
11. Red wine contains an acid that causes headaches, so people who drink more red wine probably take more aspirin. Taking aspirin may prevent heart disease. (a) In questions 9 and 10, what term do we use to refer to the amount of aspirin that people take? (b) What problem of validity pertains to this situation, and how does it affect our conclusions?

12. In question 9, describe how you would control the variable of aspirin by (a) by eliminating it, (b) by keeping it constant, and (c) by balancing it.
13. When conducting a study, a researcher wears a white "lab coat" and carries a clipboard and stopwatch. How might these details influence the internal and external validity of the study?
14. We hypothesize that a person's frequency of changing sexual partners is caused by the degree to which that person fears sexually transmitted diseases. How should we study this relationship, and what inherent research flaws must we accept?

DISCUSSION QUESTIONS

1. Consider the hypothesis that greater exposure to violence from television or movies results in more aggressive behavior. (a) For ethical reasons, what may be the best design for determining whether this relationship exists? (b) What is the trade-off involved in being ethical?
2. A nurse claims that when she wore one of those silly-looking hats, patients followed instructions better than they do now that she no longer wears it. (a) What hypothetical constructs might this situation reflect? (b) Outline an experiment for studying this situation in a laboratory. (c) Outline a correlational design for studying it in the real world.
3. A researcher reads numerous traffic accident reports and finds that brighter-colored automobiles are involved in more traffic accidents, with red autos having the worst record. He concludes that certain colors cause more accidents. (a) What type of research method has been used in this study? (b) Are the researcher's inferences correct? Why? (c) What confounding variables might have been operating? (Hint: Who drives red cars?) (d) What steps must be taken to more convincingly support this hypothesis?
4. Create a descriptive hypothesis about a behavior and decide how you would test it. What problems do you foresee?
5. Create a causal hypothesis about a behavior and decide how you would test it. What problems do you foresee?

3 Statistical Issues in Designing and Interpreting Research

As we have seen, the focus of psychological research is measuring behaviors and events. In correlational designs we examine the relationship between the scores on the variables we measure, and in experiments we attempt to produce a relationship by manipulating the independent variable and measuring the dependent variable. If we observe a relationship in our sample data, we have evidence that the variables are related. And by confirming that the variables are related as predicted, we confirm our original hypothesis about the behavior.

The evidence for testing a hypothesis hinges on the data that demonstrate a relationship between variables. Researchers use statistical procedures to examine these data and to understand the observed relationship. This chapter discusses the common statistical procedures found in psychological research. First we examine the common procedures for summarizing data and describing a relationship. Then we consider methods for drawing statistical inferences about the relationship. Throughout the chapter, remember that statistical procedures are not separate from the research process. As we will see, our statistical conclusions and our psychological conclusions are interrelated. Both ultimately depend on the design of the study.

THE PURPOSE OF STATISTICAL ANALYSIS

As we saw in the previous chapter, issues of validity and reliability concern us in every study. But statistical procedures themselves do not tell us if the data is reliable and valid. On the contrary, they take the scores at face value, treating them simply as numbers. The purpose of statistical analysis is to examine these numbers, so that we can (1) precisely describe and summarize the data for ourselves and efficiently communicate our findings to other researchers, (2) determine the mathematical relationship between the scores in the sample data, and (3) use the sample data to describe the relationship we would expect to find in the population, if we could observe it. Once we have completed this analysis, we are largely finished with statistics and can return to our conceptual questions regarding what the data reflect about the nature of behavior. Thus, statistical analysis is only one step in the research process. It has to be performed correctly, because statistical descriptions of our scores form the basis for all subsequent conclusions. However, we must not lose sight of the fact that any claim we make about scores will ultimately become a claim about behavior. Our purpose is to use statistics to help us be psychologists.

We employ two types of procedures when performing a statistical analysis: descriptive statistics and inferential statistics. **Descriptive statistics** are mathematical computations that summarize and describe the important characteristics of a sample of data. (Note that the term *descriptive research* refers to designs that describe behavior. *Descriptive statistics* describe the data from *any* type of design.) The central purpose of these procedures is to describe the observed relationship, summarizing how, as the scores on the X variable change, the scores on the Y variable also change. The goal is to understand two characteristics of the relationship, its type and its strength. The *type of relationship* is the overall direction in which the Y scores tend to change as the X scores change. The *strength of the relationship* is how consistently the Y scores change with changes in X.

REMEMBER   The important characteristics of a relationship are its *type* and its *strength.*

Once we understand the relationship in our sample data, our next step is to generalize this relationship. As we will see, however, we cannot automatically assume that a sample relationship represents a relationship that would be found in the population. To help prevent errors when making such inferences, we perform inferential statistical procedures. **Inferential statistics** are mathematical procedures for deciding if a sample relationship represents a relationship that actually exists in the population.

There are many inferential and descriptive statistical procedures to choose from, because there are many ways to describe and summarize a relationship. Therefore, when designing a study, we must consider the appropriate statistical procedures to employ.

SELECTING THE STATISTICAL PROCEDURES

Because it is possible to design a study that cannot be statistically analyzed, the type of statistical procedures to be used should be considered early in the design process. Some procedures are more prone to errors than others, and whether we can use the best procedure depends upon other decisions we make when designing the study. After a study is conducted, we have little choice as to which procedure can be used.

A statistical procedure provides accurate information only when your data and design meet the statistical rules or "assumptions" of the procedure. Use these assumptions as a checklist for selecting a procedure. The question of which statistical procedures we should employ depends on two major characteristics of the design. The first is the general method used to answer our research question: Some types of descriptive and inferential statistics are used to analyze experiments, and others are used to analyze descriptive studies.

The other major consideration when selecting a statistical procedure concerns the way that you measure subjects' behavior. Subjects' scores are produced using various *scales of measurement,* each of which has particular mathematical characteristics such that only certain procedures are appropriate. There are four scales of measurement: nominal, ordinal, interval, and ratio.

In some studies we might wish to identify membership in one or another category—for example, by assigning certain subjects a "1" to identify them as "Republican" and others a "2" to identify them as "Democrat." Such scores are called nominal data. **Nominal scores** do not measure an amount but, rather, identify a quality or category. The numbers on football jerseys, the letters representing blood-type, and a person's sex are other examples of nominal scales.

Alternatively, we might wish to rank-order a subject according to the amount of a variable the subject exhibits *relative* to other subjects. In this case we would assign one subject the score of "1" or "first" on the variable, rank another as "2," and so on. **Ordinal scores** such as these indicate a subject's rank order along a variable. The letter grade a student receives in a course and military rank are other examples of ordinal scales.

Both nominal and ordinal scales involve unusual number systems, because they do not include a meaningful zero, and the difference between and 2 is not necessarily equal to the difference between 2 and 3.

More commonly, the scores we examine reflect actual amounts of a variable, such as the amount of time subjects take to run a race or the degree of conservatism they exhibit. Here the numbers have their usual meaning, with the same constant amount separating any two adjacent scores and with zero serving as a meaningful score. Sometimes, however, a score of zero does not truly mean zero amount. In the case of **interval scores,** the data reflect an actual amount, but because this scale has no true zero, negative scores are possible. For example, temperature is usually measured on an interval scale. "Zero degrees" does not mean that a zero amount of heat is present, only that the temperature is less than 1 degree and more than -1 degree. Likewise, when measuring subjects' over- and underestimates of the weight of an object, or the amount of money in their checking account, we are using interval scales. In the case of **ratio scores,** however, the data reflect an actual amount, but zero truly means zero amount, so negative scores are *not* possible. When measuring subjects' errors on a test, calories consumed in a day, or the amount of money in their pocket we are using ratio scales.

When working with interval or ratio scores, we must also determine whether the scores are normally distributed. We must ask, Do the scores form an approximately **normal distribution**? With such scores, we can usually employ the inferential statistical procedures—and the corresponding descriptive procedures—that fall into the category known as parametric inferential statistical procedures. **Parametric statistics** are used to analyze normally distributed interval or ratio scores. Some of the procedures in this category are commonly used to analyze experiments, and others are used to analyze descriptive designs. When our interval or ratio scores are not normally distributed, or when we are measuring nominal or ordinal scores, we use the inferential statistical procedures—and the corresponding descriptive procedures—that fall into the category called **nonparametric statistics.** Here, too, some procedures are used with experiments and others are used with descriptive designs.

Psychological research usually involves interval or ratio scores that meet the requirements of parametric statistical procedures. In the following sections we will focus on the most common parametric procedures as we examine the role that statistics play in the research process.

DESCRIBING THE RELATIONSHIP IN A CORRELATIONAL DESIGN

Recall that a common descriptive research design is the correlational design. In this case, we do not manipulate the variables of interest but merely measure the behaviors and events as they occur and describe the relationship that exists between the variables. One idea for a correlational study might be to examine the rumor that "the more you study, the better you learn." Cognitive and educational psychologists have proposed hypothetical constructs of "learning," "memory," and "concept formation" to describe how people build their knowledge. One component of this process seems to be that a person must repeatedly encounter and interact with the information to be learned in order to integrate the information in memory.

Let's say we propose the descriptive hypothesis that "greater studying is at least associated with greater learning." Our operational definition of "amount of studying" is the variable of number of hours a subject studied the night before a college exam. The "amount of learning" is the number of questions a subject correctly answers on a multiple-choice test. To achieve high external validity for our data, we ask students in a research methods course to report both the number of hours they studied Chapter 2 in this book and their grade on a subsequent test of the chapter. (We also design the study to ensure reliability, content validity, and internal validity.) We predict not only that these scores are related but, more specifically, that higher test grades are associated with higher study-time scores.

Before we proceed, note the special way researchers have of phrasing and communi- cating the components of a relationship between variables. We refer to the relationship as involving an X variable and a Y variable. How do we decide which variable to call X or Y? In any study, we implicitly ask the question: For a given score on one variable, what scores occur on the other variable? The "given" variable is always called the X variable, and the "other" variable is always called the Y variable. In our present study, we are asking: For a given amount of study time, what test grades occur? Then, we describe the relationship using the format: "Y scores change *as a function of* changes in X." In our study, we predict the relationship in which test grades increase as a function of greater study times.

> REMEMBER   The "given" variable in any study is always designated as the X variable, and we phrase our description of a relationship using the format "Y scores change as a function of changes in X."

At the heart of any description of the results of a correlational design is the correlation coefficient. The term *correlation* is synonymous with *relationship,* so a correlation coefficient describes the important characteristics of a relationship. The most common, parametric correlation coefficient is the Pearson correlation coefficient. The **Pearson correlation coefficient,** symbolized as r, is a number that describes the type and strength of a linear relationship. By **linear relationship,** we mean that as the X scores increase, the Y scores change in only *one* direction, continually increasing or decreasing in a straight-line pattern. In the following sections, we will see how the correlation coefficient describes a relationship.

Perfectly Consistent Linear Relationships

Let's say that in examining study times and test grades, we tested an unrealistically small number of subjects and obtained one of the data sets presented in Figure 3.1. Looking first at the scores, we see that the type of relationship present in both sets of data is a linear relationship. The difference is that data set A shows a **positive linear relationship:** As the X scores increase, the Y scores *increase*. And data set B shows a **negative linear relationship:** As the X scores increase, the Y scores *decrease*. In both

FIGURE 3.1   Data Producing Perfect Positive and Negative Linear Relationships

Data Set (A) Perfect Positive Relationship			**Data Set (B)** Perfect Negative Relationship		
Scores			Scores		
X Hours Studied		*Y* Test Scores	*X* Hours Studied		*Y* Test Scores
1		20	1		80
1		20	1		80
1		20	1		80
3		50	3		50
3		50	3		50
3		50	3		50
5		80	5		20
5		80	5		20
5		80	5		20

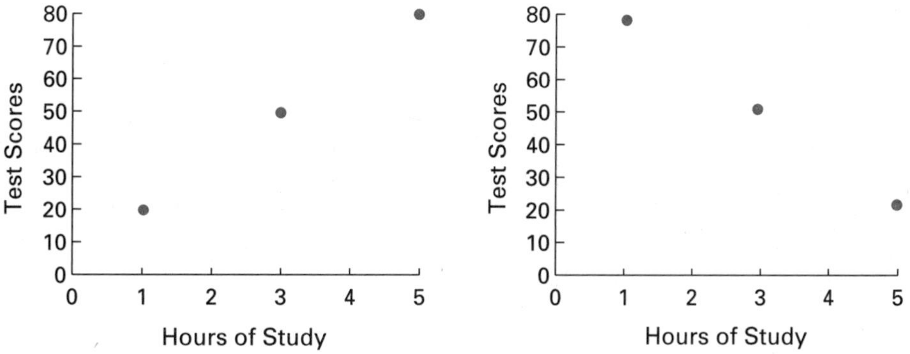

cases, we also see the strength or consistency of the relationship. All subjects with the same X score have the same Y score so when their X scores changes, the Y scores all change in a consistent way. Thus, both of these relationships are as strong as they can be, because they are perfectly consistent.

In the graphs of these data in Figure 3.1, we have placed our "given" X variable of hours studied on the X axis. Each "dot" is a *data point,* representing an X-Y pair, and each graph is called a *scatterplot.* Again, in data set A we see a positive linear relationship, because the scatterplot follows *one* straight line that is slanted upward, indicating that as the X scores increase, the Y scores also increase. Data set B shows a negative linear relationship, because the scatterplot follows *one* straight line that is slanted downward, indicating that as the X scores increase, the Y scores decrease. Each scatterplot also shows a perfectly consistent relationship, because there is only one data point above each X, indicating that all subjects at a particular X received the same Y score. (In other words, their data points are all on top of one another.) If we were to draw a straight line through each scatterplot, all of the data points would fall on the line, so these are perfect linear relationships.

These characteristics are summarized by calculating the Pearson correlation coefficient. (The formula for computing r is given in Appendix A.) The computed r will have a value between -1.0 and $+1.0$. The coefficient has a positive sign $(+)$ when the relationship is positive and a negative sign $(-)$ when the relationship is negative. The absolute value of r (ignoring the sign) indicates the strength of the relationship. Both of the data sets above produce coefficients of 1.0, indicating that the data form perfectly consistent linear relationships.

Perfect relationships, however, do not occur in the real world of research.

Intermediate-Strength Relationships

Most relationships have an intermediate strength, such that a value of Y *tends* to be paired with a value of X and, as X changes, the value of Y will *tend* to change in a consistent fashion. Figure 3.2 presents examples of intermediate-strength relationships. Looking at the scores, we see one group of different Y scores at one X and a different group of different Y scores at another X. In other words, these data sets contain some **variability,** the extent to which Y scores differ or are spread out. It is the variability in Y scores at each X that works against the strength of a relationship. Instead of consistently seeing a different value of Y at each different value of X, we see (1) different Y scores paired with the same value of X and/or (2) the same value of Y paired with a different value of X.

The way to understand any relationship is to compare it to a perfect relationship. In Figure 3.2, data set A shows a relatively stronger relationship because its pattern is closer to a perfect one: The Y scores at an X do not differ from each other by large amounts, and there are not the same values of Y at different Xs. Thus, there is "close" to one value of Y at each X. Data set B shows a weaker relationship because it is less like a perfect one: Its pattern shows more frequent and larger differences among the Y scores at a particular X, and the Ys at one X often equal the Ys at other Xs.

> *REMEMBER*   The greater the variability of the Y scores at each X, the weaker the relationship.

The same patterns can be seen in the scatterplots. In scatterplot A, different values of Y are associated with an X so a group of different data points appear above each X. Therefore, the scatterplot does not form a straight line but instead resembles a slanting ellipse. However, the ellipse is narrow and "close" to forming a straight line, so the relationship shown is a relatively stronger one. Conversely, scatterplot B shows a weaker relationship because the greater variability in Y scores produces greater vertical spread among the data points above each X. This pattern produces a rather wide ellipse that does not closely form a straight line. (Although both of these examples demonstrate positive relationships, whether a relationship is positive or negative has nothing to do with its strength.)

We can summarize the characteristics of each of these relationships by again computing an r. Since an r of ± 1.0 indicates a perfectly consistent relationship and the

FIGURE 3.2 Data Producing Intermediate-Strength Relationships

Data Set (A) Strong Positive Relationship		Data Set (B) Weak Positive Relationship	
Scores		Scores	
X Study-time	Y Test Scores	X Study-time	Y Test Scores
1	10	1	10
1	20	1	30
1	20	1	50
3	40	3	30
3	50	3	50
3	50	3	70
5	70	5	50
5	80	5	70
5	80	5	90

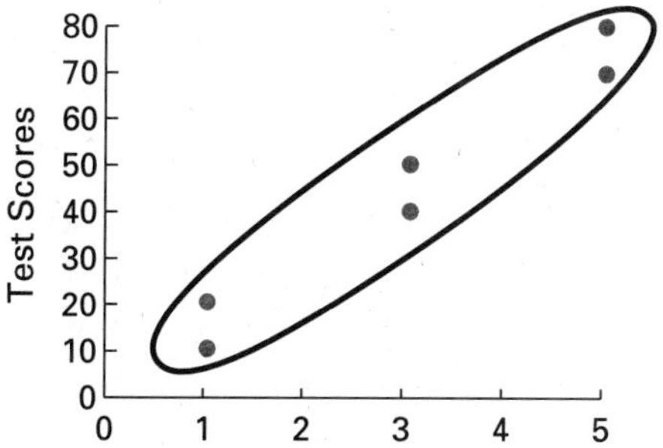

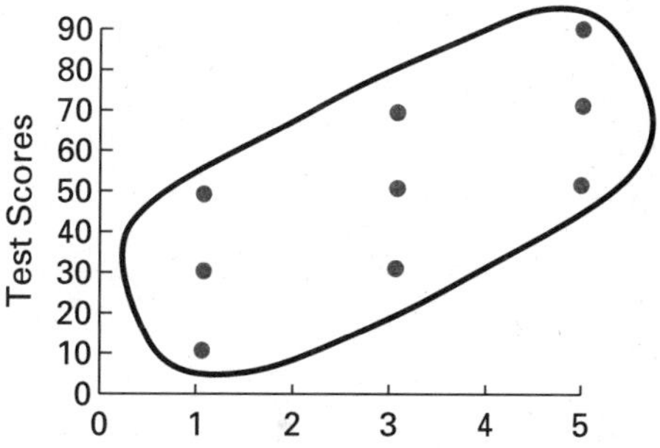

relationships shown in Figure 3.2 are not perfectly consistent, the absolute value of r will be less than 1.0. The closer the value of r is to 1.0, however, the closer the relationship comes to forming a perfect relationship, and the closer the scatterplot comes to forming a straight line. Thus, the r from data set A will only be larger than that from data set B.

No Relationship

Figure 3.3 shows data that do not form a relationship. This pattern is as far from that of a perfect relationship as we can get. There is not one, or even "close" to one, value of Y associated with only one value of X, nor is there a consistent change in the Y scores as X scores change. Instead, the same distribution of Y scores tends to show up at every X score. Further, the scatterplot in this figure is *not* slanted, indicating that the Y scores show no tendency to increase or decrease in a consistent fashion. Such data will produce a correlation coefficient of 0.0.

FIGURE 3.3   Data Producing No Relationship

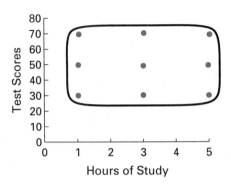

Scores

X	Y
Study-time	Test Scores
1	30
1	50
1	70
3	30
3	50
3	70
5	30
5	50
5	70

Thus, in sum, an r of ± 1.0 indicates a perfectly consistent linear relationship, and that an r of 0.0 indicates no linear relationship. For intermediate-strength relationships, the absolute value of r will be greater than 0.0 but less than 1.0. The way to interpret such values is to compare them to 1.0 and 0.0. The closer the r is to ± 1.0, then the closer to one value are the Y scores at an X, the less the same Y scores occur with different Xs, and the more the scatterplot approximates a slanted straight line. Conversely, the closer the r is to 0.0, the larger the variability in the Y scores occurring at each X, the more the same Y scores occur at different X scores, and the less the scatterplot resembles a slanted straight line.

REMEMBER   The sign of r indicates a *positive* or *negative linear relationship*, and the absolute value of r indicates the strength of the relationship.

Graphing Correlational Data

The purpose of a graph is to simplify the relationship in the data. With real data, however, the typical scatterplot contains many data points, so it is difficult to see the relationship. Therefore, we summarize the scatterplot by plotting the linear regression line. The **linear regression line** is the straight line that summarizes a linear relationship. (Appendix A describes the calculations for creating the regression line, and these calculations are reviewed in Chapter 9.) In essence, it is the straight line we expect would be formed if the data produced a perfect relationship. Figure 3.4 shows the scatterplot and regression line we might obtain from our study-time data.

Because our goal is to *summarize* data, we would normally not plot the individual data points. Figure 3.4 shows these data points, however, so you can see that the regression line passes through the center of the scatterplot, "splitting" the Y scores such that data points above the line are, on the whole, as far from the line as those below it. The fact that the scores are equally split makes the regression line the *best fitting line* for describing the linear relationship buried in the data. The "slope" of the regression line—how much it

FIGURE 3.4 Scatterplot and Regression Line Showing Test Grades as a Function of Hours Studied

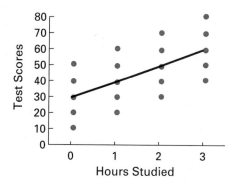

slants—indicates the rate at which Y scores change as X increases. A steeply sloped line indicates a relatively large change in Y scores for each increase in X. A mildly sloped regression line indicates a relatively small change in Y scores for each increase in X. And when the data produce no relationship, the regression line is horizontal, indicating no change in Y as X increases.

> *REMEMBER*   The *correlation coefficient* and a graph of the *linear regression line* are the primary descriptive statistics for summarizing a correlational design.

Interpreting the Sample Correlation Coefficient

As we'll see, our next step will be to perform the appropriate inferential statistical procedures. After that as you know, the study must be evaluated in terms of reliability and the various types of validity discussed in the previous chapter, to be sure that we are not being misled by flaws in the design. If our study passes these tests, our *descriptive* statistics will be the basis both for testing the hypothesis of the study and for interpreting the results.

Let's say that after collecting our study-time data, we compute an r of $+.50$. From this, we know two things. First, even without seeing the data, we know that there is a positive linear relationship between the variables: As the number of hours studied increases, test grades also tend to increase. Originally, our hypothesis led us to predict a positive linear relationship; now, a positive value of r provides evidence that confirms our hypothesis. A negative r would have been contrary to the relationship predicted by our hypothesis, thus disconfirming the hypothesis. In a different study, the hypothesis might lead us to predict only some kind of relationship, either positive or negative. Then either a positive or negative value of r would confirm our hypothesis.

Second, we also know that an r with an absolute value of .50 indicates a reasonably strong, consistent relationship, which in turn forms a relatively narrow elliptical scatterplot. The strength of the relationship is important to our hypothesis, particularly if we have predicted a relationship of a particular strength. (For example, we might state that r has to be at least $+.25$ to confirm our hypothesis.) More commonly, a nonzero relationship confirms our hypothesis. Even then, however, the strength of the relationship is important, because it gives us a *hint* about what the relationship reflects.

We assume that everything in nature has an explanation. Therefore, as we will see, we first consider whether the inconsistency in a relationship is due to problems of reliability and validity. Beyond this consideration, however, the inconsistency in the relationship suggests whether there are other variables related to test grades that we have not taken into account. An r of $+.90$, for example, indicates extreme consistency, suggesting that only a few, rather unimportant variables are related to test grades in addition to hours studied. Conversely, an r of $+.09$ would indicate great inconsistency, suggesting the presence of other important variables related to test grades that we have not considered. Following this line of reasoning, we begin to interpret our results "psychologically," considering what the consistency and inconsistency in our relationship indicate about test grades and hours studied, and how they relate to our theoretical explanations, models, and constructs involving learning and concept formation. However, we are employing a descriptive, correlational design, so we cannot infer causality. (As a frame of reference, note that a relationship in psychological research is considered reasonably strong when it produces an r in the neighborhood of $\pm.40$. An r of $\pm.60$ is downright impressive.)

It's important to realize that, although the value of r is *interpreted* as reflecting the degree of consistency in a relationship, it does not directly measure "units of consistency." Thus, for example, an r of $+.60$ indicates a more consistent relationship than, say, an r of $+.30$, but when r is .60 the relationship is *not* twice as consistent as when r is .30. The way to directly compute the amount of consistency in a relationship is to square the value of r. By squaring the correlation coefficient (r^2), we compute the proportion of variance in Y that is accounted for by the relationship with X. We'll see more of this statistic in later chapters. For now, think of the **proportion of variance accounted for** as the extent to which we can explain, predict, or "account for" differences in Y scores by using our knowledge of the relationship with X. The greater the proportion of variance accounted for, the more valuable the relationship is for understanding when subjects will have one Y score and when they will have a different Y score.

> **REMEMBER**   Research is interpreted on the basis of the type and strength of the relationship found in the sample. The value of r^2 indicates the *proportion of variance* in Y scores that can be accounted for by the relationship with X.

Nonlinear Relationships

We do not always predict a linear relationship. In a **nonlinear relationship,** as the X scores increase, the pattern of changing Y scores does not fit one straight line. Figure 3.5 shows two examples of nonlinear relationships.

In scatterplot A, as the X scores increase, the Y scores also increase at first; but beyond a certain X, the Y scores change direction and tend to decrease. Coincidentally, these data show a relatively strong relationship, in that the pattern they form is relatively

FIGURE 3.5   Scatterplots Showing Nonlinear Relationships

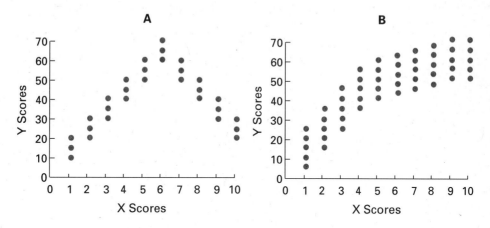

consistent. In scatterplot B, as *X* scores increase, *Y* scores at first tend to increase sharply; but beyond a certain *X*, they change their direction, tending to increase only slightly. Coincidentally, these data show a weaker relationship, in that larger variability in *Y* scores is found at each *X*.

Other nonlinear relationships may be more complex, following a wavy line that repeatedly changes direction. Regardless of the direction of change, the strength of such relationships is the consistency with which a particular value of *Y* is associated with each value of *X*. Remember, however, that the Pearson correlation coefficient describes the extent to which the data form a *linear* relationship. As we'll see, if our intent is to summarize a nonlinear relationship (or when we cannot meet other assumptions of the Pearson correlation), we compute other types of correlation coefficients.

DESCRIBING THE RELATIONSHIP IN AN EXPERIMENT

To show that greater study time *causes* higher test grades, we would conduct an experiment. Our independent variable could again be defined as the amount of time subjects study for a test, and our dependent variable could be subjects' grades on a multiple-choice test. Let's say we randomly select and randomly assign subjects to one of four conditions of study time, having them study new material in a controlled laboratory setting for either 0, 1, 2, or 3 hours. After studying for the assigned time, all subjects take the test. With the data in hand, we will look for a relationship where, as the conditions of the independent variable of study time change, scores on the dependent variable of test grades also tend to change.

Here again we have a system for identifying the *X* and *Y* variables and communicating our relationship. Since the researcher determines the time a subject will spend studying, the "given" *X* variable is the independent variable of hours of study time. In experiments, we always look for a change in scores on the dependent variable *as a function of* changes in the independent variable. In our study-time experiment, then, we examine changes in test grades as a function of changes in hours spent studying.

> *REMEMBER*   The conditions of the independent variable are the X scores, and scores from the dependent variable are the Y scores. The relationship is described as "changes in the dependent variable as a function of changes in the independent variable."

Notice that the relationship we are dealing with in our experiment is the same as that in our correlational study: In both cases we predict a positive linear relationship such that increased study time is associated with increased test grades.

You might think that our next step would be to compute the Pearson correlation coefficient in our experiment, again correlating subjects' study times and test grades. However, in experiments we do not usually limit ourselves to describing only the linear relationship formed by the X-Y pairs. Also, as we'll see, if the Pearson correlation coefficient is to accurately describe a relationship, a rather wide range of X scores is required. However, as in our experiment with only four study times, we usually deal with only a few conditions or X scores, so r will not accurately summarize the strength of the relationship. Therefore, in an experiment we must go about describing the type and strength of the relationship using different procedures than those used in a correlational design.

Describing Central Tendency

To find the pattern of increasing Y scores in our relationship, we first need to know whether the test grades in each study-time condition are generally low, medium, or high scores. Toward this end, we summarize the dependent scores in each condition by computing a **measure of central tendency.** The common measures of central tendency are the mean, the *median,* and the *mode,* and each of these is a way of indicating the score at which the center of a distribution of scores tends to be located. Which statistics we compute depends first on the way we measure the *dependent* variable. Usually, we obtain interval or ratio scores that are approximately normally distributed so that parametric statistical procedures are appropriate. Under these circumstances, the mean score is the most accurate measure of central tendency. The **mean** score, symbolized $\bar{X}$, is the average of a group of scores, interpreted as the score "around" which the scores in a distribution tend to be clustered. (Later we'll see that the mode and median are used with nonparametric procedures.)

Let's say that we've tested an unrealistically small number of subjects in each condition, obtaining the subjects' scores and the mean scores shown in Table 3.1. Inside each column are subjects' test grades—their *dependent* scores. Underneath each column is the mean test score for the condition. By examining how the mean scores change with the conditions, we determine whether a relationship is present: A study time of 0 hours results in a distribution of scores "around" the mean score of 18.33; a study time of 1 hour results in a different distribution of scores located around the mean of 20.00; study times of 2 and 3 hours result in still other distributions around 25.00 and 31.67,

TABLE 3.1   Test Scores as a Function of Hours Studied

	Independent variable: Hours studied			
	0-hour condition	*1-hour condition*	*2-hour condition*	*3-hour condition*
Test scores	10 20 25	5 25 30	15 25 35	20 35 40
	$\bar{X} = 18.33$	$\bar{X} = 20.00$	$\bar{X} = 25.00$	$\bar{X} = 31.67$

respectively. Because the mean scores tend to increase as study time increases, we know that the individual test scores tend to increase as study time increases. Thus, a relationship is present whenever we observe *differences* between the means of the conditions. Conversely, if the means in all conditions were the same value, we would conclude that virtually the same distribution of dependent scores is present in each condition and, thus, that no relationship exists.

Recognize, however, that not *all* of the mean values have to differ for a relationship to be present. For example, we might find that only the mean test score in the 0-hour condition is different from the mean test score in the 3-hour condition. We still see a relationship here, because, *at least sometimes,* as the conditions of the independent variable changed, the dependent scores also tended to change.

> *REMEMBER*   When the *mean* scores change along with changes in the conditions, we can conclude that scores on the dependent variable have changed as a function of changes in the independent variable—so a relationship is present.

Graphing the Results of an Experiment

Researchers typically graph the results of an experiment by creating a *line graph*. The above data from our study-time experiment produce the line graph shown in Figure 3.6.

Before we interpret this graph, notice how it is drawn. The X axis shows the conditions of the independent variable, and the Y axis shows the *mean* scores on the dependent variable. Each data point is the mean score for a condition, and then adjacent data points are connected with straight lines.

> *REMEMBER*   The results of an experiment are graphed with the independent variable on the X axis and the dependent variable on the Y axis.

A line graph functions in the same way as a regression line except that the line graph is not necessarily the best fitting *straight* line across the entire relationship. The

FIGURE 3.6   Line Graph Showing Mean Test Scores as a Function of Study Time
Each data point is the mean score for a condition.

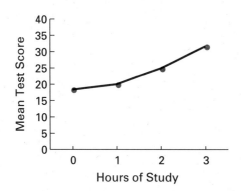

vertical location of each mean implies a distribution of Y scores around that value of Y. When the location of the mean on the Y axis changes as the conditions change, we know that there is a different distribution of scores for each condition and, thus, that a relationship exists. As in Figure 3.6, a line graph that tends to form an upward-slanting line indicates a largely positive linear relationship. Conversely, a graph that tends to slope downward indicates a largely negative linear relationship. And a line graph that fluctuates up and down indicates a nonlinear relationship. How steeply a line is sloped indicates the average rate of change in dependent scores as the conditions change. A horizontal line graph indicates no relationship, because it shows no change in means so virtually the same scores are found in each condition.

Describing Variability

To begin to see the strength of a relationship in experimental data, we can describe the variability of the Y scores in each condition. **Measures of variability** are numbers that summarize the extent to which scores in a distribution differ. When the mean is the appropriate measure of central tendency for the dependent scores we are measuring, the two appropriate measures of variability are the sample variance and the sample standard deviation. These are methods for calculating the extent to which scores in a condition differ, or "deviate," from the mean of the condition. The **sample variance** is the average of the squared deviations of the scores around the mean. Essentially, this number is interpreted such that a larger variance indicates *relatively* more variability or differences between the scores in the condition. A more direct measure is the **sample standard deviation,** which is the square root of the sample variance. Essentially, this number is interpreted as roughly indicating the "average" amount by which the scores in the condition deviate from the mean of the condition. (Computations are shown in Appendix A.) The important thing to remember is that these measures communicate how much the scores in a condition differ or are spread out, and thus indicate the inconsistency of the scores in that condition.

REMEMBER We usually summarize the relationship in an experiment by computing the *mean* and *standard deviation* in each condition and by plotting a line graph.

Interpreting the Means and Standard Deviations

As in our correlational study, we would now perform the appropriate inferential procedures and evaluate the reliability and validity of our experiment. Again, however, note that our interpretation of any experiment ultimately depends on the type and strength of the relationship in the sample data. In the case of our study-time experiment, we will examine the mean and standard deviation for each condition shown in Table 3.2.

It is by examining the differences between the mean scores that we can see how and when test grades change as study time increases. Recall that, on the basis of our hypothesis, we originally predicted test grades would increase as study time increased. Now we see that the means in Table 3.2 form a somewhat positive linear relationship, thus providing evidence that confirms our hypothesis. If instead we had insufficient information to predict a specific type of relationship, we would have predicted a relationship of some kind. In that case, a negative linear relationship or any nonlinear relationship would also have confirmed our hypothesis.

Each standard deviation in the table communicates the variability or spread of test grades in a condition. However, we must be rather subjective in describing the strength of the relationship using these numbers. Back in Table 3.1 we saw that the lowest score in the experiment was 5 and the highest was 40, so the test grades differ by as much as 35 points. Therefore, the relationship *seems* to be relatively consistent, given that the scores in each condition differ by an "average" of only 6 to 10 points. (If each standard deviation equaled 0.0, we would find the same score within each condition and a perfectly consistent relationship.)

To produce a less subjective interpretation of the strength of a relationship, we must compute it directly. As we will see in later chapters, statistical procedures similar to computing r^2 are available for this purpose. These procedures are the *only* way to *directly* measure the strength of a relationship and, thus, to determine the extent to which the independent variable accounts for differences in subjects' scores.

REMEMBER To directly measure the strength of the relationship in an experiment, we must compute the proportion of variance accounted for.

TABLE 3.2   Mean and Standard Deviation of Test Scores in Each Condition of Study-Time

	Independent variable: Hours studied			
	0-hour condition	*1-hour condition*	*2-hour condition*	*3-hour condition*
Mean	18.33	20.00	25.00	31.67
Standard deviation	6.23	10.80	8.16	8.5

Once we know the strength and type of relationship in our sample data, we can interpret the relationship by considering what its consistency and inconsistency indicate about the behaviors and constructs under study. In our study-time experiment, the extent to which test scores are consistently related to study time suggests the extent to which test grades are "caused" by study time. A highly consistent relationship would suggest that study time has a major, controlling effect on test scores: It seems to be *the* variable that determines a score. Conversely, a weak, inconsistent relationship would suggest that in addition to study time, there are other factors that cause or influence test grades (perhaps intelligence or motivation is important). Following this line of reasoning, we will interpret our results "psychologically," adding to our understanding of the relevant constructs and behaviors.

APPLYING INFERENTIAL STATISTICAL PROCEDURES

As we have seen, descriptive statistics help us decide whether there is a relationship between the scores in our sample. However, before we can generalize about what the relationship represents in terms of our variables and constructs, we must decide whether the sample relationship represents anything at all. The problem is that, even though we may find a *mathematical* relationship in our sample, it does not necessarily represent a real relationship in nature. By "real" relationship, we mean there is some underlying aspect of nature that actually associates a particular *Y* score with a particular *X* score. Here we are not considering whether the data are reliable or valid for our purposes. Regardless of what the scores may measure, our most basic inference is that there is some unseen process that actually ties the *X* and *Y* scores together, such that the relationship in the sample represents a relationship that actually exists in nature. *Inferential statistical procedures* help us to decide if a sample relationship represents a relationship that actually exists.

If the relationship does not actually exist, then how did we obtain sample data that forms a mathematical relationship? The answer is, by chance! If you drop a handful of coins, by chance they may land in such a way as to form a somewhat linear pattern. Likewise, perhaps our test grades also paired up by chance with study times to form a somewhat linear pattern. If so, we might see a relationship in our sample data even though no such relationship exists in nature. In research terminology, if there is no real relationship between the scores, then in the *population* of such scores, no relationship exists. In other words, the sample of scores may form a relationship by chance, but the data are *unrepresentative* of a population of scores where the relationship does not exist. To communicate that the scores in the sample are unrepresentative of the population to some degree, we say that the sample contains *sampling error*.

To see how sampling error might mislead us, assume that we can examine study times and test grades for the entire population using our correlational and experimental designs. Let's say we obtain the two scatterplots shown in Figure 3.7. Having measured the population using our correlational design, we might produce scatterplot A, which shows no relationship. Then the results we originally obtained in our sample are due to sampling error. What the ellipse encloses are those scores we obtained creating the

FIGURE 3.7   Hypothetical Population Scatterplots

These scatterplots show obtained sample relationships even though no such relationships exist in the population.

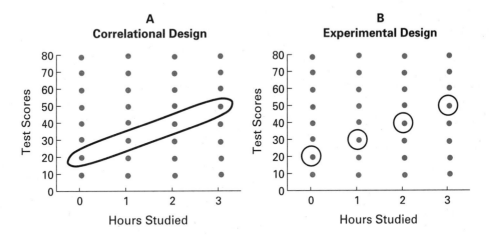

illusion of a relationship: By chance, the X and Y scores pair up in such a way as to form a linear pattern, even though the population itself does not show this pattern. Also, our original correlation coefficient of $+.50$ reflects sampling error, poorly representing a population correlation of 0.0.

Likewise, in our experiment, we might find the population of scores shown in scatter-plot B, where changes in the independent variable result in the same scores each time. In this case, the four circles enclose the scores we obtained in each condition of our original experiment: By chance, the scores in the 0-hour condition are rather low, those in the 1-hour condition are higher, and so on. Because of sampling error, our sample scores increase with amount of study time, even though they do not increase in the population. Likewise, the sample means tend to increase, even though the same population mean is found in each condition.

Thus, for any type of design, we can propose the statistical hypothesis that the predicted relationship does not exist in the population. This statement is called the null hypothesis. The **null hypothesis** implies that, because of sampling error, the sample data poorly represent the absence of the predicted relationship in the population of scores.

On the other hand, of course, our sample data may represent a real relationship. This statement is called the alternative hypothesis. In statistics, the **alternative hypothesis** implies that our sample data represent the situation where the predicted relationship exists in the population of scores.

> *REMEMBER*   The *null hypothesis* implies that the sample data poorly represent the absence of the predicted relationship in the population of scores. The *alternative hypothesis* implies that the sample data represent the predicted relationship in the population of scores.

The Logic of Inferential Statistics

Inferential statistics test the null hypothesis. Remember that by claiming the relationship exists, we ultimately support our hypothesis about a behavior. But it makes no sense to conclude that higher test grades are associated with greater study time if our results are actually due to random chance. Therefore, if sampling error can explain our results, we will *not* claim that the relationship exists. Only if we can *disconfirm* the null hypothesis do we claim that our data represent a real relationship.

The logic of inferential procedures is actually quite simple. Although we cannot know whether a sample relationship reflects a real relationship, we can determine the probability of obtaining a particular sample relationship by chance. Say we obtain a very weak, barely consistent sample relationship, in which only a few scores form anything close to a consistent pattern. The null hypothesis says that this pattern is due to chance—and, in reality, our sample poorly represents a population of scores in which no relationship exists. We can accept this explanation because intuitively the odds are very high that a few scores might pair up by chance when no real relationship exists. In this case, we "retain" the null hypothesis. Conversely, however, let's say we obtained a perfectly consistent relationship. The null hypothesis again says that this pattern is due to sampling error, but here we cannot accept this explanation. Our perfect sample relationship is "unbelievably" unrepresentative of a population in which no relationship exists, and the probability of getting such a relationship through sampling error is extremely small. Such a low probability is taken as evidence that disconfirms the null hypothesis. Because such a sample relationship is *too unlikely* to be produced by sampling error, we "reject" the null hypothesis, thus rejecting the idea that no real relationship exists. We must look for another explanation for our results. The only one left is the alternative hypothesis that our sample data represent a real relationship.

Selecting an Inferential Procedure

Every inferential procedure involves a statistical model called a *sampling distribution*. This model allows us to determine the probability of finding a particular relationship in a random sample of numbers, when the sample represents a population of similar numbers in which no relationship exists. If we treat the scores from our randomly selected subjects as a random sample of numbers, we can use a sampling distribution to determine the probability of obtaining our data by chance if they represent no real relationship. However, the probability of obtaining a particular relationship by chance depends on the characteristics of our design (the way the relationship is summarized, how many groups are involved, etc.). Therefore, our first step is to select the appropriate inferential procedure to be used for our particular study.

There is a specific inferential procedure for each type of correlation coefficient. One procedure is appropriate for the parametric Pearson correlation coefficient, other procedures are suitable for nonparametric coefficients. There are also specific parametric and nonparametric inferential procedures for different types of experiments. In these designs, our choice depends first on the scale of measurement we are using to measure the *dependent variable*. As mentioned, we usually obtain interval or ratio types of dependent scores that are approximately normally distributed, and so it is appropriate to compute the mean of each condition. With such data, the most common parametric inferential procedures are the two-sample t-test and the analysis of variance.

Two-sample t-test   We perform the **two-sample t-test** when conducting an experiment consisting of only two conditions of the independent variable. For example, we could use the t-test and compute t, if we conducted our study-time experiment by comparing only subjects who studied for 1 hour with those who studied for 2 hours.

There are two ways to calculate t. The one we use depends on the design of our experiment. The **independent samples t-test** is appropriate when we randomly select and assign subjects to one condition without regard to the subjects we assign to the other condition. This t-test would be used if we randomly selected one group to test after studying for 1 hour and another group to test after studying for 2 hours. The **dependent samples t-test,** on the other hand, would be used if we were more selective in assigning subjects. Also called the "paired samples t-test" or the "related samples t-test," this procedure is used in either of two designs. We can pair the samples by *matching* each subject in one condition with a subject in the other, creating a *matched groups design*. Or we can *repeatedly measure* one group of subjects under both conditions, creating a *repeated measures design*. (How we decide between these two designs is discussed in Chapter 7.)

In either two-sample t-test, we compare the scores in one group to the scores in the other group. Let's say we obtain the data shown in Table 3.3. Essentially, the stronger the relationship—the more consistent the differences in test scores between the conditions—then the less likely it is that our results reflect sampling error, and the more likely it is that they reflect a real relationship. (Note: when only two groups are being considered, the relationship will be either a positive or negative *linear* one, with scores going either up or down with increased study time.)

Analysis of Variance   For an experiment with three or more conditions, we perform an **analysis of variance,** or **ANOVA,** computing the value of F. (When there only two conditions, we can use *either* the t-test or ANOVA.) In ANOVA the independent variable is called a **factor** and the conditions of the independent variable are called **levels** of the

TABLE 3.3   A Two-Sample Experiment Investigating Test Scores as a Function of Hours Studied

	Independent variable: Hours studied	
	1-hour condition	*2-hour condition*
Test scores	5 25 30	15 25 35
	$\bar{X} = 20.00$	$\bar{X} = 25.00$

TABLE 3.4   Test Scores as a Function of Hours Studied

	Independent variable: Hours studied			
	0-hour condition	*1-hour condition*	*2-hour condition*	*3-hour condition*
Test scores	10 20 25	5 25 30	15 25 35	20 35 40
	$\bar{X} = 18.33$	$\bar{X} = 20.00$	$\bar{X} = 25.00$	$\bar{X} = 31.67$

factor. Thus, in our original experiment we had four levels (0, 1, 2, and 3 hours) of our factor of study time.

As with the t-test, there are two ways to calculate F. We perform the **between-subjects** ANOVA when we randomly select and assign subjects to one level without regard to the subjects we select for the other level. We perform the **within-subjects** ANOVA when we match each subject in one level with a subject in the other levels or, more commonly, when we repeatedly measure one group of subjects under all levels of the factor.

Either way, the F statistic simultaneously compares the scores in all conditions. Table 3.4 shows the original study-time data in our experiment with four levels. Here, too, the stronger the relationship—the more consistent the differences in test scores between the conditions—then the less likely it is that our results reflect sampling error, and the more likely it is that they reflect a real relationship. (Note: because more than two conditions are involved, the relationship may be linear or nonlinear.)

The formulas for t-tests and ANOVA are presented in Appendix A (along with those for other inferential procedures we will encounter). To help you select a procedure, the previous discussion is summarized in Figure 3.8.

INTERPRETING INFERENTIAL STATISTICS

In any inferential procedure, we use our sample data to calculate a statistic called the *obtained value*. This statistic summarizes the relationship in the data in a way that allows us to determine the likelihood of obtaining the results by chance. The calculated values of t, F, and r are all obtained values. The larger the obtained value, the less likely it is that sampling error alone produced the relationship in our sample data. To decide whether an obtained value is large enough to reject the null hypothesis, we compare it to a value from our statistical model called the *critical value*. This is the minimum obtained value that is needed to indicate that our results are "too unlikely" to occur by chance. Within a particular procedure, the critical value for a study depends on three things:

FIGURE 3.8 Common Inferential Procedures Used in Experiments with Normally Distributed Interval or Ratio Dependent Scores

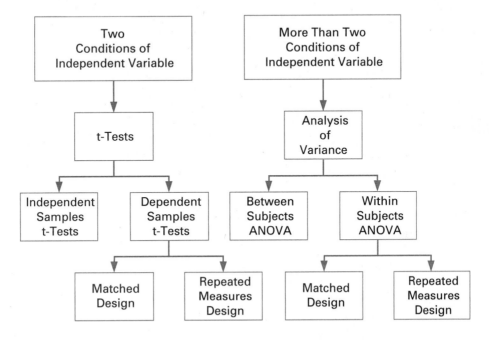

1. The *alpha level:* Symbolized by α, this is the probability we select that defines "too unlikely." Psychologists have agreed that alpha should be .05 at most (although we may set it at a smaller value). If the probability of obtaining our sample relationship by chance is *less* than alpha, it is by definition too unlikely to occur by chance.

2. The *degrees of freedom:* Symbolized by *df,* these are based upon *N,* the number of subjects in our study. The critical value and thus our decision about a relationship is influenced by our *N,* because although 2 subjects may be likely to produce a particular relationship by chance, 2,000 are not.

3. A *one-tailed* or *two-tailed test:* Both *r* and *t* describe a linear relationship, and so we may or may not predict the direction of the relationship. With *r,* we perform the one-tailed test when we specifically predict only a positive correlation coefficient or only a negative one. With *t,* we perform the one-tailed test when we predict that the mean of one condition will only be larger or only be smaller than the mean of the other condition (that is, when predicting only a positive or a negative relationship). We perform a two-tailed test with these statistics when we predict that a relationship is present but cannot predict whether it will be positive or negative. (The ANOVA is always a two-tailed test in which, for statistical purposes, we do not predict the type of linear or nonlinear relationship that our data represent.)

For whichever procedure we use, we go to the appropriate statistical tables (in Appendix B) and find the critical value for our alpha level (usually .05) and our *df*. Then, in a two-tailed test we determine whether the absolute value of our obtained value is *greater than* the critical value. And in a one-tailed test, we determine whether *t* or *r* is greater than the critical value *and* whether the positive or negative relationship we predicted is present. If the obtained value is greater than the critical value, then the probability of obtaining our results by chance is less than .05 if the relationship does not exist in the population. A probability of less than .05 is small enough to convince us that our results are not due to chance. Therefore, we reject the null hypothesis and accept the alternative hypothesis.

We communicate our decision to reject the null hypothesis by stating that our results are significant. The word **significant** indicates that the relationship found in our sample is too unlikely to occur by chance, so we assume that it represents the real, predicted relationship found in the population. Or we may find that our sample *r* of +.50 is "significantly different from zero," communicating that +.50 is too large to obtain by chance if the data represent a population coefficient of 0.0. Or we may say that the means of the conditions in our *t*-test "differ significantly," communicating that the difference between them is too large to obtain by chance if they represent the one population mean that would occur with no relationship.

If our obtained value is *not* greater than the critical value, then our results are not too unlikely to occur through sampling error. Therefore, we do not have sufficient disconfirming evidence to reject the null hypothesis, so we do not accept the alternative hypothesis that the data represent a relationship in the population. We describe such results as **nonsignificant.**

> *REMEMBER*   In every study, we must determine whether our sample relationship is *significant* or *nonsignificant.*

Comparing the Conditions in ANOVA

We are not finished with inferential procedures even when our obtained *F* is significant. A significant *F* does not indicate that *all* of the means are significantly different. Rather, it indicates that *at least two* conditions are likely to represent a real relationship. Therefore, after we find a significant *F*, our second step is usually to perform *post hoc* comparisons. ***Post hoc* comparisons** compare all possible pairs of conditions to determine which ones differ significantly from each other. As we will see, performing these procedures is similar to performing *t*-tests on all possible pairs of levels in the factor. Thus, in our study-time experiment we would compare the 0-hour and one-hour conditions, then compare the 0-hour and 2-hour conditions, then compare the 1-hour and 2-hour conditions, and so on.

We perform *post hoc* comparisons *only* when the obtained *F* is significant (and they are necessary only when there are more than two levels in the factor). Instead of computing *F* and then performing *post hoc* tests, you can take a different approach and perform planned comparisons. **Planned comparisons** are procedures for comparing only some conditions in an experiment. In our study-time experiment, for example, a hypothesis might lead us to compare the zero study-time condition to each of the other conditions—that is, without comparing the 1- and 2-hour conditions, the 2- and 3-hour conditions, etc. Planned comparisons are also called *a priori* comparisons. (In these procedures, *F* need not be computed.)

> **REMEMBER**   We perform either *post hoc* comparisons or planned comparisons to determine which levels in a factor differ significantly. Such procedures identify those conditions that form a "real" relationship.

Estimating the Population Parameters

If our results are significant, we can use the data to estimate the characteristics of the relationship we would expect to find if we studied the entire population. Numbers that describe the characteristics of a population of scores are called **parameters.** A correlation coefficient describing the relationship in the population of scores is called "rho," symbolized by ρ, and the mean of a population of scores is called "mu," symbolized by μ. Thus, if the r of $+.50$ from our correlational study is significant, we estimate that, in the population, ρ would be approximately $+.50$. We also expect that the sample's regression line reflects the regression line that would be found for the population. Likewise, in our study-time experiment we would use the means of those conditions that differ significantly to estimate the corresponding population μs. For example, if our sample mean of 18.33 for 0 hours of study time differs significantly from the other sample means, we estimate that after testing the population under this condition, the population μ would be approximately 18.33. We also expect the line graph that describes our sample data to reflect the line graph that would be found for the population. (To estimate the population values of the standard deviation and variance in a condition, we compute the *estimated population variance* or the *estimated population standard deviation,* using the formulas in Appendix A.)

Notice that we expect the population parameters to *approximate* the statistics found in our sample. Even if we now believe that the sample data form a real relationship, we may still have sampling error such that the sample data do not perfectly represent the scores that would be found in the population. To factor in the possibility of sampling error, we compute a confidence interval. A **confidence interval** describes a range of values in the population, any one of which our sample statistic is likely to represent. For example, instead of saying that 0 hours of study time would produce a population μ "around" our sample mean of 18.33, we calculate the range of values of μ that the sample mean is likely to represent. In other words, we compute those values of μ that are not significantly different from our sample mean. As shown in the following diagram, when computing a confidence interval we compute the highest and lowest values of μ that are not significantly different from our sample mean.

$$\mu \ldots \mu\ \mu\ \mu\ \mu\ 18.33\ \mu\ \mu\ \mu\ \mu \ldots \mu$$

Lowest and highest values of μ
likely to be represented by
our sample mean

Because all values of μ between these two values are also not significantly different from the sample mean, it is likely that the sample mean represents one of them. (Computations are shown in Appendix A.) Likewise, for a correlation, we can compute the highest and lowest value of ρ that is not significantly different from our sample coefficient.

> REMEMBER   A *confidence interval contains* the values of the population parameter that a sample statistic is not significantly different from and, thus, is likely to represent.

Interpreting Significant Results

When our results are significant, we are confident that the sample relationship represents a real relationship. However, even after performing the methodical statistical procedures discussed above, researchers are still cautious in their conclusions. When making inferences about a significant relationship, we must bear in mind two restrictions.

Type I Errors   A significant result does not "prove" that the relationship exists in the population. All that we have "proven" is that sampling error would be unlikely to produce our sample relationship, if the relationship does not exist in the population. But, unlikely means unlikely—not impossible. However slight, the possibility exists that the null hypothesis is true: that the relationship does not exist in the population, but sampling error produced unrepresentative data that give the appearance of a relationship. Thus, whenever our results are significant, it is possible that we have made a Type I error. A **Type I error** occurs when we reject the null hypothesis when in fact it is the correct hypothesis. In other words, we say that our data reflect a real relationship when in fact they do not.

Although we never know for sure if the null hypothesis is true, we do know the probability that we will decide to reject null when it is true: Our alpha level is the probability that we will make a Type I error. The reason psychologists have agreed that alpha can be no greater than .05 is that, when we reject the null hypothesis, the probability that we have rejected a true null hypothesis is less than .05. Then, because the probability of making a Type I error is so small, we are confident that we have not made such an error. But it is still possible that we have!

Type I errors can have an especially dangerous impact on society. For example, we would not want to conclude that a drug having potentially dangerous side-effects cures an illness if in fact our results reflect mere chance sampling error. In such situations, we may set alpha at a smaller value, such as at .01, so that we have only a 1% chance of saying the relationship exists when in fact it does not.

Interpreting the Relationship   Our second restriction is that the term "significant" indicates *only* that the relationship between the *numbers* in our data is unlikely to occur if the sample represents a population of *numbers* in which the relationship does not exist. It does not mean that our scores accurately reflect our variables, or that the behaviors and constructs are related in the way that we hypothesized. Thus, once our results are significant, our job has only just begun.

As we've seen, one of our most important tasks as researchers is to interpret and explain a relationship "psychologically," so that we understand what it tells us about the nature of behavior. First, however, we consider whether there are flaws in our design. Do we have reliable and content valid measurements, or do the scores reflect error or unintended variables? Do we have internal validity, or are there confounding variables operating? Do we have external validity so that our results generalize to other subjects and situations? Only if we have performed a well-designed study can we be confident that the relationship between our scores reflects the relationship between our variables that we have predicted. Then, to the extent that we have confidence in our results, we consider what the consistency and lack of consistency in the sample relationship indicate about the variables, constructs, and relationships as they occur in nature.

> REMEMBER   *"Significant* results" mean only that we are confident there is a "real" relationship in the population of scores, even though we may not know what it is that the scores or relationship reflect.

Interpreting Nonsignificant Results

If our results are not significant, we have not "proven" that the predicted relationship does not exist in the population. We have simply found that chance *could* reasonably produce data such as ours when the relationship does not exist. But because chance could do so does not mean that it *did* do so. For example, let's say we obtain a sample r of $+.10$ that turns out to be nonsignificant. There are three possible reasons why this might happen: (1) Maybe a population relationship does not exist and this sample relationship occurred because of sampling error; (2) maybe the sample perfectly represents a similar relationship in the population, but an r of $+.10$ is so weak that our statistics "misinterpret" it as reflecting sampling error; or (3) maybe there is a very strong relationship in the population but, because of sampling error, we have an unrepresentative sample that produced this weak r. The same arguments apply to nonsignificant differences between sample means: Maybe they really do not reflect a relationship, or maybe we have erroneously concluded that they do not reflect a relationship.

With nonsignificant results, we have merely failed to disconfirm the null hypothesis, so both it and the alternative hypothesis are still viable interpretations. Accordingly, we cannot decide whether the relationship exists in the population or not. Therefore, we play it safe: we do not consider the sample relationship as confirming or disconfirming the hypothesis of our study, and we do not even begin to interpret it psychologically.

> REMEMBER   Nonsignificant results provide no convincing evidence—one way or the other—as to whether a "real" relationship exists.

Because it is possible that a particular relationship exists in the population even though our results are nonsignificant, it is also possible that we are making an error whenever we retain the null hypothesis. This is called a **Type II error:** We retain the null hypothesis although it is false and the alternative is the correct hypothesis. In other words, we conclude that there is no evidence for the predicted relationship in the population when, in fact, the relationship exists.

STATISTICAL POWER AND RESEARCH DESIGN

Type I and Type II errors are mutually exclusive: If we've made one type of error, then we cannot have made the other type. Sometimes (although we never know when) the null hypothesis really is true; then rejecting null is a Type I error and retaining it is the correct decision. And sometimes (again, we never know when) the null hypothesis is really false; then retaining null is a Type II error and rejecting it is the correct decision.

We want to avoid Type I errors, so that we avoid considering relationships that do not exist. However, we also want to avoid Type II errors, so that we do identify those relationships that do exist and thus learn something about nature. **Power** is the probability that we will not make a Type II error. In other words, power is the probability that we will reject the null hypothesis on those occasions when null is actually false, correctly concluding that the sample data reflect a real relationship.

As researchers, we want to maximize our power.[1] After all, why bother to conduct a study if we are unlikely to reject the null hypothesis even when the predicted relationship *does* exist? The logic behind maximizing power is this: On those occasions when null is false, we "should" reject it, so our results "should" be significant. Therefore, to maximize our power, we maximize the probability that our results will be significant. Then, when null is false, we make the correct decision. However, by increasing power, we are not "rigging" the decision to reject the null hypothesis. Setting alpha at .05 or less ensures that we have minimized the probability of claiming significant results when null is *true:* Alpha protects us from making a Type I error. At the same time, by maximizing power we have minimized the probability of claiming nonsignificant results when null is *false:* Power protects us from making a Type II error.

We maximize power through our design, both through the statistical procedures it allows, and the data it produces.

Using Designs That Allow Powerful Statistical Procedures

Some inferential statistics are inherently more powerful than others. When we analyze data using a more powerful test, we are more likely to reject the null hypothesis when it is false than if we analyze the same data using a less powerful test. As we shall see in later chapters, we try to design a study in such a way that we *can* use the more powerful statistical procedures.

Obtaining Powerful Data

Our statistical decisions are only as good as the data we collect (garbage in, garbage out!). Therefore, our goal is to obtain the most powerful data. Essentially, this means

---

[1] Some introductory statistics books discuss directly calculating the power in a study, or see Cohen (1988).

obtaining the strongest sample relationship possible. The stronger the relationship, the less likely we are to misinterpret it as representing no relationship in the population. Consider the examples in Table 3.5 showing both powerful study-time data and data with reduced power. Remember that in both examples we are considering Type II errors, so we assume that the null hypothesis is actually false and that a real relationship exists. The powerful data form close to an ideal, perfect relationship with three characteristics: (1) There is a little variability or differences in scores *within* each group; (2) there are relatively large differences *between* the groups; and (3) this pattern holds for a relatively large number of subjects—for a large N. Given the consistency of scores within groups and the distinctive differences between groups for many subjects, such data would be very unlikely to occur through sampling error. Our statistical procedures consider these characteristics, producing a *larger* obtained value. Because a larger obtained value is more likely to be larger than our critical value, we are more likely to conclude that the results are significant. Therefore, we have greater power because we are more likely to reject the false null hypothesis in this situation.

TABLE 3.5 Examples of the Relationship Between Study Time and Test Scores Using Powerful Data and Data with Reduced Power

Powerful data

	0-hour condition	1-hour condition	2-hour condition	3-hour condition
Test scores	10	20	30	41
	11	20	31	40
	12	21	30	39
	8	19	28	40
	10	20	29	41
	9	22	30	39
	10	18	32	40
	$\bar{X}=10$	$\bar{X}=20$	$\bar{X}=30$	$\bar{X}=40$

Data with reduced power

	0-hour condition	1-hour condition	2-hour condition	3-hour condition
Test scores	5	4	5	23
	10	18	22	12
	27	26	24	19
	$\bar{X}=14$	$\bar{X}=16$	$\bar{X}=17$	$\bar{X}=18$

The data in Table 3.5 with reduced power, however, do not present so strong and convincing a relationship. There is greater variability among the scores *within* each group, there are relatively small differences *between* groups, and the data are from a small N. With such data we—and our statistical procedures—are more likely to miss the real relationship being represented. Logically, it would be "easier" and thus more likely to obtain such a relationship through sampling error when no real relationship exists. Statistically, this logic is translated into a *smaller* obtained value, one that is less likely to be larger than our critical value. Therefore, we are less likely to conclude that the results are significant. We have reduced power because we are less likely to reject the false null hypothesis in this situation.

Although the above example involves an ANOVA, the logic of obtaining powerful data also applies to t-tests and other analyses involving groups, as well as to correlational designs. In each, we seek the strongest, clearest depiction of a relationship. Then we maximize our power to detect a significant relationship when the null hypothesis is false.

> **REMEMBER** To increase the power of a study, we use powerful statistical procedures and obtain data that has minimum variability within groups, large differences between groups, and a sufficiently large N.

The way we obtain powerful data is by creating a powerful design. Although we seek large differences in scores between groups, statistical procedures evaluate the differences between the groups *relative* to the amount of variability within the groups. Therefore, the key issue in creating a powerful design is to minimize the variability of scores within the groups.

Researchers use an important term to refer to the variability of scores within the groups. Recall that one way to measure variability is to compute the *variance*. Also recall that, because of this variability, we have *error* in measuring a perfectly consistent relationship. The inconsistency in a relationship, then, is called **error variance.** In calculating error variance, we essentially determine the variability in the group of Y scores at each condition or X score, and then "average" this variability together. Error variance is the scourge of research, because the larger the error variance, the weaker the relationship and the less likely that the results are significant.

> **REMEMBER** *Error variance* is the variability of dependent scores within the conditions of an experiment or within the Y scores at the different X scores in a correlation.

Because we assume that nature is lawful, we assume that something must be causing subjects to produce different scores within a group. Therefore, a powerful design attempts to eliminate anything that might cause error variance. To do this, we again focus on our old friends: the issues of reliability, validity, and control. Consider our study-time studies.

First, perhaps our measurements are unreliable and contain random error. Are the exam questions open to varying interpretations? Do they promote guessing? If so, then even when several subjects actually know the material to the same degree, we will obtain different test scores within the same study-time group. Likewise, perhaps our measurement of study time is unreliable. If everyone in a study-time group did not actually study for the same length of time, we would expect their test scores to be different.

Second, perhaps our measurements lack content validity. If hours of study time do not actually and only reflect studying activity, then subjects in a particular study-time group who did not perform the same mental activities will have different test scores. Similarly, the test scores may partially reflect subjects' vocabulary or test-taking skills. If so, then within a study-time group, subjects differing in these skills will have different test scores.

Third, perhaps we lack internal validity, such that error variance is being produced by uncontrolled extraneous variables. The physical environment or the amount of sleep subjects had the night before may have changed unsystematically. If such fluctuating variables influence a subject when studying or when taking the test, they would cause differences in test scores within the same study-time group. Or perhaps the researcher inadvertently imparted a greater motivation to some subjects. If so, this would produce differences between the scores in a study-time group.

As these examples illustrate, we have yet another reason for attempting to design a study in such a way that we accurately and only measure the variables of interest, while controlling all other variables. The poorer our measurements and the less controlled our variables, the larger the error variance and the weaker the relationship, so the less powerful the design.

PUTTING IT ALL TOGETHER

The lesson that should be obvious at this point is that issues of reliability, validity, and control are *the* issues in research design. In the previous chapter, we saw how research flaws can mislead us when we're conceptually interpreting our results. In this chapter, we saw that many of these same flaws influence our statistical interpretations as well. And, clearly, our statistical interpretations influence our conceptual interpretations, because results must be significant before we can draw *any* inferences about a relationship. Thus, centering on error variance, we attempt to eliminate any flaws in the design, so that we obtain powerful data and draw the correct statistical interpretations, and so that we avoid being misled and draw the correct psychological interpretations.

When designing a study, remember that you will eventually perform descriptive and inferential statistical procedures, so you must seek the most powerful design and statistical procedures possible. Further, if your results are significant, you will then attempt to interpret the relationship psychologically and answer your original question in the clearest way possible. In the remainder of this text, you will see how researchers accomplish these two goals. Ironically, your efforts to increase confidence in your conceptual interpretations will sometimes decrease your power and vice versa. Good research balances these goals, so that from both a statistical and a conceptual perspective, you can be confident that you are accurately describing how nature operates.

CHAPTER SUMMARY

1. A relationship between variables is described using the format "changes in Y as a function of changes in X." Experiments investigate changes in the dependent variable as a function of changes in the independent variable.

2. *Descriptive statistics* summarize and describe the important characteristics of a sample of data. *Inferential statistics* are procedures for deciding whether a sample relationship represents a relationship that actually exists in the population.

3. *Nominal scores* reflect the category a subject falls in; *ordinal scores* reflect a subject's rank order; *interval scores* measure an amount on a scale in which negative numbers are possible; and *ratio scores* measure an amount on a scale in which negative numbers are not possible.

4. *Parametric statistics* are usually employed when we measure *normally distributed* interval or ratio scores. *Nonparametric statistics* are employed when these scores are not normally distributed, or when nominal or ordinal scores are being measured.

5. To describe a relationship in any type of design we determine (a) the strength of the relationship, the extent to which one value of Y is consistently associated with a value of X; and (b) the type of relationship, the direction in which the Y scores tend to change as the X scores change.

6. In a *positive linear relationship,* as the X scores increase, the Y scores also tend to increase. In a *negative linear relationship,* as the X scores increase, the Y scores tend to decrease. In a *nonlinear relationship,* as the X scores increase, the Y scores change their direction of change. When no relationship is present, the distribution of Y scores at one X is virtually the same as at other Xs.

7. The *Pearson correlation coefficient,* symbolized r, is a parametric procedure for describing the type and strength of a *linear relationship*. The *linear regression line* is the straight line that summarizes a linear relationship.

8. The squared correlation coefficient (r^2) indicates the *proportion of variance accounted for.* This statistic conveys the extent to which differences in Y scores can be predicted or accounted for by the relationship with X.

9. The common *measures of central tendency* are the *mean,* the *median,* and the *mode.* The common *measures of variability* are the *variance* and the *standard deviation.*

10. When dependent scores are normally distributed interval or ratio scores, we summarize an experiment by computing the *mean* score and the *sample variance* or the *sample standard deviation* in each condition. We also create a line graph, placing the conditions of the independent variable on the X axis and the mean score of the dependent scores on the Y axis.

11. The *null hypothesis* implies that because of sampling error, the sample data poorly represent the absence of the predicted relationship in the population of scores. The *alternative hypothesis* implies that our sample data do represent the predicted relationship in the population of scores.

12. The parametric inferential procedures that are appropriate in experiments are the *two-sample t-test*, used when there are only two conditions, and the *analysis of variance (ANOVA)*, used when there are two or more *levels* (conditions) of a *factor* (independent variable).

13. Our choice of the *independent-samples t-test* or *dependent-samples t-test* and *between-subjects* or *within-subjects* ANOVA depends upon our method of selecting subjects for each condition.

14. The alpha level (α) is the probability that defines a sample relationship as too unlikely to occur through sampling error. It is also the probability of making a Type I error.

15. Degrees of freedom (*df*) are based on N, the number of subjects in our study.

16. In a *one-tailed* inferential test of r or t, we predict that the linear relationship is only a positive or only a negative one. In a *two-tailed* test, we predict either a positive or a negative relationship.

17. The term *significant* results means that the sample relationship is too unlikely to occur if the predicted relationship does not exist in the population. When results are *nonsignificant*, we have no evidence for the predicted relationship, so we do not interpret it.

18. In ANOVA, *post hoc comparisons* are performed to compare all possible pairs of conditions to determine which ones differ significantly. *Planned comparisons* are performed to compare only some pairs of conditions.

19. Numbers that describe the characteristics of a population of scores are called *parameters*. A *confidence interval* describes a range of values of the population parameter, any one of which our sample statistic is likely to represent.

20. *Type I errors* occur when the null hypothesis is true but we reject it. *Type II errors* occur when the null hypothesis is false but we retain it.

21. *Power* is the probability that we will reject the null hypothesis when it is false.

22. The variability in Y scores at each X score is called *error variance*. Greater error variance reduces the strength of a relationship, so we are less likely to reject the null hypothesis when it is false.

23. We increase power by minimizing the error variance, by maximizing the differences in Y scores between different X groups, and by increasing N. The key to minimizing within-groups variability is to strive for reliable and valid measurements.

REVIEW QUESTIONS

1. What two major characteristics of a design determine the type of statistical procedures we should employ?
2. When do we perform parametric statistical procedures? When do we perform nonparametric procedures?
3. Summarize the steps involved in describing and interpreting the results of a correlational study.
4. Summarize the steps involved in describing and interpreting the results of an experiment.
5. (a) Why is it important to create a powerful design? (b) What two goals do we try to meet in order to achieve power?
6. A researcher examines whether amount of graffiti changes as a function of whether a restroom serves males or females. What scale of measurement is being used to measure each variable?
7. A researcher studies the relationship between students' choices to sit toward the front, middle, or back of a classroom and their grade in the class. What scale of measurement is being used to measure each variable?
8. (a) What is the difference between positive and negative linear relationships? (b) What is the difference between linear and nonlinear relationships?
9. A researcher conducts an experiment to study memory for pictures as a function of a subject's mood. Which variable is the independent variable and which is the dependent variable?
10. A researcher studies IQ as a function of hair length, finding a significant r of $+.07$. Describe this relationship in terms of IQ scores and hair-length scores.
11. Let's say the researcher in question 10 claims that, because the r is significant, hair length is somehow an important cause of IQ. What two reasons lead you to disagree with this conclusion?
12. In an experiment, a researcher observes that subjects' interest in a lecture increases as a function of whether they are paid $1.00, $5.00, or $25.00 to listen to it. What statistical procedures must be performed before we can accept that each amount of money causes a difference in interest level?
13. A commercial claims that "ultra-bleach" toothpaste significantly reduces tooth decay compared to other brands. What does this statement imply about (a) the type of research method employed and (b) the statistical procedures performed and their outcome?
14. Let's say you learn that the researcher in question 13 employed an alpha level of .25. What problems are raised by this alpha level?
15. A researcher hypothesizes that males and females are the same when it comes to intelligence, predicting a nonsignificant difference. Why is this hypothesis impossible to test?
16. Researcher A finds a significant negative relationship between increasing stress level and ability to concentrate. Researcher B replicates this study but finds a nonsignificant relationship. Identify the statistical error that each researcher may have made.

DISCUSSION QUESTIONS

1. (a) For the correlational study discussed in this chapter, should we employ a one-tailed or two-tailed test? (b) Given an N of 62, determine whether the r of $+.50$ is significant.

2. In our study-time experiment, random selection and random assignment should have resulted in a mix of different subjects for each condition. How might this mix adversely affect the power of our study?

3. A researcher obtains a large degree of error variance in an experiment on children's ability to remember a passage they read as a function of the number of hours they have previously watched television. (a) What does this statement indicate about the scores in each condition? (b) What might cause such variability? (c) What impact will this variability have on the statistical results? (d) What impact will it have on the conceptual interpretation of the importance of the variable of television watching?

4. Immediately prior to an exam, we ask students in the class the number of hours they studied. We then conduct an experiment by selecting a group of 10 subjects who studied for 1 hour and a group of 10 who studied for 2 hours. The mean exam scores for the two groups were 35 and 50, respectively. An independent samples t-test yielded an obtained $t = +1.70$. (a) For $\alpha = .05$, what conclusion do you draw from this study? (b) If t had equaled $+2.70$, what conclusion would you draw? (c) In part b, what additional information about the data would you seek? (d) What type of experiment is this? (e) How confident are you in your conclusions in part b and why?

5. (a) In our study-time experiment, should we use the actual exam from the research methods course and count subjects' test scores toward their grade? Why or why not? (b) Can we use this procedure in our correlational study?

4 Organizing and Communicating Research

From previous chapters we know that a single study is not proof of a hypothesis because of the potential for misinterpreting the data. However, recall that science is a community activity, in which we correct for any one researcher's fallibility by allowing everyone to skeptically evaluate a study. Further, scientific facts are ultimately built through literal replication (repeated confirmation using the same variables and procedures) and through conceptual replication (repeated confirmation using similar variables and procedures). To allow critical evaluation and to build evidence for a hypothesis through replication, researchers share the results of their studies with others.

Publishing a study and contributing to the "research literature" is an important part of science. This chapter discusses the literature and describes how a research article is created. By knowing the process an author uses in writing an article, you can read the literature more effectively. Also, as a psychology student, you will probably be reporting your own study sooner or later. This chapter will demonstrate what goes into the manuscript for a research report.

ORGANIZATION OF A RESEARCH ARTICLE

Most psychological research articles follow the rules set down in the ***Publication Manual of the American Psychological Association*** (1994). Now in its fourth edition, this is *the* reference source for answering any question regarding the organization, content, and style of a research manuscript. Although "APA format" may at first appear to be a very rigid, arbitrary set of rules, it is necessary. This format minimizes publishing costs by defining precisely the space and effort that a publication requires. It also specifies the information that any report should contain, how the information should be organized, and how it should be reported.

Especially for beginning researchers, APA format is a very useful organizational scheme. As a reader, you will learn where to look in an article to find certain information and how to understand the shorthand codes used to present it. As an author, you will discover how to organize your paper, what to say, and how to say it. And as a researcher, you will be provided with a framework for remembering the many design aspects of a study that must be considered. Asking yourself the question "What will I say in each section of a report of this study?" is a cue for remembering the issues that you must deal with.

The sections of an article report the various aspects of a study in the order in which they logically occur. Recall from Chapter 2 that the flow of a research study can be depicted using two funnels, as shown in Figure 4.1. In designing and conducting a study, we work from the general to the specific and then back to the general. As shown, an APA-style report is organized following these same steps. In the *Introduction* we present our hypothetical constructs as they are defined and related in relevant literature from past research, develop the hypothesized relationship between our variables for the target population, and then derive the specific predictions of the study. In the *Method* section we describe the specifics of the design and how we collected the data. In the *Results* section we report our descriptive and inferential statistics and describe the statistical

FIGURE 4.1 The Parallels Between Research Activity and APA Format

The flow of a research study is from a general hypothesis to the specifics of the study, and then back to the general hypothesis. The APA format also follows this pattern.

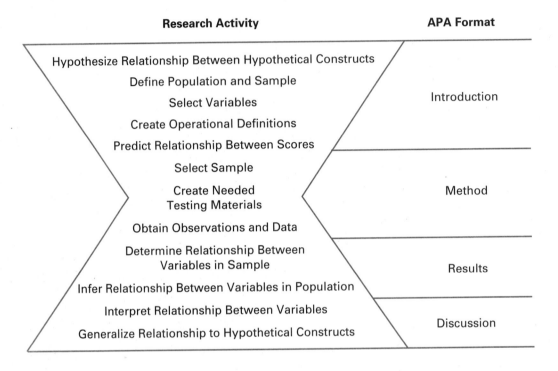

relationship we have found. Finally, in the *Discussion* section we interpret the results in terms of our variables and then generalize to the broader relationship between the hypothetical constructs with which we began.

REMEMBER   The organization of a research report follows the logical order of the steps performed in conducting the research.

To see how all of this is accomplished, let's design a study that we'll later write as the manuscript of a research report.

AN EXAMPLE STUDY

Let's say that in a Cognitive Psychology course, you read a study by Bower, Karlin, and Dueck (1975). These researchers studied short-term memory by presenting subjects with simple cartoons called "droodles." Each droodle is a meaningless geometric shape, but the neat thing is that a particular droodle will instantly become meaningful when an accompanying verbal interpretation is provided. Two examples of droodles are provided in Figure 4.2. Some subjects were told that droodle (a) shows a midget playing a trombone in a telephone booth and that droodle (b) shows an early bird that caught a very strong worm. Other subjects were not given any interpretation. Bower et al. found that after seeing 28 different droodles, those subjects who had been told the interpretations could recall (sketch) more droodles than those who had not. The authors concluded that the interpretations made the droodles more meaningful to subjects, allowing them to integrate the droodles with their knowledge in memory. Then, as the subjects recalled the droodles, this knowledge provided useful "retrieval cues."

Let's say that this strikes us as an interesting topic to investigate further. In critically evaluating the above study, we notice that the accompanying interpretations not only make the droodles meaningful but do so in a humorous way. By employing interpretations that can be seen as both humorous and meaningful, the droodle study may have been confounded: On the one hand, the interpretations may make the droodles meaningful and thus more memorable, as the authors suggested. On the other hand, the interpretations may make the droodles humorous, and their humor makes the droodles more memorable. This second idea leads us to a rival, alternative hypothesis. Although Bower et al. argued that they studied how the hypothetical constructs of "meaningfulness" and "short-term memory" are related, we can argue that the construct of "humor" was examined as well. We hypothesize that when the contexts in which stimuli occur differ in humor, differences in memory for the stimuli are produced.

Our hypothesis suggests that greater humor *causes* improved memory, so a well-controlled, internally valid laboratory experiment to test the hypothesis is in order. In fact, the design of Bower et al. seems appropriate. They compared the effects of an interpretation versus the absence of an interpretation on memory for the droodles. We can investigate our hypothesis by presenting subjects with humorous and nonhumorous interpretations. Our prediction is that droodles with humorous interpretations will be better recalled.

FIGURE 4.2 Examples of "Droodles"

These droodles were accompanied by the following interpretations: (a) "A midget playing a trombone in a telephone booth," and (b) "An early bird that caught a very strong worm."

A   B

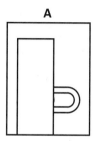 

From G. H. Bower, M. B. Karlin & A. Dueck (1975), Comprehension and memory for pictures, *Memory and Cognition,* 3(2), 216–222. Reprinted by permission of the Psychonomic Society, Inc. and the author.

Before proceeding, we need to be sure our study is rational, ethical, and practical. Rationally speaking, the idea that humor acts as a cue for recalling information seems to fit known memory processes (but we will check), and understanding memory is a worthwhile psychological study. Ethically, asking subjects to remember droodles does not appear to cause any major harm (but we will check). And practically speaking, such a study seems doable and does not require inordinate time, expense, or hard-to-find subjects or equipment.

As we begin creating the design for our study, we find that we do not yet know very much about this topic, so—to the literature!

THE RESEARCH LITERATURE

Previous research is the ultimate source for learning about a particular psychological topic. When you are designing a study, published research provides you with background in the issues that pertain to your research question so that your hypothesis fits with existing conceptualizations of your constructs and with the results of previous studies. The literature also suggests numerous ideas for interesting studies and describes established procedures that you can incorporate into your study.

Recall that defining our population early in the design process not only helps us to develop a more precise hypothesis but also directs our attention to the most relevant portions of the literature. The Bower et al. experiment studied memory in normal adults. For our droodle study, then, we need to find past research on adults regarding (1) how the constructs of "humor" and "meaningfulness" are defined and how they may influence "memory," (2) whether humorous stimuli are better retained than nonhumorous stimuli, and (3) whether other studies using the Bower et al. design have identified flaws in it, have replicated it, or (heaven forbid) have already tested the effects of humorous and nonhumorous interpretations as we will do.

What Constitutes the Research Literature?

When we refer to "the research literature," we do not mean books found in the supermarket or popular magazines such as *Time* or *Psychology Today*. At best, these contain synopses of research articles that most likely omit the details we need. For the literature of psychological research, therefore, we go to professional books and psychological journals. Books provide useful background, but because of the time required to create them, even new books may be a few years behind the latest developments. Journals contain the most current developments in a research topic, because they are published once or more a year.

Not all professional journals are of the same quality, however. In some, the primary requirement for publishing an article is that the author(s) pay the publication costs. These journals have less stringent requirements that the study provide convincing evidence. Other journals are "refereed," meaning that each article has been reviewed by several psychologists who are knowledgeable about the research topic being studied.

To gauge the quality of a journal, check the section describing its editorial policies. Also, as an indication of higher-quality articles, look for journals published by such national professional organizations of psychologists as the American Psychological Association and the Psychonomic Society. One function of these organizations is to promote the dissemination of quality research. Still, although such journals *tend* to provide convincing studies, you must continue to approach each study with a critical and skeptical eye.

Searching the Literature

To search the literature, you must begin with some idea of your research topic. Most journals are organized around a broad topic, identified by the journal's title (e.g., *Cognitive Psychology* or the *Journal of Personality and Social Psychology*). By perusing such journals, you may come across articles that you wish to read or that suggest research topics to you. However, if you have a specific idea in mind, you can consult reference sources that search the literature in an organized manner.

Psychological Abstracts   The *Psychological Abstracts* is a monthly publication that describes studies recently published in other psychology journals. Its index is organized using the variables and hypothetical constructs commonly studied by psychologists. When using this index, try to be specific, selecting terms you think would be used in the titles of relevant articles. For our droodle study, we would first look in the index of recent issues of *Psychological Abstracts* under such terms as *humor*, *meaningfulness*, and *short-term memory*. *Psychological Abstracts* provides a separate author index, so we would also look up the authors of the original droodle study to see if they have reported other similar research. For each article listed, an "abstract"—a brief synopsis—of the study is presented. By reading the abstract, we can determine whether we want to read the entire article.

Computerized Literature Searches   Many college libraries provide a user-friendly computer program that searches the literature for you. Programs such as *PsychLIT* contain a large database covering years of research literature. You simply enter the names of your constructs and variables, at which point the computer provides abstracts and the references for studies filed under those terms. Note, however, that the computer will call up many unrelated references for a general term; so carefully cross-reference your terms to ensure a more selective search. For example, merely entering *memory* as a search term will produce hundreds of unrelated studies. But entering *memory* and *humor* will call up references more directly related to our study.

Bibliographies of Research Articles   When you find an article on a topic of interest, notice that its accompanying bibliography contains references to past related studies. By reading the published articles that it cites, and then reading the references in those articles, you can work backward in time and learn about earlier research. Sometimes you will also see references to psychological conventions and meetings at which researchers verbally present their research. For a copy of a particular presentation, contact the first author cited in the reference. (For assistance, the American Psychological Association provides a directory of the addresses of its members.)

Social Science Citation Index   When you find a relevant article that is several years old, you can search for more recent articles using the ***Social Science Citation Index.*** This publication identifies a research article by authors and date, and then lists subsequent articles that have cited it. Thus, for example, we could look up the original 1975 droodle study in the index for 1993 and 1994, and perhaps find more recent related articles.

Review Articles   The purpose of a review article is to survey and summarize a large body of theoretical and empirical literature dealing with a particular topic. Such articles not only offer a useful overview but also provide references to many specific studies. The title of a review article usually contains the word *review* and some books and journals, such as *Psychological Bulletin* and *Annual Review of Psychology*, specialize in review articles.

References on Testing Materials   Researchers often use some form of paper-and-pencil test to measure subjects' intelligence, personality, creativity, attitudes, emotions, motivations, and so on. Instead of creating your own test and being uncertain of its reliability or its content and construct validity, look for acceptable tests that already exist. To find them, consult reference books that describe common psychological tests. Such books usually have titles conveying the fact that they describe tests (e.g., *The Mental Measurements Yearbook* or *Measures of Personality and Social Psychological Attitudes*).

You can also use a computerized literature search to find research articles that have employed such tests. To be efficient, cross-reference the name of the attribute to be measured with the term *assessment*. For example, if you wish to measure depression, using the terms *depression* and *assessment* will limit your search to studies involving the measurement of depression.

DESIGNING AND CONDUCTING THE DROODLE STUDY

Our literature search provided no studies that would cause us to question the original Bower et al. (1975) procedure of presenting droodles as to-be-remembered stimuli. Because we now know that this procedure produced informative and powerful results (they were significant) we can adopt it for our study.

We can find many studies that replicate the finding that, for a variety of types of stimuli, the more meaningful a stimulus is, the better it is retained. For example, when learning a list of words, subjects who use each word in a sentence will recall the words better than if they merely think of a rhyme for each word (see Lockhart & Craik, 1990).

Surprisingly, my literature search turned up little research that directly studied whether simple humorous stimuli are better remembered than nonhumorous stimuli. (But see MacAninch, Austin & Derks, 1992, and Dixon, Willingham, Strano & Chandler, 1989.)

However, there are numerous studies showing that more *distinctive* stimuli are better retained than less distinctive stimuli (e.g. Schmidt, 1985). For example, in a list of words, a word printed using a different style of print tends to be better retained than the other words that are visually similar (Hunt & Elliott, 1980). Often, we must generalize from previous findings and descriptions of constructs in the literature to apply them to our specific hypothesis. Thus, in suggesting that humor influences memory, we can propose that a humorous interpretation makes a droodle more distinctive in memory, thereby making it more memorable. Essentially, then, we have proposed that humor is one component of the construct of distinctiveness—one way to make a stimulus distinctive.

Although the meaningfulness of a stimulus may seem to be the same thing as its distinctiveness, researchers do distinguish between the two concepts. Desrochers and Begg (1987), for example, suggest that distinctiveness is the extent that unique cues are associated with the particular context in which the stimulus was encountered. In short, a distinctive event is notable and thus stands out in our memory. Therefore, greater distinctiveness enhances *access* to the stimulus, allowing us to "find" it in our memory. Meaningfulness, on the other hand, is the extent to which the components of the stimulus are organized and integrated. A meaningful event is tied together such that we know all of its "parts." Therefore, once we access our memory of a stimulus, greater meaningfulness enhances recall of the *components* of the stimulus (see also Einstein, McDaniel & Lackey, 1989).

Although the preceding discussion greatly simplifies the debate about the hypothetical constructs of distinctiveness and meaningfulness, for our study it boils down to this: On the one hand, the importance of the interpretations in the original droodle study may be that they were humorous, and thus made the droodles more distinctive and in turn more memorable. On the other hand, the importance of the interpretations may have nothing to do with the humor involved. Perhaps they simply made the droodles more meaningful and thus more memorable. Our task is to design a study that clearly shows the influence of humor, separate from the influence of meaningfulness.

By discussing the hypothetical constructs of memory, humor, and meaningfulness in terms of droodles and their interpretations, we have begun to create our operational definitions of them. Now we must "whittle down" these constructs, completing the design of the study by refining the definitions of our specific variables and procedures.

Defining the Independent Variable

Our goal is to manipulate (change) the hypothetical construct of humor. Although there are many components to this construct (slapstick, puns, etc.), we will focus on the humor produced by the interpretations. Thus, our independent variable involves changing the amount of humor attributed to the droodles by the interpretations. However, the challenge is to manipulate the amount of humor in the interpretations while producing equally meaningful interpretations. If the droodles are not equally meaningful, then humor and meaningfulness will be confounded in our study. Then we will be unable to tell whether more humor or more meaningfulness improves retention of a droodle.

What seems to make an interpretation in Bower et al. humorous is that it provides an unusual explanation involving unexpected objects, people, or animals. So if we revise the original interpretations to provide common explanations involving predictable objects, people, and animals, they should be less humorous (and less distinctive) but just as meaningful as the originals. For example, from the humorous interpretation "This is a midget playing the trombone in a telephone booth," we can derive the less humorous interpretation "This is a telephone booth with a repairman inside, repairing the broken door handle." In both cases the droodle features a telephone booth, so if a telephone booth is particularly meaningful and memorable, it is equally so in both the humorous and nonhumorous conditions. Also both interpretations involve the meaningful integration of a person, a telephone booth, and an object (either a trombone or a door handle).

By deciding how we will change the interpretations, we have operationally defined how we will measure and manipulate different amounts of humor. We have two conditions of our independent variable: In one we will provide subjects with nonhumorous interpretations (as defined above), and in the other we will provide humorous interpretations (again, as defined above). If humor is an attribute that aids memory, then the humorous interpretations should produce better recall of the droodles. If humor is *not* psychologically important in this way, then there should be no difference in retention between the two conditions.

Now, we consider all of the details involved in devising a reliable, valid, and powerful study. Remember that the key in designing an experiment is to keep the influence of all extraneous variables equal. Anything other than our independent variable that may influence retention of droodles threatens the internal validity of our experiment and, thus, our confidence that we have shown that changes in humor cause changes in memory. In addition, anything that causes scores to change *within* the humor or nonhumor group increases the error variance, resulting in a weaker relationship and less power. Therefore, we attempt to control the influence of all extraneous variables, simultaneously considering the four components of any study: researcher, subjects, environment, and measurement procedure.

First we consider the details of our stimuli, and subjects' reactions to them. How many droodles should we use? If we have only one droodle per condition, subjects might forget or remember it because of some hidden peculiarity unrelated to the interpretation we give. Then our results would yield an unreliable and invalid measure of the influence of the interpretation. The original Bower et al. study presented 28 droodles per condition, so we will use the same number of droodles.

The easiest way to obtain the droodles for our study is to use the ones from Bower et al. (To borrow stimuli not fully presented in an article, we would write to the first author of the article.) If we decide to create our own, we must attempt to control extraneous variables associated with the complexity and memorability of each droodle. Thus, we would specify rules for creating comparable stimuli: All are of equal size, all are drawn in black ink, all contain only two basic geometric shapes, and so on. Although Bower et al. handed each drawing of a droodle to subjects, for better control we can present the droodles using a slide projector with an electronic timer (or have subjects sit at a computer-controlled television monitor).

Also for consistency, all interpretations will contain roughly the same number and type of words, and all will begin with the phrase "This is a...." As in the original study, we will test subjects one at a time, reading them the interpretation as they first view a droodle. We will read all interpretations at the same speed and volume, with the same tone of voice and expressiveness. (To further ensure consistency, we might record the interpretations and time the playback to occur when subjects view each droodle.) Likewise, the humorous interpretations should all be consistently humorous for a wide range of subjects, the nonhumorous interpretations should be consistently nonhumorous, and, as a group, the humorous interpretations should be consistently more humorous than the nonhumorous interpretations. (In later chapters, we'll examine methods of ensuring that our stimuli meet these criteria.)

Finally, we must create clear and precise instructions for our subjects so that they know exactly what to do at each step, and so that we can control their extraneous behaviors. The instructions should be, to the extent possible, worded identically for all conditions consistently read or recorded, of the same duration, and so on. Further, the researcher must attempt to behave identically when testing all subjects, and the environment must be constant for them all.

Defining the Dependent Variable

Our dependent variable is recall of the droodles, but we must also decide how we will define and measure it. As in Bower et al. (1975), our subjects will study each droodle for 10 seconds, so that all subjects are given the same time to perform the mental tasks that may influence their retention and so that all subjects retain the information for the same period of time. Immediately after all droodles have been presented, we will measure subjects' recall by asking them to sketch all droodles, on sheets of paper containing a grid of approximately 3-by-3-inch squares. Subjects will sketch each droodle in a square, so that we can tell what shapes a subject believes go together to form one droodle.

As the researchers, we could score the sketches as correct or incorrect ourselves, but our judgment may not be reliable. We may be inadvertently biased, because we know when we want subjects to be recalling the droodles best. Instead, therefore, we will enlist as scorers two people who are "blind" to the purposes of our study. Then we will operationally define a response as correct if both scorers agree that it matches an original droodle. (For the time being, we'll assume that this procedure produces a reliable and content valid measurement of subjects' ability to reproduce the droodles, and that it is construct valid for measuring their "memory.")

Identifying Subjects

We must also decide on the specific subjects to be examined. Variables such as age, gender, and cultural background may influence what subjects consider humorous, and we want them all to clearly see the droodles and to understand the interpretations that accompany them. To keep such variables constant, we will randomly select as subjects Introductory Psychology students who are similar in age and background, with good eyesight, hearing, and English abilities. (Previous research will have identified other subject variables that researchers think are also important.) Recall that a relatively large N is needed for a powerful design, so we will select 40 subjects for each condition. To control the variable of gender, we will balance it, randomly selecting 20 males from the population of available males and 20 females from the population of available females to be in each condition. Because we can randomly assign subjects to either condition, we have a true experiment.

Statistical Procedures and Results

A subject's score will be the number of correctly recalled droodles. These are ratio scores, and from past research we see that it is appropriate to assume such scores are normally distributed and to compute the mean number of droodles recalled in each condition. Because we have two conditions, the t-test is the appropriate inferential procedure to perform. Because we do not have a matched groups or repeated measures design, the independent samples t-test is appropriate. Further, we have hypothesized that humor will improve memory, which leads to the prediction that as humor increases, recall scores will also tend to increase. Thus, because we predict a positive relationship, we perform a one-tailed t-test. (If we are unsure of this prediction, we may choose the two-tailed prediction that, as humor increases, recall scores will tend to either increase or decrease.)

It is important to note that there are other designs we might use to test our hypothesis. However, let's assume we conducted our two-group study and found that the mean number of droodles recalled was 15.2 with nonhumorous interpretations and 20.5 with humorous interpretations. The t-test we then performed on these scores indicated a significant difference, convincing us that the scores represent a real relationship, which confirms our hypothesis. Then we begin the task of interpreting this relationship, first inferring what it indicates about our variables of amount of humor and recall of droodles, and then working back to the broader hypothetical constructs of humor, distinctiveness, and memory.

Now, to share our results with other researchers, we will follow APA format to prepare a written report of our study.

THE GENERAL STYLE OF A RESEARCH ARTICLE

The ultimate goal of APA format (or of any scientific writing) is precision in communication. At the same time, we need to conserve space and avoid overstatements or redundancy. Thus, we strive to state each idea clearly, to say it once, and to report only the necessary information. To meet the goal of precise yet concise communication, both the author and the reader make certain implicit assumptions.

The Assumptions of the Author and Reader

The reader assumes that the author understands statistics and research methods; that the author has described any unusual or unexpected events; and that he or she is a reasonable, ethical, and competent researcher. Many things are left unsaid in a research article, because the reader can assume that commonly accepted procedures were used and that the details of the procedures are unimportant. Thus, for example, you need not state, "I compared the obtained value to the critical value" because all researchers know this must be done. Stating it would be redundant.

Likewise, an author assumes that the reader is a competent psychologist (you are now a "Pro"). Therefore, a research article does not give readers a detailed background of the topic under study, because the assumption is that they already know something about it, or at least that they will read the references provided. The author also assumes that the reader understands statistics and research methods. Do not teach statistics and design principles to the reader. Do not say "Reliable data were important because . . ." or "A *t*-test was performed to test the null hypothesis that. . . ." The reader already knows why reliability is important and why a *t*-test is performed. Finally, always use common terminology (e.g., *valid, confounding,* and *significant*), but without providing definitions. The author assumes that the reader either understands them or will find out what they mean.

As an author, you should focus on providing readers with the information they cannot get elsewhere: *your* thoughts and actions as a researcher. What conclusions did you draw from a previous article? What do you mean by essential terms such as *distinctiveness* or *meaningfulness?* What logic did you use in deriving a hypothesis or prediction? And what do you think a significant result indicates about the behavior under study? As the author, you are the expert, so give the reader the benefit of your wisdom. Your job is to clearly and concisely relate to readers all of the *important* mental and physical activities you performed in creating, conducting, and interpreting your study. The goal in reporting research is to provide readers the information necessary for (1) understanding the study, (2) evaluating the study, and (3) performing a literal replication of the study.

> *REMEMBER* A good research report allows the study to be fully understood, scientifically evaluated, and literally replicated.

Some Rules of Style

Below are some general rules for writing a research article that conforms to APA style. There are many other specific rules, so refer to the *Publication Manual.*

1. A report describes a completed study, so it is written in the past tense (e.g., "I predicted that. . ."). The exception is to state in the present tense any conclusions that apply to present or future situations (e.g., "Humor influences recall by. . .").

2. Cite all sources from which you obtained information, using only the last names of the author(s) and the date. You may use the reference as the subject of a sentence: "Smith and Jones (1992) defined distinctiveness as. . . ." Or you may state an idea and provide the reference in parentheses: "Distinctiveness is defined as . . . (Smith & Jones, 1992)." (In a parenthetical citation, "&" is used instead of "and.") When citing an article with three to six authors, include all names the first time you cite it. Thereafter, refer to it using only the first author and the Latin phrase *et al.* Thus, first we say "Bower, Karlin, and Dueck (1975)," but subsequently we say "Bower et al. (1975)." When citing an article having more than six authors, even the first time you cite it use only the first author and *et al.*

3. Refrain from directly quoting an article. Instead, paraphrase and summarize the idea, so that you tell the readers what they should understand about the idea. Also,

address a study itself, not its authors. For example, the phrase "Bower *et al.*" refers primarily to a reported experiment, not to the people who conducted it. Thus we write "The results are reported *in* Bower *et al.* (1975)" instead of "The results are reported *by* Bower et al. (1975)."

4. To distinguish your study from other studies, refer to it as "this study" or "the present study." However, do not use these phrases in a way that attributes human actions to nonhuman sources, as in "This study attempted to demonstrate that. . . ." Instead, use "I" as the subject of these verbs. (Use "we" *only* in the case of multiple authors.)

5. Use accepted psychological terminology as much as possible. When you use a nonstandard term or name a variable, define the word the first time you use it and then use that word consistently. In our droodle study we will define *humorous* and use only this term, rather than mixing in related terms such as *funny* or *entertaining*. This prevents confusion about whether we mean something slightly different by *funny* or *entertaining*. In addition, avoid using contractions or slang terms. A reader from a different part of the country or another country may not understand such terms.

6. Avoid abbreviations. They are justified only if (a) a term consists of several words, (b) it appears very frequently throughout the report, and (c) you are not using numerous different abbreviations. If you must abbreviate, do so by creating an acronym, using the first letter of each word of the term. Define the complete term the first time it is used, with its acronym in parentheses. Thus, you might say "Short-term Memory (STM) is. . . ." Then use only the acronym, except as the first word of a sentence; there, always use the complete term.

7. Use words for numbers between zero and nine, and digits for numbers that are 10 and larger. However, use digits for any size number if (a) you are writing a series of numbers in which at least one is 10 or larger, or (b) the number contains a decimal or refers to a statistical result or to a precise measurement (e.g., a specific score or the number of subjects). Thus, you would say "The three conditions, with 5 individuals per condition. . . ." Also, never begin a sentence with a number expressed in digits.

8. Although throughout this text I've used the generic term *subjects* to refer to those organisms that researchers study, APA style requires the use of less impersonal and more precise terms. The generic term to use is *participants,* but where appropriate use more descriptive terms such as *students, children, men, women, rats,* or *pigeons.*

9. Finally, use precise wording. In our droodle study, we will not say that participants "saw" or "looked at" a droodle, or that they "forgot" a droodle, because we do not know that these events occurred. We know only that participants were presented a droodle or failed to recall it. In addition, APA rules stress that we avoid biased language. Thus, refer to the gender of participants using the equivalent terms "male" and "female" and to individuals as "he" or "she." When possible, use neutral terms such as "Chairperson."

THE COMPONENTS OF AN APA-STYLE RESEARCH ARTICLE

These are the components of an APA-style manuscript in the order in which they occur:

Title page

Abstract page

Introduction

Methods

    Participants

    Materials or Apparatus

    Procedure

Results

Discussion

References

Tables and Figures

In the following sections, we examine each component, using examples from a manuscript of our droodle study. (The complete manuscript is presented in Appendix C.) Throughout this discussion, compare our previous steps in designing the study—and all that was said—to what is actually reported. Translating and summarizing our thoughts and activities are the keys to creating a research report.

The Title

A **title** allows readers to determine whether they want to read the article. It should clearly communicate the variables and relationship being studied, but it should consist of no more than 12 words. You will frequently see titles containing the phrase "as a function of." For example, "Helping Behavior as a Function of Self-Esteem" indicates that the researcher examined the relationship between participants' helping behavior and different amounts of their self-esteem. A title such as "Decreased Errors in Depth Perception as a Function of Increased Illumination Levels" provides the added information that the observed relationship is negative, such that greater illumination is associated with fewer errors. Since illumination level can easily be manipulated, this title probably describes an experiment in which "illumination level" was the independent variable and "errors," the dependent variable.

Titles also often begin with the phrase "Effect of," as in "Effect of Alcohol Consumption on Use of Sexist Language." The word *effect* means "influence." Such a title is a causal statement, implying that an experiment was conducted and that changes in the independent variable (amount of alcohol consumed) caused a change in the dependent variable (amount of sexist language used by subjects). Note the difference between *effect* (usually a noun) and *affect* (usually a verb). If *X a*ffects *Y*, then there is an *e*ffect of *X* on *Y*. (Here's a trick for remembering this distinction: *Effect* means *end result*, and both begin with *e*. *Affect* means *alter* and both begin with *a*.)

The title you create should provide sufficient information for readers to determine whether the article is relevant to their literature search. Choose terms that are specific, and never use abbreviations or terms that need to be defined. Thus, for our study, we might use the title "Effect of Humorous Interpretations on Immediate Recall of Nonsense Figures." This wording identifies our variables, specifying that we are studying short-term memory of drawings. Contrast this with such terrible titles as "A Study of Humor and Memory" (of course it's a study) and "When Does Memory Work Better?" (what does "work" mean?). Either of these would be useless for determining whether the article is relevant to a *specific* research topic.

In an APA-style manuscript, the title page is a separate page containing the title, your name, and the formal title of your college or university. A sample title page appears in Figure 4.3. The title page is page number 1, with the number placed in the upper-righthand corner of the page, as it is on all other pages (minimum margins are one inch). The title page also contains two other components. First, left of the page number is typed the "manuscript page header," consisting of the first two or three words from your title. The header appears on all subsequent pages, so if any pages become separated, the publisher can identify them as belonging to your manuscript. (This is another reason for all researchers not to use titles beginning "A Study of.") Second, on the first line below the header is typed the words "Running head:" followed by an abbreviated title. This running head will be printed at the top of each page in the published article. (On this page of your textbook, the running head is "Organizing and Communicating Research.")

The Abstract

The title page is followed by the **abstract,** which is a brief summary of the study. The abstract describes the specific variables used, the important subject characteristics, a brief description of the overall design, and the key general statistical relationship obtained. It also indicates the theoretical approach taken in interpreting the results, though often without giving the actual interpretation.

Although the abstract accompanies the article, it is also reproduced in *Psychological Abstracts,* so it must be able to stand alone, containing no abbreviations or uncommon terms (no "droodles"). It should include only details relevant to the reader's question: "Is this article relevant to my literature search?" Most authors write the abstract after they have written the report, so they can easily summarize the key points. If you find it is difficult to compress a lengthy paper into 100–120 words, think of the abstract as an elaboration of the title. Given the title, what else would you say to communicate the gist of the article?

> *REMEMBER* The *title* describes the relationship under investigation. The *abstract* summarizes the report. Together, they allow readers to determine whether the article is relevant to their literature search.

The abstract for our droodle study appears in Figure 4.4.

FIGURE 4.3 Sample Title Page of a Research Manuscript
Notice the location and spacing of the various components.

```
                                                   Effect of Humorous    1
        Running head: EFFECT OF HUMOROUS INTERPRETATIONS ON RECALL




                          Effect of Humorous Interpretations on
                          Immediate Recall of Nonsense Figures
                                  Gary W. Heiman
                                 Podunk University
```

FIGURE 4.4   Sample Abstract Page

The abstract page is page number 2, with a centered heading reading "Abstract." The abstract itself is one paragraph long. Note that the first line is not indented.

Effect of Humorous   2

Abstract

The effect of humor on the immediate recall of simple visual stimuli was investigated. Eighty college students (20 men and 20 women per condition) viewed 28 nonsensical line drawings that were each accompanied by either a humorous or nonhumorous verbal interpretation. Although the interpretations were comparable in the meaningfulness they conveyed, those participants presented with humorous interpretations correctly recalled significantly more drawings than those presented nonhumorous interpretations. The results suggest that a meaningful and humorous context provides additional retrieval cues beyond those cues provided by a meaningful yet nonhumorous context. The effect of the cues produced by humor is interpreted as creating a more distinctive and thus more accessible memory trace.

The Introduction

The **Introduction** to a research article should *reproduce* the logic we used to derive our hypothesis and design our study to test it. It is in the Introduction that we work through the "whittling down" process, beginning with broad descriptions of behaviors and hypothetical constructs and translating them into the specific variables of our study. We then describe the predicted relationship between scores that will be measured using our operational definitions.

Researchers read an introduction with two goals in mind. First, we want to understand the logic of the study. Thus, the author should introduce us to the hypothesis and the psychological explanations being tested, the general design (e.g., whether correlational or experimental), the reasons that certain operational definitions are employed, and the logic used by the author in stating that certain results would support the predictions and hypothesis of the study. Both the purpose of the study and the population under study should be clear. (Unless specified, we assume that the relationship between variables applies to the broadest population.) As readers, we also evaluate the hypothesis of the study and its logic. Are the explanations circular pseudo-explanations? Are there alternative hypotheses and extraneous variables to be considered?

Second, we look for empirical evidence that supports the hypothesis. Remember, we do not accept opinions or beliefs as evidence but, rather, we weigh the confirming and disconfirming empirical evidence. The Introduction is where virtually all references to past research occur, including those studies that do and do not support the hypothesis. Further, if the study is successful, the author will attempt to interpret and explain the findings in psychological terms, so the Introduction must also contain the conceptual and theoretical issues to be discussed later in the paper.

The reader assumes that, unless otherwise noted, a study cited in support of a hypothesis is reasonably convincing. Previous studies are reported very briefly; often the author merely cites them (rather than explaining them in detail) to indicate that they provide support. If discussed at all, previous studies are described in terms of the specific information the author judged to be important when deriving his or her hypotheses. The details of a study are provided only when (1) they are necessary for the reader to understand the author's comments about that study, or (2) they are necessary for showing support for the author's position. Therefore, the Introduction does not usually contain such details as the *N,* the statistical tests used, or the specifics of the design employed in the cited research.

A portion of the Introduction for our droodle study appears in Figure 4.5. Although we know how the study turns out, the Introduction is written as if we do not, describing the process we went through *before* we collected the data.

We begin the Introduction within the larger context of the hypothetical constructs of meaningfulness and its influence on memory. Then we will work logically from the broad ideas to the specific example of the droodle study. However, we immediately focus on the perspective we have taken in studying the hypothetical construct. We orient the reader, providing the major relevant conclusions from past research and their references. We also identify when we are merely speculating. Note that the purpose of the study is stated *early* in the Introduction—in this case, at the end of the first paragraph. In subsequent

FIGURE 4.5   A Sample Introduction

Note that the title is repeated, and that we do not label this section as the Introduction.

Effect of Humorous Interpretations

on Immediate Recall of Nonsense Figures

Researchers have consistently demonstrated that retention of to-be-learned material improves when the material is presented in a context that leads to meaningful processing (Lockhart & Craik, 1990). In particular, Bower, Karlin, and Dueck (1975) presented college students with a series of "droodles," which are each a meaningless line drawing that can be made meaningful by presentation of an accompanying verbal interpretation. Those individuals who were provided the interpretations correctly recalled (sketched) significantly more of the droodles immediately following their presentation than did those individuals given no interpretations. However, each interpretation in Bower et al. (1975) defined a droodle in a humorous fashion, using unexpected and incongruent actors and actions. Thus, differences in the meaningfulness attributed to

paragraphs, we further retrace our logic, defining what we mean by the constructs of meaningfulness and distinctiveness and explaining how humor might influence memory. Then we describe how we define and manipulate humor while keeping meaningfulness constant.

Notice that, in the process, we must make a logical connection between past research literature and the present study. Usually, after presenting previous research findings, we point out a question or flaw that has not been addressed. Once we have provided the background and important issues, we might say something like "However, this interpretation does not consider...." or "However, this variable was not studied...." Then, we address the problem we have raised.

A good strategy is to logically lead up to a final paragraph that says something like "Therefore, in the present study...." Then we state the specific hypothesis and relationship to be studied, describe our general approach to defining and manipulating our variables, and specify our prediction. The details regarding how we will collect the data to test the prediction are provided in the next section.

REMEMBER   The *Introduction* presents all information that will be used to interpret the results: the conceptual and theoretical logic of the study, relevant past research, and the predictions of the study.

The Method

The **Method** section contains the information needed to understand, critique, and literally replicate the data-collection procedures. To collect data we need subjects, testing materials and equipment, and a specific testing procedure and design. APA style requires that these categories be presented in three separate subsections, in this order: (1) *Participants,* (2) *Materials or Apparatus,* and (3) *Procedure.* The beginning of our Method section is shown in Figure 4.6.

Participants   Here we simply describe the type of subjects we've enlisted so that other researchers can obtain comparable participants and look for uncontrolled subject variables. Thus, we identify important subject characteristics (e.g., gender, age, school affiliation) and specify any criteria we imposed when selecting participants. Because our statistical power is important, we always report the number of individuals tested. And because their motivation is important, we describe any form of reimbursement that was

FIGURE 4.6   Sample Method Section

Notice the placement of the headings, as well as the use of capital letters and underlining.

```
            humorous interpretations should be more frequently recalled

            than those accompanied by nonhumorous interpretations.

                                Method
        Participants
                Forty female and 40 male undergraduate students from an

        introductory psychology course at Podunk University each

        received $3.00 for their voluntary participation. All were

        between 20 and 22 years of age (mean age = 20.7 years), were

        born in the United States, were raised in English speaking

        families, and had normal or corrected eyesight and hearing.

        Participants were randomly assigned to either the humorous or

        nonhumorous condition, with 20 males and 20 females in each

        condition.
        Materials
                The 28 droodles from Bower et al. (1975) were reproduced,

        each consisting of a black-ink line drawing involving two
```

used. Also in this section (or in a letter sent to the journal editor) an author must certify that the participants were treated in accordance with the ethical principles of the APA, which we discuss in the next chapter.

Materials or Apparatus   This section immediately follows the Participants section (see Figure 4.6). Usually it is called _Materials_ because most studies involve mainly testing materials such as stimulus objects, tests and printed material, slides, drawings, and so on. We may call this section _Apparatus_ if testing mainly involves equipment such as computers, recording devices, and the like. (If extensive discussion is required, we may divide this section into two sections.) Regardless of its title, we describe both the relevant materials and apparatus we prepared, but without explaining how they are used. Again organize the information according to the logical order in which the components occur: we present a droodle, we give an interpretation and then we measure retention.

Supplies must be described clearly so that the reader can understand, evaluate, and reproduce them. Therefore, if supplies are purchased, indicate the manufacturer and model, or the edition or version. If materials are borrowed from previous research, briefly describe them and provide the citation. If you build equipment, describe it so a researcher can produce equipment that is similar in operation. If you create visual stimuli, describe the rules used to create them in terms of their dimensions, their color, and so on. If you create verbal stimuli, describe the rules used to select them, such as the length of words or sentences, their meaning and content, their difficulty level, and so on. For any paper-and-pencil tests, describe the number of questions, the format of each question, and the way in which participants indicate their responses. Also report information about the reliability and validity of a procedure. For example, the speed and error rates of equipment should be indicated because such rates affect reliability. With paper-and-pencil tests, either note their previously demonstrated validity and reliability or briefly report any procedures you performed to determine this.

Note that all physical dimensions are reported using the _metric_ system, and that common units of measurement are abbreviated. Table 4.1 provides the most common abbreviations used in psychological research. If you measure in nonmetric units, report the measurement both in the nonmetric units and in converted metric units.

Keep in mind that, throughout this section, only _important_ elements are reported. The reader knows the necessary steps in designing a study, and generally understands why and how each component is chosen. Therefore, we do not specify how subjects were

TABLE 4.1   Common Abbreviations Used in the APA Format
Notice that these abbreviations do not take periods.

Unit	Symbol	Unit	Symbol
centimeters	cm	meters	m
grams	g	milliliters	mL
hours	hr	millimeters	mm
kilograms	kg	minutes	min
liters	L	seconds	s

randomly selected or how we determined their age, eyesight, and so on. Likewise, we do not describe obvious equipment (e.g., whether participants used a pencil or a pen to complete a questionnaire, or what furniture was present in the room where testing took place). We note a detail only if it (1) would not be expected by a reasonable researcher or (2) would seriously influence the reliability or validity of our measurements.

Procedure   In the **Procedure** section, we describe how we brought the participants, materials, and apparatus together to actually perform the study. A portion of the Procedure section for our droodle study is presented in Figure 4.7.

The best way to organize this section is to follow the temporal sequence as it actually occurred in the study. The first thing we do is give participants their instructions, so we first summarize these instructions. Then we proceed through the tasks performed by the participants in the order they were performed. A useful strategy is to initially describe those aspects of the procedure that are common to all participants and then to distinguish one condition from another. (Always work from the general to the specific.)

Along the way, the various parts of our Method section should have communicated the complete design of our study. If the complete design has not been communicated in an understandable way by this point, an optional *Design* section may be added. Here we would describe the layout of the study in terms of the conditions, subjects, and

FIGURE 4.7   Sample Portion of the Procedure Section

```
with a loop attached to the lower right side. The humorous
interpretation was "This shows a midget playing a trombone in a
telephone booth." The nonhumorous interpretation was "This shows
a telephone booth with a repairman inside fixing the broken door
handle."
     Response forms for recalling the droodles consisted of a
grid of 3 by 3 in. (7.62 cm by 7.62 cm) squares printed on
standard sheets of paper.
Procedure
     Participants were tested individually and viewed all 28
droodles accompanied by either the humorous or nonhumorous
interpretations. Participants were instructed to study each
droodle during its presentation for later recall and were told
that the accompanying interpretation would be helpful in
remembering it. A timer in the slide projector presented each
```

variables used. But note that this section would be necessary only if we are describing a very complicated study, involving numerous groups or variables, or elaborate steps in testing subjects. (In some instances, still other sections can be created —but, again, only if they're truly necessary. For example, if we took extensive steps to determine the reliability of a procedure and this element was central to our study, we might describe these steps in a *Reliability of Measures* section.)

> REMEMBER   In the *Participants* section, we describe the important characteristics of subjects. In the *Materials or Apparatus* section, we describe the characteristics of the testing materials and equipment. And in the *Procedure* section, we describe the testing situation and design.

The Results

In the **Results** section we report the statistical procedures we performed and the statistical outcomes we obtained. We do *not*, however, interpret the results in this section. A portion of the Results section for our droodle study appears in Figure 4.8.

In describing our results, we follow the order in which the steps of an analysis are performed. First, we must produce some scores to analyze, so we describe how we operationally defined and tabulated each subject's score. Thus, we describe how

FIGURE 4.8   Sample Portion of the Results Section

Notice that the heading is centered.

```
          instructed to recall the droodles in any order, sketching each

          droodle within one grid on the response sheet.

                                 Results

               Two assistants who were unaware of the purposes of the

          study scored the participants' sketches. A sketch was considered

          to indicate correct recall if both scorers agreed that it

          depicted a droodle. (On only 2% of the responses did the scorers

          disagree.) Each participant's score was then the total number of

          correctly recalled droodles.

               The mean number of droodles correctly recalled was 20.50 in

          the humorous interpretation condition (SD = 3.25) and 15.20 in

          the nonhumorous interpretation condition (SD = 4.19). With an

          alpha level of .05, a one-tailed independent samples t-test

          indicated a significant difference between the conditions,

          t(78) = 6.32, p <.05. The relationship between amount of humor
```

we score each droodle as correct or incorrect. We also describe any transformations performed on scores, such as if we determined the mean number correct as the score for each participant, or converted them to percentages. It is in this section that we also note any data we have regarding the reliability of our scores. (In our droodle study, disagreements between our scorers would influence the reliability of the scores.)

Our analysis then involves first computing the descriptive statistics that summarize the scores and relationship. Whenever we report means, we must also report a measure of variability, so we next report the mean and standard deviation for each condition. Note that the symbol for a mean is "M" and for a standard deviation it is "SD." However, we say, "The mean number of droodles," not "the *M* number of droodles."

Our next step is to perform the appropriate inferential procedure, so next we provide the formal name for our procedure and show how it was applied to our data. Then we report the results of the analysis. You must indicate the alpha level you employed, and the terms *significant* or *not significant* must appear for each result.

For any statistic, we must report the symbol for the obtained value (r, t, or F), the degrees of freedom in parentheses, the obtained value, and the probability of your result. In our droodle study, for example, we reported:

$$\underline{t}(78) = 6.32, \underline{p} < .05$$

This sequence indicates that we performed the *t*-test with 78 degrees of freedom and obtained a value of 6.32, and that the probability is less than .05 that such data would occur by chance if there is no actual relationship in the population. (Slightly different formatting rules are used when reporting a statistic whose symbol is from the Greek alphabet. See the *Publication Manual*.) We report "$\underline{p} < .05$" when a result is significant and "$\underline{p} > .05$" (or whatever our alpha is) when a result is not significant. (Note too that statistical symbols to be italicized when published, such as "$\underline{t}$" or "$\underline{p}$," are underlined in the manuscript.)

If the results of our inferential procedure are significant, we have convincing evidence of a relationship. At this point, we conduct any secondary analyses that allow us to describe that relationship. Recall, for example, that with a significant correlation we summarize and describe the relationship by computing the regression line. And with a significant *F*, we perform *post hoc* comparisons to determine which specific conditions differ from one another. Also, we should always indicate the strength of the relationship and using procedures we'll discuss later, we report the proportion of variance accounted for by our relationship. For each secondary analysis, we again first identify the procedure and then report the results.

Remember that for any inferential procedure, we decide either yes, we reject the null hypothesis, or no, we do not reject it. Therefore, one result cannot be "more significant" than another, and there is no such thing as a "very significant" or "highly significant" result. (That would be like saying "more yes" or "highly yes.") Results are simply significant or nonsignificant, period! Also, we do not attribute human actions to statistical procedures, saying such things as "according to the ANOVA . . ." or "the *t* gave significance." Instead, we say that "there were significant differences between the means" or that "there was a significant effect of the independent variable."

Figures   Because of cost and space considerations, we include graphs, tables, or other artwork only when the information is complicated enough that the reader will benefit from a visual presentation. Usually, graphs—called **"Figures"**— provide the clearest way to summarize the *pattern* in a relationship. Note, however, that the author should also have something to say about each figure, telling readers what they should see in it. (For illustrative purposes, a figure is included in our droodle study manuscript, although, technically, the relationship is so simple that a figure is unnecessary.)

Every figure needs to be numbered (even if there is only one). At the point in the narrative where the reader should look at the figure, we direct their attention to it, saying something like "As can be seen in Figure 1...." Refer to Figure 4.9 for the wording as it appears in our manuscript.

We do not physically place the figure here, and an important change in the most recent (fourth) edition of the *Publication Manual* is that we do *not* indicate where the figure should be placed (the printer will decide that). The graph itself is drawn on a separate page and placed after the references at the end of the manuscript. The sample figure from our manuscript appears in Figure 4.10.

There are numerous rules for preparing a figure, so check the *Publication Manual*. In general, the height of the Y axis should be about 60 to 75 percent of the length of the X axis. Fully label each axis, using the names of the variables and their amounts. Use black ink, because color is expensive to publish, and a reader might be color blind. If the figure contains more than one line in the body of the graph, use different symbols for each (e.g., one line is solid and one is dashed). Then, to the side of the figure, provide a "legend" or "key" to the symbols. (Such figures are discussed further in Chapter 8.)

Every figure has an explanatory title, called the "figure caption," which briefly identifies the variables and relationship depicted. (For the figure in our manuscript we used the caption "Mean number of droodles correctly recalled as a function of nonhumorous and humorous interpretations.") However, instead of positioning each caption on the cor-

FIGURE 4.9   Sample Portion of Results Section Showing Reference to a Figure

$\underline{t}(78) = 6.32$, $\underline{p} <.05$. The relationship between amount of humor and recall scores can be seen in Figure 1. Although a positive relationship was obtained, the slope of this curve indicates that the rate of change in recall scores as a function of increased humor was not large.

Discussion

The results of the present study indicate that humorous interpretations lead to greater retention of droodles than do

FIGURE 4.10   Sample Figure

The caption for our graph reads: "Mean number of droodles correctly recalled as a function of nonhumorous and humorous interpretations."

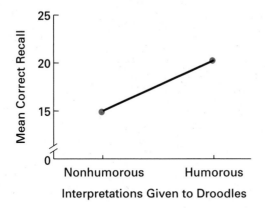

responding figure (the printer does that), we place all captions on the **Figure Caption page,** a separate page at the end of the manuscript.

Tables   We create a table of our results, rather than a figure, when it is important for the reader to compare the actual numerical values of means, percentages, and so on. However, a **table** is called for only when there are too many numbers to efficiently include in the narrative. All tables are numbered consecutively, and, as with figures, the reader is directed to them at appropriate points in the Results section. The actual tables are placed at the end of the manuscript. Note that we place the title for each table *on* the table itself. (The *Publication Manual* provides detailed instructions for laying out a table.)

> *REMEMBER*   The *Results* section summarizes the data and the relationship obtained in our study, and reports the outcomes of the inferential procedures we perform.

The Discussion

The purpose of the **Discussion** section is to interpret our results and draw our conclusions. Here we answer the questions originally posed in the Introduction. The Discussion section begins at the point where we have already reported a significant relationship, so our first question is, "Do the results confirm (1) our predictions, and thus (2) our hypothesis? We can almost always answer this question by beginning our discussion with the phrase "The results of the present study. . ."

As the term *Discussion* implies, however, we do not merely state our conclusions; we discuss them. Our task, after answering the original research question, is to use the answer to explain what we have learned about behavior. Recall from the funnel diagram in Figure 4.2 that, in the Discussion section, we work backward, from the specific to the general. Beginning with the narrowly defined relationship in our study, we generalize to the relationship between our variables that might be found with other subjects or situations. Then we generalize the findings based on our variables to the constructs we originally set out to study. Figures 4.9 and 4.11 show a portion of our discussion.

We begin our discussion by focusing on the descriptive statistics we reported (t or F are no help here). Our job is to become psychologists again, translating the numbers and statistics into descriptions of behaviors and explanations of the variables that influence them. For example, we obtained a significantly higher mean for humorous interpretations. This higher mean reflects higher recall scores, which in turn indicate better *retention,* a mental *behavior* that is different from the behavior that occurs when nonhumorous interpretations are given. Thus, based on the scores in each condition, we propose how manipulating humor influences the memory system. Of course, we must not discount those droodles given nonhumorous interpretations, because they were frequently recalled, and the addition of humor had no great effect. Then, as we saw in the previous chapter, we consider what the direction and rate of change in scores, and the consistency or inconsistency in the relationship indicate. Also, the proportion of variance accounted for by this relationship gives us a perspective on the importance of humor as a variable affecting memory. (Recall that, in studies with more than two conditions, only some conditions may differ significantly and represent an actual relationship. In such cases we would also consider why and how this result occurs.)

FIGURE 4.11 Sample Portion of the Discussion Section

```
                                      Effect of Humorous      8

        nonhumorous interpretations. Because the meaningfulness of the

        droodles provided by the interpretations was presumably constant

        in both conditions, it appears that humor provides an additional

        source of retrieval cues. This conclusion is consistent with the

        proposal that humor increases the distinctiveness of a stimulus,

        thereby facilitating recall by increasing the accessibility of

        the stimulus in memory.

            The improvement in recall produced by humor, however, was

        relatively small. This result may be due to the fact that all

        droodles were made meaningful, although sometimes by a

        nonhumorous interpretation. As in other research (Lockhart &
```

Throughout our discussion, our explanations must rationally fit with previous findings and theoretical explanations. Thus, we attempt to provide an integrated and consistent explanation, answering the question, "Given our findings *and* past findings, what is the present state of our knowledge about a behavior or construct?" In our droodle study, for example, we relate our findings to current explanations of the role of distinctiveness and meaningfulness in memory. Notice, however, that in our sample Discussion section we use such words as *presumably, probably,* and *appears.* We do not say *prove,* or provide explanations as if they are fact. And although we can say *causes* or *influences,* the difficulty in identifying causal variables leads us to use these words cautiously.

Of course, we must also consider any *major* flaws in the design that limit our interpretations or our confidence in them. When discussing such flaws do not use the tired old argument that the data may not be representative or that a larger N is needed. Your significant results have *confidently* eliminated these arguments. Instead, any questions you raise about your study are based on these important design issues:

1. Reliability and content validity: Did our way of changing the interpretations consistently manipulate the variable of humor? Did we consistently and only measure subjects' recall of the droodles? (Or did we measure their drawing ability?)

2. Internal validity: Were the humorous and nonhumorous interpretations truly equal in meaningfulness? Perhaps the unusual elements in a humorous interpretation yield a broader, more wide-ranging meaning. If so, then by manipulating humor we have also manipulated meaningfulness, and greater meaningfulness may have increased recall scores. It is possible that this (or another) confounding occurred, and that we have reduced internal validity because of it.

3. External validity: Is it appropriate to generalize this relationship to other subjects and situations? Did our subjects have an unusual sense of humor, so that our results are unique? Droodles are simple visual stimuli, so can we generalize the effect of humor to verbal material or for complex visual material?

4. Construct validity: Do the subjects' recall scores actually reflect their "memory" of the droodles? Have we correctly defined "meaningfulness" and "humor"? In particular, we have no empirical evidence that humor produces "distinctiveness." Rather, we have only proposed that humor has this effect.

Although you should attempt to prevent potential flaws when designing a study, they are sometimes unavoidable. Do not try to hide a major flaw. Instead, evaluate the study and either provide counterarguments to explain why a potential flaw does not seriously reduce your confidence in your conclusions, or qualify and limit your conclusions in lieu of the troubling flaw.

Clearly, further research is needed before we can be confident that humor aids memory in the way we have proposed. We often conclude the Discussion section by pointing out the *specific* next step to be taken in the research area. Remember, as authors we are the experts, so we indicate what hypotheses should be tested next. (For example, we would note the lack of evidence that humor makes a stimulus more distinctive, and suggest that researchers attempt to confirm this hypothesis.)

REMEMBER   The *Discussion* section answers the questions posed by the study, interpreting the results in terms of what we now know about the underlying behavior.

The Reference Page

The final section following the discussion is the **Reference** page(s). Here are listed alphabetically the complete reference for all sources cited in the article. Each source should be one that you have read. If, for example, you learn about Jones' article from reading Smith's report, it is best that you read Jones too (because Smith may be misleading). If you do not, then your reference to Jones should indicate that it is "as cited in" Smith.

As shown in Figure 4.12, each reference is typed as a paragraph. (The published version will be converted to the normal hanging-indent format, as shown in the bibliography in this textbook.) For a journal article, provide the last name and first initials of all authors, listed in the same order as they appear in the article. Listed next are the year of publication, the article's title, and the title of the journal, its volume number, and the

FIGURE 4.12   Sample Reference Page
Notice the punctuation and underlining.

```
                                      Effect of Humorous   10
                           References
     Bower, G. H., Karlin, M. B., & Dueck, A. (1975).
Comprehension and memory for pictures. Memory and Cognition, 3,
216-220.
     Desrochers, A., & Begg, I. (1987). A theoretical account of
encoding and retrieval processes in the use of imagery-based
mnemonic techniques: The special case of the keyword method. In
M. A. McDaniel & M. Pressley (Eds.), Imagery and related
mnemonic processes: Theories, individual differences, and
applications (pp. 56-77). New York: Springer-Verlag.
     Einstein, G. O., McDaniel, M. A., & Lackey, S. (1989).
Bizarre imagery, interference, and distinctiveness. Journal of
Experimental Psychology: Learning, Memory, and Cognition, 15,
137-146.
     Hunt, R. R., & Elliott, J. M. (1980). The role of
```

page numbers of the article. The *Publication Manual* provides slightly different rules for referencing books, book chapters, monthly magazines, and so on.

PUTTING IT ALL TOGETHER

By now, you have probably gathered that most research ideas come from the literature. Authors suggest rival, alternative explanations for their results, point out untested hypotheses, or indicate the direction future research should go. Also, no study is perfect, so as a reader, you may find flaws that suggest a research hypothesis. Or you may discover two published studies in which the data or theoretical interpretations directly contradict each other, so design a study to help resolve the debate.

You may also choose to literally replicate any study, but it is more interesting and informative to add a new twist or perspective to the design that simultaneously expands our knowledge. For example, in replicating the above droodle study, you might add a third, no-interpretation condition, or change the humor in the interpretations using a different approach. Alternatively, you might identify a technique used to study one behavior and design a study to determine whether it can be used to examine a different behavior. (Since humorous droodles may elevate a person's mood, perhaps you could adapt the droodle experiment to the study of mood.)

Be creative when selecting a research idea. When reading about any model or theory, ask, "If the behavior operates as proposed, then what should the behavior be in a specific situation?" By identifying the situation and answering this question, you will have generated a hypothesis—so test it! Also, for any existing area of research there will always be a multitude of additional variables to consider, including environmental factors or subject variables. And, finally, you can study a behavior from many perspectives. For example, you might ask, "How do motivational, cognitive, emotional, or social factors influence or alter the results of our droodle study? "

Developing your research ideas will be easier if you recognize that any published article describes a much smoother, more intelligent, and more organized process than actually occurred during the study itself. An article will not report the number of subjects who volunteered for the study but never showed up. It will gloss over the difficulty the researcher had in finding an artist who could draw droodles or the hours it took to invent their interpretations. And it will not mention the number of prior attempts, using different stimuli or procedures, that failed to produce a significant relationship. Thus, although an article may give you the impression that the researcher is omniscient and the study ran like clockwork, do not be fooled. Research is much more challenging—and fun—than that.

CHAPTER SUMMARY

1. A research report is organized according to the logical sequence in which the various aspects of a study occur.

2. Most psychological articles follow the rules set down in the *Publication Manual of the American Psychological Association*, so that they conform to "APA format."

3. The *Psychological Abstracts* contains the abstracts of articles recently published in other psychological journals.

4. The *Social Science Citation Index* is used to identify recent articles that cite a previous article.

5. A research report should not present information that is redundant with a reader's knowledge or other reference sources. Rather, its focus is to provide to readers the necessary information for (a) understanding the study, (b) evaluating it, and (c) literally replicating it.

6. A report's *Title* should clearly communicate the variables and relationship being studied. The *Abstract* should summarize the report. Together these elements allow readers to determine whether they want to read the article.

7. The *Introduction* presents all information that will be used to interpret the results. It is here that we reconstruct the logic and cite the literature we used in working from the hypothetical constructs to the specific predicted relationship between scores.

8. The *Method* section provides the information needed to understand, critique, and literally replicate the data-collection procedures. It consists of three subsections: *Participants, Materials or Apparatus,* and *Procedure.*

9. The *Participants* section defines the subjects of a study in terms of their characteristics, their total number (*N*), and the reimbursement given.

10. The *Materials or Apparatus* section describes the characteristics of the stimuli, the response materials, and the equipment used to test participants. Any information about the reliability and validity of the material and apparatus is also included here.

11. The *Procedure* section describes the situation(s) in which participants were tested. It should summarize the instructions given to subjects and the task(s) performed by them, and complete the description of the design.

12. The *Results* section describes the statistical procedures performed and the outcomes obtained. In this order, we (a) describe the scores, (b) report the descriptive statistics, (c) identify the inferential procedure performed, and (d) report the results of the procedure. We report primary procedures first, followed by secondary analyses.

13. We always indicate the alpha level we used and include "$p < .05$" when results are significant or "$p > .05$" (or whatever alpha is) when results are nonsignificant.

14. In the *Discussion* section we interpret the results and draw our conclusions. We answer the initial questions posed by the study and relate our findings to past findings, providing an integrated description of a behavior or construct. It is here that we also deal with any major potential flaws in the study.

15. In an APA-style manuscript, after the discussion section comes the *References,* the *Tables,* the *Figure Caption Page,* and the *Figures.*

REVIEW QUESTIONS

1. Why is it necessary to conduct a literature search?
2. How would you go about finding literature that investigates the possible connection between violence on television and heightened aggressiveness in adolescents?
3. Let's say you find an article related to the topic of television and aggressiveness in adolescents. How can you use this article to find relevant research that occurred prior to it?
4. The article you find was published in 1980. How would you use this article to find more recent related research?
5. Let's say you wish to measure the aggressiveness of a sample of adolescents. Other than creating your own test, what two approaches can you take to obtain a valid and reliable test of aggressiveness?
6. What information should you include in the title of a research article?
7. What information should you include in the abstract of a research article?
8. From another researcher's perspective, what is the purpose of reading your title and abstract?
9. (a) How do you create the "manuscript page header" that appears at the top of each page of a manuscript? (b) What is the "running head," and how is it used?
10. (a) Summarize the information that is presented in the Introduction. (b) In general terms, what information about a study is not included here?
11. (a) What are the three standard components of the Method section? (b) What information is contained in each subsection? (c) In general terms, what information about a study is not reported in the Methods section?
12. (a) How is the Results section organized? (b) In general terms, what information about a study is not reported here?
13. (a) When should you include a figure in a research report? (b) When should you include a table in a research report?
14. (a) How is the Discussion section related to the Introduction? (b) In addition to drawing a conclusion about your specific prediction, what concerns are addressed in the Discussion section?
15. For each of the following statements, indicate two reasons that it is incorrect: (a) "40 students will hear the music and be tested." (b) "Because the critical value is 2.45 and the obtained value is 24.7, the results are very significant." (c) "The mean scores in the respective conditions for men were 1.4, 3.0, 2.7, 6.9, 11.8, 14.77, 22.31, 25.6, 33.7, and 41.2. For girls, the mean scores were. . . ." (d) "To create the groups, the participants were split in half, with five individuals in each." (e) "The results were significant, indicating the null hypothesis should be rejected. Therefore, I concluded that the relationship demonstrates. . . ." (f) Title: "Type of Interpretation as a Function of Remembering Funny Droodles."

DISCUSSION QUESTIONS

1. In question 15 above, revise each statement so that it employs correct APA format.
2. Examine a published research article and discuss how it follows the funnel diagram originally presented in Figure 4.1.
3. (a) What practical application might the droodle study have, for example, in the preparation of lectures or textbooks? (b) Why might your confidence in such a generalization be limited? (c) How would you use the literature to increase your confidence?
4. A researcher obtains a correlation coefficient of $r = .434$, which is not quite significant (the critical value is .44). Several participants, however, behaved contrary to the researcher's predictions. The study has potential life-saving applications, so to produce a significant r the researcher eliminates the data from these "bad" subjects and publishes the study. What is your reaction to this decision?

PART **II**

Designing and Conducting Laboratory Experiments

As we have seen, researchers have many issues to deal with when designing a controlled and systematic study. Laboratory experiments typically yield the greatest control, since we solicit subjects to come to our controlled environment and be tested under situations we determine. The following chapters examine each of the major components of a laboratory experiment. However, don't for a moment think that laboratory experiments are the only research method used by psychologists. Because experiments involve so much control, discussing them is a way to learn about the many issues involved in designing and evaluating any type of study. Therefore, Chapter 5 focuses on the decisions we make regarding the independent variable, Chapter 6 explains how to measure the dependent variable, and Chapter 7 examines how to control subject variables. Then, in Chapter 8, after looking at experiments involving only one independent variable, we will see how these considerations combine when creating a complex experiment involving more than one independent variable.

Although this discussion will simplify the decision-making process by examining each major topic in a separate chapter, remember that, as a researcher, you must consider all of these issues simultaneously. A decision about one aspect of an experiment often affects many other decisions.

5 Selecting and Controlling the Independent Variable

One of the first steps taken in designing a study is to create operational definitions of the variables. As noted earlier, an operational definition specifies a variable in terms of how it is measured. This chapter focuses on the decisions involved in developing an operational definition of an independent variable. The process of defining how we measure and then manipulate the variable allows us to create the specific conditions under which we will observe subjects and measure them using the dependent variable.

We have four major objectives when defining an independent variable: (1) to select procedures that reflect the hypothetical construct and variable we intend to investigate, (2) to design the conditions in such a way that we detect and adequately describe the predicted relationship, (3) to create a controlled and reliable procedure that eliminates the influence of extraneous variables, and (4) to ensure that our procedure is ethical.

SELECTING AN INDEPENDENT VARIABLE

It is pointless to design a study merely by grabbing some variables out of the blue to see if they are related: In so doing, we end up with a design in search of a question to answer. *Research proceeds well only if the question you want to answer determines the design of your study*. Therefore, the first step in designing a study is to formulate a hypothesis. For help we turn to the literature, where we find theories, models, and hypothetical constructs that guide our research, ensuring that our hypothesis rationally and parsimoniously fits known psychological processes.

To confidently answer a question about the causes of or influences on a behavior, we design an experiment. Then we select an independent variable that we will systematically change, as well as a dependent variable that measures changes in a behavior. For example, our interest might be in the environmental factors that influence people's stress level. In particular, we might ask whether subjects' stress level will differ after they have experienced various types of music. From this, it logically follows that we should select different types of music—classical, jazz, rock and roll, and so on—as the conditions of our independent variable. After playing one type of music to some subjects, we will measure their scores on a dependent variable that reflects their stress level. We can envision this design using the diagram in Table 5.1.

Recall that an independent variable is also called a *factor*. Each column represents a condition of the independent variable, also called a "level" or a "treatment," under which subjects are tested. The Xs represent each subject's score on the dependent variable in that condition.

Completing the design of the study requires that we decide on all of the details that constitute this procedure, using the four components of any study. That is, we must determine the number and type of *subjects,* the specific behavior of the *researcher,* the *environment* in which testing will occur, and the details of the *measurement procedure.* Then, in defining the independent variable, we must decide how many music conditions

TABLE 5.1   Diagram of an Experiment Studying Stress Level as a Function of Type of Music Presented

	Conditions of the independent variable (Type of music)		
	Condition 1 (Classical)	*Condition 2 (Jazz)*	*Condition 3 (Rock and Roll)*
Scores on dependent variable (Stress)	X X X . .	X X X . .	X X X . .
Mean scores	$\overline{X}$	$\overline{X}$	$\overline{X}$

we will present, what example of each type of music we will present, the duration and loudness of the music, and any other consideration that pertains to playing different types of music to subjects in a controlled fashion.

After we collect the data, we use our design and statistical procedures to answer our original question. We look for a relationship in which scores on the dependent variable (stress) consistently change "as a function of" changes in the independent variable (type of music). So that we can more easily see these changes, we summarize the dependent scores in each condition, usually by computing the mean of the scores ($\overline{X}$) in each column. Of course, there is always the possibility that differences between the scores in the conditions are the result of sampling error, so we perform the appropriate inferential statistics. If the means for the conditions differ significantly, we have evidence that type of music influences stress level. In reporting our research, we then propose how and why this relationship occurs psychologically.

Recall that the above design is a **true experiment** having a true independent variable, because we can randomly assign any subject to any condition. In addition, recognize that there are two important terms for describing the characteristics of the above design.

1. This is a **one-way design** because we are manipulating one independent variable or factor.

2. This is a **between-subjects design** because we randomly assign subjects to each condition without regard for the subjects in the other conditions, and each subject serves in only one condition.

Our focus in this and the next chapter will be on true experiments with one-way, between-subjects designs.

> **REMEMBER**   In a *between-subjects design,* we randomly select and assign subjects to one condition without regard to the subjects assigned to other conditions, and each subject serves in only one condition.

Approaches to Manipulating the Independent Variable

Broadly speaking, the manipulation of a true independent variable involves changing a stimulus to which subjects respond. Yet the stimulus may be as simple as a flash of light or as complex as a social situation. Therefore, there are few hard and fast rules for operationally defining a particular independent variable. The specifics of our treatments will depend on the specific behavior, variables, and subjects we seek to study. The research literature describes many creative ways of presenting and manipulating a stimulus, so it is a great help during the process of defining an independent variable. A manipulation typically involves one of the following approaches.

Presenting Different Stimuli   Researchers often create the conditions of an independent variable by presenting subjects with different stimuli or changing the characteristics of a stimulus. For example, researchers studying "psychophysics" have presented stimuli that differ along some physical dimension (e.g., loudness, brightness, weight), and the dependent variable is a measure of subjects' detection or recognition of the stimuli (e.g., Stevens, 1975). Researchers in developmental psychology have presented various sex-stereotyped toys to see whether children are stereotypical in their manner of play (Blakemore, LaRue & Olejnik, 1979). In studying aggression, Green (1978) exposed subjects to films in an experiment for which the conditions consisted of different amounts of violence depicted and the dependent measure was the aggressiveness subsequently shown by subjects. And researchers in social psychology have measured the effect of various furniture arrangements on social interactions (Campbell & Herren, 1978).

Manipulating Context   Often the independent variable is the context in which a stimulus is presented, while the stimulus itself is kept constant. For example, environmental psychologists have presented various amounts of background noise while measuring subjects' performance on a set of mental problems (Hockey, 1970). Researchers studying learning processes have examined the effect of different types and amounts of rewards or punishments on subjects' ability to learn a task (e.g., Bower & Hilgard, 1981). Other researchers have induced different moods in subjects through hypnosis and then examined subjects' memory and thought processes (e.g., Bower, 1981). And still others have examined broad contextual variables, such as studying subjects' emotional states as a function of the seasons of the year (Rosenthal et al., 1986).

Manipulating Information Given Subjects   The independent variable may consist of the instructions or information given to subjects in each condition. For example, to study how diligently people work in a group, Weldon and Mustari (1988) created conditions by telling some subjects that they were working alone and other subjects that they were working with unseen others. To study memory, Loftus (1975) examined how different information conveyed in questions about an event affected subjects' recall of the event. And to study attitudes, Phesterson, Kiesler, and Goldberg (1971) presented a painting to subjects who were told that the supposed painter was a male or female, to see whether the subjects would evaluate the painting in a sexist manner.

Manipulating Social Settings Using Confederates   **Confederates** are people enlisted by a researcher to act as other subjects or "accidental" passers-by, thus creating a particular social situation to which the "real" subjects can then respond. For example, Deutsch and Krauss (1960) created a supposed game between a subject and a confederate, in order to study the subjects' cooperativeness as the costs of cooperation increased. Darley and Latané (1968) had a confederate fake a seizure and measured a subject's willingness to help as a function of the number of other people present. And Asch (1951) manipulated the number of confederates present along with a subject who, when asked to judge the length of a line, drastically overestimated its length. In this last instance, the dependent variable was the overestimate produced by the subject, showing the extent to which the subject conformed to social pressure.

Stressing a Psychological System   One interesting approach to the creation of experimental conditions is to stress or overload a psychological system and then to infer from subjects' responses how the system normally operates. For example, researchers studying the psychology of language ("psycholinguistics") have developed procedures for inducing speech errors—getting your "mords wixed"—to infer speech-production processes (Fromkin, 1980). Researchers studying attention have presented two "dichotic" messages simultaneously, one to each ear. In this case, the conditions consisted of varied instructions or message content, and the dependent variable was the way in which each message was perceived (Gray and Wedderburn, 1960). Other researchers have stressed subjects socially or emotionally—for example, by having them produce a behavior that conflicts with an attitude they advocate and measuring how they resolve the conflict (Sherman & Gorkin, 1980). Still others have created conditions under which subjects fail various tasks, to study how the subjects attribute blame (Whitley & Frieze, 1985).

Physiological Investigations   Some researchers manipulate internal, physiological processes. Here the conditions may involve giving subjects different amounts of alcohol or other drugs (Taylor & Leonard, 1983), manipulating the amount of sleep subjects get (Horne, 1978), or varying the "sensory deprivation" they receive (e.g., Suedfield, Ballard, Baker-Brown, & Borrie, 1986). Using animal subjects, researchers may employ surgical techniques to create different conditions in which parts of the brain are removed or altered (e.g., Tokunaga, Fukushima, Kemnitz & Bray, 1986). The dependent variables in such studies indicate whether these manipulations produce differences in subjects' behavior, motivation, memory, and so on. And in neurological research the conditions have involved the visual presentation of words such that they fall on different locations on the eye. Here the dependent variable is the time needed to recognize each stimulus, allowing researchers to map the flow of information through the hemispheres of the brain (Gazzaniga, 1985).

Manipulating Intervening Variables   Often, researchers will employ the above techniques to manipulate a variable because they believe it changes an internal psychological state, which then influences a behavior. This internal state is called an intervening variable. An **intervening variable** is influenced by the independent variable, which in turn influences the dependent variable. It "intervenes" or comes between the independent and·

dependent variable. For example, let's say we hypothesize that being frustrated makes subjects angry, and that greater anger leads to greater amounts of aggressive behavior. Here we manipulate the independent variable of frustration—for example, by sometimes blocking subjects from obtaining a desirable reward. In doing so, we presumably change the intervening variable of anger, which will then influence subjects' scores on the dependent variable of aggressiveness—for example, the degree to which they punish a confederate.

Recognize that psychologists distinguish between two types of internal psychological states. A **state characteristic** is a temporary, changeable attribute that is influenced by situational factors. For example, you have a certain "state anxiety," the level of anxiety you experience depending on the situation you are in. (Suddenly realizing you are unprepared for an exam will raise your state anxiety.) Conversely, a **trait characteristic** is stable over time and not easily influenced by situational factors. (Think in terms of "personality traits," here.) For example, self-esteem is generally defined as a trait characteristic, because it is relatively immune to influence by the situation you are in. Some attributes have both state and trait components: A person's momentary state anxiety can be described in conjunction with his or her "trait anxiety," the general level of anxiety the person experiences regardless of the situation. Other attributes, such as self-esteem, are considered to have only a trait component.

State characteristics can be manipulated and studied as intervening variables, because they will change in response to the conditions of an independent variable. Trait characteristics are *not* studied in this way, because, being rather permanent, they are not influenced by most manipulations.

> **REMEMBER** *State characteristics* are transient and can be experimentally manipulated. *Trait characteristics* are rather permanent and cannot easily be manipulated.

Drawing Construct- and Content-Valid Inferences

In selecting from any of the above approaches, bear in mind that if you find a significant relationship, you will want to infer that your study demonstrates an aspect of nature. In Chapter 2 we discussed several types of *validity*, the degree to which we can be confident in our inferences. Each of these types is a concern when selecting and creating an operational definition of our independent variable.

First, when defining the independent variable, we must consider whether our manipulation has *construct validity*, thus allowing valid inferences about the underlying construct as we conceptualize it. For example, are we truly increasing the "social pressure" a subject experiences by increasing the number of confederates in a room? Are we erroneously claiming to influence the construct of self-esteem, which, by definition, is actually a rather immutable trait characteristic? If our study lacks construct validity, then any inferences we draw about underlying psychological processes will be in error.

Likewise, we are concerned with *content validity*, the degree to which a procedure allows accurate inferences about a variable of interest. If, for example, our objective is to expose subjects to films featuring different amounts of violence, then we must measure and manipulate this variable. But if we inadvertently select different films based on their humorous content or their plots, then we are not actually and only studying the influence of the variable of a film's violent content.

Questions of construct and content validity are ultimately resolved by theoretical discussion as well as by research showing that a procedure is valid because it produces the same results as other procedures that are already accepted as valid. If as a beginning researcher you are too inventive when defining your variables, you run the risk of threatening the construct and content validity of your study. Instead, it is best to adopt procedures that are commonly accepted as valid in the literature. Or, at the very least, when being inventive you must be concerned with demonstrating that a procedure allows for valid inferences. (The procedures for demonstrating construct and content validity are discussed in Chapter 9.)

Drawing Externally Valid Inferences

Recall that, when interpreting our results, we also seek *external validity,* so that we can confidently generalize our results to other subjects and other situations. The key point here is that our independent variable and other components of the experiment should not be so atypical that they generalize in a very restricted way to a very limited type of subject. Because there are several perspectives from which we can generalize our results, researchers refer to two additional aspects of external validity.

Temporal Validity   One aspect of external validity is **temporal validity,** the extent to which our results can be generalized to other time periods. Temporal validity has two applications. First, a treatment will last for a particular period of time and there will be a fixed period of time between a treatment and measurement of the dependent variable. Temporal validity is the extent to which an observed relationship can be generalized to other time frames. Second, a study occurs at a specific time occurring in a particular month, in a particular year. Here, temporal validity is the extent to which results can be generalized to other months or years.

For temporal validity, we define our independent variable and procedures so that they are representative in terms of time. We seek internal temporal components of the study that should generalize well, we choose stimuli and procedures that should generalize to different eras, we conduct the study over a period of time that encompasses important seasonal variations, and so on.

> **REMEMBER**   *Temporal validity* is the extent to which our generalizations are accurate across different time periods.

Recognize that many past research findings do have temporal validity for generalizing to present times. Therefore, when you find a research article in the literature that was published a number of years ago, do not automatically dismiss it as outdated. Instead, consider the specific behaviors involved: Studies of basic psychological processes (e.g., thinking, memory, or emotion) tend to apply to past and present generations, whereas studies of social processes, attitudes, and other behaviors that are influenced by societal changes over time may generalize less well.

Ecological Validity   When generalizing our results, we must consider whether the independent and dependent variables, and the entire context of the experiment, represent natural behaviors and natural situations. This component of external validity is called ecological validity. **Ecological validity** is the extent to which an experimental situation can be generalized to natural settings and behaviors. If a design does not have ecological validity, we end up focusing on what subjects *can* do in an experiment, not what they *usually* do in real life. For example, years of psychological research were directed at "paired-associate learning" in which subjects learned pairs of nonsense syllables (e.g., they were instructed that BIM and YOB go together). But nonsense syllables are not an everyday experience for most people, and this learning process is an unusual one that occurs only in the laboratory. Such research thus lacks ecological validity: We cannot be confident that it accurately generalizes to and describes natural, everyday learning processes.

Researchers often lose ecological validity in their quest for internal validity. For example, they may develop a rather unusual task for subjects in order to simplify the stimuli and the behavior. (Paired associate learning allows for much more controlled and objective observations than, say, classroom learning.) However, where possible, a balance between both types of validity is desirable; the challenge is to maintain control while creating a research situation that bears some resemblance to the real world. Essentially, therefore, to the extent that we can, we seek both to provide realistic stimuli and to require that subjects perform realistic, everyday tasks.

> **REMEMBER**   *Ecological validity* is the extent to which the situation and behaviors in a study are those that are found in the natural environment.

TWO EXAMPLE STUDIES

To illustrate the decisions we must make when defining an independent variable, the following discussions will refer to two example studies. The first comes from research investigating emotions. One hypothesis is that the facial muscles people use when smiling provide feedback to the brain that further improves their mood. (In other words, not only does being happy make you smile, but smiling also makes you happy.) To test this "facial-feedback" hypothesis, Strack, Martin, and Stepper (1988) had subjects hold a pen in their mouths, using either their teeth (which mimics smiling) or their puckered lips (which does not mimic smiling). The researchers then measured subjects' mood as the dependent variable.

The second study, from environmental psychology, tested the hypothesis that when the temperature in the environment is "hot," people become more aggressive. Bell (1980) placed subjects in a laboratory under various temperature conditions. The experimenter intentionally provoked subjects and then provided a situation in which subjects could retaliate through their evaluation of him. The degree of negative evaluations was the dependent variable for measuring aggressiveness.

In creating these studies, the researchers had to develop operational definitions for measuring and manipulating the independent variable. What constitutes "smiling" as opposed to "not smiling"? How can a smile be induced? What is a "hot" temperature? How is room temperature measured and changed? Many of the decisions we make when creating definitions are arbitrary, because there is often more than one approach to take. "Hot" can be defined as a certain arbitrary temperature *or* as the temperature each subject subjectively judges as hot. A smile can be formed by manually manipulating a subject's face *or* by instructing the subject to smile.

Of the possible operational definitions for a variable, the one we select depends on a combination of considerations. First, our operational definition depends on the purposes of the study. Second, we must consider the various aspects of validity discussed above, attempting to select a definition that best allows for the inferences we wish to draw. Third, we may have to settle for inherent weaknesses, given the nature of the behavior under study. (After all, our procedures for measuring temperature are likely to be more precisely and objectively defined than those for measuring smiling, and thus have potentially greater content validity.) Finally, our definition must allow for a controlled study. (For example, the mere act of instructing subjects to smile might cause an elevation of their mood, separate from any facial feedback.) As we will see in the discussions that follow, design decisions are always made in response to the questions "What is it we wish to study?" and "What aspects must we control?"

SELECTING THE CONDITIONS OF THE INDEPENDENT VARIABLE

Defining the independent variable requires selecting the particular conditions we will present to subjects. Specifically, we must decide on the number of conditions and on the specific amount or category of the independent variable that each condition will present.

Selecting the Number of Conditions

The simplest research design typically compares the effect of one condition of the independent variable to the effect of another condition. For example, in the smile study, subjects may be asked to mimic smiling in one condition and to not mimic smiling in the other. In the temperature study, the two temperatures of 70 and 90 degrees Fahrenheit might arbitrarily be selected. Because the design and interpretation of a study are inseparable, we evaluate our design decision in terms of the interpretation it allows. Figure 5.1 shows some possible results for each of these studies.

Before we interpret these results, notice that the type of graph we create depends upon the characteristics of the *independent variable*. Graph A is a **line graph,** in which adjacent data points are joined by straight lines. We create a line graph when the independent variable implies a continuous, ordered amount. (A continuous variable allows for fractional amounts, at least theoretically.) Temperature is a continuous, ordered

FIGURE 5.1   Possible Temperature-Study and Smile-Study Results

(A) a line graph showing data for the temperature study, and (B) a bar graph showing data for the smile study.

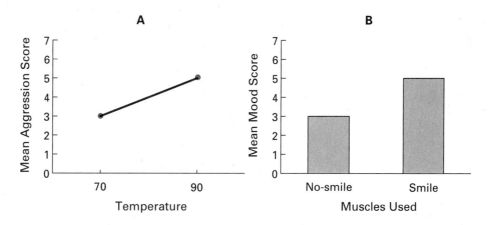

variable because 90 degrees is more than 70 degrees, and because there are other, potentially fractional amounts falling between 70 and 90 degrees. Thus, there is only one place on the *X* axis to place a third condition of 80 degrees. Graph B is a **bar graph,** in which the height of each bar reflects a data point and the bars do not touch. We create a bar graph when the independent variable implies discrete categories and the categories follow no set order. (A discrete variable does *not* allow for fractional amounts.) Our "smile" variable is unordered because the two conditions are merely different: Smiling is not more of something than not smiling. Further, smiling cannot be broken down into fractional amounts, and the location we would place a third category—such as frowning—would be arbitrary.

> *REMEMBER*   Data obtained with an ordered, continuous independent variable are plotted on a *line graph*. Data obtained with an unordered, discrete independent variable are plotted on a *bar graph*.

Let's now interpret the graphs in Figure 5.1. Both graphs depict a relationship: The mean scores for the conditions are located at different positions on the *Y* axis, thus indicating a different set of dependent scores for each condition. These data appear to show that a temperature of 90 degrees results in greater aggressiveness than does one of 70 degrees, and that mood is heightened by mimicking a smile compared to not mimicking a smile. If the results are significant, we say there is a *significant effect* of the independent variable. If we find a significant effect of the temperature manipulation, then within the limitations of our design we can argue that increasing temperature causes an increase in aggressiveness. Similarly, with a significant effect of the smile manipulation, we can argue that using the smile muscles results in an increase in mood.

Although these designs seem to adequately test our hypotheses, it is important to ask whether only two conditions are sufficient to accurately describe the *type* of relationship between the variables. Recall that a relationship may be either *linear* (following a straight line) or *nonlinear* (following a line that changes direction). In a study with just two conditions, one group's mean can be only higher or lower than the other group's mean, so the data can depict only a linear relationship, even if the relationship in nature is nonlinear. We must have at least three conditions to see a nonlinear relationship. Consider the graphs we might obtain with two and then four temperature conditions, as shown in Figure 5.2.

When interpreting graph A, we assume that aggression scores at other, untested temperatures (such as at 80 and 100 degrees) would change in the same way as did those at the temperatures we observed, such that all means would fall on the straight line. But this is an assumption! By testing the additional temperature conditions, we might confirm this linear relationship. However, as in graph B, we might instead find a nonlinear relationship showing that increasing temperature does not always result in a consistent linear increase in aggression: The 70- and 80-degree conditions have the same mean score, thus showing no effect on aggression—no relationship—when the temperature changes from 70 to 80 degrees. Increases beyond 80 degrees produce increases in aggression, with the rate of increase greater for 100 degrees than for 90 degrees.

Thus, to be sure we are accurately describing the type of relationship formed between our independent and dependent variables, we may want to add more conditions. When practical, research typically involves at least three conditions, in case the relationship is nonlinear. The maximum tends to be six to eight conditions, which is considered more than adequate for describing most relationships.

> **REMEMBER** To demonstrate a nonlinear relationship, we must have at least three conditions.

FIGURE 5.2 Two-Condition and Four-Condition Temperature-Study Results

(A) The inferred linear relationship with two conditions, and (B) the demonstrated nonlinear relationship with four conditions.

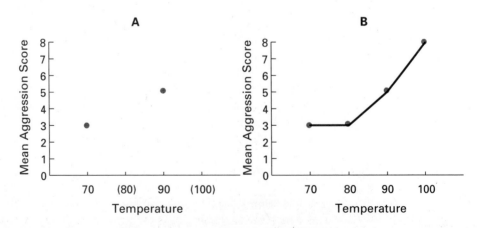

Specifying Each Condition of the Independent Variable

In addition to deciding on the number of conditions, we must specify the particular amount or category of the independent variable to be presented in each condition. Should we use temperatures of 75, 80, and 85 degrees, or temperatures of 50, 100, and 150 degrees? The answer depends in part on our hypothesis: Here we are studying "hot" temperatures, so, by definition, we do not want cold ones. Also, we must provide for the ethical and safe treatment of our subjects, so we would avoid employing a very high temperature that might cause heat stroke. Likewise, from the various types of facial expressions—broad smiling, grinning, smirking, frowning, or a neutral face—we must select the specific categories we will investigate. Based on physiological and anatomical research, we specify those facial expressions that do and those that do not engage the muscles used in smiling. (And, of course, we induce all expressions in an ethical and safe manner.)

When selecting the conditions of the independent variable, we need to consider two important issues: control groups and strong manipulations.

Control Conditions   A **control group** is measured on the dependent variable but receives zero amount of the independent variable, or otherwise does not receive the treatment. Control groups are distinguished from **experimental groups,** which receive a nonzero amount of the independent variable or otherwise do experience the treatment. A control condition reflects how subjects behave without the treatment, providing a *baseline* or starting point for evaluating the influence of the variable when it is present. For example, it strikes me that being in either condition of the smile study is pretty funny: Imagine sitting in a room with an experimenter watching you hold a pen in your mouth. Regardless of how the pen is held, the situation itself may elevate subjects' mood. Thus, we might include a third condition, a control group of subjects who don't hold anything in their mouths. Then, let's say we obtain either of the results shown in Figure 5.3.

The data in bar graph A show that the no-smile condition elevated mood compared to doing nothing, and that smiling improved mood even more. The data in graph B show that the no-smile condition lowered mood relative to doing nothing, having the opposite effect of smiling. The important point to recognize is that, without the control condition, we would not be able to identify either influence of the no-smile conditions. Compared to our original graph in Figure 5.1, which involves only two conditions, the graphs that include a control condition provide much more information and a clearer picture of how our manipulation affected subjects.

A control group is not always essential to a design—its inclusion depends on the question being asked. Do note, however, that control groups are especially useful for eliminating alternative hypotheses about what causes the dependent scores to change. For example, let's say that in a different study we present a loud background noise to subjects while they read a story, and find that they poorly remember the story. It appears that the noise interferes with memory, but only if we assume that subjects would otherwise retain the story well. Perhaps the story is intrinsically difficult to recall. To eliminate this rival hypothesis, we compare the noise condition to a control condition, an otherwise identical condition but with no noise. If retention is poor in both conditions,

FIGURE 5.3   Two Possible Smile-Study Results That Include a Control Condition

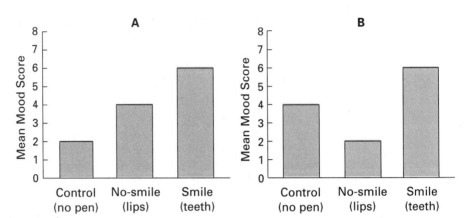

we could conclude that this result is due to the story and that the presence of noise literally does not make a difference. But if retention is lower with noise, then we'd have support for the hypothesis that noise lowers retention.

Sometimes it is not possible to administer zero amount of the independent variable. In such cases, the control group is often tested under a condition considered "normal" or "neutral." For example, in our temperature study there must be *some* temperature present, so our control condition is normal room temperature. Or, say we presented subjects with cheerful or sad statements to alter their mood (Cunningham, Shaffer, Barbee, Wolff & Kelley, 1990). In this instance, the control condition would involve emotionally neutral statements.

Sometimes the equivalent of a control condition involves comparing subjects' performance to the result we would expect if they were guessing. For example, to study "psychic abilities," researchers test subjects claiming to receive telepathic messages by "sending" them a message about a card drawn from a deck of playing cards. The number of cards correctly selected by a subject is compared to the number we would expect if the subject was merely relying on chance guessing. As it turns out, so-called psychics do not perform significantly above a chance level (Hanssel, 1980).

> **REMEMBER**   *Control conditions* provide a clearer indication of the influence
> of a manipulation and of the causes of subjects' responses.

Selecting strong manipulations   As you know, we cannot claim to have demonstrated anything about a behavior unless we find a statistically significant relationship in the sample data. Therefore, in the design of a study we are always concerned with maximizing statistical *power,* the probability of rejecting the null hypothesis when it is false. One way to maximize power is to produce large differences in scores *between* the conditions. We assume that differences in our conditions cause differences in scores, so to produce large differences in scores, we select conditions that differ substantially. A **strong manipulation** involves creating conditions that will greatly differentiate subjects' behavior, producing large differences in scores between the conditions. We create strong manipulations in two ways.

First, we select amounts or categories of the independent variable that are substantially different from one another. For example, a strong manipulation of temperature is to have the conditions differ by large amounts—say, by 20 degrees. Then, if different temperatures influence aggression, we should see large differences in aggression. Or, in a study presenting happy or sad words to influence mood, the happy words should be very happy and the sad ones should be very sad.

Second, we ensure that subjects sufficiently experience a condition to dramatically influence their behavior. In our smiling study, for example, we would have subjects hold the pen for more than 10 seconds, because this amount of time is hardly enough to influence anything. Or, say we are studying how different speaking styles influence the persuasiveness of a message. Rather than presenting a short message with only one example of the style, we'd present a longer message with many aspects conveying that style.

Any time research fails to find significant differences in scores between the conditions, this result may be due to a weak manipulation that produced only minuscule differences.

> **REMEMBER** For power, we create a *strong manipulation* so that the conditions differ substantially and we are likely to obtain large differences in dependent scores.

CONTROLLING THREATS TO RELIABILITY AND VALIDITY

Once we select the conditions of the independent variable, we must precisely define how we will create and present them. In so doing, we must consider the four components of an experiment: the subjects, the researcher, the measurement procedure, and the environment. For each, we try to anticipate and eliminate anything that may threaten the reliability and validity of our results.

Creating a Reliable Manipulation

Recall that reliability means that our results are consistent and contain no error. We seek reliability not only in terms of measuring subject's scores but also in terms reliably manipulating the independent variable: All subjects in a condition should receive the same amount or category of the variable, and when we change to another condition, all subjects there should receive the same, new amount. Thus, if in our temperature study the conditions are 70 and 90 degrees, then we want precisely 70 degrees for all subjects in one condition and precisely 90 degrees for all subjects in the other condition.

If there is inconsistency in our manipulation, then we are not always presenting the condition we think we are, and our conclusions will be based on the wrong amounts of the independent variable. Also, if the experimental situation is in any way different for each subject, we will end up with different responses and thus variability among the scores within each condition. Recall that such variability is called *error variance,* and that greater error variance reduces the strength of the relationship and decreases power.

Controlling Confounding Variables

Although we are concerned with all aspects of validity, once an independent variable has been created our concern is focused on *internal validity,* the degree to which we can draw accurate inferences about the observed relationship in our study. In experiments, internal validity is of paramount importance, because we seek to draw a causal inference. We must be confident that it is *only* the changes in the independent variable that cause changes in the dependent scores. Therefore, it is especially important that our manipulation of the independent variable does not introduce a *confounding*. Recall that a confounding occurs when systematic differences between the conditions exist, in addition to the independent variable.

In our smile study, for example, let's say that holding a pen between the teeth not only makes subjects smile but also makes them laugh. Holding the pen in their lips does neither. The results of such a study can be diagrammed as shown in Table 5.2. Note that what we are *calling* the smile condition produced a higher average mood score. The problem is that there are two ways to describe our conditions: either in terms of the intended manipulation of mimicking or not mimicking a smile, or in terms of the confounding variable of laughing or not laughing. Because of this confounding we don't know which variable is causing the elevated mood, so we cannot be confident that we have confirmed the hypothesis that facial feedback from smiling increases mood.

A confounding can also work to cover up the predicted relationship. If subjects holding the pen with puckered lips laughed more often and thus experienced a higher mood, this confounding could produce results directly opposite to those we predicted, causing us to think that mood improves with *less* use of the smile muscles. Or, let's say that

TABLE 5.2   Diagram of a Confounded Smile Study

	Condition 1 *(Pen in teeth)*	*Condition 2* *(Pen in lips)*
Independent variable	Smile	No-smile
Confounding variable	Laughter	No-laughter
Mood scores	X X X	X X X

High $\overline{X}$ mood   Low $\overline{X}$ mood

the researcher inadvertently made those subjects in the smile conditions more anxious. Then, although smiling might actually tend to increase mood, increased anxiety might tend to decrease mood. These effects could cancel out so that we find no difference in mood between our conditions. But without this confounding, our results might confirm our original hypothesis.

A confounding could also occur in our temperature study. Given that we must provide an experimenter for subjects to be aggressive toward, anything that consistently differentiates that experimenter from one temperature condition to the next is a potential confounding variable. Let's say that we carelessly employ a male experimenter when the room is 70 degrees and a female experimenter when the room is 90 degrees. In this case, we cannot know whether differences in subject aggressiveness are due to differences in room temperature or to differences in the sex of the experimenter.

Different confounding variables arise with the use of different independent variables. We have a confounding variable if we are presenting examples of different types of music, but one song contains lyrics and another does not, the volume of one is greater than that of another, or one is familiar and another is obscure. The same is true if we are presenting lists of happy or sad words, but one list consists of words that contain more syllables, are less familiar, or are more socially acceptable. Or, we have a confounding if we employ a confederate who is friendlier, more attractive, or more disorganized in one condition than in another.

Remember, for any study, you won't know whether subjects are being influenced by such extraneous variables instead of by your independent variable. Rather you must anticipate potential confoundings and attempt to eliminate them, so that to your knowledge, the only thing that systematically differentiates the conditions is your independent variable.

> **REMEMBER** Every design must be scrupulously examined to eliminate potential confounding.

As discussed in Chapter 2, we may control extraneous variables that produce confounding by trying to eliminate them. Thus, ideally, we would design a procedure for the smile study in which no subjects will laugh. If, however, we're unable to eliminate them, we may keep the extraneous variables constant across all conditions. For example, we could select happy and sad words that all have the same length, the same familiarity, and so on.

If we do not eliminate or keep an extraneous variable constant, then we may balance it, allowing its influence to be evenly spread across subjects within every condition. For example, we could employ a male experimenter with half of the subjects in each temperature condition and a female experimenter with the other half. A diagram of such a balanced study is shown in Table 5.3. To summarize the scores, we ignore the gender of the researcher and obtain an overall mean aggression score in each column. By ignoring gender, we are **collapsing** across that variable—that is, combining the scores from the different amounts or categories of that variable. Above, we would say that we "collapsed across gender" because we combined the two groups in a column into one group.

TABLE 5.3   Diagram of Temperature Study in Which Experimenter Gender is Balanced

	Temperature Conditions	
	70 degrees	*90 degrees*
Scores obtained with male experimenter	X X X X	X X X X
Scores obtained with female experimenter	X X X X	X X X X
	Low mean aggression	High mean aggression

REMEMBER   *Collapsing* across a variable means that we combine the scores from the different levels of the variable.

By balancing experimenter gender, we evenly distribute its influence in each temperature condition. Then, if the 90-degree condition produces greater aggression in subjects, this result cannot be attributed to the particular sex of the experimenter present, because each sex is equally represented in each condition. (As we'll see in Chapter 8, we can also analyze the influence of a balanced variable; so, for example, we could see what differences arise due to the presence of a male or female experimenter.)

Diffusion of Treatment

Another threat to internal validity associated with the independent variable is diffusion of treatment. **Diffusion of treatment** occurs when subjects in one condition are aware of the treatment given in other conditions. In a between-subjects design, for example, let's say the subjects who have participated in one condition tell other potential subjects about their experience. Because the latter subjects are now aware of the treatment, the strength of our manipulations may be reduced. Diffusion of treatment is especially a problem when we manipulate the information given to subjects in each condition, or when we surprise them with some event. Not only will the strength or impact of our treatment be reduced, but the internal validity of the design will be threatened as well: Instead of being influenced only by the condition of our independent variable, subjects' responses will be influenced by extraneous information they have about the conditions and the study.

Our first line of defense against diffusion of treatment is to explain to subjects why it is important that they not tell other potential subjects about the details of the study. Second, we can conduct the entire study over a brief period, to minimize the time during which subjects might communicate with each other. Third, we can test subjects from different locations so that they have little physical contact with each other. Finally, as we'll see, we can also endeavor to disguise our treatments.

Creating Consistent Procedures

In addition to presenting a reliable manipulation and eliminating any obvious confoundings, a key issue in designing the remainder of the procedure is the need to achieve *consistency*. To accomplish this objective, we standardize our procedures, preventing any extraneous variables from randomly fluctuating within and between the conditions. Thus, in each condition of the smile study, all subjects should hold the same type of pen in their mouths, for the same period of time, all the while maintaining the same posture and performing the same tasks. In the temperature study, all subjects should be warmly dressed to the same degree, seated the same distance from the heater, acclimated to the temperature to the same extent, and so on. If we have not achieved such consistency, fluctuating variables may cause subjects to respond differently within a condition, producing greater error variance and reducing our statistical power. Further, such fluctuations might cause one condition to differ from another, thus confounding the independent variable.

> *REMEMBER*   A key issue in designing our procedures is the need to produce consistency within and between conditions.

Instructions   Our instructions should clearly explain the task so that subjects consistently attend to the stimulus and respond appropriately. In particular, we describe the sequence of events, identify the stimuli they should attend to, and explain how to indicate a response. We also anticipate subjects' questions. (Should they guess when making a response? Should they hurry?) Further, we use instructions to prevent unwanted subject behaviors: We tell them not to look around, fidget, or talk, so they don't miss crucial aspects of the task. The goal is to have all subjects perform precisely the same intended task, without introducing extraneous stimuli or behaviors that make the task different for different subjects.

When creating instructions, we make sure they're clear for the least sophisticated subjects, avoiding psychological jargon and using words that subjects will easily understand (especially if they are children). Then, we present the same instructions to all subjects. If we are manipulating a variable through instructions, we change only the necessary parts and avoid a confounding by keeping all other aspects (e.g., length, duration, and wording) constant. We never "ad lib" instructions; instead, we may read them aloud, using a neutral voice that can be consistently reproduced, or play a tape recording of them.

Of course, there are no guarantees that our instructions will have the desired effect. We can encourage subjects to ask questions if they don't understand us, but the more they do so, the more their testing experience differs from those who do not ask questions. For clarity we can add more detail, but experienced or bored subjects may not listen, especially when instructions are presented in a dry, neutral manner. Finally, we can have subjects read the instructions themselves, but in that case we must be sure they actually do read and understand them. The creation of effective yet efficient instructions requires considerable effort on the part of the researcher.

Automation At the outset of any study, we must consider the mechanics of how we will present a stimulus and determine whether it will introduce inconsistency. For example, use of a stopwatch to time the presentation of visual stimuli can be unreliable, and variation in presentation times is an extraneous, potentially confounding variable. The alternative is to rely on automated equipment—electronic timers, slide projectors, and the like—to control and present stimuli. Likewise, when presenting auditory stimuli, we can use headphones to keep the volume constant for all subjects (rather than risk having them sit near or far from speakers) and exclude distracting environmental noises. When creating a situation for subjects to react to, we might videotape the situation so that all subjects in a condition see exactly the same event. We can also benefit from the availability of personal computers, which present many opportunities for providing reliable presentation of stimuli through **automation.**

Testing Subjects in Groups An important question to ask ourselves when designing a study is whether to test subjects individually or in groups. Group testing is more common when the task requires subjects' written responses, such as on a test or questionnaire. The advantage of group testing is greater efficiency in collecting the data. Also, if we can test an entire condition at one time, all subjects will experience the same condition consistently presented. The disadvantage is that subjects may make noise, block one another's view, or otherwise distract each other. As a result, the situation for some subjects may be slightly different from that for other subjects, especially for those tested in another group. Therefore, we need to be especially careful to control subjects' extraneous behaviors, so as to prevent potential confoundings. Usually, this issue can be handled with particularly explicit instructions, but it also depends on the experiment and how susceptible the subjects are to the presence of other subjects.

Pilot Studies To be sure that our procedures are appropriate and reliable and that we have anticipated all major extraneous variables, we conduct a pilot study before conducting our actual study. A **pilot study** is a miniature version of a study in which we test our procedures. Using a sample of the type of subjects we will test in our actual study, we determine such matters as whether the instructions are clear and subjects perform appropriately, whether the task is doable given time constraints or other demands, and whether the manipulation actually works and is strong. Rather than just measuring the dependent variable, we may ask subjects questions and talk with them about the procedure to determine what they are actually experiencing. In addition, a pilot study allows the experimenter to work out any bugs in the equipment or procedure. (In the smile study, for example, the experimenter should not giggle!)

Pilot studies are also used to create and validate our stimuli. Let's say our conditions involve showing films that contain different amounts of violence. Our personal judgment is of little help in determining the amount of violence in a film (perhaps we're particularly insensitive to violence). Therefore, we would show the films to pilot subjects and have them rate the amount of violence each contains.

For any problems we identify during a pilot study, we alter the stimuli, task, or instructions and conduct more pilot studies until we have the desired situation in each condition. (In APA-style reports, pilot studies are briefly described in the Materials section.)

Manipulation Checks   Although pilot studies are very useful, to increase internal validity we may also want to "check" whether our manipulation actually influenced our subjects in the experiment. A **manipulation check** is a measurement, in addition to the dependent variable, that determines whether the independent variable had its intended effect. Usually this check is made after subjects have performed the task. It is especially useful for ensuring that an independent variable has the intended influence on an intervening variable. For example, in a study where we manipulate frustration to influence subjects' intervening anger and then measure aggressiveness, we can check the manipulation by directly measuring subjects' anger (e.g., by determining their physiological responses or having them complete a questionnaire). If subjects make the desired responses, we have greater confidence that differences in aggression are the result of differences in anger. If they do not, we go back to the drawing board to redesign the study.

> *REMEMBER*   Instructions, *automation,* group testing, *pilot studies,* and *manipulation checks* are important considerations for creating a reliable and valid design.

CONTROLLING DEMAND CHARACTERISTICS

Imagine you are a subject in an "experiment" that is taking place in a "laboratory" full of timers, cameras, and who-knows-what. A "psychologist" with lab coat and clipboard puts a plate of cookies in front of you. He says, "Normal people crave cookies at this time of day, so eat if you want." I'll bet you eat one. If he says, "Only people who have no self-control eat at this time, but eat if you want," I'll bet you don't. In any situation the social and physical surroundings provide cues that essentially "demand" that we behave in a certain way. In research these cues are called demand characteristics. A **demand characteristic** is a cue provided by the research context that guides or biases a subject's behavior. Subjects rely on demand characteristics to answer such questions as "What's really going on here? What am I supposed to do? How will my response be interpreted?" These cues arise in addition to—or despite—the explicit instructions we give subjects, and their use is not necessarily the result of an intentional, conscious process.

Demand characteristics can be grouped in terms of the four components of a study. First, *subjects* bring with them certain attitudes that influence their behavior. Research procedures are mysterious, and rumor has it that psychologists do strange things to subjects and study only intelligence, sexual deviance, and crazy people. Therefore, while subjects are trying to determine what is expected of them, they are also on guard, sensitive to portraying themselves in a bad light or appearing "abnormal." Because of these concerns, different subjects will react differently to the same situation. Some subjects tend to be overly cooperative (Adair, 1973), doing and saying what they think they are "supposed" to. In our smile study, some subjects may laugh and act happy, not so much because they want to but because they think it is expected. Other subjects may be overly cautious: They may want to laugh but inhibit this response because they're afraid it's inappropriate. Still other subjects may be overly defensive: They may feel happy but intentionally act sad and controlled to hide this fact.

Second, the *environment* in which a study takes place can feed into such reactions. The surroundings may distract subjects or cause them to react to extraneous factors. Indeed, subjects often use such things as random noises, changes in lighting, or a broken pencil point as cues for erroneously concluding what is being studied and how they should respond. This is especially true in fancy laboratories with one-way mirrors and complex equipment that can play upon subjects' fears. (Once, in a study involving a bank of electronic timers, I had to convince subjects they would not be electrocuted by having them look under their chair to see there were no wires!)

Third, the *measurement procedure* subjects must perform also communicates demand characteristics that subjects use to modify their responses. For example, in studies of mental imagery, subjects envision a previously presented map, and the time they take to mentally travel between different locations on the map is measured. Subjects take longer when the locations on the map are more distant. However, this result may occur not because it reflects how subjects travel along mental maps, but because subjects know that longer distances should take longer, so they "oblige" (Intons-Peterson, 1983).

Finally, the *experimenter* is an important source of demand characteristics. Researchers usually dress and behave rather formally to inspire serious cooperation from subjects. But our formality may inhibit subjects' normal reactions. If we act and dress too informally, we may encourage inattentiveness and sloppy performance. Further, subjects are very sensitive to **experimenter expectancies,** subtle cues the experimenter provides about the responses that subjects should give in a particular condition. These expectancies occur because, as researchers, we know the predictions of the study and may inadvertently communicate them to subjects. Then the ultimate self-fulfilling prophecy is produced. In our smile study, for example, we expect subjects to be happier when mimicking a smile. A subtle action on our part can register on subjects, and, sure enough, they'll respond with the predicted mood.

As these examples illustrate, demand characteristics cause subjects to play a role, being good (or not so good) subjects who perform on cue. The problem is, subjects respond to these cues, instead of responding solely to our treatment. We lose internal validity when the cues themselves cause a subject to coincidentally behave in the manner we predict, making it appear that our manipulation influences their behavior. Or the cues may cause subjects to behave contrary to our predictions, making it appear that our manipulation does not influence their behavior. We also lose external validity when subjects are not responding to the independent variable and are not behaving naturally, so our results do not generalize to other situations in which the demand characteristics are not present. Demand characteristics also reduce reliability, because not all subjects react to them in the same way, in which case we have inconsistency in subjects' reactions to the intended stimulus and greater error variance in their scores.

> *REMEMBER*   *Demand characteristics* are cues that bias subjects, resulting in
> responses that are not valid, reliable reactions to our variables.

In later chapters, we'll see the names for particular types of demand characteristics. For now, however, we look at several general techniques that researchers use to control demand characteristics.

General Controls for Demand Characteristics

There are three general strategies for controlling demand characteristics. First, we provide as few cues as possible. If subjects have no cues, their only recourse is to act naturally. Thus, in our instructions we do not divulge our specific purpose, manipulation, or predictions. Likewise, we do not include extraneous, distracting information. (For example, telling subjects they have 5 minutes for a task may raise their anxiety and make them concentrate on the clock.) Also, we hide threatening equipment, and we avoid extraneous behaviors or comments by the experimenter.

Our second strategy is to make those cues that must be present as neutral as possible. Thus, the researcher tries to be rather bland, being neither overly friendly nor unfriendly. We present the task without implying that it is difficult or easy, and without indicating what is a normal response. We also try to neutralize subjects' fears and suspicions. (For example, when conducting a memory study we tell them that their performance does not reflect on their personality or intelligence.)

Our third strategy is to seek experimental realism. **Experimental realism** is the extent to which the measurement task engages subjects psychologically. The goal is to define the independent variable (and other aspects of the experimental task) in such a way that subjects find the task interesting, challenging, or engrossing. Then they should actually respond to the task as we intend, instead of responding as they think is expected. However, we do not mean the task is like real life, so experimental realism is different from ecological validity. Rather, the point is that regardless of how strange the task may be, subjects' responses are real and actual responses to it. Ideally, by being realistically engaged in the task, subjects will "forget" about demand characteristics.

Use of Deception to Control Demand Characteristics

Sometimes, a straightforward presentation of a measurement procedure produces very strong demand characteristics that cannot be eliminated or neutralized. Then we may rely on deception. *Deception* involves the creation of an artificial situation, a "cover story" that disguises our procedures. Subjects are then unaware of the independent variable being manipulated or the behavior being studied, so they do not feel pressured to respond in a certain way.

For example, in our smile study, what would you do if a researcher simply said, "Here, hold this pen in your lips?" It's likely that you would try to come up with a reason for this task, that you would feel very self-conscious, and that your behavior and mood would be constrained. To reduce these demand characteristics in the original smile study, Strack et al. (1988) told subjects that the study was investigating how physically impaired people use their mouths to do tasks that are normally done by hand. Subjects were thus placed in the role of physically impaired people, and while holding the pen in either their lips or teeth, they were asked to draw and to use the pen to mark various stimuli. Among the tasks given them was one in which they rated how humorous they found several cartoons. Their responses here constituted the dependent variable for measuring mood. Thus, what might have been a bizarre task producing biased, unnatural behaviors was transformed into a rational, experimentally real task in which subjects were less self-conscious and responded in a more natural way.

Conversely, we sometimes use demand characteristics to our advantage, disguising a task by incorporating elaborate scientific-looking procedures. For example, Duclos et al. (1989) manipulated the posture that subjects adopted in order to determine how posture influences mood. So that the subjects would maintain a posture without being overly conscious or suspicious of it, fake electrodes for measuring "brain activity" were attached to them, and they were told that their posture was important for accurate measurements.

Deception is not always necessary (as with everything in research, we must balance the pros and cons). In the temperature study, we might attempt to control demand characteristics by off-handedly telling subjects that the room's heat control is broken. However, as Bell and Baron (1976) found, subjects in a hot room are likely to guess that the study deals with temperature anyway, and catching the researcher in a lie will worsen the impact of demand characteristics.

Placebos to Control Demand Characteristics

One problem with demand characteristics occurs in conjunction with a control condition. If an experimental group is exposed to stimuli, tasks, or instructions that are not presented to the control condition, then we have a confounding: We are not sure whether the experimental group behaves differently because of the treatment or because of the demand characteristics that accompany it. For example, let's say we give an experimental group a drink of alcohol while a control group receives nothing. Any impairment the experimental group exhibits may be due to the alcohol, *or* it may arise because giving subjects alcohol implies that we expect them to act drunkardly, so they do.

To keep such demand characteristics constant, we give control groups a placebo. A **placebo** provides the demand characteristics of a manipulation while presenting zero amount of the independent variable. Thus, we would give the above control group something we call alcohol, with the smell and taste of alcohol, but that in reality contains no alcohol. Because we communicate to *both groups* the same demand characteristics for acting drunkardly, we can be more confident that any differences in their behavior are due to the real alcohol given the experimental group. Note, too, that placebos help to reduce diffusion of treatment. On the surface, at least, all subjects think they are being given the same treatment, so it is more difficult for subjects to identify, and thus become aware of, the various conditions of the study.

Similarly, when testing other drugs, we give placebo pills or injections to the control group so that all subjects experience the same procedure and form the same expectations. And in experimental conditions requiring subjects to perform a long or involved task prior to making a response, we give a similar placebo task to the control group to eliminate differences between the groups in terms of expectations, motivation, or fatigue.

> **REMEMBER** *Placebos* are given to control groups so that they will experience the same demand characteristics as experimental groups.

Controlling Subject and Experimenter Expectancies

The previous strategies are designed to keep subjects from developing their own expectations about the influence of a particular condition. Anytime we keep subjects in the dark regarding the condition they receive, we are using a single-blind procedure. In a **single-blind procedure,** subjects are unaware of the specific condition they are receiving.

In addition, we need to prevent experimenters from communicating expectations to subjects. Another reason for using automation, for example, is to eliminate experimenter cues: The more we can rely on equipment to perform our job, the less we risk influencing subjects' responses. When automation is not possible because the study requires substantial interaction with the subjects, we can eliminate experimenter expectations by using a double blind. In a **double-blind procedure,** both the researcher who interacts with the subjects and the subjects themselves are unaware of the specific condition being presented. The original experimenter trains other researchers to actually conduct the study, but they are "blind" to the condition a subject is in and to the predictions. For example, say we are testing the effects of a drug or medicine. If the experimenter knows when a placebo, or the drug itself, is being administered, our expectations about the effects of each treatment may be communicated to subjects. These expectations *alone* can produce specific physical reactions or influence recovery from an illness. However, if the experimenter is blind to such information, no expectations can be communicated to subjects that may influence the study's outcome.

> **REMEMBER** A *double-blind procedure* keeps both the researcher and the subjects blind to the conditions and predictions of a study, so that their expectations do not influence the results.

ETHICAL TREATMENT OF HUMAN SUBJECTS

From the preceding discussions, you can see that psychological research is often rather tricky and devious. As such, it gives rise to an ethical dilemma that reflects the conflict between two points of view. On the one hand, we want a well-controlled study of our subjects, even though this goal may require us to be deceptive, to elicit responses that subjects want to keep private, or to cause subjects discomfort. We justify these actions on the grounds that scientific knowledge will ultimately benefit humanity. On the other hand, subjects have basic rights to privacy, to respect, and to safety. To resolve this conflict in an ethical manner means that we try to balance our right as researchers to study a behavior with the rights of subjects to be protected from abuse. In the following sections, we will discuss how researchers achieve this balance when subjects volunteer for an experiment. (In a later chapter, we will consider the treatment of subjects who unknowingly participate in a study.)

The Cooperativeness of Subjects

To understand how subjects may be mistreated by researchers, consider how subjects approach an experiment. First, as researchers we are often viewed as authority figures; and, as with all authority figures, subjects tend to think that we are benevolent and honest, that we know what we are doing, and that we will not hurt them. Second, they assume that research is valuable for society, so they believe their participation is important and that they have a stake in the study's outcome.

The result is that subjects respect our research and trust the researcher. An example of how this respect and trust motivate subjects was demonstrated by Orne (1962), who attempted to create an obnoxious task that subjects would refuse to perform. Every subject was given 2,000 sheets of paper, each of which contained 224 addition problems. No justification for the task was given, and subjects were merely told that the researcher would return "sometime." Five and one-half hours later, the *experimenter* gave up! In the next attempt, subjects were told that, after completing each sheet, they should tear it into a minimum of 32 pieces and then continue with the next sheet. Subjects performed this task for *several hours* until, again, the experimenter gave up. Instead of recognizing this as a meaningless task, subjects responded to demand characteristics that made them persevere, reporting that they assumed it was some sort of important psychological endurance test.

As the above example illustrates, an overriding demand characteristic of any study is for subjects to be cooperative. In fact, subjects respond in this way *even to their own detriment*. A classic example of this phenomenon is Milgram (1963), in which people's obedience to authority figures was studied. Subjects believed they were assisting the experimenter to train a "learner" to learn verbal stimuli. Each time the learner made an error, the subject pressed a switch that he or she believed administered an increasingly larger electrical shock to the learner. Despite protests from the learner (who could be heard but not seen, and who eventually emitted deathly silence), and despite the fact that the electrical switches were labeled "DANGER: SEVERE SHOCK," a *majority* of subjects delivered what they believed was as much as 450 volts of electricity! (The typical electrical outlet in your home delivers "only" 110 volts.)

Milgram applied no coercion other than to tell subjects to continue, using the implicit authority that the subjects had given him. Yet subjects administered the shocks, even though they believed they were harming another person, and in many cases became very emotionally and physically distressed themselves. And these were not impressionable freshman college students, but adults of various ages and backgrounds!

Milgram was soundly criticized for his tactics, but there are many studies suggesting that, given the way subjects approach a study, researchers can probably get them to do almost anything: Subjects are willing to suffer great mental or physical discomfort, and they are reluctant to protest or to protect themselves. However, merely because subjects volunteer for a study does not mean that we have the right to take advantage of them. In essence, there is an implicit contract between subjects and researchers. Their side of the contract is to help in our study and to trust us. Our side of the contract is to not abuse their trust. Being ethical means living up to our part of the contract.

> *REMEMBER*   We must treat subjects ethically, because they are helping us and trust us not to harm them.

Principles of Ethical Conduct

To assist researchers when dealing with ethical issues, the American Psychological Association in 1992 adopted the *Ethical Principles of Psychologists and Code of Conduct*. These principles govern the full range of a psychologist's activities, including scientific and professional integrity, treatment of clients in therapy, and the care of human and nonhuman subjects in research. The principles regarding human subjects apply to any type of study (not just to experiments) and can be summarized as follows.

Identify Potential Risks   First, we identify potential physical risks: Is there anything in the study that could physically endanger subjects? We ensure that equipment is working properly and safely, and do not present stimuli that may cause pain or physical damage. We also adhere to all accepted health procedures when injecting drugs, drawing blood, and the like. Second, identify potential psychological risks: Will subjects experience undue anxiety, depression, or other unpleasantness as a result of our procedures? Distress could occur directly as the result of our manipulation, as when we intentionally lower subjects' mood, or it could result indirectly. For example, you might think Milgram's study was not so unethical, because subjects did not actually hurt anyone. But if Milgram had not initially disconnected the electrical wires, the subjects would have killed— murdered—the learner! Think about how they felt when *that* dawned on them.

When identifying potential risks, we consider not only our particular procedure and variables but our *subjects* as well. Having subjects perform strenuous exercise may not be risky for healthy teenagers, but it is risky for the elderly and for people with heart conditions. Likewise, films containing sex, violence, and mayhem are standard fare for some adult moviegoers, but they may be emotionally upsetting for children.

Dealing with deception is a particularly difficult issue. On the one hand, Christensen (1988) surveyed subjects who had participated in both deceptive and nondeceptive experiments, finding that those in the deceptive studies enjoyed the experience more, became better educated about psychological research, and did not mind being deceived. On the other hand, however, we are not free to incorporate just any degree of deception. Deception may be psychologically harmful because, when subjects learn of it, they may feel foolish, depressed, or angry. Therefore, the APA guidelines explicitly require that deception be used only when it is a necessary component of a design. Thus, in evaluating the ethics of deception, first consider whether it is necessary for producing the desired study. (It is doubtful, for example, that Milgram could have observed subjects' extreme obedience to authority without employing deception.) Second, consider how much deception is actually involved. The greater the deception—the bigger the lie—the more objectionable it tends to be. Finally, and most important, consider the potential psychological impact of the deception in terms of its severity and duration. The extreme emotional reactions potentially resulting from Milgram's deception are a serious ethical concern; the more minor reactions that might arise from the deception in our smile study are less objectionable.

Ethical issues are not always clearcut, so we should seek the advice of other researchers. In fact, to conform to the APA's *Ethical Principles* (as well as to federal and state regulations), colleges and research institutions maintain a **Human Subjects Review Committee** (also called an Institutional Review Board, or IRB). This committee consists of individuals from various disciplines and professions, so a broad perspective is represented. The committee's job is to review all research procedures to ensure the ethical and safe treatment of subjects. Every researcher submits to such review *prior* to conducting a study.

Protect Subjects from Physical and Psychological Harm   Once we have determined the potential risks of a study, they must be addressed from two perspectives: First, can we eliminate or minimize the risks? If subjects will be needlessly stressed or embarrassed by our design, can we alter it to eliminate these feelings and still get at the behaviors we seek? Can we "tone down" our manipulation to reduce such feelings? The challenge is to strike a balance between seeking a strong manipulation that dramatically impacts on subjects and limiting its effect for ethical reasons. (If we want to make one group more depressed than another group, we don't need to make the first group suicidal! In fact, we might consider whether the study will work if, instead, we make one group happier than another.) We can also minimize risks by screening out high-risk subjects before they participate. If the study involves exercise, for example, we can screen out subjects having a heart condition; if we are manipulating depression, we can screen out people who are already clinically depressed and thus may react dangerously to our study.

Second, with respect to any risks that remain, we determine whether they are justified in terms of the study's scientific worth. Does the knowledge we may potentially develop from a study justify the risks we will expose subjects to? As the risk of physical or psychological harm becomes more serious, the scientific justification for a study is less convincing. As we have seen, one study is never considered the definitive proof of a hypothesis; therefore, conducting an unethical or dangerous study is just not worth it.

> *REMEMBER*   Our primary ethical concern is to minimize potential harm to subjects and to ensure that any remaining potential harm is justified.

Obtain Informed Consent   Out of respect for subjects' rights to control what happens to them, we inform subjects about the study *prior* to their participation. Then we explicitly let them decide whether they wish to participate. That is, we obtain **informed consent**. The APA's *Ethical Principles* state that informed consent is required unless there is minimal risk, as when we are merely observing anonymous people in a natural setting. But we should always obtain informed consent when conducting laboratory experiments. The usual procedure is to provide subjects with a written description that contains four components.

First, we describe the purpose and procedures of the study. Sometimes we must withhold specific details because of demand characteristics, but usually we can provide general information without biasing subjects. We tell them as much as we can.

Second, we explicitly warn subjects of any potential physical or psychological risks associated with the procedure, describing any details that could reasonably be expected to weigh in a subject's decision to participate in the study. Even if we cannot divulge all aspects of a procedure, we must warn subjects of any negative consequences of it. (For example, it was appropriate for Milgram to warn his subjects that they might learn some unpleasant things about themselves.)

Third, we inform subjects that they are free to discontinue their participation at any time during the study, without any penalty. Volunteering for a study produces such strong demand characteristics to be cooperative that this option does not often occur to subjects. Further, we must make this a realistic option, being sensitive to any hidden coercion that may arise because subjects are enrolled in a class or have a job where the study is being conducted, or are experiencing peer pressure.

Finally, we obtain each subject's signature as explicit consent to participate. In the case of minors and others who are not capable of making this decision, we obtain informed consent from their parents or guardians.

Take Care of Subjects after the Experiment After a study, we are responsible for removing any negative consequences of the procedure, so that subjects feel as good about themselves and their participation as they did when they first entered the study. First, we remove any questions by providing a **debriefing**. That is, we fully inform subjects about all aspects of the study, including the manipulations we employed and any deception used and why. (It is usually during the debriefing that we also ask subjects not to divulge the details of the study, in order to minimize diffusion of treatment.) Second, we remove any adverse physical or emotional reactions in subjects that we may have created. Thus, if we tested the effects of alcohol, we care for our subjects until they are sober. If we created anxiety or depression, we try to reverse these feelings, explaining why we think they're a normal reaction to our manipulation. If follow-up counseling or check-ups are possibly needed, we provide qualified, professional help. Finally, we give subjects a means of contacting us later in case unforeseen problems arise.

> *REMEMBER* To conduct an acceptable psychological study, we obtain *informed consent*, we *debrief* subjects, and we care for them after the study.

PUTTING IT ALL TOGETHER

As we have seen, the challenge in designing a good study is to anticipate and eliminate potential flaws so that the results are reliable and our conclusions are valid. However, remember to be skeptical. Even with all of our precautions, we cannot *prove* that changes in the independent variable actually cause the dependent scores to change as predicted. If, for example, we find that mimicking a smile does elevate subjects' mood, we have only *confirmed our hypothesis* that the smile muscles provide feedback to the emotional system. This hypothesis may be incorrect, but our results coincidentally confirm it. Meanwhile, the correct, alternative hypothesis may involve some unknown confounding variable—a variable in the environment or a demand characteristic—that is actually causing the higher mood scores. And, we have not yet considered either the potential flaws in our technique for measuring the dependent variable or any characteristics of our subjects that may be responsible for the results. Or, in performing our statistical analysis, we may have made a Type I error and the results are really due to sampling error, a chance coincidence. Thus, do not develop a false sense of security about the "proof" that a controlled experiment provides. *We are still only collecting evidence.* The techniques discussed in this chapter are necessary simply for producing "good," convincing evidence.

On the basis of this chapter, you may think that producing good evidence calls for remembering an overwhelming number of details, a vast recipe to memorize. However, the design and evaluation of any study is actually a thoughtful, logical, and creative process. What makes research design challenging is that, in each study, we create a complete social and physical environment having its own set of influences on subjects. Therefore, instead of approaching these issues as a list to memorize, view them as a way to think about the research setting. To assist you in this endeavor, Table 5.4 presents a checklist of the major issues we have discussed. After each of the following chapters, a few more items will be added to this list.

TABLE 5.4   Checklist of Major Issues to Consider When Designing an Experiment

- Hypothesis about relationship
- Operational definitions
  - Construct and content validity
  - Internal and external validity
  - Temporal and ecological validity
- Specify conditions
  - Linear or nonlinear relationship
  - Control groups and a strong manipulation
- Validity and reliability of independent variable
  - Confounding
  - Diffusion of treatment
  - Consistency of procedures: instructions, automation
  - Pilot study, manipulation check
- Demand characteristics
  - Experimental realism, deception
  - Placebos, blind procedures
- Ethical concerns
  - Physical and psychological risks
  - Informed consent and debriefing

CHAPTER SUMMARY

1. In a *one-way design* we manipulate one independent variable or factor.

2. In a *between-subjects design,* we randomly select and assign subjects to one condition without regard to the subjects assigned to the other conditions, and each subject serves in only one condition.

3. *Confederates* are people enlisted by a researcher to create a particular social situation for subjects.

4. An *intervening variable* is an internal subject characteristic that is influenced by the independent variable, which in turn influences the dependent variable.

5. A subject's *state characteristic* is transient and can be experimentally manipulated. A subject's *trait characteristic* is rather permanent and is not easily manipulated.

6. *Temporal validity* is the extent to which our results can be generalized to other time frames. *Ecological validity* is the extent to which an experimental situation can be generalized to natural settings and behaviors.

7. We create a *line graph* when the independent variable implies ordered, continuous amounts. We create a *bar graph* when the independent variable implies unordered, discrete categories.

8. A *control group* is measured on the dependent variable but receives zero amount of the independent variable, or otherwise does not receive the treatment. Thus it provides a baseline for determining the variable's influence in the *experimental groups* and helps to eliminate competing, alternative hypotheses.

9. A *strong manipulation* of the independent variable is intended to strongly differentiate subjects' behavior, producing large differences in dependent scores between the conditions.

10. A confounding occurs when, in addition to the independent variable, an extraneous variable systematically differentiates the conditions.

11. We *collapse* across a variable by combining the scores from the different amounts or levels of that variable.

12. *Diffusion of treatment* occurs when subjects in one condition are aware of the treatment given in other conditions.

13. Instructions, *automation,* group testing, *pilot studies,* and *manipulation checks* are procedures for ensuring validity and reliability.

14. *Demand characteristics* are the cues in a study that guide or bias a subject's behavior.

15. *Experimenter expectancies* are subtle cues the researcher provides about the responses subjects should give.

16. With *experimental realism,* subjects are psychologically engaged by the measurement task and thus less concerned with demand characteristics.

17. A *placebo* presents zero amount of the independent variable while still providing the demand characteristics of the variable.

18. In a *single-blind procedure,* subjects are unaware of the treatment they are receiving. In a *double-blind procedure,* both the researcher who interacts with the subjects and the subjects themselves are unaware of the specific treatment being presented.

19. The primary ethical issue in research is to balance the right of a researcher to adequately study a behavior with the rights of subjects to be protected from abuse.

20. The APA's *Ethical Principles of Psychologists and Code of Conduct* require that we protect subjects from physical or psychological harm.

21. To conduct an acceptable psychological study, we obtain *informed consent, debrief* our subjects, and take care of them after the study.

22. All research projects are first reviewed by an institution's *Human Subjects Review Committee* to ensure the ethical and safe treatment of subjects.

REVIEW QUESTIONS

1. What question about a study is raised by the term *ecological validity?*
2. What two questions about a study are raised by the term *temporal validity?*
3. Researcher A manipulates whether subjects study for a test in a room with either red, blue, or green walls and then measures test scores. Researcher B manipulates whether subjects are paid $1, $2, or $3 an hour to study for a test and then measures test scores. How should the results of each study be graphed?
4. In question 3, the colors and payments are intended to alter subjects' mood when taking the test. What name do researchers have for the variable of mood in this context?
5. What statistical reason is there for creating more than two conditions of the independent variable?
6. (a) What is a strong manipulation? (b) Why do we seek strong manipulations?
7. (a) What is a control group? (b) What is an experimental group? (c) Why do we employ control groups?
8. (a) What is meant by reliable manipulation of the independent variable? (b) Why is reliable manipulation important?
9. In the smile study discussed in this chapter, should subjects in a condition be tested individually or in groups? Why?
10. While testing one condition of the smile experiment, you are in a good mood. Coincidentally, while testing the other condition, you are depressed. (a) What do we call the variable of your mood? (b) What two techniques could you use to control this variable?
11. In question 10, your happy mood engages subjects so they try harder. Your depressed mood makes subjects passive and they become marginally attentive. (a) Your moods communicate messages to the subjects. What are these messages called ? (b) How do they threaten internal validity? (c) How do they threaten external validity?

12. (a) Draw a diagram of the smile design and show how you would balance the variable of sex of subject. (b) What does it mean to "collapse" across this variable? (c) Why does this procedure improve internal and external validity?

13. In terms of fluctuating variables, what is our key concern when developing instructions, considering automation, and designing all other aspects of a testing procedure?

14. What is the difference between a pilot study and a manipulation check?

15. (a) In terms of demand characteristics, what potential confounding occurs between a control group and an experimental group? (b) How do we attempt to eliminate this confounding?

16. (a) What is the difference between ecological validity and experimental realism? (b) Why is experimental realism important?

17. In study 1, the researcher is intentionally either friendly or unfriendly, predicting that being friendly will induce greater levels of cooperation from subjects. In study 2, the researcher reads a list of either similar or dissimilar words and measures subjects' memory for the list. (a) How might the researcher bias the outcome of each study? (b) How can this bias be eliminated in each study?

18. You create different conditions by playing different types of music to subjects. After a while, you suddenly pull out and shoot a (blank) pistol. You then measure subjects' anxiety level in order to determine whether different types of music cause subjects to remain more or less calm in the face of startling stimuli. What threat to internal validity may arise as you test more and more subjects?

19. In question 18, (a) What ethical problem is present? (b) How can you reduce the risks? (c) What should you do to ensure that subjects are willing to endure any remaining risks?

DISCUSSION QUESTIONS

1. You compare the number of typing errors that subjects produce when copying material onto a computer as a function of using a black-and-white or color monitor. (a) What potential confounding variables are present? (b) How would you control such variables?

2. You wish to study how hard subjects will work for food as a function of how hungry they are. (a) Create an operational definition for manipulating the independent variable, and diagram your design. (b) Evaluate your definition in terms of construct, content, and internal and external validity.

3. You provide subjects with different types of speeches designed to make them more or less sexist, to see how sexism influences whether they help a confederate of the opposite sex. (a) Why is it that your manipulation could appear to work even though it does not really alter subjects' views? (b) Why could your manipulation appear not to have worked although it really did alter subject's views?

4. You have discovered a new drug treatment for a serious mental illness that you wish to test. What conflicting ethical and design principles do you face when considering whether to include a control condition with a placebo?

6 Selecting and Designing the Dependent Variable

As you know by now, in each condition of the independent variable, we examine subjects' behavior by obtaining their scores on the dependent variable. Then we interpret differences in scores between conditions as indicating that changing the conditions causes the underlying behavior to change. This chapter discusses the special concerns we face when developing an operational definition for the dependent variable. First it examines the various approaches we can use; then it describes how we deal with demand characteristics, ethics, and other issues that arise in obtaining valid and reliable scores. Finally, it discusses how our measurement procedure affects the conceptual and statistical interpretations of the data.

SELECTING THE DEPENDENT VARIABLE

Most of the time, the dependent scores *quantify* the behavior under study. In some way we measure the amount or degree of a behavior—how strongly it is exhibited, or its frequency or rate of occurrence. At other times, the scores may *qualify* the behavior, distinguishing one behavior from another in terms of a quality, characteristic, or attribute. Either way, differences in scores should accurately reflect differences in subjects' behavior.

Methods of Measuring the Dependent Variable

The dependent variable we select and the operational definition we develop for it depend upon the hypothesis and behavior we are investigating, our subject population, and the perspective we seek to study. Most dependent variables employ one of the following approaches.

Direct Observation of the Behavior of Interest   The dependent variable may involve direct observation and measurement of the behavior under study. For example, in studying eating behavior, Schacter (1968) measured the quantity of food eaten by subjects as a function of different eating cues present. In a classic learning study, Greenspoon (1955) said "mmmmm hmmmm" after subjects spoke certain words, counting the frequency with which these words were then emitted. And Cunningham, Shaffer, Barbee, Wolff, and Kelley (1990) studied how mood influences our willingness to help others. After presenting subjects with cheerful or sad statements, they observed whether subjects would help a confederate.

Indirect Measures of Unseen Processes   Frequently, the behavior we observe is a more indirect indication of an unseen, internal process. The dependent variable measures an observable response that we think is correlated with the unseen process, so we use changes in the response to make inferences about changes in the unseen process. For example, researchers take physiological measurements of breathing, heart rate, and perspiration level to make inferences about subjects' anxiety or stress level (e.g., Zimbardo et al., 1966). Or we measure subjects' pupil dilations (whether the subjects were "wide-eyed or not") as an indication of how pleasant they perceive a stimulus to be (Mudd, Conway & Schindler, 1990). In memory research, the number of words correctly or incorrectly recalled or recognized under various conditions is used to infer the cognitive processes of retention and forgetting (e.g. Craik & Lockhart, 1972). Or the number of associations between objects or words that subjects provide is used as a measure of their creativity (Isen, Johnson, Metz & Robinson, 1985). In studying social processes, Latané, Williams, and Harkins (1979) inferred a subject's response to peer pressure by measuring the amount of cheering and clapping that subjects exhibited as a function of the number of other people present.

A common indirect measure is **reaction time,** the amount of time a subject takes to respond to a stimulus. After presenting stimuli that differ along a physical or mental dimension, we use differences in reaction time to infer the underlying cognitive or emotional processes involved. For example, Sternberg (1969) measured subjects' reaction time to a "probe word" that either was or was not part of a previous list, to infer how subjects search through the information in their memory.

The use of indirect measures is especially common in studies of young children, because they cannot directly tell us about their reactions. Thus, we may measure the length of time a baby stares at a stimulus, or note when a baby smiles at it, to infer a positive emotional reaction to the stimulus (Tronick, 1989). We may measure the duration and intensity of a baby's sucking response (with an electronic nipple) to infer whether a stimulus is recognized (Lippsit, Kaye & Bosack, 1966). And to determine whether young children understand various types of sentences, we may have them act out each message using dolls, trucks, and other toys.

Judgments about a Stimulus   Another measurement approach is to ask subjects to make judgments about a stimulus, and then to observe how the judgments change as function of the conditions. Often, this approach involves a **forced-choice** procedure, in which subjects must select from the possible choices we provide (e.g., a multiple-choice test). The simplest of these is a **yes-no task.** Researchers in perception, for example, may manipulate characteristics of a visual illusion and have subjects indicate whether or not they still perceive the illusion (Stuart & Day, 1991). Note that any recognition judgment about a stimulus actually reflects two components: a basic ability to detect the stimulus and a bias toward making a particular response. (For example, are we cautious or liberal when saying yes?) Be aware that researchers often use a statistical procedure, called "signal detection analysis," to separate these two components of a subject's judgments. (Many introductory perception texts discuss this procedure.)

Sometimes, instead of an all-or-none choice, researchers may obtain more refined judgments. For example, in studying how people perceive the passage of time, we may ask subjects to judge the duration of an interval in seconds after a certain type of activity has occurred. If, however, the judgments are not easily verbalized, we may use more symbolic responses. For example, Block (1978) had subjects draw a line to indicate the perceived duration of an interval. Or we may use a **sorting task,** in which subjects indicate their judgments by sorting cards containing stimuli into different groups, thus showing the categories they are using to organize them mentally (e.g., Flowers, Warner & Polansky, 1979).

Self-reports   Of course, if we wish to determine the internal processes occurring in subjects, we can explicitly ask subjects to describe these processes. When subjects provide descriptions about their own feelings or thoughts, they are providing what are called **self-reports.** Often, self-reports involve completing a rating scale called a **Likert-type question.** In this procedure, a statement is presented to subjects who then rate their response to it (typically using a scale of 1 to 5, where 1 indicates "strongly agree" and 5 indicates "strongly disagree"). For example, Schwarz and Clore (1983) manipulated the description that subjects heard about their physical surroundings, and then had them rate statements about their mood level and the causes for it. Similar rating scales can be used to measure such things as subjects' attitudes, their perceptions of an event, or their confidence in their memory for an event (e.g., Brandsford & Franks, 1971). In another form of self-reports, researchers ask subjects to provide a running commentary of the mental steps they perform in problem solving or making judgments. In Ekman and O'Sullivan (1991), for example, subjects described their approach when identifying liars.

Evaluating the Dependent Variable

Ultimately, our conclusions from a study hinge on the scores we obtain and the differences in scores we find between the conditions. Remember, however, that all we actually *see* is a set of scores from each condition. Just because we obtain a particular set of scores in a condition does not necessarily mean that the behavior occurs as we propose, and differences between the conditions do not necessarily mean that the behavior or internal process changes as we think it does. Therefore, we must critically evaluate the operational definition of our dependent variable using the same criteria we previously used when evaluating the independent variable.

In evaluating our dependent variable, we first determine whether it provides *construct validity,* reflecting the hypothetical construct as we conceptualize it. In particular, recall that we distinguish between "state" and "trait" characteristics. State characteristics are transient attributes that we can change by manipulating an independent variable, so it is appropriate to study them as a dependent variable. Trait characteristics, however, are rather stable and immune to momentary situational events. Therefore, we must be careful not to claim that manipulating our independent variable causes differences in a trait characteristic. ("Quasi-experiments" involving the study of trait characteristics will be discussed in a later chapter.)

Our dependent variable should provide *content validity* as well, such that we actually and only measure the variable of interest. Thus, for example, our scores should not depend on subjects' abilities and experiences unrelated to the behavior we are studying. We also seek *internal validity,* such that changes in scores reflect the influence of the independent variable but do not reflect changes in extraneous variables. And we seek *external validity,* such that our observed relationship generalizes to other subjects and settings. This includes considering whether the measurement task has ecological validity, in that we measure a subject's real-world behaviors so that we can generalize to real-world psychological processes. And we seek *reliability,* of course, so that there is no error or inconsistency in our measurements of the behavior.

Any approach to defining a dependent variable will have some weakness in terms of reliability and validity. When directly observing a behavior, we may observe an unreliable example of the behavior; in the eating study mentioned earlier, for example, subjects may eat differently because we are watching them. Self-reports can be unreliable and invalid because subjects may not know or care to divulge their true feelings. A study involving the sorting of words into categories may lose content validity because the sorting process may partially be a test of subjects' vocabulary. Similarly, asking subjects to indicate a response by drawing may partially be a test of their drawing ability. We also must be careful when making inferences about any internal construct: If subjects fail to recall a stimulus, is it because they initially "stored" it poorly or because they cannot "locate" it in memory? Likewise, with physiological measurements we do not always know which psychological response is being reflected: For example, anger and fear produce very similar physiological reactions.

The process of selecting and designing a dependent variable depends upon the aspects of reliability and validity we are willing to sacrifice. When studying physiology, we recognize that we may not positively know the underlying emotion being reflected in a response and thus direct our efforts toward more clearly identifying it. When studying unseen cognitive processes, we recognize the difficulty of drawing valid inferences and therefore attempt to build in controls that increase our confidence in these inferences. And when asking subjects questions about their behavior, we recognize the problem of potential unreliability in subjects' self-reports and attempt to minimize its impact on the scores. As with the independent variable, our design is guided by the questions "What is it we wish to study?" and then "What potential flaws must we deal with?"

> *REMEMBER*   We select a procedure for its strengths and then try to minimize its weaknesses.

Recall that an operational definition of any variable gives us a limited and potentially biased perspective, and may provide results different from those encountered when another definition is employed. As we saw in Chapter 2, one strategy for bolstering our conclusions from one approach is to use *converging operations*—employing different approaches that "converge" on the same behavior. Researchers can employ this strategy by testing subjects on multiple dependent variables within a single study. For example, let's say we obtain physiological measurements and self-reports of subjects' emotional state. If the subjects report greater anxiety when they are physiologically more anxious, we have greater confidence in the validity of inferences drawn from either variable. Measuring subjects on more than one dependent variable is also very cost-effective, yielding considerably more information for the effort involved in a study. However, researchers do not always employ multiple measures. A single variable—especially if it is an established, accepted measure—can be satisfactory. The use of just one variable is particularly beneficial when we do not want to actually weaken reliability and validity by overloading subjects with many confusing tasks or making their participation in a study too tedious.

Two Example Studies

Different dependent variables require different procedures. In the discussions that follow, we'll examine these procedures in the context of the following studies.

Modeling of Aggression   Sometimes there is no concrete way to precisely quantify a behavior—no "ruler" for measuring it. How, for example, should we measure a subject's aggressiveness, sexism, or motivation? One approach is to create a situation in which we can subjectively evaluate a subject's behavior. For example, in a classic study, Bandura, Ross, and Ross (1961) studied whether children would imitate the aggressive actions of others. First, while in a playroom, experimental subjects watched an adult model kick, punch, and yell at a "Bobo the Clown" punching-bag doll. With control subjects, however, the model was passive and ignored Bobo. Then, after frustrating each child by preventing access to desirable toys, the researchers subjectively rated how aggressively the child acted toward Bobo. The design for this study can be envisioned using the diagram in Table 6.1.

Before proceeding, recall our terminology for describing a design. Because only one independent variable is being manipulated here, this is a *one-way design*. Because the subjects are participating in only one condition, this is a *between-subjects* design. And because the subjects can be randomly assigned to either condition, this is a *true experiment* having a true independent variable.

If we were to conduct this study firsthand, we'd find that all of the issues discussed in the previous chapter for designing the independent variable still apply: In planning the study, we would evaluate the ethics of the design and obtain informed consent from the children's parents; we would ensure a strong manipulation by employing a model who is distinctly aggressive; we would eliminate potential confoundings by keeping all other aspects of the model and environment constant. And we would consider all aspects of the dependent variable so that we have a reliable and valid measurement procedure.

We would also plan the inferential and descriptive statistical procedures to be used. First and foremost, which statistical procedures we should use depends on the "scale of

TABLE 6.1   Diagram of One-Way Aggression Experiment, Showing Control and Experimental Conditions

	Conditions of aggressiveness of model	
	Control group (Passive model)	*Experimental group (Aggressive model)*
Child's aggression score	X X X " "	X X X " "
	Mean aggression	Mean aggression

measurement" used to measure the *dependent variable*. Recall from Chapter 3 that we use *parametric inferential procedures* if we measure the "amount" of a behavior that is exhibited, using either an interval scale, which allows for negative numbers (e.g., as when measuring positive and negative mood), or a ratio scale, which does not allow for negative scores (e.g., when measuring the number of errors made on a test). Further, recall that if we intend to use parametric procedures, the interval or ratio scores must be *normally distributed:* If we measured all potential subjects in each condition of our study, would the populations each form an approximately normal distribution?

One other requirement of the dependent scores must be fulfilled in order to employ parametric procedures: We should be able to assume that if we calculated the variance in each population represented by our data, all variances would be equal. If so, the data have the characteristic known as **homogeneity of variance.** (A check of the literature will indicate whether other researchers think your type of scores are normally distributed with homogeneous variance. Also, statistical procedures for confirming homogeneity of variance are described in many introductory statistics texts.)

> **REMEMBER**   Parametric procedures require normally distributed interval or ratio scores that have *homogeneity of variance.*

If our dependent variable meets the criteria for parametric inferential procedures, the *mean* is the measure of central tendency that is appropriate for telling us how the subjects in each condition behaved. The appropriate measures of variability are the *standard deviation* and the *variance,* which tell us how much the scores differed within each condition. The particular parametric inferential procedures we use depends on *the number of conditions* and whether or not we have a *between-subjects* design. For the above aggression study, the independent samples *t*-test is a parametric inferential procedure applied to a between-groups design having two conditions of the independent variable. We would perform a one-tailed *t*-test if we can confidently predict the direction of the relationship that will be produced or, more commonly, a two-tailed *t*-test if we cannot make such a prediction.

If after collecting the data we find that the calculated *t* is significant, we will conclude that there is a significant effect of manipulating a model's aggressiveness. We will have evidence that children mimic aggressive models if their aggression scores are significantly higher in the experimental group. Then we will examine the size of the means and the amount that they differ to see how aggressive the subjects were in each condition. Also, we will consider the strength of the relationship, create confidence intervals, and so on, to more precisely describe and understand how modeling influences aggressiveness.

Word-color Interference   Different design considerations arise when the dependent variable entails a more concrete, objectively measurable response. Consider the classic "Stroop interference task" (Stroop, 1935) in which the researcher measured subjects' reaction time to identify the colors of ink they saw. In the control condition, color patches were presented. In the experimental condition, the word name for one color was superimposed on a different colored patch. Thus, for example, subjects might have viewed the word *yellow* printed in green ink. To see yourself how this works, quickly identify the color of the *ink* used to print the word below.

red

Identification of the ink color is interfered with by processing of the word, so that reaction times for reporting ink color tend to be slower when a color name is present than when no name is present.

In studying such interference, Klein (1964) varied the meanings of the stimulus words. As part of the study, he compared conditions in which the word was either a nonsense syllable (e.g., *BJB*), a word that implied a color (e.g., *grass*), or the name for a color (e.g., *red*). Then he measured the reaction time required for identifying the ink color in each condition. The outline of this one-factor, between-subjects design is shown in Table 6.2.

Here again, if conducting this study ourselves, we design it such that the only difference between the conditions is the type of word presented. We design the dependent variable to reliably and validly measure reaction times. And we consider whether parametric statistical procedures are appropriate. Measuring the amount of time subjects take to react involves a ratio variable. If reaction times are normally distributed, we will summarize the scores in each level of our factor by computing the mean and standard deviation. Further, this is a between-subjects design with three levels of one factor. If the scores have homogeneous variance, the *one-way, between-subjects ANOVA* is the parametric inferential procedure to employ in a between-subjects design having two or more levels of one factor. If after collecting the data we find that the F is significant, we will be confident that the relationship between our conditions and reaction time scores is not merely due to sampling error.

Don't forget, however, that when we have three or more levels of a factor, a significant F indicates only that somewhere in the study we produced one or more significant differences between the conditions. To determine which means differ from which other

TABLE 6.2   Diagram of the One-Factor "Stroop" Interference Task

	Factor of type of word presented		
	Nonsense word (e.g., BJB)	*Implied color word* (e.g., grass)	*Color name* (e.g., red)
Subject's reaction time in identifying ink color	X X X " "	X X X " "	X X X " "
	Mean reaction time	Mean reaction time	Mean reaction time

means, we can perform *post hoc* comparisons (or planned comparisons). Statisticians have developed several versions of *post hoc* tests, each of which essentially involves performing special *t*-tests that compare every possible pair of means. However, some of these procedures (e.g., the "Scheffé Test") are rather conservative, meaning they are biased toward avoiding Type I errors, even at the risk of making Type II errors. Others (e.g., the "Newman Keuls" or "Duncan" tests) are rather liberal, meaning they are biased toward avoiding Type II errors, even at the risk of making Type I errors. An in-between procedure that gives good protection from both types of errors is the "Tukey HSD test" (shown in Appendix A). In the experiment just described, this procedure will identify where, among the three conditions, significant differences in reaction time occur.

For those conditions that differ significantly, we will infer differences in the amount of interference that is produced: A larger mean reaction time indicates that subjects responded slower under that condition, presumably because of greater interference in recognizing an ink color due to the word that was also present. Then we will examine the size of each mean and the differences between them, determine the strength of the relationship, create confidence intervals, and so on, in order to more precisely describe and understand how this interference occurs and impacts on recognizing stimuli.

In designing each of the above studies, once the dependent variable has been identified, the next step is to completely define our procedure for measuring it. As usual, we seek a valid and reliable approach, and we seek statistical power for rejecting the null hypothesis when it is false. Based on our statistical plans, we also seek scores that meet the criteria for our parametric procedures.

We will deal first with the issue of validity.

THREATS TO A VALID MEASUREMENT PROCEDURE

If we are to make the most valid inferences about a behavior being studied, the operational definition of our dependent variable should anticipate anything that might prevent the scores from accurately reflecting the behavior we seek to study, as well as anything that might prevent them from showing differences in the behavior under the different conditions.

Sensitivity of the Dependent Measure

To accurately reflect the effects of our manipulation, the dependent variable should be sensitive. A **sensitive measure** produces different scores for small differences in behavior. Only when two subjects exhibit the identical behavior should they obtain the same score. Even a slight difference in behavior should produce a different score. Then we can observe even a small effect on responses that is produced by our manipulation. Also, recall that for statistical power, we want to produce relatively large differences in scores between groups. A sensitive measure improves power because it increases the likelihood of observing such differences. Conversely, since an insensitive measure gives the same score for different behaviors, it may cause us to miss subtle changes in behavior due to our manipulation. In this case, we would be less likely to obtain significant results.

Sensitivity is increased through observing responses that can differ subtly. For example, measuring subjects' reaction time in a Stroop interference task is more sensitive than merely seeing if they correctly name the ink color: Measuring correct responses glosses over subtle differences in what subjects are mentally experiencing. Measuring reaction time is sensitive to these differences because a slow correct response indicates more interference than a fast one.

Sensitivity is also increased through increased precision in measurement. Thus, reaction time is measured in milliseconds (thousandths of a second) because this level of precision is sensitive to very small differences caused by interference. Likewise, rating scales increase precision, so instead of merely judging whether or not a child acts aggressively toward "Bobo," we would rate the degree of aggression exhibited. Always try to precisely measure the amount or degree of a behavior, as opposed to merely noting whether it occurs or not. In other words, as we originally planned, try to use interval or ratio scales of measurement: These are generally more precise and sensitive for measuring the influence of our manipulation, and they provide greater power.

To increase the sensitivity of a procedure, we also attempt to avoid any aspects of the design that might artificially limit subjects' scores.

Avoiding the Restriction of Range Problem   The experimental task must realistically allow subjects to obtain any of the different scores that occur on the variable. Therefore, when designing a measurement procedure, we should envision the range of scores it will produce. If all subjects can actually get only a few of the possible scores, then we have the problem of restricted range. **Restriction of range** occurs when the range of scores on a variable is limited by the researcher. For example, there is a wide range of aggressiveness that a subject might exhibit. Therefore, our procedure should allow subjects to score anywhere within that wide range. If it does not, we have restricted the range. Then, because we have limited the scores that subjects may obtain, it is more difficult to see the actual influence of our independent variable. At the same time, because it is now more difficult to obtain relatively large differences between the groups, we have reduced our statistical power.

To avoid restriction of range, first consider the method you will use to assign scores. In our aggression study, we want a system that allows a wide range of scores to occur. If our system allows subjects to get an aggression score of only 1, 2, or 3, the range is restricted; if subjects can score between 0 and 100, the range is not restricted. Second, consider demand characteristics, subject characteristics, or task requirements that will restrict the behaviors that subjects exhibit and, thus, inherently restrict the range of scores they receive. In our reaction-time study, for example, we avoid testing only exceptionally coordinated athletes who may produce the same scores regardless of conditions. In our aggression study, we avoid communicating the expectation that our subjects should "behave themselves" so that all children do not produce the same low aggression score in the different conditions.

Avoiding Ceiling and Floor Effects   One aspect of a task that restricts the range occurs when the task is too easy or otherwise biased so that all scores are likely to be near the highest possible score. In that case, the data will show ceiling effects. When

ceiling effects occur, the lowest potential scores—from the worst-scoring subjects—are very high, so scores cannot differ much because the better-scoring subjects cannot get much higher (everyone's scores are "hitting the ceiling"). For example, let's say we are studying memory for lists of words. If we present subjects with three-word lists to recall, this is hardly a challenge, and everyone may get perfect recall scores regardless of our conditions. Then we will not see the differential influence of our independent variable that might otherwise occur.

The range is also restricted if the task is too hard or otherwise biased toward producing low scores. Here the data will show floor effects. When **floor effects** occur, the highest potential scores—from the best-scoring subjects—are very low, so scores cannot differ much because lower-scoring subjects cannot get much lower (everyone's scores are "hitting the floor"). For example, let's say we are studying problem-solving abilities by having subjects solve anagrams. If the anagrams are so difficult that virtually no subjects can solve any of them, then everyone will tend to have a low score around zero, and again we may not see an effect of our treatments.

The goal is to create a task that starts off in the middle between very low scores and very high scores. Then, as our conditions change, subjects *can* obtain higher or lower scores.

> *REMEMBER* We want a *sensitive* procedure that will reflect slight differences in behavior and that will produce an *unrestricted range* of scores.

Recall from Chapter 5 that we conduct a "pilot study" to be sure that our design meets our goals. A pilot study allows us to confirm that we have a sensitive measurement procedure.

Demand Characteristics Associated with the Dependent Variable

As you know, to be able to draw valid inferences about a behavior, we should make sure that our subjects' responses have not been influenced by demand characteristics. *Demand characteristics* are cues that guide or bias a subject's response. Therefore, we try to identify and eliminate serious demand characteristics associated with the dependent variable. A subject's response should reflect the variable and behavior of interest; it should not reflect responses to cues arising from subjects, the experimenter, the environment, or the task.

Perhaps the greatest single threat to the validity of the dependent variable is the demand characteristic called "reactivity." **Reactivity** is the bias in responses that occurs when subjects are aware that they are being observed. Subjects "react" to the mere presence of an experimenter who observes, records, and potentially "analyzes" their behavior. Subjects know they're under the gun, so they may respond in unusual ways, become nervous and giddy, concentrate on a task and try harder, or make more errors than they would if the experimenter was not present. In a difficult condition of the Stroop interference study, for example, subjects are especially likely to make errors. If our presence causes them embarrassment or anxiety, their reaction times may be even longer than if we were not present. Although we would interpret these longer response times as reflecting interference in cognitive processing, such inferences are not valid, because they at least partially reflect subject anxiety.

Reactivity can also decrease reliability. For example, when we are measuring blood pressure, the mere act of attaching the measuring cuff to a subject raises pressure, so we would have error in our measurement of normal blood pressure.

Part of a subject's reactivity to being observed is the tendency to avoid responses that are potentially embarrassing or that make the subject appear weird or abnormal. This demand characteristic is called social desirability. **Social desirability** is the demand characteristic that causes subjects to provide what they consider to be the socially acceptable response. For example self-reports from subjects about their emotions, beliefs, or desires may be "edited" for public consumption. Likewise overt behaviors may be altered to avoid negative judgments. Thus, children who know they are being watched while playing with "Bobo" may stifle their natural aggressiveness because they don't want to look "bad."

Notice that in addition to reducing validity and reliability, reactivity and social desirability may lead to a restricted range. If all subjects restrict their aggressiveness, they will all score low, producing floor effects. Conversely, if we are measuring "niceness," we are likely to see ceiling effects. Or if we measure how much subjects agree or disagree with a statement, we may find that they don't express a strong opinion either way so as not to appear extreme. Such restrictions reduce the differences between conditions that might occur if subjects were not conscious of being observed and evaluated.

> *REMEMBER* For valid and reliable measurements, it's important that we reduce the demand characteristics of *reactivity* and *social desirability*.

General Controls for Demand Characteristics Our first approach is to recognize that *any* measurement procedure may produce reactivity and social desirability. In our instructions, therefore, we encourage subjects to respond naturally and honestly, and tell them that they should not be upset if they make errors. We assure subjects that their responses will be kept confidential, and we try to allow subjects to remain anonymous, assigning each of them a number instead of recording their names. Also, we try to provide subjects with a response format they are comfortable with: We have children act out responses using toys, we give college students a paper-and-pencil test, or we observe professors giving a lecture.

In addition, recall that we attempt to reduce the influence of demand characteristics by creating *experimental realism,* so that subjects are engaged by the task. If we can develop and present the task in such a way that subjects concentrate on responding to the *stimuli* we present (as when children concentrate on playing with "Bobo," rather than on their concern about being observed), the results will be less influenced by reactivity and other demand characteristics.

When responses are especially likely to be influenced by reactivity and social desirability (e.g., in a study of sexual fantasies), it is especially important to control researcher variables, such as gender or age. Whether people will alter their behavior depends in part on the nature of the other people present—we generally behave very differently in a locker room than when meeting a date's parents. Thus, a subject's willingness to risk making mistakes or to honestly divulge personal information may depend upon the characteristics of the experimenter. Also, in studies involving an unavoidable bias toward a restricted range of responses, we seek an especially sensitive measure. For example, if we think that all of our subjects will tend to exhibit the same level of aggression, then we want a very sensitive measure so that we can still detect slight differences in the behavior.

Habituation   We also attempt to reduce reactivity through habituation. **Habituation** refers to familiarizing subjects with a procedure before we begin actual data collection. For example, we may first have subjects perform a practice task until the researcher's presence becomes a "habit" and is no longer disruptive. Likewise, when testing children, who often respond poorly to strangers, we may play with them and get to know them before testing begins. We also allow subjects to habituate to any equipment being used. If we intend to videotape responses, for example, we allow subjects to become comfortable with being recorded.

Unobtrusive Measures and Deception   When measuring the dependent variable will strongly encourages reactivity and social desirability, researchers employ unobtrusive measures. With an **unobtrusive measure** we measure subjects' behavior without making them aware the measurement is being made. Thus, an unobtrusive measurement of children's aggressiveness toward "Bobo" might involve observing the children through a one-way mirror. Other unobtrusive measures may include the use of hidden cameras and recorders, or the observation of telltale evidence left by subjects. For example, to measure how far subjects sit from others, we may measure the distance separating their chairs after subjects have left the room.

Unobtrusive measures are often combined with some form of deception that hides the dependent variable. For example, Schacter, Goldman, and Gordon (1968) sought to measure how much food subjects would eat under different conditions. Because blatant observation was likely to make subjects highly reactive, the researchers told subjects they were in a taste experiment. They asked subjects to rate the taste of different crackers and to "taste" as many of each type of cracker as was necessary for an accurate rating. The real dependent variable was the number of crackers eaten.

Note: Anytime we have subjects perform a task that conceals or reduces demand characteristics or otherwise distracts subjects from making undesirable extraneous responses, it is referred to as a *distractor task*.

Another way of controlling reactivity is to conceal the entire experiment. For example, many studies are performed while subjects sit in a waiting room, supposedly waiting to be taken into the experiment. Using this technique, Mathews and Cannon (1975) studied how the noise level in a room influenced a subject's willingness to help another. The stimulus for eliciting helping was a confederate dropping some books. Doing this in a formal laboratory with the experimenter watching might have communicated that helping behavior was being studied and that the socially acceptable behavior was to help. Instead, a confederate dropped the books while walking past the subject in a noisy "waiting room," and the subject's response was unobtrusively observed.

Still another approach for reducing reactivity and other demand characteristics is to move out of the laboratory and conduct a *field experiment*. Here, we can unobtrusively conduct the entire experiment in the natural environment, observing people in shopping malls, student unions, and so on. For example, Mathews and Cannon (1975) also studied helping behavior by having a confederate drop books on a sidewalk in front of random passers-by, while another confederate operated a noisy lawn mower. (The special issues involving field experiments are discussed in chapter 10.)

> *REMEMBER* We reduce *reactivity* and *social desirability* through instructions, experimental realism, *habituation, unobtrusive measures,* and deception.

ETHICAL ISSUES WITH THE DEPENDENT VARIABLE

Because of the stress, embarrassment, or deception involved in measuring a dependent variable, we must again consider our ethical responsibilities when designing this part of our procedure. Remember, as researchers we are responsible for protecting subjects from abuse. Here the concern is whether subjects will be psychologically or physically distressed by making the response we elicit: Are we invading their privacy, producing unpleasant emotions, or lowering their self-esteem and feelings of competence? As usual, if a problem is identified, we try to eliminate it, or at least tone it down. Any stress that remains must be justified in terms of the scientific value of the study and dealt with through informed consent and debriefing. One important rule is to keep confidential all information regarding subjects. Never identify a subject in publications or even during casual conversation.

With unobtrusive measures it is especially important that we determine whether we are violating subjects' rights. In a laboratory setting, subjects are generally aware that they will be observed even if they cannot see the observer, so the use of one-way mirrors and such is usually acceptable. In a waiting-room situation, subjects have given their tacit agreement to be observed, simply by showing up for the study. However, the APA's *Ethical Principles* require informed consent unless there is *minimal* risk to subjects. If an unobtrusive procedure might embarrass, victimize, or otherwise harm a subject, then explicit *prior* informed consent is needed.

Role Playing and Simulations

If our independent or dependent variable is potentially very harmful to subjects, one possible solution is to have subjects simulate being in the experiment through *role playing*. In this case, we have subjects play the role of people in a particular situation. Then we either observe their behavior or have them describe the behaviors that they predict they would exhibit. Because the situation is not real, no physical or psychological harm is likely to occur. However, caution must still be exercised. For example, Haney, Banks, and Zimbardo (1973) created a prison simulation that unexpectedly turned sinister: Subjects pretending to be guards or prisoners exhibited the worst, most dangerous behaviors associated with a real prison!

In practice, role playing is used infrequently because we have so little confidence in the validity and reliability of the results. First, demand characteristics can run rampant in such studies. Subjects may alter their reactions or descriptions to conform to perceived expectations or to keep such behaviors private. (Would subjects simulating the Milgram [1963] electric-shock study actually admit that they'd electrocute someone?) Second, pretending to be in a particular situation usually produces little ecological validity. In other words, subjects are unlikely either to make realistic responses to the role-playing situation or to accurately report how they would actually respond. For example, in studies measuring the "personal space" that people use to separate themselves from others in social settings, subjects have given verbal descriptions, manipulated dolls, or drawn lines on paper to indicate how far they would stand from someone else. Yet even with such a nonthreatening task, subjects' predictions did not match their actual behavior under more realistic conditions (Hayduk, 1983).

THREATS TO A RELIABLE MEASUREMENT PROCEDURE

In addition to drawing valid inferences, we seek to show a reliable effect of the independent variable on the dependent variable, and to measure the behavior of interest in a reliable manner. After the data are collected, we will see unreliability in the form of variability among the scores within each condition. Recall that this variability is called error variance. We can see different amounts of error variance in the data in Table 6.3.

Ideally, we seek a highly consistent relationship between the conditions of the independent variable and the dependent variable. The data in experiment A reflect such consistency, because there is little error variance. In experiment B, however, there are larger differences among the scores within each condition. This greater error variance may be due either to fluctuating extraneous variables that cause the behavior and scores

TABLE 6.3 Error Variance

These diagrams show (A) a consistent relationship with little error variance, and (B) an inconsistent relationship with greater error variance.

	Experiment A			Experiment B	
Condition 1	Condition 2	Condition 3	Condition 1	Condition 2	Condition 3
4	7	9	2	5	7
5	8	10	5	8	9
6	9	11	8	11	14
$\bar{X}=5$	$\bar{X}=8$	$\bar{X}=10$	$\bar{X}=5$	$\bar{X}=8$	$\bar{X}=10$

to fluctuate, or to sloppiness and error in measuring the behavior. Regardless, greater error variance reduces the strength of the relationship, so we may not be able to accurately describe the actual effect of the independent variable on the dependent variable. Also, greater error variance decreases our statistical power, thus increasing the chances that we will erroneously conclude that the relationship results from sampling error.

As discussed in the previous chapter, we reduce error variance by presenting the conditions of the independent variable consistently to all subjects, and by controlling extraneous variables that can cause subjects to behave differently within a condition. To further reduce error variance, we design the dependent variable so that we measure the behavior consistently. We discuss how to do this in the following sections.

Defining the Scoring Criteria

The reliability of scores depends upon how *completely* we define the measurement procedure. Let's say we define a child's aggression score as the number of physically aggressive acts exhibited toward the "Bobo" doll. But what do we mean by an aggressive act? The general strategy to follow is to minimize inconsistency and bias by minimizing the interpretation we must give to a behavior. In this case, then, we want to define aggressive acts in terms of observable behaviors such as slapping, punching, kicking, or yelling at Bobo.

However, for completeness, we must also define how we will assign scores when we observe such behaviors. Do we count each time a child kicks Bobo as one aggressive act, or do we count each uninterrupted series of kicks as one aggressive act? Does a slap receive the same aggression score as a punch? By answering such questions, we develop that part of our operational definition called the scoring criteria. The **scoring criteria** define the system for assigning scores to different responses. In particular, we define the beginning and end of a response, distinguish one response from another, and determine how we will consistently assign a particular score to a particular response.

Subjects do not always behave in a way that nicely fits our intended procedure, so the scoring criteria must anticipate variations on the expected responses. If a child puts Bobo on top of another toy, or hugs him very hard, are these aggressive acts? In the Stroop interference task, do we include subjects' reaction times when they name the wrong ink color? In a memory study, if subjects see the word *bare* but write down *bear*, is this a correct or an incorrect response? If we are observing whether subjects smile in response to a stimulus, how shortly after the stimulus must the smile occur in order to be considered a response to that stimulus? How long must a smile last for it to be counted? (Is a momentary twitch a smile?)

Some answers to these questions depend upon our particular hypothesis, and we refer to the literature to suggest acceptable criteria. Beyond this, our decisions are usually arbitrary: We simply define one way in which we will measure and score a behavior, so that we eliminate inconsistency, sloppiness, and error. Then, as usual, we confirm through a pilot study that we have anticipated unexpected behaviors and developed a workable procedure.

REMEMBER Precise *scoring criteria* are necessary for reliably measuring a behavior.

Automation and Instrumentation Effects

Once the scoring system is defined, we want to ensure that it is consistently and accurately applied. For precise and consistent measurement of the dependent variable, we consider *automation* of the data-collection process. A stopwatch would not be sufficiently reliable or sensitive for measuring very small differences in reaction time. Thus, for timing responses in the Stroop interference task, we could use a voice-activated electronic timer that begins when a stimulus is presented and is stopped when a subject names a color. Or we might provide several different colored levers, one of which can be pressed by a subject to indicate the ink color and to stop a timer (as in Pritchatt, 1968). Automation can also be used to record subjects' behaviors, thus preventing errors that occur because we miss part of the behavior. For example, we could unobtrusively videotape the children with Bobo, leisurely scoring their aggressive behaviors later.

Automation also improves reliability because it eliminates the experimenter error and inconsistency that sometimes result when we are writing down each subject's score. Mistakes may occur because the experimenter is trying to record responses while also directing the study, and also because the experimenter has expectancies that cause scores to be erroneously recorded in a way that confirms the predictions. To solve all of these problems in the Stroop interference task, automation through a computer and monitor would be ideal for reliably presenting stimuli, measuring reaction times, and recording the data. In a different task, we even consider "low-tech" automation by having subjects record their own responses using paper and pencil.

> *REMEMBER*   Automation reduces imprecision, experimenter bias, and errors in recording scores.

On the other hand, because materials and apparatus wear out over time, we must guard against instrumentation effects. **Instrumentation effects** are changes in the measurement procedure that occur because of use, making the measurements less reliable. Such stimulus materials as slides, films, and videotapes become scratched and blurred, paper materials get worn and mutilated. Equipment becomes worn, so that levers are easier or harder to operate, toys become damaged, and timers break. And part of the "instrumentation" is the experimenter who may become more experienced, more bored, (or more crazed) and change the procedure. Because of such changes, the components used late in the study are different from those used early on, making for inconsistent presentation of stimuli and measurement of responses over the course of the experiment.

To minimize instrumentation effects, always keep equipment in order and make copies of materials so that all subjects can be presented with pristine stimuli. Also, be vigilant in keeping the experimenter's behavior constant. Finally, do not test all of the subjects in one condition before testing any in the other conditions, because changes due to instrumentation effects will be confounded with changes in your independent variable. Instead, test some subjects from each condition during the early, middle, and late stages of the study. In this way, potential instrumentation effects are represented in all conditions in a balanced fashion, thus eliminating confounding and keeping the overall reliability in each condition equal. Statistically speaking, this method also helps to keep the variance equal or homogeneous in each condition.

> *REMEMBER* *Instrumentation effects* refer to changes in the measurement procedure that occur through extended use.

Inter-Rater Reliability

We have special reliability concerns when a score is based on our subjective judgment of a behavior. Because of experimenter expectancies, a researcher cannot be relied upon to produce objective, valid, and reliable judgments. Therefore, we enlist the aid of others, called *raters,* who are usually "blind" to the conditions and are trained to assign scores using our scoring criteria. For example, there has been considerable study of chimpanzees who learn American Sign Language. One test of signing ability is to see whether a chimp can correctly name objects. The potential problem is that experimenters might cue the chimp to give the correct sign or, because chimps are sloppy signers, might erroneously give the chimp credit for a sign because it was "close enough" to the desired sign. To eliminate these biases, the researcher shows the object, and the rater, who cannot see the object, observes and records the chimp's sign. Raters are also commonly used in studies that involve the subjective scoring of such behaviors as creativity, nonverbal communication, and emotional displays (e.g., aggressiveness).

Of course, the rater may not reliably score a given behavior. At times the rater might miss or forget part of a subject's action. Over the course of a study, the rater may become more attuned and sensitive, or become fatigued and less motivated. And, finally, because subjective interpretations are often called for, one rater might judge a behavior differently than another. (What you consider a hug, I may consider an aggressive squeeze.) Any rater may introduce such measurement errors, and we usually cannot eliminate them.

When we cannot eliminate an extraneous influence, we try to balance it out. A common approach with raters is to employ **multiple raters,** so that we have more than one rater judging each subject's behavior. Then we combine the ratings from the different judges, usually computing the mean of the ratings given to a subject. The average rating should balance out the biases of each individual rater, giving us a more reliable measure of the subject's behavior. Further, multiple raters form a sample of observers from which we can infer that any observer would judge the behavior in roughly the same way, so we can generalize our results with greater confidence.

To be convinced that the raters are consistent, we determine their inter-rater reliability. **Inter-rater reliability** is the extent to which raters agree in the scores they assign to a subject's behavior. To ensure high inter-rater reliability, we may conduct a pilot study. In addition, we usually determine the inter-rater reliability in the actual completed experiment. Statistically, we can determine inter-rater reliability by computing the percentage of agreements between raters—for example, the percentage of times that raters agreed on the sign a chimp produced. (Better than 90% agreement is usually considered reliable.) Or we may correlate the ratings of two raters, seeking a large positive correlation coefficient. Thus, in our aggression study we should find that low aggression scores assigned by one rater were consistently matched by another, while high scores given by one were also given by the other. (An r in the neighborhood of +.90 is considered reliable.) Inter-rater reliability is usually reported in the Results section of APA-style reports.

REMEMBER The use of *multiple raters,* with high *inter-rater reliability,* improves the reliability of scores.

OBSERVING RELIABLE BEHAVIORS

Unreliability comes not only from inconsistency in measuring behaviors but also from inconsistency in the *behavior* we are measuring. When drawing conclusions from the data, we use subjects' scores as an estimate of the typical score—and behavioral response—that subjects produce under that condition. For this to be an accurate estimate, each subject's score should reflect a reliable, representative example of the subject's typical response.

We approach the goal of observing reliable responses by considering the number of **trials** on which we will observe a subject within a condition. (Measuring a subject's reaction time to one Stroop word-ink pair is a trial, and exposing a child to an aggressive model and then measuring aggressiveness is a trial.) Then, there are two important techniques for ensuring the reliability of the behavioral responses we observe: practice trials and multiple trials.

Practice Trials

A subject's response may be unrepresentative because he or she is rusty and not warmed up to the task. When this is a possibility, we give subjects **practice trials** before we begin actual data collection. That is, we present stimuli and measure responses as in the real portion of our study, but the data are not included in our analyses. Practice trials are especially useful when the response involves physical actions, as in a reaction-time task. They are also useful if the task is complicated or involves elaborate equipment, to ensure that subjects understand and perform the task correctly. In addition, practice trials "habituate" subjects to being observed, so that they can get over their reactivity before we collect the real data.

Multiple Trials

If we measure a subject on only one trial, the score may reflect all sorts of extraneous factors: Subjects may be momentarily distracted, be exceptionally lucky in a guess, be particularly reactive, or make an error they usually would not make. Also, the one stimulus we present may have unique characteristics that bias the response: if we present only the word *yellow* printed in green ink, this may coincidentally be the one word color combination that makes the task especially easy or especially difficult for subjects. In fact, any aspect of the situation—whether due to the subjects, the behavior of the experimenter, the environment, or the task—may coincidentally make one trial peculiar such that a subject's response and score are not representative of his or her typical response and score. Further, because such aspects may influence each subject differently, any one score is likely to differ from other scores within the condition, producing a relatively large error variance.

When a response is likely to be influenced by such factors, we again use the strategy of balancing, or canceling out, their influence. We do so by observing each subject in a condition on **multiple trials.** For example, we might present 10 different word-ink pairs in each condition of our interference study. Then we can assume that differences in a subject's motivation or attention on different trials balance out, that easy stimuli are balanced by hard ones, and so on.

To summarize the data for each subject, we can *collapse* across the multiple trials. Sometimes it makes sense to report each subject's total score: For a series of memory trials, we could count the total number of correct or incorrect responses each subject made. At other times, it may be more appropriate to compute a measure of central tendency to summarize each subject's trials. If the scores for the trials are normally distributed interval or ratio scores, we would compute a mean score. In our interference study, then, each subject's score might be the mean of his or her 10 reaction times in the condition.

By collapsing across multiple trials, we are more confident that each subject's summary score reliably reflects his or her typical level of responding to our condition. Further, by balancing out the random fluctuations found throughout individual trials, a subject's summary score is likely to be closer to other subjects' scores in the condition, producing less error variance.

> *REMEMBER*   Testing subjects over *multiple trials* per condition tends to increase the reliability of the data.

There is no magic number of trials to observe per condition, although to prevent confounding, all conditions should have the same number of trials. We observe a greater number of trials when each single trial is more easily influenced by extraneous variables and likely to be unreliable. For example, because reaction time is measured in milliseconds, it is likely to be highly variable over trials. Therefore, procedures like the Stroop interference task usually involve many trials per condition (in the range of 40 to 200) so that we can obtain a reliable estimate of a subject's typical reaction time. On the other hand, since imitating an aggressive model is less influenced by momentary, extraneous variables, only one trial with "Bobo" per condition seems appropriate.

We should also consider the influence that multiple trials have on our subjects. Although several reaction-time trials can be performed quickly and easily without unduly fatiguing or stressing subjects, trials that consist of observing a young child cannot be run for hours on end. (If many trials are necessary and mental or physical fatigue is a problem, we break up the testing so that it is conducted over a series of days.) Of course, in studies calling for a surprise response from subjects or a deceptive procedure of some sort, multiple trials may not be possible. As with everything in research, we weigh the pros and cons of our design decisions (and check the literature to see how others have weighed these concerns).

A major disadvantage of observing subjects over multiple trials in a condition is "order effects."

CONTROLLING ORDER EFFECTS WITHIN A CONDITION

The moment we observe a subject more than once, we are introducing a new extraneous variable called order effects. **Order effects** are the influence on a particular trial that arises from its position in the sequence of trials. (These are also called *sequence effects.*)

Order effects have two sources. First, a series of trials may produce **practice effects,** the influence on performing each trial that arises from practicing the task. Even after a practice session, subjects may perform initial trials poorly because they are not warmed up. After more trials, however, subjects tend to get into the rhythm, becoming quicker and more accurate in their responses. With even more trials, subjects may become fatigued, bored, or overloaded so that performance decreases.

The other source of order effects is known as carry-over effects. **Carry-over effects** occur when a subject's experience of a particular trial biases his or her performance on subsequent trials. These effects may be created when subjects experience particular stimuli. For example, in the Stroop study, the first word-and-ink-color combination presented may happen to be especially difficult, so that the resulting frustration or stress carries over and makes subsequent trials especially difficult. Also, carry-over effects may be created when subjects make particular responses, resulting in a response set. A **response set** is a bias toward responding in a particular way because of previous responses made. After a while, a response reflects a habit instead of being a natural reaction to the stimulus. For example, let's say our subjects indicate a color by pushing one of two colored levers and, coincidentally, the correct response is the left lever on the first few trials. This coincidence may bias subjects toward always selecting the left lever, either out of habit or because they superstitiously believe that it will be the correct choice.

Response sets are even more of a problem when a response is influenced by complex cognitive strategies. Let's say we are studying subjects' ability to solve anagrams. Try this yourself by unscrambling each of the words below:

ookb
reet
oatc
oabt

You can solve the second and third words quickly because of the response set that leads you to always place the final letter first. If you stumble on the fourth word, however, it's because this strategy no longer works. Thus, because of the response set, your solution of each word is faster or slower than it would be if the word was in a different location in the sequence.

You might think that collapsing across trials and obtaining a summary score per subject will balance out order effects. However, it is always possible for a researcher to use the one order that produces peculiar practice or carry-over effects. Then all subjects' scores will be an *un*reliable indication of the typical response, because they are tied to the unique order used. Therefore, we usually control for order effects, using one of two approaches: counterbalancing and randomizing.

Counterbalancing Order Effects

As you know, we can eliminate the bias from a variable by systematically balancing its effects in each condition. When we balance order effects, this procedure is called counterbalancing. **Counterbalancing** is the process of systematically changing the order of trials for different subjects in a *balanced* way, so that we *counter* the biasing influence of any one order. For example, say we have 10 trials per condition in the Stroop study and we number the stimuli 1 through 10. A simple way to counterbalance order is to present the stimuli to half of the subjects in each condition in the order 1 through 10, and to present the stimuli to the remaining subjects in the order 10 through 1. This design can be diagrammed as shown in Table 6.4.

Here, each subject's score is the mean reaction time for the 10 trials. Then we can *collapse* across the different orders that subjects experienced, averaging vertically all of the scores in a column to obtain the mean reaction time for each level. Although any subject's score may be influenced by a particular order, each overall mean for a condition is not, because no one particular order predominates. Thus, each level's mean is a more reliable, typical reaction time for subjects in that condition than it would be if we had not counterbalanced. (If we tested additional subjects using other orders, we would have even more confidence that a level's mean was not unduly biased by the order of trials.)

TABLE 6.4   Diagram of the One-Factor Interference Experiment with the Order of Trials Within Each Condition Counterbalanced

Each *X* represents a subject's mean reaction time for 10 trials.

	Factor of type of word presented		
	Nonsense word (e.g., BJB)	*Implied color word (e.g., grass)*	*Color name (e.g., red)*
Subject mean scores obtained with order 1–10	X X " "	X X " "	X X " "
Subject mean scores obtained with order 10–1	X X " "	X X " "	X X " "
	Mean reaction time	Mean reaction time	Mean reaction time

The above example illustrates the type of counterbalancing procedure known as partial counterbalancing. **Partial counterbalancing** is the process of balancing order effects by presenting only some of the possible orders. (Above, we did not test some subjects using the order 5 through 10 followed by 1 through 5, and so on, so we've only "partially" represented all orders.) Partially counterbalancing the order of trials within each condition is usually sufficient to confidently eliminate order effects. Sometimes, however, order effects may be so strong that we want all possible orders represented. **Complete counterbalancing** is the process of balancing order effects by testing different subjects under every possible order.

Note that some researchers use the term *counterbalancing* to refer to the systematic balancing of any extraneous variable, in addition to the variable of order. Thus, as we saw in previous chapters, if a male experimenter tests half of the subjects in each condition and a female tests the remainder, we have "counterbalanced" for experimenter gender. And if half the subjects in each condition are male and half are female, we have counterbalanced for subject gender.

Randomizing Order Effects

Typically we counterbalance when there are only a few possible orders, so that we can efficiently handle order effects systematically. When there are many possible orders, and the goal is simply to include some different sequences in an unsystematic way, we use randomization. With **randomization,** we randomly create different orders under which different subjects are tested. In the Stroop interference task, for example, before each subject is presented the series of 10 trials, we might shuffle the stimuli. Then each subject would be tested under a more or less distinct order of trials, as shown in Table 6.5.

TABLE 6.5 Diagram of the One-Factor Interference Experiment with the Order of Trials for Each Subject Randomized

Each *X* represents a subject's mean reaction time for 10 trials.

	Factor of type of word presented	
Nonsense word (e.g., BJB)	*Implied color word (e.g., grass)*	*Color name (e.g., red)*
Order 1 X	Order 2 X	Order 3 X
Order 4 X	Order 5 X	Order 6 X
Order 7 X	Order 8 X	Order 9 X
"	"	"
"	"	"
Mean reaction time	Mean reaction time	Mean reaction time

Each subject's score is the mean of that subject's reaction times for the 10 trials, and again we can collapse across the different orders that subjects experienced to obtain the mean reaction time for each level. Because there are many different orders present in each condition, each condition's mean score is a more representative, typical reaction time.

The drawback to this procedure is that it is not systematic: It does not ensure that the bias from any one order is balanced by a reverse order. Therefore, you should examine your various sequences to be sure that randomizing has not coincidentally produced a set of similar and thus potentially biasing orders. You should also examine each individual sequence and use it only if it does not exhibit a predictable pattern that might produce a response set.

> **REMEMBER** We balance order effects from multiple trials by *partially counterbalancing, completely counterbalancing,* or *randomizing* the order of trials within each condition.

Pros and Cons of Counterbalancing and Randomization

Counterbalancing and randomization can be used to control many potentially biasing or confounding variables. For example, if subjects must press a lever to indicate the ink color presented in each of 10 trials, we would want the correct response to be the left lever on 5 trials and the right lever on 5 trials. In this way, we would counterbalance any biases due to location of the correct lever. To avoid a response set, we would also randomize the sequence of left and right trials. To create a random sequence, we could write the words left and right on 10 slips of paper and draw the slips from a hat. We could create a random sequence for each subject or create only a few random sequences and counterbalance their use in each condition. Further, we could counterbalance the color of ink with the words they are printed in. For example, half of the subjects might see a series with the word *blue* printed in red ink and *yellow* printed in green ink, and the other half would see a series with *blue* printed in green ink and *yellow* printed in red ink.

The advantage of such procedures is that they greatly increase the control we have over extraneous variables. In the study just discussed, different inks and words would be combined in each condition, trials would be performed in different orders, levers would be pressed in unbiased locations, and so on. Thus, we would have greater confidence that the mean of each condition reliably reflects the typical reaction time to stimuli in that condition. We also would have increased internal validity for claiming that the results truly reflect the influence of the independent variable, because potential confounding variables have been eliminated. And we would have increased external validity for claiming that the effect of the independent variable will be found in other situations, because this effect was demonstrated even when various extraneous variables were fluctuating.

There are, however, several disadvantages to randomizing and counterbalancing extraneous variables. If you think about it long enough, you can identify an unlimited number of variables to counterbalance in any study. But extensive counterbalancing greatly complicates the design of a study, thus also increasing the potential for experimenter errors. In addition, since different subjects must be tested with each order, counterbalancing may prohibit testing subjects in large groups. Further, testing subjects under various orders of trials or with other balanced variables can increase the number of subjects required in each condition. Yet sometimes only a limited number of subjects is available.

The biggest drawback associated with counterbalancing and randomizing extraneous variables is that these procedures can increase the *error variance*. This is the case because, within each condition, we are changing an extraneous variable that produces *differences* in scores. In the Stroop interference task, for example, we would use two orders of trials because we assume that one order might tend to produce, say, low reaction times, while the other order might produce high reaction times. By counterbalancing and including both orders, we would expect to produce some higher and some lower scores *within* each condition. Thus, we'd have an increase in error variance that would not occur if we used only one order. The larger the number of variables that we counterbalance or randomize, the more we are changing variables that influence scores, so we are likely to obtain a wider variety of different scores within each condition.

In making decisions about counterbalancing, we face two conflicting goals. First, by increasing the error variance, counterbalancing weakens both the strength of the relationship and our statistical power. This is a problem because we must first have a strong, significant relationship before we can conclude anything. The best way to achieve a strong, significant relationship is to balance extraneous variables as little as possible, instead eliminating them or keeping them constant. By using one order of trials, one experimenter, and so on, we keep the task and situation more consistent, so that scores in a condition are less likely to vary and we observe a more consistent relationship.

On the other hand, if we do find a significant relationship, our goal is to argue that we have internal and external validity. Without counterbalancing, however, we do not meet this goal as well, because our results are tied to a unique situation, with one order of trials, one experimenter, one combination of words and ink colors, etc. In this case, internal validity would be reduced because we could not be sure that differences in scores between conditions were caused by our manipulation. That is, we could not know whether differences in reaction times were due to the type of word presented or to differences in response sets produced in each condition. External validity would be reduced as well, because a unique situation does not generalize well: If we test subjects only with a male experimenter, we cannot confidently generalize the results to a situation in which a female experimenter is present.

As usual, there is no easy solution to this predicament. We strive for a happy medium, but, if pushed, we will risk producing a unique situation. We counterbalance only those few variables that are *likely* to confound the independent variable or to seriously bias the dependent scores. We control other, more minor variables by keeping them constant.

> *REMEMBER* By randomizing and counterbalancing extraneous variables we increase internal and external validity, but at the cost of increased error variance.

NONPARAMETRIC STATISTICAL PROCEDURES

Thus far, we have focused on studies that allow us to use parametric inferential procedures—the *t*-test or ANOVA. However, the design issues involved in experiments discussed previously are the same issues that are involved in *any* experiment. Sometimes, though, our procedure for measuring the dependent variable does not produce interval or ratio scores that form normally distributed populations having homogeneous variance. In such cases, we use different types of descriptive statistics, as well as nonparametric inferential procedures.

Nonparametric Statistics Used with Ordinal Scales

Sometimes we measure the dependent variable by indicating the *relative* amount of the behavior that subjects exhibit; in other words, we rank-order them. Then our scale of measurement is an ordinal scale, as discussed in Chapter 3. On an *ordinal scale,* a subject's score indicates his or her rank-order position. For example, let's say we have raters rank-order *all* children in the aggression study, with 1 referring to the least aggressive of the subjects, 2 referring to the second least aggressive, and so on. We might obtain the data shown in Table 6.6. Looking at the ranked scores, we see what appears to be a relationship: Higher ranks—and thus greater aggressiveness—are found with the aggressive model.

   To summarize the central tendency of ordinal scores, we do not compute the mean. Instead, we compute the median in each condition. The **median** is the score located at the 50th percentile, and the 50th percentile indicates that 50%of the scores are at or below this point (computations shown in Appendix A). This is simply another way of summarizing subjects' scores in a condition. Look again at Table 6.6. With the passive model, the lower 50% of the scores occur at a rank of only 3, so there are many low ranks here. But with the aggressive model, the lower 50% of the scores include ranks as high

TABLE 6.6   The Aggression Experiment Showing the Ranks of Subjects on Aggressiveness in Each Condition

Conditions of Independent Variable

Control	*Experimental*
Passive model	*Aggressive model*
2	6
3	9
4	8
1	7
5	10

Median = 3   Median = 7

as 7, so there are few low-ranked subjects and more with higher ranks here. Thus, we have a different median in each condition, indicating that as we change the conditions, subjects' aggressiveness tends to increase.

To summarize the variability of ranks in a condition, we use the range. The **range** is the difference between the highest and lowest score. The smaller the range, the more consistent the relationship, with subjects in a condition obtaining close to the same rank or often being tied. The larger the range, the less consistent the relationship.

With ordinal data, we use nonparametric inferential procedures to determine whether the conditions result in significantly different scores. These procedures are analogous to the *t*-test and the one-way ANOVA.

1. When we have two conditions in a between-subjects design, a procedure that is analogous to the *t*-test for ranked scores is the **Mann-Whitney test** (computations can be found in Appendix A). If the results are significant, we conclude that the ranks in one sample are significantly different from the ranks in the other sample. (This procedure may be conducted as a one-tailed or a two-tailed test.)

2. When we have three or more conditions, the procedure that is analogous to the one-way between-subjects ANOVA for ranks is the **Kruskal Wallis test** (again, see Appendix A for computations). If the results are significant, then at least two of our conditions differ significantly. Then, we perform nonparametric *post hoc* comparisons between all pairs of conditions, to determine which specific conditions differ significantly.

> *REMEMBER*   For ordinal (ranked) data, the *Mann-Whitney test* is the nonparametric version of the between-subjects *t*-test and the *Kruskal-Wallis test* is the nonparametric version of the one-way between-subjects ANOVA.

Nonparametric Statistics Used with Interval and Ratio Scales

We also use these nonparametric procedures for ranks when our dependent variable is initially measured on an interval or ratio scale but the scores do not meet the other requirements of a parametric procedure. Sometimes, interval or ratio scores are not normally distributed. For example, reaction-time scores would form a *positively skewed distribution* if most scores are rather low (fast) but a few trials produce very high (slow) reaction times. To summarize a skewed distribution, we compute the median and range in each condition. (If we are collapsing across multiple trials per subject and each subject's trials produce such a distribution, then each subject's summary score is the median of his or her scores.) At other times, the scores may form a normal distribution but without producing homogeneous variance. For example, reaction times may be rather consistent in one condition but exhibit a great deal of variability in another. Here again we can summarize the scores by computing the mean and standard deviation.

To perform inferential procedures with such data, we first transform each subject's score or summary score on the original interval or ratio scale by assigning it a rank. For example, we could assign the subject with the fastest reaction times in the entire study the rank of 1, the next fastest a rank of 2, and so on. Then we use the appropriate nonparametric procedure for ranked data (either the Mann-Whitney or the Kruskal-Wallis test, depending on the number of conditions). If the conditions differ significantly in terms of ranks, the conditions also differ significantly in terms of the underlying interval or ratio scores they contain. (In the Stroop interference task, for example, the original reaction-time scores would also differ significantly.)

Nonparametric Statistics Used with Nominal Scales

Sometimes, measuring the dependent variable involves determining which category a subject falls into. Is the subject male or female? Left- or right-handed? Here we are measuring not an amount but, rather, a quality. As a shorthand code, we may arbitrarily assign each category a number ("1" for each male and "2" for each female), but the numbers do not reflect an amount the way numbers usually do. In this case, our scale of measurement is a nominal scale. On a *nominal scale,* each score is a label that identifies a category or quality.

For example, let's say that as part of our aggression study we examine only those subjects whose ratings meet our definition of being aggressive. Then we might count the frequency with which males and females were aggressive, obtaining the data shown in Table 6.7. It looks as if there is a relationship here, because the frequency of aggressiveness changes as gender changes.

For nominal scores, the appropriate measure of central tendency is the **mode,** the most frequently occurring score. By communicating that the mode is "male", we indicate that more males than females were classified as aggressive. To summarize the variability of such data, we report the percentage of subjects in each category. If 99% of the aggressive subjects were male, we would conclude that a very consistent relationship exists between aggressiveness and gender. But Table 6.7 shows that only 60% are male, so here we see a less consistent, weaker relationship.

Of course, we would also ask if there is a *significant* difference in the frequency with which male and females are aggressive. The nonparametric inferential procedure used with nominal data is the **chi square procedure.** We perform the **one-way chi square** when (1) we count the frequency with which subjects fall into different categories of one variable, and (2) we have a between-subjects design. (This procedure is also called the "goodness of fit test." Computations are shown in Appendix A.) If the obtained "χ^2" is significant, then we have confidence that the differences in the frequencies are not due to sampling error and, thus, that there is a "real" relationship between gender and the frequency of aggressiveness. (In APA-style reports, we use a special format

TABLE 6.7   The Frequency with Which Male and Female Children Were Aggressive

| *Conditions* | |
Male	*Female*
30	20

for reporting an obtained value of χ^2; see the *Publication Manual of the American Psychological Association.*)

> REMEMBER   The *one-way chi square* is the nonparametric procedure used when we count the frequency with which subjects fall into each category along one variable.

To help you when selecting from the various parametric and nonparametric procedures, Table 6.8 summarizes our previous discussions.

Selecting Powerful Statistical Procedure

Recall that we always seek statistical power, so that we have the greatest chance of rejecting the null hypothesis when it is false. All inferential procedures, however, are not equally powerful. Therefore, we try to design a study that permits us to use the most powerful statistics.

First, because of their theoretical foundations, parametric inferential procedures are more powerful than nonparametric procedures: Data that are analyzed using a parametric procedure are more likely to be significant than if the same data are transformed and analyzed using a nonparametric procedure. Therefore, so that we can use parametric statistics, we prefer to measure the dependent variable in a way that produces interval or ratio scores.

Note that we can use parametric procedures even if the interval or ratio scores then produce only approximately normal distributions or not-quite-homogeneous variance. These procedures are "robust," meaning that when the data somewhat violate these requirements, we only marginally increase the probability of making an incorrect inference. Thus, we tend to use nonparametric procedures only when interval/ratio scores dramatically violate the requirements of parametric procedures, or when we must measure a variable by rank-ordering subjects or by categorizing them.

Second, with parametric *t*-tests or their nonparametric equivalents, a one-tailed test is more powerful than a two-tailed test. However, we should use one-tailed tests only

TABLE 6.8   Parametric Procedures and Their Nonparametric Counterparts Used in One-Way, Between-Subjects Experiments

Number of conditions	*Parametric scores (Interval or ratio)*	*Nonparametric scores*	
		Ordinal	*Nominal*
Two samples	Independent samples *t*-test	Mann-Whitney test	Chi square
Three or more samples	Between-Subjects ANOVA (Parametric *post hoc* test)	Kruskal-Wallis test (Nonparametric *post hoc* test)	Chi square

when we can *confidently* predict the direction of the differences that will be produced. If the data turn out to form a relationship opposite to that predicted, the relationship is *not* significant, so we cannot draw any inferences from our study. Therefore, if we are unsure of our prediction, we should choose the two-tailed test. This option is safer because it potentially allows us to find a significant positive or negative relationship, so that, either way, we can still draw inferences from our study.

> *REMEMBER* The power of a design is increased by the use of parametric inferential procedures and/or one-tailed tests.

PUTTING IT ALL TOGETHER

All of the design techniques discussed in this chapter and the previous one boil down to meeting two goals. First, we seek to create a situation in which the hypothesized relationship can and will occur. Therefore, we consider the number of conditions needed, produce a strong manipulation of the independent variable, design a sensitive measure of the dependent variable, and employ powerful statistics. Second, to the degree possible, we seek to know what is happening to subjects and what their scores really reflect. Therefore, we attempt to eliminate confounding variables, reduce demand characteristics, develop consistent manipulations, and minimize error in our measurements.

Of course, we will always have questions about what the results of a study really indicate. In our reaction-time study, for example, are the differing reaction times due to differences in interference, as we think? Or is there a confounding, perhaps because of demand characteristics or because of different amounts of time needed to read the words? Does longer reaction time actually reflect greater mental "interference"? Because subjects seldom perform such a task, does our relationship have ecological validity for describing real-life interference? Likewise, in our aggression study, did subjects even notice the model, or are differences in aggression due to some unknown confounding? (Maybe the children in the experimental group were naturally more aggressive.) Did subjects imitate the model for the benefit of the adults who were present, even though they would not normally copy this behavior? And since aggressiveness toward a toy doll may be very different from aggressiveness toward other people, have we measured what we really mean by aggressiveness?

As you now know, these are the types of questions we ask when planning the design of a study, so that we can identify potential problems and correct them. Then, after the study, we revisit such questions, to be sure that the study was conducted as planned, to verify the conclusions we have drawn, and to gauge our confidence in them. To help you remember all of the issues researchers consider when designing or evaluating an experiment, Table 6.9 presents the checklist from the previous chapter, amended to reflect our additional concerns about the dependent variable.

In the next chapter, we will examine the final critical component of experimental design: the subjects.

TABLE 6.9   Checklist of Major Issues to Consider When Designing an Experiment

The items in bold type were discussed in this chapter.

- Hypothesis about relationship
- Operational definitions
  - Construct and content validity
  - Internal and external validity
  - Temporal and ecological validity
- Specify conditions
  - Linear or nonlinear relationship
  - Control groups and a strong manipulation
- Validity and reliability of independent variable
  - Confounding
  - Diffusion of treatment
  - Consistency of procedures: instructions, automation
  - Pilot study, manipulation check
- **Validity and reliability of dependent variable**
  - **Sensitivity and restriction of range**
  - **Scoring criteria**
  - **Automation, instrumentation effects**
  - **Inter-rater reliability**
  - **Practice trials and multiple trials per condition**
  - **Order effects, and counterbalancing or randomizing order**
  - **Error variance**
- Demand characteristics
  - Experimental realism, deception
  - Placebos, blind procedures
  - **Reactivity, habituation, and unobtrusive measures**
- Ethical concerns
  - Physical and psychological risks
  - Informed consent and debriefing
- **Statistical procedures**
  - Between-subjects design
  - **Scale of measurement and type of descriptive statistics**
  - **Parametric or nonparametric inferential procedure**
  - **Number of conditions**
  - **Power**

CHAPTER SUMMARY

1. When operationally defining the dependent variable, the goal is to maximize our confidence that scores validly and reliably measure the behavior we wish to study.

2. A common indirect measure of the dependent variable is *reaction time*. Other methods include *forced-choice* procedures (including *yes-no* and *sorting tasks*) and *self-reports* (including *Likert-type* questions).

3. A *sensitive* dependent measure will produce different scores for small or subtle differences in behavior.

4. The *restriction of range* problem occurs when the range of scores on a variable is limited or restricted by the researcher. *Ceiling effects* occur when scores in all conditions are very high, and *floor effects* occur when scores in all conditions are very low.

5. *Reactivity* is the demand characteristic that influences responses through subjects' awareness that they are being observed. *Social desirability* is the demand characteristic that influences responses through subjects' behaving in a socially acceptable manner.

6. We attempt to prevent reactivity through (a) *habituation,* by familiarizing subjects with a procedure before we begin actual data collection, and (b) *unobtrusive measures,* by measuring subjects' behavior without making them aware that the measurement is being made.

7. To increase reliability (and decrease error variance) we use (a) *scoring criteria* that define the system for assigning a particular score to a particular response; (b) *automation,* which provides for precise and consistent measurement and recording of scores; and (c) *multiple raters,* who have high *inter-rater reliability,* the extent to which raters agree in the scores they assign a particular behavior. We also attempt to limit *instrumentation effects,* which are changes in the measurement procedure that occur through use.

8. An important consideration in experimental design is the number of *trials* on which we will observe a subject within a condition. To ensure the reliability of the behavioral response under study, we provide *practice trials* and observe subjects on *multiple trials* within each condition.

9. Multiple trials may introduce *order effects,* the influence on a particular trial that arises from its position in the sequence of trials. These include *practice effects,* the influence on performance that comes from practicing the task; and *carry-over effects,* the influence that a subject's experience of a trial has on his or her performance of subsequent trials. A *response set* is a bias toward responding in a particular way because of previous responses made.

10. To control for order effects, we can use the technique known as *counterbalancing.* *Partial counterbalancing* involves the presentation of only some of the possible orders; *complete counterbalancing* includes all possible orders.

11. We can also control order effects through *randomization,* creating different random orders of trials for different subjects.

12. Counterbalancing and randomization tend to increase validity, because the effect of the independent variable occurs even when fluctuating extraneous variables are present. Yet these procedures tend to increase error variance because the presence of the fluctuating variables produces different scores within each condition.

13. The statistical procedures we employ depend on the measurement scale used to measure the dependent variable, the number of conditions tested, and whether the design is a between-subjects design.

14. Parametric procedures (the *t*-test and ANOVA) are used with interval or ratio scores that form normal distributions having homogeneous variance. The data are summarized using the mean and standard deviation or variance.

15. The nonparametric procedures used with ordinal (ranked) scores for between-subjects designs with one independent variable are the *Mann-Whitney test* (with two conditions) and the *Kruskal-Wallis test* (with more than two conditions). The data are summarized using the *median* (50th percentile) and the *range.*

16. For *nominal* scores, the appropriate measure of central tendency is the *mode,* the most frequently occurring score in a sample. The nonparametric procedure used with nominal data is the *chi square procedure.* When we count the frequency of category membership along one variable in a between-subjects design, we use the *one-way chi square* procedure.

17. When possible, we prefer a procedure that produces interval or ratio scores, both because they are more precise and sensitive, and because they usually permit the use of parametric inferential procedures, which have the most statistical power. When appropriate, one-tailed tests are more powerful than two-tailed tests.

REVIEW QUESTIONS

1. What does it mean to use (a) a "forced-choice" procedure? (b) "Likert-type" questions? (c) a "sorting task"?

2. (a) What does the term *self-reports* mean? (b) What is the major disadvantage of this procedure?

3. What are the three major aspects of a design that determine the specific statistical procedures you should employ?

4. To study nonverbal communication, your conditions involve showing subjects a picture of a person making different kinds of faces (smiling, frowning, smirking). You ask subjects to indicate the person's emotional state as either happy or sad. (a) What flaws are built into the scores you obtain? (b) How can you improve this procedure?

5. To study how practice influences physical ability, you manipulate three conditions of the amount of practice that subjects have playing basketball; then you measure the number of baskets they make out of 50 tries. Your subjects are physical education majors. (a) What flaw is built into these scores? (b) How can you improve this procedure?

6. (a) In question 5, what scale of measurement are you using? (b) What other criteria must the data meet to permit the use of a parametric procedure? (c) Assuming that the data do meet these criteria, describe the statistical procedures you would perform, and indicate what each tells you about your results.

7. In question 5, to make the task challenging to subjects, you have them stand at the far end of the basketball court when testing their basket-shooting. What flaw is built into this procedure?

8. In question 5, when testing subjects' shooting ability, you stand beside them, recording on a clipboard whether they make each basket. (a) What bias may influence the subjects' responses? (b) What two procedures can you use to reduce the impact of this flaw?

9. (a) What is "role playing"? (b) What is the advantage of this approach? (c) What is the disadvantage of this approach?

10. To study how background noise influences memory, you read one list of eight words to subjects under conditions of either soft, medium, or loud noise. Then you ask subjects to write down the list of words. (a) To reliably score subjects' recall, what decisions should you make? (b) How would you ensure unbiased scoring? (c) How would you determine whether the scoring was reliable?

11. In question 10, (a) what problem affects the reliability of the memory behavior you are observing? (b) What preliminary task can you add to the design to improve reliability? (c) How can you expand your observations of a subject to improve reliability?

12. Let's say you now test subjects' memory on each of *several* lists in each condition. (a) What extraneous variable may influence recall of each list? (b) What two approaches can you use to eliminate the influence of this variable?

13. In question 12, (a) how might your reading of the lists to subjects influence their recall scores? (b) How can you eliminate this problem? (c) What problem may then arise over the course of testing many subjects?

14. (a) What is the difference between partial counterbalancing and complete counterbalancing? (b) What is the advantage of counterbalancing compared to randomization?

15. (a) What is the advantage of counterbalancing or randomizing variables in terms of internal and external validity? (b) Statistically, what is the disadvantage of both procedures? (c) How do we resolve this conflict?

16. You manipulate motivation by paying subjects different amounts of money; then you measure the impact of this manipulation on subjects' position in a race to finish a series of math problems. (a) How would you summarize the data? (b) With two conditions, how would you test for significant differences? (c) With three conditions, how would you test for significant differences?

17. If a researcher summarizes scores using the mode and computes a chi square, how has he or she measured the dependent variable?

DISCUSSION QUESTIONS

1. For a study of sex-role stereotypes, you measure the subjects' sexist attitudes using a questionnaire titled "Survey of Sexist Attitudes." (a) Why might you fail to observe differences in attitudes under the different conditions? (b) How would you attempt to avoid this problem? (c) Before the study is actually under way, how would you confirm that you have a reliable and valid procedure? (d) How would you increase your confidence in the reliability and validity of your measurements?

2. In a study involving differing conditions of illumination, you wait until your subjects have left and then determine the distance that they were comfortable sitting from a confederate by measuring the distance they placed their chair from the confederate's. (a) How will you get subjects to place their chairs? (b) What demand characteristics should concern you? (c) After the subjects have participated, what actions might they take that can decrease the accuracy of your measurements? (d) How can you increase your confidence that you know how comfortable the subject's actually felt?

3. Your conditions consist of three types of instructions on how to be logical. The dependent variable is subjects' ability to solve three brain-teaser problems of this sort: "You go to a

stream with a three-quart bucket and a five-quart bucket. How would you come back with exactly two quarts of water?" (a) What major threat to reliability and validity is present in this study? (b) Diagram how you would partially counterbalance for this problem. (c) You are also concerned about the influence of the sex of the experimenter. Diagram how you would counterbalance for this variable along with that in part A.

4. You wish to test the proposal that females become more sexually aroused by erotic films when the plot has a stronger theme of love and romance. (a) After selecting different types of films, how would you measure the dependent variable? (b) What demand characteristics are a major problem? (c) How would you reduce these demand characteristics? (d) What ethical problems might arise with this study?

7 Controlling Subject Variables

The controls that we discussed in the previous two chapters are essentially designed to limit subjects' responses to only our independent variable using the response built into our dependent variable. So far, however, we have taken the subjects for granted. Yet, in addition to any external stimuli, a response depends on the inherent characteristics of a subject. Subjects are observing, thinking, and feeling organisms who can modify any measurement procedure. Thus, differences among subjects constitute a multitude of extraneous variables that can decrease the validity and reliability of a study.

In this chapter we will see how to recognize subject variables that can influence our results, examine techniques for controlling subject variables, and consider the impact that such controls have on our statistical and conceptual interpretation of a study.

HOW SUBJECT VARIABLES INFLUENCE A STUDY

Subjects respond differently to a manipulation because no two individuals are identical. **Subject variables** are inherent, personal characteristics that distinguish one subject from another. Physically, subjects differ in gender, age, metabolism, hormones, the speed their neurons fire, musculature, coordination, height, and weight. Because their physical machinery is not identical, their physical reactions are not identical. Cognitively, because they differ in style, strategies, intelligence, and memory, they do not all process a stimulus identically. They also differ in terms of personal histories and experiences, social and economic standing, and so on, so some are more familiar with a task than others. Emotionally, they are influenced by moods in different ways, and they have different motivations. Socially, their attitudes and personality differ, so some will be more reactive, more competitive, or more attentive.

To communicate all of these differences, we sometimes use the catch-all phrase **individual differences,** by which we mean the characteristics that make individuals different from one another and thus produce different responses to the same situation. When discussing subject variables, we really mean any variable that makes one individual different from another.

Selecting the Population

Remember it is the external validity of a design that allows us to accurately generalize our results to the population, describing how all subjects would behave in the conditions of our experiment. Subject variables are extremely important to external validity, because they define the population we can generalize to. We define the population by creating our selection criteria. **Selection criteria** form the operational definition of our subjects in terms of the characteristics we require for allowing them to participate in our study. The criteria that define the sample also define the population it represents. Therefore, we create our selection criteria so that, ideally, the sample is *representative* of our target population: It is a good example, accurately reflecting the characteristics of subjects and, thus, the behaviors and scores that are found in the population.

Defining the sample first depends on the constructs and hypothesis being investigated. If, for instance, we are studying the behavior of children, then the sample and population should be composed of children of a specified age. Recognize, however, that a population is not a fixed entity defined by one variable. Members of a population may differ along many subject variables: The population of children, for example, contains males and females from different cultures and backgrounds, with different abilities, and so on. How well our results generalize to the population depends on how much the sample has in common with the population in terms of *all* of the subject variables that can influence responses. If we exclude subjects having a particular characteristic, we may end up with a biased and unrepresentative example of the population, thus creating a biased picture of how all members of the population behave. In short, our selection criteria should give rise to a sample that is similar to the population along all relevant subject variables—a sample that is essentially a miniature version of the population we will generalize to.

> **REMEMBER**   The sample of subjects we observe should reflect the important characteristics of the population to which we will generalize our results.

Limitations on the Representativeness of a Sample

Recall that we randomly select subjects so that every subject in the defined population has the same chances of being selected. As discussed in Chapter 2, we may use *simple random sampling* (similar to drawing names from a hat) or *systematic random sampling* (selecting every *n*th name from a list). By selecting subjects in an unbiased and unselective manner, we allow the diverse characteristics of the population to occur in the sample as often, and to the same degree, as they occur in the population. Therefore, as a whole, the subjects in our experiment should be representative of our population. However, there will always be certain *de facto* limitations on our sampling that prevent some members of the population (and thus some subject variables) from being selected. First, the entire population may not be identifiable. For example, if you peruse the research on alcoholism and its treatment, you will find that it is largely limited to males. Historically, female alcoholics have been unwilling to identify themselves, so many are not available as subjects.

Second, we are unable to contact all identifiable subjects. Usually our sample will be limited to those people living near us. If we then solicit subjects using the telephone directory, the represented population is further limited, excluding the rich and famous with unlisted numbers, as well as poor people who have no phone. Many psychological experiments are even more limited, because the samples in such cases are made up of students at the researcher's university. Further, we are often able to reach only certain students—namely, those enrolled in psychology courses.

Because of such limitations, we usually cannot obtain a truly random sample from the population. In practice, many researchers solicit subjects by announcing an experiment in college classes or by posting announcements on bulletin boards or in the newspaper. Under these circumstances, subject selection is random only to the extent that we try to give every potential subject in the available portion of the population an equal opportunity to volunteer for the study. Often we will then test all volunteers who meet our selection criteria, or we may use simple or systematic random sampling to select from those who constitute the volunteer pool.

By excluding some subjects in the population from our sampling procedures, we may overrepresent some subject variables and fail to represent others, so that the sample is unrepresentative of the population. For example, because of its admission standards, cost, and so on, a particular college will attract a certain type of student. Whether such limitations seriously reduce external validity depends upon the behavior under study. If we are studying consumer attitudes toward a product and exclude poor people from our sample, we have left out an important segment of the population and thus reduced the external validity of our results. However, if poor people cannot afford the product, then they *should* be excluded from the sample. Likewise, some behaviors of college students, such as memory or other cognitive processes, may not generalize well to the adult population as a whole, because college students may be better educated and smarter than adults in general.

The reason researchers so often use college students as subjects is that they are conveniently available and we assume that findings about many of their basic behaviors do generalize reasonably well to the larger population. However, for some behaviors, we may need to broaden both the population and the sample. Milgram's infamous electric-shock study did not rely on college students, because, given their age and position, such students might have been especially responsive to authority figures. Instead, the general adult population was sampled. Always give thoughtful consideration to the population you wish to generalize your results to, and determine whether any limitations in your sample will seriously reduce the validity of your conclusions. If they are likely to do so, take the necessary steps to obtain a more representative sample. (In Chapter 10, we'll examine techniques that researchers use to identify and contact a wider range of subjects.)

Sample Size and Representativeness

Working within the limited available population, we seek to adequately represent it. An important aspect of this process is deciding on our target N, the number of subjects we plan to observe. Typically, the symbol N stands for the number of subjects in a study, and n stands for the number of subjects in a condition (adding all of the ns equals N). To maximize external validity, the general rule is "the more the merrier": The larger our sample, the more likely it is to accurately represent the population, because we are actually observing more of the population. And by observing more of the population, we are more likely to include all relevant subject variables, so that we are less likely to obtain a biased sample and to make errors in our inferences. Conversely, with only a few subjects, we are more likely to obtain a sample having rather atypical characteristics, such that it is not representative of the population.

"The more the merrier" does not mean that we need to test hundreds of subjects per condition. The range of N in laboratory experiments is often between 50 and 100, with ns in the range of 15 to 30. The results of such studies are replicated with considerable frequency, at least in terms of the general pattern of results. This suggests that, with Ns in this range, one random sample is roughly comparable to another and the findings they produce are externally valid. Of course, if more subjects can easily be tested, they will only further increase the external validity of our study.

We are not required to have the same number of subjects—"equal ns"—in all conditions. However, remember that we want to generalize the results of each condition, and that we seek the same level of confidence in our results for each. Therefore, we should avoid having only a few subjects in a particular condition. Instead, we evenly divide the subjects so we have at least close to the same number of subjects per condition and therefore an adequate, comparable representation of the population in each. (Note, too, that inferential statistics are most accurate with close to equal ns, and they are often much easier to perform, with equal ns.)

Limitations on the Representativeness of Volunteer Subjects

Even with a large N from a not-too-limited portion of the population, the representativeness of our sample can be further limited because only some subjects will end up participating in our study. Then the external validity of our results suffers because of the peculiar characteristics of these subjects.

First, external validity is limited because of the volunteer bias. The **volunteer bias** is the bias that arises from the fact that our sample contains only those subjects who are willing to participate in our study. There are considerable differences between people who volunteer for a study and those who do not (Rosenthal & Rosnow, 1975). Among other things, volunteers tend to have a higher social status and intelligence, to exhibit a greater need for approval, and to be less authoritarian and conforming. Also, participants who find the research topic interesting or personally relevant are more likely to volunteer, as are those who expect to be positively evaluated.

The generality of our results may also be limited by the fact that, among those who initially volunteer, some subjects will not complete the study. Then the sample suffers from subject mortality. This doesn't mean that subjects literally die (usually). Rather, **subject mortality** refers to the loss of subjects because their participation dies out. Subjects may fail to show up for the study, or they may discontinue their participation before the study is completed. Subject mortality is especially prevalent when we schedule multiple testing sessions for each subject. In such cases, some subjects show up for initial sessions but do not return for later ones. The problem is, mortality effects are selective: Subjects who continue to participate may find the study more interesting, perform better at the task, be more committed to helping science, or be more desperate for college credit or money. Therefore, our results may be biased, because they are based on only a certain type of subject.

Finally, the subjects who complete our study may be biased because they are not naive about psychological research. **Subject sophistication** is a bias in our results that occurs when subjects are knowledgeable about research. Subjects may have participated in previous experiments, or they may have studied research methods or the psychological topic under investigation. Subjects also gain experience and knowledge about our manipulations over the course of their participation. Because of their knowledge, these subjects may be more or less susceptible to reactivity and other demand characteristics, or they may be aware of our deceptions or predictions. Then, of course, their behavior does not represent that of the general, unsophisticated population.

REMEMBER   The subjects we study may differ from nonsubjects in terms of *volunteer bias, subject mortality,* and *subject sophistication.*

Although these threats to the external validity of a study are not entirely controllable, we can try to limit them. We attempt to make the mechanics of volunteering and participating in the study easy for subjects, with a minimum of effort on their part. We try to design the task so that it is interesting, easy, and brief, so that its completion does not require extremely dedicated volunteers. And we initially solicit a wide range of both sophisticated and unsophisticated subjects. As usual, we also consider a study's possible flaws when interpreting it. Thus, we pay attention to the degree of subject mortality, and during debriefing we may question subjects about their sophistication or their reasons for volunteering, so that we can gauge how biased our sample may be.

Eliminating Subjects from the Data

There is one other aspect of subject selection that influences the external validity of our results (as well as the internal validity and reliability of the study). Even with all our precautions, research never runs as smoothly as we plan: Murphy's law always applies. Some subjects may behave strangely (I've had subjects go to sleep!). Through a manipulation check, we may find some subjects who were unduly biased by a demand characteristic or discover others who were told the details of the study by a previous subject. A fire drill may occur while we're testing a subject. Or our tape-recorder may blow a fuse.

In such situations, the subjects are not participating in the study that we designed: They are not being reliably exposed to our independent variable, they are not responding as directed, or they are being influenced by uncontrolled extraneous variables. Therefore, we may exclude from our analysis the data produced by such subjects. Of course, we need to be *sure* that these subjects do not belong in the study. We cannot exclude them just because their scores do not confirm our prediction. If we exclude subjects on this basis, we are rigging the results and committing fraud: We might as well make up the data. When in doubt, therefore, we include a subject's data. It is only when scores are *clearly* inappropriate because of extraneous influences that we can exclude them. (Usually, such exclusions are noted in the Participants section of a report.)

To maintain external validity, we test additional subjects to fill in for excluded subjects so that we have at least close to the same number of subjects in each condition. Of course, any study that produces many excluded subjects may contain a hidden factor that is affecting a certain type of subject. As a consequence, the sample will be biased and external validity will be reduced. To ensure a minimum of excluded subjects, we must sometimes redesign the procedure and conduct additional pilot studies.

Subject Variables That Threaten Internal Validity and Reliability

Once we have identified the sample's characteristics that we seek for maximizing external validity, we consider any additional subject variables that may influence our results. Remember, we want to control any extraneous variable that may fluctuate within a condition or between our conditions. Subject variables that fluctuate within conditions can threaten reliability because differences in subject variables cause subjects to respond differently, producing differences in scores within each condition and increasing error variance. Subject variables that fluctuate between conditions produce confoundings and we lose internal validity, because we cannot know whether differences between the scores in the conditions are due to our manipulation or to the subject variables. Ideally, therefore, we seek to control *all* extraneous subject variables so that subjects are equivalent on any variable that may influence our results.

To identify subject variables that must be controlled, look for any subject characteristic that is substantially correlated with the independent and dependent variables: A correlation may indicate a causal influence. First, look for differences among subjects that may influence the impact of your treatments. For example, let's say we are studying the effects of alcohol. Because of differences in weight, metabolism, or tolerance, some subjects may be more or less debilitated by a particular amount of alcohol. Then we will have an inconsistent effect of each condition of our independent variable. Second, look for differences among subjects that may influence how a response on the dependent variable is made. For example, let's say that we're studying how differences in the organization of a written paragraph influence retention of it. A subject's vocabulary and reading skills are correlated with, and thus may influence, his or her comprehension and retention of *any* paragraph. These variables will produce differences in recall scores despite any effect of the manipulation.

Generally, when the stimulus is rather concrete and elicits a physical, performance response, we look for subject variables that influence the "machinery." These may be physical, such as a subject's height or degree of coordination, or they may be psychological, such as a subject's cognitive abilities or motivation. For stimuli and responses that involve social behaviors or attitudes, we look for variables that influence social processes, such as personality or cultural differences. Of course, the research literature is helpful in identifying important subject variables that we should control. Research specifically related to our study will indicate variables that others have felt needed controlling. And general research investigating individual differences will indicate subject variables that can influence the behavior we are studying.

> *REMEMBER*   A subject variable that is correlated with the influence of the independent variable or with performance on the dependent variable is a potential subject variable to control.

Two Example Studies

We will discuss the various ways we control subject variables in the context of two example studies. The first is taken from research on "subliminal perception." Typically this research involves presenting a stimulus that is visible to subjects only very briefly—say, for about 5 milliseconds. (It takes about 150 milliseconds to blink.) The hypothesis is that the stimulus can in some way be processed, even though subjects do not consciously recognize that it was even present.

Let's debunk some misconceptions regarding subliminal perception. There is *no* accepted evidence that brief messages hidden in advertisements make you buy a product, or that other types of hidden messages in music or in photographs control your behavior. These misconceptions can be traced to a *rumor* about a study from the 1950s (relayed in McConnell, Cutler & McNeil, 1958). The subliminal messages "Buy popcorn" and "Drink Coca Cola" were supposedly inserted in a film being shown at a theater, and the sale of refreshments at the theater's concession stand supposedly increased dramatically. However, the duration of each message was—again, supposedly—only 1/3000 of a second (an impossible speed for a 1950s movie projector), *no* control group was used, and *no* distinction was made between refreshments bought during the movie and those bought *before* the movie started. Further, these results were never reported in any journal, and there are no published replications of this or similar claims under controlled conditions. (To understand how such misconceptions become part of the folklore, consider two possible explanations: [1] the public's fear of brainwashing and other such mysteries, and [2] self-proclaimed "experts" who claim that subliminal messages are effective, and who will *sell* you a book or technique to "prove" it.)

There is, however, well-controlled experimental evidence that a subliminal stimulus can register. For example, in cognitive research, flashing the word *doctor* allows faster recognition of *nurse* when the latter is subsequently presented at normal speed, than does flashing the word *bread* (Meyer & Schvanveldt, 1971). In social research, flashing words that describe honesty or meanness produce a corresponding bias in subjects' later description of a confederate (Erdley & D'Agostino, 1988).

In clinical research, too, numerous studies have shown a positive influence of the subliminal message "Mommy and I are one" (see Silverman & Weinberger [1985] for a review). Presumably, the message in some way resolves subjects' unconscious conflicts with their Mom, allowing them to perform better on a variety of tasks. For example, Parker (1982) exposed subjects in a college law course to the message "Mommy and I are one," the message "My Prof and I are one," or the control message "People are walking." The dependent variable was a subject's grade on the final exam. We can envision this design as shown in Table 7.1. There are three levels of one factor in this "one-way" design, and because we can randomly assign subjects to any condition, it is a true experiment.

In this study, reliable manipulation was produced by presenting the messages using a computer, a reliable scoring method was employed by giving an objective, multiple-choice final exam; and demand characteristics were controlled by the instructor/experimenter being "blind" to the condition a subject was in. The study produced the means shown in Table 7.1, indicating that after repeated exposure throughout the semester, subjects seeing the "Mommy message" obtained significantly higher final-exam grades.

A different sort of mysterious psychological effect is found in the study of memory. Sometimes we know a word or the answer to a question, but we cannot quite get it out: The answer seems to be "stuck" on the tip of our tongue. This experience is referred to as the tip-of-the tongue state, or TOT. Brennen, Bagley, Bright, and Bruce (1990) produced TOTs in the laboratory by providing subjects with questions about somewhat famous people, such as "Who is the actor who played TV's 'Bionic Man'?"[1] The researchers compared the effectiveness of three types of cues that subjects could use to resolve and

---

[1]Lee Majors

TABLE 7.1 Diagram of the Subliminal Message Experiment

X's represent each student's final-examination grade. Overall means indicate the mean final exam scores from Parker (1982).

	Conditions of independent variable *(Content of subliminal messages)*	
"Mommy and I are one"	*"My prof and I are one"*	*"People are walking"*
X	X	X
X	X	X
X	X	X
"	"	"
"	"	"
$\overline{X} = 90$	$\overline{X} = 88$	$\overline{X} = 83$

From K. A. Parker (1982), Effects of subliminal symbiotic stimulation on academic performance: Further evidence on the adaptation-enhancing effects of oneness fantasies, *Journal of Counseling Psychology,* 29, 19–28. Copyright ©1982 by the American Psychological Association. Reprinted by permission.

recall the TOT—a picture of the famous person, the person's initials, or a repetition of question (the control condition). This design is shown in Table 7.2. Again, note that it is a one-way design of a true experiment, with three levels of the factor. Each X represents the percentage of TOTs that a subject resolved.

For reliability, the scoring criteria required a time-limit for solving each TOT, each subject performed multiple trials in each condition (for each of 50 questions one type of cue was provided.), and the order of trials in each condition was counterbalanced. The study produced the means shown in Table 7.2, indicating that a significantly greater percentage of TOTs were resolved when the famous person's initials were the cue. This finding suggests that the information in memory that subjects use to overcome a TOT is more accessible to verbal cues than to pictorial cues or to the mere repetition of the question.

In designing these two studies we would also consider the statistical procedures to be employed. Before we could do that, however, we'd have to consider what important subject variables come to mind and how we would control them. In the study of subliminal messages, the dependent variable is the final-exam grade in a college law course. Exam grades are correlated with a subjects' general academic skills. Therefore, we want to control differences in the academic abilities of subjects in each condition, so that we can say that any differences in grades between the conditions are not due to this variable. In the TOT study, we want to control any subject variables that influence whether subjects will experience a TOT and how they overcome it. Therefore, we want to say that any differences in scores between conditions are not due to differences in subjects' knowledge of famous people, memory strategies, or anxiety reactions to a TOT.

As we will see below, such variables can be controlled in either a between-subjects design or a within-subjects design.

TABLE 7.2   Diagram of the TOT Experiment

*X*s represent the percentage of TOTs resolved by a subject in a condition. Overall means indicate the percentage of TOTs resolved in Brennen et al. (1990).

*Conditions of the independent variable
(Type of cue for overcoming a TOT)*

Initials cue	Picture cue	Repeated question
X	X	X
X	X	X
X	X	X
"	"	"
"	"	"

$\overline{X} = 46.6\%$ $\overline{X} = 14.5\%$ $\overline{X} = 10.7\%$

CONTROLLING SUBJECT VARIABLES IN BETWEEN-SUBJECTS DESIGNS

In a **between-subjects design,** we select a different group of subjects to serve in each condition, without considering the subjects selected in the other conditions. With this design, our first (and last) line of defense for controlling subject variables is random assignment.

Random Assignment

Random sampling only helps to ensure that the characteristics of the population are represented somewhere in the study as a whole. Therefore, in a between-subjects design involving a true independent variable, we randomly assign subjects to each condition. In doing so, we control subject variables by randomly mixing them, so that differences in any subject variable are balanced out in *each* condition. For example, by randomly assigning subjects to our subliminal-message conditions, some subjects who are academically skilled and some who are not should end up in each condition. Then, differences between the conditions should not be due to differences in the academic skills of the subjects in each condition. Overall, each condition should reflect the same mix of academic skills, so we should eliminate this potential confounding.

We must be careful to assign subjects to conditions in a truly random way, however, and to avoid allowing a hidden subject variable to determine each subject's assignment. Let's say we make the mistake of assigning students who sit in the first row in the law class to one level of our subliminal messages, those in the second row to another level, and those in the back row to the third. The problem is that students select where in a classroom they wish to sit, and that this decision is influenced by individual differences. Hillmann, Brooks, and O'Brien (1991), for example, found that self-esteem tends to be lower in those students sitting farther from the front of the room. Thus, our independent variable would be confounded by differences in self-esteem. Subject mortality may produce another such confounding, because those subjects who complete one condition may be consistently different from those who complete another condition. Then differences in scores between our conditions may actually be due to differences in the characteristics of the types of subjects who "survived" each condition. Finally, do not think that you have random assignment if you assign to the same condition all of the subjects who first volunteer or show up for a study. Those who participate early in the course of a study may bias a particular condition simply because they are inherently more prompt, compulsive, or ambitious than later subjects. Instead, randomly alternate the assignment of subjects to different conditions as they arrive. As these examples illustrate, be sure throughout that your random assignment distributes subject characteristics over all conditions in a truly random way.

Pros and Cons of Random Assignment   Given how frequently research findings can be replicated, random assignment—and random selection—are powerful tools for producing balanced, representative samples in each condition. This is especially heartening because we often cannot identify the important subject variables to be controlled. But with random assignment, we don't need to know the subject variables that are being controlled, because whatever they are in the population, we allow them to occur in a balanced way in each condition.

However, there are three potential problems with random assignment. First, it is not systematic, so it does not match each positive influence of a variable with a negative influence of the same degree. Therefore, random assignment does not guarantee a balance of subject variables within each condition. Thus, for example, we may by chance have subjects in one condition who are more academically skilled than those in another, so that our independent variable is confounded by skill level.

The second problem is that random assignment works less well with small samples. Sometimes, the available pool of potential subjects is rather small; or because of other design considerations, we can test only a few subjects. In such cases we are more likely to assign a group of subjects to one condition whose characteristics tend to be different from those in another condition.

The third problem with controlling subject variables through random assignment is that if it does work, we are including the influence of extraneous subject variables, allowing them to fluctuate *within* each condition. For example, differences in subjects' academic ability can cause any two subjects in the same condition to have different final-exam scores. As we saw in the previous chapter, changing extraneous variables within a condition produces increased variability in scores, thus increasing the error variance. This increased error variance, in turn, reduces both the strength of the relationship and our statistical power for rejecting the null hypothesis when it is false.

Because of these potential problems with random assignment, researchers sometimes choose to actively control subject variables. Toward this end, one approach is to apply the counterbalancing techniques discussed in the previous chapter.

Counterbalancing Subject Variables

Usually, we do not leave the balancing of a critical subject variable to random chance, because the possibility of a serious confounding is too great. Instead, we control the subject variable by systematically *counterbalancing* its influence within each condition. To counterbalance a subject variable, we first make the variable part of our selection criteria. For obvious physical or personal characteristics (gender, age), we merely solicit subjects who meet the criteria. For less obvious characteristics, we **pretest** subjects: Prior to conducting the study, we measure potential subjects on the subject variable we wish to control. For example, we may measure a physical attribute (subjects' strength), a cognitive skill (reading ability), or a personality trait (self-reported anxiety level).

Notice that conducting a pretest is no different than measuring subjects on a dependent variable, so we need a valid and reliable measurement technique: We must be concerned with the usual issues of scoring criteria, sensitivity, automation and instrumentation, practice trials, inter-rater reliability, multiple trials, and order effects.

Using the pretest information, we create a separate subject "pool" for each aspect of the subject variable we wish to balance. For example, in the subliminal message study, we could create a pool of males and a pool of females to control the subject variable of gender. And to control academic ability, we could identify good students and poor students using our operational definition of academic ability. Then we would randomly select subjects from the pools and randomly assign them so that each pool is represented in each condition in a balanced way. For example, we could randomly select and assign subjects so that 25% of the subjects assigned to a condition are from the male–good student pool, 25% are from the female–good student pool, and so on. This design is shown in Table 7.3.

Each row in this table represents subjects selected for their scores on the subject variables we are balancing. Otherwise, we still employ random selection and assignment when selecting subjects from each pool, to balance out any other subject variables as well. To determine the effect of our subliminal message manipulation, we collapse across

TABLE 7.3   Diagram of the Subliminal Message Experiment, Showing Counterbalancing of Gender and Academic Ability

*X*s represent each student's final examination grade.

	Levels		
Subject pools	*"Mommy and I are one"*	*"My prof and I are one"*	*"People are walking"*
Male–Good students	$XXX\cdots$	$XXX\cdots$	$XXX\cdots$
Female–Good students	$XXX\cdots$	$XXX\cdots$	$XXX\cdots$
Male–Poor students	$XXX\cdots$	$XXX\cdots$	$XXX\cdots$
Female–Poor students	$XXX\cdots$	$XXX\cdots$	$XXX\cdots$
	$\overline{X}$	$\overline{X}$	$\overline{X}$

the rows, averaging all scores vertically in a condition. Then the mean score in each condition should be equally influenced by differences in academic ability and gender, so that any differences between conditions cannot be confounded by these variables. To test for significant differences, we have created a between-subjects design so we employ the one-way, between-subjects ANOVA.

Pros and Cons of Counterbalancing   If we find a significant relationship, then having counterbalanced a subject variable alleviates one potential problem of random assignment: We can be sure that the influence of each variable *is* balanced in each condition, so we have greater internal validity. We also have greater external validity, because we demonstrate the relationship even when different genders and academic abilities are present.

Of course, that's *if* we find a significant relationship. As with random assignment, the drawback to counterbalancing is that a subject variable is changing within each condition, so there may be greater variability in scores within each condition. By including in each condition the scores of males and females, who are academically good and poor, we are likely to see a relatively large error variance, so we obtain a less consistent relationship and have less power.

In addition, a drawback of counterbalancing is that a pretest may alert subjects to the variables we are examining or to the purpose and predictions of our study. This knowledge can produce a diffusion of treatment, which, as you may recall, reduces the impact of each condition. It may also decrease the experimental realism of the actual testing task, such that subjects are less realistically engaged than if they were not conscious of the pretest variable. Further, the pretest may communicate demand characteristics that subjects respond to during the experiment proper, instead of responding to our treatments. Thus, pretesting in order to counterbalance for one variable may actually decrease internal and external validity by creating other flaws. (To avoid such problems, we may have to use some form of deception in the pretest.)

> *REMEMBER*   Counterbalancing a subject variable ensures that it cannot confound the results, but it may result in increased error variance. Pretesting may also create problems.

Limiting the Population

An alternative to counterbalancing a subject variable is to limit the population based on that variable. The broader our population, the more heterogeneous it is in terms of subject variables. But if we intentionally limit the population, defining it more narrowly, we exclude or keep constant certain subject variables, thus preventing them from influencing our results. For example, if we expect males and females to differ greatly in anxiety level when experiencing TOTs, we might limit the population to males only. Or, in the subliminal message study, we could limit the population to good students only.

We limit the population through our selection criteria. If necessary, we pretest subjects to identify those who meet our criteria and whose scores are approximately the same (e.g., only males having high academic skills). Then, from this pool, we randomly select and assign subjects to our conditions.

Pros and Cons of Limiting the Population   There are two advantages to selecting subjects from a more limited population. First, we increase internal validity by eliminating a potential confounding that might occur with random assignment: By testing only good students, we need not be concerned about whether academic skill is balanced in each condition. Second, we reduce the error variance because, the more similar the subjects, the less variable the scores are likely to be within each condition. For example, differences in scores within a condition that might occur between males and females will not occur when all subjects are males.

There are also two drawbacks to limiting the population. First, if we become too selective, we may produce ceiling or floor effects or otherwise restrict the range of scores. For example, by limiting our study to just the best students, we are likely to see little or no difference in subjects' final-exam grades, despite the different subliminal messages. Second, because we are more selective in choosing subjects, they represent a more select, limited population and our external validity is reduced. Thus, if we test only males, we will have no evidence for generalizing our results to females.

In most situations, researchers consider the advantages of limiting the population to outweigh the disadvantages. As with other design decisions we've discussed, we usually opt for increased internal validity, even at the expense of external validity.

> *REMEMBER*   Sampling from a limited population eliminates potential confounding by a subject variable and reduces error variance, but at the possible cost of restricted range and reduced external validity.

Selecting the Approach for Dealing with Subject Variables

We now have three procedures for controlling subject variables in a between-subjects design: We may rely on random assignment to balance variables, we may counterbalance specific subject variables, or we may limit the population so that a subject variable is excluded or held constant. Notice that these procedures are not mutually exclusive. We could, for example, limit the population in terms of sex of subject and then counterbalance academic skill level. And regardless of the extent to which we counterbalance or limit the population, we would still rely on random selection and random assignment to balance any other differences in subject variables within and between the conditions.

In selecting a procedure or combination of procedures, we are faced with two considerations. First, how important is the subject variable? The more it might potentially influence the impact of the independent variable or the way that subjects respond on the dependent variable, the more we must actively control it. Never leave the control of an identified, highly influential variable to random assignment: Either counterbalance it or limit the population to keep it constant. Second, as we saw in previous chapters, our decisions should strike a balance between the goal of having the statistical power to find a significant relationship and the goal of making internally and externally valid inferences about the relationship. By selecting from a broader population and counterbalancing variables we increase validity, but we also increase error variance and thus reduce power. Conversely, by limiting the population and not counterbalancing we decrease validity, but we also minimize error variance and thus increase power.

When thinking about power, remember that for a strong, significant relationship we seek large differences in scores between the conditions and reduced error variance within conditions. We are especially concerned with error variance when responses and scores are likely to be inherently variable, or when we cannot produce a strong enough manipulation or a sensitive enough measure to bring about large differences between conditions. In such cases we would want to avoid producing additional error variance, so we limit the population and counterbalance only the most critical potentially confounding variables. When inherent error variance is less of a concern, however, we can risk reduced power by selecting from a broader population and counterbalancing more subject variables.

> *REMEMBER*   Limiting the population and counterbalancing fewer variables may be necessary with highly variable data.

If we cannot produce relatively large differences between conditions and/or we must use techniques that produce large error variance, we can compensate for the expected weak relationship by testing a larger N (and ns). Recall that the greater the N (and ns), the greater our statistical power. The reason for this is that we might, by chance, obtain a few subjects whose scores produce a particular relationship when there is no relationship in the population. The more inconsistent the relationship, the more it appears to be due to such sampling error. However, if we show that the relationship holds for many subjects, then it is not so likely to be due to chance. Generally, for minimum acceptable power, we should observe at least 15 to 30 subjects in each condition. Increasing the n tends to substantially increase power, until we obtain about 60 scores per condition. Beyond this point, increasing n results in a modest increase in power.

Reading the literature related to your research will show you the N that other researchers find acceptable. And for help in making decisions regarding power, you can utilize certain advanced statistical procedures called "power analysis" (e.g., Cohen, 1988).

> *REMEMBER*   We seek a larger N when differences in scores between conditions may be small, or when the error variance is likely to be large.

CONTROLLING SUBJECT VARIABLES THROUGH MATCHED-GROUPS DESIGNS

In the between-subjects designs discussed previously, the approach has been to accept the possibility that individuals may differ but to hope that the *group* in one condition is comparable to the *groups* in the other conditions. However, there is still a lot of room for subjects to differ within each condition (producing error variance) and between conditions (producing confoundings). To gain greater control of subject variables, we can attempt to ensure that each *individual* in one condition is comparable to an individual in the other conditions. One way to accomplish this is to create a matched-groups design.

In a **matched-groups design,** each subject in one condition "matches" a subject in every other condition in terms of selected extraneous subject variables. (If there are only two conditions of the independent variable, we match pairs of subjects and have a *matched-pairs design.*) Essentially, we try to ensure that in every condition there is a subject with virtually the same score on the subject variable(s) we wish to control. Then we keep subject variables constant across the conditions, so that we have greater control for eliminating potential confounding and reducing error variance.

To create a matched-groups design, we pretest subjects and identify those who have the same "matching" score on the subject variable we wish to control. For example, in the subliminal message study we could control subjects' academic ability and gender by matching subjects who have the same college average and gender. Thus, we might create one pool of males all having an A+ average, one pool of females all having an A+ average, and so on. Then we would randomly select and assign one member of the pool to each condition of our independent variable. We can envision this design as shown in Table 7.4.

Each row in this table contains the scores for a matched triplet of subjects: The first triplet consists of three males all having an A+ average, the second triplet consists of three females all having an A+ average, and so on. In every other respect, we conduct this experiment as we would any experiment.

This design again involves a one-way ANOVA. But as we'll see, the calculations for analyzing a matched-groups design are different from those for analyzing a between-subjects design. The logic is to always keep the matched scores together. Think of a row as representing a very small experiment (with one subject per condition). Any differences between exam grades in the row cannot be due to differences in subjects' academic ability or gender, because these variables have been held constant. Of course, an experiment with one subject per condition is not a reliable approach. Therefore, we replicate this study with other triplets of matched subjects. When we collapse the data by

TABLE 7.4 Diagram of a Matched-Groups Design for the Subliminal Message Experiment

Each row represents three subjects who have a matching college average and a matching gender. Xs represent each student's final examination grade.

	Levels		
Subject pools	*"Mommy and I are one"*	*"My prof and I are one"*	*"People are walking"*
Triplet 1: A+; Male	X	X	X
Triplet 2: A+; Female	X	X	X
Triplet 3: C−; Male	X	X	X
Triplet 4: C−; Female	X	X	X
"	"	"	"
	$\overline{X} = 90$	$\overline{X} = 88$	$\overline{X} = 83$

averaging vertically, the overall mean for each level becomes a reliable estimate of the typical final-exam grade obtained with each message. However, the potential influence of different academic abilities and gender is equally represented in each condition, so any differences between conditions cannot be due to these variables.

If it is difficult to find subjects who have the same score on the matching variable, we can rank-order subjects' scores on this variable from highest to lowest. Thus, in the design shown in Table 7.4, male subjects who are ranked 1, 2, and 3 on college grade average could form a triplet, one of whom is randomly assigned to each condition. Then, males ranked 4, 5, and 6 could form another triplet, and so on. Also, we may rely on natural groupings to match subjects. For example, roommates or husband and wife teams are already matched in terms of having the same housing arrangements. Another common approach is to test identical twins, assigning one of the twins to each condition. In this case, because genetic influences can be equated, any differences in a behavior between groups must be due to environmental causes.

There is also a technique for creating a control group and experimental group that results in matched pairs. When we wish to match the experiences of each control subject to that of a corresponding experimental subject, we create a *yoked control group*. Like two oxen pulling a cart, a control subject and an experimental subject are figuratively "yoked" together, so that whatever one experiences the other also experiences. For example, in studying how control of the environment influences emotionality, Joffee, Rawson, and Mulick (1973) allowed rats in the experimental group to press levers to control the food, water, and lighting in their cages. Each control rat's cage was electronically yoked to that of an experimental rat, so that the same environment created by the experimental animal was also experienced by the control animal.

> **REMEMBER** In a *matched-groups design,* each subject in one condition matches a subject in every other condition in terms of one or more extraneous variables.

Pros and Cons of Matched Groups

The advantage to matching subjects is that we eliminate the potential influence of the subject variable. By controlling academic ability in the subliminal message experiment, we have greater internal validity for inferring that differences between the conditions are due to our treatments. Further, by controlling one source of differences in scores—academic ability—we reduce error variance and create a more sensitive and powerful design. In this way, we are better able to detect subtle differences due to the type of subliminal message that might otherwise be hidden by differences in academic ability.

There are, however, limitations to a matched-groups design. Again, we have the problem that pretesting may increase demand characteristics or cause diffusion of treatment. Also, to find matching subjects we may have to pretest many subjects and/or settle for a very small number of subjects who match. And, with a design involving numerous conditions, matching quadruplets or larger numbers can be very difficult. Our biggest problem is the difficulty involved in measuring and matching important subject variables. First, we may not even know the relevant variables on which to match subjects.

Second, we may not have a valid and reliable method for measuring the matching variable. Finally, if there are many subject variables we wish to control, it may be almost impossible to find subjects who match on all variables.

When matching is unworkable but the study calls for tightly controlling subject variables, we employ a repeated-measures design.

CONTROLLING SUBJECT VARIABLES THROUGH REPEATED-MEASURES DESIGNS

The more variables we can match subjects on, the more we eliminate potential confounding and the more we reduce error variance. The ideal is to have subjects in all conditions who are identical in every respect. The way to have identical subjects is to place the same subjects in each condition. In a **repeated-measures design,** each subject is tested under all conditions of an independent variable. Notice that repeated measures are different from the "multiple trials" discussed in the previous chapter. Multiple trials involve repeated observation of subjects in a condition. Repeated measures involve observation of the same subjects under all conditions, regardless of the number of trials per condition.

As an example, consider the TOT study and all of the experiential, motivational, cognitive, and intellectual differences between subjects that might influence their memory. We're not sure which of these differences are most important to control, and even if we were, counterbalancing in a between-subjects design would not control so many differences, limiting the population would limit generalizability, and finding subjects who match on so many variables would be impossible. The solution is to test the same subjects under every condition, thus providing the "perfect" control of these subject variables. This design is shown in Table 7.5.

Each row in this table represents the scores from one subject tested under all conditions. Otherwise, all other design requirements apply, so for example, the sex of subjects is counterbalanced, as is the order of the 50 trials in each condition (indicated in the table as order 1 and order 2). This design also involves a one-way ANOVA that is analyzed in the same way as the matched-groups design. Again, think of each row as a miniature study. Because the same person is being observed, virtually all subject variables should be constant in all levels. Then, for reliability, we replicate this study with different subjects. After we have collapsed vertically in each column, the mean score for each level is the typical percentage of TOTs resolved with each type of cue. Differences between the means cannot be due to differences in subjects' memory abilities and so on, because such subject variables are equally represented in all levels.

Repeated measures are used whenever responses are likely to be strongly influenced by individual differences in cognitive strategies, physical abilities, or experiences—that is, whenever the responses of different subjects are likely to be very different, regardless of the effect of the independent variable. Thus, studies involving reaction time, such as the Stroop interference task described in the previous chapter, are usually conducted in this way. Repeated measures are also used to examine the influence of a sequence on an individual, as when we are studying the effects of practice or maturation.

TABLE 7.5 Diagram of the TOT Experiment Using a Repeated-Measures Design

Each row represents one subject tested under all conditions. The *X*s represent the percentage of TOTs resolved by a subject in each condition.

	Levels		
Subject pools	*Initials cue*	*Picture cue*	*Repeated question*
Subject 1 (male, order 1)	X	X	X
Subject 2 (male, order 2)	X	X	X
Subject 3 (female, order 1)	X	X	X
Subject 4 (female, order 2)	X	X	X
" "	"	"	"
	$\overline{X} = 46.6\%$	$\overline{X} = 14.5\%$	$\overline{X} = 10.7\%$

A special type of repeated-measures design is employed when we measure subjects before and after a treatment. This is called a **pretest-posttest design**. Thus, for example, to test whether meditation reduces physical stress, we might measure the same subjects' blood pressure before and after a period of meditation. Or to determine the effectiveness of a new weight-loss diet, we could measure subjects' weight before and after a period of dieting. Because there are special design and statistical concerns for creating a well-controlled pretest and posttest design, we will hold off further discussion of this procedure until the next chapter.

> *REMEMBER*   We match subjects along all subject variables by using a *repeated-measures design,* in which we measure each subject under all conditions of an independent variable.

Pros and Cons of Repeated Measures

The strength of repeated measures is that they should eliminate the potential confounding that might result from virtually any subject variable: Differences between the conditions cannot be due to differences in subject variables because the same subjects, with the same characteristics, are in every condition. By keeping subject variables very constant, we also greatly limit the error variance and increase our statistical power for detecting differences due to the influence of our independent variable. However, as is usual in research, any good idea has its shortcomings. When considering the use of a repeated-measures design, we need to be aware of several such problems.

As noted above, repeated measures "should" keep subject variables constant. But because we must test the various conditions in a sequence that occurs over time, our scores are influenced by a **subject history,** the continuing experiences between measurements that can change an individual and influence responses. Similarly, our scores are influenced by **subject maturation;** as a subject grows older and more mature, he or she develops different attitudes and abilities that may influence responses. Thus, a difference between a response to one condition measured now and a response to another condition measured later may be confounded by changes in a subject due to history and maturation. To control for these influences, we try to obtain repeated measures (and multiple trials) within a short time span. However, because individuals change from moment to moment, we cannot keep all subject variables perfectly constant.

A second problem is that, by serving under all conditions, subjects eventually become aware of all our different treatments. Therefore, a diffusion of treatment may occur, such that subsequent conditions have a relatively smaller impact on subjects because of their knowledge of and experience with previous conditions. Such knowledge may also cause subjects to identify what they think is the purpose and hypothesis of the study, creating demand characteristics that lead subjects to behave either according to or contrary to what they think is expected of them.

A third problem is that repeated measures usually require a considerable amount of testing per subject, so to eliminate the effects of fatigue and overload that might occur, we schedule each subject for multiple testing sessions spread out over several days. Yet for this reason, repeated-measures designs may be especially susceptible to *subject mortality,* because only a certain type of subject will return or participate in a committed way. Therefore, we may end up with a very select, biased sample of subjects who complete the study. Further, subject mortality may produce a confounding. In testing a new diet, for example, those subjects who give up on dieting are likely to disappear. Those who stay may be so motivated that *any* diet would work well. Then, what is apparently the influence of the diet may actually be due to a characteristic of our subjects.

Finally, a major problem is *order effects*. In Chapter 6, we discussed order effects (practice effects and carry-over effects) that occur over multiple trials within a condition. With repeated measures, these effects can also occur *between* conditions. In the TOT study, for example, by the time subjects get to the third condition they may be tired and inattentive, they may be very good at resolving TOTs, or they may have developed a strong response set. If this third condition were performed first, however, these influences might not be present.

> *REMEMBER*   A subject's *history* and *maturation, subject mortality,* and *order effects* are threats to validity and reliability that occur with repeated measures.

Any of these problems may confound our results depending on the order in which the conditions are performed. We cannot know the extent to which the differences in dependent scores between the conditions are due to our independent variable or to the subject's maturation or history. We cannot know whether subject mortality would have selected a different type of subject who would produce different results if other, perhaps less boring conditions were performed first. And we cannot know whether performance in one condition is higher or lower than in another condition just because of the order effects operating on that condition.

Since we cannot eliminate these influences, we attempt to control them through randomization or counterbalancing.

Randomizing the Order of Conditions

Randomization is generally used when manipulation involves changing an aspect of the stimuli while giving subjects the same instructions and requiring the same type of response in each condition. Under these circumstances, we can randomize order effects by randomly mixing the trials from different conditions. Thus, in the TOT study we have 3 conditions with 50 trials per condition, for a total of 150 trials. Rather than have subjects complete all 50 trials in a condition at once, we may intermix the 150 trials. In this way, we ensure that each condition is equally represented in each portion of the sequence. For example, for every 12 trials, we can randomly intermix 4 trials in which we provide an initials cue, 4 in which we provide a picture cue, and 4 in which we provide a control cue.

To be sure that we have not created a unique sequence of 150 trials that may have a peculiar impact on subjects, we can test some subjects using one overall order of trials and test other subjects using a different order. For example, in one order the "Bionic Man" question could be early in the sequence, and in another order it could be late in the sequence. (Alternatively, if we are using multiple testing sessions per subject, we could give give each subject a different order at each session.) When we unscramble subjects' responses to each condition and combine their scores, the mean for each condition will contain trials performed at the beginning, middle, and end of the subjects' participation. Each particular question will be sometimes performed early in the sequence and sometimes performed later in the sequence. Thus, there is no consistent bias due to the time at which each question or each condition was completed.

We usually do not intermix conditions when each condition requires us to stop and change the instructions or procedure. Instead, we have subjects complete all trials in one condition before going on to the next condition. This method is known as "blocking" trials, in that trials from a condition are performed as a group or "block." Here we control order by having different subjects perform the conditions in different orders. Rather than randomizing the order of conditions, however, we typically use the more systematic method of either "complete" or "partial" counterbalancing.

Complete Counterbalancing between Conditions

As we saw in Chapter 6, *complete counterbalancing* means that every possible order is included. For example, let's call the three conditions of the TOT study A, B, and C. In this case we would have six possible orders of conditions:

ABC

ACB

BCA

BAC

CAB

CBA

Notice two things about these orders. First, each condition appears in every position within the sequence: A appears twice as the first condition, twice as the second condition, and twice as the third condition (likewise for B and C). Second, every possible sequence is included: For the sequence beginning with A, we specify the two possible orders ABC and ACB; for that beginning with B, there are BCA and BAC; and so on. Thus, with complete counterbalancing we balance both a condition's position in the sequence and the order of the conditions coming before and after it. Applying this technique to the TOT study, we have the diagram of our repeated-measures study (see Table 7.6).

Note that within each order of conditions, we can still balance other variables of concern. For example, we can counterbalance subject gender, so that both males and females perform each order. Likewise we can randomize or counterbalance the order in which the trials in each level are performed. When we collapse vertically in each column, each level's mean reflects the typical response to each cue, with no confounding (1) by sex of subject and other subject variables, (2) by order effects occurring while the 50 trials per condition were being performed, or (3) by history, maturation, mortality or order effects occurring because of the time, within the sequence, at which each condition was performed.

Partial Counterbalancing

You may have noticed that the design shown in Table 7.6 has evolved into a seriously complex one! With more conditions, the number of possible orders increases astronomically: Just one more condition, for a total of 4, would produce 24 possible orders. Complete counterbalancing tends to create a design that becomes unworkable, especially if we are counterbalancing many other variables. We also lose any advantage associated with testing subjects in one large group, because now we must test a different group with each order. And we need many more subjects so that we can test some subjects under each order.

TABLE 7.6   Diagram of the TOT experiment using complete counterbalancing

Each row represents those subjects tested under a particular sequence of all three conditions.

	Levels		
Orders	*A* *Initials* *cue*	*B* *Picture* *cue*	*C* *Repeated* *question*
Subjects tested using ABC	$XXX\cdots$	$XXX\cdots$	$XXX\cdots$
Subjects tested using ACB	$XXX\cdots$	$XXX\cdots$	$XXX\cdots$
Subjects tested using BCA	$XXX\cdots$	$XXX\cdots$	$XXX\cdots$
Subjects tested using BAC	$XXX\cdots$	$XXX\cdots$	$XXX\cdots$
Subjects tested using CAB	$XXX\cdots$	$XXX\cdots$	$XXX\cdots$
Subjects tested using CBA	$XXX\cdots$	$XXX\cdots$	$XXX\cdots$
	$\overline{X}=46.6\%$	$\overline{X}=14.5\%$	$\overline{X}=10.7\%$

Such problems suggest that we may be going overboard by completely counterbalancing order effects between conditions. After all, our goal is simply to ensure that the results are not confounded or unduly influenced by one particular order of conditions. Therefore, we often only *partially counterbalance,* presenting only some of the possible orders of conditions. In the TOT study, for example, we could use the following three orders of conditions:

ABC

BCA

CAB

As shown here, typically a partial counterbalancing scheme systematically changes the *position* at which a condition occurs in the sequence, but it does not change the conditions coming *before* or *after* the condition. (Note: The procedure for creating this type of counterbalancing scheme is sometimes called a "Latin square design.")

Applying this scheme to the TOT study, we have the diagram shown in Table 7.7. Much better! For one-third of the subjects, condition A is first, so performance under this condition may be biased because of its location in the sequence. However, conditions B also occurs first for one-third of the subjects, as does condition C, so these conditions are equally biased. Likewise, each condition occurs second at times, and third at times.

Notice that we have balanced only practice effects or other biases that occur because of where in the sequence a condition occurs (first, second, or third). Partial counterbalancing does not control for carry-over effects. Carry-over effects occur between conditions if performance under condition A biases the way in which subjects then perform condition B, and so on. With the scheme shown in Table 7.7, we do not *balance* potential carry-over effects, because B follows A and C follows B in two-thirds of the sequences, but C never immediately follows A. Therefore, when carry-over effects are likely to occur between conditions, we include all orders using complete counterbalancing.

TABLE 7.7 Diagram of the TOT Experiment Using Partial Counterbalancing

Each row represents those subjects tested under one partial counterbalancing sequence of the three conditions.

	Levels		
Orders	*A* *Initials* *cue*	*B* *Picture* *cue*	*C* *Repeated* *question*
Subjects tested using ABC	$XXX\cdots$	$XXX\cdots$	$XXX\cdots$
Subjects tested using BCA	$XXX\cdots$	$XXX\cdots$	$XXX\cdots$
Subjects tested using CAB	$XXX\cdots$	$XXX\cdots$	$XXX\cdots$
	$\overline{X} = 46.6\%$	$\overline{X} = 14.5\%$	$\overline{X} = 10.7\%$

> *REMEMBER*   With *partial counterbalancing,* we present some of the possible orders of conditions to control practice effects. With *complete counterbalancing,* we include all possible orders to control practice and carry over effects.

CHOOSING A DESIGN

Obviously whether we will employ a between-subjects, matched-groups, or repeated measures design is an important decision. Usually the choice is between using a repeated measures or a between-subjects designs. Matched groups are typically used for controlling only one subject variable—and when subject variables are an issue, there are usually many that are critical.

A repeated-measures design is preferred when differences due to subject variables are a potentially serious problem. Essentially, this design is used when it makes most sense to compare a person in one condition to the same person in the other conditions. (As always, reading the relevant research literature will help you to make this decision.) Also, because they provide greater control of subject variables, repeated measures—and matched groups—reduce error variance and produce a more sensitive design for detecting small differences due to our manipulation. Therefore, these two designs are generally more powerful than a comparable between-subjects design. Likewise, the statistical procedures associated with repeated-measures and matched-groups designs are more powerful: A relationship analyzed using these procedures is more likely to be significant than if analyzed using a between-subjects procedure.

However, there are other design considerations that may prevent you from using repeated measures. First, consider whether a particular condition may produce rather permanent changes in behavior so that the condition has unique carry-over effects. For example, showing subjects the message "Mommy and I are one" may have lasting effects. If so, then with repeated measures the effect of experiencing the control condition after this message is very different from that of experiencing the control condition first. **Nonsymmetrical carry-over effects** occur when the carry-over effects from one order of conditions do not balance out those of another order. We encounter such effects whenever performing task A and then task B is not the same as performing task B and then task A. When counterbalancing will not effectively balance a bias produced by one of the orders of conditions, we may be better off with a between-subjects design, where no carry-over effect is possible.

Second, consider the effect that performing all conditions has on the subjects. If testing the same subjects under many different conditions cannot be done in one setting, breaking up the testing sessions may produce maturation and mortality effects that are more detrimental than the lessened control occurring in a between-subjects design. Also, do not underestimate the influence of diffusion of treatment and demand characteristics that can occur when subjects experience all conditions of a study.

Third, consider the demands that a repeated measures design places on the stimuli. If, for example, we conducted the TOT study as a repeated-measures design, we'd need a different set of 50 questions for each condition or else subjects would have practice with the same TOT questions. To prevent confounding, all 150 questions would have to elicit the same type of TOT, exhibit the same degree of difficulty, familiarity, pronounceability, and so on. But we may not be able to create so many different yet comparable stimuli. Also, we cannot be sure that the stimuli are comparable. And to be confident that performance is not tied to the particular 50 items presented in a condition, we would have to counterbalance: Some subjects would be given a set of 50 items with initials cues, others would be given the same items with picture cues, and vice versa. Conversely, if we conducted the TOT study as a between-subjects design, we would present the same 50 questions under each condition and vary only the type of cue given.

Finally, consider the advantages of repeated measures versus the disadvantages of counterbalancing. On one hand, controlling subject variables through repeated measures reduces error variance and increases statistical power. On the other hand, repeated measures almost always require extensive counterbalancing, so we must intentionally change extraneous variables within a condition. By including the influence of these changing variables, we tend to increase error variance and reduce power.

The key to selecting your design depends primarily on the number and importance of subject variables that must be controlled. If numerous subject variables could seriously reduce reliability and validity, then we prefer repeated measures despite the difficulties they entail. However, if repeated measures create more problems than they solve, a better choice may be to identify the one most serious subject variable to control and match subjects on that variable in a matched-groups design. Alternatively, we can still obtain valid and reliable results from a between-subjects design, especially if we balance subject variables and/or limit the population.

Don't forget that the size of your N is another very important design decision. The increased power of a repeated measures design will help to compensate if you can reach a small sample of subjects, or if for practical reasons the design requires that you test only a small sample. For comparable power in a between-subjects designs, you need a larger N. In essence, the strategy is either to observe a few subjects many times or to observe many subjects on fewer occasions.

> *REMEMBER* Between-subjects designs are preferred if carry-over effects are nonsymmetrical, if the task does not allow repeated testing, or if extensive counterbalancing is unwise.

STATISTICAL PROCEDURES FOR WITHIN-SUBJECTS DESIGNS

From a statistical point of view, there are two types of designs. As we have seen, in a between-subjects design we select a different group of subjects to serve in each condition, without considering the subjects selected in the other conditions. In a **within-subjects design,** for each subject in one condition there is a comparable subject in the other conditions. Thus, a matched-groups design and a repeated-measures design are the two subtypes of within-subjects procedures: as we saw, in both designs we essentially compare the effect of our manipulation "within" each row of uniquely comparable scores.

Recognize, however, that researchers use the term *within-subjects* in a slightly confusing way. In research terminology, a matched-groups design is technically a between-subjects design, because it involves comparing different subjects in each condition. A within-subjects design is technically defined as only a repeated-measures design. In statistical terminology, however, both the matched-groups and the repeated-measures designs are within-subjects designs. For simplicity's sake, subsequent discussions will use the statistical definition of within-subjects design to refer to either a matched-groups or repeated-measures design.

The inferential statistical procedure we choose to employ in an experiment depends on whether we have a within-subjects or a between-subjects design. Matching or repeatedly measuring subjects violates the underlying statistical bases for the between-subjects procedures discussed previously. Instead, we should employ analogous, within-subjects procedures.

Parametric Inferential Procedures for Within-Subjects Designs

Recall that when dependent scores measure an actual amount of the dependent variable, they are interval or ratio scores. If these scores are normally distributed, and if we can assume that their populations have homogeneous variance, then parametric inferential procedures are appropriate. For a within-subjects design (whether matched groups or repeated measures), the most common parametric procedures are the dependent samples *t*-test and the within-subjects ANOVA.

We perform the **dependent samples *t*-test** when our scores meet the requirements of a parametric test, we have matched groups or repeated measures, and we have *two* conditions of the independent variable. For example, we would use this procedure in the study of subliminal messages if we matched pairs of students on the variable of academic ability and tested them under either the message "Mommy and I are one" or the message "People are walking." Final-exam grades are normally distributed ratio scores (you cannot receive a negative score on a final exam). The mean grades per condition are shown in Table 7.8(A).

The **one-way within-subjects analysis of variance** is performed when we have one factor with two or more levels, the scores meet the requirements of a parametric procedure, and the design is either repeated measures or matched groups. Thus, our original matched-groups study with three types of subliminal messages is appropriate for this ANOVA. The means from this study are shown in Table 7.8(B).

In the two-sample study, as is usual with a *t*-test, we may use a one-tailed test if we are predicting the direction of the differences, or a two-tailed test if we are making no prediction. Note that the *t*-test calculations for a within-subjects design are different from those for a between-subjects design (as shown in Appendix A). Nonetheless, if the *t* is significant, we conclude that the mean exam score of 90 with the "Mommy message" differs significantly from the mean score of 83 found with the control message.

With three levels of the factor, we compute the within-subjects *F*. (Again, calculations are presented in Appendix A.) As usual, if *F* is significant, then at least two of the means from our factor differ significantly. Next, we perform *post hoc* comparisons to identify which levels differ significantly.

TABLE 7.8 Within-Subjects Designs

Shown here are (A) mean final-exam grades in the two-sample, subliminal message experiment, and (B) mean final-exam grades in the subliminal message experiment with three levels.

A

Conditions

"Mommy and I are one" $\overline{X} = 90$	"People are walking" $\overline{X} = 83$

B

Levels

"Mommy and I are one" $\overline{X} = 90$	"My Prof and I are one" $\overline{X} = 88$	"People are walking" $\overline{X} = 83$

For both the two-sample and three-level experiments, we interpret our results in the same way as we previously interpreted the results of between-subjects designs: We consider the size of each mean and the differences between them, the strength and type of the relationship, and so on. We then attempt to rationally and parsimoniously explain how our manipulation influences internal psychological processes such that we further understand the impact of subliminal messages.

> *REMEMBER* The *dependent samples* t-*test* and the *within-subjects ANOVA* are the appropriate parametric procedures used for within-subjects designs.

Nonparametric Procedures for Within-Subjects Designs

There are also nonparametric procedures for use with matched-groups or repeated-measures designs. As discussed in the previous chapter, we employ nonparametric procedures when the scores are ordinal (i.e., when a subject's score is a rank of 1st, 2nd, 3rd, etc., on the dependent variable). Also, we use such procedures if we originally collected interval or ratio scores but they form very non-normal distributions or the conditions do not have homogeneous variance. In either case we rank-order subjects using their interval/ratio scores.

For example, in our TOT study we present subjects with 50 questions that we hope will bring about a tip-of-the-tongue state. Then, from the total number of TOTs produced per subject, we calculate the percentage that are resolved by a particular type of cue. Because of the variability in the number of TOTs experienced or resolved, the scores may not form normal distributions with homogeneous variance. If that is the case, we transform the scores by rank-ordering each subject's performance in the three conditions, as shown in Table 7.9.

TABLE 7.9   The TOT Experiment with the Performance of Each Subject Rank-Ordered Across the Three Levels

| | *Levels* | | |
| | *Initials cue* | *Picture cue* | *Repeated question* |
Subjects			
Subject 1	1	2	3
Subject 2	2	1	3
Subject 3	1	3	3
Subject	"	"	"
	$\overline{X} = 46.6\%$	$\overline{X} = 14.5\%$	$\overline{X} = 10.7\%$

Note that subject 1 resolved the greatest percentage of TOTs with the initials cues, was second best with the picture cues, and least successful with the repeated question. Subject 2 was best with the picture cues, second best with the initials, and so on. Thus, we see a relationship in that, overall, subjects had the greatest success with the initials cues, less success with the picture cues, and least success when the question was repeated. This relationship is mirrored by the mean percentage of TOTs resolved in each level.

Because this design is analogous to a one-way ANOVA design, we determine whether the levels differ significantly using the Friedman Test. The **Friedman test** is the one-way within-subjects ANOVA for ordinal scores (calculations provided in Appendix A). As with any ANOVA, if the results are significant, then at least two of the levels produced significant differences in scores. To determine which of the levels differ significantly, we perform nonparametric *post hoc* comparisons, comparing each level with every other level (calculations given in Appendix A). For those pairs of levels in which the ranks differ significantly, the underlying raw scores (the percentages of TOTs resolved) also differ significantly.

Let's say that instead, we originally tested only two conditions of our independent variable, not including the control message. Then the appropriate procedure would be the **Wilcoxon test,** which is analogous to the dependent samples *t*-test for ranked data (calculations presented in Appendix A). If the results are significant, then the ranks in the two conditions differ significantly. And if the ranks differ significantly, then the underlying raw scores in each condition (the percentages of TOTs resolved) also differ significantly.

In both the Friedman test and the Wilcoxan test, we interpret our results as we have done previously: We examine each mean percentage of TOTs resolved and the differences between them, the strength and type of relationship, and so on. We then attempt to rationally and parsimoniously explain how our different types of cues influence internal psychological processes such that we further understand TOTs and memory processes.

Note: In the previous chapter we examined one other type of nonparametric procedure, the chi square. This is used when we count the frequency that subjects fall into different categories of a variable. A requirement of the chi square procedure is that each subject is counted only once and there can be no inherent matching of subjects between the different categories. Therefore, we cannot use the one-way chi square procedure for a one-way, within-subjects design.

> *REMEMBER* The inferential procedures for within-subjects designs with ranked scores are the *Wilcoxon test* (for use with two conditions) and the *Friedman test* (for use with more than two conditions).

To help you select a statistical procedure, Table 7.10 summarizes all of those discussed in this and the previous chapter.

TABLE 7.10 Parametric Procedures and Their Nonparametric Counterparts Used in Experiments with One Independent Variable

Between-subjects design

Number of conditions	*Parametric scores (Interval or ratio)*	*Nonparametric scores*	
		Ordinal	*Nominal*
Two Samples	Independent samples *t*-test	Mann-Whitney test	Chi square
Three or more samples	Between-subjects ANOVA (Parametric *post hoc* test)	Kruskal-Wallis test (Nonparametric *post hoc* test)	Chi square

Within-subjects design (Matched groups or repeated measures)

Number of conditions	*Parametric scores (Interval or ratio)*	*Nonparametric scores*	
		Ordinal	*Nominal*
Two samples	Dependent samples *t*-test	Wilcoxon test	none
Three or more samples	Within-subjects ANOVA (Parametric *post hoc* test)	Friedman test (Nonparametric *post hoc* test)	none

PUTTING IT ALL TOGETHER

Although it has taken some time to get here, you now understand what is meant by the term *controlled experiment.* You reliably present the independent variable, while eliminating other variables that subjects may respond to. You reliably measure scores on the dependent variable, so that different scores reflect different responses to your manipulation and are not biased by extraneous factors. At the same time, you control the characteristics of subjects so that the relationship between the independent variable and the dependent variable is not the result of or overly influenced by individual differences. In this way, you attempt to find the typical response of the typical subject to a typical stimulus in each condition. Then, with the help of statistical analysis, you begin to build a case that the observed relationship reflects a relationship found in the relevant population.

The process of designing a study may seem overwhelming. As a friend once remarked, "First you have to consider everything!" This is true, but you don't have to *control* everything. You want data from a well-controlled experiment, but you must also concentrate on *getting* the data! Do not concern yourself with controlling so many variables that you cannot conduct the study. Therefore, control those variables that are likely to confound the results or severely reduce reliability. But, keep in mind that when you institute a control to eliminate one problem, you may produce other problems. You are never going to produce the perfect study, so produce the best study you can *within practical limits.* Remember, the final support for any hypothesis comes not from the definitive study but from repeated replication.

To help you recall "everything" you need to consider when designing or evaluating an experiment, Table 7.11 presents the checklist from previous chapters, now amended to reflect this chapter's discussion of subject variables. Although this checklist is long, the good news is that you are now familiar with most of the basic issues in research. The remainder of our discussions will largely be variations on these themes that arise in other types of designs.

CHAPTER SUMMARY

1. A *subject variable* is a personal characteristic that distinguishes one subject from another. It results in *individual differences,* which reflect the differences in individuals' responses to the same situation.

2. *Selection criteria* form the operational definition of our subjects in terms of the characteristics we require for allowing them to participate in our study.

3. External validity depends on the sample size (N), on whether subjects are drawn from a limited portion of the population, and on whether subjects differ from nonsubjects due to *volunteer bias, subject mortality,* or *subject sophistication.*

TABLE 7.11 Checklist of Major Issues to Consider When Designing an Experiment

The items in bold type were discussed in this chapter.

- Hypothesis about relationship
    - **Appropriate population for generalizing**
- Operational definitions
    - Construct and content validity
    - Internal and external validity
    - Temporal and ecological validity
- Specify conditions
    - Linear or nonlinear relationship
    - Control groups and a strong manipulation
- Validity and reliability of independent variable
    - Confounding
    - Diffusion of treatment
    - Consistency of procedures: Instructions, automation
    - Pilot study, manipulation check
- Validity and reliability of dependent variable
    - Sensitivity and restriction of range
    - Scoring criteria
    - Automation, instrumentation effects
    - Inter-rater reliability
    - Practice trials and multiple trials per condition
    - Order effects, and counterbalancing or randomizing order
    - Error variance
- **Possible confounding by subject variables**
    - **Counterbalancing and limiting the population**
    - **Pretesting and matched groups**
    - **Repeated measures**
    - **Counterbalancing order effects between conditions**
- Demand characteristics
    - Experimental realism, deception
    - Placebos, blind procedures
    - Reactivity, habituation and unobtrusive measures
- Ethical concerns
    - Physical and psychological risks
    - Informed consent and debriefing
- **Selection of N and n**
    - **Variability and power**
- Statistical procedures
    - Scale of measurement and type of descriptive statistics
    - **Between-subjects or within-subjects design**
    - Parametric or nonparametric inferential procedure
    - Number of conditions
    - Power

4. An uncontrolled subject variable that is correlated with the influence of the independent variable or with performance on the dependent variable can reduce reliability and internal validity.

5. In a *between-subjects design* we control subject variables by balancing them through random assignment, by systematically counterbalancing them, and by keeping them constant through limitation of the population being sampled.

6. We *pretest* subjects to identify those who have particular characteristics we wish to control. However, pretesting may increase diffusion of treatment and demand characteristics.

7. Counterbalancing subject variables tends to increase internal and external validity, but it may also increase error variance and reduce power. Limiting the population reduces error variance and increases power, but it may also reduce external validity.

8. Statistically, in a *within-subjects design,* for each subject in one condition there is a comparable subject in the other conditions. In a *matched-groups design,* each subject in one condition is matched with a subject in every other condition along an extraneous variable. In a *repeated-measures design,* each subject is measured under all conditions of an independent variable. In design terminology, only a repeated-measures design is a within-subjects design.

9. A repeated-measures design that entails measuring subjects before and after some event is called a *pretest-posttest design.*

10. Within-subjects designs reduce the influence of extraneous variables, so they tend to produce more consistent, stronger relationships. These designs (and their inferential statistical procedures) tend to be more powerful than between-subjects designs.

11. Repeated measures are especially prone to confounding by a subject's *history* and *maturation,* by *subject mortality,* and by *order effects.* We control these effects by *randomizing* or *counterbalancing* the order in which conditions are performed.

12. With *complete counterbalancing,* a portion of the subjects are tested under using every possible order of the conditions. With *partial counterbalancing,* subjects are tested using only some of the possible orders of conditions.

13. *Nonsymmetrical carry-over effects* occur when the carry-over effects from one order of conditions do not balance out those of another order.

14. The *dependent samples* t-*test* and the *within-subjects analysis of variance* are the appropriate parametric statistics for within-subjects designs.

15. The nonparametric procedures for ranked scores in a within-subjects design are the *Friedman test,* used with more than two levels of one factor, and the *Wilcoxon test,* used with two conditions.

REVIEW QUESTIONS

1. What is meant by the term *selection criteria?*
2. (a) How can subject variables influence the external validity of a study? (b) How can they influence its internal validity?
3. (a) In a study involving students from a college law course, what limitation on external validity might arise? (b) Why might this limitation not arise?
4. (a) When is it acceptable to exclude a subject's data? (b) How might you reduce external validity by doing so?
5. What is meant by the terms (a) *volunteer bias,* (b) *subject mortality,* and (c) *subject sophistication*? (d) How do these effects bias our results?
6. (a) Why is a larger N important for external validity and power? (b) What is the range of n that is usually adequate?
7. You conduct a study in which the dependent variable is the degree of subjects' helpfulness in aiding a confederate to study for an exam in psychology. In each condition, subjects are tested on five consecutive days. What characteristics of the subjects who complete the study may bias your results?
8. How do you identify subject variables that may confound a study?
9. (a) How does random assignment to conditions control subject variables in a between-subjects design? (b) Why is counterbalancing subject variables more effective than random assignment?
10. What problems arise when we pretest subjects?
11. (a) What positive impact does counterbalancing subject variables have on internal and external validity? (b) What negative impact does it have on our results?
12. (a) What positive impact does limiting the population have on the results of a study? (b) What negative impact does it have?
13. (a) What is the difference between a between-subjects design and a within-subjects design? (b) What are the two types of within-subjects designs? (c) Why would we choose to employ a within-subjects design?
14. (a) How is a matched-groups design created, and how does it control for confounding subject variables? (b) How is a repeated-measures design created, and how does it control for confounding subject variables?
15. What are the problems produced by repeated-measures designs?
16. You conduct a repeated-measures design, comparing a condition in which you train subjects to improve their memory to a control condition. What problem will counterbalancing order of conditions *not* solve?
17. The abstract of a research article specifies that a Wilcoxon test was performed. (a) What does this test indicate about the design and scores used in the study? (b) What would be indicated if a Freidman test had been performed?
18. A rather dim student proposes testing the conditions of "male" and "female" as a repeated measures study. (a) What's wrong with this idea? (b) What control techniques can be applied instead?

DISCUSSION QUESTIONS

1. Let's say you employ a repeated-measures design for the Stroop interference task (discussed in the previous chapter), in which subjects identify the color of ink present in

conjunction with one of three types of words (10 trials per condition). (a) What subject variables would you limit through your selection criteria? (b) How would you randomize order effects within and between conditions? (c) How would you counterbalance order effects within and between conditions? (d) Which statistical procedure would you use to analyze this study?

2. A student with appendicitis was absent for four weeks from the law course during the subliminal message study discussed in this chapter. (a) What should the researcher do about this subject? (b) Why? (c) Given this explanation, what added selection criterion should the researcher ultimately employ? (d) What impact might this criterion have on the strength of the observed relationship? (e) How does this criterion affect external validity?

3. In the subliminal message study, (a) why did subjects see the message "People are walking" instead of seeing nothing as the control? (b) Why was the instructor "blind" to the condition a subject was in? (c) Why was a multiple-choice test given as the final exam instead of an essay test? (d) If an essay test had been given, how would the experimenter ensure valid and reliable scoring?

4. After presenting different subliminal messages, the researcher measured the dependent variable of subjects' final-exam grade. (a) What ethical problem(s) arise with this design? (b) How should the researcher deal with them?

8 Multifactor Experiments

Believe it or not, so far we have discussed *simple* experiments. They are simple because they involve manipulating only one independent variable and performing only the most basic statistical analyses. In actual practice, however, experimental psychologists often manipulate more than one independent variable. In the terminology of ANOVA, an independent variable is a factor, so when we manipulate more than one independent variable in a study, we have a **multifactor experiment.**

To introduce you to multifactor experiments, this chapter first discusses between-and within-subjects experiments containing two factors. It then briefly discusses designs involving more than two factors, concluding with an examination of some additional statistical procedures found with many types of experiment.

THE REASON FOR MULTIFACTOR STUDIES

A multifactor design has two advantages over a single-factor design. First, in most natural settings there are varying amounts of many variables present that combine to influence a behavior. By manipulating more than one independent variable in our experiment, we can examine the influence of a combination of variables on a behavior. When each combination of the different amounts of our independent variables produces a different effect on dependent scores, we have an *interaction*. The primary reason for conducting multifactor studies is to observe the interaction between independent variables.

A second advantage of multifactor designs is that, once we have created a design for studying one independent variable, often only a minimum of additional effort is required to study additional factors. Indeed, multifactor studies can be an efficient and cost-effective way of determining the main effect of—and interactions among—several independent variables.

THE TWO-WAY BETWEEN-SUBJECTS DESIGN

Recall that when we manipulate only one independent variable, we have a *one-way design*. Not surprisingly, in a **two-way design** the researcher simultaneously manipulates two independent variables within one study. The logic in selecting the variables for a two-way study is the same as that for a one way-design: For each variable, we formulate hypotheses and make predictions regarding the effect of the manipulation on the dependent variable. For example, as part of a multifactor design, Berkowitz (1987) examined the hypothesis that the more positive a subject's mood, the more that person will be willing to help others. Berkowitz induced either a positive, negative, or neutral mood in subjects by having them read 50 mood-influencing statements. The experimenter then asked each subject for help in scoring data sheets from a fictitious experiment. The number of columns of data scored within a five-minute period was the dependent measure of helping.

This factor was examined in a between-subjects design, because matching seems unnecessary, and because repeated measures of the same subjects under all three moods

TABLE 8.1 Diagram of a Between-Subjects Design with the Factor of Mood

Each X represents a subject's helping score, and each $\overline{X}$ represents the mean helping score in a condition.

Mood factor		
Negative	*Neutral*	*Positive*
X	X	X
X	X	X
"	"	"
"	"	"
$\overline{X}$	$\overline{X}$	$\overline{X}$

might produce uncontrollable carry-over effects. The design of this factor is shown in Table 8.1.

All of the principles we've discussed for designing the independent and dependent variable and controlling extraneous variables also apply to a multifactor design: Berkowitz limited the population and sample to females, devised a plausible request for help that minimized reactivity and other demand characteristics kept the experimenter's behavior constant, and developed scoring criteria. Because the amount of help that a subject provides—the number of columns scored for the experimenter—is a ratio score, computing the mean helping score in each condition is appropriate. Averaging vertically across the subjects' scores in each column yields the mean for each mood level, showing how the typical helping score changes as a function of improving mood.

Another of Berkowitz's hypotheses about helping behavior is that heightened self-awareness increases helpfulness. To test this hypothesis, the researcher manipulated subjects' self-awareness by having some subjects see their reflection in a mirror throughout the experiment, while others did not. This portion of the design can be envisioned as shown in Table 8.2.

TABLE 8.2 Diagram of a Between-Subjects Design with the Factor of Self-Awareness

Here, each each row represents a level of self-awareness, each X represents a subject's helping score, and each $\overline{X}$ represents the mean helping score in a condition.

Self-awareness factor

High self-awareness (Mirror)	X X X X X X X X X	$\overline{X}$
Low self-awareness (No-mirror)	X X X X X X X X X	$\overline{X}$

For reasons that will become clear in a moment, the novelty in this diagram is that the two conditions are arranged horizontally, so that each row identifies a different level of awareness. Again we apply the necessary controls: We reduce demand characteristics by explaining that the mirror is part of another study being conducted in our lab; and, in the no-mirror condition, we have the mirror present but turn it away from subjects. Averaging horizontally across the scores in each row then yields the mean helping score for each level of self-awareness.

To create a two-way design, Berkowitz systematically manipulated both mood and self-awareness. The complete design for this study is shown in Table 8.3. Note that the columns still represent the levels of mood, and the rows still represent the levels of self-awareness. Each small square in the diagram is called a cell. A *cell* is produced by the particular combination of a level of one factor with a level of the other. For example, the upper left cell in Table 8.3 contains the scores of subjects who received the combination of high self-awareness and negative mood treatments. Their mean helping score, the *cell mean,* is 2.0.

REMEMBER   In a *two-way between-subjects design,* we randomly assign *different* subjects to each cell formed by the levels of two independent variables.

Researchers have a code for communicating the layout of a multifactor design. The design diagrammed in Table 8.3, having one factor with three levels and another factor with two levels, is called a "three by two" design, which we write as "3 × 2" (or "2 × 3"). The number of digits indicates the number of factors in the study, and each digit indicates the number of levels in that factor. Thus, if we are dealing with two factors, each with two levels, we'd have a 2 × 2 design. Also, because our design combines all of our levels of one factor with all of our levels of the other factor, it is called a **complete factorial design** (or simply a factorial design). If for some reason we did not include the

TABLE 8.3 Two-Way Design for Studying the Factors of Type of Mood and Level of Self-Awareness

The mean scores shown here are similar to those found in Berkowitz (1987). See Experiment 2 (Table 3) in that study.

		Negative	Neutral	Positive	
		Mood factor			
Awareness factor	High self-awareness (Mirror)	$\overline{X} = 2.0$	$\overline{X} = 8.9$	$\overline{X} = 16.8$	$\overline{X} = 13.9$
	Low self-awareness (No-mirror)	$\overline{X} = 2.4$	$\overline{X} = 9.6$	$\overline{X} = 9.5$	$\overline{X} = 7.2$
		$\overline{X} = 2.2$	$\overline{X} = 9.3$	$\overline{X} = 13.2$	

positive mood–low self-awareness cell, we would have an *incomplete* factorial design. (Incomplete factorial designs require special statistical procedures.)

> REMEMBER In a *complete factorial design,* all of our levels of one factor are combined with all of our levels of the other factor.

All of the controls we devise for each single independent variable still apply in the two-way design. The major difference in multifactor designs lies in the way we statistically analyze and interpret our results. As always, our goal is to determine whether a significant relationship exists between our independent and dependent variables. Usually, our dependent variable is measured with interval or ratio scores that form normal distributions with homogeneous variance. The parametric inferential procedure for a two-way between-subjects design is the **two-way between-subjects** ANOVA (calculations are shown in Appendix A). As we'll see, the two-way ANOVA essentially creates a series of one-way ANOVAs. First, we examine the relationship produced by each individual independent variable.

Main Effects

When we examine the effect of an individual independent variable, we examine its main effect. The **main effect** of a factor is the influence that changing its levels has on the dependent scores, ignoring any other factors in the study. In the two-way design of our helping study, for example, we determine the main effects on helping behavior produced by (1) changing the levels of mood and (2) changing the levels of self-awareness.

To find the main effect of mood, we examine our scores as if they were from the one-way design shown in Table 8.4. The small box is our original 3 × 2 diagram. Just as we previously collapsed across counterbalanced variables in prior chapters, we now collapse vertically, averaging across the different awareness levels. To compute the overall mean helping score in a column, we can either average all scores in the column, or as shown,

TABLE 8.4 Diagram of the Main Effect of Mood

In each column are the two cell means from the original diagram in Table 8.3

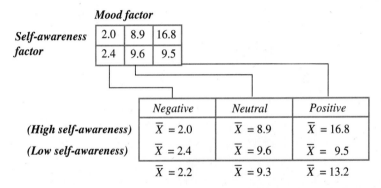

average the original cell means in that column. The means we obtain from the columns are the *main effect means* for that factor. In Table 8.4, the main effect means are 2.2 for negative mood, 9.3 for neutral mood, and 13.2 for positive mood.

Although these means appear to show a relationship between mood and helping, when performing the two-way ANOVA we compute a "main effect F" to test whether the main effect means of for the columns differ significantly. If the F is significant, we would then conclude that changing a subject's mood produces significant differences in helping scores. Remember, however, that a significant F indicates only that, somewhere in the factor, at least two of the levels differ significantly. Therefore, as we did previously with one-way designs, we perform *post hoc* comparisons such as the Tukey HSD test discussed in Chapter 6. From this, we will determine whether our main effect means of 2.2, 9.3, and 13.2 differ significantly from each other. Then, as usual, we examine the means, determine the type and strength of relationship they form, compute confidence intervals, and so on, to describe and interpret how changing mood level influences helping behavior.

Once we have analyzed the main effect of one factor, we analyze the main effect of the next. To find the main effect of self-awareness, we examine our scores as if they were from the one-way design shown in Table 8.5. Here, we collapse horizontally across the mood factor ignoring whether subjects had a negative, neutral, or positive mood to obtain the overall mean helping score of each row. To compute each mean, we can either average subjects' scores in the row, or as shown here, average the cell means in the row. These means are the main effect means for high self-awareness (13.9) and low self-awareness (7.2).

Although these means appear to reflect a relationship between awareness level and helping, we compute a second, separate main effect F to test the differences between the means of the rows. If it is significant, then at least two of these main effect means differ significantly. In this design, the self-awareness factor contains only two levels, so the significant difference must be between the levels of low and high self-awareness. If there had been more than two levels, *post hoc* comparisons would be performed to

TABLE 8.5   Diagram of the Main Effect of Self-Awareness

In each row are the cell means from the original diagram in Table 8.3.

Self-awareness factor	(Negative)	(Neutral)	(Positive)	
High self-awareness (Mirror)	$\overline{X} = 2.0$	$\overline{X} = 8.9$	$\overline{X} = 16.8$	$\overline{X} = 13.9$
Low self-awareness (No-mirror)	$\overline{X} = 2.4$	$\overline{X} = 9.6$	$\overline{X} = 9.5$	$\overline{X} = 7.2$

determine which specific means differ significantly. In either case, we then examine and interpret the relationship as we have done previously.

After examining the main effects for each variable, we examine the interaction effect.

Interaction Effects

An **interaction effect** is the influence that the combination of levels from the factors has on dependent scores. In a sense, an interaction is an artificial variable created by combining the factors. In the helping study, for example, we examine how a particular mood level combined with a particular self-awareness level influences scores, compared to the influence on scores when other levels of mood or awareness are present. The interaction of two factors is called a **two-way interaction.** It is identified using the number of levels in each factor. Here, one factor has three levels and one has two, so we have a "three by two" ("3×2") interaction.

To examine a two-way interaction, we do not collapse across or ignore either of our original factors. Instead, we treat each *cell* in the study as a level of the interaction factor. We can think of this factor as the original six cell means arranged in the one-way design shown in Table 8.6.

The relationship in an interaction is a complex one because it involves three variables that are changing: two independent variables (in this case, mood and self-awareness) and the dependent variable (helping). *To interpret an interaction, look at the relationship between one factor and the dependent scores, and see how that relationship changes as the levels of the other variable change.* As shown in the left portion of Table 8.6, under low self-awareness, changing mood from negative to neutral increases helping scores, but changing mood from neutral to positive slightly decreases them. However, this is not the pattern found on the right, under high self-awareness, where mean helping scores consistently increase as mood improves. These data form an interaction for the following reasons:

1. The effect of changing one factor is not consistent for each level of the other factor. As shown in Table 8.6, the effect of improving mood under high self-awareness is not the same as that under low self-awareness.

TABLE 8.6   Interaction of Type of Mood and Self-Awareness Level

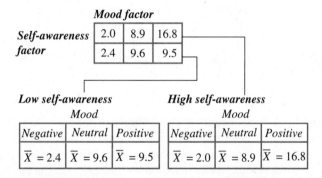

2. Our conclusion about the effect of changing the levels of one factor *depends on* the level of the other factor we examine. In other words, whether we should conclude that improving subjects' mood always increases their helping behavior depends on whether we are talking about subjects having high or low self-awareness. Or, whether we should conclude that helping is greater with high or low self-awareness depends on which mood level we are talking about.

> **REMEMBER** A *two-way interaction* indicates that the relationship between one factor and the dependent scores changes as we change the levels of the other factor.

Conversely, an interaction would *not* be present if the pattern of cell means produced by changing mood for high self-awareness is the same as that for low self-awareness. When there is no interaction present: (1) the effect of changing one factor is the same for all levels of the other factor, and (2) the influence of changing the levels of one factor does not depend on which level of the other variable is present.

Of course, although these six means appear to show an interaction, this result may be due to sampling error. Therefore, in the two-way ANOVA we calculate another, separate *F* for the interaction. (We can think of the interaction as a one-way ANOVA for the six levels of the interaction. Statistically, however, we are testing the difference between the cell means *after* those differences related to each main effect have been removed.) As usual, if the interaction *F* is significant, then somewhere among the cell means there are significant differences. As we'll see, researchers perform additional statistical procedures (either special *post hoc* tests or analysis of *simple main effects*) to discover where these differences lie.

But first, recognize that, because of its complexity, an interaction can be a beast to interpret. Therefore, to clarify the pattern produced by the data, always graph the interaction effect.

Graphing the Interaction Effect   An interaction is graphed on a *single* graph. As usual, we label the *Y* axis as the mean of the dependent variable, (and we'll plot the *cell* means). We label the *X* axis as the levels of one factor (usually placing the factor with the most levels here). We show the second factor by drawing a separate line for each of its levels. Thus, in our helping study, we'll label the *X* axis with the three mood levels and draw a separate line for each level of self-awareness, as shown in Figure 8.1.

Note that we connect the datapoints from the three cell means for high self-awareness with one line and those from the three cell means for low self-awareness with a different line. (A legend is always included in such graphs to define the different lines.) To read the graph, look at one line at a time. Because we have two differently shaped and oriented lines, the *type* of relationship between mood and helping we see *depends* on whether the subjects are in the high or low self-awareness condition.

It's important to recognize that an interaction may produce any pattern of lines *except* parallel lines. Such non-parallel lines can depict a variety of different types of relationships. For example, let's say our data turned out to produce one of the graphs in Figure 8.2. On the left, changing mood level has an opposite effect depending on the self-awareness condition. On the right, the slopes of the lines are different, indicating that

FIGURE 8.1 Graph of an Interaction, Showing Mean Helping Scores as a Function of Mood and Self-Awareness Level

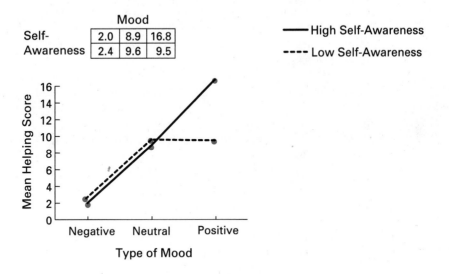

FIGURE 8.2 Two Graphs Showing That an Interaction Is Present

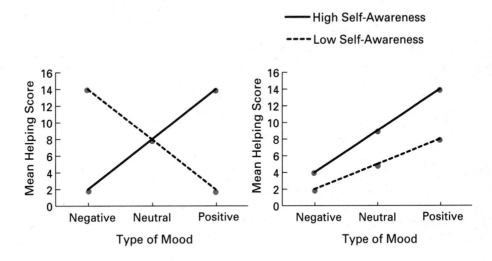

improving mood with high self-awareness more dramatically increases helping scores than does improving mood with low self-awareness.

When *no* interaction exists, the lines are parallel. Say that our data produced one of the graphs in Figure 8.3. In both of these graphs, the lines indicate that as mood level changes, the scores change in the same way *regardless of* level of self-awareness. Thus, neither graph shows an interaction.

Think of a significant interaction *F* as indicating that somewhere in the graph, the lines significantly differ from parallel. A nonsignificant *F* indicates that any deviance from parallel is likely to be due to sampling error in representing parallel lines—no interaction—in the population.

We can also graph the means from any main effect using the same procedures for graphing a one-way design that were discussed in Chapter 5. Note, however, that when reading a research article, we are generally expected to visualize the main effects from a graph of the interaction. Since cell means are averaged together to obtain main effect means, we envision the data points for graphing the main effect of a factor as the average of the appropriate data points in the interaction graph. To see how this is done, assume that we obtained the data in Figure 8.4.

On the graph at the left, the asterisks show where the overall mean for each level of mood is located after we have collapsed vertically across high and low self-awareness (averaging the two data points in each circle). Plotting the line formed by these points on a separate graph (with the *X* axis labeled for mood level) would show the main effect of type of mood. On the graph at the right, the asterisks show where the overall mean for each level of self-awareness is located after we have collapsed across levels of mood (averaging the three data points in each circle). Plotting the line formed by these points

FIGURE 8.3   Two Graphs Showing No Interaction

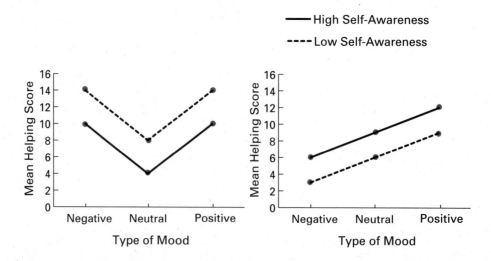

FIGURE 8.4 Main Effects Seen in the Graph of an Interaction

Here, the dots are cell means and the asterisks are visualized main effect means.

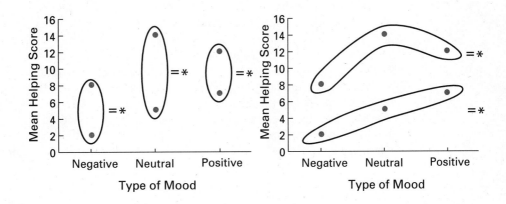

on a separate graph (with the X axis labeled for low and high self-awareness) would show the main effect of self-awareness.

All of the cell means may not differ significantly when the F for the interaction is significant. Therefore we must identify where the significant differences lie.

Simple Main Effects   One technique for investigating an interaction deals with simple main effects. A **simple main effect** is the effect of one independent variable at one level of a second independent variable. Essentially we examine the overall relationship within any row or any column in the diagram of our interaction. For example, we might examine the simple main effect of changing mood under the high self-awareness condition, looking only at these cell means from our original interaction:

	Negative	*Neutral*	*Positive*
High self-awareness	$\overline{X} = 2.0$	$\overline{X} = 8.9$	$\overline{X} = 16.8$

The simple main effect is analyzed as a one-way ANOVA on these cell means, but with somewhat different computations. (See, for example, Hinkle, Wiersma & Jurs, 1988.) If the F is significant, it indicates that in the high self-awareness condition, changing mood produces a significant relationship, and that somewhere among these three means there are significant differences. This information is helpful if, for example, we do not obtain a significant simple main effect for mood in the low self-awareness conditions. Then we'd know that the interaction reflects a relationship for high self-awareness and no relationship for low self-awareness.

Post Hoc **Comparisons in the Interaction**   A more general approach is to examine all means in the interaction by performing *post hoc* comparisons. While a simple main effect is similar to performing an *F* in a row or column of our diagram, *post hoc* comparisons directly compare pairs of cell means in a row or column (similar to performing *t*-tests). We can again perform the Tukey HSD test discussed previously, but the computations for an interaction are different from those for a main effect (as shown in Appendix A). To begin, we examine the interaction cell means from our helping study shown in Table 8.7.

Note that we do *not* compare every cell mean to every other cell mean. For example, we would not compare the cell mean for negative mood–high self-awareness to the mean for neutral mood–low self-awareness. Doing so would create a *confounded comparison:* Because the cells differ along more than one factor, we cannot identify which factor produced the difference in scores (the change in mood or the change in awareness?). Thus, in our diagram of a study, we do not compare cells that are diagonally positioned. Instead, *post hoc* comparisons in the interaction should involve only **unconfounded comparisons**—comparisons of cell means that differ along only one factor. In short, we compare all possible pairs of cell means that are in the *same row,* and we compare all possible pairs of cell means that are in the *same column.*

> *REMEMBER*   A *simple main effect* involves a one-way ANOVA performed on a row or column of cell means. *Post hoc* comparisons compare all pairs of means within all rows and columns.

Interpreting the Results of a Two-Way Experiment

In a multifactor ANOVA, whether any one *F* is significant is not influenced by whether the other *F*s are significant. (In the Results section of an APA-style report, both significant and nonsignificant *F*s are reported.) Also, after we have performed *post hoc* comparisons on the main effect means and the cell means, any combination of significant differences between means is possible. So that we can see the results of our various *post hoc* comparisons, Table 8.8 shows a way to identify the significant differences that we might find in our helping study.

Outside the diagram, main effect means that differ significantly are connected by a line. Inside the diagram, interaction cell means that differ significantly are connected

TABLE 8.7   Cell Means as a Function of Type of Mood and Level of Self-Awareness

		Negative	*Neutral*	*Positive*
Self-awareness factor	High self-awareness (Mirror)	$\overline{X} = 2.0$	$\overline{X} = 8.9$	$\overline{X} = 16.8$
	Low self-awareness (No-mirror)	$\overline{X} = 2.4$	$\overline{X} = 9.6$	$\overline{X} = 9.5$

Mood factor

TABLE 8.8 Summary of Significant Differences in the Helping Study

Each line connects two means that differ significantly.

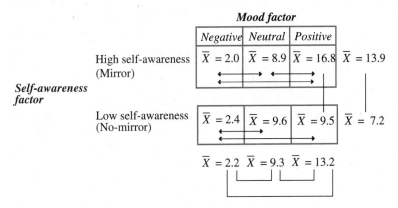

by a line. We interpret main effects in this study the same way we would in a one-way design. Thus, from Table 8.8, we would *like* to conclude that, overall, the main effect for awareness indicates that subjects with high self-awareness help more than those with low awareness. Likewise we would like to claim that overall, the main effect of each improvement in mood is to produce higher scores.

The problem is that main effect means are based on an average across the cell means of the interaction. But when we examine these cell means, the interaction contradicts the overall conclusions suggested by the main effects. Literally, the effect of one factor *depends* on the other factor and vice versa. Thus, looking at the cell means, high self-awareness does not always produce significantly higher scores than low self-awareness; rather, it does so only in the positive mood condition. Likewise, improving mood does not always increase scores: With high self-awareness it does, but there is no significant difference between neutral and positive mood in the low self-awareness condition.

Because a significant interaction indicates that the effect of one factor depends on the level of the other, we usually *cannot* make an overall, general conclusion about any main effects. Instead, we focus our interpretation of the study on the significant interaction. In our helping study, therefore, our interpretation would center on explaining why, regardless of self-awareness level, negative mood produced less helping than neutral mood, but positive mood increased helping only when subjects also experienced high self-awareness. We might propose that whether they pay attention to their feelings or not, a negative mood is sufficiently aversive to make subjects unwilling to help. For a positive mood to increase helpfulness, subjects must also have a high level of self-awareness so that they attend to their mood.

Had the interaction not been significant, our interpretation would be based on any significant main effects we obtained.

> **REMEMBER** The two-way ANOVA produces an *F* for each main effect as well as an *F* for the interaction. When the interaction is significant, we usually do not draw conclusions about each main effect.

Using Counterbalanced Variables to Produce Two-Way Designs

Sometimes we can *analyze* a design as a multifactor experiment, even when we are not intentionally studying multiple independent variables. Instead, we may create an additional factor because we have counterbalanced an extraneous variable. For example, let's say that in a different study we examine the influence of positive or negative mood on subjects' ratings of how helpful others are. In each condition, subjects read descriptions of several fictitious people and then rate each one's perceived helpfulness. We might wish to counterbalance for subject gender, such that half of the subjects in each condition are male and half are female. Or, we might control order effects by testing some subjects with different orders of trials. Both designs are shown in Table 8.9.

By analyzing these studies as two-way designs we obtain more information than we would if, as in previous chapters, we ignored subject gender or order and created a one-way design. In addition to obtaining an *F* for the influence of mood, we also obtain an *F* for subject gender, to see whether the overall means for males and females differ. We can obtain an *F* for order of trials, to see whether one order produced a difference in scores relative to the other. Moreover, we can examine the interaction between these control variables and mood. If the interaction is significant, then we may discover that the effect of manipulating mood depends on a subject's sex, or that it depends on the order in which trials are performed.

A further advantage of treating these designs as two-way designs involves error variance. Recall that a problem with counterbalancing is that it may add error variance: Combining males and females produces greater differences in scores within each column than does testing only one sex. By treating gender as a separate factor, however, the ANOVA removes the differences between males and females that contribute to error variance, instead treating them as differences in scores that are related to gender. This procedure reduces the amount of error variance that is present when the mood factor is being analyzed, so there should be a stronger relationship between mood and subjects' scores, that is more likely to be significant.

Thus, always consider whether you should analyze any single-factor study as a multifactor design involving counterbalanced variables. You will obtain considerably more information from a study that, regardless, you are going to conduct in the same way. Likewise, remember that your goal as a researcher is not only to demonstrate a relation-

TABLE 8.9   Examples of Two-Way Designs That Arise From Counterbalancing Variables

	Mood factor				*Mood factor*		
	Positive	*Negative*			*Positive*	*Negative*	
Males	$\overline{X}$	$\overline{X}$	$\overline{X}$	*Order 1*	$\overline{X}$	$\overline{X}$	$\overline{X}$
Females	$\overline{X}$	$\overline{X}$	$\overline{X}$	*Order 2*	$\overline{X}$	$\overline{X}$	$\overline{X}$
	$\overline{X}$	$\overline{X}$			$\overline{X}$	$\overline{X}$	

ship but to understand it. Therefore, after you have performed your primary analyses, explore the data. You may group scores along any potentially relevant variables. (For example, did the time of day during which subjects were tested produce differences?) Or, you may correlate scores with personal information collected from subjects. (Does their age relate to their performance?) The more precisely you examine the data and subjects, the more precisely you will be able to explain how a behavior operates and to describe the variables that influence it.

THE TWO-WAY WITHIN-SUBJECTS DESIGN

As you know, in a within-subjects design we control subject variables by measuring the same subjects repeatedly in all levels of a factor, or by matching different subjects along an extraneous variable. We have a **two-way within-subjects design** if (1) we repeatedly measure the same group of subjects in all conditions of two independent variables, (2) we match subjects in all cells, or (3) we have matched groups on one variable and repeated measures on the other. If our data fit the criteria for parametric statistics, we analyze the results using the *two-way within-subjects ANOVA.* Although the calculations for this procedure are different from those for a two-way between-subjects design, its logic and interpretation are identical.

For example, Flowers, Warner, and Polansky (1979) developed a variation on the Stroop interference task discussed in Chapter 6. To gain a sense of their manipulation, quickly indicate the *number* of numbers indicated in each row:

2 2 2
three three

As in Flowers et al., we will present one row of numbers at a time. Let's say that, in one factor, interference is created because the number present is incongruent with the number of numbers present (e.g., 2 2 2), or interference is not created because the number present is congruent with the number of numbers present (e.g., 2 2). In a second factor, let's say we present a row of digits (e.g., 2 2 2) versus a row of words (e.g., two two two). Our dependent variable is a subject's reaction time to report the number of numbers present in a row. We test each subject in all conditions of this 2×2 repeated-measures design. We can envision this factorial design as shown in Table 8.10.

As usual, we apply the appropriate controls, such as creating comparable stimuli for each condition, testing multiple trials per condition, and counterbalancing order effects due to the order of trials per condition and the order of conditions.

For now, we will collapse across the different orders, computing each subject's mean reaction time in each of the four cells. We again view the two-way within-subjects ANOVA as a series of one-way ANOVAs. First, we collapse vertically across the conditions of whether words or digits were presented, so that we examine the main effect for the factor of type of pairing. Apparently, as Table 8.10 shows, incongruent pairings produced interference, resulting in a slower mean reaction time (.542 seconds) than that

TABLE 8.10 2 × 2 Repeated-Measures Design for the Factors of Digit-Word and Congruent-Incongruent Pairings

Each X represents a subject's mean reaction time. Cell means are taken from Flowers et al. (1979), Table 1.

		Type of Pairing		
		Congruent (2 2)	*Incongruent* (2 2 2)	
Type of number	Digit	X X $\overline{X} = .493$ X "	X X $\overline{X} = .543$ X "	$\overline{X} = .518$
	Word	X X $\overline{X} = .505$ X "	X X $\overline{X} = .542$ X "	$\overline{X} = .524$
		$\overline{X} = .499$	$\overline{X} = .542$	

associated with congruent pairings (.499 seconds). Next, we collapse horizontally across type of pairing, examining the main effect for the type of number presented. Apparently, mean reaction time for digits (.518 seconds) was faster than that for words (.524 seconds). Finally, we examine the interaction, comparing the four cell means. Apparently, when congruent numbers producing no interference were presented, subjects responded to digits more quickly than to words (.493 seconds versus .505 seconds, respectively). But when incongruent numbers producing interference were presented, there was virtually no difference in reaction time between digits and words (.543 seconds versus .542 seconds respectively.)

In such a design, we compute an F for each main effect as well as an F for the interaction effect. We perform *post hoc* comparisons for those main effects that are significant and have more than two levels. If the interaction is significant, we perform *post hoc* comparisons or analyze the simple main effects. Then we focus on explaining why the difference between digits and words disappears when the incongruent, interfering stimuli were presented. If the interaction is not significant, we focus on any significant main effects: Why, overall, did subjects respond more quickly to digits than to words, and why did any type of incongruent pairing (using words or digits) produce interference?

REMEMBER   In a *two-way within-subjects design,* we create matched groups or repeatedly measure the same subjects in all conditions of two independent variables.

THE TWO-WAY MIXED DESIGN

In the previous chapter, where the one-way within-subjects design was discussed, we saw the difficulty involved in matching many subjects or many variables, as well as the problems of order and carry-over effects with repeated measures. These drawbacks become even greater with a two-way design. Therefore, we may prefer to create a within-subjects factor only when it critically requires control of subject variables, and test the other factor as a between-subjects factor. When a design features a "mix" involving one within-subjects factor and one between-subjects factors, it is called a **two-way mixed design.**

One common mixed design arises when we begin with one factor that is set up as a *pretest-posttest design.* Recall that here, we measure the same subjects both before and then again after we have presented our treatment. As an example, consider the study of subliminal messages conducted by Silverman, Ross, Adler, and Lustig (1978). They tested males' ability at dart-throwing before and after presentation of the subliminal message "Beating Dad is OK." The message was hypothesized to reduce residual guilt developed from childhood feelings of competition with father figures.

A *poor* way to design this study is shown in Table 8.11. If the mean dart scores are significantly higher after the message, we'd *like* to conclude that the message improved performance. But! There is something seriously wrong with this design in terms of potential confoundings. Here's a hint: Remember maturation, history, reactivity, and practice effects? Perhaps the "After-message" scores improved because of changes in these variables. Perhaps the subjects acclimated to being tested, developed better eye-hand coordination, or improved because of the practice at dart-throwing provided by the "Before-message" condition.

To eliminate these competing alternative hypotheses, we need a control group that does everything the experimental group does but, instead of seeing the message "Beating Dad is OK," sees a placebo message that does not alleviate guilt. By adding a control group, we create a between-subjects factor, with some subjects tested with the experimental message, and others are tested with the control message. Now we have the much-better, two-way mixed design shown in Table 8.12.

If the dependent variable meets the criteria for parametric procedures, we compute *a two-way mixed design ANOVA* (calculations are provided in Appendix A). This, too, we

TABLE 8.11   Diagram of a One-Way Dart-Throwing Experiment

X's represent each subject's dart score.

Before message	*After message*
X	X
X	X
"	"
$\overline{X}$	$\overline{X}$

TABLE 8.12   Diagram of the Two-Way, Mixed-Design Dart-Throwing Experiment

		Repeated-measures factor		
		Before message	*After message*	
Between-subjects factor	Subjects with "DAD" message	X X X "	X X X "	$\overline{X}$
	Subjects with control message	X X X "	X X X "	$\overline{X}$
		$\overline{X}$	$\overline{X}$	

treat as a series of one-way ANOVAs. When we collapse vertically and obtain the main effect means of "Before message" versus "After message," both types of messages will be included, so we will see the changes in scores that occur between the two testings, regardless of the message. When we collapse horizontally across Before and After, the main effect mean with the "Dad" message may be higher than with the control, but we will not know whether this occurred because the Before scores were higher and/or because the After scores were higher.

The specific test of the hypothesis that the "Dad" message increases performance comes from the interaction, comparing the four cell means. Ideally, we would predict a significant interaction that produces the graph shown in Figure 8.5. This graph shows an interaction (the lines are not parallel), and ideally the *post hoc* comparisons will confirm the following: (1) that there is no difference in the Before scores for the two groups, suggesting that our study is not contaminated by initial differences in dart-throwing skills between the two groups of subjects; and (2) that there is no change in scores from Before to After for the control group, suggesting that maturation, acclimation to testing, practice, and so on are not likely to produce a Before-After difference in the experimental group. With these findings in hand, the dramatic rise in posttest scores for the experimental group would support the hypothesis that the "Dad" message does improve dart-throwing. As this example illustrates, with a little thought you can predict and understand interaction effects, so, regardless of the type of design, don't think solely in terms of main effects.

A mixed design arises whenever we set out to investigate two independent variables, one of which is best suited to a within-subjects design while the other is best suited to a between-subjects design. In addition, though we may originally seek to investigate only one within-subjects factor, we may wish to determine the effects due to counter-balancing a second, between-subjects variable. Or, with a between-subjects variable, we

FIGURE 8.5   Ideal Interaction Between Pretest Vs. Posttest and Control Vs. Experimental Cells

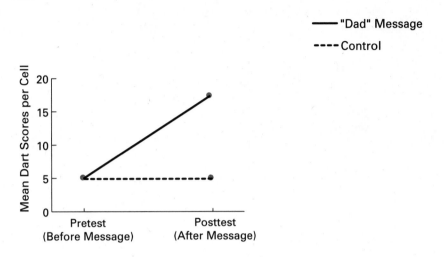

may also include the within-subjects factor of multiple trials, so that we can examine practice effects.

> *REMEMBER*   In a *two-way mixed design,* we have one within-subjects factor and one between-subjects factor.

THREE-WAY DESIGNS AND BEYOND

The beauty of ANOVA is that it can be applied to even more complex experiments with as many factors as we wish, regardless of whether we have a between-subjects, a within-subjects, or a mixed design. We may add more independent variables, or we may analyze more counterbalanced control factors.

For example, say that we add the variable of subject gender (male versus female) to the above two-way dart study. With three factors, we have a **three-way design.** And because there are two levels of each factor, we also have a $2 \times 2 \times 2$ design. We can conceptualize this mixed design as shown in Table 8.13. On the left, we have the previous 2×2 design for males. On the right, we replicate that design but test female subjects. If the data fit the criteria of a parametric procedure, then a *three-way mixed design ANOVA* is appropriate.

Main Effects

Because we have three independent variables, the ANOVA produces separate *F*s for three main effects. Thus, to find the main effect of subject gender, we average all of

TABLE 8.13   Diagram of a Three-Way Design for the Factors of Before and After Messages, Type of Messages, and Subject Gender

Each mean is the mean dart score of subjects in that cell.

	Males		**Females**	
	Before message	*After message*	*Before message*	*After message*
"Dad" message	$\overline{X} = 10$	$\overline{X} = 20$	$\overline{X} = 8$	$\overline{X} = 12$
Control message	$\overline{X} = 10$	$\overline{X} = 10$	$\overline{X} = 8$	$\overline{X} = 10$

the males' scores together (for the lefthand box in Table 8.13, $\overline{X} = 12.5$) and all of the females' scores together (in the righthand box, $\overline{X} = 9.5$). These means indicate that, overall, males were better at throwing darts than females. To find the main effect of "Before message" versus "After message," we average together the columns containing Before scores, regardless of gender ($\overline{X} = 9.0$), and then compare that mean with the mean from the columns containing After scores ($\overline{X} = 13.0$). These means show that, overall, subjects scored higher on the posttest than on the pretest. Finally, to find the main effect of type of message, we average the scores in the rows of the "Dad" message ($\overline{X} = 12.5$) and compare that mean with the mean of the rows of the control message ($\overline{X} = 9.5$). These means show that, overall, subjects who saw the "Dad" message scored higher than those who saw the control message.

Two-Way Interactions

With three factors, we obtain separate Fs for three, two-way interactions. We collapse across gender, producing the interaction of Before versus After and the "Dad" versus control messages. This interaction is shown in the diagram below:

	Before	**After**
"Dad"	$\overline{X} = 9$	$\overline{X} = 14$
Control	$\overline{X} = 9$	$\overline{X} = 10$

Each cell contains the mean score of both males and females. Note that, the difference between the "Dad" and control messages is greater in the after condition. (Or, to put it another way, the difference between Before and After depends on the type of message.)

To produce each of the other two-way interactions, we collapse across the third factor as shown below.

Gender and type of message interaction				Gender and Before-After interaction		
	Male	*Female*			*Male*	*Female*
"Dad"	$\overline{X} = 15$	$\overline{X} = 10$		*Before*	$\overline{X} = 10$	$\overline{X} = 8$
Control	$\overline{X} = 10$	$\overline{X} = 9$		*After*	$\overline{X} = 15$	$\overline{X} = 11$

On the left, we collapse across Before-After, producing the interaction between gender and type of message. Note that the difference between the "Dad" and control messages is greater for males than it is for females. (Or to put it another way, the difference in scores between males and females depends upon which message they receive.) On the right, we collapse across type of message to produce the interaction between gender and Before-After. Here, males show a greater increase from Before to After than do females. (In other words, the difference between males and females depends on whether we examine the Before scores or the After scores.)

The Three-Way Interaction

Finally, we do not collapse across any factor, computing an *F* for the three-way interaction that reflects the combined effect of all three factors. Previously, we saw that in a two-way interaction, the effect of one variable is different depending on the levels of the second factor we examine. In a **three-way interaction,** the two-way interaction of two variables is different depending on which level of the third factor we examine. (Conversely, if the three-way interaction is not significant, then we have basically the same two-way interaction regardless of the levels of the third factor we examine.) By graphing the original cells means we saw in Table 8.13, we have the three-way interaction shown in Figure 8.6.

As this shows, the interaction between Before-After and "Dad"-control depends upon whether subjects are male or female. For males, we find a dramatic change from pre- to posttest scores with the "Dad" message, but control subjects show no change. For females, we see a different two-way interaction: There is slight improvement in dart-throwing following the control message, suggesting that the control females benefited from their practice throwing darts. Following the "Dad" message, experimental females showed a slight, additional improvement beyond the practice effects of the control females. Thus, the "Dad" message had a minimal positive influence, suggesting that females are not intensely guilty about competition because of feelings toward their fathers. The dramatic improvement after the "Dad" message among males, however, confirms that they may feel guilty about this competition, such that the message reduces an otherwise serious restriction on their performance.

In an APA-style report, we would graph this interaction on *one* set of *X-Y* axes. As shown in the legend for Figure 8.6, we create the four different lines by combining two types of symbols: solid lines for experimental groups and dashed lines for controls, and solid dots for males and open dots for females. Thus, ●——● connects the means

FIGURE 8.6 Graphs Showing How the Two-Way Interaction Between Pretest and Posttest and "Dad"-Control Message Changes as a Function of Subject's Gender

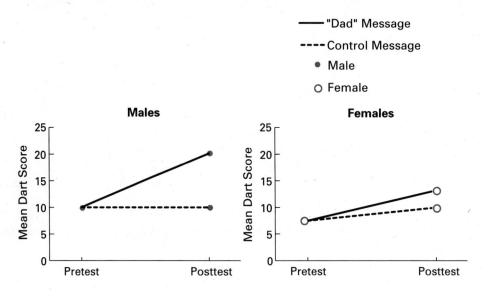

of the male-experimental group, ○——○ connects the means of the female-experimental group, ●‑ ‑ ‑● connects those of the male-control group, and ○——○ connects those of the female-control group.

Of course, we consider only main effects and interactions that are significant, and for each, we perform *post hoc* comparisons to determine which means differ significantly. To interpret the results of such a study, we follow the same logic used with a two-way design: We focus on significant interactions because they contradict main effects. However, a significant three-way interaction also contradicts any two-way interactions: Above, we saw that the two-way interaction between type of message and Before-After change between males and females. Therefore, our interpretation of a three-way design focuses on the significant three-way interaction. Based on Figure 8.6, we would attempt to explain the psychological reasons why the "Dad" message produced a dramatic improvement in scores for males, but produced a small improvement for females. Note that if the three-way interaction is not significant, we focus on significant two-way interactions. And if these interactions are not significant, we focus on significant main effects.

Limitations of the Multifactor Design

There is no limit to the number of possible factors in an ANOVA. We can conduct a four-way design containing four independent variables or a five-way design containing five variables. There are, however, practical limits to such designs. The number of subjects needed becomes quite large, and the counterbalancing scheme or stimulus requirements may be impossibly complex. Although with effort these problems can be solved, we are also limited in our ability to *interpret* such studies. If we conduct a "simple" four-way study—a $2 \times 2 \times 2 \times 2$ design—the ANOVA provides separate *F*s for four main effects, six two-way interactions, four three-way interactions, and one monster four-way interaction (there would be *eight* lines on its graph). If this sounds very complicated, it's because it *is* very complicated. Three-way interactions are difficult to interpret, and interactions containing more than three factors are practically impossible to interpret.

Remember that a major concern of science is to simplify the complexity found in nature. Duplicating this complexity in the laboratory is counterproductive. Therefore, unless you have a good reason for including many factors in one study, it is best to examine only two or at most three factors. Then conduct additional studies to investigate the influence of other variables. In each, you will not learn of the simultaneous interactions of many variables, but what you do learn you will understand. In addition, when conducting each study you can perform a literal replication of portions of your previous studies, thus greatly increasing their internal and external validity.

THE TWO-WAY CHI SQUARE

Recall that there are times when we do not measure the *amount* of a variable but, rather, we count whether a subject falls in one or another *category* of a variable. In Chapter 6 we used the one-way chi square to determine whether the frequency of category membership differed significantly along one variable. If we have two such variables, we use the **two-way chi square procedure.** This procedure requires a between-subjects design, with each subject falling into only one category of each variable. Thus, for example, we might categorize subjects in terms of their gender and political party, counting the frequency of male Republicans, female Republicans, and so on.

The two-way chi square is used if there are two variables on which we are categorizing subjects, regardless of whether we call each an independent or dependent variable. Often, we end up with a two-way design because there are different categories of one independent variable and different categories of our dependent variable. To illustrate, let's say that, in our original study of mood and helping behavior, we conduct a manipulation check and categorize those subjects who report having either a negative or positive mood after testing. Then, we could simply count the number of subjects who helped as a function of type of mood. It would be wrong, however, to envision this study as the one-way design shown below.

Mood

Positive	*Negative*
Number who helped	Number who helped

This design is incomplete: A requirement of the chi square procedure is that the responses of *all* subjects in the sample be included. Therefore, we must count the frequency both of the subjects who helped *and* of those who did not. Then we would have a two-way chi square design. Let's say we obtain the data shown in Table 8.14. Here we have a complete factorial 2 × 2 design in which we categorize subjects along two variables: whether they were in a positive or negative mood and whether they were helpful or not. (Other designs might be a 2 × 3, a 4 × 3, etc.)

Although this design looks like a two-way ANOVA, the two-way chi square examines only the *interaction* of these two variables. That is, we determine whether the frequencies in the categories of one variable *depend* on which category of the other variable we examine. For this reason, the two-way chi square is also known as a "test of independence": Here we will determine whether the frequency of helping or not helping is independent of subjects' mood. Essentially, we are asking whether a relationship or correlation exists between the two variables. When the variables are independent, there is no correlation or relationship between category membership on one variable and category membership on the other variable. In the example in Table 8.14, however, the two variables appear somewhat dependent or correlated: Saying "No" is more often associated with being in a negative mood, and saying "Yes" is more often associated with being in a positive mood.

The null hypothesis in a two-way chi square is that the variables are independent in the population, and that any appearance of a relationship is due to sampling error. If the obtained χ^2 is significant (calculations in Appendix A), we conclude that the variables are dependent or correlated. Thus, for our above helping study we would conclude that the frequency of helping or not helping depends upon a subject's mood. As in any other study, we then summarize the data in each mood condition (using the mode); we examine the type and strength relationship; and, using this information, we attempt to explain why those subjects in a positive mood were more likely to help.

> **REMEMBER** A significant *two-way chi square* indicates that category membership along one variable is dependent upon, or correlated with, category membership along the other variable.

Note that procedures exist that are analogous to a three-way chi square design. For example, say that we categorized subjects along the variable of being a male or female, as well as along the variables of helping versus not helping and positive versus negative mood. Here, a significant result would indicate that helping or not helping was dependent upon both mood and gender.

TABLE 8.14 Frequency of Subjects Who Helped or Did Not Help as a Function of Their Reported Mood

| | | Mood | |
		Negative	Positive
Helping	Yes	5	18
	No	20	2

DESCRIBING EFFECT SIZE

Throughout our discussions, we have treated all independent variables as being of equal importance. In nature however, some variables are more important than others. Therefore, a critical question in any experiment is "How important is this independent variable?" In answering this question, do not confuse importance with significance. "Significant" only indicates that we are confident that the data reflect a "real" relationship and not a chance pattern of scores produced by sampling error. To be important, a variable must first produce a significant relationship. But a significant relationship is not necessarily important.

In experiments, we determine a variable's importance by measuring its effect size. **Effect size** is an indication of how dramatically an independent variable influences a dependent variable. Presumably, manipulating our independent variable causes subjects scores—and behavior—to change. The effect size indicates the extent to which the manipulation causes this change.

One crude measure of effect size is the size of the difference between the means of the conditions. For example, say that after manipulating mood we obtain the helping scores shown below.

Mood level

Neg	Neut	Pos
0	5	12
4	13	19
8	18	29
$\overline{X} = 4$	$\overline{X} = 12$	$\overline{X} = 20$

The difference between the mood level means averages out to 8 points. Because this factor seems to produce relatively large differences in helping scores, we can argue that it is important in determining a subject's helping behavior.

The problem with this approach, however, is that we have no way of knowing whether a difference of 8 points is really a large difference in nature, so we must be very subjective when evaluating the difference. Further, an important variable need *not* produce large differences in the behavior. Rather, a scientifically important variable will tightly control and consistently influence the behavior in question. From this perspective, the variable of mood is not so important, because there is considerable variability— error variance—in the scores *within* each condition. Since we assume that differences between scores must have a cause, there must be *other* subject variables, environmental influences, and so on, that are exerting an influence here. Thus, mood level is only one of the variables we should consider when trying to understand helping behavior.

When describing an independent variable's effect size, we usually compute how *consistently* the variable influences the behavior. We refer to this computation as the proportion of variance accounted for.

The Proportion of Variance Accounted For

To evaluate the importance of a relationship, we must have something to compare it to. Our approach is to determine how informative the relationship is, compared to the information we'd have if we were not aware of the relationship. To do this, we examine the scores from an experiment from two perspectives. First, we examine the dependent scores as if there were no independent variable: as if we had simply measured our entire sample of subjects on the dependent variable. Then, we determine how much information is gained if we do not ignore the independent variable.

In an experiment, the term *proportion of variance accounted for* is a shortened version of *the proportion of total variance in the dependent scores that is accounted for by the relationship with the independent variable.* The total variance in dependent scores is simply a measure of how much all of the scores in the study differ from each other when we ignore the independent variable. For example, let's say we perform a simple version of our mood study, comparing the helping scores of subjects in the conditions of positive or negative mood. We obtain the scores shown below.

*Finding the
total variance in
dependent scores*

*Finding the
systematic variance
in dependent scores*

		Neg	Pos
4	8	4	8
4	8	4	8
4	8	4	8
Overall	$\overline{X} = 6$	$\overline{X} = 4$	$\overline{X} = 8$

On the left, we ignore the conditions of the independent variable and simply compute the total variance in the scores—how much the six scores differ from the overall mean of the study. To determine the proportion of variance accounted for, as shown on the right, we do not ignore the independent variable but, instead, group scores according to the conditions. Look what happens: All of the differences in scores occur *between* the conditions with no differences in scores *within* a condition. In other words, there is no error variance. Rather, all of the differences between scores form systematic variance. **Systematic variance** refers to the differences in scores that occur with changes in our independent variable. It is changes in scores that are associated with—correlated with—changes in our conditions.

Because this is a perfectly consistent relationship, all of the total variance is systematic variance. Thus, the mood factor accounts for 100% of the variance. Or, as a proportion, it accounts for 1.0 of the total variance in helping scores. In an experiment, the **proportion of variance accounted for** is the proportion of total variance in dependent scores that is systematic variance. In other words, it is the proportion of total variance in scores that is associated or correlated with changes in the independent variable.

We "account" for the variance in helping scores in that we know when and why different scores occur. Subjects will have a score of 4 when their mood is negative. They will have a *different* score of 8 when their mood is positive. Assuming that we have no confounding, these differences are caused by our independent variable. Thus, the effect size of our mood manipulation is 1.0: it produces or accounts for *all* of the observed differences in helping behavior.

Since a perfectly consistent relationship does not normally occur, we usually cannot account for 100% of the variance. For example, we might obtain the following helping scores.

Total variance in dependent scores		*Systematic variance due to mood*	
		Neg	*Pos*
2	6	2	6
4	8	4	8
6	10	6	10
Overall $\overline{X} = 6$		$\overline{X} = 4$	$\overline{X} = 8$
Total variance = 6.67		Error variance = 2.67	

Again, on the left, we ignore the relationship with our independent variable and obtain the total variance, the amount by which all scores differ from the overall mean of the experiment. Calculating the total variance, we find a value of 6.67. On the right, when we do not ignore the independent variable, we see that although there is a relationship, there is also some error variance. With negative mood, subjects score around the mean of 4, but some are above and some are below. With positive mood, subjects score *around* the mean of 8. Essentially, we compute the error variance by determining the amount the scores in each condition differ from the mean of the condition, and then average together the different conditions. Here, we calculate the error variance to be 2.67.

Of all the differences between the scores in a study, to some extent the differences are associated with changing the independent variable, and to some extent they are not. In other words, the total variance is the sum of the systematic variance plus the error variance. Thus, out of a total variance of 6.67, about 2.67 is error variance and the remainder is systematic variance. Whether 2.67 represents a large amount is difficult to judge, so to make this number easier to interpret, we transform it into a proportion of the total: 2.67 divided by 6.67 equals .40. In this study, then, 40% of the total variance in helping scores is error variance. This means that 60% of the total variance is not error variance, so it must be systematic variance. Thus, the effect size of this independent variable is .60: Of all the differences in this study, 60% of them are associated with and presumably caused by changing our independent variable.

One way to interpret the proportion of variance accounted for is in terms of how well a relationship allows us to predict each subject's score and thus to predict his or her behavior. When we ignore the independent variable, we would predict each subject's score as the overall mean score, and be in error —be "off" —by whatever amount the actual scores differ from the mean. The differences between the actual scores and the overall mean is the total variance. In the example above, using the overall mean of helping scores (6), our predictions of subjects' score are off by an "average" of 6.67. When we consider the conditions of the independent variable, our best estimate of subjects' scores is the mean of the condition. By predicting that subjects will score around 4 when in a negative mood and around 8 when in a positive mood, we are closer to their actual scores than if we predicted a score of 6 for everyone in the experiment. How much closer? Using the mean of each condition, our predictions are still off by an average of 2.67, the amount of error variance or differences within the conditions. But our predictions are only "off" by an average of 40% of what they would be if we ignored the independent variable. In other words we are, on average, 60% closer—60% more accurate—when we use the mean of the condition to predict scores than when we use the overall mean of scores. Thus, by using our knowledge of the relationship between helping and mood, we are 60% more accurate in predicting, explaining, and understanding the differences in helping scores than if we do not consider this relationship.

> **REMEMBER** The *proportion of variance accounted for* communicates the proportional improvement in our understanding of differences in dependent scores that occurs when we consider the relationship with the independent variable.

The proportion of variance accounted for provides us with a way to evaluate the importance of different independent variables. Because of the many extraneous variables that can cause differences among scores, the effect size of any single variable in actual research is usually in the neighborhood of .15 to .30. Let's say that variable A accounts for .10 of the variance in a particular behavior, while variable B accounts for .20 of the variance. Variable B is twice as important for understanding the behavior as variable A: we are twice as accurate in knowing when and why subjects will exhibit a particular score and behavior under the conditions of B than we are by knowing their condition under variable A. Essentially, by studying variable B we are 20% better at understanding the behavior than if we had not studied this variable. By studying variable A, we are only 10% better off than if we had not bothered. (Recognize, however, that effect size indicates importance in a statistical sense, not in a practical sense: A variable that accounts for only 3% of *deaths* is, practically speaking, very important. Scientifically, though, it does not advance our knowledge greatly.)

Anytime you obtain a *significant* effect of an independent variable in an experiment, you should determine the proportion of variance accounted for. (With a nonsignificant result, you cannot believe that a "real" relationship even exists, so a nonsignificant effect always accounts for zero proportion of the variance.) The proportion of variance accounted for is *the* way to determine whether a relationship is scientifically important or merely much ado about nothing. Effect size is not always reported in the literature, although it should be. Huge, elaborate experiments are often performed to study what are actually very minor variables. By computing effect size, you can gauge the importance of your variables.

> *REMEMBER* The *effect size* of a manipulation indicates how dramatically it influences dependent scores and, thus, how important it is for understanding the underlying behavior.

Computing the Proportion of Variance Accounted For

As we saw above, the less consistent a relationship, the smaller the proportion of variance accounted for. A correlation coefficient reflects this degree of consistency. The preceding steps in finding the proportion of variance accounted for are mathematically equal to computing a correlation coefficient and then *squaring* it. Because there are different formulas for calculating a correlation coefficient depending on the scale of measurement of our scores and the nature of our design, we also have different ways of calculating the proportion of variance accounted for.

The Point-Biserial Correlation Coefficent When we have only two conditions of the independent variable and perform either an independent- or dependent-samples t-test, it is appropriate to compute the **point-biserial correlation coefficient.** Symbolized as r_{pb}, this statistic describes the strength of the relationship between two conditions of the independent variable and an interval or ratio dependent variable. For example, consider our previous example comparing negative and positive moods. The helping data are presented again in Figure 8.7.

In this figure is a scatterplot like those we first saw in Chapter 3, except that, with only two conditions of the independent variable, there are only two points on the X axis. Here we see a positive linear relationship, which is summarized by an r_{pb} of .77. (The value of r_{pb} can be computed directly from our obtained value of t, as shown in Appendix A.) The value of r_{pb} is interpreted in the same way that any other correlation is. A value of ± 1.0 indicates a perfectly consistent relationship between the conditions and the scores on the dependent variable. As the value approaches 0, it indicates a weaker and less consistent relationship.

The proportion of variance accounted for equals the squared correlation coefficient. In this case, our r_{pb} is .77, so r_{pb}^2 equals .60. Thus, as we saw originally, mood accounts for .60 of the variance in these helping scores. (In APA-style reports, this statistic is given in the Results section, just after the obtained t.)

Eta Squared When we perform either a between- or within-subjects ANOVA, the appropriate correlation to compute is *eta*. This statistic describes the strength of a linear or nonlinear relationship between a dependent variable and the independent variable, and it can be used regardless of the number of levels in a factor. The proportion of variance accounted for is equal to **eta squared,** symbolized as η^2. (Calculations are shown in Appendix A.) In multifactor designs, a separate η^2 is computed for each significant main effect and interaction. By describing the effect size of each factor in this way, we determine which factor is most important and should be emphasized in our interpretations. In essence, a small η^2 tells us the factor or interaction was not a big deal in *producing* consistent differences in scores, so we should not make a big deal out of it

FIGURE 8.7 Data and Scatterplot Employing a Point-Biserial Correlation Coefficient

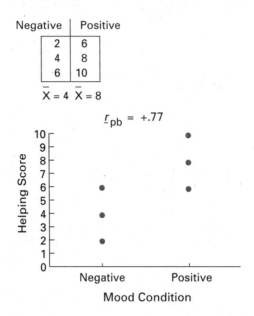

when *explaining* the differences in scores. (There are also nonparametric versions of η^2 for use with ranked scores, as shown in Appendix A.)

Effect size is especially important when we are dealing with interactions. The one exception to the rule of always focusing our interpretation on the significant interaction is when it has a very small effect size. An interaction contradicts the general, overall pattern shown in a main effect. However, if the interaction has a very small effect size (say, only .02), then it only slightly and inconsistently contradicts the overall main effect. In this case, we can focus our interpretation on any substantial significant main effects instead.

Notice that the procedures we are discussing involve descriptive statistics that indicate the proportion of variance accounted for by the relationship in our *sample data*. There are other approaches for inferring or estimating the effect size an independent variable would have if the study could be performed on the entire population. One common method for doing so is called *omega squared.*

The Phi and Contingency Coefficients   There is no measure of effect size for a one-way chi square. But with the two-way chi square, we describe the sample relationship by computing special correlation coefficients (shown in Appendix A). Which procedure we use depends on our design. For example, let's say we counted the number of subjects who helped or did not help as a function of their mood, using either of the two designs shown in Table 8.15.

When dealing with a 2×2 design, as on the left, we compute the **phi coefficient.** But when, as on the right, we have a two-way design that is *not* a 2×2 (e.g., a 3×2, a 3×3,

TABLE 8.15 Frequency of Subjects Who Helped or Did Not Help as a Function of Their Reported Mood

2 × 2 Design

		Mood	
		Neg	*Pos*
Helping	Yes	5	18
	No	20	2

2 × 3 Design

		Mood		
		Neg	*Neut*	*Pos*
Helping	Yes	5	13	20
	No	20	12	3

etc.), we compute the **contingency coefficient.** Like any correlation coefficient, these indicate the consistency of the relationship between the two variables. If we square these coefficients, we describe the proportion of variance accounted for, indicating how much we can account for or predict the frequency of category membership on one variable by considering category membership on the other variable. In the study described in Table 8.15, for example, we would see the degree to which the frequency of helping behavior is determined by subjects' mood.

ADDITIONAL STATISTICAL PROCEDURES FOUND IN EXPERIMENTS

In addition to the statistics we have discussed, you will come across other, advanced procedures in the literature. Although some of these procedures may be unknown to you, remember that all statistics are used to describe a relationship and determine whether it is significant. (Remember, too, that the Discussion section of any research report will explain what the statistical analysis indicates about the behavior under study.) Two important types of procedures you will encounter are multivariate statistics and meta-analysis.

Multivariate Statistics

All of the studies discussed so far have involved *one* dependent variable, for which the appropriate statistics have been *univariate statistics.* Recall, however, that researchers sometimes measure subjects on more than one dependent variable, both to bolster their confidence in their interpretations and to obtain more information. For example, to check our manipulation of subjects' mood, we might directly measure their mood using self-reports or physiological measurements, as well as examining their helping behavior. The inferential statistical procedures that we use when a study involves multiple dependent variables are called **multivariate statistics.** These include the multivariate *t*-test when we have two conditions and the multivariate analysis of variance (MANOVA) when we have more than two conditions and/or more than one factor.

Even though these procedures are very complex, the basic logic still holds: If the results are significant, the observed relationship between our independent variables and dependent variables is unlikely to be the result of chance, or sampling error. Given these significant results, we would then examine the influence of our manipulations on each individual dependent variable, using the *t*-tests or ANOVAs we have discussed previously.

Meta-Analysis

Recall that ultimately, confidence in the external validity of our findings is developed through repeated studies that literally and conceptually replicate the findings. Rather than subjectively evaluating the extent to which these studies support a particular hypothesis, researchers analyze the studies using meta-analysis. **Meta-analysis** refers to statistical procedures for combining, testing, and describing the results from different studies. For example, Carlson, Marcus-Newhall, and Miller (1990) performed a meta-analysis of some 22 published studies that investigated the influence of cues for aggression (e.g., weapons) on subjects' aggressive behavior. In such meta-analytic studies, researchers generally take one of two approaches: Either they determine whether the experiments taken together consistently show a significant effect of a particular variable, or they estimate the effect size of a variable based on all of the studies.

On the one hand, a meta-analysis provides objective methods for generalizing a variable's effect, and because the results are based on many subjects tested under varying procedures, we can have a high degree of confidence in our conclusions. On the other hand, a meta-analysis glosses over many differences in operational definitions, controls, and measurement procedures. Therefore, although any meta-analysis (and any review of the literature) will add to our understanding of a behavior, we must necessarily speak in *very* general terms.

PUTTING IT ALL TOGETHER

Previous chapters have stressed the importance of creating a well-controlled study, but the statistical topics discussed throughout are just as important. The best-designed study in the world is useless if you cannot make sense out of the data. Therefore, for any significant main effect or interaction, always fully describe the effect: Graph the effect, understand the pattern depicted, and compute the effect size.

Remember, however, that finding a significant result does not conclude the study. Your purpose is to describe and explain how a variable influences a behavior. Therefore, in your reporting always interpret the relationship and specify what it tells us about the psychology of the behavior. Focus on the mean (or other appropriate measure) that indicates the "typical" score in each condition. Translate this score into the typical behavioral response and describe how it changes as a function of your manipulation. Then, incorporating the relevant literature, explain in a parsimonious and rational manner the psychological mechanisms that can account for why and how each typical response occurs. At each step, consider what you did or did not do in conducting the experiment that may bias or confound your results and thus restrict your conclusions.

CHAPTER SUMMARY

1. In a *multifactor experiment,* the researcher examines several independent variables and their interactions. In a *complete factorial design,* all levels of one factor are combined with all levels of the other factor.

2. In a *two-way between-subjects design,* a different group of subjects is tested under each condition of two independent variables. In a *two-way within-subjects design,* matched groups or the same repeatedly measured subjects are tested in all conditions of two independent variables. In a *two-way mixed design,* one within-subjects and one between-subjects factor is examined.

3. In any two-way ANOVA, we compute an F for the *main effect* of each factor and an F for the *interaction.*

4. A *main effect* of a factor is the effect that changing the levels of that factor has on dependent scores, while collapsing across all other factors in the study.

5. An *interaction effect* is the influence that the combination of levels from the factors has on the dependent scores. In a *two-way interaction,* the relationship between one factor and the dependent scores is different for and depends on each level of the other factor. When the cell means of a significant interaction are graphed, the lines are not parallel.

6. A *simple main effect* is the effect of one factor at one level of a second factor within the interaction. *Post hoc* comparisons in an interaction should involve only *unconfounded comparisons*—comparisons of cell means that differ along only one factor.

7. Because an interaction contradicts the overall pattern suggested by the main effects, we usually focus our interpretation of a study on the significant interaction.

8. A *three-way design* produces three main effects, three two-way interactions, and a three-way interaction. In a *three-way interaction,* the two-way interaction between two factors changes as the levels of the third factor change.

9. The *two-way chi square procedure* is used when the data consist of the frequency with which subjects fall into the categories of two variables. If χ^2 is significant, the frequency of subjects in the different categories of one variable depends upon their category membership along the other variable.

10. For any significant main effect or interaction, we describe its *effect size,* an indication of how dramatically the variable influences the dependent scores.

11. The total variance in dependent scores is a measure of how much all of the scores in the study differ, and it equals the error variance plus the systematic variance. *Systematic variance* refers to the differences in scores that occur with, or are associated with, changes in the conditions.

12. Calculating effect size as the *proportion of variance accounted for* indicates the proportion of total variance in dependent scores that is systematic variance. It reflects the proportional improvement in our understanding of differences in the dependent scores that occurs when we examine the relationship with the independent variable.

13. The effect size is calculated as (1) the squared value of the *point-biserial correlation coefficient* when we perform a *t*-test, or (2) *eta squared* for each significant factor or interaction effect when we perform ANOVA.

14. The effect size in a significant 2×2 chi square is calculated as the squared value of the *phi coefficient*. With a two-way design that is not a 2×2, effect size is the squared *contingency coefficient*.

15. *Multivariate statistics* are the inferential statistical procedures used when a study involves more than one dependent variable.

16. *Meta-analysis* involves statistical procedures for combining, testing, and describing the results from different studies.

REVIEW QUESTIONS

1. (a) What are the reasons for conducting multifactor designs? (b) What is a complete factorial design?
2. A student hears that a 2×3 design was conducted and concludes that six factors were examined. Is this conclusion correct? Why or why not?
3. What is the difference between a two-way within-subjects design and (a) a two-way between-subjects design? (b) a two-way mixed design?
4. Identify the *F*s that are computed in a two-way ANOVA involving factors *A* and *B*.
5. What is the difference between a main effect mean and a cell mean?
6. (a) A significant main effect indicates what about an independent variable? (b) A significant interaction indicates what about an independent variable?
7. A researcher studies subjects' frustration levels when solving problems both as a function of the difficulty of the problem and as a function of whether they are math or logic problems. She finds that logic problems produce more frustration than math problems, that greater difficulty leads to greater frustration, and that more difficult logic problems produce much greater frustration than more difficult math problems. In the ANOVA performed for this study, what effects are significant?
8. In question 7, let's say the researcher instead found that math and logic problems lead to the same frustration levels, that frustration consistently increases with greater difficulty, and that this is true for both math and logic problems. In the ANOVA performed for this study, what effects are significant?
9. You are studying the volunteer bias. You advertise your experiment first as a memory study and again later as an attitude study. For each, you pass around a sign-up sheet in some psychology courses and then count the number of volunteers who actually show up for the experiment. (a) What statistical procedure should you use? (b) What factor (or factors) do you examine?

10. A researcher examines subjects' performance on an eye-hand coordination task as a function of three levels of reward and three levels of practice, obtaining the following cell means.

		Reward		
		Low	Medium	High
Practice	Low	4	10	7
	Medium	5	5	14
	High	15	15	15

(a) What are the main effect means for reward, and what do they indicate about this factor?
(b) What are the main effect means for practice, and what do they indicate?

11. (a) In question 10, is an interaction likely? (b) How would you perform unconfounded *post hoc* comparisons of the cell means?

12. (a) In question 10, why does the interaction contradict your conclusions about the effect of reward? (b) Why does the interaction contradict your conclusions about practice?

13. (a) What is a simple main effect? (b) In question 10, what will the simple main effects of reward (at each practice level) apparently indicate?

14. In question 10, the researcher reports that the effect size of reward is .14, that the effect size of practice is .31, and that the interaction accounts for .01 of the variance. What does each value indicate about the influence of these effects?

15. (a) What is the difference between systematic variance and error variance? (b) What does the total variance refer to? (c) What does the proportion of variance accounted for refer to?

16. Why does the proportion of variance accounted for indicate how important a variable is?

17. What statistic indicates proportion of variance accounted for in (a) a *t*-test design? (b) an ANOVA? (c) a chi square?

18. The abstract for a research article reports (a) a meta-analysis or (b) a multivariate statistic. Based on this information, what do you know about the procedure undertaken by the researchers in each study?

DISCUSSION QUESTIONS

1. Create a graph of the interaction in the reaction time study shown in Table 8.10, placing "type of number" on the *X* axis.

2. Design a two-way study, diagram it, and place mean scores in each cell that appear to produce the predicted main effects and interactions.

3. In a between-subjects design, you investigate subjects' hypnotic suggestibility as a function of whether they meditate before being tested, and whether they were shown a film containing a low, medium, or high amount of fantasy. For the following data, perform all appropriate statistical analyses, and determine what you should conclude about this study.

	Amount of fantasy		
	Low	*Medium*	*High*
Meditation	5	7	9
	6	5	8
	2	6	10
	2	9	10
	5	5	10
No meditation	10	2	5
	10	5	6
	9	4	5
	10	3	7
	10	2	6

4. When designing a two- or three-way repeated measures with many trials and conditions:
   (a) What potential biases and confoundings due to subjects may be especially prominent?
   (b) What ethical concern arises regarding the demands you place on subjects?

PART **III**

BEYOND THE TYPICAL LABORATORY EXPERIMENT

Our previous discussions have focused on true laboratory experiments involving groups of human subjects. Such experiments are common in psychological research, because they usually produce the greatest internal validity for arguing that a particular variable causes people's behavior to change. However, in any research, the goal is to design the best study we can, so that we can most clearly and confidently answer the research question at hand. Therefore, psychologists often have reasons for choosing an alternative to the typical laboratory design. In some cases, the reason may be that the laboratory setting creates an artificial setting and the observed behavior is too unnatural. At other times, the variables cannot be manipulated or measured in a way that conforms to an experimental design. And sometimes the hypothesis being tested and the goals of the research require a different approach. In these situations, other designs—or a combination of designs—are better suited for answering our research questions. In the following chapters, we examine these other designs.

9 Correlational Research and Questionnaire Construction

Recall that researchers do not test only experimental or causal hypotheses but also descriptive hypotheses. A common descriptive approach in psychological research is the **correlational design.** Here we test the hypothesis that a relationship between the variables is present. The term *correlation* is synonymous with *relationship,* so in using a correlational design we are describing a relationship—examining the correlation—between variables.

In this chapter, we first discuss the logic of correlational designs and contrast them with experimental designs. Then we review basic correlational statistics and discuss a number of ways they are used. We will also cover two major tools for gathering data that are often involved in correlational designs: interviews and questionnaires.

THE DIFFERENCE BETWEEN TRUE EXPERIMENTS AND CORRELATIONAL STUDIES

Experimental and correlational designs differ in terms of *how* a researcher demonstrates a relationship. To illustrate, consider a research hypothesis from the area of industrial-organizational psychology: Supposedly "job satisfaction," the degree to which workers find their jobs satisfying, is related to their wages (e.g., Pritchard, Dunnette & Jorgenson, 1972). In a true experiment, we might attempt to demonstrate this relationship by manipulating the independent variable of amount of pay that subjects receive while performing a laboratory task. Thus, we randomly assign subjects to various pay levels and have them perform a "job" of assembling "widgets" out of toy building-blocks. Then, after an interval, we obtain subjects' answers to a series of questions that measure job satisfaction. Our research hypothesis implies the question, "For a given pay rate, what is a subject's job satisfaction?" Recall that the "given" variable is always graphed as the X variable, and that we examine Y scores as a function of X. To graph our results, we place the different conditions of the independent variable of pay rate on the X axis and the dependent variable of subjects' job satisfaction scores on the Y axis. By way of illustration, we will break with tradition and create a *scatterplot* of the individual data points from this experiment. Let's say we obtain the results shown in scatterplot A of Figure 9.1.

The important thing to recognize about an experiment here is that, by randomly assigning subjects to a pay condition, we, the *researchers*, determine each subject's X score—that is, we decide whether their "score" will be \$3, \$6, or \$9. Then, we show that, for an *assigned X,* subjects tend to produce a certain Y score.

The distinguishing aspect of a correlational design is that we do not manipulate the X variable: We do not determine subjects' X scores by randomly assigning subjects an amount of the variable to experience. Rather, the scores on both variables reflect an amount or category of a variable that a subject has *already* experienced. Thus, to conduct our study using a correlational design, we might randomly select some subjects who are already employed at jobs and then measure their hourly pay as well as their job satisfaction. As shown in scatterplot B of Figure 9.1, we again examine the same relationship, but here we show that for a *reported X* score of pay rate, subjects tend to produce a certain Y score of job satisfaction.

FIGURE 9.1   Job Satisfaction Scores as a Function of Pay Rate

The results in scatterplot A were gathered in a true experiment; those in scatterplot B were gathered in a correlational study.

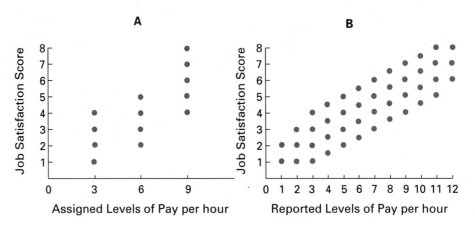

Thus, in a correlational design the X variable is not a *true* independent variable, although subjects' scores on the X variable are analogous to the levels of a factor in an experiment. The reason pay rate is the X variable in scatterplot B is that we are again asking the question "For a given pay rate, what is a subject's job satisfaction?"—so pay rate is the X variable. In both of these graphs we examine job satisfaction as a function of pay rate. (Conversely, if our correlational design had asked the question "What is a subject's pay rate for a given satisfaction level?" then pay rate would be the Y variable and satisfaction level would be the X variable.)

Sources of Data for a Correlational Design

Any of the approaches to measuring variables in experiments can also be used in correlational designs. A common approach is to measure subjects' scores using various tests. For example, Runco and Albert (1986) correlated subjects' intelligence test scores with their creativity test scores. Alternatively, questions measuring several variables may be included in one test, from which we relate subjects' scores on each variable. Such questionnaires are often referred to as "inventories" or "batteries"; one example is the Minnesota Multiphasic Personality Inventory or MMPI (Butcher et al., 1989). We may also examine the relationship between test scores and a physical or physiological attribute. For example, Martinez and Dukes (1987) related subjects' self-esteem scores to their gender. Or we may obtain scores from subjects' records: Fridell (1989) correlated information from police shooting incidents to examine the use of deadly force, and Firth and Britton (1989) correlated the attendance factors relating to psychological "burnout" in nurses. We may have subjects create the record themselves, as did Burk, Mackay, Wortheley and Wade (1991). They studied subjects' records of their TOTs (tip-of-the-tongue experiences) and how they resolved them. Similarly, Cann and Donderi (1986) examined dream journals, in which subjects recorded the contents of the previous night's dreams every morning. We may also correlate environmental events and behavior. For example, Anderson and Anderson (1984) determined the relationship between daily temperature in a large city and the daily incidence of crime, and Osborn (1988) correlated subjects' personality characteristics with the physical arrangement of their living rooms. In other studies, we may measure a variable in a laboratory procedure, as did Jenson (1993) when correlating reaction times with intelligence test scores. As these examples illustrate, a correlational design can examine the relationship between the scores from virtually any variables, regardless of how we obtain them.

Interpreting Correlational Designs

Our confidence in the conclusions drawn from correlational designs is influenced by the same concerns we've raised previously in relation to experiments. Thus, the procedures for measuring each variable should have construct and content validity. They should be reliable and provide sensitive measurements so that we can detect subtle differences between subjects. Extraneous influences such as demand characteristics, response sets, and the volunteer bias should be eliminated. And, as always, we address such concerns by considering the four components of any study—the subjects, environment, researcher, and measurement task — looking for any aspect that may threaten reliability and validity.

However, recall that, compared to experiments, correlational designs have two additional flaws that severely reduce internal validity for concluding that differences in the X variable *cause* differences in Y scores. The first flaw is that we do not randomly assign subjects to a score on the X variable. Therefore, we do not control subject variables by randomizing and thus balancing them across the different X scores. Because of this, differences between subjects on the X variable are very likely to be confounded by differences in extraneous subject variables. In our job-satisfaction study, for example, subjects who differ in their existing pay rates may also differ in job type, length of employment, or education level. Since the variable of pay rate is confounded with these variables, we cannot say that it is pay that *causes* job satisfaction.

The second flaw in correlational designs is that, often, we cannot be certain that X occured before Y. Yet to conclude that X causes Y, we must know that X occurred first. In our example above, we cannot know for sure that a worker's low pay rate occurred first, such that it could have caused low job satisfaction. Perhaps for some reason subjects were first dissatisfied with their job and, because of poor motivation and performance, they then received low pay. Or perhaps a third variable was first operating: perhaps some workers suffered discrimination, and this caused both low pay and low job satisfaction.

Thus, the relationship found in a correlational design may mean that changes in X cause changes in Y, as we think. The problem is that changes in Y may cause changes in X, or some third variable may produce differences in both the X and Y scores. Therefore, a single correlational study is, at best, only interpreted as *suggesting* that changes in X *may* cause changes in Y. Because of our lack of confidence in such a statement, correlational designs are best for testing a descriptive hypothesis that a relationship exists between the variables. Conversely, in a true experiment, we do randomly assign subjects to conditions and subjects do experience a condition before the dependent variable. Therefore, this design is best for testing a hypothesis about a causal variable.

> *REMEMBER*   Causal relationships are not inferred from a correlational design, because (1) the absence of random assignment allows for potential confoundings and (2) the order of occurrence of the variables is unknown.

Reasons for Using the Correlational Approach

Though we must accept the limited evidence for causality found in a correlational design, it is still a legitimate research approach that allows us to learn about behavior. In fact, a correlational design may be preferable for several reasons.

Ethical and Practical Reasons   Because of ethical and practical considerations, some relationships can be studied only through a correlational design. For example, physical and sexual abuse, accidents, crime, and recreational drug use are important psychological variables. Ethically, however, we cannot study such variables by randomly assigning subjects to experience them in a true experiment. Likewise, there are many variables we simply cannot manipulate, such as deciding a subject's career, race, gender, personality traits, or mental and physical illness. Yet because such variables and behaviors do occur in the real world, we *can* study them through correlational methods. Thus, for example, we can measure the amount of abuse subjects have experienced and relate it to other behaviors or characteristics. Further, through repeated literal and conceptual replication of such relationships, together with experimental studies of relevant constructs, researchers may eventually develop some degree of confidence that the variable of abuse has a causal influence.

Discovering Relationships   Correlational procedures are useful because they allow us to discover relationships. For example, we may measure workers on numerous variables that we suspect may be related (their work history, training level, motivation, pay, job satisfaction, and so on) and then discover which variables do produce relationships. Such descriptive research is useful not only for describing behavior but also for identifying relationships that may later turn out to be causal. Thus, once we discover the variables related to job satisfaction, we may study them using experimental designs to determine whether they are causal factors.

External Validity   As we've seen, a laboratory experiment creates a rather artificial situation and involves only subjects who will come to us. An advantage of the correlational approach is that often it can be conducted *outside* of the laboratory. Potentially, therefore, we have greater ecological validity, external validity, and construct validity with a correlational study. For example, measuring the pay and job satisfaction of employed workers is a more valid way to study this relationship than studying laboratory subjects who make widgets (but see Pritchard, Dunnette & Jorgenson [1972] for a surprisingly realistic laboratory task).

Prediction and Selection   As you know, part of understanding a behavior is being able to predict when it will occur. The relationship found in a correlational study may be better for predicting behaviors than that found in an experiment, because correlational designs usually provide a more complete description of the relationship. Typically, an experiment involves a limited set of conditions (X scores) with gaps between them. As shown in scatterplot A of Figure 9.1, for example, we studied only the three pay rates of $3, $6, and $9 dollars per hour. Therefore, we have no data for predicting satisfaction levels for a $5 or $7 rate. In a correlational study, however, we can obtain a wider variety of X scores to relate to Y, thus possibly improving our predictions. Look again at scatterplot B of Figure 9.1. Here, actual workers reported pay rates between $3 and $12 per hour, so we have data for predicting job satisfaction scores when a worker earns $5 or $7.

A correlational design is especially preferred in applied research involving the creation of a "selection test." If, for example, people must take a test when applying for a job, they are taking a selection test. Previous correlational research may have shown that those employed workers who score higher on the test also tend to be better workers. Therefore, only those job applicants who perform above a certain score on the test will be hired, because we predict that they will also be better workers. Similar selection tests are being used when people take college entrance exams, which allow us to predict their future college performance. Or when clinical patients take diagnostic tests, which allow us to identify those who are at risk of developing emotional problems.

> *REMEMBER*   Correlational designs are useful for discovering relationships, they solve ethical and practical problems, and they may provide better validity and accuracy in predictions.

ANALYZING DATA WITH CORRELATIONAL STATISTICS

Usually we analyze data from correlational research by computing a correlation coefficient. However, computing a correlation coefficient does *not* automatically create a correlational *design*. A correlational design occurs whenever we do not randomly assign subjects to the levels of either variable, *regardless* of how the data is analyzed. As we saw in Chapter 8, we can compute correlations within experimental designs, and we can apply ANOVAs or *t*-tests to correlational designs. Generally the rule is this: On the one hand, we employ ANOVA, *t*-tests, and similar procedures as our primary method of analysis when the X variable consists of a few *discrete* points. Then we examine the Y scores paired with each X by computing the mean score per condition and so on. On the other hand, we employ correlational statistics as our primary method of analysis when the X variable *continues* over a wide range of scores. Then we examine the overall relationship between all pairs of X-Y scores. For example, using an ANOVA to compare the mean job-satisfaction score for each of 20 different pay rates would be overwhelming. Instead, when a design produces such a wide variety of X scores, we use the correlation coefficient as an efficient way to summarize the data.

Recall from Chapter 3 that the correlation coefficient communicates the type and strength of a relationship between variables. Let's say that we correlate subjects' overall job satisfaction scores with their corresponding pay rates, as shown in the scatterplots of Figure 9.2. In a study of this sort, we would typically compute the **Pearson correlation coefficient** (technically this statistic is called the "Pearson Product Moment Correlation Coefficient"). Symbolized by r, the Pearson coefficient is the parametric statistical procedure used to describe the linear relationship between X and Y scores that are normally distributed interval or ratio scores (calculations are shown in Appendix A). Summarizing the data in this way is usually the starting point for most correlational research, because a straight-line relationship is the simplest type. A positive coefficient indicates a generally positive linear relationship (as in scatterplot A of Figure 9.2), and a negative value indicates a generally negative linear relationship (as in scatterplot B). The absolute value of the coefficient communicates the strength of the relationship. A value of ± 1.0 indicates a perfectly consistent relationship, with *one* value of Y associated with only one value of X so that all data points fall on a straight line. A value less than ± 1.0 is essentially the degree to which the data *approximate* a perfect linear relationship. As the coefficient approaches 0, it indicates a less consistent linear relationship, with greater variability in Y scores at each value of X. Since the components of a relationship in a correlation are analogous to those in an experiment, the variability in Y scores at each X is again called the *error variance*. In Figure 9.2, scatterplot A shows greater error variance and thus a less consistent relationship, which produces a lower correlation coefficient than that in scatterplot B.

A correlation coefficient describes the relationship found in our sample. As usual, however, the sample relationship may be the result of sampling error—a coincidental pairing of X-Y scores that happen to form a linear pattern. Therefore, we must determine whether the coefficient is significant. We perform a *one-tailed test* if we are predicting a positive or a negative relationship, and we perform a *two-tailed test* if we are predicting a linear relationship but do not specify whether it is positive or negative.

FIGURE 9.2   Two Scatterplots Showing Possible Relationships Between Job Satisfaction Scores and Hourly Pay Rate

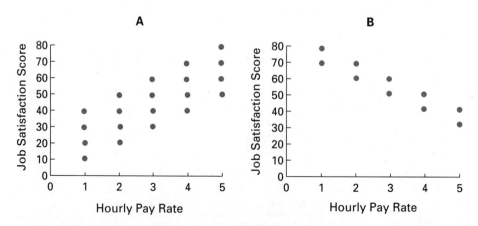

A common nonparametric procedure is the **Spearman correlation coefficient** (calculations are shown in Appendix A). This coefficient is employed when both variables are measured using an ordinal scale, showing subjects' relative rank order. Other types of correlation coefficients are used when we have other types of data (including the *point-biserial, phi,* and *contingency* coefficients discussed in Chapter 8). We interpret every coefficient, however, in the same way as we interpret the Pearson r.

If the correlation coefficient is significant, we are confident that the relationship in our data is not a chance occurrence. Then we go on to explain the relationship psychologically. In our example above, we would focus on the question of why, as pay rate increases, job satisfaction tends to change. We would also consider why the relationship is inconsistent to some degree and what other variables may more consistently relate to job satisfaction. To help us describe and understand the observed relationship, we employ the additional procedure of linear regression and examine the errors in prediction.

Linear Regression

When the Pearson r is significant, we perform linear regression. **Linear regression** is the procedure for predicting subjects' scores on one variable based on the linear relationship with subjects' scores on another variable. Thus, once we know the relationship between pay and job satisfaction, we can predict a worker's job satisfaction by knowing his or her pay rate. Simultaneously, the linear regression procedure allows us to describe the straight line that summarizes a scatterplot, indicating the linear relationship that is hidden in the data.

We perform regression procedures by using our sample data to calculate the **linear regression equation** (shown in Appendix A). This equation allows us to graph a straight line that summarizes the scatterplot, called the **linear regression line.** To draw this line, we perform the following steps: (1) We select some values of X and, using the regression equation, calculate the corresponding values of Y; (2) we plot these X-Y data points; and (3) we connect the data points with a straight line.

An idealized scatterplot and its corresponding regression line are shown in Figure 9.3. The regression line fits the scatterplot so that, with respect to all X-Y pairs, the distance some Y scores are above the line equals the distance other Y scores are below the line. Essentially, we envision this line as the one that would be obtained if the data formed a perfect linear relationship.

The value of Y that falls on the regression line above any X is called "Y prime," symbolized as Y'. Each Y prime is a summary of the Y scores at an X based on the overall linear relationship in the sample. By entering the value of any X into the regression equation, we can calculate the corresponding Y' score. As with other summary statistics—such as the mean—Y prime not only indicates the typical Y score at an X but also represents our best prediction of a subject's Y score at a value of X. Thus, **Y prime** is the predicted value of Y for subjects scoring at a particular value of X. In Figure 9.3, for example, we predict a Y' of 30 for an X of \$1. Because the sample's Y scores are evenly spread out *around* (above and below) the regression line, the Y scores are evenly spread out *around* (more or less than) each value of Y prime. Thus, considering the entire linear relationship, our subjects with an X of \$1

FIGURE 9.3   Idealized Scatterplot Showing a Linear Regression Line

The arrow indicates Y' for $X = 1$.

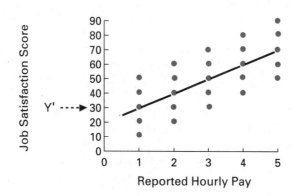

scored around a Y of 30, so 30 is our best prediction and summary for any subject scoring an X of \$1.

> *REMEMBER*   The *linear regression equation* summarizes the linear relationship in a sample of data, producing the *linear regression line.* From this, we use the relationship to predict the Y score—Y'—at any X.

The above procedure allows us to summarize the linear relationship in our sample and to see the Y scores we would predict for our subjects based on this relationship. It is by using such procedures that we create selection tests. First we test a sample of subjects on both the X and Y variables so that we can determine the regression equation. Then we test new subjects on the X variable. We enter these subjects' X scores into the regression equation and calculate the corresponding values of Y prime. If a subject's predicted Y score meets our "criterion," he or she is selected for the job, admitted to a college, and so on. Because of this procedure, in correlational designs the X variable is also called the *predictor variable* and the Y variable is also called the *criterion variable.*

Errors in Prediction and the Variance Accounted For

It is not enough merely to say that a relationship can be used to predict unknown scores. We should know the amount of error we can expect in such predictions so that we know how much credence to give them. To estimate the amount of error we will have when predicting unknown scores, we examine how well we can predict the scores in our sample. As an example, let's say that we conduct three different studies showing three different relationships. As shown in Table 9.1, we perform the linear regression procedure for each study and obtain the predicted Y scores for two different X scores.

TABLE 9.1 Errors in Prediction Using Two Values of X

Here, the relationship has a correlation coefficient of $+1.0$, $+.60$, or $+.20$.

Strength of relationship		Predicted Y score	Actual Y scores	Error prediction
Perfect	$X = 1$	5	5, 5, 5, 5	0, 0, 0, 0
$(r = +1.0)$	$X = 2$	8	8, 8, 8, 8	0, 0, 0, 0
Medium	$X = 1$	5	3, 4, 6, 7	$-2, -1, +1, +2$
$(r = +.60)$	$X = 2$	8	6, 7, 9, 10	$-2, -1, +1, +2$
Weak	$X = 1$	5	1, 2, 8, 9	$-4, -3, +3, +4$
$(r = +.20)$	$X = 2$	8	4, 5, 11, 12	$-4, -3, +3, +4$

The amount of error in a single prediction is the difference between a subject's actual Y score and the predicted Y' score. A correlation of ± 1.0 indicates a perfect linear relationship, so, as shown in the top row of Table 9.1, every subject's predicted Y score equals his or her actual Y score and we have no prediction error. Alternatively, a correlation of less than ± 1.0 indicates some error variance in the Y scores at each X, such that the actual Y scores are *around* the predicted Y score. Thus, as shown in the middle row of the table, when $r = +.60$ our predictions of Y are close to the actual Y scores found at that X, but our predictions of Y are 1 or 2 points off. When $r = +.20$ (see the bottom row of the table), the actual Y scores found at each X vary considerably, so our predictions in this case are off by 3 or 4 points. As these data illustrate, the closer r is to 0, then the greater the variability in the Y scores at each X, the farther subjects' actual Y scores are from the predicted Y score, and the larger our prediction error.

Although the size of the correlation coefficient indirectly communicates the amount of prediction error, we also have two direct methods for describing it. The first is called the standard error of the estimate. The **standard error of the estimate** communicates the amount by which the actual Y scores in a sample differ from their corresponding predicted Y' scores. For example, let's say that when $r = +.60$, the standard error of the estimate equals 2.0 (calculations shown in Appendix A). We interpret this number as indicating that "on average" our predicted Y's differ from subjects' actual Y scores by about 2 points. (The standard error of the estimate is reported in the Results section of APA-style reports.)

> *REMEMBER* Whenever we compute a correlation coefficient, it is appropriate to compute the standard error of the estimate to describe the prediction error we would have if we performed the linear regression procedure.

It is difficult to determine whether being off by an average of 2 points is a lot, so it is still difficult to evaluate the prediction errors occurring with this relationship. Instead, a less subjective way of evaluating the accuracy of our predictions is to determine the *proportion of variance accounted for*. In Chapter 8, we saw that this statistic is the proportion of the total variance in Y scores that we can predict or account for by knowing the condition a subject was tested under. Because a condition of the independent variable is simply a special type of a subject's X score, the proportion of variance accounted for is *always* the proportion of the total variance in Y scores that we can account for by knowing subjects' X scores.

Recall that the proportion of variance accounted for is the proportion of total variance in Y that is *systematic variance*—the extent to which differences in Y are systematically related to changes in X. In making this calculation, we again determine the improvement in predictions we have when we use the relationship to predict scores, as compared to when we do not use the relationship. For example, let's say that we obtained the job satisfaction scores shown in Figure 9.4.

On the left of this figure are the scores we obtained. All of the differences between them constitute the total variance. Without utilizing the relationship with pay rate, we cannot predict any of these differences. On the right, we have created the regression line for this study. To the extent that the satisfaction scores tend to increase with pay, some differences in satisfaction scores are now predictable. To this extent the scores exhibit systematic variance. At the same time, to some extent, the Y scores do not follow this trend. Thus, the scores exhibit error variance. That is, a predicted Y score only gets us in the neighborhood of the actual Y scores: We know that subjects tend to score around 20 when paid \$1 and around 30 when paid \$2, but we don't know precisely when they score 10, 20, 30, or 40. Compared to the situation in which we do not utilize the relationship, then, using a subject's pay rate improves our accuracy in predicting job satisfaction by some proportion.

The proportion of variance accounted for in a correlational design equals the **squared correlation coefficient.** Thus, after a Pearson r has been computed, the value of r^2

FIGURE 9.4 Proportion of Variance Accounted For in a Job Satisfaction Study

Differences between scores on the left constitute the total variance. By correlating the scores with pay rates on the right, we identify both systematic and error variance.

Y scores
10 20 20
30 30 30
40 40 40
50 50 50
60 60 70

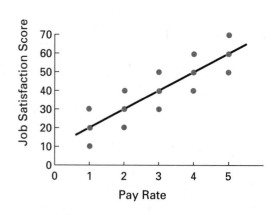

indicates the proportion of total variance in Y scores that is systematically associated with changing X scores. This value of r^2 essentially communicates the proportional improvement in predicting Y scores that occurs when we calculate the regression equation and use it to predict Y scores, compared to when we do not use this procedure. (Likewise, squaring other types of correlation coefficients provides the same kind of information about the relationship found in those situations.)

> *REMEMBER*   Squaring a correlation coefficient indicates the proportion of variance in Y that is accounted for by the relationship with X.

In a correlational design, r^2 is *not* called a measure of effect size: To say that the X variable has an effect would be to imply causality. However, as with effect size, we compare the values of r^2 from different relationships to evaluate which is the most useful, scientifically important relationship. Let's say that the correlation between pay rate and job satisfaction is $r = +.40$, producing an r^2 of .16. Let's also say that the correlation between years on the job and satisfaction is $r = +.20$, producing an r^2 of $= .04$. Since .16 is four times .04, the relationship involving pay rate is four times as systematic as that involving years on the job. In these data, then, pay rate is four times as useful for predicting scores and, thus, four times more important for understanding differences in job satisfaction. (A squared coefficient is only a rough estimate of the actual variance that would be accounted for in the population, but it is still a useful statistic for evaluating different relationships.)

Maximizing the Power of the Correlation Coefficient

If a correlation coefficient is not significant, then we draw no conclusions about the relationship, we do not perform linear regression, and we do not compute the proportion of variance accounted for. Therefore, to ensure that we will not miss such information about a relationship that actually exists in the population, we seek a correlational design that maximizes our statistical power.

Remember, the discussion of power is confined to those times when the null hypothesis is false, so our goal here is to obtain a significant coefficient. We maximize power by creating a design that will produce a strong relationship and thus a large coefficient. To illustrate, let's say that the graphs in Figure 9.5 depict the results of two studies investigating the relationship between hourly pay and job satisfaction. As shown, study A produces a pattern that closely approximates a straight line, forming a relatively long, narrow ellipse. This pattern, in turn, produces a relatively large correlation coefficient that is likely to be significant. Study B, however, produces a less elliptical and more circular pattern. This pattern will produce a smaller coefficient that is less likely to be significant, so we may miss finding the relationship. Study B had two problems that led to this less elliptical pattern of scores.

First, study B reflects greater variability in Y scores at each X. The fact that the Y scores do not closely fit a straight (regression) line is precisely what a low correlation coefficient indicates. Thus, to increase our power, we seek to control any extraneous variables that might produce error variance. Further, we seek a precise and sensitive

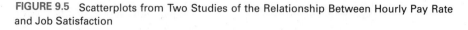

FIGURE 9.5 Scatterplots from Two Studies of the Relationship Between Hourly Pay Rate and Job Satisfaction

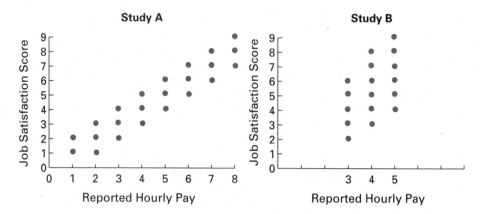

measurement of each variable. If, for example, we round off the pay rates to whole-dollar amounts, then we may be forcing different job satisfaction scores to occur at the same pay score, artificially increasing error variance.

Second, study B suffers from *restriction of range.* The researcher obtained a limited range of pay scores, so a scatterplot with so much error variance is not very elliptical. These data are misleading, causing us to underestimate the strength of the relationship that would be found if the range were not restricted. Had study B included pay scores below $3 and above $5, even with the same variability in Y scores, the overall pattern would be more elliptical (more linear), producing a larger coefficient that was more likely to be significant. (Since we can place either variable on the X axis, restricting the range of either will produce a truncated, circular scatterplot and an artificially low correlation coefficient.)

Often, restriction of range in a correlational study is due to the subjects we select. For example, when correlating pay with job satisfaction, we should avoid selecting only those subjects who have the same specific job because they all will receive very close to the same pay rate. Similarly, if we wish to correlate subjects' overall college grade-point average with later job success, our selection criteria should not limit us to honor students only or to students taking a particular course: Such selectivity could produce *ceiling* or *floor* effects, or otherwise restrict the range of grade-point averages observed.

In addition, we have three general principles for increasing the power of correlational designs. First, we can increase power by increasing N. Correlational designs frequently entail less control of extraneous variables, which in turn may produce error variance and weaken the relationship. When using such designs, therefore, we often compensate by employing larger Ns than those found in experiments, often in the range of several hundred subjects. Second, recall that parametric statistical procedures are more powerful than nonparametric procedures. When possible, we prefer to measure scores using an interval or ratio scale that meets the requirements of the parametric Pearson correlation coefficient. Finally, remember that the Pearson correlation coefficient describes the extent to which the data form a *linear* relationship. We compute r when we predict a linear relationship, or when we wish to determine the degree to which a linear relationship is present. However, we always create a scatterplot of the data to see whether they form a distinctly nonlinear pattern. If they do, they will not fit a straight line very well, and the coefficient may not be significant. Then we lose power because we conclude that there is no relationship when, in fact, a consistent and significant nonlinear relationship exists. Therefore, to maximize power, we compute the coefficient that is appropriate for the type of relationship found in the data.

> *REMEMBER*   Maximize the size of the correlation coefficient by minimizing error variance, avoiding restricted range, testing a large N, and computing parametric, linear statistics when appropriate.

ADDITIONAL USES OF CORRELATIONAL STATISTICS

In addition to their use in describing the overall results of a study, correlation and regression are the statistical procedures we use to determine reliability and validity in any experimental or correlational design.

Ascertaining Reliability

If a measurement procedure is reliable, then whenever a subject consistently exhibits a particular behavior, he or she should receive the same score. **Test-retest reliability** indicates that subjects tend to obtain the same score when tested at different times. For example, if a college exam has test-retest reliability, a student who produces a low score now should also produce a low score later, and a student scoring high now should also score high later. In other words, test-retest reliability is evident when there is a high, positive correlation between the scores obtained from the two testings. Likewise, we would demonstrate the test-retest reliability of a physiological measurement if scores from the same subjects tested under the same condition were positively correlated. Researchers generally consider "high" test-retest reliability to be indicated when the coefficient is significant and at a value of $+.80$ or higher.

Test-retest reliability reflects the reliablity of a subject's overall score. However, we may also determine whether individual trials are reliable. **Split-half reliability** indicates that subjects' scores on some trials consistently match their scores on other trials. Typically we make this determination by computing each subject's summary score for the odd-numbered trials and correlating it with the scores for the even-numbered trials (thus balancing order effects). For example, if the questions on a college examination have split-half reliability, then subjects producing a low score on the odd questions should also obtain a low score on the even questions, and so on. Likewise, we might determine the split-half reliability of a series of reaction-time trials by correlating times from even- and odd-numbered trials. (In APA-style articles, both types of reliability are reported in the Methods section in the case of a pilot study or in the Results section when the actual data have been used.)

> *REMEMBER*   *Test-retest reliability* is the correlation between repeated test-ings, and *split-half reliability* is the correlation between different trials within a test.

Ascertaining Validity

There are several ways of providing evidence that a particular measurement procedure allows for valid inferences about a construct, variable, or behavior. One simple approach is face validity. **Face validity** is the extent to which a measurement procedure appears to measure what we seek to measure. This is a judgment made by researchers as one *very* limited way of arguing that they are using valid procedures. Thus, for example, a reaction-time task has face validity if it appears to measure the time taken by subjects to perform a mental operation. Similarly, an intelligence test has face validity if it appears to measure intelligence.

> *REMEMBER*   When we say that a procedure has *face validity,* we mean that it is valid because it looks valid.

In addition, we can use correlational procedures to bolster our confidence in the validity of a procedure. On the one hand, we may determine the convergent validity of our measurement procedure. **Convergent validity** is the extent to which the scores obtained from one procedure are positively correlated with scores obtained from another procedure that is already accepted as valid. For example, say we develop a new test for measuring job satisfaction. If the test is valid, then after giving the same subjects our test along with another accepted test, we should find a strong, positive correlation between the scores from the two tests. If so, we can argue that both procedures "converge" on and measure job satisfaction. On the other hand, **discriminant validity** is the extent to which the scores obtained from one procedure are *not* correlated with the scores from another procedure that measures other variables or constructs. Thus, we can argue that our job satisfaction test is valid if it does not correlate with accepted measures of personality or motivation. In this case we would argue that our procedure "discriminates" between what it is intended to measure and what it is not intended to measure.

> *REMEMBER*   We demonstrate *convergent validity* when our procedure corre-lates with other procedures that are valid. We demonstrate *discriminant validity* when our procedure does not correlate with other, unintended measures.

Even when two procedures correlate with each other, this does not necessarily mean that they reflect the behaviors that we think they do. Therefore, another approach for demonstrating validity is to correlate the scores from a procedure with an observable behavior. **Criterion validity** is the extent to which a procedure can distinguish between subjects on the basis of some behavior. There are two subtypes of criterion validity.

Concurrent validity is the extent to which a procedure correlates with the present behavior of subjects. For example, let's say our definition of job satisfaction is such that it should be negatively related to job absenteeism. Here, concurrent validity would be demonstrated if those workers who reported low satisfaction were actually absent more frequently than those reporting high job satisfaction.

The other type of criterion validity is predictive validity. **Predictive validity** is the extent to which a procedure allows accurate predictions about a subject's future behavior. We would determine the predictive validity of our job satisfaction test by testing subjects and predicting their future absenteeism. Then, we would later measure their actual absentee rates and determine the extent to which their actual scores are positively correlated with their predicted scores.

Not surprisingly, predictive validity is of paramount importance when we are creating selection tests. What *is* surprising is the fact that a measurement can lack construct, content, and even face validity but still have predictive (and concurrent) validity. Essentially, in such cases, the procedure does distinguish subjects' behavior, but we don't understand why. Consider, for example, that some clinical therapies are based on Freudian interview techniques even though many of the constructs proposed by Freud have been repudiated. Information gleaned from Freudian techniques may allow us to predict a subject's behavior and responsiveness to treatment, however, so these techniques have predictive validity.

> **REMEMBER** *Criterion validity* is the extent to which a procedure relates to a specific behavior, either distinguishing the behavior concurrently or predicting future behavior.

To remember the various approaches to reliability and validity, consult Table 9.2.

TABLE 9.2 Summary of Methods for Ascertaining Reliability and Validity

Reliability

Test-retest:	Each subject's test and retest scores are correlated positively.
Split-half:	Subjects' scores from half of the trials positively correlate with their scores from the other half of the trials.

Validity

Face:	Procedure appears valid.
Convergent:	Procedure correlates with other accepted measures.
Discriminant:	Procedure does not correlate with other unintended measures.
Criterion	
Concurrent:	procedure correlates with a present behavior.
Predictive:	procedure correlates with a future behavior.

ASKING SUBJECTS QUESTIONS THROUGH INTERVIEWS AND QUESTIONNAIRES

A common method of gathering data in a correlational design is to ask subjects self-report questions, using interviews and questionnaires. (The preceding procedures for ascertaining validity and reliability are especially common in the development of such questions.) In the following sections, we will examine the basics involved in creating questions and the issues we consider when presenting them to subjects. However, don't make the mistake of thinking that questionnaires and interviews are used solely within correlational designs, or that correlational designs employ only such techniques. As we have seen, self-reports are often used to measure the dependent variable in experiments or to serve as a manipulation check, and we can measure the predictor and criterion variables in a correlational design using any appropriate technique. Remember, there are no set rules for designing a study, so researchers often mix and match their procedures.

Selecting an Existing Test

Rather than creating your own questions, your first step should be to search the literature for existing questionnaires and tests. Typically, the term *questionnaire* implies that there are no correct or incorrect answers, while *test* implies that there are correct and incorrect answers or that, based on previous research, there are at least typical and atypical answers. In either case, the material may be administered by an interviewer who asks subjects the questions and records responses, or subjects may read the questions and record their own responses.

We can find many existing procedures by searching previous research or examining reference books that describe various psychological tests and questionnaires (e.g., Robinson, Shaver & Wrightsman, 1991). The advantage of using established procedures is that their reliability and validity have been established, so from the start, we know their appropriateness for measuring a specific variable. Thus, for example, we would find that some widely accepted questionnaires for measuring job satisfaction already exist, such as the "Job Descriptive Index" (Smith, Kendall & Hulin, 1969).

When selecting a questionnaire, remember that researchers distinguish between state and trait characteristics. As discussed in Chapter 5, a *state characteristic* is a temporary, changeable attribute that is influenced by situational factors. Conversely, a *trait characteristic* is stable over time and not easily influenced by situational factors. In the literature, you'll find many questionnaires that measure a specific state or trait characteristic.

Goals of Question Construction

If you choose to develop your own questions, recognize that a question is essentially a stimulus and that a subject's answer is his or her response. Therefore, you must exercise the same concerns when designing a question as when presenting an independent variable and measuring a dependent variable.

Validity   A question should have construct validity, reflecting the hypothetical construct as we define it. It should also have content validity, such that the "contents" of the question and the "contents" of the response actually and only reflect the variable or behavior we seek to measure. In addition, we consider the face validity of a question as well as its temporal validity, ecological validity, concurrent validity, and predictive validity.

Demand Characteristics   Take care to avoid questions that create demand characteristics, which may elicit certain responses because of reactivity, social desirability, or perceived experimenter expectancies. Realize that this goal may contradict the goal of having face validity. The problem is that the more obvious it is to a researcher that a question measures a particular variable, the more obvious it also is to subjects. Because this situation may increase demand characteristics, researchers sometimes sacrifice face validity by disguising questions or less directly measuring a behavior.

Sensitivity   Design questions that are sensitive to the subtle differences that exist between subjects. After all, we create a question to *discriminate* (i.e., differentiate) between subjects on the variable being measured. We assume that there are differences between subjects on the variable because, otherwise, why bother to measure it? Therefore, we seek questions that subjects will answer differently, to reflect such differences. We design a sensitive measure by asking precise questions and by avoiding questions that produce ceiling effects, floor effects, or any other restriction on the range of scores.

Reliability and Standardization   The way a question is asked and the way responses are scored should be consistent for all subjects so that we introduce no bias. Also recognize that subjects must interpret the meaning of a question and that we must interpret the meaning of their response. Be on guard for the possibility of misinterpretations that lead to inconsistency and error.

   As you know, a subject's score should reflect his or her "typical" response. However, a subject's response to a question may be atypical because of a question's unique wording or perspective, or because the subject experiences a momentary distraction, has not previously thought about the issue being addressed, misinterprets the question, or makes an error in responding. As usual, we increase reliability through multiple trials: We create a number of different questions designed to measure the same variable or behavior. By varying the wording, perspective, and choices that subjects may select from in answering the questions, we attempt to balance out the unique characteristics of each. We then produce a summary score for each subject, such as the subject's total number correct or mean score. This method provides a more reliable estimate of a subject's typical response to such items. Computing a summary score from many questions also increases sensitivity, because the summary scores will tend to span a wide range of scores and will allow us to discriminate between subjects more clearly.

   REMEMBER   The goal of questionnaire construction is to reliably and validly discriminate between subjects on the variable of interest.

With such goals in mind, our first step is to consider the type of questions we will ask.

Using Closed-End Versus Open-End Questions

In a **closed-end question,** the researcher provides alternatives from which the subject must select when responding. Multiple-choice, true-false, yes-no, and rating scale questions are closed-end questions. Some closed-end questions that might be used to measure aspects of job satisfaction are:

(a) At work, my favorite activity is
    1. working with my hands.
    2. solving mental problems.
    3. supervising others.
    4. completing paperwork.

(b) At work I become angry
    1. never.
    2. once in a while.
    3. frequently.
    4. most of the time.

(c) Select the words that describe your co-workers:
    — stimulating
    — stupid
    — helpful
    — boring

(d) On most days, do you look forward to going to work?
    1. yes
    2. no

Closed-end questions are often referred to as "objective" questions, and this is their overwhelming strength: A response can be assigned a score objectively and reliably, with no subjective interpretation or error. For the first two questions above, when subjects select choice 1, we can directly assign them a score of 1 on that question. Thus, we can reliably assign the same score to all subjects who gave the same response of "working with my hands" or "never angry." Likewise, we can consistently score the way subjects describe co-workers and whether they look forward to going to work.

The disadvantage of closed-end questions is that they may yield limited information. Since we can measure subjects only on the variable(s) we have selected, we may miss other relevant variables. In question (b) above, we ask subjects about their anger at work, but subjects may feel that happiness is the relevant emotion. And within each question, subjects can select only from the choices provided, even if they would like to give a different response. In question (a) above, perhaps a worker's favorite activity is socializing with friends. For these reasons, we may miss measuring important responses and variables. Typically, therefore, closed-end questions are used when reliability is a major concern but we are not interested in discovering new variables that may be relevant.

Conversely, in an **open-end question,** the subject determines both the alternatives to choose from and the response. Any question equivalent to an essay question, whether written or oral, is open-ended. Thus, we might ask the open-end questions "Describe your favorite activities at work" and "How often do you become angry at work?"

Open-end questions may also be projective. In **projective tests,** the researcher asks subjects to create a description or interpretation of an ambiguous stimulus. This approach is used when subjects may not be conscious of their attitudes or feelings, or when social desirability is likely to prevent them from explicitly revealing them. Instead, subjects will "project" their feelings into the ambiguous situation. Two classic examples of projective tests are the *Rorschach test,* in which subjects interpret ambiguous inkblots (e.g., Exner, 1974), and the *Thematic Apperception Test,* in which subjects interpret ambiguous pictures (e.g., McClelland, 1961).

The advantages and disadvantages of open-end questions are the opposite of those of closed-end questions. The advantages of open-end questions are that they allow subjects to provide a wide range of detailed responses and permit researchers to potentially discover many relevant attitudes, experiences, or behaviors. Such questions also allow subjects to respond in their own words, so they are not limited to just the one perspective or phrasing that is present in a closed-end question. The disadvantage of open-end questions, however, is that assigning a score to a subject's responses requires subjective interpretation by the researcher, so scoring may not be reliable or valid. Two subjects who should be given the same score because their attitude or behavior is the same may be given different scores because of differences in the wording of their responses or in our interpretations of them. (How would you score the responses "The paperwork is easy" versus "The paperwork is very easy"?) Further, the scoring of open-end questions is highly susceptible to experimenter biases and expectations.

As usual, we counteract problems of subjective scoring by using double blinds and multiple scorers who demonstrate high inter-rater reliability (as discussed in Chapter 6). The crucial components, however, are our scoring criteria. Researchers structure the scoring of open-end questions by using a technique called content analysis. In **content analysis,** we score a subject's written or spoken answer by counting certain types of responses. For example, we may assign a score based on the number of times a certain word, a certain feeling, or a particular perspective occurs in a subject's response. Thus, a subject's score might be the number of positive references made to paperwork, regardless of whether the word *very* occurs. (See Holsti, 1969, or Krippendorf, 1980, for further information on content analysis.)

Even with strict scoring criteria, open-end questions tend to provide less reliable and objective data, so they are used less frequently in psychological research. They are most appropriate when reliability is not a major concern and is outweighed by a need to obtain responses in a subject's own words. In particular, open-end questions are used when we are beginning research into some unexplored behavior so that we can identify relevant variables, or when each subject's response is likely to be unique.

Of course, in any questionnaire we may employ both open- and closed-end questions. A mixture of the two has the advantage of providing both some reliable questions that are narrow in scope and some less reliable but wider-ranging questions.

Using Interviews Versus Questionnaires

We must also decide whether to use an interviewer to ask the questions or simply to provide subjects with a questionnaire to complete. The advantage of interviewers is that they ensure that subjects complete the questions as instructed. In addition, an interviewer can react to the information provided by a subject, either requesting clarifying information so a response can be reliably scored or exploring additional, unanticipated topics brought up by the subject. The drawback to interviewers, however, is that their presence and actions can greatly bias a subject's responses. An interviewer may inadvertently heighten the demand characteristics of reactivity and social desirability, or communicate expectancies about the desired response.

This drawback of interviewers is precisely the advantage of questionnaires; that is, the interaction between the researcher and subject is minimal. Thus, there is less risk of biasing subjects with experimenter expectations. Likewise reactivity and social desirability may be reduced, because completing a questionnaire anonymously can be much less threatening than talking to another person. Questionnaires also provide more efficient data collection, because many subjects can be tested at one time. The main disadvantages of questionnaires, however, are that subjects may not complete them as instructed and the information we obtain is necessarily limited to the questions we have created.

The decision to involve an interviewer, however, is not all-or-nothing. We can ensure that subjects complete the questions as instructed, but with a minimum of interviewer bias, by conducting a structured interview. In a **structured interview,** we ask subjects a specific set of predetermined questions in a controlled manner. The most structured interview is one with closed-end questions. Here, the interviewer simply reads a questionnaire to subjects and mechanically records their responses. This approach is common, for example, when testing young children or other subjects who are unable to satisfactorily complete a written questionnaire themselves.

If we want to place fewer restrictions on subjects' responses by asking open-end questions, we can structure the interview in such a way that subjects are asked the same specific questions, with a minimum of extraneous discussion on the part of the interviewer. (This approach is commonly used in intelligence tests.) Although interviewer biases are potentially always present, we can use a script for the interview to ensure that all subjects are asked the same questions in a reasonably consistent, unbiasing fashion.

The more structured the interview, the less we can explore issues that subjects might otherwise bring up. To avoid this limitation, we may conduct an unstructured interview. In an **unstructured interview,** the researcher has a general idea of the open-end questions that will be asked, but there is substantial discussion and interaction between subject and interviewer. Such interviews are commonly used when a researcher begins to study a behavior and wishes to discuss with subjects the many variables that may be related to it. Unstructured interviews are also used when the researcher wants to develop a complete, personalized description of an individual, such as during a clinical diagnosis. The lack of structure allows us to explore a wide range of issues raised by subjects, but the trade-off is that we lose some consistency and reliability between subjects, and the interviewer must be careful not to lead subjects into saying things they do not mean. (To increase the reliability of interviews, we can use a double-blind procedure and/or record the interviews and score them with multiple raters.)

REMEMBER   Interviews are preferred when the researcher must be present to oversee or react to subjects' responses, but questionnaires are more reliable and less susceptible to demand characteristics.

CONSTRUCTING QUESTIONS

The principles for creating open- or closed-end questions in interviews and question-naires are largely the same. Above all, our goal is to minimize the extent to which subjects must provide their own interpretations. The question "Are you satisfied with your job?" is open to subjects' interpretation of what we mean by job satisfaction. Instead, we focus on asking subjects to report specific *behaviors*. If job satisfaction is related to feeling monetarily rewarded by the job, then we ask subjects to indicate the degree or frequency they feel rewarded. Essentially, subjects report identifiable behaviors and the researcher interprets and translates the behaviors into psychological variables and constructs.

When generating questions, try to identify many examples and perspectives that reflect a variable. Begin with a long list and then select those questions that are best suited to your purposes. The elimination process is based on the following criteria.

Wording Questions

The vocabulary and sentence structure of each question must be understood by all subjects, so do not use psychological jargon or slang. The wording should also be clear and unambiguous: Always ask precisely what you mean to ask. Most importantly, word each question so that you are confident you know what subjects are communicating by their response and so that you can discriminate between different subjects. To succeed at this endeavor, you should avoid certain types of questions.

First, avoid **double-barreled questions.** These are questions that have more than one component. Consider the question "Should you be given more flexibility and less supervision on your job?" What if a subject agrees to one part but not the other? The meaning of any response here will not be clear, so you should ask two separate questions instead. Phrase any question so that it states just one idea to which subjects can respond, avoiding the use of such words as *or, and,* or *but.*

Second, avoid **leading questions.** These are questions that are so loaded with social desirability or experimenter expectancies that there is only one obvious response. Consider the question "Should very bad workers who are always late receive low pay?" You'd be unable to discriminate between subjects with this question, because everyone knows what the correct answer "should be." Such a built-in response bias not only prevents you from measuring the intended variable but also restricts the range. Phrase a question in a neutral manner, avoiding biased and inflammatory statements.

Third, avoid **Barnum statements.** These are questions that are so global and vague that everyone would agree with them or select the same response for them. (They are named after P. T Barnum, the showman who was famous for such statements.) For example, asking "Do you sometimes worry?" or "Have you had difficulty in some college courses?" will elicit the same answer from virtually every subject. This is the problem with horoscopes and palm readings that claim to be "individualized": The descriptions are so general that people can always think of personal situations or feelings that seem to fit.

Finally, avoid questions that contain **undefined terms.** For example, asking "Should workers who are always late receive low pay?" will leave you wondering how subjects interpret "always" and "low pay." Instead, either define such terms for subjects, or have the subjects provide the definition in their response. Thus, you might ask "What pay should a worker receive who is late for work an average of twice a week?" This version defines what you mean by "always late" and allows subjects to define "low pay" in their response.

> *REMEMBER*   A question should be a clear, precise, and unbiased statement of one idea, to which different subjects are likely to respond differently.

Creating the Responses for Closed-End Questions

The above guidelines also apply to the wording of the response choices we provide for closed-end questions. The choices should be precise and unbiased, should convey one idea each, and should be mutually exclusive. The wording of the responses should be appropriate to the wording of the question (don't phrase a question implying a "yes" or "no" response and then provide four choices). Also, subjects should not have to fill in a missing link to get from the question to the responses. If, for example, you mean to ask subjects about their hourly pay, then in either the question or the choices you must explicitly indicate an *hourly* pay rate.

> *REMEMBER*   Response alternatives should be constructed to maximize your confidence that you know what subjects wish to communicate when they select a particular response.

You must also determine the **response scale,** the number and type of choices you provide for each question. This is a very important decision, because it determines both the manner in which you will score subjects on their answers and the sensitivity of your measurement procedure.

For example, you may choose to ask yes-no (or true-false) questions, such as "Do you deserve a raise in hourly pay for the job you perform?" Then you can assign subjects a score of 1 for "yes" and a score of 2 for "no" (or arbitrarily pick any other two numbers). However, with only two scores, you cannot finely discriminate between subjects: You'd be glossing over differences between those subjects who firmly believe a statement is true and those who think it is somewhat or sometimes true. Also, if you are scoring a test for correct answers, subjects' apparent performance may actually be the result of lucky guesses. (After all, the reasons many students prefer true-false questions on exams is that they have a good chance of correctly guessing answers, and those who know only the basics cannot be discriminated from those who know more.)

We alleviate problems of restricted range and guessing by increasing the number of response choices. Multiple-choice questions are most appropriate for measuring factual information or discrete responses. For example, by employing a multiple-choice format with four choices, we can obtain finer discrimination between subjects. Thus, we might ask:

> Do you deserve a raise in hourly pay for the job you perform?
> 1. No
> 2. Yes, a $1 raise
> 3. Yes, a $2 raise
> 4. Yes, more than a $2 raise

Now that we have four choices, we can discriminate among four categories of subjects based on their response. But notice that the fourth choice does not allow us to distinguish between those who seek a $3 raise and those who seek a $4 or $5 raise. To obtain finer discriminations, we can provide additional choices specifying these amounts.

When measuring subjective responses that fall along a continuum, we often employ *Likert-type questions.* These usually consist of a declarative statement accompanied by a rating scale. Most often, the scale is "anchored" at each end by the words *agree* and *disagree.* Thus, we might ask:

> My hourly salary is sufficient for me.
>
>   1   2   3   4   5
> Strongly   Strongly
> agree   disagree

We can also change the wording of the question to measure other experiences and attitudes, using such anchors as *seldom-frequently* or *like-dislike.*

Notice that the above example reflects three decisions we must make. First, by placing the word *strongly* at both anchors, we imply rather extreme feelings. But because of social desirability, subjects may be less likely to select the extreme positions, so our range may be limited to the center scores of 2, 3, and 4. Had we labeled the anchors with only *agree-disagree,* we would have implied less extreme feelings and thus would be more likely to get a wider range of scores. In that case, however, we would be leaving the definition of the anchors to our subjects, so we'd have less confidence in how strongly subjects felt when choosing a 1 or 5. The way we resolve this issue depends on how threatening the question is that we are asking. Usually we clearly define the anchors and attempt to minimize demand characteristics by our wording of the declarative statement being rated.

Second, the above rating scale allows us to discriminate between only five levels of agreement. When greater sensitivity is needed, we can expand the scale to include more alternatives. (We do not allow subjects to place responses between the points on the scale, because of the great difficulty involved in reliably assigning subjects a fractional score.) How large a scale we select depends on subjects' ability to actually differentiate their feelings. On a scale that ranges from 1 to 20, for instance, subjects probably cannot distinguish between a score of 17 and one of 18. Instead, they are likely to respond unreliably, haphazardly guessing between the two. Then our interpretation of what a 17 or 18 indicates is in error. Selecting this aspect of a scale also depends on the particular question, but we usually employ scales consisting of between 5 and 7 points.

Finally, note that with five, seven, or any odd number of choices, there is one neutral "middle of the road" choice. Here again we must consider demand characteristics. The more threatening an issue, the more likely it is that subjects will play it safe and choose the midpoint. In doing so, however, they defeat our primary purpose of discriminating between subjects. The solution in such cases is to use an even number of choices. With six alternatives, for example, there is no middle ground, so subjects must commit one way or the other. In general, we use an odd-numbered scale when we assume that subjects can be legitimately neutral on an issue, and we use an even-numbered scale to counter strong demand characteristics or to force subjects to take a stand.

> **REMEMBER**   A rating scale should be anchored so that it does not bias subjects, does not contain choices that subjects cannot distinguish between, and does not gloss over differences between subjects.

CONDUCTING QUESTIONNAIRE AND INTERVIEW RESEARCH

Once we have identified the basic questions to ask, we often can generate multiple questions merely by changing the wording and perspective. For example, to measure how interesting workers find their job, we can ask them to rate their agreement with the statement "My job is interesting" and with the statement "My job is boring." We can also have them rate the frequency with which they find that "My mind wanders when performing my job," and "Performing my job is mentally stimulating." Likewise, we may include multiple questions that measure subjects' satisfaction with their specific work tasks, with their supervisor, and so on.

In creating the final questionnaire, test, or structured interview that subjects will respond to, we must consider all of the components necessary for completing the study.

Scoring and Analyzing the Data

First, we must give some thought to how we will score each subject's responses. We create our scoring criteria to allow us to "code" responses so that they are comparable across related questions. To understand this procedure, consider the following two questions:

My job is interesting.	My job is boring.
1 2 3 4 5	1 2 3 4 5
Strongly agree Strongly disagree	Strongly agree Strongly disagree

By our definitions, strongly agreeing with "My job is interesting" is equivalent to strongly disagreeing with "My job is boring." Therefore, we can score a subject's response of 1 on the "boring" question as a 5, a 2 as a 4, and so on. On *both* questions, then, the higher the score, the more interesting the job. Likewise, with multiple-choice questions we score the choices so that each score reflects the same response (e.g., a 1 is assigned to any choice describing minimum job satisfaction). Of course, we must carefully examine our definitions and the questions we have created, to be sure that those responses we see as equivalent are also equivalent for subjects. One indication of this equivalence would be a strong correlation between two questions we think are equivalent.

We must also plan the statistical techniques we will use to analyze the data. For the Likert-type questions above, we can summarize each subject's responses by computing a mean rating per subject; for a test, we can sum the total number of correct responses; and for multiple-choice or open-end questions, we can count the frequency of certain responses. We then combine such scores to summarize a sample. If we are testing different samples or conditions of an experiment, we can perform t-tests, ANOVA, and the like to identify significant differences between the groups. Instead, we can correlate a subject's summary score on a questionnaire with a score measured by another questionnaire or by some other procedure. If our questionnaire measures several variables, we can correlate the subjects' scores on these "subtests." And when testing different samples or conditions of an experiment, we can determine whether the correlations for the groups differ significantly.

Dealing with Order Effects

By employing multiple questions, we again face the problem of *order effects*. Subjects beginning a questionnaire or interview may find the style and content of the questions to be novel, or they may show great reactivity. Then, after more questions, they may become habituated or fatigued and bored. In addition, at any point subjects may be biased by earlier questions, or they may develop response sets. We have several techniques for dealing with order effects, which may be used singly or in combination, depending on the nature of the questions we are asking.

1. *Using funnel questions:* **Funnel questions** are general questions that lead to more specific questions. Just as a funnel opens large and then narrows, we order questions from the general to the specific. Often we use an initial open-end funnel question that is followed by more specific, closed-end questions. In this way, we create a "block" of questions that all pertain to the same issue. This order introduces subjects to a topic and gets them thinking about it, so that they can establish their feelings before they can be biased by the specific choices provided in subsequent closed-end questions. Thus, for example, we might first ask subjects to describe their general satisfaction with their pay, and then follow up with specific multiple choice or Likert-type questions.

2. *Using filter questions:* **Filter questions** are general questions that allow us to determine whether subjects should be asked more detailed questions. Thus, for example, we might ask a worker whether he or she has experienced sexual harassment on the job. If the answer is "no," the interviewer would not ask detailed follow-up questions about harassment. (Similarly, on a questionnaire the subject would be instructed to skip the following section.) In this way we "filter out" those subjects who would be needlessly fatigued, annoyed, or biased by answering a number of subsequent, irrelevant questions. In addition, we can more easily and clearly phrase the follow-up questions, because they will be directed only at those subjects who have experienced harassment.

3. *Providing practice questions:* By providing *practice questions* prior to presenting our actual questions of interest, we allow subjects to warm up to our questions and to habituate to their content, without contaminating our data.

4. *Counterbalancing order effects:* We counterbalance order effects by creating different orders of the questions or blocks of questions, so that, for example, those questions that appear early in some questionnaires appear later in others, and vice versa. Then, when we collapse the scores from subjects completing the different versions, the total sample will not be biased by one unique order of questions.

Sometimes we may have subjects complete two questionnaires that may produce order effects between them. In such cases, we also counterbalance the order of questionnaires between subjects. However, *nonsymmetrical carry-over effects* may occur, so that counterbalancing will be ineffective. For example, Council (1993) found such carry-over effects in a study designed to correlate traumatic childhood experiences with psychopathology. When the trauma test was completed first, there was a positive correlation. When the psychopathology test was completed first, there was no correlation. One possible solution here would be to intermix the questions from the tests and present subjects one large questionnaire. Then their responses could be separated after the fact.

5. *Preventing response sets:* A *response set*—a habit of responding in a certain way—can easily develop over repeated questioning, especially with closed-end questions. If, for example, initial multiple-choice questions consistently call for choice 1, subjects may superstitiously select choice 1 for subsequent questions. Or if subjects strongly agreed on the initial Likert-type questions, they may subsequently select this option automatically. To prevent such rote responding, we try to force subjects to read and think about each question by varying the question format. Thus, in multiple-choice questions, we randomly vary which choice is correct. In Likert-type questions, we present both positive and negative statements to be rated, and we vary the scale by mixing *agree-disagree* with *frequently-infrequently,* and so on. And we may intermix multiple-choice with Likert-type questions.

Note, however, that we do not drastically change the format from question to question. Rather, we generally present a block of one type of question (containing, say, 10 questions) before changing to a different format for the next block of questions. In this way, we avoid confusing subjects and increasing their errors, while still minimizing the development of response sets.

6. *Using alternate forms:* **Alternate forms** are different versions of the same questionnaire. Here we change the order, wording, and perspective of questions so that the questionnaires appear to be different, yet still measure the same variables. Alternate forms are necessary for dealing with order and carry-over effects when the design involves repeated measures, as in a pretest-posttest design. If, for example, we were to measure workers' job satisfaction immediately before and after giving them a raise, we would not use the identical questionnaire both times. If we were to do so, subjects might duplicate their previous responses on the second testing in order to appear consistent. Or they might intentionally change their responses to conform to perceived experimenter expectations. Ideally, the alternate forms will hide the similarity of subjects' past and present responses so that they honestly answer the second version.

Of course, alternate forms involve questionnaires that *differ* from each other, so we must take care to ensure that they are comparable in terms of validity and reliability.

Creating Catch Trials

A problem with any questionnaire is that subjects may not follow instructions when completing it. Some subjects may give no thought to the questions and select answers randomly, just so they can be done with it. Other subjects may be untruthful, responding solely to demand characteristics. Still other subjects may make errors when responding. We can incorporate specific questions to "catch" such subjects.

To identify subjects who may be answering questions randomly, we can include a specific question several times throughout the questionnaire, but reorder the choices. Consider these examples:

When working I prefer to be	When working I prefer to be
1. left alone.	1. supervised occasionally.
2. supervised occasionally.	2. supervised frequently.
3. supervised frequently.	3. left alone.

A subject's preference should be the same on both questions. Any subject who fails to give a consistent response is either randomly completing questions or erroneously recording responses.

To identify subjects who may be responding to demand characteristics, we can create questions for which we know the truthful response. Say that we are questioning teenagers about the extent of their drug use, but we are concerned that peer pressure may cause some subjects to overstate their drug involvement. To identify these subjects we might ask the following:

> I have taken the pill known as a "watermelon"
> 1. never.
> 2. between 1 and 5 times.
> 3. between 5 and 10 times.
> 4. more than 10 times.

There is no pill known as a watermelon. All subjects should select response 1, unless they are untruthful or made an error when recording their response.

With such questions, we can estimate the frequency with which subjects were untruthful or made errors when responding to other questions. Also, we can identify subjects who meet our operational definition of not following instructions and then eliminate their data from our analysis.

Pilot Studies

Pilot studies are extremely valuable when developing questionnaires and interviews. Instead of having pilot subjects complete our questions, we ask them questions about our questions to confirm any assumptions we might have. We ask subjects to interpret our questions to be sure they convey our intended meaning. We ask whether the range of a rating scale is appropriate for differentiating their feelings. We have subjects rate how well the response scale fits the nature and wording of the question, or have them rate the degree of demand characteristics present. And we ask whether the questions that we see as equivalent are also equivalent for them. Based on their responses, we alter problem questions and conduct additional pilot studies until we are confident that we have constructed the desired questions.

We can also test pilot subjects to determine whether a questionnaire has convergent or discriminant validity compared with other questionnaires, or to determine criterion validity by correlating scores with a present or future behavior. Likewise, we can determine whether alternate forms of a questionnaire have comparable reliability and validity. For example, we can ask subjects to complete each separate version in a test-retest procedure, or to complete a combined version that we then separate in a split-half procedure. Either way, subjects' scores from the two forms should produce a high, positive correlation. In addition, both forms should show high convergent and criterion validity with other measures.

Administering the Questionnaire or Interview

Administering a questionnaire or interview requires the same controls that are found in experiments. You should limit or balance subject variables and control the environment so that there are no extraneous distractions. You should avoid complicated and tiring questions so that subjects do not make errors in responding. You should always provide unbiased instructions for completing the questions (even if they seem self-explanatory). And, finally, you should keep the behaviors of the researcher neutral and consistent.

To minimize demand characteristics, first be careful when creating a title for your questionnaire. Ask yourself, Is a title really neccesary? Does it bias subjects? (Think about how you would respond to a questionnaire titled "Survey of Deviant Sexual Fantasies." What if it were titled "Survey of Common Sexual Fantasies"?) Second, consider whether deception is needed, in the form of "filler" or "distracter" questions. These are not scored, but they alter the overall appearance of the questionnaire and disguise its actual purpose. (For example, you might include filler questions about other, non-sexual fantasies to reduce reactivity to sexually oriented questions, and title the questionnaire "Survey of Common Fantasies.")

Ethical considerations are always important. A questionnaire or interview should not be unduly stressful for subjects, and, as with all research, your procedure should be approved by your institution's Human Subjects Review Committee. Subjects' responses must always be kept confidential, and care should be taken to alleviate their fears about what the questions will divulge about them or what the data will be used for. As always, you must obtain explicit informed consent: The fact that a subject completes a questionnaire or interview is *not* informed consent, because subjects may feel coerced in the same way they might during an experiment. Upon completion of testing, be sure to provide a debriefing.

Finally, remember that you are obtaining subjects' self-reports about their behaviors or feelings, instead of directly observing them. Even with all of the above controls, there is always room for skepticism about whether subjects' responses actually reflect the variables we are attempting to measure.

To help you remember the various considerations when constructing questions, Table 9.3 presents a summary of the above discussions.

TABLE 9.3   Checklist for Question Construction

- Closed- versus open-end questions
  - Reliability and objective scoring
  - Breadth of information needed
- Interview versus questionnaire format
  - Demand characteristics
  - Need for structure
  - Breadth of information needed
- Wording of questions
  - Double-barreled questions
  - Leading questions
  - Barnum statements
  - Undefined terms
- Response scale
  - Sensitivity
  - Likert scales
    - Anchors
    - Range of scale
    - Odd/even number of points
- Administering questions
  - Funnel and filter questions
  - Order effects
  - Response sets
  - Alternate forms
  - Catch trials
  - Instructions and informed consent
  - Pilot study
  - Determining reliability and validity using correlations

ADVANCED CORRELATIONAL PROCEDURES

Advanced correlation and regression procedures are used when we examine relationships involving more than two variables. Although these procedures are appropriate regardless of how the variables are measured, they are frequently found in questionnaire and interview research. Four specific methods that you will commonly find in the literature are multiple correlation and regression, discriminant analysis, partial correlation, and factor analysis.

Multiple Correlation and Regression

Often, researchers discover more than one variable that predicts a behavior. For example, let's say that we can predict job satisfaction based on workers' pay rate, and that we can also predict job satisfaction based on workers' feelings toward their supervisor. If we want the most accurate prediction of job satisfaction, therefore, we should simultaneously consider *both* a worker's pay and his or her feelings toward a supervisor. **Multiple correlation** and **multiple regression** are the appropriate procedures when we use *multiple* predictor (X) variables to predict one criterion (Y) variable. Conceptually, these procedures are similar to those discussed above. The multiple correlation coefficient, called the multiple R, indicates the strength of the relationship between the multiple predictors and the criterion variable. The multiple regression equation allows us to predict a subject's Y score by simultaneously considering the subject's scores on the X variables. And the squared multiple R is the proportion of variance in the Y variable accounted for by using the X variables to predict Y scores.

Discriminant Analysis

A variation of multiple correlation is used when the Y variable reflects *qualitative* differences between subjects. This procedure is common in clinical research, for example, when we wish to use test scores to categorize subjects who are schizophrenic versus borderline personality versus paranoid, and so on. **Discriminant analysis** allows us to categorize subjects along a qualitative Y variable using several quantitative predictor (X) variables. Simultaneously the procedure calculates what are essentially selection criteria or "cutoff" scores. Subjects whose combined scores fall below a cutoff score are categorized in group A of the Y variable (e.g., as borderline personality). Those whose scores are above the cutoff score are classified in group B (e.g., as paranoid). And those with scores beyond a higher cutoff score are categorized in group C (e.g., schizophrenic). By using this technique, we can determine the best X variables and the best cutoff scores for maximally separating or "discriminating" between subjects so that there is a minimum of overlap or similarity between the groups.

Partial Correlation

Sometimes instead of employing multiple predictors, we take the opposite approach: We wish to examine the relationship between one X variable and the Y variable, without including other X variables. For example, say we wish to examine the relationship between job satisfaction and pay rate. However, this relationship may be tinged by subjects' feelings toward their supervisor. Essentially, there may be an *interaction,* such that the relationship between workers' pay and job satisfaction *depends* on their feelings toward their supervisor. The ideal would be to find workers who all feel the same way toward their supervisor, so that, with this variable constant, we can examine just the relationship between job satisfaction and pay rate. Unfortunately, it may be impossible to keep such an extraneous variable constant in the real world. It *is* possible mathematically, however, to keep its influence constant. A **partial correlation** indicates the correlation between two variables while keeping the influence of other variables constant. Essentially, this procedure removes the correlation between subjects' job satisfaction and their feelings toward their supervisor from the data. What are left are only the differences in job satisfaction that are correlated with pay rate.

Factor Analysis

So far, our approach has been to begin with a specific hypothesized relationship and then to create questions to test whether two or more variables are related. A more exploratory approach, however, is to create a variety of questions that address many aspects of a general behavior, and then to determine which are correlated. From such relationships, we attempt to identify the common, underlying component that they measure. The statistical procedure used in this process is called factor analysis. In **factor analysis** we use the intercorrelations between responses to discover the common aspect or component they reflect.

For example, in a general questionnaire about the workplace, say we find that a question about being absent from work is positively correlated with a question about taking long lunches: Subjects who are frequently absent also tend to frequently take long lunches. Both questions appear to tap the same underlying attitude about work—call it the "dedication" factor. At the same time, say that these two questions are not correlated with questions about the importance of friendly co-workers or the time spent in casual conversation, but that these latter questions are highly correlated with each other. These questions appear to tap another aspect of the workplace—call this one the "sociability" factor. Likewise, we may find an "ambition" factor, because questions about how hard subjects work, how much they desire promotion, and how much they seek added responsibility are found to be correlated. From such results, the factors of dedication, sociability, and ambition become the constructs of interest when we describe workers. Further, these factors may then be related to other behaviors, such as workers' overall job satisfaction.

> **REMEMBER**   *Multiple correlation, discriminant analysis, partial correlation,* and *factor analysis* are used when we examine relationships involving several variables.

PUTTING IT ALL TOGETHER

In this chapter, we discussed a number of complex issues that arise when creating questionnaires, as well as several fancy statistical procedures that may be used in correlational research. Regardless of how elaborate it is, however, remember that a correlational study cannot be used to infer the causal variable in a relationship. Recall that even with all of the controls employed in an experiment, you must be cautious in inferring causality because there may be a hidden confounding. In a correlational design with no random assignment, there is almost certain to be a confounding. Therefore, always be on guard for identifying this approach. In the newspaper, for example, you may read about teenagers who committed suicide after listening to a particular rock and roll album, or about serial killers who were abused as children. If you think about it, these statements involve a correlational approach, because the "subjects" were not randomly assigned to the levels of either variable. Therefore, the apparent causal variable is confounded with other potential causes. The apparent cause may be the actual cause (we're open-minded, remember), but such reports do not indicate this.

CHAPTER SUMMARY

1. In a *correlational design,* the researcher measures subjects' scores on two or more variables to observe a relationship. We cannot infer causality with such a design because subjects are not randomly assigned to the levels of a variable, and which variable occurred first is unknown.

2. The *Pearson correlation coefficient* is the parametric procedure we employ when the X and Y scores are normally distributed and measured using either an interval or ratio scale. The *Spearman correlation coefficient* is the nonparametric procedure we employ when both variables are measured using an ordinal scale.

3. *Linear regression* is the procedure we use for predicting subjects' scores on one variable based on the linear relationship with subjects' scores on another variable. The *linear regression equation* is used to predict a Y score, called Y *prime* (Y'), for a particular X. The *linear regression line* summarizes a linear relationship, with the values of Y prime falling on the line.

4. The *standard error of the estimate* communicates the amount by which the Y scores in a sample differ from the corresponding predicted Y scores. The *squared correlation coefficient* is the proportion of total variance in Y scores that is accounted for by the relationship with X.

5. We maximize the size and power of a correlation coefficient by minimizing error variance, avoiding restricted range, testing a large N, and using parametric, linear procedures when appropriate.

6. *Test-retest reliability* indicates that subjects tend to obtain the same overall score when repeatedly tested at different times. *Split-half reliability* indicates that subjects' scores on some trials consistently match their scores on other trials.

7. *Face validity* is the extent to which a procedure appears to be valid. *Convergent validity* is the extent to which a procedure is correlated with other procedures that are already accepted as valid. *Discriminant validity* is the extent to which a procedure is not correlated with procedures that measure other things.

8. *Criterion validity* is the extent to which the scores from a procedure correlate with an observable behavior. *Concurrent validity* is the extent to which a procedure correlates with the present behavior of subjects. *Predictive validity* is the extent to which a procedure accurately predicts a behavior.

9. The goal of psychological questions is to reliably and validly discriminate between subjects on the variable of interest.

10. With *closed-end questions,* subjects select from alternatives provided by the researcher. With *open-end questions,* subjects determine the alternatives to choose from.

11. With *projective tests,* subjects create a description or interpretation of an ambiguous stimulus, thus projecting their hidden feelings or attributes.

12. *Content analysis* is the procedure we use for scoring open-end questions by looking for specific words or themes.

13. In a *structured interview,* subjects are asked specific, predetermined questions. In an *unstructured interview,* the questions are less rigidly predetermined.

14. When creating questions we avoid (a) *double-barreled questions,* which have more than one component; (b) *leading questions,* which are biased so that there is only one obvious response; (c) *Barnum statements,* which are global truisms to which everyone responds in the same way; and (d) questions containing *undefined terms.*

15. A *response scale* is the number and type of choices provided for each question.

16. When using Likert-type questions, we consider whether the rating scale (a) has anchors that overly bias subjects, (b) contains choices that subjects can discriminate between, and (c) forces subjects to indicate a preference.

17. When asking subjects a series of questions, we must take care to eliminate order effects, especially those due to response sets.

18. *Funnel questions* are general questions that lead to more specific follow-up questions. *Filter questions* are general questions that allow us to determine whether subjects should be asked more detailed follow-up questions.

19. *Alternate forms* of a questionnaire contain differently worded questions that measure the same variables. They are especially important when testing in a repeated-measures design.

20. With *multiple regression* and *multiple correlation,* we predict subjects' scores on a Y variable by using their scores from multiple X variables. With *discriminant analysis,* we categorize subjects along a qualitative criterion variable using several predictor variables. With *partial correlation,* we determine the correlation between two variables while keeping the influence of other variables constant. And with *factor analysis,* we discover a common underlying factor by determining which questions are correlated.

REVIEW QUESTIONS

1. (a) What is the major difference between a correlational design and an experimental design? (b) What is the usual purpose of each?

2. (a) How do we decide which variable to call X in a correlation? (b) What other names are given to the X and Y variables?

3. (a) When do we compute a Pearson correlation coefficient? (b) When do we compute a Spearman coefficient?

4. (a) Why do we perform linear regression? (b) What is Y'? (c) What does the standard error of the estimate indicate?

5. (a) Conceptually, why is the proportion of variance accounted for equal to 1.0 with a perfect correlation? (b) Why is it 0 when there is no relationship? (c) Why don't we compute r^2 when the correlation is not significant?

6. A student complains that it is unfair to use scores from the Scholastic Aptitude Test (SAT) to determine college admittance because she might do much better in college than predicted. (a) What statistic(s) will indicate whether her complaint is correct? (b) What concern about the test's validity is she actually addressing?

7. A researcher measures both how loudly students play music when studying and their exam grades. She tests a very large N, obtaining a significant r of $+.10$. She concludes that playing loud music has a dramatic impact on exam grades. What two errors has she made?

8. A researcher uses mathematical ability to predict subjects' sense of humor. He measures creativity in terms of how funny a subject finds three puns to be. He tests 10 math majors and finds a nonsignificant r. (a) What characteristic of his subjects may account for this result? (b) What problem with his criterion variable may account for this result? (c) What other obvious improvement in power can he achieve?

9. In question 8, say that previous research has shown that people with very high or very low math skills tend to find puns humorous, but those with intermediate skills do not. How can this finding account for the nonsignificant r?

10. (a) What is the difference between test-retest reliability and split-half reliability? (b) Why would we prefer to show the split-half reliability instead of the test-retest reliability of a college exam?

11. (a) What is the difference between convergent and divergent validity? (b) How does criterion validity differ from the two previous types of validity? (c) What are the two types of criterion validity, and how is each determined?

12. (a) What are the advantages and disadvantages of open-end questions? (b) of closed-end questions?

13. For each of the following, indicate whether you should use a written questionnaire, a structured interview, or an unstructured interview: (a) when measuring the attitudes of first-graders, (b) when measuring the contents of people's day-dreams, (c) when measuring people's attitudes toward researchers.

14. I ask my students to rate their agreement with the following statements. What is wrong with the wording of each statement? (a) The material in this book is sometimes difficult. (b) I like reading this book, but I dislike the statistics. (c) A good student will like this book. (d) With this book I can get an acceptable grade.

15. A friend says that his reactions to inkblots couldn't possibly indicate anything about him. (a) What aspect of the test's validity is he reacting to? (b) Why is the test doing what it is intended to do?

16. On a personality test, the question "Do you prefer cooked carrots or raw carrots?" is asked several times. (a) Why might a researcher include the responses to this question when predicting someone's personality? (b) For what other reason(s) might the researcher ask this question?

17. (a) What are alternate forms? (b) What is our design concern about them? (c) When are they necessary?

18. As you read a research article's abstract, what can you determine about the research when you see that (a) multiple correlation and regression procedures were performed, (b) a discriminant analysis was performed, (c) a partial correlation was performed?

19. From a factor analysis of a personality questionnaire, a researcher identifies the factors of sociability, extroversion, and depression as constituting personality. How were these factors identified?

DISCUSSION QUESTIONS

1. You wish to examine how well people do on a test of problem solving ability as a function of how anxious they are. (a) Why and how would you conduct this as an experiment? (b) Why and how would you conduct this as a correlational design? (c) How would you analyze the relationship in each case?

2. The original research into smoking and lung cancer showed that people who smoked more often also developed lung cancer more often. (a) Tobacco companies deny that this finding is evidence that smoking causes cancer. Are they correct? (b) This finding has been replicated numerous times in human studies, and other research shows that white rats exposed to cigarette smoke develop lung cancer. Are tobacco companies still correct in disputing the above claim?

3. A student complains that a college exam was unfair because it contained some questions that only a few students answered correctly. How would a researcher justify the inclusion of such questions?

4. Research has found that people from certain races score an average of as much as 15 points lower on standard intelligence tests than do people from other races. This finding has been used as evidence that some races are inherently less intelligent than others. (a) What considerations would cause you to qualify such a conclusion? (b) What would you say to those people who dismiss this conclusion as blatant racism? (c) What are the ethical issues involved in disseminating these findings to the general public?

10

Field Experiments, Animal Research, and Single-Subject Designs

In addition to correlational studies, psychological research involves other designs that are different from the standard laboratory study with groups of human subjects. Sometimes an experiment is conducted outside of a laboratory, sometimes the research does not involve human subjects, and sometimes we study only one subject. In the present chapter, we examine these three common alternatives: field experiments, animal research, and single-subject designs.

FIELD EXPERIMENTS

Throughout this book, we have seen that controlled laboratory experiments provide the greatest *internal validity*: At the conclusion of such experiments we are confident that we know what occurred within them, so we can confidently conclude that changes in the independent variable caused changes in the dependent variable. Yet, although laboratory experiments increase internal validity, they simultaneously limit *external validity*, the extent to which findings generalize to other subjects or settings.

The problem is that a laboratory setting is not a slice of real life. The situation is artificial because subjects know they are being studied—and, of course, a researcher is present who does not behave the way people in real life behave. Therefore, we are faced with the problems discussed in previous chapters. The results may suffer from reduced *experimental realism*, because subjects cannot forget they are involved in a study and thus cannot be totally engaged by the task. The results may be biased by *demand characteristics* such as *experimenter effects* and subjects' *reactivity* to being observed. The results may lack *ecological validity* because we observe what subjects can do and not necessarily what they typically do. And our subjects may be unrepresentative because of *volunteer bias, mortality effects*, and a *limited population*. The bottom line is that the results of a laboratory experiment may be peculiar to our procedure, such that the observed relationship is found only in a literal replication of our experiment with a very similar situation and very similar subjects.

Sometimes this is an acceptable state of affairs. In cases where our hypothesis involves basic research into hypothetical constructs and basic behaviors, we are usually most concerned with internal validity and so conduct a laboratory experiment. When studying mental tasks, for example, we conduct reaction-time experiments under laboratory conditions, because we are concerned with a basic component of cognitive processing rather than with the way in which the mental tasks translate into everyday behaviors.

As you know, however, it is the conflict between the goals of internal and external validity that often influences the design decisions a researcher makes. When we seek greater external validity, we leave the laboratory and conduct the study in the real world. In doing so, we are conducting what is collectively called field research. More specifically, when we seek to demonstrate a causal relationship, we perform a field experiment. A **field experiment** is an experiment conducted in a natural setting. Field experiments are common when the research is more applied or seeks to examine complex behaviors that occur in a natural setting. The setting may be a factory, a school, a shopping mall, a street corner, or any place in which the behavior can be studied. There are four advantages to conducting field experiments.

1. We can make our observations in natural settings, so such studies generally have a high degree of external and ecological validity. Our findings should generalize to the real world because they are obtained in the real world.

2. We can take the experiment to the subjects, so the sample can be taken from either a select target population or from the general population.

3. We can observe behavior when subjects are psychologically engaged by a real situation, so we have greater experimental realism. This advantage may be especially important because, instead of relying on potentially unreliable self-reports of what subjects say they do, we can observe what they actually do.

4. We can go out into the real world and replicate laboratory studies to ensure the generality of their findings. After supposedly learning about a behavior in the lab, we go out and see whether it operates the way we think it does.

Note that a field experiment still incorporates the procedures of an experiment. As much as possible, we assign subjects to conditions randomly, systematically manipulate the conditions of an independent variable, control extraneous variables, and measure the dependent variable in a reliable, sensitive, and powerful manner. We analyze the results using *t*-tests, ANOVAs, or nonparametric procedures. If the results are significant, we examine the summary scores from each condition as well as the differences between them, and we consider the type and strength of the relationship observed. We then attempt to explain the psychological processes reflected by our results. Because we conduct an experiment, we have controls for making an internally valid argument that changes in the independent variable caused the dependent scores to change. Because we conduct the experiment in the field, we also have high external validity for concluding that our findings apply to common, realistic situations and actually reflect natural behaviors.

> **REMEMBER**   *Field experiments* are conducted to show a causal relationship in a natural setting.

Additional Sampling Techniques

In previous examples of experiments, we have relied on the random selection of subjects from the available pool, often consisting of college students. Given our emphasis on internal validity when conducting such research, however, we accept that our samples are not truly "random" because we are restricted to only those subjects we can solicit and bring to our laboratory. This "pseudo-randomness" may weaken our external validity, because we may be observing an unrepresentative sample, a sample whose characteristics do not reflect those found in the population. An unrepresentative sample is different from the population, leading us to make inaccurate estimates of the typical responses that would occur in the population.

There are additional sampling techniques, however, that we can use when select-ing a sample for *any* type of experimental, correlational, or descriptive design. These techniques are especially common in field research, because, by taking the study to the subjects, we can be more selective in defining our target population and/or we can potentially expand the size of the available population from which to draw subjects. Recognize, however, that although these procedures are described here in rather abstract, ideal terms, in practice they may be used individually or in combination, and may only somewhat serve their intended purpose. There are two general types of sampling techniques we can use: probability sampling and nonprobability sampling.

Probability Sampling Techniques   In **probability sampling**, every potential subject has an equal likelihood of being asked to participate. By giving every subject an equal chance, we allow each subject characteristic that occurs with a certain frequency in the population to occur with that same frequency in the sample. One form of probability sampling, discussed in Chapter 2, is *simple random sampling*, in which we randomly select subjects from a list of the population members. Another form we have seen is *systematic random sampling*, in which we select every *n*th subject from the population list.

Both simple and systematic random sampling rely on chance, so we may not contact all of the types of subjects in the population, especially those who constitute a small proportion of it. To ensure that the various subgroups of the population are represented in our study, we may also employ the technique called stratified sampling. In **stratified random sampling** we identify the important subgroups in the population and then randomly select subjects from each group. We select a proportion of our total N from each group so that we proportionally represent the important "strata" in the population. So, for example, if government records reveal that 70% of the target population is female, then we want 70% of our sample to be female. If our sample N is to be 100, then from the identified females we randomly select 70 females (and thus 30 males). If a subject declines to participate, we select another appropriate subject to replace her. We may also combine selection criteria—for example, by selecting a certain proportion of females from a specific race. Notice that by randomly selecting subjects from within a stratum, we also hope to balance out other unidentified subject variables, so that we have a representative sample in terms of all variables.

Sometimes it is too time consuming, expensive, or difficult to identify the individuals in a population so that we can then randomly select them. In such cases we might use an alternative sampling technique called cluster sampling. In **cluster sampling** we randomly select certain groups, or "clusters," and then observe all subjects in each. To study homeless people, for example, we can randomly select from areas in a city where homeless people are found and then study all the subjects we can locate in each area. Similarly, to study workers at a large factory, we can select departments randomly and study the workers in each. Since the clusters are randomly selected, we assume that there is no bias in our subject selection, so the sample should be reasonably representative.

> *REMEMBER*   Simple random sampling, systematic sampling, *stratified sampling,* and *cluster sampling* are *probability sampling* techniques that provide all subjects in the population an equal change of being selected.

Nonprobability Sampling Techniques   In **nonprobability sampling**, every member of the population does *not* have an equal opportunity to be selected. Therefore, we are likely to miss certain types of subjects, so the sample is unlikely to be representative of the population. A common form of this approach is **convenience sampling**, in which we study the subjects that are conveniently available. Studying the students sitting in the student union or the people riding on a bus involve convenience samples. These are not random samples, unless we have randomly selected the location and time as in cluster sampling. Otherwise, only those people who are present at the one place and time of the study have any chance of being selected, and the reason they are present is usually not a random event. Therefore, a convenience sample is representative of a very limited population, composed of only the same types of people found in the same situation as that of our study.

To at least some extent, most "random" samples are convenience samples: Given researchers' limitations in travel, cost, and so on, there will always be some members of the population who have no chance of being selected. For example, we may have permission to conduct a study only in one portion of a factory so the resulting sample is not representative of all workers. Similarly, we are relying on convenience sampling when we sample from among college-level, introductory psychology students; our subjects are, at best, representative of the population of introductory psychology students.

One type of nonprobability sampling that may produce a more representative sample is **quota sampling**. As in stratified sampling, with this technique we ensure that the sample has the same percentage (i.e., the same "quota") of each subgroup as that found in the population. However, unlike stratified sampling, in quota sampling we do not select from the subgroup randomly. Instead, we rely on convenience samples to fulfill each quota. Thus, for example, say that we want to have 20 six-year-olds and 20 seven-year olds in our sample. If we obtain these subjects by testing a convenient class of first-graders and a convenient class of second-graders, we are using quota sampling.

Sometimes we seek to study a "hidden" population which is not easily identifiable, as when research deals with drug addicts, prostitutes, and so on. In such cases, we may use **snowball sampling**. Here we identify one potential subject, and from him or her we obtain the names and addresses of other subjects, and from them we obtain still other potential subjects, so that the growth of the sample tends to build or "snowball." With this technique too we have less confidence that the sample is representative, because only those people within a specific network of acquaintances have any chance of being selected, and they are likely to be different from other people in the population.

> **REMEMBER** *Convenience sampling, quota sampling,* and *snowball sampling* are *nonprobability sampling* techniques that are likely to produce unrepresentative samples.

For a summary of these sampling techniques, consult Table 10.1.

Both probability and nonprobability sampling techniques play a role in the two general types of field experiments: those involving the general population, and those involving selected groups.

TABLE 10.1   Summary of Sampling Techniques

Probability Sampling

Simple:	Randomly select subjects from list of population.
Systematic:	Select every nth name from list of population.
Stratified:	Randomly select from subgroups, proportionate to each group's representation in population.
Cluster:	Randomly select clusters and test all subjects per cluster.

Nonprobability Sampling

Convenience:	Select subjects who are conveniently available.
Quota:	Obtain convenience samples to represent subgroups, proportionate to each group's representation in the population.
Snowball:	Locate each subject through contacts with previous subjects.

Field Experiments with the General Public

One approach to field experiments is to conduct the study in an unrestricted public area so that we can generalize to the "typical citizen." We usually conduct this kind of study in one of two ways: Either the researcher targets certain subjects and observes their response to a condition of an environmental independent variable, or the researcher (or a confederate) creates a condition by approaching subjects and exhibiting a behavior to elicit a response. Essentially, we are conducting the study we would like to conduct in the laboratory, except that the demand characteristics associated with a formal laboratory and experimenter would lead us to seriously doubt the validity and reliability of our results. In the field, therefore, we disguise the fact that an experiment is being conducted, employing deception and unobtrusively measuring the behavior.

Such field experiments are especially common when we study a social behavior. For example, Isen and Levin (1972) studied helping behavior—or "bystander intervention"—as a function of subjects' mood. They manipulated mood by allowing some subjects the pleasant experience of finding money in the change return of a pay phone. Then a passing confederate dropped a manila folder, and the dependent variable was whether subjects helped the confederate. Similarly, Shaffer, Rogel, and Hendrick (1975) staged a theft at a college library. A confederate (the "victim") sat with a subject and then left, presenting the conditions of either asking or not asking the subject to watch his belongings. Another confederate then approached, searched the belongings, and stole the victim's wallet. The dependent variable was whether the subject tried to stop the thief.

In the area of environmental psychology, Barefoot, Hoople, and McClay (1972) investigated how people react when they must violate another's "personal space." The researchers manipulated the conditions of how far a confederate sat from a public drinking fountain and measured two dependent variables: the number of passers-by who stopped to drink, and the amount of time each spent drinking. Similarly, Albas and Albas (1989) conducted a fictitious opinion poll measuring the dependent variable of how far a subject came to stop from a pollster. The study investigated whether this distance varied as a function of the safety of the environment (a safe shopping mall or a less safe city park) and as a function of whether subjects were able to make eye contact (depending on whether the pollster wore dark sunglasses).

Other social behaviors have also been studied in field experiments. Crusco and Wetzel (1984) examined the influence of physical touching on restaurant patrons by having a confederate waitress present conditions of no touch, a fleeting touch on the hand, or a lingering shoulder touch. The dependent variable was the size of the tip a subject left for the waitress. Ellsworth, Carlsmith, and Henson (1972) studied how being stared at causes people to take flight: When drivers were stopped at an intersection, a stare from a researcher standing on the corner prompted them to depart more rapidly than did the absence of staring. Similarly, Kleinke and Singer (1979) studied the influence of making eye contact, using the common technique of having a confederate distribute leaflets, with the dependent variable defined as whether subjects accepted the leaflet.

Limitations of Studies with the General Public   As with any study, field experiments are not perfect. We still lack construct and content validity because our operational definition of a variable may not measure what we intend. (The amount of time that people linger at a drinking fountain may in part reflect how thirsty they are.) We still fall short of perfect ecological validity, because the situation may be somewhat contrived. (Would a real thief riffle through someone's belongings when another person is sitting at the same table watching?) Our external validity is still limited to situations similar to the ones we are studying. (Helping was studied when a *nonviolent* theft occurred in a *library*.) And, finally, demand characteristics may still be present: Our subjects may be suspicious and uncooperative (thinking "What kind of weirdo is this?"), or they may give socially desirable responses instead of natural ones.

Our ability to generalize the results of field experiments is also limited due to limited random selection of subjects. Such experiments entail some degree of convenience sampling, because we can select subjects only from among those people who are present at the time and location of the experiment: People in the park or mall may not represent people who are seldom found there. We may have to impose selection criteria that further limit random selection: In the library study, subjects must be sitting alone, and people sitting alone may act differently from those who are not. Convenience sampling may also be imposed by experimenter bias: Perhaps the pollsters in the park conveniently avoided a potential subject who seemed threatening to them! And we continue to rely on volunteer subjects, who may be unrepresentative of nonvolunteers. People who stop for the pollster may be different from those who do not including exhibiting a different sense of personal space.

Most important, field experiments allow less control of potentially confounding variables that reduce internal validity. We lose our ability to balance subject variables because our random assignment of subjects to conditions is limited. For example, personal-space differences supposedly due to the safety of a park or mall may actually be due to differences between the types of subjects found in the park and mall. Other confoundings may also be present: Whether subjects stop and help a pollster or drink from a fountain may actually be due to the time of day and where they are going. Or, the size of the tip left may depend on how much money a subject has or the perceived quality of the waitress's service. And often there can be no control group in field experiments: We cannot measure the personal space of those subjects who did not stop to talk to the pollster.

Field experiments also allow a less consistent testing situation. In the real world, it is difficult to consistently manipulate an independent variable. (Consider how hard it would be to maintain the same degree of eye contact when staring at different drivers.) A confederate's behavior may also be inconsistent, since he or she must react to a subjects's more natural, uncontrolled behavior. (Some subjects may be gabby, some not.) Finally, we have less control over environmental variables, such as the number of other people present, wind and temperature conditions, or horns blowing and other distractions.

Our loss of control also reduces the reliability of scores and the statistical power we can achieve. In field experiments we provide no instructions to guide subjects, so we may encounter a wide variety of responses. (For example, subjects may pace while talking with the pollster, so that we cannot reliably measure their personal space.) Obtaining multiple trials per subject to increase reliability is usually not possible, because a deception works only once, or a passer-by may volunteer only if a task is brief. Likewise, repeated-measures designs are usually not possible. Further, we are often able to obtain only gross measurements of a behavior. (To time drinking-fountain behavior we must use a stopwatch, and we can indicate only whether a subject did or did not attempt to stop the thief instead of measuring how much he or she wanted to help.) Not only do such measurements reduce precision and sensitivity, but the data must often be recorded in terms of categorizing or rank-ordering subjects, so we are limited to the use of less powerful, nonparametric statistical procedures (e.g., the chi square).

Controlling Experiments with the General Public   We employ the usual methods to deal with the above problems. To improve random selection and generality, for example, we may use the equivalent of cluster sampling, testing at several locations (e.g., several randomly selected drinking fountains) in a counterbalanced way. We also usually employ systematic sampling, selecting every nth subject who meets our selection criteria in the mall, or timing every nth subject who stops at a drinking fountain. We can also stratify the sampling—for example, by observing every nth female until we have the desired proportion of females in our sample. Systematic and stratified sampling makes selection more random and eliminates experimenter biases in selecting subjects. And we balance subject variables, time of day, and other potential confoundings by randomly alternating the treatment condition assigned as each subject is encountered.

For consistency, we set criteria for selecting a subject (doing so only when a certain number of people are present, when no major momentary distractions are occurring, etc.). We control for effects due to different confederates, for example, by having each test a portion of the subjects in each condition, and we attempt to keep the appearance and behavior of all confederates consistent. Finally, we try to develop sensitive scoring criteria using quantitative measurements and parametric procedures where possible. For even greater reliability and validity, we can ask subjects questions directly as a manipulation check following our unobtrusive observation of them, we can employ multiple raters, and we can test a relatively large N.

Even with such controls, however, we must be especially careful to critically evaluate all field experiments, and to temper our conclusions that the independent variable caused the dependent variable to change. The trade-off of internal validity for external validity means that we do obtain a general idea about the influence of a variable on a behavior in a natural setting, but we lose precision and confidence in our description of exactly how the variable caused the behavior, and how the behavior was exhibited.

Field Experiments with Selected Groups

The other approach to field experiments involves entering the field to study a specific group of subjects that already exists. Sometimes we may be unable to disguise the study, especially when we have to provide instructions and incorporate the same trappings as those in a laboratory experiment. At other times we may operate more unobtrusively. Either way, however, there is some existing factor that creates the group we wish to study, and this factor provides greater external validity. Usually this is the case because we are studying a behavior that occurs only in certain situations or with certain subjects.

For example, Neri, Shappell, and DeJohn (1992) studied the problem of errors made by airplane pilots by measuring errors as a function of different conditions of fatigue. (To avoid too much realism by causing airplane crashes, they tested subjects using flight simulators.) Rosenfeld, Tenenbaum, Ruskin, and Halfron (1989) studied the effect that an exercise program had on worker productivity, comparing the productivity of workers who exercised to that of workers who did not. Likewise, we may study police officers or nurses on the job, because they exhibit specific types of behavior, operate in a role of authority, and normally wear uniforms (e.g., Lavender, 1987).

Selected groups can also be found outside of the work setting. In one of the first studies of personal space, Felipe and Sommer (1966) felt that the effects of invading an individual's personal space could not be examined unless it occurred in an environment where such "crazy behavior" would not be viewed as bizarre. Therefore, their manipulation involved whether a confederate sat very close to patients in a mental institution! Similarly, educational research often involves existing groups of students. For example, Fisher and Harris (1973) manipulated different note-taking and review styles in college classes. Another way of gaining access to a select group is to study young children at a daycare center or elderly subjects at a senior citizen's home. In an interesting twist on this selected group approach, Gladue and Delaney (1990) investigated the hypothesis that men and women become more attractive to one another as the closing time of a bar approaches by studying an existing group of patrons at a bar. Using a repeated-measures design, the researchers asked the subjects to rate the attractiveness of the other patrons on several occasions during the evening. They confirmed that attractiveness increased as time wore on. (Interestingly, the ratings were not positively correlated with alcohol consumption, so alcohol was not the reason for this increase!)

Limitations of Studies with Selected Groups   In addition to the usual loss of control that frequently occurs with field experiments, there are several special problems in testing selected groups. One problem is that we are often limited to convenience sampling of those groups that we can obtain permission to test. Another major problem occurs if we use cluster sampling but assign one intact group to each condition. In that case we are not randomly assigning subjects, so our manipulation is probably confounded. If, for instance, a condition contains all workers from the same department, the reason they are in that department—rather than our manipulation—may cause them to behave differently from workers in another condition. Also, the general public may not be as obedient or adventurous as the typical college student subject. Some workers may refuse to try a particular working condition, or parents may object to their children being in a control or mildly aversive condition. The resistance of such subjects is not random, so subject selection and assignment to conditions is likewise not random. Also, in a repeated-measures design we may see substantial subject mortality, further reducing the randomness of our selection.

Another limitation of studies involving selected groups is that a researcher entering an established field setting may render the situation artificial and thus bias subjects' responses. Ideally, to preserve the natural environment we prefer to use an unobtrusive measure, but this may not be possible. Most nursery schools, for example, do not have a one-way mirror, and the management or union authorities at most companies will not allow us to videotape workers. As an alternative, we can ask the subjects' regular supervisor or teacher to act as the experimenter. But such people are not trained researchers, so they may greatly bias the results. The data may not be valid or reliable for our purposes if a substitute experimenter scores the dependent behavior (the purpose and criteria of a supervisor's rating may be very different from those of a researcher). Also, supervisors' or teachers' expectations, as well as subtle variations in their treatment of subjects, can produce a self-fulfilling prophecy. In a classic study, Rosenthal and Jacobson (1966) found that when a student was identified as about to "bloom" intellectually, the teacher's expectations produced greater intellectual development scores, despite the fact that the identified students had originally been randomly selected and were not expected to bloom at anything.

Existing-group designs are especially prone to *diffusion of treatment*. Recall from Chapter 5 that this problem occurs when subjects in one condition are aware of the treatment received by subjects in other conditions. Thus, for example, group membership may overlap or change during the course of a study: Shift workers may at times work a different shift and thus be exposed to another condition. Or subjects in an existing group may gossip about the experiment: Senior citizens may talk to others who have not been tested, or children in one class may learn of a desirable treatment given to another class. Such information may lead subjects to react to their conditions in a biased, unnatural manner.

Finally, note that a special kind of demand characteristic may be operating among subjects who have formed a cohesive group. This phenomenon was discovered when six female assembly workers at Western Electric's "Hawthorne" factory were placed in a separate room so that worker productivity could be studied (Roethlisberger & Dickson, 1939). Over the course of a year, the researchers manipulated such variables as the illumination in the room, the length of the work day, the number of rest periods, and the method of pay. However, regardless of the manipulation and whether it was predicted to increase or decrease productivity, the subjects' continuously increased their productivity! Afterward, subjects indicated that they felt honored that their employer had taken special notice of them and that they had received special attention from the researchers. Apparently a team spirit had developed, compelling subjects to be cooperative and to continuously increase their productivity.

The term **Hawthorne effect** has come to refer to a change in subjects' performance—usually an improvement—that occurs simply because a researcher shows a special interest in them. (Note that this is different from reactivity, which refers to a change in subjects' behavior because they know they are being observed.) Although the Hawthorne effect can be found in any study, it is especially prevalent in those involving subjects from a coherent, relatively permanent group.

> *REMEMBER*   The *Hawthorne effect* is a bias in subjects' performance due to the apparently special treatment and interest shown by a researcher.

Controlling Experiments with Selected Groups   By now, you are familiar with the methods we use to overcome the above limitations. We seek random assignment of subjects to conditions, so in a factory study, for example, we would try to ensure that some workers from each department experienced each condition. To minimize diffusion of treatment, we explain to subjects why they should not talk to each other, and we test all conditions close together in time. We also give all conditions the same appearance, by disguising the control condition with a placebo or by using deception. Then, if subjects learn about another condition, it will sound the same as their own. Testing at different locations not only improves generalizability but also helps prevent diffusion of treatment because subjects from different localities are unlikely to have contact with each other. Further, if supervisors or teachers must serve as the researchers, we give them explicit instructions, train them, and employ a double-blind procedure. And, finally, to counter demand characteristics such as the Hawthorne effect, we instruct subjects to behave naturally, and not in the way they think the experimenter wants them to.

Ethics and Field Experiments

As with any other type of research we must evaluate the ethics of a field experiment to ensure that subjects experience a minimum of psychological and physical stress, and to protect their rights. When conducting a field experiment in which subjects are aware they are participating in a study, we deal with issues of risky variables, deception, unobtrusive measures, debriefing, and informed consent in the usual ways. Of particular concern is the need to avoid any implicit coercion of subjects; we do not want them to participate because they think they must in order to keep their job or to be viewed favorably by their boss, teacher, or peers.

Unobtrusive field experiments involving the general public present the additional question of whether it is ethical to even conduct such research. After all, they involve the ultimate deception, because subjects are not even aware a study is being conducted! They have not formally volunteered, nor have they been given a chance to provide informed consent. At issue, therefore, is whether we are violating subjects' rights. A classic example of this dilemma is a study by Middlemist, Knowles, and Matter (1976). They wanted to measure whether an invasion of one's personal space created physical tension by using a physiological measure of tension that would be free of any laboratory demand characteristics. Their solution was to conduct a field experiment in a public restroom, observing males as they visited the urinal. They invaded personal space by having a confederate use the adjacent urinal. They determined that tension increased by measuring the greater amount of time that subjects took to urinate. To be unobtrusive, the experimenter occupied one of the stalls and used a periscope to observe and time each subject, recording the interval between unzipping and rezipping.

How do we evaluate the ethics of such a design? We might justify the secret observation of this behavior by claiming that we are conducting scientific research for the "good of humanity." But is this really any different from justifying the covert spying of a government agency or the police by claiming that it helps catch criminals? Some would say that it is not, arguing that such research is an invasion of subjects' privacy and a violation of their rights: spying is spying, whether it is intended for scientific advancement and the good of humanity, or for national security and rooting out evil. However, others would argue that a public behavior is just that—public—and is thus open to the scrutiny of any observer. Thus, if someone stops on the street to help a pollster, that person has tacitly agreed to produce behaviors that anyone can observe. Conversely, if a male wishes to keep his urinal behavior strictly private, he should not use a public restroom. From this perspective, some researchers claim that it is *un*ethical for scientists *not* to conduct field research, and potentially miss valuable information that may benefit society.

There is no easy resolution to this debate. You might think that obtaining informed consent after the fact would help, but doing so would violate the spirit of allowing subjects to provide *prior* informed consent (and might be more upsetting than not informing them at all). Instead, the responsibility falls on the researcher and involves weighing the violation of subjects' rights against the potential importance of the scientific information we may gain. Toward this end, first consider just how "public" a particular behavior might be considered by subjects. Are we invading their expected privacy? How strenuously would they object if we asked their permission? How upset would they be if they found out about our spying after the fact? (If we are unsure of the answers here, we can conduct a pilot study of potential subjects in which, without any spying, we directly approach them and ask these questions.)

We then weigh the invasion of privacy in a study against the potential scientific benefits of the results. Are the potential findings important, or have they already become known through other methods? Koocher (1977) argued that the above urinal study needlessly invaded subjects' privacy, replicating conclusions already demonstrated by other, less questionable techniques. (But see the reply of Middlemist et al. [1977].) Also consider whether the procedure really needs to be conducted as an unobtrusive field experiment. Do the benefits of a field experiment outweigh the accompanying ethical issues and lessened control that would not be problems in a laboratory study? Finally, the APA's *Ethical Principles* (1992) state that informed consent is needed unless the risk to subjects is *minimal* and that deception must be *necessary*. The more the behavior being studied is an innocuous, mundane public behavior, and the greater the necessity for an unobtrusive field experiment, the more the study can be justified ethically.

Another ethical concern raised by field experiments is that they open up the range of variables we can manipulate. Therefore, we must consider the limits of our right to conduct studies that impose upon others and cause real-life events to occur. (We do *not* have the right to yell "fire" in a crowded theater simply to see what happens!) Thus, always determine whether a study's context is ethical. Are we justified in taking up the valuable time of police or medical personnel? Also consider the unintended effects of a manipulation. Is it ethical to frighten subjects by causing them to believe that they are confronting a possibly dangerous thief while alone in the library? Finally, recognize that we are predicting an impact of the independent variable on the dependent behavior. Is it ethical to manipulate treatments that we suspect will decrease a student's classroom learning, or to manipulate factors which may cause traffic accidents?

In short, we cannot be cavalier about what we do in the real world. In a laboratory setting, informed consent and the lack of experimental realism are protection for subjects: Because they have volunteered to experience our artificial situation, it has less of a real impact on them. In field experiments, however, this is not the case. Researchers therefore have a much greater responsibility when it comes to balancing their right to study a behavior with the rights of subjects. And, as usual, after we think we have resolved these ethical issues, we submit our procedures for review by our institution's Human Subjects Review Committee.

> *REMEMBER*   Researchers must be particularly sensitive to the ethics of a field experiment.

RESEARCH INVOLVING ANIMAL SUBJECTS

Another type of psychological research involves animals because psychology is not limited to the study of human behavior. Animal subjects are involved in approximately 7% of psychological research, and the majority of subjects are mice, rats, and birds (Gallup & Suarez, 1985). Animal and comparative psychologists study animals in part because they demonstrate interesting behaviors. For example, we can create laboratory and field experiments of migratory birds to test whether they navigate using the earth's magnetic field (Able & Able, 1990). We can study the social dominance hierarchies among animals, determining, for example, whether submissive mice remember other mice who have previously beat them up, or describing the characteristics of mice in tests of exploration, maze-running, and even swimming (e.g., Hilakivi-Clarke & Lister, 1992). Or we can examine the cognitive capabilities of different species. From such research, for example, we have learned that a gorilla will use American Sign Language to tell lies (Patterson, 1978), and that sea lions demonstrate an ability to understand symbolic relationships (Gisner & Schusterman, 1992).

Researchers also study animals to test an "animal model" of some basic aspect of behavior that can then be generalized to all species, including humans. For example, much of what we know about the basic functioning of the brain is based on biological models that were tested through animal research. A common approach is to create conditions of the independent variable by surgically eliminating an area of the brain in experimental groups, and comparing the behavior of altered animals to that of unaltered control animals. This approach was taken by researchers who observed the eating behavior of white rats in which various parts of the hypothalamus had been surgically damaged.

The studies revealed one area that controls initiating and another that terminates eating behavior (e.g., Tokunaga, Fukushima, Kemnitz & Bray, 1986). Other animal models of the biology of behavior do not involve surgical procedures. In studying behavior genetics, for example, Ebert and Hyde (1976) selected mice that exhibited high or low aggression. Then, after breeding the animals, they determined the level of aggression in the offspring, as an indication of whether this trait is genetically carried.

We also create behavioral models based on animal research. The most common of these occur in the area of learning and conditioning. Ivan Pavlov's development of the principles of classical conditioning was based on the behavior of dogs, and B. F. Skinner's work on operant or instrumental conditioning was based on the behavior of rats and pigeons. Such research yielded models of how learning occurs, and how reinforcement and punishment govern the behavior. Other animal models have been developed to explain such basic mechanisms as pain, aggression, frustration, and emotional development. For example, researchers developed a model of emotional development by studying the effects of raising young monkeys with or apart from their mothers (e.g., Harlow & Harlow, 1962).

Though some people are incensed by the comparisons, animal research often has substantial external validity, generalizing very well to many aspects of human psychology, including such uniquely human endeavors as education, clinical therapy, and the workplace. Humans *are* animals themselves, and some laws of nature apply to all animals in the same ways. For example, Schachter (1971) provided a classic—and entertaining—description of the convergence of animal and human research in the study of obesity. A hypothalamus is a hypothalamus, and the model of how a white rat's hypothalamus influences eating behavior has generalized well to humans. Likewise, animal research is often the first step researchers take when testing a new medicinal drug or physical treatment. When the treatment works with animal subjects, it often works with human subjects as well.

> *REMEMBER* Animal research is conducted either to directly study animal behavior or to create a model that can be generalized to other species, including humans.

Controls Used with Animal Research

In the laboratory, many animal studies are designed as a typical true experiment: We obtain a random sample of animals (sometimes trapped in the wild but usually purchased from commercial suppliers who breed them), randomly assign them to conditions, and apply all of the typical controls for consistently, validly, and strongly manipulating the independent variable. Because we seek a valid and reliable measurement of the dependent variable, we create scoring criteria to distinguish between different types of overt behaviors. We may count the frequency of a certain behavior or time its duration. We may even present forced-choice trials (by having a rat press one of several levers) or score for correct-incorrect responses (by having cats and primates solve problems). To maximize reliability, we observe multiple trials and counterbalance for order effects. (Rats demonstrate carry-over effects just like humans.)

As usual, we are concerned with internal validity, so we keep constant all of the extraneous variables that might confound the independent variable. We maintain the cages and environment in the same way for all subjects and handle each animal in the same, careful manner. Note that control groups are often necessary to identify the influences of merely handling and testing the animals. With drug testing or surgical procedures, control animals are injected with a placebo or undergo the anesthesia and surgery without receiving the actual treatment. In this manner, they experience the same trauma that experimental animals experience.

Believe it or not, experimenter expectancies and demand characteristics are a problem even in animal studies. A researcher can inadvertently make recording and scoring errors that are biased toward confirming the research hypothesis. And a researcher's expectations can produce subtle differences in the way that animals are handled and tested, again biasing the results so that they confirm the hypothesis. These problems can occur even when a researcher is dealing with something as simple as a rat learning a response (Rosenthal, 1976), but they are especially serious when dealing with more social animals, such as dogs and primates. In particular, great care must be taken to prevent the experimenter from communicating demand characteristics through facial expressions and body movements so that we avoid the problem demonstrated by "Clever Hans" (Pfungst, 1911). Hans was a horse who his owner claimed could perform addition. If asked to give the sum of 2 plus 2, Hans pawed the ground 4 times; if asked 3 plus 3, he pawed 6 times. However, when Hans was blindfolded, he mysteriously lost his mathematical abilities! Apparently, Hans produced correct answers by watching his owner. At the point when the correct sum was reached, the owner showed a relaxed look and Hans stopped pawing the ground. To minimize such experimenter biases, researchers handle all animals in the same way, automate response collection and scoring as much as possible, employ multiple raters when responses must be subjectively scored, and employ double-blind procedures.

> *REMEMBER* In research involving animals, we control extraneous variables, including demand characteristics, in the same ways as in research involving humans.

Ethics and Animal Research

There is an ongoing debate among scientists and the general public about the ethics of conducting laboratory research with animals. It is true that research often exposes animals to unpleasant and harmful manipulations. In addition to surgical procedures, animals experience independent variables involving electric shock, food or water deprivation, exposure to toxins, and other aversive conditions. Further, the way to conduct a manipulation check of a surgical procedure is to perform an autopsy. Also, because animals are physically or psychologically altered by the manipulation (they are *sophisticated* subjects), they usually cannot be studied again and are destroyed.

On the one hand, animal rights groups say that such research is unethical because it violates the right of animals to live free and unharmed. They argue that even though humans have the ability to exploit other animals, they do not have the right to do so.

Some make the more radical argument that laboratory studies of animals do not even provide useful information, so there is no justification for what is seen as essentially animal abuse. From these perspectives, it is the reponsibility of researchers to protect the rights of animal subjects, and to treat them with the same respect they show human subjects. Therefore, because the equivalent of informed consent cannot be obtained, they should study animals only by observing them in field research.

On the other hand, animal researchers argue that the use of animal subjects is justified by the knowledge it produces. Granted, some animal research seems frivolous (such as testing animals' skin reactions to new perfumes so that humans will smell better), but much of this research has been discontinued. Contrary to the argument above, however, animal research *has* added substantially to the well-being of humans in important ways: Animal research has been the basis for virtually all modern drugs and surgical techniques, for the identification of numerous toxins and carcinogens, and for many psychological principles. From this perspective, it would be *un*ethical if we did not conduct animal research to benefit humans (and often other animals as well). Thus, the argument here is that researchers have the right—*and the responsibility*—to pursue any useful scientific information.

This issue boils down to whether the goal of benefiting humans takes precedence over the rights of other animals. If it does, then animal research is justified, because *there is no other way to obtain the data.* It would be more unethical to perform experimental surgical or medical procedures on humans: We cannot undo surgical alterations, and, when first testing a drug, we may have no idea of the harmful side-effects that can occur. Likewise, we cannot control the breeding practices of humans in order to study genetics, nor can we administer to humans many of the aversive conditions that have led to important discoveries with animals.

In addition, there are scientific and practical reasons for conducting animal laboratory studies. Field research limits the variables we can control and manipulate, so this approach is an inadequate substitute. Also, laboratory research with animals can be conducted quickly and efficiently. Animals are easily obtained and housed, their environment can be easily controlled and manipulated, and, with respect to genetic studies, animals have a short gestation period.

Regardless of where your personal feelings fall in this debate, it is inaccurate to think of animal research as involving the mindless torture of abused animals. As with all human endeavors, some researchers are less than ethical and may mistreat their animals. For the vast majority of researchers, however, laboratory animals are valued subjects in whom much time, energy, and expense have been invested. Also, it is in the researchers' interest to treat them well, because animals who are physically and emotionally distressed make poor subjects for a reliable and valid study. Furthermore, the APA's *Ethical Principles* (1992) provide guidelines for the treatment of research animals, and all animal laboratories must conform to federal, state, and local regulations for the housing and care of animals as well. Because of such rules, animals are well cared for, undergo surgery in sterile settings with anesthesia, and are disposed of in a humane manner.

The APA's guidelines essentially call for the same ethical evaluation of animal research as that performed in human research. First, we attempt to minimize the harm we may cause an animal. That is, we prefer designs that provide positive events as opposed to aversive events, we prefer mildly aversive events to drastic ones, and we prefer temporary physical alterations over permanent surgical ones. Second, we should not be frivolous in our treatment of animal subjects, so every aspect of a procedure must be necessary. As usual, the key issue is whether the procedure is justified by the scientific importance of the information that may be learned. Finally, every research institution must have a review board that approves animal studies on the basis of the ethical treatment of the subjects.

> *REMEMBER*   Acceptable animal research minimizes the harm done to subjects and must be justified as scientifically important.

SINGLE-SUBJECT DESIGNS

So far, all of our discussions have concerned the study of groups of human or animal subjects. However, there is an entirely different kind of experiment in which we study only one subject. A **single-subject design** is a repeated-measures experiment conducted on one subject. This means, of course, that our N is 1.

Before considering the particulars of such designs, let's discuss why we would want to use them.

The Argument for Single-Subject Designs

Some researchers argue that there are three unacceptable flaws in the group experiment (Sidman, 1960). The first pertains to error variance, the random differences between scores found within a condition. When we study groups in an experiment, we employ random assignment of subjects and counterbalancing of extraneous variables. Because we include fluctuating subject and other variables within each condition, the design itself produces much of the error variance. The inconsistency in scores then makes it difficult to see a consistent relationship hidden in the data. Even if the relationship is statistically significant, the error variance may render it barely perceptible, so that we cannot tell whether the independent variable is actually important in causing the dependent behavior. This is especially a problem given how often researchers fail to report the variable's effect size (the proportion of variance accounted for). Further, group designs ignore the differences in behavior reflected by error variance. They ignore "intersubject" differences, leading us to conclude that "more or less, this is how all subjects tend to behave." They also ignore intrasubject variations, differences in a particular subject's behavior that occur when he or she is repeatedly measured in the same situation. Implicitly, then, group designs ignore variables that cause differences in scores, even though these variables are potentially important aspects of the behavior under study.

The second flaw in group designs is that, because of the variation in individual scores, we are forced to compute the mean score (or similar measures) in each condition. Yet a mean score may misrepresent the behavior of any and all individuals. A classic example of this problem occurred when Eysenck (1952) examined group means and found that neurotic patients undergoing psychotherapy showed no improvement compared to neurotics who had never entered therapy. He then concluded that therapy is basically useless! Later, however, Bergin (1966) demonstrated that, individually, some subjects do improve while others worsen, and that this is why Eysenck's means showed no change. Furthermore, after using group means to describe a relationship, we turn around and generalize our findings to individuals! Psychology studies the laws of behavior as they apply to the individual, but in group designs we do not examine a relationship in terms of the individual.

The third flaw in group designs involves the problem of demonstrating a consistent, reliable effect of the independent variable. Usually, we demonstrate a relationship only once in a particular study, by testing subjects briefly under the various conditions. Then, we rely on inferential statistics to conclude that the study is reliable. That is, if our results are significant, the relationship is unlikely to be due to random chance. Therefore, it is likely to be reproducible, so a significant relationship is also described as a reliable relationship. However, we do not have any *empirical* evidence that the relationship is reproducible. Other researchers may replicate a study, but their situation and subjects inevitably differ from ours. In replicated studies, too, researchers seldom empirically demonstrate that the relationship is reliable.

> *REMEMBER* Group designs ignore the causes of error variance, they rely on mean scores for describing individuals, and they do not empirically show that an effect is reliable.

Single-subject designs address these problems in the following ways.

1. We control subject variables and individual differences not by balancing them but by keeping them constant. With just one subject, there can be no differences in scores due to differences between subjects. At any point, if we see an inconsistency in the subject's response (i.e., intrasubject variability), we know that some extraneous variable is responsible, so we can attempt to identify and control it.

2. Our "analysis" of the data is usually accomplished by visual inspection: We do not perform inferential statistics when $N = 1$. Instead, we look at a graph of the data to see whether there is a relationship between changes in the independent variable and changes in the dependent scores. Since we rely on visual inspection, we accept that the independent variable has an effect only when it is obvious. The size of the effect will be clearly reflected in the extent to which the subject's response changes between conditions.

3. To be sure that the effect of the independent variable is reliable, we perform our manipulations repeatedly on the same subject, or we perform a replication of the experiment on additional subjects (usually involving only a few). We view each replication as a separate study, however, and we do not "gloss over" individuals by combining their results. Ultimately, then, because the relationship we describe is based on an individual subject, we are studying the psychology of individuals.

Baseline Designs

If an experiment contains only one subject, then of course the subject must be repeatedly measured under all conditions. Typically, however, a study involves only two levels of the independent variable: a *control* condition with zero amount of the variable present and a *treatment* condition with some nonzero amount of the variable present. Under each condition, we measure a dependent variable that usually reflects the quantity of responding, such as the rate of responding over time or the magnitude of responses.

By observing a subject under a control condition, we establish a baseline. A **baseline** is the level of performance on the dependent variable when the independent variable is not present. It is used as a comparison to the level of performance when the variable *is* present. To establish the baseline, we observe the subject in the control condition for a specific period of time, providing numerous opportunities for the subject to respond. Once the subject has habituated to the procedure so that the baseline is stable, we can determine the subject's typical response rate when our treatment is not present. Then we introduce the experimental treatment condition and establish the subject's response rate in this new situation. If the subject's response rate with the treatment is different from that without the treatment, we have demonstrated an effect of the independent variable.

Because of the flaws in group studies, baseline designs became the mainstay of B. F. Skinner and others who study instrumental conditioning. This approach is often referred to as the "experimental analysis of behavior" (and the *Journal of the Experimental Analysis of Behavior* is devoted to it). In a typical baseline experiment, for example, a researcher might place a rat in a cage containing a lever and then establish the baseline rate of lever-pressing. Or a pigeon might be trained to peck at a target to receive food, in which case the baseline rate of pecking is established. A particular reward, punishment, or environmental stimulus is then introduced. Once responding is again stable, the response rate with the treatment is compared to the baseline response rate. Often the procedure is then replicated on several other animals, with the results from all published as one research report.

Although baseline designs are most often associated with animal research, they are also performed with humans. In applied studies involving behavior modification, for example, researchers establish baselines for anxiety attacks, phobias, psychotic episodes, eating disorders, and other dysfunctional behaviors. They then introduce rewards, punishments, or other forms of treatment and observe the change in the frequency or magnitude of the behavior. Similar designs are also used in industrial settings to demonstrate the effects of various treatments on a worker's productivity, or in educational settings to study factors that improve a child's performance.

The fundamental logic of baseline designs is to compare the baseline response rate with the treatment response rate, but there are two general design approaches we may take.

Reversal Designs   The simplest approach would be to test the subject first when the independent variable is not present, in order to obtain the baseline (call this condition A). Then we could observe the subject after the variable is present (call this condition B). This simple "AB" design could be used to show that rats, for example, will press a lever more often when food is dispensed to reward this response than in a baseline condition when food is not dispensed.

By showing that responding is different with the treatment, we may be tempted to conclude that the treatment has an effect. *But*, if this is all we do, we leave ourselves open to the rival, alternative hypothesis that it was not our independent variable but some other, confounding factor that produced the change in responding. Recall, for example, that changes in subjects due to ongoing history and maturation may confound a repeated-measures design. In our example above, perhaps a change in the rat's age or experience coincidentally caused the increased lever-pressing (or maybe the rat got bored and started pressing to entertain itself). Then again, maybe some confounding environmental stimulus led to the increased lever-pressing.

To demonstrate that it is the presence of the treatment and not some other variable that controls the subject's behavior, we return the subject to the control condition after the treatment condition is over. If the responding "reverses" to the baseline rate, we have evidence that the behavior is controlled by our treatment. This approach is called a reversal design. In a **reversal design**, the researcher repeatedly alternates between the baseline condition and the treatment condition. When we present the baseline phase, the treatment phase, and then the baseline phase again, the design is described as an *ABA reversal design*. For even more convincing evidence we may reintroduce the treatment condition again, employing an *ABAB design* (or any extended sequence, such as an ABABAB design).

To see the effects of our manipulation, we would graph the results, as shown in Figure 10.1. Going from testing sessions under condition A to those under condition B, we see that the introduction of food leads to increased responding. Then, after removing the reward and returning to condition A, we find that the response "extinguishes," eventually returning to its original baseline rate. Reintroducing the reward reinstates the response rate. Since it is unlikely that a confounding subject or environmental variable

FIGURE 10.1   Ideal Results from an ABAB Reversal Design

Here, lever-pressing rate is shown to be a function of the presence or absence of a food reinforcer.

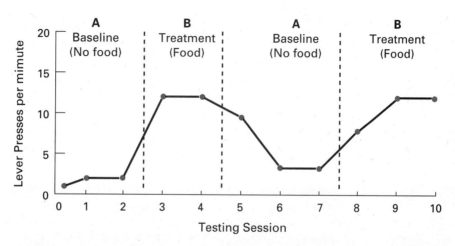

would repeatedly change *simultaneously* with each of our alternating conditions, we are confident that the treatment has caused the behavioral change. We may then replicate this study on a few other subjects, reducing the possibility that the change in behavior was due to a unique aspect of one subject, and even further reducing the possibility that a confounding variable coincidentally changed with our treatment.

> *REMEMBER*   With a *reversal design*, we demonstrate the effect of a variable by repeatedly alternating between testing with and without the treatment condition.

Multiple-Baseline Designs   Recall that, when using any repeated-measures design, we face the problem of carry-over effects from one condition to the other. If the above reversal designs are to work, the carry-over effect of the treatment must be reversible. However, many treatments involve a permanent, irrevocable change. For example, we cannot use an ABA design to study the effect of removing part of the hypothalamus because we cannot return the animal to its normal state. Likewise, once a rat has been electrically shocked, some learning may remain such that, after the treatment, the animal's responding never returns to the original baseline rate. Further, some clinical treatments are not reversible for ethical reasons. For example, a researcher may believe that it is unethical to discontinue a treatment that reduces a subject's phobic reactions, just for the sake of the research.

Because we do not reverse the treatment in such situations, we do not eliminate the possibility that the change in behavior is due to maturation, to history, or to environmental effects that occurred coincidentally with the treatment phase. The solution to this problem is to employ a multiple-baseline design instead. With a **multiple-baseline design** we reduce the possibility of confounding factors by examining more than one baseline.

There are three general variations of the multiple-baseline design. One approach is to establish *multiple baselines across subjects*. Here, we measure a baseline for several individuals on the same behavior but we introduce the treatment for each at a different time. For example, the argument that maturation, history, or some other variable might cause a rat to increase lever-pressing relies on the idea that the variable changed at the precise moment that we introduced the treatment phase. To counter this argument, we might obtain the baselines for several subjects, but for each one introduce the food reward at a different point in time. Let's say we obtain the data shown in Figure 10.2.

Note that by starting the treatment at a different time for each subject, but still showing that the treatment alters the behavior, we effectively eliminate the argument that some other variable produced the results. An incredible coincidence would be required for a confounding variable to change simultaneously with the onset of each treatment phase. (This approach is also incorporated when replicating the previous reversal design with different subjects: we vary the time at which the ABA conditions are instituted for each subject.)

A second approach is to collect *multiple baselines across behaviors*. Here, we measure a baseline for several behaviors from *one* subject and apply the treatment for each behavior at a different time. If our study concerns a child who is disruptive in school, for example, we might establish baselines for aggressive acts, for temper tantrums,

FIGURE 10.2 Idealized Data from a Multiple-Baseline Design Across Subjects
Note the different points in time at which a food reward was introduced.

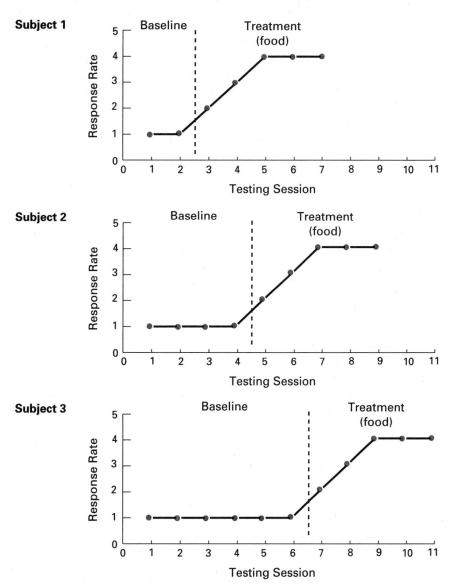

and for attention-seeking behavior. Let's say we hypothesize that a treatment involving verbal feedback is effective for all of these behaviors. The treatment is applied first to one behavior, later to the second behavior, and still later to the third. If the rate of each type of behavior drops only when the treatment is introduced, it is implausible that an extraneous confounding variable coincidentally caused the change in each behavior. Alternatively, let's say we hypothesize that a treatment will affect only one of the behaviors. After introducing the treatment, we should find that the target behavior changes but that the other behaviors remain at their baseline rate. If so, we can be confident that it was not changes in some extraneous variable that produced the change because it then should have changed all of the behaviors.

A third approach is to establish *multiple baselines across situations*. In this case, we establish baselines for one behavior on the same subject, but in different situations. For example, we might establish a baseline for a child's temper tantrums when at school and also when at home. Then, at different points in time we might apply a treatment phase consisting of quiet, time-out periods after each tantrum. It is unlikely that an extraneous variable that decreases tantrums would coincidentally occur with our treatment at different times, and both at school and at home. (Notice that such a design would be conducted as a field experiment with lessened environmental control, and with parents and teachers acting as researchers.)

> *REMEMBER* With a *multiple-baseline design*, we show the effect of a variable by demonstrating a change in the target behavior only when the treatment is introduced.

Design Concerns with Baseline Research   In any baseline design, the behavior and procedure we use to observe it must first produce a stable or consistent baseline. Therefore, we try to operationally define the dependent variable in a way that minimizes variability, and we observe the baseline condition for a sufficient period of time so that there are no clear increasing or decreasing trends in responding. Likewise, each treatment condition should be observed until the behavior is stable, so that we can clearly compare the effects of the presence and absence of the variable.

As usual, we must be careful to avoid any confounding. In particular, to balance changes in subjects due to their ongoing history and maturation, we ensure that each baseline phase has the same duration as each treatment phase. Also, given that some behaviors are influenced by a physiological or seasonal cycle (e.g., by the menstrual cycle in females), we prevent confounding due to cyclic changes by balancing the cycle's effect. We do so either by extending the baseline and treatment phases so that each encompasses the complete cycle or, when replicating with other subjects, by testing each at a different point in the cycle.

In multiple-baseline studies involving different behaviors from the same subjects, it is important that the behaviors be independent of one another. If they are not, then an extraneous variable (rather than our treatment) might actually cause one behavior to change, leading to changes in the other related behaviors. Therefore, we seek to examine behaviors that are not highly correlated with each other—and we must be sure that once the treatment is applied to one behavior, the baseline rate of the other behaviors does not change until we introduce the treatment.

Other Approaches to Single-Subject Designs

There are many variations to the single-subject approach (see for example Barlow & Hernsen, 1984). Although baseline studies usually compare the control condition to one treatment condition, we can also use this design to study the effects of several levels of a variable. For example, Kosten, Silverman, Fleming, and Kosten (1992) studied the effects of a cocaine substitute on cocaine abusers. They observed first the control baseline condition (A), then a subject under one dose level (B), then the same subject under a different dose level (C), and so on. (To reverse the effects of the treatment, we may insert a control condition between each treatment condition, producing an ABACAD design.)

It is also possible to investigate an interaction effect—the combined effect of two independent variables. However, in a baseline design, we investigate the effect of combining *one* specific level from one variable with *one* specific level of another. For example, we can determine whether there is a particular combined effect of presenting one amount of food with one amount of water as a reinforcer. In addition to control conditions, we test one animal with only food as a reward, then with both food and water, and then with only food again. In testing another animal, we present only water first, then food and water, and then only water. By comparing performance in the food-only and water-only conditions to the control conditions, we see their respective effects. And by comparing performance in the food-plus-water conditions to performance with water-only and food-only, we see whether there is a combined effect that is different from either individual effect. If there is, we have an interaction, a particular influence on responding that occurs with the combination of food and water.

In addition to the baseline designs we have discussed, the term *single-subject design* can also refer to the kinds of repeated-measures experiments described in previous chapters. We test only one subject, but we measure the dependent variable in terms of discrete trials, compute a mean or other summary score per condition, and so on. This approach is common when we are studying a subject with an extraordinary ability. In cognitive psychology, for example, Ericsson & Polson (1988) performed experiments on a waiter with an astounding memory for customer's dinner orders. They measured the errors in recalling an order as a function of manipulating the number of complete dinner orders taken or the length of time before recall. Likewise, in neuropsychology we may study "split-brain" patients (in whom the two hemispheres of the brain are not connected). For example, Gazzaniga (1983) examined recognition of visual or auditory stimuli in such patients as a function of the side of the brain to which stimuli were presented. Single-subject experiments are also common in psychophysics, where the objective is to quantify the relationship between the amount of physical stimulation presented and the psychological sensation of the stimulus. Here, one or a few subjects are tested over many trials to describe individual reactions to different amounts of weight, loudness, or brightness (e.g., Schiffman, 1990). Single-subject designs are often used in clinical research as well, because the symptoms of each patient are unique (e.g., Sacks, 1985).

Choosing Between Single-Subject and Group Designs

The major advantage of single-subject designs is that they allow us to closely examine a relationship between variables in a single individual. Further, sometimes they are necessary because the behavior of interest is found in an extremely small percentage of the population, and a researcher can find only one or two subjects to study. Sometimes, too, a design entails so much time and effort per subject that a single or small N is required. And single-subject designs are useful for initially exploring a behavior, or for studying variables that cause error variance in group studies.

The disadvantages of these designs stem from the fact that they involve repeated measures. They become less feasible the more that carry-over effects occur. In addition, they are not commonly used for studying an interaction involving several levels of each factor, because they create impossibly complex schemes. Finally, any single-subject design is wiped out by mortality effects: Rats may die during a study, and humans require extreme patience and motivation for long-term participation. To avoid such problems, we may find that a between-subjects group design works best. Between-group designs also can be conducted more quickly, and they allow for the use of deception and other procedures that may not be feasible with repeated measures.

As usual, we must also balance our concerns about internal and external validity. On the one hand, the potentially great control of variables in a single-subject design achieves a high degree of internal validity. So we would select a single-subject design especially when the possible influence of fluctuating subject variables is of primary concern. On the other hand, a major drawback of single-subject research is its limited external validity for generalizing to other subjects and situations. Since our results are tied to a unique subject (or to a very small N), *individual differences* may make our results very different from those we would find with other subjects. At the same time, our results are tied to a highly controlled and individualized setting, so generalizability is limited to only similar specific procedures. With a group design, however, we have greater confidence that our conclusions generalize to other subjects and settings.

> **REMEMBER** *Single-subject designs* provide substantial internal validity but have limited external validity.

The pros and cons of a single-subject design boil down to those shown in Table 10.2.

TABLE 10.2   Pros and Cons of a Single-Subjects Design

Pros	*Cons*
High internal validity	Limited external validity
Eliminates intersubject variance and examines intrasubject variance	Repeated measures influenced by mortality and carry-over effects
Describes relationship for an individual	Biased by characteristics of individual studied
Empirically demonstrates reliability of effect	Not practical for studying interactions

PUTTING IT ALL TOGETHER

The typical laboratory study of groups of humans is the most common in psychology, because it is practical and efficient, it provides a relatively high degree of internal validity, and it provides some external validity for generalizing our conclusions to other situations and human subjects. The question of whether to take this approach, however, depends on your reasons for conducting the study. You should conduct field research when you seek increased generalizability to real-world behaviors and subjects, which the generic laboratory study does not provide. You should conduct a single-subject design when you seek to eliminate error variance, especially variability due to differences in subjects, which group designs incorporate. And you should conduct research with animals either when you want to study animal behavior or when it is the only way to even remotely study a human behavior.

The variations on the typical experiment that we've seen in this chapter are a strength of psychological methods, because they provide a form of *converging operations* that allow us to study a behavior using different perspectives and procedures. Ideally, to form a complete body of knowledge, psychology needs both laboratory experiments and field experiments, since the reduced internal or external validity of one is made up for by the other. Likewise, researchers need group studies and single-subject designs to confidently build our understanding of a behavior. Single-subject designs give a specific description of a relationship as it applies to one case. Group designs give a general description of how a relationship tends to operate over numerous cases.

CHAPTER SUMMARY

1. A *field experiment* is an experiment conducted in a real-life setting in order to increase external validity.

2. Simple and systematic random sampling are types of *probability sampling* techniques, in which every potential subject has an equal likelihood of being selected. Additionally, with *stratified random sampling* we identify the important subgroups in the population and then proportionately randomly select from each group. With *cluster sampling* we randomly select certain groups and then observe the subjects in each group.

3. In *nonprobability sampling*, every member of the population does *not* have an equal opportunity to be selected. With *convenience sampling*, we study the subjects who are conveniently available. With *quota sampling*, we proportionately sample from the population but rely on convenience sampling to fill each quota. And with *snowball sampling*, we contact potential subjects who have been identified by previously tested subjects.

4. Field experiments may lose internal validity because extraneous variables are difficult to control in such settings. They may lose reliability because

subjects' behaviors are unreliable and measurements are imprecise and lack sensitivity.

5. A special demand characteristic that may occur in field experiments is the *Hawthorne effect*, a bias in subjects' behavior resulting from the special treatment and interest shown by a researcher.

6. When conducting field experiments we consider the ethics of invading subjects' privacy and manipulating variables that may have a real impact.

7. Laboratory research with animals is conducted when we wish to study an animal's behavior, to compare the behaviors of different species, or to create a model of behavior that generally applies to all animals, including humans.

8. Research with animals requires the same control of extraneous variables, including demand characteristics, that is found in research with humans.

9. Ethical animal research should minimize potential harm and be justified in terms of the scientific importance of the study.

10. Group designs have been criticized on the grounds that (a) they ignore the variables that cause inter- and intrasubject differences reflected by error variance, (b) they rely on mean scores that may barely show an effect and are inaccurate for describing any individual, and (c) they do not empirically show that an effect is reliable.

11. A *single-subject design* is a repeated-measures experiment conducted on one subject. The advantages of this type of design are that it (a) keeps subject variables constant, (b) allows the researcher to clearly see the size of the effect of a variable, and (c) demonstrates the reliability of the effect within the experiment.

12. A *baseline* is the level of performance on the dependent variable when the independent variable is not present. It is used as a comparison to performance when the variable is present.

13. In a *reversal design* (such as an ABA design), the researcher alternates between the baseline condition and the condition in which the independent variable is present.

14. When the influence of a manipulation cannot be reversed, we may employ a *multiple-baseline design*. With this design, a baseline is established for one behavior from several subjects, for several behaviors from one subject, or for one behavior from one subject in several situations.

15. Single-subject designs are most common when we are seeking a detailed description of one subject, when the treatment does not produce large carry-over effects, and when many observations per subject are necessary. Otherwise, a group design may be preferable.

REVIEW QUESTIONS

1. (a) What is the difference between a laboratory experiment and a field experiment? (b) What is the difference between correlational field research and a field experiment?

2. In terms of validity, (a) what is the major advantage of field experiments over laboratory experiments? (b) What is the major disadvantage?

3. What are the disadvantages of field experiments in terms of (a) the consistency of your procedures? (b) the reliability of your scoring? (c) power?

4. (a) What is the advantage of probability sampling over nonprobability sampling? (b) Why is the "randomness" and thus the representativeness of any random sample limited?

5. (a) What is the difference between simple and systematic random sampling? (b) What is stratified random sampling? (c) What is cluster sampling?

6. (a) What advantage and disadvantage are associated with convenience sampling? (b) What is quota sampling? (c) What is snowball sampling?

7. You test the effectiveness of motivational training by providing it to half of your college's football team during training camp. The remaining members form the control group, and the dependent variable is the coach's evaluation of each player. (a) Why might diffusion of treatment influence your results? (b) How could the Hawthorne effect influence your results? (c) How could the coach bias your results?

8. In question 7, why would you test the football team, instead of conducting a laboratory study of random psychology students?

9. To determine whether attractiveness influences a pledge's acceptability to a sorority, you present subjects from one sorority with descriptions of potential pledges accompanied by photos of unattractive females. Subjects from another sorority are given the same descriptions along with photos of pledges of medium attractiveness, and so on. (a) What confounding is present in this study? (b) How would you eliminate it?

10. In question 9, (a) why would you choose this design over randomly selecting females from a psychology course? (b) Compared to a laboratory study, what flaws are *not* eliminated by this design?

11. (a) What is a reversal design? (b) What is the logic for eliminating confoundings in this design? (c) What is the major factor that prohibits its use?

12. (a) What is a multiple-baseline design involving one behavior from several subjects? (b) What is the logic for eliminating confoundings in this design?

13. (a) What is a multiple-baseline design involving several behaviors from one subject? (b) involving one behavior for one subject in several situations?

14. Let's say you conduct a single-subject study of the influence of relaxation training on "state" anxiety (measured on the basis of heart rate). (a) Should this study involve an ABA reversal design or a multiple-baseline design? (b) Describe the specific design to use.

15. (a) In question 14, what are three advantages to using a single-subject design? (b) What are two disadvantages?

16. Several researchers claim that a procedure developed from an animal model has high criterion validity when applied to humans. What do they mean?

DISCUSSION QUESTIONS

1. You wish to examine the influence of wall color on people's mood. (a) How would you conduct this as a laboratory study? (b) As a field experiment on the general public? (c) As a field experiment on existing groups? (d) Discuss the pros and cons of each design.

2. Using the food-plus-water example of a reversal design discussed on page 331, sketch graphs that would show an interaction.

3. (a) How would you answer people who criticize field experiments as an invasion of people's privacy? (b) How would you feel after learning that you had participated in a study like the one by Middlemist et al. (1976) discussed in this chapter?

4. (a) How would you answer critics of laboratory animal research? (b) Do their arguments also lead to the conclusion that we should all be vegetarians?

11 Quasi-Experiments and Descriptive Designs

So far we have examined correlational designs and various types of true experiments. But psychological research also investigates hypotheses and variables using two other techniques: quasi-experiments and descriptive designs. These are legitimate research methods, although, as we will see, they have both strengths and weaknesses. As usual, our approach is to recognize the inherent weakness of a procedure but, otherwise, to design the best study we can.

QUASI-EXPERIMENTS

Recall that in a *true* experiment the researcher randomly assigns subjects to the conditions of the independent variable, so it is the researcher who determines each subject's "score" on the *X* variable. Sometimes, however, the nature of our independent variable is such that we cannot impose it on subjects, and thus we cannot randomly assign subjects to conditions. For example, let's say we think that gender influences memory ability. We obviously cannot randomly assign a *person* to be male or female, so, instead, we compare a group of existing males to a group of existing females, examining the memory abilities of each. In such a situation, we have a *quasi-experiment.* As discussed in Chapter 2, the subjects in a **quasi-experiment** are assigned to a particular condition because they have already experienced or currently exhibit that level of the variable. The term *quasi* means "seemingly," so this design has the appearance of a true experiment. Likewise, we do not truly manipulate the independent variable, so a quasi-experiment involves a **quasi-independent variable:** We lay out the design and compare the scores between conditions as in a true experiment, but we only appear to administer the variable.

You may have noticed that quasi-experiments bear a remarkable resemblance to correlational designs. In both, subjects have a score on the *X* variable because they have already experienced or now exhibit that level of the variable. Technically, a quasi-experiment *is* a descriptive, correlational design in that it tests the hypothesis that a relationship between certain variables exists. After all, whether we call it an experiment or not, the above example is equivalent to a study in which we merely approach a number of people, measure their gender and memory, and then correlate their scores. However, researchers use the name "quasi-experiment" to express two important differences between this type of design and the typical correlational design.

First, in a correlational design, subjects determine the range or variety of *X* scores we obtain, and we examine the relationship across the full range. For example, we might give subjects a personality test and correlate the full range of personality scores we obtain with their creativity scores. In a quasi-experiment, however, the researcher chooses or is forced to examine a few, specific values of the *X* variable. Thus, a researcher might first identify a few, specific personality scores, each defining a condition of the quasi-independent variable. Then, after measuring subjects' creativity, the researcher would examine the relationship between creativity and only these personality scores.

The second distinction is that a correlational design usually implies that there is little control of extraneous variables, while a quasi-experiment usually implies that the relationship between our variables is examined under more controlled conditions, with control groups and the like. Ideally, the latter will yield a more reliable and internally valid study for describing the relationship.

Essentially, then, a quasi-experiment is a more controlled version of a correlational design, in which we focus on certain levels of the X variable and arrange the design as if it were an experiment. However, like correlational designs, quasi-experiments still have two major limitations. First, their greater internal validity does *not* extend to extraneous *subject* variables. In other words, because we do not randomly assign subjects to conditions, we do not attempt to balance subject variables between and within conditions. Therefore, the conditions may be confounded by subject variables. For example, people differing in personality may also differ in intelligence, physiology, genetics, or experiences, any one of which may cause differences in creativity. Second, we may not be able to identify the true temporal order in which the variables occur. For example, someone's personality may cause a certain creativity level to develop, but it is possible that one's creativity level causes a certain personality to develop. Because of these restrictions, even a quasi-experiment conducted in a highly controlled laboratory setting provides little confidence that differences in the quasi-independent variable cause differences in the dependent variable.

> *REMEMBER* A *quasi-independent variable* is confounded by subject variables, so it severely restricts internal validity for inferring the cause of a behavior.

Still, a quasi-experiment is a common research approach that is necessitated by the variables or settings we wish to study. We must simply accept that the results of any single study only suggest a causal variable. And as usual, we ultimately build our confidence in a conclusion through *replication* and *converging operations*. Let's say, for example, that through repeated literal and conceptual replications—using correlational designs, quasi-experiments, and true experiments where possible—we consistently found a relationship between personality and creativity, yet failed to find other variables that relate to creativity. If this outcome fits our understanding of the constructs, then we will eventually develop a fair degree of confidence that personality has a causal influence on creativity.

Quasi-experiments generally occur in one of three situations: when the independent variable involves a subject variable, when it involves an uncontrollable, environmental event, and when it involves the passage of time.

QUASI-INDEPENDENT VARIABLES INVOLVING SUBJECT VARIABLES

Researchers are studying a quasi-independent variable whenever they study differences in behavior as a function of a subject variable. Often this variable involves a "trait characteristic," such as a subject's general level of anxiety, depression, or self-esteem. It may also involve such variables as the specific attitudes that subjects hold, their cognitive or physical abilities, their history and experiences, their social or work activities, their physiology, or their membership in a particular social, ethnic, or economic group. We "manipulate" such variables to the extent that we select the different types of subjects that are present in the experiment. Thus, for example, Russel (1976) compared the conditions of males and females in terms of their ability to recognize sex-specific body odors (by smelling a person's well worn t-shirt!). Burke, Chrisler, and Devlin (1989) studied brain organization by comparing left- and right-handed subjects on the dependent variable of creativity. In studies of personality, intelligence, and the like, researchers test identical twins in the quasi-conditions of those raised together and those raised apart (e.g., Tellegen et al., 1988). And in field research, researchers use quasi-independent variables when they examine, for example, factory workers whose jobs differ in level of responsibility and the resulting stress they produce (Martin & Wall, 1989). Likewise, the study in Chapter 10 comparing subjects in a shopping mall to subjects in a city park was a quasi-experiment. And quasi-independent variables occur in animal research when we compare the behaviors of different species or compare animals who differ in innate aggressiveness or dominance.

Also, a quasi-independent variable is involved any time the conditions compare "normal" to "abnormal" subjects. This is the predominant approach in clinical research, where the conditions are defined in terms of subjects having differing emotional disorders or degrees of a disorder, and the dependent variables reflect differences in behaviors, perceptions, or responsiveness to treatment. Likewise, in neurological research we can compare the cognitive abilities of healthy subjects with those having Korsakoff's syndrome or Alzheimer's disease (e.g., Janowsky, Shimamura, Kritchevsky & Squire, 1989).

Creating the Conditions of a Quasi-Independent Subject Variable

Identifying the subjects for each condition requires that we first measure subjects on the quasi-independent variable. Sometimes the variable is an obvious characteristic such as gender. At other times, we must pretest subjects with some type of selection device, perhaps observing their overt behavior or administering a questionnaire that measures a characteristic. Using the scores from the pretest, we operationally define each condition. For example, let's say we hypothesize a relationship between a subject's having low, medium, or high self-esteem and his or her willingness to take risks. From the research literature we can obtain any number of existing self-esteem tests, and one classic measure of risk-taking is the distance at which subjects stand from the target in a ring-toss game (Atkinson & Litwin, 1960). After administering the self-esteem test to a large pool of potential subjects, we use their scores to select subjects for each condition. Since few subjects are likely to exhibit an identical level of self-esteem, we can define low self-esteem as a test score of between 0 and 10, medium self-esteem as a score between 45 and 55, and high self-esteem as a score between 90 and 100. The design for this study is shown in Table 11.1.

Except for the absence of random assignment to conditions, this design is the same as it might be in a true experiment. We face all of the usual concerns, such as ethics, instructions, standardized procedures, demand characteristics, double blinds, reliable scoring,

TABLE 11.1   Diagram of a One-Way Experiment with a Quasi-Independent Variable

	Self-esteem level		
	Low (0–10)	*Medium (45–55)*	*High (90–100)*
Risk-taking scores	X	X	X
	X	X	X
	X	X	X
	.	.	.
	.	.	.
	$\overline{X}$	$\overline{X}$	$\overline{X}$

and pilot studies. Also, the factor of self-esteem may be combined with other variables in a factorial design—for example, we might manipulate the number of confederates present when a subject tosses rings. Note that in a multifactor design, we may employ any combination of true and quasi-independent variables.

How effectively we manipulate the conditions of our quasi-independent variable hinges on our selection pretest. Since this test is itself a measurement procedure, we have the usual design concerns to consider, such as scoring criteria, sensitivity, reliability, and demand characteristics. We must also consider the conditions that it will create. As always, we seek a valid manipulation of our independent variable, so, for example, the previous selection test must validly identify differences in self-esteem. Also, we seek a reliable, consistent manipulation, so the self-esteem scores should reliably reflect differences in self-esteem. Finally, we seek to maximize our power to find a significant relationship by creating a *strong manipulation.* We therefore select subjects having very distinctly low, medium, and high self-esteem scores so that our groups are very different from one another. We should then see large, significant differences in risk-taking.

> REMEMBER   The subjects within each condition of a quasi-independent variable should differ dramatically from subjects in other conditions.

Regression Toward the Mean

There is a potential flaw in reliability that can occur whenever we seek to identify subjects who are relatively extreme on a variable. Recall that any measurement technique may be unreliable to some extent and contain measurement error because random distractions and flukes can occur. Simply by chance, these influences may conspire in such a way that some subjects obtain extreme scores: Some subjects will be particularly lucky or unlucky at guessing answers, some may feel particularly good while others might be having a bad day, or there may be quirks in our measurement procedure that cause subjects to score especially well or especially poorly. Such random, momentary influences will not always be present, however, and they do have a way of averaging out. If we measured the subjects again, their scores will tend to be less extreme, simply by chance. This time, the high scores aren't so high and the lows aren't so low, but tend more toward the middle. Since the mean of a sample of scores falls in the middle of the scores, another way to say this is that a subject's typical score will tend to be closer to the mean. This outcome is known as regression toward the mean. **Regression toward the mean** occurs when, because of inconsistent random factors, extreme scores tend to change in the direction of coming closer to the mean.

Regression toward the mean can reduce the strength of our manipulations. Subjects identified by our selection pretest as having very high or very low self-esteem scores are likely to typically exhibit a more average level of self-esteem. Therefore, our three conditions may not actually differ in self-esteem as much as we think. If self-esteem does cause risk-taking, then with smaller differences between the levels of self esteem, we may find smaller, possibly nonsignificant differences in risk taking.

Regression toward the mean can also threaten internal validity, because what appears to be a change in scores due to our treatment may actually be nothing more than a change in random measurement error. For example, let's say we set out to test a counseling treatment for raising subjects' low self-esteem, using a pretest-posttest design. We measure and select people having low self-esteem, then apply the treatment, and then measure their self-esteem again. To some extent the peculiarities that produced very low self-esteem when we tested subjects the first time will not be present the second time. Therefore, the subjects' second score will tend to be higher (closer to the mean), regardless of whether our treatment works or not.

We counteract regression toward the mean by employing multiple trials from the most reliable selection tests possible. Also, as usual, we include a control group—another group that is measured at the same times as the experimental group but does not experience the treatment. The extent to which the control group's scores change will show the extent of extraneous influences, including that of regression toward the mean.

> **REMEMBER**   *Regression toward the mean* is a change in an extreme score toward a less extreme score that occurs because random influences are not consistently present.

Controlling Extraneous Variables

Even in a quasi-experiment, we attempt to control extraneous subject variables. We can select subjects from a limited population or match them on relevant variables (e.g., we might select only young subjects and match them across the conditions on their ring-tossing ability). We may control other subject variables by counterbalancing them (e.g., by selecting an equal number of males and females for each level of self-esteem). And, of course, we use random sampling (e.g., we randomly select subjects to pretest, and if enough people meet the criteria for a condition, we randomly select from among them the subjects we will actually study). Recognize, however, that such controls do not eliminate the problem that a quasi-independent variable is still likely to be confounded by other extraneous subject variables.

We are especially concerned with demand characteristics produced by the selection pretest: It may alert subjects to the variables and hypothesis we are studying and thus cause them to behave differently than they would if they were not conscious of our variables. Therefore, we may employ deception to disguise both the pretest and the purpose of the study. Or we may measure many subjects on the dependent variable first, and *then* give subjects the selection test to determine which subjects will be placed in each condition when we analyze the data. In any correlational study, we can capitalize on the fact that one variable does not truly precede the other by testing the variables in the order that is least biasing to subjects.

Recall that we also seek to eliminate differences on dependent scores within each group, so that we minimize error variance. In particular, the more that subjects differ on the independent variable *within* a condition, the greater the variability in dependent scores that we may see. Therefore, we try to narrowly define the range of selection scores that create each condition. In our self-esteem study above, the goal is to select very similar subjects in terms of self-esteem within a condition, because then they should score consistently in terms of risk-taking. Finally, recall that whenever we have lessened control and potentially large error variance, we can compensate by testing a relatively large N.

From the preceding discussion, you can see that there are four major threats to internal validity in a quasi-experiment of subject variables:

1. Lack of random assignment may lead to confounding by other subject variables.

2. Regression toward the mean may yield misleading results.

3. The selection device may produce demand characteristics.

4. Differences between subjects on the independent variable within conditions may produce error variance and reduce the apparent effect of the independent variable.

Analyzing the Results

As in previous experiments, we first examine the scores in each condition by computing the mean or other summary measure. We then perform parametric or nonparametric versions of the *t*-test or ANOVA, depending upon the characteristics of the dependent variable and the number of levels of the independent variable. Note, however, that unless we have created matched-groups or a pretest-posttest design, a quasi-independent variable is virtually always a between-subjects factor. With a multifactor design, we examine each variable's main effect as well as their interaction. For any significant effect, we perform *post hoc* tests and compute confidence intervals. And it is again appropriate to compute the effect size—the proportion of variance in dependent scores that is accounted for, or predicted, by knowing the condition a subject was in.

As usual, our final step is to attempt to explain psychologically how and why the independent and dependent variables are related in nature. But we tread softly around the issue of causality. In our example above, we know only that subjects who differ in their level of self-esteem—and possibly also differ on some hidden subject variable—show different levels of risk-taking.

QUASI-INDEPENDENT VARIABLES INVOLVING ENVIRONMENTAL EVENTS

A second type of quasi-experiment arises when we investigate the effect that an uncontrollable, environmental event has on behavior. Natural disasters (e.g., floods, hurricanes, and earthquakes) can dramatically affect an individual's mental health. Governments, schools, and industries institute programs that can influence a person's productivity and satisfaction. And societal events, such as wars, riots, and economic recessions, can alter individuals' expectations and attitudes.

Usually such variables cannot be studied in the laboratory (how do you create a war?), and when they can be, often the setting is so unrealistic that we have little experimental realism or ecological and external validity. Instead, researchers study such events using the general quasi-experimental approach known as a time-series design. A **time-series design** is a repeated-measures design in which we sample subjects' behavior prior to the occurrence of an event and again after it has occurred. Although this sounds like the typical pretest-posttest design, it is a quasi-experiment because we cannot randomly assign subjects to receive the treatment: We cannot randomly select those subjects who will experience an earthquake or who will have their school adopt a new program. We also have difficulty in creating control groups, and we cannot control the occurrence of the independent variable (in a city hit by a hurricane, not everybody experiences the same ferocity). We therefore have considerably less internal validity for concluding that the independent variable causes the dependent behavior, as well as less external validity for concluding that the same relationship is found with other subjects and settings.

While there are numerous approaches to time-series designs, the four major types are discussed below. (See Campbell & Stanley [1963] for the definitive brief text on such designs.)

One-Group Pretest-Posttest Designs

In the **one-group pretest-posttest design,** we obtain a single pretest measure on a group and then, after the treatment, obtain a single posttest measure of the group. For example, Frank and Gilovich (1988) hypothesized that wearing black uniforms leads to more aggressive behavior. Noting that more aggressive hockey players tend to spend more time in the penalty box, the researchers examined the number of penalty minutes incurred by a National Hockey League team before and after it changed to black uniforms. If we chose to replicate this study, we could use a repeated measures *t*-test design, comparing players' penalties immediately before and again immediately after the uniform change.

Note, however, that a one-group pretest-posttest design provides extremely weak internal validity for inferring the causes of a behavioral change. The overwhelming problem is that it lacks a control group. Without knowing the penalty scores of another control team that is repeatedly measured, we have no idea whether penalty scores might have changed in the experimental group, even if the uniforms *hadn't* been changed. To illustrate, consider the two graphs in Figure 11.1.

FIGURE 11.1 Graphs Showing the Potentially Missing Information When a Control Group Is Not Present in a Pretest-Posttest Design

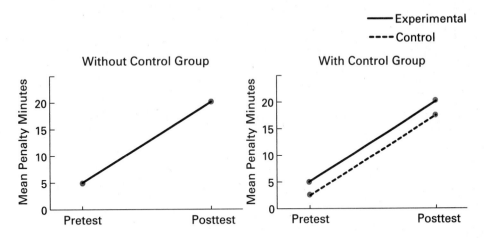

On the left, the one-group design appears to show that changing uniforms produced an increase in penalties. However, with a control group, we might have obtained the data on the right, which shows that with or without the uniform change, penalty minutes increased. This outcome would suggest that some other, confounding factor simultaneously changed which actually produced the increase in penalties: Maybe all teams became more aggressive, or the referees began calling more penalties than they had previously. Alternatively, since these measurements are separated by a period of time, there is always the possibility that the scores changed because of subjects' ongoing history and maturation: Maybe aggressiveness naturally increases as players become older and more experienced. Maybe the results reflect mortality effects, with less aggressive players leaving the team between measurements. Or, if researchers interviewed subjects, maybe they introduced a confounding through experimenter expectations or created a Hawthorne effect that altered later scores. And maybe the results reflect regression toward the mean: Perhaps at the pretest, players were coincidentally experiencing very low penalty rates, and the increase at the posttest merely reflects natural fluctuations in scores.

Similar problems arise if we study the job satisfaction of workers before and after a major change in a factory's production schedule or, as in Nolen-Hoeksema and Morrow (1991), if we examine the mental stress of people before and after an earthquake. Because our conclusions from a one-group pretest-posttest design are so weak, this design is typically used only when no alternative design is possible.

> **REMEMBER** In the *one group pretest-posttest design,* the absence of a control group means that we cannot eliminate the possibility that extraneous variables caused the dependent scores to change.

Nonequivalent Control Group Designs

You may think that the solution to the problems with the one-group design is simply to add a control group. However, implicitly we have always sought an *equivalent* control group. By *equivalent* we mean subjects who are similar to the experimental group in terms of their subject variables and their experiences between the pretest and the posttest. In true experiments we attempt to obtain an equivalent control group by (1) randomly assigning subjects to conditions, thus balancing subject variables, and (2) keeping all experiences the same for both groups. Thus, the ideal would be to randomly select half of a team to change uniforms and the other half not to or half of a city to experience an earthquake and the other half not to. Then the experimental and control groups would have similar characteristics and similar experiences between pre- and posttesting. Ideally, the only difference between the groups would be that one group experiences the treatment, so any differences in their posttest scores could be attributed to it.

The problem, of course, is that we cannot create the above control groups. In a time-series design, we usually cannot randomly select an equivalent control group because *all* members of the relevant subject pool automatically experience the treatment. The best we can do is to obtain a **nonequivalent control group,** a group that has different subject characteristics and different experiences during the study. For example, we might observe another hockey team that did not change to black uniforms during the same season as our experimental team. But this would be a nonequivalent control group because different teams have players with different styles of play, different coaches, different game strategies, and different experiences during the season. Likewise, if we selected people living in a different locale as the control group for people who experience an earthquake, this too would be a nonequivalent group, because people living in another region may be different and have different daily experiences.

If we simply compare the posttest scores of the experimental and control groups, any difference is confounded by initial differences between the groups and by differences in experiences during the study. Instead, therefore, we can compute the *difference* between the pre- and posttest scores for the subjects in each group. By computing the mean difference score for each group, we can see the *relative* change occurring with and without the treatment. To illustrate, let's say that with our control hockey team we obtain the data shown in Figure 11.2.

As you can see, the experimental team showed an increase in penalty minutes from 4 to 10 minutes (a difference of 6), while the control team showed an increase from 10 to 12 (a shift of only 2). Regardless of the actual number of penalties in each group, the important finding is that, over the same time period, there was a larger increase for the team that changed uniforms. To determine whether this difference is significant, we could perform the between-subject's *t*-test, comparing the *difference scores* for subjects in the control group with those in the experimental group.

Alternatively, we could perform a two-way ANOVA on the penalty scores and examine the interaction. As Figure 11.2 shows, the relationship between pretest-posttest scores and penalty minutes should *depend* on whether we examine the control group or the experimental group.

A nonequivalent control group design provides some degree of improvement in internal validity compared to the previous single-group design. The nonequivalent control

FIGURE 11.2 Data for a Nonequivalent Control Group Design

These data show penalties for both experimental and control groups over the same pre- and posttest period.

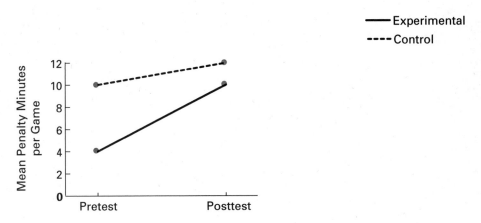

group helps us to eliminate potential confounding from only the factors *common* to different locales and subjects. In our hockey study, for example, the results suggest that there were no broad confounding factors common to both teams that produced the increase in penalties. If any maturation, history, or environmental effects common to all hockey players had been responsible for the results, then the difference between pre- and posttest would be the same for both groups. Because the experimental group exhibited a larger change, something else was present for only that group which produced the change. However, it is still possible that this "something else" was *not* the treatment. A nonequivalent groups design does not eliminate the possibility of a unique confounding influence or a random fluctuation that occurred only in the experimental group. Thus, it might have been some *localized* confounding event or a random fluctuation in yearly scores specific to our experimental team that actually brought about the increase in penalties. (Maybe the change was produced by a new coach who actively promoted more aggressive play.)

> *REMEMBER* A *nonequivalent control group design* eliminates only potential confoundings by variables that are common to both the experimental and control groups.

Interrupted Time-Series Designs

Sometimes, we do not have access to even an approximately equivalent control group. For example, it is difficult to imagine the control group for survivors of an airplane crash or for the men who have served as president of the United States. In such cases, we test whether the pretest-to-posttest changes in scores would have occurred without the treatment by examining scores at other times before and after the treatment. In an **interrupted time-series design,** we make observations at several spaced times prior to the occurrence of the independent variable and at several times after it. In fact, this was the approach taken by Frank and Gilovich (1988), who examined the penalty records for 10 years before and 6 years after a hockey team changed to black uniforms. Their results were similar to those shown in Figure 11.3

The researchers also incorporated the idea of a nonequivalent control group by comparing the team to the entire league. To do this, they transformed the team's yearly total penalty minutes to a z-**score.** This statistic describes the team's score relative to the average penalty time for the entire league (an average score produces a z of 0, a below-average score produces a negative z, and an above-average score produces a positive z). As you can see in Figure 11.3, before the uniform change the team was consistently below the league average in penalties but after the change it was consistently above average.

From such a pattern we see two things. First, the many pretest and posttest observations demonstrate the normal random fluctuations in scores from year to year. These are not as large as the change from before to after the treatment, so our treatment effect is apparently not a random fluctuation. Second, since we see a long-term stable type of response before the treatment and then a different long-term stable response after the treatment, it is unlikely that subject history, maturation, or environmental variables produced the observed change. These variables would be expected to operate over the entire 16-year period, producing similar changes in responses at other points in time. Yet the change occurred only after the treatment was introduced. (Advanced statistical procedures are available for determining whether this is a significant change; see Cook and Campbell, 1979.)

The interrupted time-series design allows us to conclude confidently that the pretest-to-posttest change in dependent scores has not resulted from a random fluctuation in scores or from a repeatedly occurring confounding variable. The one weakness in the design is

FIGURE 11.3   Data for Interrupted Time-Series Design

Shown here are the yearly penalty records (in z-scores) of a hockey team before and after changing to black uniforms.

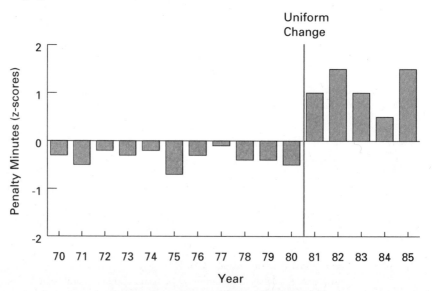

that some variable may have coincidentally changed once, at the same time as our treatment was introduced. For example, hockey teams change players yearly, and perhaps by chance more penalty-prone players were acquired at the same time as the uniform change. However, such an explanation would require a rather exceptional coincidence, considering all of the continual changes in the makeup and experiences of the team over this 16-year period. Therefore, we have substantial confidence that the change in behavior is due to the treatment. (Frank and Gilovich (1988) provide additional confidence by also reporting a laboratory study demonstrating that wearing black does increase aggressiveness.)

> **REMEMBER** The numerous pre- and posttest observations of an *interrupted time-series design* reduce, but do not eliminate, the possibility that the treatment is confounded with some other event.

Multiple Time-Series Designs

To further increase our confidence in the conclusions from a quasi-experiment, we can combine the interrupted time-series design and the nonequivalent control group design, creating a **multiple time-series design.** Here, we observe an experimental and nonequivalent control group, and for each we obtain several spaced pretest scores and several spaced posttest scores. Thus, for example, we might examine several years of penalty records both for the team that changes uniforms and for another team that does not, as shown in Figure 11.4.

FIGURE 11.4 Data for a Multiple Time-Series Design

The yearly penalty record of hockey team before and after changing to black uniforms, and of a nonequivalent control team.

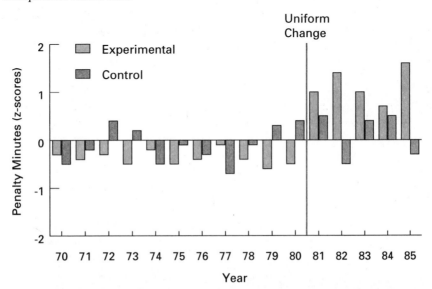

This figure shows the effect of the treatment in two ways. First, within the experimental group we see that the change in behavior occurs only after the treatment has been introduced, and that otherwise we have one stable behavior before and a different stable behavior after the treatment. Second, comparing the experimental and control groups, we see that the change from pre- to posttest scores in the experimental group is larger than that in the control group.

Although there may still be some factor that occurred simultaneously with our treatment, the fact that it does not produce the same results in the control group means that it is localized and specific to the experimental group. Further, the fact that throughout all these years it occurs only once and simultaneously with the treatment means that it would have to be a most exceptional coincidence. Together, these findings make it very unlikely that a confounding variable produced the change in the experimental group.

> REMEMBER   *In a multiple time-series design* we examine numerous pretest and posttest observations for both an experimental and nonequivalent control group as two ways of eliminating potential confounding variables.

THE QUASI-INDEPENDENT VARIABLE OF THE PASSAGE OF TIME

One very important quasi-independent variable in psychology is the passage of time. The entire field of developmental psychology is built around the variable of age, focusing on how it relates to changes in social, emotional, and cognitive behavior. We also study the passage of time in other settings, as when we compare experienced with inexperienced workers or follow an individual's change in memory ability over the course of a day. These are quasi-independent variables, because we cannot randomly assign people to be a certain age or to experience only a certain amount of work. Therefore, such studies are essentially time-series designs, in that we sample subjects' behavior at different points, before and after the passage of a certain amount of time. They differ from the previous time-series designs in one important way, however. In the previous designs, an environmental event was the variable of interest, while the accompanying passage of time between measurements allowed for potential confoundings from maturation and history. In the present designs, the passage of time with the accompanying maturation and history is the variable of interest, while environmental events are potential confoundings.

There are three general approaches to studying the passage of time: longitudinal designs, cross-sectional designs, and cohort designs.

Longitudinal Designs

In a **longitudinal design,** we repeatedly measure a group of subjects in order to observe the effect of the passage of time. For example, we might study vocabulary development in a group of children by testing them yearly from ages four to eight (Gathercole, Willis, Emslie & Baddeley, 1992). As shown in Table 11.2, such a design is set up and analyzed

TABLE 11.2   Diagram of a One-Way Longitudinal Study, Showing Repeated Observations of Each Subject at Different Ages

Xs represent vocabulary scores.

	Age (in years)				
	4	*5*	*6*	*7*	*8*
Subject 1	X	X	X	X	X
Subject 2	X	X	X	X	X
Subject 3	X	X	X	X	X
"	.	.	.	.	.
"	.	.	.	.	.
	$\overline{X}$	$\overline{X}$	$\overline{X}$	$\overline{X}$	$\overline{X}$

in the same way as any other repeated-measures experiment. Collapsing vertically, any differences between the mean scores for the conditions will reflect changes in vocabulary skills as a function of age. As usual, this factor may be part of a multifactor design, in which we also examine other true or quasi-independent variables.

We might also study briefer periods of time. For example, Nelson and Sutton (1990) examined white-collar workers over a nine-month period to determine how they coped with work-related stress. And, as discussed in Chapter 10, Gladue and Delaney (1990) technically used a longitudinal design when they questioned patrons in a bar repeatedly to see whether they rated others as more attractive as closing time approached. (See also Pennebaker et al., 1979.)

The overriding advantage of a longitudinal study is that, as a repeated-measures design, it keeps subject variables reasonably constant between the conditions. Thus, in the example above, by observing the same children as they age, we keep constant such variables as their genetic makeup, their parents, and so on. The disadvantages of longitudinal designs are, first, that just keeping in touch with subjects over a lengthy period can be difficult, so these studies often involve a small N. Second, because they involve repeated measures, successive responses may be confounded by carry-over effects or by response sets, and the results may be misleading because of subject mortality during the study. Third, and most important, a longitudinal study is inherently confounded by any extraneous variable that subjects experience during the study. (For example, an increase in a boy's vocabulary between ages four and five might appear to reflect normal development but may actually be due to his learning to read or watching certain television shows.) Finally, a lengthy longitudinal study may not generalize well to future generations, because the society and culture are constantly changing. Recall that a concern about our inferences is *temporal validity,* the extent to which our results generalize to different time periods. A study of language development in the 1950s, for example, may not generalize well to children in the 1990s, because of such changes as modern educational television and preschool education.

REMEMBER *Longitudinal designs* are confounded by extraneous events that occur during the course of the study, and they may not generalize over time.

Cross-Sectional Designs

We can also study the passage of time using a **cross-sectional design.** This design is a between-subjects quasi-experiment in which subjects are observed at different ages or at different points in a temporal sequence. Thus, for example, we might select a "cross-section" of ages, testing the vocabulary of a group of four-year-olds, a different group of five-year-olds, and so on, as shown in Table 11.3. Similarly, we may obtain a cross-section of workers having different amounts of job experience. Basically, these are examples of the design we examined earlier, in which the researcher selects subjects for each condition using a subject variable—except that the variable here is based on time. (And again, these factors may be part of a multifactor design, in which we also examine other true or quasi-independent variables in a factorial design.)

The major advantage of a cross-sectional design is that the study can be conducted rather quickly and easily. The major disadvantage is that the conditions may differ not just in terms of age or amount of experience but also in terms of many confounding variables. For example, our five-year-old subjects will also differ from our four-year-olds in genetic makeup, family environment, and other variables that may cause differences in dependent scores. Further, given the general societal experiences of the subjects we study, our conclusions may not generalize well to future four- and five-year-olds.

A special confounding in cross-sectional studies occurs because of differences in subject history. For example, let's say we study memory ability as a function of age by testing subjects born in the United States in 1930, 1950, and 1970. These groups differ not only in age but also in that each group grew up during a different era. Their backgrounds therefore differ in terms of health and nutritional care, educational programs, and cultural experiences. (One group reached adolescence during World War II, another during the birth of television, and the third when recreational drugs were

TABLE 11.3 Diagram of a One-Way Cross-Sectional Study, Showing Observations of a Different Group of Subjects at Each Age

Xs represent vocabulary scores.

Age (in years)				
4	5	6	7	8
X	X	X	X	X
X	X	X	X	X
X	X	X	X	X
.	.	.	.	.
.	.	.	.	.
$\overline{X}$	$\overline{X}$	$\overline{X}$	$\overline{X}$	$\overline{X}$

common.) Thus, any differences in memory ability that we find may actually be due to these differences in history. This confounding is called a cohort effect. **Cohort effects** occur when age differences are confounded by differences in subject history. The larger the differences in age, the greater the potential for cohort effects.

> *REMEMBER*   *Cohort effects* confound age differences with differences between each generation's unique history.

A more subtle but equally detrimental problem is that our testing procedures and stimulus materials may not be appropriate for widely divergent age groups. If we test subjects' knowledge of common popular culture, for example, older people may be unable to identify the names of current rock-and-roll bands or to understand electronic games. But if we test knowledge of political or historical events, older people may perform better, because they lived through the events.[1] Likewise, different age groups will not be equally motivated and engaged by a particular procedure, nor will they obey our instructions to the same extent. It is difficult enough to get college students to memorize "droodles" or to hold a pen in their mouths to make them smile. Faced with such tasks, the elderly may be disinclined to participate altogether or, at a minimum, may experience little experimental realism. Great care must be taken, therefore, to ensure that differences in the mental and physical abilities, experiences, and motivations of different age groups do not confound the variable of age.

Because of the greater likelihood of potential confoundings, cross-sectional designs are generally considered to be less effective than longitudinal designs. However, they do provide an immediate snapshot comparison of subjects who differ in age or time-related experiences. To the extent that we are able to match subjects across conditions and eliminate confoundings in a cross-sectional design, we can determine how temporal differences affect a dependent variable.

> *REMEMBER*   *Cross-sectional designs* involve a between-subjects comparison of different age groups. They may be confounded by any other variable that also distinguishes the groups.

Cohort Designs

Although we cannot completely prevent cohort effects, we can identify whether they are present. To do this, we employ a cohort design. In a **cohort design** we perform a longitudinal study of several groups, each from a different generation. Let's say, for example, that we repeatedly study the vocabulary development in one generation of children beginning when they are four years old in 1990 and in another generation of children beginning when they are four in 1994. As shown in Table 11.4, this design is set up and analyzed in the same way as any other two-way experiment.

---

[1] As a demonstration of how people remember information about an unusual event, I used to ask students to recall what they were doing when President John F. Kennedy was assassinated. Now they answer, "I wasn't born yet!"

TABLE 11.4   Diagram of a Two-Way Cohort Study

*X*s represent vocabulary scores.

		Repeated measures over age					
		4	5	6	7	8	
1990	1	X	X	X	X	X	
Subjects	2	X	X	X	X	X	$\overline{X}$ ←
	3	:	:	:	:	:	
1994	1	X	X	X	X	X	
Subjects	2	X	X	X	X	X	$\overline{X}$ ←
	3	:	:	:	:	:	
Age main effect →		$\overline{X}$	$\overline{X}$	$\overline{X}$	$\overline{X}$	$\overline{X}$	

Generation main effect

In this table, the columns represent the repeated testing of a child at different ages, and the upper and lower portions represent the two respective generations. Collapsing vertically over the two generations, we obtain the mean score for each age, and differences between the means show the main effect of different ages, regardless of a subject's generation. This factor provides the longitudinal, developmental information. Next, by collapsing scores horizontally, we obtain the main effect mean of each generation, regardless of age. If there is no significant difference between these means, then there is no evidence that the scores differ on the basis of a subject's generation. However, if there is a difference between the two groups, then cohort effects may be present and our developmental results are less likely to generalize to other generations. Likewise, the absence of a significant interaction between generation and age would suggest that changes in scores as a function of age are basically similar—*parallel*—regardless of each generation's unique history. A significant interaction, however, would indicate that the type of changes with age that we see *depends* on which generation we examine—in which case we have a cohort effect.

> REMEMBER   A *cohort design* is the longitudinal study of several groups, each from a different generation.

To help you remember the names and procedures of all the preceding quasi-experimental designs, they are summarized in Table 11.5.

DESCRIPTIVE RESEARCH

The final general research approach for us to discuss is descriptive research: studies designed to describe a behavior, the situation it occurs in, or the subjects exhibiting it. You already know that, in demonstrating causality, true experiments involve some description of the behavior under study. Likewise, correlational designs—including quasi-experiments—are descriptive procedures used to test a hypothesis that a rela-

TABLE 11.5   Summary of Quasi-Experimental Designs

Type of design	*Procedure*
Designs involving subject variables	Create conditions on the basis of a subject characteristic
Time-series designs	
One-group pretest-posttest design	Measure one group once before and once after event.
Nonequivalent control group design	Conduct pretest and posttest on both an experimental and nonequivalent control group
Interrupted time-series design	Obtain repeated measurements of one group, both before and after event.
Multiple time-series design	Conduct interrupted time-series measurements on both an experimental and control group
Designs involving temporal variables	
Longitudinal design	Obtain repeated measures as a function of age or experience.
Cross-sectional design	Use a between-subjects design based on age or experience.
Cohort design	Examine repeated-measures factor based on age with between-subjects factor based on generation.

tionship exists between two or more variables. Outside of these contexts, however, the term **descriptive research** usually conveys the intention only to observe and describe subjects or their behavior, usually in natural settings where we do not manipulate or control any variables. Further, since descriptive studies may describe only one subject or measure only one variable, we neither correlate changing variables nor look for specific, hypothesized relationships. Instead, our goal is literally, and simply, to describe a certain behavior or type of subject.

On the one hand, the disadvantage of such descriptions is that we examine a behavior while the full complexity of nature is present. Without the controls that simplify nature, we may miss hidden influences on the behavior or misinterpret what we see. Thus, with descriptive research we can only speculate on the causes of a behavior. On the other hand, there are three advantages of descriptive research:

1. We conduct descriptive research because descriptions are informative. Thus, for example, we might describe the mating rituals of frogs in the wild or the actions of drivers in a large city, because these are interesting behaviors. Also, for applied research, we may need descriptions of consumer attitudes or of the behaviors of drug addicts.

2. Because we examine the full complexity of nature, describing a behavior can be the starting point for identifying variables and building hypothetical constructs that will later be tested using other methods. For example, much research in clinical psychology developed from the constructs of Sigmund Freud, even though he never conducted an experiment but rather described the behaviors he

observed. Likewise, descriptions can provide an indirect test of a theory or model. (A researcher might ask, for example, Are the predictions from a Freudian model confirmed by a description of a schizophrenic?)

3. Some behaviors and situations cannot be studied any other way than through description, either because there are ethical restrictions, because artificialness would otherwise be introduced by the researcher, or because the behavior cannot be produced on demand. The only way to learn about the migratory behaviors of whales or the childhood experiences of a serial killer, for example, is by observing and describing them.

REMEMBER   The focus of *descriptive research* is to describe a behavior, the situation in which it occurs, or the subjects who exhibit it.

Descriptive research designs fall into two general categories: field surveys and observational studies.

Field Surveys

A **field survey** is a procedure in which subjects complete a questionnaire or interview in a natural setting. Note that this is different from having subjects complete a questionnaire in a field experiment, because the term *survey* conveys that we do not manipulate factors. Instead, the focus of such a study is to poll a sample so that we may infer the responses we'd see if we could poll the population. Field surveys may apply to a particular population, as in George, Reed, Ballard, Colin, and Fielding's (1993) survey of nurses who treat AIDS patients. They are also used to describe the general population. For example, we might determine the public's reactions to drug use and criminal behavior (Harrison & Gfroerer, 1992), describe general consumer attitudes (Fornell, 1992), or determine the frequency of a certain characteristic, such as that of homosexuality (Harry, 1990). Field surveys may also describe subjects' common experiences, as in Conlon's (1993) study of people's feelings about justice after appealing their parking violations. The Roper Organization (1992) even polled 6,000 Americans to gauge whether people have experiences associated with ghosts and UFOs: More than 1,800 people reported that they had!

All of the considerations about questionnaires discussed in previous chapters should be applied to a field survey: construct and content validity, reliable scoring, clear questions with precise, mutually exclusive choices, and controlled consistent behavior on the part of the interviewer. In particular, since we often deal with unsophisticated subjects, we want to focus on having them describe concrete behaviors. Also, because in the real world subjects may be frazzled and busy, we counterbalance the order of questions across different subjects and include "catch questions." In this way we control for and identify response biases that occur when subjects half-heartedly respond in order to finish the task quickly.

In addition to a good questionnaire, the key to field surveys is our sample. Because we are especially concerned about the external validity provided by survey research, we want to obtain a representative sample, a sample that truly reflects the characteristics and responses found in the population. To improve our chances of doing so, we typically survey a rather large N, often involving hundreds of subjects. We may sometimes conduct a survey at a particular location, such as a shopping mall or other public place, because we believe members of the target population frequent that place. At other times, we may be unable to reach a representative sample at any one location. Then we reach a broader segment of the population either by mailing the survey or by conducting it over the telephone.

Mailed Surveys   Mailing a survey to subjects is most useful when a large sample is needed and/or a lengthy questionnaire is being used—and when the researcher is not in a hurry to get the data. A major problem with mailed surveys, however, is that some subjects may not bother to complete and mail them back to us (even though we always include a stamped, addressed return envelope). The "return rate" can be very low, with only 10% or 20% of the surveys being returned. In such a case, we may have a sample that is very unrepresentative of the population. Therefore, some researchers use the rule of thumb that we can have confidence in a mailed survey when the return rate is at least 50%.

There are many techniques for improving return rates (see Kanuk & Berenson [1975] for a review). First, include a cover letter with the survey that explains its purpose and why it is important for subjects to complete it, and provides complete information about the researchers and how they can be contacted. Second, make sure that the survey presents the appropriate *face validity:* It should be well organized, neat, and professional, and should look like a serious, precision psychological instrument. Third, both for reliability and to increase return rates, rely on closed-end or brief open-end questions so that it is easy for subjects to follow the instructions and to accurately and rapidly complete the survey. Sometimes researchers include a small reward for subject participation, or they mail a follow-up letter to remind subjects to complete the survey. The goal is to convince subjects that you are conducting legitimate research and to engage their interest and cooperation.

Telephone Surveys   Surveys can also be conducted over the telephone (see Lavrakas, 1993). These usually consist of structured interviews, in which the interviewer reads the subject a series of closed-end questions. With only one interviewer, a telephone survey can be a *very* lengthy enterprise. If the researcher has sufficient funds to hire many interviewers, however, the data collection can be compressed into a short time frame. For this reason, telephone surveys are used, for example, during election campaigns to get the momentary "pulse" of the voters. Also, telephone surveys may achieve a higher response rate than mailed surveys because some people are less likely to refuse when a person directly requests their help. Conversely, some people may *not* participate because they consider such surveys to be demanding interruptions in their lives. And many subjects may be wary because "psychological surveys" have frequently been used as a cover for obscene phone calls and for telemarketing scams.

Again, the key to enlisting subjects is an effective initial introduction. A professional, straightforward, yet friendly manner will add to your credibility and engage your subjects. Clearly identify yourself and allow subjects to verify who you are (e.g., give them your phone number). Describe the survey, the time needed to complete it, its purpose, and the way in which responses will be handled. Keep the length of the questioning brief (subjects tend to be more receptive to lengthy surveys when they are received by mail).

To improve the reliability of a telephone survey, keep each question and the response choices brief and simple: Subjects do not have the questions in front of them, so they must rely on their memory, and thus subject errors are likely. Further, remember that the interviewer's behavior is important. By calling subjects at their homes, we increase the likelihood of biasing, informal interactions. Therefore interviewers are trained to stick to the script, reading the questions in an unbiased manner and providing no additional information or hints. To the degree possible, the interviewer should respond to a subject's comments by politely repeating the survey question.

Once we have identified the method for conducting the survey, we must decide how to assemble a representative sample. In doing so, we consider how we will identify and select subjects from the appropriate population.

Identifying the Population   As with *any* type of research, surveys may be biased by the manner in which we identify the population of potential subjects. The members of a population are often identified from government and commercially available mailing lists or from membership lists of relevant social or civic groups. On the one hand, we want to avoid including people from outside of the target population. In a survey of voter attitudes, for example, we should survey only those people who vote, so we may use a list of people who voted in the last election (although this doesn't mean they'll vote in the next election). Similarly, to contact senior citizens, we might obtain addresses from senior citizen groups. On the other hand, we do not want to exclude any important segments of the population. Some senior citizens do not belong to any groups, and a list of voters from the last election does not include people who are going to vote for the first time. Likewise, a survey of opinions about gun control should not be based solely on registered gun owners—but it should not exclude them totally either. Thus, our first goal is to identify all of the important subgroups in the target population that should be represented in the sample.

Selecting the Sample   A survey can still be biased by the manner in which we select our sample from the target population. From a mailing list, we may simply contact every subject. If this is not feasible, we can employ any of the sampling techniques discussed in Chapter 10.

When we have a large list of potential subjects, *probability sampling*—simple and systematic random sampling—can be very effective. To ensure that the various subgroups of the population are accurately represented, however, we often employ *stratified random sampling.* That is, we identify the important subgroups in the population and then randomly select subjects from each of them, so that the proportion of our total N made up by each subgroup matches the corresponding proportion found in the population. For example, if government records reveal that 10% of the population own guns and our sample N is to be 1,000, we randomly select 100 subjects from the pool of registered gun owners. To be even more precise, if 2% of the population are females who own guns, we randomly select 20 subjects from the pool of female gun owners. (This technique is used in professional telephone surveys at election time, and though each survey typically involves only about 1,000 subjects, the pollsters are extremely accurate in predicting the outcome of an election involving some 50 million voters!)

If we cannot obtain a list of individuals in the population from which to randomly select, we may employ *cluster sampling* and randomly select certain locations or groups to survey. Or we may employ *nonprobability sampling* techniques, such as *convenience sampling, quota sampling,* or *snowball sampling.*

With any of the above approaches, a survey can still be biased, because our procedures may involve hidden criteria that eliminate certain subjects. For example, the time of day we telephone is an important consideration. At noon on weekdays we may find only a certain type of subject at home, and calling at dinner time may be biased against parents who are busy with small children to feed. Likewise, when we distribute surveys at a public place, we must remember that the time and place we select, our manner of dress, and our approach to subjects may produce a biased sample.

Subjects have their own reasons for participating, so, as usual, our results are prone to the volunteer bias. Those who do not participate may be a certain type (e.g., very busy or very lazy) and those who do participate may be a different type (e.g., very inactive or bored). An especially important bias is how strongly subjects feel about the issues being raised in the survey. For example, a mailed survey about abortion in the United States is most likely to be completed by those who very strongly favor abortion or very strongly oppose it. This is the danger with radio and television call-in surveys: The callers are probably a biased sample, consisting of those people who, for some reason, are especially motivated to make the call. In field surveys, always consider whether you have missed the "silent majority."

> *REMEMBER* As in any research, we must take care to identify the target population to be surveyed and to obtain a representative sample.

Analyzing Survey Results To summarize the results of a survey, we employ many of the statistical techniques already discussed. Usually we rely on descriptive statistics, computing summary statistics such as the mean rating for questions, counting the frequency of certain responses, and describing the variability in scores. We may also correlate scores from different questions that measure different variables. As usual, we determine whether correlations are significant and use t-tests, ANOVA, and the chi square procedure to identify significant differences between the groups we've surveyed.

Since we conduct field surveys to describe the population, we frequently compute a confidence interval. Recall that a confidence interval is a range of values, one of which we would expect to find if we could test the entire population. Thus, for example, if a sample of nurses produces a certain mean rating about dealing with AIDS patients, a confidence interval would provide a range of values within which we expect the average rating of the population of nurses to fall. Likewise, confidence intervals are involved when we report the frequency of a certain response, In this context, however, they are usually called the **margin of error.** If, for example, pollsters report that 45% of a sample support the president's policies, they may also report a margin of error of plus-or-minus

3%. This number communicates that if we could poll the entire population, the actual percentage of people who support the president is expected to be within 3 percentage points of 45%, or between 42% and 48%.

Recognize, however, that even if we use sophisticated sampling techniques and have a large N, the results of our survey will lack external validity to some degree. Any sample we select is likely to be different from any other sample we might have selected. Also, the more we use convenience and other nonprobability sampling techniques, the less representative our sample will be. Finally, because surveys reflect how people feel at the time of the survey, they may have little *predictive validity* for describing how people will feel later.

Observational Studies

In a field survey, subjects know they are being surveyed and there is some interaction between the researcher and subjects, even if it is only through the mail. A different approach to descriptive research is to employ observational techniques. In **observational research,** we do not directly ask subjects to respond. Rather, we observe them in an unobtrusive manner. In this case, then, our description is based simply on our observations of the subjects.

There are three general observational methods. In **naturalistic observation,** the researcher observes a wide variety of subjects' behaviors in an unobtrusive manner. Usually, the term *naturalistic observation* implies a rather unstructured and unsystematic approach in which we have not identified a specific, limited behavior or situation to study. To be unobtrusive, we may use hidden cameras, observe from camouflaged hiding places, or simply blend in with the crowd in a public place. If unobtrusive techniques are not possible, then at a minimum we *habituate* subjects to our presence before beginning the study, so that they are not self-conscious about our observing them. For example, the famous studies performed by Jane Goodall (1986, 1990) involved naturalistic observation of chimpanzees. After they had habituated to her presence, she was able to observe their general lifestyles in the wild. Likewise, Mastrofski and Parks (1990) performed an observational study of police officers in action by riding with the officers on patrol.

More commonly, researchers perform **systematic naturalistic observation.** Here again we are unobtrusive and noninvasive, but in this case we identify a particular behavior and a specific situation to observe so that we are more "systematic" in our observations. For example, Heslin and Boss (1980) observed the nonverbal interactions of people being met at an airport, and Pellegrini (1992) observed the "rough and tumble" games of children at a playground. This approach is also common in studies of animals in the wild; Boesch-Acherman and Boesch (1993), for example, observed the use of natural tools by wild chimpanzees.

Sometimes, the behavior of interest involves private interactions between members of a group that cannot be seen from afar. Then we may perform **participant observation,** in which the researcher is an active member of the group being observed. Usually, this is a form of systematic observation, but the researcher's purposes and activities remain hidden from subjects. In a classic example, Rosenhan (1973) arranged for "normal" observers to be admitted to a psychiatric hospital to observe the way the staff treated and diagnosed patients. Likewise, Rafaeli and Sutton (1991) conducted participant observation of the intimidation strategies of bill collectors by working alongside experienced collectors.

> *REMEMBER* The basic approaches in observational studies are *naturalistic observation, systematic observation,* and *participant observation.*

The overriding advantage of these approaches is that, through unobtrusive observation with no intervention by the researcher, we are describing behaviors in a natural setting that are not influenced by subject reactivity or other demand characteristics. There are, however, several disadvantages.

1. Our descriptions are highly susceptible to experimenter expectations, so that we sometimes see only what we expect to see. This is especially a problem with participant observation because the researcher can inadvertently influence the group, causing the subjects to behave in the expected way.

2. We do not obtain informed consent. Especially with participant observation, there is the ethical question of violating a subject's expectation of privacy.

3. Usually we do not have a list of the population from which to randomly sample, so we must often rely largely on convenience samples of those subjects we can find to observe.

4. Instead of measuring or quantifying subjects' responses, we often have only our verbal descriptions of a given behavior based on our visual observations. Such *qualitative data* may lack precision and accuracy, and they are not very sensitive for reliably discriminating subtle differences in behavior.

For the above reasons, observational designs are generally considered to have little validity for identifying the presence of relationships between variables, let alone for identifying causal relationships. However, they can be very useful as a starting point for identifying potentially important variables, and they provide the ultimate natural setting for testing models or predictions about a behavior that are derived from more controlled research settings.

To minimize biases and to create more reliable and precise observations, we usually employ an assortment of systematic techniques. For example, we may develop scoring criteria using *content analysis* as discussed in Chapter 9, looking for certain movements, speech patterns, facial expressions, and so on (see Holsti [1969] or Krippendorf [1980]). We may count the frequency of each specific behavior or measure its duration. We may employ *time sampling,* in which we break the observation period into intervals and then determine whether the behavior occurs during each interval. And, when observing groups, we may observe the entire group all at once, or we may observe only one subject for a certain time, then observe another, and so on.

To facilitate accurate data recording and to minimize the time spent not observing, we may produce structured scoring sheets so that we can simply check off categories of behaviors. Or we may automate by tape-recording subjects or our verbal descriptions of them for later scoring. To reduce experimenter biases, we may employ multiple observers and double-blind procedures. And, finally, to improve external validity, we may attempt to obtain more "random" samples, either through systematic random sampling of every *n*th subject or through random selection of clusters to observe.

Additional Sources of Data in Descriptive Approaches

When we use the term *observational research,* we generally mean that a researcher was physically present to observe a number of subjects. In the research literature, however, you will encounter different terms communicating that other procedures were employed to collect the data. Whether the researcher's goal is simply to describe subjects or their behavior, or to test a hypothesis about a specific relationship, the three common terms that further identify a design are archival research, *ex post facto* research, and case studies.

Archival Research   The term **archival research** communicates that written records constitute the source of our data on one or more variables. Typically, these records come from schools, hospitals, government agencies, or police. For example, Faustman and White (1989) examined medical and psychiatric records to describe the posttraumatic stress disorder found in some war veterans. Leenaars (1991) examined suicide notes to identify their common themes. And in applied archival research, Kiesler (1993) described the extent to which nonpsychiatric hospitals are actually involved in the treatment of psychiatric cases. Archival research is also used to describe social trends and events, as in Connors and Alpher's (1989) analysis of the alcohol-related themes in country-western songs. The researchers concluded that alcohol is usually used for drowning one's sorrows. (Does this finding suggest something about the people who write such songs, or about the people who listen to them?)

The advantage of archival research is that it allows access to behaviors that would otherwise be unobservable. It also allows us to verify subjects' self-reports (e.g., we can check subjects' actual college-grade records as opposed to relying on their reports). However, archival research also presents some practical disadvantages. First, we may not have access to all pertinent records, because obtaining permission from those who keep the records may not be easily accomplished. Second, we are obliged, whenever possible, to obtain informed consent from the people described in the records, because our examination of their private records may cause them distress.

A third major disadvantage of archival research is that the accuracy and appropriateness of our data depend entirely on the people who created the records. Usually the records are not made with a researcher's question in mind, so they may not address important variables. Further, they may contain verbose, open-ended descriptions, requiring much interpretation on our part. Of course, we would attempt to quantify such descriptions using content analysis, but different record-keepers may give such different types of descriptions that we may not be able to adopt a consistent approach. Often, too, there are few controls in place to prevent errors, or to prevent the inclusion of the record-keeper's personal biases. Thus, we may have considerably less confidence in archival data than in data derived from our own direct observations.

Ex Post Facto **Research**   The term *ex post facto* **research** means that we have conducted the study after the events of interest have occurred. (The phrase *ex post facto* means "after the fact.") The most common approach in such studies is archival research, involving the examination of written records. Thus, the study of hockey team penalties was *ex post facto* because it involved past penalty records. Anderson and Anderson (1984) conducted an *ex post facto* correlational study when they examined police records and meteorological records to determine whether aggressiveness (defined in terms of number of criminal assaults) increases with increased daily temperature. Less commonly, in *ex post facto* research we may have subjects provide reports about their past behaviors, as when researchers ask subjects to complete a questionnaire regarding their childhood development or to describe their stress levels before and after experiencing a earthquake.

Because we usually cannot randomly assign subjects to conditions after the fact, we cannot infer that a cause-and-effect relationship is present. In addition, this method provides potentially unreliable data. Often we can neither precisely quantify the variables and events that occurred nor ensure that they reliably occurred for all subjects. Likewise, written records are only as good as the accuracy of the people keeping them, and subjects' self-reports may be biased and erroneous.

> REMEMBER   *Archival* research is conducted using written records, and *ex post facto* research is conducted after a phenomenon has occurred. Both may provide unreliable and invalid descriptions.

Case Studies   The term **case study** refers to an in-depth study of one situation or "case." Usually, the case is a person, but a case study is different from a single-subject experiment, in that it does not involve manipulation of any independent variables. Some researchers distinguish between a case study, implying a prospective, longitudinal approach, and a case *history,* implying a retrospective, archival approach. Case studies are frequently found in clinical research, describing the many aspects of a particular patient, especially those relating to his or her clinical symptoms and reactions during the course of therapy (e.g., Martorano, 1991; Stagray & Truitt, 1992). Case studies may also involve normal behavior. For example, Neisser (1981) studied the memory distortions of a government witness by comparing records of the events to records of the witness's testimony. A case may also involve a specific event, as in Anderson's (1983) study of the decision-making procedures involved in the "case" of the Cuban missile crisis. And lastly, case studies may focus on a social or business organization, as in Harris and Sutton's (1986) examination of the influence of closing ceremonies on the members of organizations that have been disbanded.

The advantage of case studies is that they provide an in-depth, rather complete description of a subject or event. The disadvantages are that, as longitudinal studies they are confounded by the occurrence of many factors, and as archival studies they may yield data with poor reliability and validity. Further, the selection of a subject or case that can be studied is often a convenience and not truly random. Therefore, we have special concerns about the generalizability of case studies, because any one case probably does not typify other cases.

REMEMBER   Although *case studies* provide in-depth descriptions of one subject or event, they may lead to inaccurate and unrepresentative findings.

A summary of the various terms we use in descriptive research is presented in Table 11.6.

TABLE 11.6   Summary of Terminology Used in Descriptive Research

Field Survey	Involves polling of subjects in the field
Observational research	Involves observation of subjects in the field, characterized by:
Naturalistic observation	Unobtrusive, rather unstructured observation
Systematic observation	Unobtrusive but rather structured observations of specific behaviors
Participant observation	Unobtrusive, rather systematic observations, but researcher is member of group being observed
Archival research	Involves any type of design in which data are collected from formal records
Ex post facto research	Involves any type of design in which data are collected after events have occurred
Case study	Involves in-depth description of one subject, group, or event

PROGRAM EVALUATION

There is one other type of design that should be mentioned which incorporates a combination of the various procedures we have already discussed. Sometimes researchers conduct studies on community human services programs, such as programs for preventing or treating drug and alcohol abuse (e.g., Werch, Meers, & Hallan, 1992; McCusker et al., 1992) or educational programs like Project Head Start (e.g., McKey et al., 1985). **Program evaluation** refers to a variety of procedures for developing and evaluating social programs. This is the ultimate applied research because such programs are essentially grand experiments in social change (Campbell, 1969). They are based on the experimental principle that if we provide some form of intervention to subjects—*to society*—we will see a corresponding change in behavior.

Program evaluation provides feedback to administrators and service providers, as well as providing scientific information about the effect of a program as a quasi-independent variable. Although this research encompasses many procedures (see Posavac & Carey, 1989), it usually consists of four basic phases.

1. *Need assessment:* We perform this phase when designing a particular program to identify the services that are needed and to determine whether potential users of the program will use it.

2. *Program planning:* During this phase we design the program to meet the community's needs, applying findings from the literature that suggest the best methods to implement for the behavior and situation being addressed.

3. *Program monitoring:* During this phase, we monitor the program to ensure that service providers have implemented the intended program and that clients are availing themselves of it.

4. *Outcome evaluation:* Finally, we evaluate whether the program is having its intended effect. This phase is actually a quasi-experimental time-series study in which we hope to demonstrate a change in behavior by comparing behaviors before and after the program's implementation. To fulfill the role of nonequivalent control groups, we may find roughly comparable cities or regions of the country that do not offer the program.

For the data in each of these phases, we rely on such sources as field surveys of the community; archival studies of hospital, school, and police records; and interviews, unobtrusive observations, and case studies of service providers and clients. On the one hand, our procedures suffer from all of the flaws we have discussed, especially because these are quasi-experiments. On the other hand, program evaluation serves a very real applied need and flawed data are generally considered better than no data.

REMEMBER   *Program evaluation* involves procedures for creating and evaluating social programs.

PUTTING IT ALL TOGETHER

The names of the designs discussed in this chapter communicate different procedures, but they are not always rigidly defined, either-or terms. Think of them as approaches that can be mixed and matched to suit your particular research question or to identify a characteristic of your study. For example, the hockey penalty study discussed earlier was simultaneously an archival, *ex post facto,* quasi-experimental, interrupted time-series study of one case. Each of these terms communicates different strengths and weaknesses of the study, so they should cause you to think about the reliability of scores, potential confoundings, and the generality of the conclusions that are drawn.

Perhaps the most important thing to remember about these designs is that they often look like true experiments, especially when a quasi-independent subject variable is being studied in a laboratory setting. When evaluating your own research or that designed by others, remember that you won't find a red flag signaling the underlying nature of the design. Therefore, you must carefully examine whether the subjects are truly randomly assigned to the conditions of a variable. If they are not, the results will only *suggest* the causes of the behavior under study.

CHAPTER SUMMARY

1. In a *quasi-experiment* involving a *quasi-independent variable,* subjects are not randomly assigned to conditions.

2. Effective manipulation of a quasi-independent variable involving a subject variable hinges on the selection of subjects for each condition who are similar to each other but very different from those in other conditions.

3. *Regression toward the mean* occurs when, because of inconsistent random factors, extreme scores tend to change in the direction of coming closer to the mean.

4. A *time-series design* is a quasi-experimental repeated-measures design in which we sample subjects' behavior at different times. A *one-group pretest-posttest design* has no control group.

5. In a *nonequivalent control group* design, the control group has different subject characteristics and different experiences during the study than the experimental group has.

6. In an *interrupted time-series design,* we make observations at several spaced times prior to the treatment and at several times after it.

7. In a *multiple time-series design,* we observe an experimental group and a nonequivalent control group; for each, we obtain several observations before the treatment and several after it.

8. In a *longitudinal design,* we repeatedly measure a group of subjects to observe the effect of the passage of time.

9. A *cross-sectional design* is a between-subjects experiment in which subjects are observed at different ages or at different points in a temporal sequence.

10. *Cohort effects* occur when differences in age are confounded by differences in subject history.

11. A *cohort design* is a factorial design consisting of a longitudinal study of several groups, each from a different generation.

12. In some *descriptive research,* the goal is to describe a behavior, the situation it occurs in, or the subjects exhibiting it.

13. A *field survey* involves having subjects complete a questionnaire or interview in the field, either in person, by mail, or over the telephone.

14. A confidence interval or the *margin of error* is computed when estimating the population's responses to a field survey.

15. In a field survey, we often increase the representativeness of the sample by employing stratified sampling.

16. *Naturalistic observation* means that we observe a wide variety of subjects' behaviors in an unobtrusive and unsystematic manner. *Systematic naturalistic observation* means that we unobtrusively observe a particular behavior or situation in a systematic manner. And *participant observation* means that the researcher is an active member of the group being unobtrusively observed.

17. *Ex post facto* research is conducted after a phenomenon has occurred. *Archival research* is conducted using subjects' existing records. And a *case study* involves an in-depth description of one subject, organization, or event.

18. *Program evaluation* involves procedures for developing and evaluating social programs.

REVIEW QUESTIONS

1. (a) What is the difference between a true experiment and a quasi-experiment? (b) In what ways are quasi-experiments and correlational designs similar? (c) In what way(s) are they different?
2. (a) What three types of variables are studied as quasi independent variables? (b) Why can't we confidently infer causality from a quasi-experiment?
3. (a) How do we design a quasi-independent variable in order to study a subject variable? (b) What is the goal when using the scores from a selection pretest to create conditions? (c) What bias may be produced by a pretest?
4. At the beginning of a gym class, you obtain the highest score on a physical-fitness test. During the semester, however, your scores get worse, while the really unfit students tend to score higher. You conclude that the gym class helps unfit people but harms the most fit. (a) What alternative explanation involving random factors might explain these results? (b) How would it cause the changes in scores? (c) How would you test your hypothesis?
5. (a) What is a one group pretest-posttest design? (b) What is missing from this design? (c) What extraneous variables may confound this design?
6. (a) What is a nonequivalent control group design? (b) What potential confounding variables does it eliminate? (c) What potential confounding variables are not eliminated?
7. (a) What is an interrupted time-series design? (b) What potential confounding variables does it eliminate? (c) What potential confoundings does it not eliminate?
8. (a) What is a multiple time-series design? (b) What potential confounding variables does it eliminate? (c) What potential confoundings does it not eliminate?
9. (a) What is a longitudinal design? (b) What is the major advantage of this design? (c) What is the major flaw in this design?
10. (a) What is a cross-sectional design? (b) What is its major strength? (c) What is its major weakness?
11. (a) What are cohort effects? (b) What is a cohort design? (c) What is the advantage of this design? (d) How do we determine whether cohort effects are present?
12. What does the term *descriptive research* convey?
13. (a) When do researchers mail surveys? (b) When do they employ telephone surveys? (c) Why is it important to ensure high subject-participation rates in both types of surveys?
14. (a) What is the difference between naturalistic observation, systematic observation, and participant observation? (b) What are the strengths of observational designs? (c) What are their weaknesses?
15. (a) What is archival research? (b) What is *ex post facto* research? (c) What are the major weaknesses of these designs? (d) Why do researchers employ them?
16. (a) What is a case study? (b) What is the strength of this approach? (c) What is its weakness?
17. What is program evaluation?

DISCUSSION QUESTIONS

1. You wish to conduct a field survey to describe the nation's attitudes toward gun control. With a closed-end questionnaire in hand: (a) How would you identify the population? (b) How would you contact subjects and have them complete the questionnaire? (c) How would you select your sample? (d) How would you summarize the data? (e) Evaluate your design.

2. Using the questionnaire in question 1 above, how would you conduct a quasi-experiment to determine whether people who differ in their attitudes toward gun control also differ in terms of how frightened they become when confronted by a thief? (You might adapt the study from Chapter 10 in which subjects are confronted by a supposed thief in a college library. Or you might create a study in which subjects are in a waiting room, thinking that they are waiting an experiment to begin.)

3. Why do the designs discussed in this chapter have potentially less temporal validity than the typical true experiment conducted in a laboratory? (Hint: Think about the behaviors typically under study in these designs.)

4. (a) What important ethical issue pertains to observational research, especially participant observation? (b) According to the APA's *Ethical Principles,* when do we not need to obtain informed consent with these approaches?

12 Designing and Evaluating Research

You are now familiar with the basic concepts and techniques found in psychological research. What will make you a good researcher is your ability to apply these techniques. In this chapter, you'll practice using research methods by "performing" some studies of selected topics. For each, you will encounter questions that put you in the role of the researcher who designs, evaluates, and replicates a specific study. To get the most out of these passages, don't just read along passively. Instead, actively and thoughtfully participate as if you really were the researcher conducting the study. At some point, you also may want to design and conduct your own study, and these topics may give you ideas. (Some references are provided, and you can use the *Science Citation Index* to track down more recent ones.)

First you will examine four research topics in depth, focusing on a specific study and the additional studies that develop from it. Then, in the second part of the chapter you will briefly review five other research topics that suggest various designs. For each, the numerous details in evaluating and designing studies that we have discussed boil down to the following key questions:

1. *Purpose of study?* Is it to test a causal hypothesis, to demonstrate a correlation, or to describe subjects or a behavior?

2. *Type of behavior studied?* Does it involve a subject characteristic, a response to concrete stimuli, or a response to a social interaction?

3. *Type of design?* Is the study a true experiment or a quasi-experiment? Does it involve a single-subject, correlational, or observational design? Should it be conducted in the field or laboratory?

4. *Type of subject and sampling?* Will you generalize to a specific population? What selection criteria are needed? How will you sample the population? Will subjects be representative?

5. *Control of subject variables?* What confounding subject variables are present? Should you counterbalance with a between-subjects design or use a within-subjects design?

6. *How to manipulate variables?* Should you vary instructions or stimuli? Should you employ confederates? Do you have a strong, consistent, and valid manipulation? Do you need a manipulation check? Are there confounding variables present?

7. *How to measure variables?* Will you examine overt behaviors or self-reports? Will subjects be tested individually? Are the scoring criteria sensitive? Are you reliably and validly scoring subjects' typical behavior?

8. *Procedural problems?* Is there experimental realism? Are there order effects, demand characteristics, or other biases present? Should you conduct a pilot study?

9. *Materials needed?* What materials and apparatus do you need for consistent and comparable stimuli and for reliable measurements?

10. *Ethical problems?* Are we harming subjects or violating their rights? Is deception justified? Have you obtained informed consent and provided a debriefing?

11. *Statistical analysis?* What is your *N*? Have you maximized power and minimized error variance? Do your scores fit a parametric or nonparametric procedure? Have you employed a between-subjects or a within-subjects design?

12. *Validity of conclusions?* Do the results clearly confirm your hypothesis? Are there alternative hypotheses that reduce your internal validity? Do you have external, construct, ecological, and temporal validity?

Refer to this list as you consider each example throughout the chapter. Also, bear in mind the major components of a study (and an APA-style report) discussed at the beginning of the book.

Remember that every research design contains flaws. Although various techniques are available for dealing with them, each solution often comes at the cost of creating a new flaw. Therefore, for each study discussed below, there are other approaches a researcher might take.

TOPIC 1: ATTRIBUTION OF AROUSAL

Schachter and Singer (1962) proposed that when people become physiologically aroused by one stimulus, their emotional response to another stimulus is heightened. In particular, this notion has been applied to the topic of romantic love and sexual attraction. For example, like Romeo and Juliet, some couples exhibit greater attraction for each other when their parents produce arousal by interfering with the relationship (Driscall, Davis & Lipetz, 1972). Researchers have proposed that the heightened physiological arousal due to an extraneous source is "misattributed" (misdiagnosed) as an especially strong romantic attraction toward the member of the opposite sex. Dutton and Aron (1974) tested this proposal in several studies, asking whether subjects would misattribute arousal due to fear as being heightened sexual attraction to a member of the opposite sex.

What are the hypothesis and purpose of this study?

What are the variables to be studied, and which design is appropriate?

How would you elicit the dependent behavior?

What sampling would you use, and should you control subject variables?

The hypothesis is that greater attraction to a member of the opposite sex occurs when subjects simultaneously experience fear from some other source. Since causation is the issue here, you should conduct a true experiment. The independent variable is amount of fear, a temporary "state" characteristic. The dependent variable is the amount of attraction a subject experiences. Although you might perform a field experiment, let's first discuss a laboratory setting. (See Experiment 3 in Dutton & Aron, 1974.)

This study clearly calls for a confederate who will be the object of attraction. Thus, the manipulation is to create conditions of different levels of fear in subjects while a confederate is present. The dependent measure is subjects' attraction to the confederate.

Because each subject's attraction is not likely to change from one condition to the next, a between-subjects design with a single trial per subject is appropriate.

Subjects are tested individually, since in a group they might be inhibited and not show misattribution. To keep the inherent attractiveness of the confederate constant, one confederate serves for all conditions. Regarding subject variables, Dutton and Aron employed a female confederate, thus requiring the testing of male subjects. Also, subjects should not know the confederate and ideally should have a minimum of other romantic entanglements (engaged or married people may resist feeling, or at least reporting, any attraction). Subjects should be the same age as the confederate, and you might limit or balance race and nationality. Otherwise, there is no unique population here, so a random sample from available college students is sufficient.

You must now define how to manipulate subjects' fear. You could arrange for an "accident" that raises anxiety or concoct an "experiment" that directly harms subjects to make them fearful. But all you really need to do is threaten them with something that will make them fearful. At the same time, the aversive treatment must seem realistic within the context of a scientific experiment, and also allow you to manipulate only the amount of fear. You might threaten to hit subjects or to embarrass them, for example, but you might bring about effects in addition to fear, such as anger or refusal to participate. Instead, Dutton and Aron capitalized on the reputation of psychology experiments by telling subjects that they would be electrically shocked as part of the study.

How would you create the conditions to manipulate fear?

How would you confirm that the intended effect occurred?

Dutton and Aron manipulated fear by threatening subjects with different levels of shock. The shock was described as either small (low fear condition) or large (high fear condition). To produce a strong manipulation, they described the small shock as "a minor tingle which some people actually find pleasant" and the large shock as "quite painful." (You might add a control group threatened with no shock.)

A manipulation check is required to ensure that the procedure actually influences subjects' fear, so at some point you will actually measure subjects' anxiety level as a function of their assigned shock level.

How would you measure the dependent variable?

Instead of observing an overt behavior from which to infer a subjects' attraction, Dutton and Aron asked subjects how sexually attracted they were to the confederate. But rather than asking "Is she attractive?" they achieved greater sensitivity by presenting a 5-point Likert scale with the questions "How much would you like to ask her out?" and "How much would you like to kiss her?" They also included an additional, less threatening measure of arousal by having subjects describe an ambiguous picture in a projective test. Each description was examined for sexual content using content analysis and, for reliability, was scored by two scorers. Included in the questionnaire was the manipulation check in the form of the question: "How do you feel about being shocked?" Subjects responded with ratings, and the researchers interpreted "greater dislike" as indicating "greater fear."

How would you ensure experimental realism?

A deceptive cover story is needed so that subjects encounter the confederate and are assigned a shock level in a convincing and realistic way. Dutton and Aron introduced the confederate to the subject as a second "subject." Both were ostensibly there for an experiment in which two people would be tested simultaneously, to study the effects of punishment (shock) on learning. The researcher then tossed a coin supposedly to determine which of the two would receive the high or low shock condition (but actually to randomly assign the real subjects to their conditions). At this point, since it was not necessary to actually administer the shock, the experimenters had subjects complete the questionnaire.

How would you address demand characteristics?

To reduce reactivity and social desirability, Dutton and Aron presented the questionnaire under the guise that personality characteristics and feelings between subjects have an important influence in this type of learning study. The confederate and subject were taken to separate cubicles while the experimenter "set up the shock equipment." For face validity, the questionnaire contained several "filler" questions about the subjects, along with the attraction and fear questions and the projective test.

What procedural or ethical problems must be addressed?

Because any subtle differences in the behaviors or demeanor of the confederate may alter her attractiveness, her behavior must be "scripted" so that she acts the same way with all subjects. Keeping where she sits constant is also important because subjects need to see her and yet not be too near or far away. Keeping her "blind" to the hypothesis is advisable, because she might otherwise emit subtle cues that could confound conditions. Of course, the experimenter must behave consistently as well. A pilot study to practice and de-bug the procedure is definitely needed.

Ethically there is a problem if subjects feel coerced into receiving shock and experiencing fear. Dutton and Aron solved this problem by telling subjects they would be shocked and then obtaining informed consent, thus giving subjects the opportunity to leave before the study continued. Although the researcher lied to the subjects because they were not actually shocked, the lie would cause them to expect more harm than they experienced—ethically a much better situation than causing them to expect less harm than they experienced.

Select *N*, and diagram the study.

What statistical procedures will you perform?

Because of the very controlled setting and the small variability of rating scores, Dutton and Aron had sufficient power to obtain significant results with 20 subjects per condition. A diagram of the study is shown in Table 12.1. Ratings from the "date" and "kiss" questions were averaged together, producing each subject's score. These scores are ratio scores, and they seem to fit the requirements of a parametric procedure. The study

TABLE 12.1   Diagram of the Misattribution Study

	Conditions		
	Low shock (low fear)	High shock (high fear)	
Each X represents subject's mean rating score	X X " " "	X X " " "	N = 40
Mean attraction	$\overline{X} = 2.8$	$\overline{X} = 3.5$	

involves a between-subjects design, and with two conditions, an independent samples *t*-test is appropriate. (If you included a control group or other levels, or if you included additional factors, you would perform a between-subjects ANOVA.) With higher ratings indicating greater attraction, Dutton and Aron obtained an overall mean attraction rating of 2.8 in the low fear condition, which differed significantly from the mean rating of 3.5 in the high fear condition.

Another analysis is also required: The manipulation check must confirm that the shock conditions produced high and low anxiety levels. Using subjects' rating scores from the question about "disliking the shock" produces a between-subjects design with parametric data, so the independent samples *t*-test is again appropriate. Dutton and Aron found that the mean dislike rating for the high shock group was significantly larger than for the low shock group, suggesting that their manipulation altered subjects' fear levels as intended.

What conclusions can you draw from this study?

What issues of validity need to be addressed?

Significantly higher attraction scores in the high fear group confirm the hypothesis that attraction is heightened by fear from an extraneous source.

One important concern, however, is whether demand characteristics have limited internal validity for concluding that greater fear causes greater attraction. Maybe the subjects were dishonest because of reactivity, social desirability, and experimenter expectations. (After all, it doesn't take a genius to realize that if a "psychologist" tells you that a shock is very unpleasant, you should then indicate that you dislike the idea of being shocked!) It is therefore possible that subjects were *not* more or less fearful. Also, you must ask whether there is external validity for concluding that this relationship occurs in other settings. Clearly, participating in an experiment is not the usual context in which you think about one's sexual attraction to another person. This setting is very contrived, and everything depends on how convincing the confederate and experimenter were.

How would you replicate this study under more natural conditions?

You need a field experiment to test this hypothesis in a more naturalistic setting. Dutton and Aron sought a setting in which subjects were made anxious by a natural fear-arousing stimulus or activity. The idea was to catch subjects after they had experienced some positive yet fear-arousing event, so any thrill-seeking activity would suffice. For example, you could test at a "bungee cord–jumping" event or at a roller-coaster ride. Dutton and Aron selected a narrow, wobbly, foot-bridge suspended high above a scenic canyon to create the experimental condition of high fear. Nearby, was a wide, solid, and sturdy bridge over the canyon, which served as the "control bridge" for the low (no) fear condition.

How would you conduct this experiment?

You might strategically place the confederate so that subjects walk by her, and then question them to determine their attraction to her. However, subjects might not even notice her. Dutton and Aron solved this problem with the following procedure: After a male had crossed the bridge, a female interviewer approached him to answer a questionnaire for a "study" about the effects of scenic attractions on creativity. Among the filler items was a brief projective test, which was later scored for sexual imagery by two trained raters. In addition, subjects were offered the interviewer's phone number, so they could later call to discuss the study. Whether subjects accepted the phone number and whether they called were taken as indications of greater attraction to the interviewer. As a control, a male interviewer also tested some male subjects and offered his phone number.

How would you analyze these results?

Dutton and Aron employed three dependent variables here. First, the sexual imagery scores from the projective test produced an inter-rater reliability coefficient of +.87. Each subject's average score was a ratio score, so the data were entered into two between-subjects t-tests using the conditions of high and low fear. When the interviewer was female, subjects who crossed the scary bridge provided significantly greater sexual imagery than did subjects who crossed the control bridge. When the interviewer was male, no significant difference was found.

Second, the scores for accepting the interviewer's telephone number and for actually calling consist of two yes-no, categorical or nominal variables. Dutton and Aron found that 9 out of the 18 high-fear subjects who took the female interviewer's phone number actually called her. Only 2 out of the 16 low-fear subjects called. The male interviewer received 2 calls out of the 7 high fear subjects who took his number, and 1 call out of 6 from the low-fear group. To determine whether calling rates for the control and experimental groups differed significantly, Dutton and Aron performed one chi square procedure for the female interviewer and one for the male interviewer. They reported significant differences only for the female interviewer.

What procedural and control problems exist?

First, you must confirm that the two bridges actually produce high and low fear, respectively. Because directly asking subjects about their fear might have caused suspicion, Dutton and Aron relied on a pilot study in which other, similar subjects who crossed each bridge answered a questionnaire and confirmed the effect of the bridges.

A second problem is that random sampling was not possible here, because only those subjects who actually crossed a bridge and who volunteered to complete the questionnaire were tested. (Also, only those of a certain age who were unaccompanied by a female were approached.) Most critical is the fact that the subjects themselves decided which bridge to cross. Given that subjects were not randomly assigned to the conditions, this study involves a quasi-experimental design. Thus, in addition to the bridge they crossed, subjects may have differed along all sorts of other variables. In particular, subjects who crossed the scary bridge were probably more adventurous and thus perhaps more likely to call the interviewer and to project more sexual imagery in their stories. In a replication, Dutton and Aron created a more comparable control group by selecting subjects who had crossed the scary bridge, but who then loitered about until (presumably) the fear had dissipated. They found results similar to those reported above. Nonetheless, it is inappropriate to say that greater fear *caused* the higher attraction scores.

What additional research on this topic would you suggest?

A general question concerns the construct validity of arguing that subjects actually misattribute or misinterpret extraneous arousal as heightened sexual attraction. Do they not know that they were scared by the bridge or electric shock? If subjects identify the actual source of their physiological arousal, then they are not misattributing it and some other factor is responsible for heightened sexual attraction. Because of this question, several alternative explanations for these results have been proposed (see Allen, Kendrick, Linder & McCall, 1989).

Conceptual replications of misattribution effects would also be appropriate. For example, Cohen, Waugh, and Place (1989) observed couples entering and leaving a movie theater, and noted that more touching occurred after a suspenseful movie than after a dull one. White and Knight (1984) demonstrated heightened attraction due to misattribution of arousal from physical exercise (running in place). However, misattribution has not always been successfully replicated (e.g., Kendrick, Cialdini & Linder, 1979). To extend this research, consider that most studies involve male subjects. But would the same results occur with female subjects and a male confederate? Would they occur with homosexual male or female subjects and a same-sex confederate? Also, studies have been conducted regarding the effects of alcohol consumption on sexual arousal (e.g., McCarty, Diamond & Kaye, 1982), and on the dynamics of people meeting in bars, reacting to "opening lines," and so on (e.g., Cunnigham, 1989). Both topics would seem relevant to the situation where fear and sexual attraction converge. Further, little evidence is available regarding misattribution of other emotions, such as anger. And, finally, it is unclear whether this process works in reverse such that increased sexual attraction might be misattributed and result in an increased response to a fearful situation.

TOPIC 2: TIME PERCEPTION

Have you ever taken a long car-trip, and noticed that the drive home seemed to take less time than the drive to your destination, even though on the clock both trips took the same amount of time? This experience may be an example of the observation that the more a time interval is "filled" with stimuli, the longer in retrospect it seems to have lasted. As you go toward your destination, the scenery and sights are novel, so that the travel time is mentally "filled" with many interesting stimuli. Then, although only 30 minutes have elapsed, they are overestimated as "feeling like 40." On the return trip, however, you've seen all the sights, so the interval is mentally unfilled. Then the elapsed 30 minutes feel like 30 or perhaps even 20 minutes.

Based on such observations, Ornstein (1969) hypothesized that people judge the duration of an interval using their memory for the stimuli that occurred during the interval. When the memory is in some sense "larger," the interval is perceived as longer. He therefore set out to show that the more stimuli a person encounters during an interval, the longer the interval is judged in retrospect.

What are the hypothesis and purpose of this study?

What are the variables to be studied, and which design is appropriate?

How would you elicit the dependent behavior?

What sampling would you use, and should you control subject variables?

The purpose of this study is to test the hypothesis that filling an interval with more stimuli causes it to be perceived as lasting longer. Because any extraneous event during an interval helps to "fill" it and thus confounds the study, you should conduct a controlled laboratory experiment. In particular, you can create a true experiment by randomly assigning subjects to conditions of the independent variable, which is the number of stimuli filling an interval. The dependent behavior is a subject's estimate of the duration of the interval. Presumably, time perception is similar in all normal humans, so you can randomly sample from available college students.

When studying any cognitive process, you are likely to find large individual differences, but you can control subject variables by performing a repeated-measures design, testing the same subjects under each condition. In our case, however, once subjects know that they will be estimating an interval, they may count or otherwise mentally time it. One solution to this problem is to employ repeated measures but also to disguise and deemphasize the time-estimate response. Ornstein, for example, buried the request for a time estimate in a questionnaire that subjects completed after each interval. Alternatively, you might employ a between-subjects design so that you can truly surprise subjects with a request to estimate the interval after it is over. Although this approach is better because it guarantees that subjects are not prepared for a time estimate, let's assume that you adopt Ornstein's repeated-measures design.

How would you define your conditions and institute needed controls?

The obvious approach is to directly vary the number of stimuli presented to subjects during an interval. Ornstein varied the number of tones that subjects heard. In similar studies, Schiffman and Bobko (1977) varied the number of visual stimuli subjects viewed, and Kowal (1987) varied the number of musical notes in a melody. Taking a somewhat different approach, Hicks, Miller, and Kinsbourne (1976) varied subjects' activities by having them sort cards and perform different mental tasks. Let's assume that you employ the tones used by Ornstein.

You must also define the duration of the interval. Although there is research literature on the perception of very brief, millisecond intervals, Ornstein defined an ecologically realistic interval of 9 minutes and 20 seconds. (You wouldn't want an interval as obvious as 60 seconds or 5 minutes, because subjects would be likely to guess these.) The key, then, is to create a strong manipulation by filling the interval with a substantially different number of tones in each condition. Ornstein created three conditions, with the tones occurring at the rate of 40, 80, or 120 tones per minute throughout the interval. The duration of the tones was constant regardless of the condition, but the pauses between them was varied so that the tones occurred regularly throughout the interval.

How would you measure the dependent variable?

Here, direct estimates of the interval's duration from subjects are needed. Thus, Ornstein asked subjects to estimate the duration in minutes and seconds. This score is objective and subjects can easily record their estimates. Alternatively, if you believed that subjects would be unable to translate their subjective impressions of time into these terms reliably, you could ask them to estimate the interval nonverbally by drawing a line to represent its length (Mulligan & Schiffman, 1979).

What procedure for testing subjects and what materials are needed?

As long as the experimenter does not communicate expectations or create undue pressure and thus reactivity, the researcher can be present to test subjects. For reliability, you can produce an audio tape recording of the three intervals, using electronic clocks and tone generators to create the stimuli. To eliminate distractions, you can play the recording over headphones, at a constant volume for all subjects. (Be sure to select only subjects with normal hearing.)

To create a realistic situation and prevent subjects from forming hypotheses that might bias their estimates, you need a cover story to "explain" why they are listening to recorded tones. For example, in your instructions you might say that you're studying the relaxing effect of these stimuli, and that subjects are to merely relax and sit quietly during the interval. In this way you also minimize any extraneous stimulation that might otherwise "fill" the interval and influence time estimates. Further, this "relaxation therapy" could require the removal of any jewelry, to ensure that subjects do not look at their watches during the interval.

For consistency, all subjects should estimate an interval immediately after being exposed to it, without any distractions between the interval and subjects' responses.

Thus, you might tell subjects that, immediately after the interval, they should turn over the paper in front of them to answer the questions provided there. What they will find on the reverse side is a questionnaire that includes a question asking them to estimate the interval's length in minutes and seconds, along with other distracting questions regarding subjects' thoughts and relaxation responses. These "other" questions not only add credence to your cover story but also allow you to determine what subjects were doing during the interval and to obtain a manipulation check of whether they attended to the tones. Afterwards, in your debriefing, stress that subjects are not to tell other potential subjects about the time-estimation task.

A major procedural problem concerns the order effects produced by repeated exposure to all three conditions: Whether an interval is *relatively* filled may depend on which intervals were previously heard. Likewise, listening to over 9 minutes of tones is a long, boring task, so fatigue effects are likely. However, by testing each third of your subjects under the order of conditions ABC, BCA, or CAB, you can adequately counterbalance for order.

What are the prediction of the study, and the *N* to be tested?

Diagram the study, and determine the statistical procedures to be performed.

The prediction is that intervals containing more tones will be estimated as having lasted longer. Because of possibly large error variance due to obtaining estimates in minutes and seconds, a relatively large N is needed. Based on similar time perception research, you can assume that approximately 50 subjects per condition will provide substantial power.

Time-estimate scores are ratio scores that meet the requirements of a parametric procedure. Since this study has three levels of one within-subjects factor, you perform a one-way within-subjects ANOVA of the design shown in Table 12.2.

After computing a significant F, you perform *post hoc* comparisons to determine which means differ significantly. Ornstein found that the interval with 120 tones per minute was judged to be significantly longer than that with 80, and that both of these were judged to be longer than that with 40 tones per minute. Unfortunately, he did not

TABLE 12.2   Diagram of the Time Perception Experiment

The means are from Ornstein (1969), Table 3, p. 56. Each row of Xs represents the time estimates from the same subject.

Conditions of number of tones in the interval		
40	*80*	*120*
X	X	X
X	X	X
X	X	X
.	.	.
.	.	.
$\overline{X} = 6.42$	$\overline{X} = 7.99$	$\overline{X} = 9.00$

report eta squared to indicate the effect size of his manipulation, so we do not know how consistently his varying the number of tones determined time estimates.

The above analysis merely deals with whether the subjective impression of an interval increases as it becomes more filled. The estimates may increase as predicted, but none of them may have any resemblance to the actual duration of the interval. To see a subject's time estimate in relation to the interval's actual duration, you can subtract the actual duration of the interval from each estimate. Any positive difference indicates that subjects have overestimated the duration, saying that it seems longer than it actually was. Any negative difference indicates that subjects have underestimated the duration, saying that it seems shorter than it actually was. An analysis of the means of scores obtained using this procedure indicates the effect that filling an interval has on *errors* when estimating time.

What conclusions can you draw from this study?

What are the limitations on your conclusions?

Unless unknown confoundings are present, this finding confirms the hypothesis that a greater number of stimuli in an interval causes the interval to be perceived as longer.

A limitation is that such tone-filled intervals are never encountered in the real world, so you have limited external validity beyond this study. You also have reduced generalizability, because your ultimate purpose is to understand the general perception of the passage of *any* time interval. With this latter problem in mind, consider the next question.

What factor could be added to this study to increase its generalizability?

The effect of varying the stimuli in an interval should be tested with intervals of different lengths, so that the findings are not tied to just one interval. Specifically you could create a second factor, by presenting both the condition containing the above interval (to replicate Ornstein's study) and another condition containing a different sized interval. Let's say that you include the interval of 4 minutes 40 seconds, which is one-half the size of Ornstein's (but you could add intervals of any size that make sense).

How would you analyze this design, and what may it indicate?

Because you now have the two factors of number of tones per minute and the length of the interval, a two-way ANOVA is appropriate. However, you should not analyze subjects' actual estimates of the duration of the interval. If their estimates bear any resemblance to reality, then the two interval sizes would automatically produce differences in time estimates (you'd expect about a 4-minute difference). To equate the different length of the intervals, again subtract the actual duration from subjects' estimates and look at their estimation errors. Let's say that you obtain the mean difference scores shown in Table 12.3.

The average error in subjects' estimates in each cell is positive, so subjects consistently overestimated all intervals. The main effect of increasing the number of tones (as seen by comparing the column means) still tests the original hypothesis that filling the interval

TABLE 12.3 Example of Mean Differences Between the Actual Interval and Subjects' Estimates

A 3 × 2 design for the factors of number of tones and interval duration.

		Number of tones per minute			
		40	80	120	
Duration of interval	4 min 40 sec	$\overline{X} = +.33$	$\overline{X} = +1.50$	$\overline{X} = +2.00$	$\overline{X} = +1.28$
	9 min 20 sec	$\overline{X} = +.50$	$\overline{X} = +1.70$	$\overline{X} = +2.80$	$\overline{X} = +1.67$
		$\overline{X} = +.44$	$\overline{X} = +1.60$	$\overline{X} = +2.4$	

with more stimuli increases its perceived duration: With more tones, overestimates increase indicating that the interval is perceived as increasingly longer than it actually was. The main effect of duration (as seen by comparing the row means) indicates that, overall, the two intervals produced differences in estimation error. Of most interest will be whether there is a significant interaction.

Graph this interaction, labeling the X axis as the conditions of number of tones per minute.

How will a significant or nonsignificant interaction be interpreted?

The interaction is graphed in Figure 12.1. If the interaction is significant, you can conclude that the way in which estimates change with more filled intervals *depends* on

FIGURE 12.1 Interaction Between Number of Tones per Minute and Interval Duration

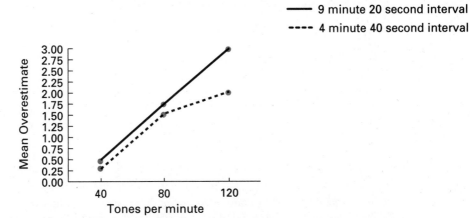

the duration of the interval. Note that this conclusion would limit your generalizability of the filled-interval hypothesis, since you would find that it applies differently depending on the interval's length. A nonsignificant interaction, however, would suggest that the influence of increasing the number of tones is similar—that is, parallel—for both short and long intervals.

So far the results seem to support the hypothesis that subjects judge an interval as longer when they have a "larger" memory for the contents of the interval. However, there are at least two additional explanations to consider when conceptualizing the constructs underlying a subject's memory of an interval. First, the greater number of tones per minute also creates an interval containing more *complex* stimulation. Perhaps a subject's time perception is actually determined by the degree of complexity characterizing the overall event that fills an interval, not merely by the amount of stimulation.

How might you manipulate the complexity of the stimuli during an interval, and what variable must you keep constant?

For a given interval size, the variable to keep constant is the *number* of stimuli presented during the interval. You then vary the complexity of the stimuli presented. (In fact, Ornstein [1969] conducted a second study in which subjects viewed drawings of geometric shapes that varied in their complexity.) You may also vary the complexity of the response that subjects make to a stimulus, as in Brown (1985) who had subjects physically trace patterns that varied in complexity. These studies showed that increased complexity did increase the perceived duration of the interval.

The second explanation to consider when conceptualizing memory for an interval is that given either a larger number of stimuli or more complex stimulation, the result may be to produce a less organized memory for the contents of the interval. Stimuli that are simple to us—that we understand—are organized in our memory; stimuli that are complex are not. Thus, anytime we organize the stimuli in memory, the interval may seem shorter, while with less organization it may seem longer. Mulligan and Schiffman (1979) tested this hypothesis by manipulating whether subjects could make the stimuli more meaningful and organized. The procedure adopted for making a stimulus more or less meaningful was discussed in a previous chapter.

How would you manipulate the meaningfulness of stimuli occurring in an interval?

There are a number of ways you might give more or less meaning to a stimulus. Believe it or not, Mulligan and Schiffman (1979) adopted the procedure discussed in Chapter 4, in which subjects were presented "droodles" (the cartoons with the funny, disambiguating captions). Subjects viewed a droodle for a fixed period, either with or without a caption, and then estimated the viewing interval. Estimates were shorter when a caption was provided, presumably because it allowed better organization and simplification of the components of the droodle in memory.

The current literature suggests that the perceived duration of an interval *is* influenced by the nature of the mental stimulation and processing occurring during the interval. There are, however, two paradoxes reported in this literature. First, it follows that the more stimuli we can recall from an interval, the more our memory is filled and thus the longer the interval is judged to be. (For example, Ornstein found that hearing neutral words that were well recalled produced longer estimates than hearing unpleasant words that were poorly recalled.) Paradoxically, increased organization of stimuli is usually a prime cause of increased retention. Thus, contrary to Mulligan and Schiffman (1979), increased organization of droodles should lead to better retention and *longer* estimates. These researchers found that it led to shorter estimates, and produced no differences in retention of the droodles! To further study this phenomenon, cognitive psychologists have many ways of producing differences in a subject's retention and organization. You might, for example, ask subjects different types of questions about a word (Craik and Tulving, 1975) or you might make an ambiguous paragraph easier to understand by presenting a title (Brandsford & Johnson, 1972).

The above research involves retrospective judgements, in which subjects consider the interval only after it has ended. The second paradox occurs when subjects are aware that they will estimate the interval at its start (making a "prospective" estimate). Here the amount of stimulation in the interval has the opposite effect, such that the more an interval is filled, the *shorter* the interval is judged to be (Hicks, Miller & Kinsbourne, 1976; but see Brown, 1985). In this setting, "time flies when you're having fun" because the fun mentally fills the interval, so time passes quickly. Conversely, "a watched pot never boils" because we ignore ongoing events, so the interval is mentally unfilled and time drags by. In fact, Cahoon and Edmunds (1980) had subjects watch a pot of water come to a boil. They found that the more that subjects concentrated on waiting for the water to boil, the longer the interval was judged to be. One possible explanation for this paradox is that when making a prospective time estimate, subjects do not rely on the amount of stimulation experienced during the interval. Instead, they rely directly on their experience of time. Time estimates become shorter when more stimuli are encountered because greater stimulation directs subjects' attention away from their experience of time. To test whether less attention to time makes it pass rapidly, you can take any established procedure for consuming more or less of a subject's attention and incorporate it into a study in which subjects estimate an interval's duration.

TOPIC 3: FEAR OF SUCCESS IN FEMALES

Some people argue that the most insidious effect of racism and sexism is that the victims of such biases are conditioned by society to behave in certain ways that match the stereotype. For example, Horner (1972) proposed that women who avoid striving for success in school or occupations may be motivated by "fear of success," or FOS. Given the society of the 1970s, it was reasonable to suggest that women were conditioned by society to avoid seeking success because they had learned to fear the negative consequences associated with it. In particular, they may have anticipated being perceived as "unfeminine" and socially undesirable if they were successful. Men, Horner proposed, generally exhibit less FOS because, for them, there are fewer negative consequences associated with success. Horner conducted a study to demonstrate that men and women exhibit different levels of FOS.

What are the hypothesis and purpose of this study?

What are the variables to be studied, and which design is appropriate?

What sampling would you use, and should you control subject variables?

The purpose of this study is to demonstrate the existence of FOS. Because it would be premature to test variables that cause FOS, you should turn to a correlational, descriptive study. The basic proposal is that men and women exhibit different levels of FOS, so at most the design is a quasi-experiment, with the quasi-independent variable consisting of the conditions of male or female. The dependent behavior is FOS, presumably a relatively stable "trait" characteristic. The study does not require a specific field setting, so conducting it in a laboratory provides the best control. Presumably, FOS is found throughout the general population, so you can select subjects randomly from available college students. Note that the quasi-independent variable of gender is a between-subjects factor, which may be confounded by many subject variables, including race, age, college experience, and so on. To control these variables, you might either limit the population to a more homogeneous group or produce matched groups of males and females.

How would you measure the dependent variable?

The key is to operationally define and then measure behaviors that are construct-valid and actually reflect FOS. You might design a situation to cause subjects to strive for success, but if they don't, you cannot be sure that this result reflects FOS. But you can measure subjects' motives more directly using their self-reports from interviews or questionnaires. Closed-end questions, however, would be unworkable here, because (1) this is exploratory research, so you do not necessarily know the appropriate questions to ask, (2) subjects may be unaware of their FOS, and (3) demand characteristics may prevent them from giving honest responses. To avoid such problems, Horner (1972) employed a projective test from which she could infer high or low FOS from subjects' responses. Female subjects completed a story that began "After first-term finals, Anne finds herself at the head of her medical school class." Males completed a corresponding story about "John."

What procedure, instructions, and materials are needed?

To ensure reliability, subjects completed the story in writing. To focus subjects on dealing with the success of the characters, Horner asked subjects to comment on Anne's or John's reactions to their grades, other people's reactions, and their past and future lives. Since only one story was completed per subject, order effects were not a problem.

By counterbalancing the gender of the researcher within each group, you could control for experimenter-produced demand characteristics. (A double-blind procedure would probably not be necessary if you can minimize the interaction between subjects and researcher.) Also note that subjects can be tested in groups. To minimize subject reactivity to divulging personal information, you might frame the experiment as a creativity test, English composition test, or as a test of knowledge about social interactions. The materials you would use consist of a sheet of paper with the appropriate description of

John or Anne typed across the top. (By providing more sheets you imply that subjects can or should write more.)

The design is ethically acceptable because subjects are knowing volunteers, and informed consent can provide straightforward information about the task and situation. However, the hypothesis would not be conveyed until the debriefing.

How would you determine each subject's score and ensure a powerful design?

The major problem with a projective, open-ended question concerns the reliable scoring of subjects' responses. Horner performed a content analysis, operationally defining FOS to be present when a subject's described Anne or John as having negative feelings or negative experiences as a result of achieving high grades. Horner found, for example, that Anne was described as the stereotypical lonely, unattractive "egghead" who was disliked (and even beat up by classmates when the grades were published). Multiple scorers would be appropriate here and you should check for high inter-rater reliability. A relatively large N is warranted because of potentially high variability in subject responses and scoring. With so simple a task, you could easily test upwards of 50 subjects per condition.

You might think that, after scoring the stories, you could assign each subject a score reflecting the number of FOS images in his or her story. However, you do not know that a greater number of FOS images in a story indicates a greater degree of FOS. (Some subjects may simply write a more detailed story.) Horner solved this problem by viewing FOS as an all-or-none characteristic. She categorized each subject's story as either exhibiting or not exhibiting FOS, and then determined whether more females exhibited FOS than males.

What statistical analysis should you perform?

This is a between-subjects design with nonparametric, nominal, or categorical data, so performing a chi square procedure is appropriate. You could perform a one-way procedure to determine whether, among those with FOS stories, there is a greater frequency of females than males, But technically you should compute the two-way chi square to determine whether the frequency of FOS and non-FOS is independent of subjects' gender. This design and the results of Horner's study are shown in Table 12.4.

Here, a significant result indicates whether the frequency that subjects produced an FOS story *depends* on whether they are male or female. Horner reported that females produced a significantly greater number of FOS stories, although, unfortunately, she did not compute the phi correlation to indicate the strength or consistency of this relationship.

What conclusions can you draw, and are they valid?

Because this is a quasi-experiment, you cannot confidently conclude that gender *causes* the differences in FOS stories. Rather, you can only speculate as to how FOS develops in males and females and how it operates to influence behavior. It is reasonable to expect that other subjects in similar settings would produce similar results, so there is some external validity for this specific relationship. But you won't know whether FOS

TABLE 12.4 Diagram of Two-Way Design and Results of Horner (1972)

	Conditions	
	Males (John story)	Females (Anne story)
FOS stories	10%	65%
Non-FOS stories	90%	35%

actually operates in the real world, whether it actually motivates people, or what all its components are, so ecological, construct, and broad external validity are limited. (Then again, this is just the first study.)

Even your tentative conclusions hinge, however, on whether there are any confoundings between the two gender conditions. Again, look carefully at Table 12.4.

What is the major confounding between the above conditions?

The difference in FOS scores between the conditions may be due to the sex of the subjects in each group or it may be due to the sex of the *character* in each story: In short, the sex of John and Anne is confounded with the quasi-independent variable of sex of subject. To test this alternative hypothesis, Monahan, Kuhn, and Shaver (1974) had both males and females complete stories about both John and Anne. They found that women *and* men showed greater FOS when describing Anne! Thus, there is something about completing the Anne story that produces greater FOS imagery. What is it about Anne's success in medical school that causes both males and females to imagine her as having negative feelings and experiences because of that success?

What bias is built into the stimuli?

The bias is that Anne is in *medical* school, stereotypically a "male" situation. Thus, Horner's study was also confounded because the two conditions differ in terms of whether the sex of the character fits the stereotype of the school. This conclusion was confirmed by Cherry and Deaux (1978), who had males and females describe John and Anne as being either at the head of their *medical*-school class or at the head of their *nursing*-school class. In the medical-school setting, 60% of the Anne stories indicated FOS, compared to only 30% of the John stories. But in the nursing-school setting the shoe was on the other foot: 64% of the John stories but only 30% of the Anne stories indicated FOS. Further, both men and women provided more negative descriptions of John in nursing school and of Anne in medical school.

What do these results indicate about the construct of FOS?

If FOS exists, Horner did not measure it. Essentially her study lacked construct validity: Subjects never actually stated that they feared success, and, instead of reflecting some intrinsic motivation, their negative descriptions depended entirely on the context of the story. Apparently, we are all aware of stereotypes and tend to predict unpleasant consequences for someone who violates a stereotype. In particular, when describing someone who is successful at something that is uncommon for their gender, we expect the social consequences of that success to be negative.

Recall that research explanations are supposed to be *parsimonious*; that is, they should not be complicated by unnecessary constructs. Because the above study (and similar research), has not demonstrated that FOS is necessary for explaining behavior, the construct has largely been discarded.

What suggestions do you have for further research?

To retain the construct of FOS, you would have to measure it in an objective, valid, and unconfounded manner. For example, you might develop a closed-end questionnaire to measure FOS and also seek to identify a concrete behavior that reflects avoiding success in real life. Then you could show both *concurrent* and *predictive* validity by determining the correlation between questionnaire scores and actual avoidance of success. Also, since very young children would not be expected to have learned the negative consequences of violating sex-role stereotypes, you might eliminate the bias in Horner's study by testing young children for FOS. And finally, because society and sex stereotypes presumably have changed since the early 1970s, a replication of the above FOS studies could determine whether there is a generational or "cohort" effect between Horner's subjects and those of today.

TOPIC 4: CREATIVITY

Creativity is often examined in terms of problem solving. In this context, being creative is defined as making new, uncommon associations between ideas to solve a problem. Isen, Daubman, and Nowicki (1987) suggested that one variable that influences creative problem solving is mood or "affect." When experiencing positive affect, subjects may organize information into broader, more all-inclusive categories, such that they combine highly divergent information. Because of this new organization, subjects may see unusual connections or novel associations, thus facilitating problem solving.

What are the hypothesis and purpose of this study?

What are the variables to be studied, and which design is appropriate?

What procedure and subjects would you employ?

The purpose here is to show that more positive affect causes greater creativity, so a laboratory experiment involving college students is appropriate. Any manipulation that influences a subject's "state" characteristic of mood is appropriate. For example, you could present different mood-inducing words or vary the amount of reward that subjects receive. In a series of studies, Isen et al. (1987) employed several such procedures, including showing subjects either a five-minute comedy film (consisting of television "bloopers"), a neutral control film (about the normal curve!), and a negative film (a documentary on World War II Nazi concentration camps). Let's say you choose to employ this procedure. Accordingly, your independent variable is the type of film shown to subjects. (Technically, a subject's mood is an intervening variable, which, presumably, is influenced by the type of film viewed.) Because of potential carry-over effects, the films should be presented as a between-subjects factor.

The dependent variable is a subject's score on creative problem solving. Isen et al. employed a number of "brain-teaser" problems to measure creative problem solving, among them, the Remote Associates Test (Mendrick, Mendrick, & Mendrick, 1964). Here, each test question contains three words for which there is one "remote" association. The questions are presented in a questionnaire, and subjects fill in the word that provides the association. For example, given the stimuli *mower, atomic,* and *foreign,* the correct answer is *power* (since it may occur logically with each stimulus word).

How would you ensure that the manipulation worked?

How would you ensure reliable measurement of creativity?

A manipulation check is necessary to be sure that the films had the desired effect. Isen et al. accomplished this check by telling subjects that the film they were about to see was being pretested for another experiment. Then, after the film was over, they asked subjects either to rate the pleasantness of several unfamiliar, neutral words or to rate statements describing how the film made them feel. Subjects' responses confirmed that the films had produced the intended differences in mood. Following these tasks, subjects performed the Remote Associates Test, under the cover story that norms were being established for another study.

To reliably measure creativity, Isen et al. had subjects complete 21 Remote Associates questions. To control the difficulty of the questions, the researchers used pilot data to select 7 easy, 7 medium, and 7 difficult items. A subject's score was the total number of questions correctly answered. Further, to reliably demonstrate the relationship, the researchers tested between 50 and 100 subjects in each of their studies, roughly counterbalancing for sex of subject.

Diagram this study, and select the statistical procedures you should use.

The study is diagrammed as shown in Table 12.5. Such scores fit a parametric procedure, and the one-way, between-subjects ANOVA is appropriate. If the *F* is significant, *post hoc* comparisons and eta squared are computed. Based on Isen et al. (1978), the number of items correctly solved should be significantly higher when subjects experience the positive-mood condition than when they experience the neutral condition. Negative mood should not, however, produce a significant difference in creative problem solving compared to the neutral condition.

To obtain greater information from the above design, you could analyze an additional, hidden factor.

TABLE 12.5   Diagram of Affect and Creativity Experiment

	Conditions of mood		
	Negative	*Neutral*	*Positive*
Each	X	X	X
subject's	X	X	X
total	X	X	X
creativity	.	.	.
score	.	.	.
	$\overline{X}$	$\overline{X}$	$\overline{X}$

What additional factor can be analyzed?

What statistical procedure should be used, and what will it show?

The additional factor to be analyzed is the difficulty of the Remote Associates items. Instead of computing an overall total-correct score per subject, you can examine the number correct for each subject when answering the easy, medium, and difficult questions, respectively. In doing so, you create a two-way mixed design. You still have the between-subjects factor containing the three levels of mood, but you also have the repeated-measures factor consisting of easy, medium, or difficult questions. This results in a 3×3 mixed ANOVA. From this, you will see the main effect of the mood conditions as well as the main effect of the difficulty of problems. Most interestingly, you will see the interaction between difficulty and mood. This interaction will indicate whether the relationship between a person's mood and his or her creative problem solving *depends* on how difficult the problems are. Notably, when Isen et al. (1987) performed a similar analysis, they found that, regardless of mood level, the difficult questions were so difficult they tended to produce a *floor effect*, while the easy items were so easy they tended to produce a *ceiling effect*. Therefore, the interaction of mood and difficulty was not significant.

Although Isen et al. found that positive mood conditions produced higher creativity scores, there is a potentially serious problem in inferring that subjects truly experienced the different moods. Consider the order in which subjects performed the various tasks described previously.

What demand characteristics might have biased this study?

After presenting a film, Isen et al. conducted a manipulation check to determine subjects' moods. But imagine you are a subject who watches a brief film that is rather obviously light-hearted or depressing. And that you are then asked to rate the pleasantness of words or, worse, to describe how the film made you feel. Wouldn't you suspect that the film was *supposed* to produce a positive or negative mood? This procedure may have communicated experimenter expectations about the mood that subjects were supposed to indicate, and the subjects may simply have complied. If this were the case, the researchers could not identify the cause of the differences in creativity, because they could not be sure that the intended differences in mood even existed.

To solve this problem, the researchers might present the manipulation check after the creativity test, but having a difficult or easy time in performing the creativity test might change subjects' mood from what it was at the beginning of the test. Likewise, they might use different stimuli, but any manipulation that is strong enough to influence mood may also communicate experimenter expectations or bias subjects. Thus, a better design might be to describe the relationship between mood and creativity, but without actively manipulating mood so that demand characteristics are avoided.

A further problem is that the above manipulation check, at best, showed that the *average* mood score differed between the conditions, but there was undoubtedly variability in the moods of subjects within each condition. Therefore, this procedure is not a very precise or sensitive way of examining how specific differences in mood relate to differences in creativity.

Given these criticisms, when designing an extension of this research you might seek a description of the relationship between subjects' specific mood level and their creativity, but without actively manipulating mood.

What other design might you employ to study this relationship?

What are the hypothesis and purpose of this study?

How would you define and measure the variables?

Given the goals described above, the obvious choice is a correlational study: After measuring subjects' present mood when they enter the study, you can correlate these scores with subjects' scores on a subsequent creativity test. The hypothesis is that mood and creativity are related. The purpose is to show that the relationship exists, but you are no longer trying to show that a positive mood *causes* greater creativity.

To perform a more literal replication of the Isen et al. procedure, you might again operationally define creativity in terms of subjects' ability to solve Remote Associates problems. To measure the state characteristic of mood, you could again have subjects rate the pleasantness of uncommon, emotionally neutral words. (By checking the literature, you can obtain previously used lists of such words.) Your operational definition here is that the higher the pleasantness ratings of the words, the better a subject's overall mood.

How would you create the rating scale for items measuring mood?

Because rating a neutral word as *very* pleasant or unpleasant may seem an unnatural task for subjects, the rating scale can be anchored with only the words *pleasant* and *unpleasant.* Likewise, because subjects may have a hard time making fine discriminations in the pleasantness of a word, it is appropriate to provide only a 5-point scale. With an odd number of points, you allow subjects a middle or neutral rating, which in this context is also appropriate. In your instructions, however, stress that subjects should consider all points on the scale.

A pilot study is called for here to determine whether the words are neutral, whether their pleasantness can be rated, and whether the scale is appropriate. You would ask subjects to rate each word on these dimensions and then include only those words in the mood test that are consistently judged to meet these criteria.

How would you construct the mood questionnaire?

To reflect a subject's mood reliably, you would want to get a sufficient number of words rated—say, 24 words total. To cancel out any potential response biases, you can counterbalance the placement of *pleasant* and *unpleasant* at the left end of the scale for half of the words and at the right end for the other half.

You might intermix the mood questions with the Remote Associates Test and present them as one questionnaire, but this arrangement could be very confusing for subjects. A better approach is to keep the two measurement procedures separate, with individual printed instructions for each.

How would you administer the mood and creativity tests?

There are two reasons that you might have all subjects complete the mood questionnaire before completing the Remote Associates Test. First, you would avoid any possible influence that the Remote Associates Test might have on a subject's mood. (Remember, your goal in this design is to *not* manipulate or influence subjects' mood.) Second, although your emphasis is definitely *not* on causality, you can strengthen such an inference by having what you believe is the causal variable occur first.

What subjects will you select, and how will you sample?

It is most important to obtain subjects who may differ greatly in their moods and in their abilities to solve the Remote Associates Test. Since observing this relationship across a wide range of scores both provides more information and increases statistical power, you want to avoid a restricted range of scores on either variable. A target N of 100 subjects would provide sufficient power.

The hypothesized relationship applies to the general population, so you can randomly select college students. Doing so also allows you the advantage of collecting data in a quiet, controlled laboratory setting. If you had reason to believe that college students would produce a restricted range of scores, however, you might instead conduct a field study in several randomly selected public locations or a mailed survey, using systematic and/or stratified random sampling techniques.

What specific steps will you follow to analyze the data?

First, you must determine each subject's score on each test. For the Remote Associates Test, you total the number of correct answers. For the mood test, you initially code all questions so that a higher rating always indicates that the word is rated as more pleasant, implying a more positive affect. Then, each subject's mood score can be either the total or the mean of the ratings that he or she selected.

Both of these variables reflect ratio scales of measurement that seem approximately normally distributed. Implicitly, you have assumed a linear relationship between the variables, so you would compute the Pearson correlation coefficient using each subject's pair of scores. Next, you would determine whether the coefficient is significant. Your prediction is that there will be a positive correlation between mood and creativity, with higher pleasantness ratings associated with higher creativity scores. Because you are predicting a specific relationship, you perform a one-tailed test of significance.

If r is significant, you can compute the linear regression equation, and then graph the regression line to summarize this relationship. Since you have essentially hypothesized that subjects' mood predicts their creativity, word ratings would be the predictor (X) variable and Remote Associates scores the criterion (Y) variable. You would also compute the standard error of the estimate. This calculation communicates the "average" amount that subjects' creativity scores differ from the score that was predicted using their mood score and the regression equation. You would also compute r^2 to describe the proportion of variance in creativity scores that is accounted for by the relationship with mood. The larger this statistic, the more important mood is for understanding differences in creativity.

What are the important issues of validity in this study?

The first issue is content validity. You want to be sure that pleasantness ratings actually and only reflect the pleasantness that subjects attribute to the words. Any flaws in the rating task, or any words that subjects have experienced in a way that biases them, will mean that you are not measuring pleasantness as intended. Likewise, the Remote Associates Test must measure subjects' ability to make remote associations. If, for example, subjects do not know a word's definition, then they will give an incorrect answer for that question because of a variable having nothing to do with making associations.

Your other major concern is construct validity. You have defined creativity as the ability to associate diverse elements in an uncommon way. But creativity may be more than this. Also, your operational definition of being creative is "producing the correct remote associate." But subjects who are creative and ingenious might see a unique association that the test does not anticipate, so they would be scored as incorrect. Likewise, the word-pleasantness ratings may reflect a subject's mood, but then again they may not. It is possible to be in a very poor mood and still think a word has a pleasant ring to it (*aardvark* springs to mind). Also, there are many aspects to a person's mood (anger, elation, sadness) and you cannot know which, if any, are reflected by these ratings.

For these reasons, you might select any number of published, objective (closed-end) mood tests from the literature (e.g., the "Profile of Mood States"; Schackman, 1983). An established mood test is usually supported by considerable research showing its validity (e.g., McNair, Loor & Droppleman, 1984). Further, such tests often contain subscales, each of which measures a certain component of mood: The items in one scale would measure the factor of "depression," those in another "anxiety," in yet another "vigor," and so on. In fact, if you had employed such a test in the above study, you could use a subject's score from each subscale as one measure of mood, which you could then correlate with creativity. (In this case, the techniques of "multiple correlation and multiple regression" as well as "partial correlation" would be appropriate.)

Of course, the above concerns about validity also apply to the Isen et al. (1987) experiments discussed initially. The advantages of your correlational study are that it conceptually replicates their laboratory study while reducing their demand characteristics, and, especially if conducted as a field study, it adds to the external validity and generalizability of the relationship between mood and creativity.

In designing this correlational study, you assumed that if subjects performed the Remote Associates Test first, their performance might influence their subsequent mood scores. As an additional research question, you could actually test whether word pleasantness ratings are changed by the Remote Associates Test.

How would you design this study and create the stimuli?

You would create a pretest-posttest design, with subjects performing a word-pleasantness rating test once before the Remote Associates Test and then once after. To prevent subjects from merely reproducing earlier ratings, you would create alternate forms, providing two different sets of words to be rated. You would need to demonstrate high test-retest reliability between the two sets and also to counterbalance their use, using each set as the pretest or posttest for one-half of the subjects. Then you would examine the difference between the overall (mean) pleasantness ratings before and after the Remote Associates Test.

However, if you merely test a group of subjects before and after the Remote Associates Test, you will encounter the problems of a one-group pretest-posttest design, having no idea why pleasantness ratings might change between the two testings. After all, you are measuring mood as a state characteristic that, by definition, changes from moment to moment. Therefore, you should also test a control group, measuring mood twice using the same intervening interval as that for the experimental group, but without the Remote Associates Test. Then you would analyze the pleasantness ratings in a 2×2 mixed-design ANOVA for the between-subjects factor of experimental-control group and the repeated-measures factor of pre- and posttest. If the interaction is significant, then differences in the pre- and posttest mood scores depend on, and are thus influenced by, whether subjects perform the intervening Remote Associates Test.

ADDITIONAL RESEARCH TOPICS

In the research literature, you will find studies that deal with almost every behavior imaginable. Below are some common and not so common research topics with which you can become involved rather easily.

Belief in Astrology

Astrological horoscopes and personality descriptions contain *Barnum statements* such as "You are generally a happy person, although you sometimes become angry." A person's reactions to such descriptions tells us not only about the popularity of astrology but also about general belief systems. For example, Glick, Gottesman, and Jolton (1989) studied "believers" and "skeptics" to determine how they deal with positive and negative descriptions in horoscopes. The researchers proposed that both types of subjects would be impressed with the accuracy of positive descriptions (e.g., "You are intelligent"), presumably because such descriptions affirm positive self-perceptions. But they also suggested that only believers in astrology would accept negative descriptions (e.g., "You are indecisive"), because their faith in astrology overrides their self-perceptions. In addition, the researchers tested whether a description not attributed to astrology would be accepted as more accurate, and whether experiencing positive or negative descriptions would alter subjects' belief in astrology.

What type of design would you use to study these factors?

Testing any of these factors involves first the quasi-independent variable of creating conditions by selecting subjects who are astrology believers or skeptics. Additional factors then include favorable versus unfavorable personality descriptions, and/or whether or not the descriptions are attributed to astrology. The dependent variable would be subjects' rating of the accuracy of the descriptions. In their study, Glick et al. (1989) manipulated these factors as between-subjects factors, so that they could also examine the influence of a particular type of experience on subjects' attitude toward astrology. They tested this influence with a pretest-posttest design, measuring subjects' attitudes toward astrology before and then after they participated in the above conditions.

The researchers found that (1) skeptics accept positive personality descriptions as more accurate than negative ones, but believers accept a negative description as being equal in accuracy to a positive one, (2) believers and skeptics alike rated astrological descriptions as more accurate than nonastrological descriptions, and (3) skeptics, more so than believers, became more positive in their feelings toward astrology after receiving favorable horoscopes. Glick et al. proposed that skeptics are more open-minded, so they are more likely to change their opinion about astrology after receiving a positive description. Believers, however, seem to ignore the contradictions from a negative description, thus suggesting that believers and skeptics differ in terms of how they test these descriptions and evaluate the evidence that may support them.

What suggestions for additional research can you make?

First, it would be interesting to examine how believers and skeptics test astrological predictions. For example, you might present them with a horoscope that is ultimately confirmed or disconfirmed by what "coincidentally" happens later in an experimental setting. Then you could measure how the outcome of a prediction is evaluated by skeptics and believers, and how this evaluation influences their attitudes toward astrology.

Second, when believers are confronted with a negative statement that *disconfirms* their self-perceptions, they continue to maintain their original opinion. The implication is that believers in astrology do not apply the correct logic for testing hypotheses. Recall from Chapter 1 that we discussed using a deck of cards for testing a hypothesis about letters and numbers printed on the cards. Such procedures could be adapted to test for differences in logic and hypothesis testing between skeptics and believers.

Serial-Position Effects

A highly reliable finding in the study of memory is that when subjects recall a list of words, they tend to recall the first few and the last few items in the list best. Because recall changes as a function of an item's serial position in the list, this effect is called the *serial position effect*. Often in these studies, a list is spoken to subjects which consists of a random string of single digits, and, for reliability, each subject is tested with a number of lists. To see this effect, we graph the subjects' recall scores for the words in a list as a function of where in the list the words occurred. The graph produces a *serial-position curve*, as shown in Figure 12.2. Note that the higher recall of the first items in the list is called the "primacy effect" and the higher recall of the final items is called the "recency effect."

To study the memory processes that produce these effects, researchers have employed numerous techniques that alter recall of the list. From the impact of a particular manipulation, they infer a characteristic of memory. For example, the final few items in a list are most recently entered into memory, so they may be in some sense "fresher." Some researchers (e.g., Crowder, 1982) have proposed that these items are better recalled because there is an "echo" in memory of the most recent spoken words. The final word in the list is recalled best because no words come after it that might otherwise interfere with its echo.

How would you test this explanation?

Researchers have tested this proposal by speaking an additional word at the end of the list, called a "stimulus suffix." When the lists consist of digits, the suffix for every list is usually the digit *zero*. So as not to increase the effort that subjects must apply to remembering the list, they are told not to remember the zero; it is merely the signal to recall the list, and they are to otherwise "ignore" it. In control conditions, a tone is

FIGURE 12.2   Idealized Serial Position Curve

Shown here is subjects' recall of 8-item lists as a function of each item's position in the list.

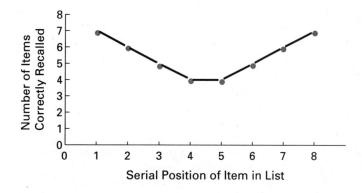

the recall signal. Because the tone is so different from the list of words, it should not produce interference, so recall of the list in the control group should exhibit the typical high recency. Conversely, because the zero is heard, it should reduce the freshness of the final list items and fill the echo, so recall of the list in the experimental group should exhibit reduced recency relative to the tone condition. In fact, it does, and the lowered recency is called the "suffix effect." (See Turner et al. [1987] for an overview.)

The reason that the suffix disrupts recency is not known. Originally, its effect was thought to be limited to spoken words only. Yet suffix effects have also been found when the zero is silently mouthed by the experimenter or by the subject, and among deaf subjects when the list and suffix is presented using sign language. In addition, suffix effects have been shown to occur when spoken words in the list have different vowels (*gap, got, gut*) but not when they have different consonants (*gap, tap, map*). Thus, the suffix effect is not restricted to auditory stimuli, yet it does not always work with auditory stimuli. This inconsistency makes the notion of an "echo" very suspect.

Although there have been many explanations of this effect, one that has received virtually no attention concerns the assumption that subjects can in fact "ignore" the zero at the end of the list. Subjects are presumably equally able to ignore a tone and "zero," and both readily signal that the list is over. Then the suffix has its effect simply because in some way it fills the echo, decreasing the freshness of the final items in the list. But how do subjects know that the word *zero* is the one to ignore unless they first pay attention to it? They must identify this word to recognize that it is *not* part of the list to be remembered. A tone, by contrast, can be ignored instantly, because it is so obviously different from the preceding list of words. Can (or do) subjects ignore the zero? If not, is the zero at first treated as part of the list, thereby confusing subjects? Does a list followed by a zero require greater attention than a list followed by a tone, and does this greater attention come at the expense of recalling the list?

How would you study whether subjects do ignore the suffix?

You might measure the reaction time of subjects to determine whether there are differences in their ability to recognize the end of a list when it is signaled by a tone or zero. If the zero takes longer to recognize, then there is something about it, in terms of the attention it requires, that is different from the control condition. If so, then a confounding has occurred, because the tone and the zero are not equivalent signals for the end of the list.

Alternatively, you might first identify some words that are easy to recognize and some that are difficult to recognize. Then, using these words in place of the zero, you can see whether they alter the recency effect. Or you might give subjects a cue to forewarn them that the zero or tone is about to occur. For example, you might ring a bell just prior to the zero. If reading the list aloud, you could change your tone of voice and inflection, or make a movement, to signal that the zero is about to occur. If such cues eliminate the suffix effect, then you have evidence that the zero normally reduces the recency effect because of the attention it demands or the confusion that it produces.

Attractiveness and Height

Evidence suggests that, in our society, taller men are perceived as more honest, competent, and attractive. For example, men described as tall when advertising in the "Personals" column of a newspaper tend to receive more responses (Lynn & Shurgot, 1984). Accordingly, Shepard and Strathman (1989) investigated whether women prefer to date taller men and whether they consider taller men more attractive. They also investigated whether men prefer to date shorter women and whether they consider shorter women more attractive.

How would you study the relationship between height and attraction?

Shepard and Strathman conducted a correlational study, presenting males and females with a questionnaire that asked for the number and height of their recent dates as well as for a rating of each date's attractiveness. Subjects were also asked whether they preferred to date a person who was shorter than, taller than, or the same height as themselves. The researcher's found that females reported that they dated tall males more frequently than short or medium males. They also reported a preference for taller men, but they did not rate their taller dates as more attractive. Interestingly, short and medium-height males reported that they went out on dates just as often as did tall males. Overall, the males preferred shorter female dates, rated them as more attractive, and dated them more frequently.

What problem do these self-reports present?

These subjects' self-reports may have been unreliable for several reasons: (1) The subjects might have inaccurately estimated a date's height, especially after the fact; (2) the date's personality and compatibility might have influenced subjects' perception of the date's attractiveness; and (3) a "bad" date might have biased subjects so that they remembered their dates as shorter or taller than they actually were. Further, as Shepard and Strathman noted, the females reported fewer dates with short or medium-height men, but the males, regardless of their height, reported the same frequency of dates. Since the shorter males were dating *somebody*, the self-reports of either the males or the females must have been in error.

What suggestions for additional research can you make?

Rather than relying on self-reports about subjects' past dating experiences, Shepard and Strathman conducted an additional experiment in which they manipulated height and measured attractiveness. Here, they presented subjects with a photograph of the upper bodies of a male and female facing each other. In the photograph, the male was either 5 inches taller, the same height, or 5 inches shorter than the female. Females rated the man as more attractive when he was taller. Males, however, did not rate females differently depending on her height.

You might also determine why the females' reports of seldom dating short men does not correspond to the high frequency of dating reported by short men. Perhaps the males or females are erroneous in their reports because of pressure to give the socially desirable response. If so, the number of erroneous reports should increase when the researcher strongly implies such demand characteristics through instructions or the task. Also, you might investigate whether the contradictory results occur because of a definitional problem, having to do with the term *taller*. Stereotypically, most people would agree that a man whose height is 7 feet is "tall," and that one who is 5 feet is "short." However, taller can be a relative personal term, because for a woman whose height is 4 feet 6 inches, a man with height of 5 feet is "taller." To what extent do males and females use a stereotypic or personal definition when selecting or describing dates?

There is an ecological issue here as well: Women *are*, on average, shorter than men. The opportunities for dates are greater, then, if women accept taller men and men accept shorter women, so their "preferences" may simply reflect the facts of life. Does the fact that most men are taller than most women lead to a stereotype of the ideal date? As we saw when we discussed Horner (1972), people tend to anticipate negative consequences when violating a sex-role stereotype. To what extent do the above studies measure stereotyped responses instead of actual attraction? And, finally, is it appropriate to conclude that being taller always makes a male more attractive to a woman? Is there a point where taller is not better but becomes "too tall"?

Influence of Color

Research from environmental psychology suggests that the color of walls, furniture, or floors has an influence on various aspects of behavior. For example, "warm" colors (those close to red) are often believed to be arousing, to increase physical performance, and to improve mood. And "cool" colors (those close to blue) are believed to be soothing, to lower performance, and to have a dulling effect on mood.

How would you design a study to test these beliefs?

One obvious way to manipulate the color in the environment is to test subjects in different rooms that are painted a different color. In each room, you can have subjects perform a physical task and/or provide responses that indicate their mood. For example, Kwallek, Lewis, and Robbins (1988) asked subjects to type business forms for 20 minutes after placing them in either a red or blue "office," and then had them complete a questionnaire describing their anxiety, mood, and general arousal. After resting in another room, subjects either returned to the same colored office or were switched to the different colored office, performed additional typing, and completed another questionnaire. As it turns out, the subjects who were moved to the different colored office made significantly more typing errors. And the interaction showed that more errors occurred when subjects moved from the blue to the red office than when they moved from red to blue. The mood data indicated that subjects remaining in the red office showed greater anxiety and stress, subjects remaining in the blue office showed greater depression, and subjects who were moved to different colored offices showed the greatest level of general arousal.

Since moving subjects into a different colored room influences their behavior, a problem with this study is that placing subjects in the first office constitutes changing rooms in an uncontrolled manner. As an alternative approach, you might include a control condition that allows you to "reverse" the influence of any previous colored room.

How would you design this alternative study?

Hamid and Newport (1989) studied how the color of a room influences behavior using an ABACAB reversal design. The control or baseline—condition A—was a gray room that presumably neutralized the influence of other colors. A pink room was condition B, and a blue room was condition C. The researchers measured hand-strength and mood in six young children after they had experienced each colored room. Greater physical strength and more positive mood was found in the pink conditions.

What suggestions for additional research can you make?

If there is an influence of color on arousal and performance, then it should extend to a variety of colored objects and situations. Would similar effects on typing errors occur depending on the color of the paper in a typewriter or the color of a computer display screen? In the previous chapter we saw the influence of black uniforms on aggression, but the present research suggests that other colors of clothing may also affect behavior. Certainly the idea behind "dressing for success" is that a worker's or job applicant's clothing style influences how that person is perceived and judged by supervisors and co-workers (e.g., Forsythe, 1990). Does wearing reddish or bluish clothes also influence perceptions? We also discussed how subjects misattribute their arousal due to fear as being due to sexual attraction. Is it possible that arousal from wall color or the color of clothing could be misattributed as sexual attraction? As an applied topic, the colors in business environments may be important for maximizing worker productivity. Similarly, given that maximum arousal is sought in athletic events, does wall color influence, for example, weight-training success? And, finally, do certain colors play a role when we become overaroused, as discussed below?

Self-Consciousness and "Choking Under Pressure"

An unusual behavior to study is the phenomenon of "choking under pressure." Baumeister (1984) proposed that inferior performance ("choking") occurs when we feel so pressured to perform well that we focus too much attention on the process of performing a task and not enough attention on the outcome of the task. Thus, in a self-fulfilling prophecy, the more we worry that things are going badly, the worse they go. Baumeister also proposed that personality characteristics play a role, such that, for example, a person who is more self-conscious should exhibit greater "choking."

How would you design a study to test these proposals?

In an experimental setting, you could create a task for subjects in which you manipulate the amount of pressure they feel. The task should be a simple one in which errors are easily measured. For example, you can have subjects quickly trace a pencil maze, solve simple math problems, or perform a reaction-time task in which they press one of several buttons to make a correct response. Consider Heaton and Sigall (1991) who first identified subjects along the quasi-independent variable of high or low self-consciousness. For experimental realism, they had subjects in each condition form a "team." Then they manipulated the pressure situation through the additional factors of: (1) indicating that the subject's team was behind or ahead, and (2) having subjects perform when alone, when watched by their team, or when watched by the opposing team. Choking was measured by the time it took to place variously shaped pegs in their corresponding holes. Subjects low in self-consciousness choked depending upon the audience characteristics, while those high in self-consciousness choked when their team was behind.

What suggestions for additional research can you make?

Apparently, people differing in self-consciousness perceive the source of pressure differently. The results for subjects with high self-consciousness suggest that they choked because of competitive pressure, so you might manipulate the situation for them in terms of the amount of competition involved. The results for subjects with low self-consciousness suggest that they choked because of their need for social approval, so for them you might manipulate the social setting. Also consider the possibility of replicating the above relationship between choking and pressure in a field setting: Perhaps a "stranger" could watch someone playing a game in a video arcade. As extensions of this research, the above results suggest that other personality traits, in terms of whether a person is task or socially oriented, may play a role in choking. Thus, for example, you might correlate subjects' scores on these traits with how much they choke or, as above, examine how these traits interact with different conditions that promote choking. Alternatively, given that high pressure is a form of arousal, you might ask whether the color of the room in which a subject is being tested influences choking. Finally, you might ask whether a "lucky charm," such as a lucky shirt, is considered lucky because a subject did *not* choke when wearing it. (And what color is it?)

PUTTING IT ALL TOGETHER

At this point, you *have* put it all together. By now you understand the basic logic of the studies we have discussed, so you understand the basic logic of most psychological research. Congratulations on mastering a complicated topic. If you still feel that you cannot evaluate and conduct the sophisticated research found in the psychological literature, remember that you are at a temporary disadvantage. The major difference between beginning student researchers and professional-level researchers is their knowledge of the psychological issues involved in any topic. You are probably not all that familiar with the existing theory and research on a particular behavior. If you read the literature, however, you will learn the details of how a construct is conceptualized, along with the commonly used, successful methods of studying it. By filling in these gaps in your knowledge, you will discover not only that you *can* evaluate and conduct real research, but also that it is a very enjoyable experience.

A Appendix: Statistical Procedures

A.1. MEASURES OF CENTRAL TENDENCY

These procedures are discussed in Chapters 3 and 6.

The Mean

The mean, $\overline{X}$, is found using the formula

$$\overline{X} = \frac{\Sigma X}{N}$$

where ΣX is the sum of the scores, and N is the number of scores in the sample. For the scores 2, 1, 3, 7, 4, 5,

$$\overline{X} = \frac{\Sigma X}{N} = \frac{22}{6} = 3.667$$

The Median

The median, *Mdn*, is calculated by arranging all scores in the sample from lowest to highest. If N is an odd number, the median is the score that divides the distribution in two, with an equal number of scores below and above it. If N is an even number, the median is the average of the two middle scores. For the scores 7, 7, 9, 10, 12, 13, 13, 14, 18, the median score is 12.

The Mode

The mode is calculated by counting the most frequently occurring score or scores in the sample. For the scores 1, 2, 2, 2, 3, 3, 4, 4, 4, 4, 4, 5, 5, 6, the mode is 4. For the scores 1, 2, 2, 2, 2, 3, 3, 4, 4, 4, 4, 5, 5, 6, the modes are 2 and 4.

A.2. MEASURES OF VARIABILITY

Below are formulas for calculating the sample and estimated population variance, the sample and estimated population standard deviation, and the range. Measures of variability are discussed in Chapters 3 and 6.

The Variance

There are two ways to calculate variance.

The Sample Variance   The sample variance S_x^2, describes how far the sample scores are spread out around the sample mean. The formula is

$$S_x^2 = \frac{\Sigma X^2 - \frac{(\Sigma X)^2}{N}}{N}$$

where ΣX is the sum of the scores and then $(\Sigma X)^2$ is the squared sum of the scores, ΣX^2 is the sum of squared scores, and N is the number of scores in the sample. For the scores 2, 3, 4, 5, 6, 7, 8,

$$S_x^2 = \frac{\Sigma X^2 - \frac{(\Sigma X)^2}{N}}{N} = \frac{203 - \frac{(35)^2}{7}}{7} = 4.0$$

The Estimated Population Variance   The estimated population variance, s_x^2, is computed using sample data, but it is an estimate of how far the scores in the population would be spread out around the population mean. The formula is

$$s_x^2 = \frac{\Sigma X^2 - \frac{(\Sigma X)^2}{N}}{N - 1}$$

where ΣX is the sum of the scores and then $(\Sigma X)^2$ is the squared sum of the scores, ΣX^2 is the sum of the squared scores and $N - 1$ is the number of scores in the sample minus 1. For the scores of 2, 3, 4, 5, 6, 7, 8,

$$s_x^2 = \frac{\Sigma X^2 - \frac{(\Sigma X)^2}{N}}{N - 1} = \frac{203 - \frac{(35)^2}{7}}{6} = 4.67$$

The Standard Deviation

There are two ways to calculate the standard deviation.

The Sample Standard Deviation   The sample standard deviation, S_x, describes how far the sample scores are spread out around the sample mean. It is calculated as the square root of the sample variance. For the above scores of 2, 3, 4, 5, 6, 7, 8,

$$S_x = \sqrt{\frac{\Sigma X^2 - \frac{(\Sigma X)^2}{N}}{N}} = \sqrt{\frac{203 - \frac{(35)^2}{7}}{7}} = 2.0$$

The Estimated Population Standard Deviation   The estimated population standard deviation, s_x, is computed using sample data, but it is an estimate of how far the scores in the population would be spread out around the population mean. It is calculated as the square root of the estimated population variance. For the above scores of 2, 3, 4, 5, 6, 7, 8,

$$s_x = \sqrt{\frac{\Sigma X^2 - \frac{(\Sigma X)^2}{N}}{N - 1}} = \sqrt{\frac{203 - \frac{(35)^2}{7}}{6}} = 2.16$$

The Range

The range is the distance between the two most extreme scores in a sample. The formula is:

range = highest score − lowest score

For the scores 2, 3, 4, 5, 6, 7, 8, the range equals 8 − 2, which is 6.

A.3.   THE TWO-SAMPLE *t*-TEST

Below are the procedures for performing the independent samples (between-subjects) *t*-test and the dependent samples (within-subjects) *t*-test.

The Independent Samples *t*-Test

This procedure is discussed in Chapters 3 and 6. Example data are shown in Table A.1.

Step 1   Determine the sum of scores (ΣX), the sum of squared scores (ΣX^2), the n, and the $\overline{X}$ in each condition.

Step 2   Calculate s_1^2, the estimated population variance based on the scores in the first condition, and s_2^2, the estimated population variance based on the scores of the second condition. Use the formula for the estimated population variance given in section A.2.

TABLE A.1   Data from Two-Sample Between-Subjects Design

Condition 1	*Condition 2*
11	13
14	16
10	14
12	17
8	11
15	14
12	15
13	18
9	12
11	11
$\Sigma X = 115$	$\Sigma X = 141$
$\Sigma X^2 = 1365$	$\Sigma X^2 = 2041$
$\overline{X}_1 = 11.5$	$\overline{X}_2 = 14.1$
$n_1 = 10$	$n_2 = 10$
$s_1^2 = 4.72$	$s_2^2 = 5.88$

Step 3 Calculate t:

$$t = \frac{(\overline{X}_1 - \overline{X}_2) - (\mu_1 - \mu_2)}{\sqrt{\left(\frac{(n_1-1)s_1^2+(n_2-1)s_2^2}{(n_1-1)+(n_2-1)}\right)\left(\frac{1}{n_1} + \frac{1}{n_2}\right)}}$$

where $\overline{X}_1$ and $\overline{X}_2$ are the means of the two conditions, $(\mu_1 - \mu_2)$ is the difference between the means predicted by the null hypothesis (usually this difference is zero), n_1 is the number of scores in the first condition, n_2 is the number of scores in the second condition, and s_1^2 and s_2^2 are from Step 2.

$$t = \frac{(11.5 - 14.1) - 0}{\sqrt{\left(\frac{(10-1)4.72+(10-1)5.88}{(10-1)+(10-1)}\right)\left(\frac{1}{10} + \frac{1}{10}\right)}}$$

$$t = \frac{-2.6}{\sqrt{(5.30)(.20)}} = \frac{-2.6}{1.030} = -2.524$$

Step 4 Find the critical value of t in Table B.1 of Appendix B. Degrees of freedom, df, equal $(n_1 - 1) + (n_2 - 1)$. Above, for $df = 18$ and $\sigma = .05$, the two-tailed critical value is ± 2.101. Here the obtained t is beyond the critical value, so it is significant. If t is *not* significant, do not perform Step 5.

Step 5 See section A.8 for computing effect size and section A.9 for computing confidence intervals.

The Dependent Samples t-Test

This procedure is discussed in Chapter 7. Example data are shown in Table A.2.

Step 1 Calculate the difference, D, between the two scores in each pair of scores formed by matching two subjects or repeatedly measuring the same subject in both conditions.

TABLE A.2   Data from Two-Sample Within-Subjects Design

Subject	Condition I	−	Condition II	=	Difference D	D^2
1	11		8		+3	9
2	16		11		+5	25
3	20		15		+5	25
4	17		11		+6	36
5	10		11		−1	1
	$\overline{X} = 14.80$		$\overline{X} = 11.20$		$\Sigma D = +18$	$\Sigma D^2 = 96$

Step 2 Calculate $\overline{D}$, the mean of the difference scores. Above, $\overline{D} = 18/5 = 3.6$.

Step 3 Calculate s_D^2, the estimated variance of the population of difference scores, found by entering the differences scores into the formula for s_x^2 in section A.2. Above, $s_D^2 = 7.80$.

Step 4 Calculate t:

$$t_{obt} = \frac{\overline{D} - \mu_D}{\sqrt{(s_D^2)\frac{1}{N}}}$$

where μ_D is the average difference score between the conditions described by the null hypothesis (usually this is zero), N is the number of pairs of scores, and s_D^2 is from Step 3.

$$t = \frac{\overline{D} - \mu_D}{\sqrt{(s_D^2)\frac{1}{N}}} = \frac{+3.6 - 0}{\sqrt{(7.80)\left(\frac{1}{5}\right)}} = \frac{+3.6}{1.249} = 2.88$$

Step 5 Find the critical value of t in Table B.1 of Appendix B. Degrees of freedom, df, equal $N - 1$, where N is the number of difference scores. Above, for $df = 4$ and $\alpha = .05$, the two-tailed critical value is ± 2.776. If the obtained t is significant, the mean scores in each condition (above, $\overline{X}_1 = 14.80$ and $\overline{X}_2 = 11.20$) also differ significantly. If t is *not* significant, do not perform Step 7.

Step 6 See section A.8 for computing effect size and section A.9 for computing confidence intervals.

A.4. THE ONE-WAY ANALYSIS OF VARIANCE

Below are the procedures for performing a one-way between-subjects ANOVA and a one-way within-subjects ANOVA.

The One-Way Between-Subjects ANOVA

This procedure is discussed in Chapters 3 and 6. Example data for a one-way design having three levels (with five subjects per level) are shown in Table A.3.

Step 1 Determine k, the number of levels in the factor; then determine the sum of scores (ΣX), the sum of squared scores (ΣX^2), the n, and the $\overline{X}$ in each level.

TABLE A.3   Data from One-Way Between-Subjects Design

	Factor **A**		
Level A_1	*Level* A_2	*Level* A_3	
9	4	1	
12	6	3	
4	8	4	
8	2	5	
7	10	2	*Totals*
$\Sigma X = 40$	$\Sigma X = 30$	$\Sigma X = 15$	$\Sigma X_{\text{tot}} = 85$
$\Sigma X^2 = 354$	$\Sigma X^2 = 220$	$\Sigma X^2 = 55$	$\Sigma X_{\text{tot}}^2 = 629$
$n_1 = 5$	$n_2 = 5$	$n_3 = 5$	$N = 15$
$\overline{X}_1 = 8$	$\overline{X}_2 = 6$	$\overline{X}_3 = 3$	$k = 3$

Step 2   Also calculate the totals:

$$\Sigma X_{\text{tot}} = 40 + 30 + 15 = 85$$
$$\Sigma X_{\text{tot}}^2 = 354 + 220 + 55 = 629$$
$$N = 5 + 5 + 5 = 15$$

Step 3   Compute the correction term:

$$\text{Correction term} = \left(\frac{(\Sigma X_{\text{tot}})^2}{N} \right) = \frac{85^2}{15} = 481.67$$

Step 4   As you perform the following calculations, create the Analysis of Variance Summary Table shown in Table A.4.

TABLE A.4   Summary Table of One-Way Between-Subjects ANOVA

Source	*Sum of Squares*	*df*	*Mean Square*	*F*
Factor A				
(Between Groups)	63.33	2	31.67	4.52
Within Groups	84.00	12	7.0	
Total	147.33	14		

Step 5   Compute the total sum of squares:

$$SS_{\text{tot}} = \Sigma X_{\text{tot}}^2 - \text{Step 3}$$
$$SS_{\text{tot}} = 629 - 481.67 = 147.33$$

Step 6 Compute the sum of squares between groups for factor A:

$$SS_A = \sum \left(\frac{(\text{sum of scores in each column})^2}{n \text{ of scores in the column}} \right) - \text{Step 3}$$

$$SS_A = \left(\frac{(40)^2}{5} + \frac{(30)^2}{5} + \frac{(15)^2}{5} \right) - 481.67 = 63.33$$

Step 7 Compute the sum of squares within groups:

$$SS_{wn} = SS_{tot} - SS_A = \text{Step 4} - \text{Step 5}$$

$$SS_{wn} = 147.33 - 63.33 = 84$$

Step 8 Compute the degrees of freedom.

a. For factor A: $df_A = k - 1$

$$df_A = 3 - 1 = 2$$

b. Within groups: $df_{wn} = N - k$

$$df_{wn} = 15 - 3 = 12$$

c. Total: $df_{tot} = N - 1$

$$df_{tot} = 15 - 1 = 14$$

Step 9 Compute the mean square for factor A:

$$MS_A = \frac{SS_A}{df_A} = \frac{\text{Step 6}}{\text{Step 8.a}}$$

$$MS_A = \frac{63.33}{2} = 31.67$$

Step 10 Compute the mean square within groups:

$$MS_{wn} = \frac{SS_{wn}}{df_{wn}} = \frac{\text{Step 7}}{\text{Step 8.b}}$$

$$MS_{wn} = \frac{84}{12} = 7.0$$

Step 11 Compute F:

$$F = \frac{MS_A}{MS_{wn}} = \frac{\text{Step 9}}{\text{Step 10}}$$

$$F = \frac{31.67}{7.0} = 4.52$$

Step 12 Find the critical value of F in Table B.2 of Appendix B, using df_A and df_{wn}. Above, for $df_A = 2$, $df_{wn} = 12$, and $\alpha = .05$, the critical value is 3.88. Here the obtained F is beyond the critical value, so it is significant. When F is significant, perform Step 13.

Step 13   See section A.7 for *post hoc* procedures, section A.8 for computing effect size, and section A.9 for computing confidence intervals.

The One-Way Within-Subjects ANOVA

This procedure is discussed in Chapter 7. Example data from a one-way repeated measures design (with five subjects) are shown in Table A.5.

TABLE A.5   Data from One-Way Repeated Measures Design

	Level A₁	*Level A₂*	*Level A₃*	ΣX_{sub}
		Factor A		
Subject 1	2	7	9	18
Subject 2	6	8	11	25
Subject 3	3	5	8	16
Subject 4	2	7	10	19
Subject 5	4	7	10	21

			Totals
$\Sigma X = 17$	$\Sigma X = 34$	$\Sigma X = 48$	$\Sigma X_{tot} = 99$
$\Sigma X^2 = 69$	$\Sigma X^2 = 236$	$\Sigma X^2 = 466$	$\Sigma X^2_{tot} = 771$
$n_1 = 5$	$n_2 = 5$	$n_3 = 5$	$N = 15$
$\overline{X}_1 = 3.4$	$\overline{X}_2 = 6.8$	$\overline{X}_3 = 9.6$	$k = 3$

Step 1   Determine k, the number of levels of the factor; then determine the sum of scores (ΣX), the sum of squared scores (ΣX^2), the n, and the $\overline{X}$ in each level. Also calculate the sum of the scores obtained by each subject, ΣX_{sub} (the sum of each row).

Step 2   Also determine the totals:

$$\Sigma X_{tot} = 17 + 34 + 48 = 99$$
$$\Sigma X^2_{tot} = 69 + 236 + 466 = 771$$
$$N = 5 + 5 + 5 = 15$$

Step 3   Compute the correction term:

$$\text{Correction term} = \frac{(\Sigma X_{tot})^2}{N} = \frac{99^2}{15} = 653.4$$

Step 4   As you perform the following calculations, create the Analysis of Variance Summary Table shown in Table A.6.

TABLE A.6 Summary Table of One-Way Within-Subjects ANOVA

Source	Sum of Squares	df	Mean Square	F
Factor A				
(Between Groups)	96.40	2	48.20	68.86
Subjects	15.60			
A × Subjects	5.60	8	0.70	
Total	117.60	14		

Step 5 Compute the total sum of squares:

$$SS_{tot} = \Sigma X_{tot}^2 - \text{Step 3}$$
$$SS_{tot} = 771 - 653.4 = 117.6$$

Step 6 Compute the sum of squares for factor A:

$$SS_A = \Sigma \left(\frac{(\text{sum of scores in each column})^2}{n \text{ of scores in the column}} \right) - \text{Step 3}$$

$$SS_A = \left(\frac{(17)^2}{5} + \frac{(34)^2}{5} + \frac{(48)^2}{5} \right) - 653.4 = 96.4$$

Step 7 Compute the sum of squares for subjects:

$$SS_{subs} = \frac{(\Sigma X_{sub1})^2 + (\Sigma X_{sub2})^2 + \cdots (\Sigma X_{subn})^2}{k} - \text{Step 3}$$

$$SS_{subs} = \frac{(18)^2 + (25)^2 + (16)^2 + (19)^2 + (21)^2}{3} - 653.4$$

$$SS_{subs} = 15.6$$

Step 8 Compute the sum of squares for the interaction of A by subjects:

$$SS_{A \times subs} = SS_{tot} - SS_A - SS_{subs} = \text{Step 5} - \text{Step 6} - \text{Step 7}$$
$$SS_{A \times subs} = 117.6 - 96.4 - 15.6 = 5.6$$

Step 9 Compute the degrees of freedom.

a. Factor A: $df_A = k - 1$

$$df_A = 3 - 1 = 2$$

b. For A by subjects: $df_{A \times subs} = (k - 1) (\text{number of subjects} - 1)$

$$df_{A \times subs} = (3 - 1)(5 - 1) = 8$$

c. Total: $df_{tot} = N - 1$

$$df_{tot} = 15 - 1 = 14$$

Step 10   Compute the mean square for factor A:

$$MS_A = \frac{SS_A}{df_A} = \frac{\text{Step 6}}{\text{Step 9.a}}$$

$$MS_A = \frac{96.4}{2} = 48.2$$

Step 11   Compute the mean square for A by subjects:

$$MS_{A \times subs} = \frac{SS_{A \times subs}}{df_{A \times subs}} = \frac{\text{Step 8}}{\text{Step 9.b}}$$

$$MS_{A \times subs} = \frac{5.6}{8} = .7$$

Step 12   Compute F

$$F = \frac{MS_A}{MS_{A \times subs}} = \frac{\text{Step 10}}{\text{Step 11}}$$

$$F = \frac{48.2}{.7} = 68.86$$

Step 13   Find the critical value of F in Table B.2 of Appendix B, with df_A as the degrees of freedom between groups and $df_{A \times subs}$ as the degrees of freedom within groups. Above, for $\alpha = .05$, $df_A = 2$, and $df_{A \times subs} = 8$, the critical value is 4.46, so the obtained F is significant. When F is significant, perform Step 14.

Step 14   See section A.7 for *post hoc* procedures, section A.8 for computing effect size, and section A.9 for computing confidence intervals.

A.5.   THE TWO-WAY BETWEEN-SUBJECTS ANALYSIS OF VARIANCE

This procedure is discussed in Chapter 8. Table A.7 shows example data from a 3×2 between-subjects design, with three scores per cell.

Step 1   In each cell, compute the sum of the scores (ΣX), the sum of the squared scores (ΣX^2), n, and the mean (the interaction means). Determine k_A, the number of levels of factor A; and, for each column, compute ΣX, n, and the mean (the main effect means of factor A). Then determine k_B, the number of levels of factor B; and, for each row, compute ΣX, n, and the mean (the main effect means of factor B).

Step 2   Also determine the totals:

$$\Sigma X_{tot} = 36 + 69 + 68 = 173$$
$$\Sigma X_{tot}^2 = 218 + 377 + 838 + 56 + 470 + 116 = 2075$$
$$N = 3 + 3 + 3 + 3 + 3 + 3 = 18$$

TABLE A.7   Data from Two-Way Between-Subjects Design

		Factor A			
		A_1	A_2	A_3	$k_A = 3$
		4 9 11	8 12 13	18 17 15	
	B_1	$\overline{X} = 8$ $\Sigma X = 24$ $\Sigma X^2 = 218$ $n = 3$	$\overline{X} = 11$ $\Sigma X = 33$ $\Sigma X^2 = 377$ $n = 3$	$\overline{X} = 16.7$ $\Sigma X = 50$ $\Sigma X^2 = 838$ $n = 3$	$\overline{X} = 11.89$ $\Sigma X = 107$ $n = 9$
Factor B $k_B = 2$		2 6 4	9 10 17	6 8 4	
	B_2	$\overline{X} = 4$ $\Sigma X = 12$ $\Sigma X^2 = 56$ $n = 3$	$\overline{X} = 12$ $\Sigma X = 36$ $\Sigma X^2 = 470$ $n = 3$	$\overline{X} = 6$ $\Sigma X = 18$ $\Sigma X^2 = 116$ $n = 3$	$\overline{X} = 7.33$ $\Sigma X = 66$ $n = 9$
		$\Sigma X = 36$ $n = 6$ $\overline{X} = 6$	$\Sigma X = 69$ $n = 6$ $\overline{X} = 11.5$	$\Sigma X = 68$ $n = 6$ $\overline{X} = 11.33$	$\Sigma X_{tot} = 173$ $\Sigma X_{tot}^2 = 2075$ $N = 18$

Step 3   Compute the correction term:

$$\text{Correction term} = \left(\frac{(\Sigma X_{tot})^2}{N} \right) = \frac{173^2}{18} = 1662.72$$

Step 4   As you perform the following calculations, create the analysis of variance summary table shown in Table A.8.

TABLE A.8   Summary Table of Two-Way, Between Subjects ANOVA

Source	*Sum of Squares*	*df*	*Mean Square*	*F*
Factor A	117.45	2	58.73	7.14
Factor B	93.39	1	93.39	11.36
A × B Interaction	102.77	2	51.39	6.25
Within Groups	98.67	12	8.22	
Total	412.28	17		

Step 5   Compute the total sum of squares:

$$SS_{tot} = \Sigma X^2_{tot} - \text{Step 3}$$
$$SS_{tot} = 2075 - 1662.72 = 412.28$$

Step 6   Compute the sum of squares for the column factor A:

$$SS_A = \Sigma \left(\frac{(\text{sum of scores in each column})^2}{n \text{ of scores in the column}} \right) - \text{Step 3}$$
$$SS_A = \left(\frac{(36)^2}{6} + \frac{(69)^2}{6} + \frac{(68)^2}{6} \right) - 1662.72 = 117.45$$

Step 7   Compute the sum of squares for the row factor B:

$$SS_B = \Sigma \left(\frac{(\text{sum of scores in each row})^2}{n \text{ of scores in the row}} \right) - \text{Step 3}$$
$$SS_B = \left(\frac{(107)^2}{9} + \frac{(66)^2}{9} \right) - 1662.72 = 93.39$$

Step 8   Compute the total sum of squares between groups (not reported in Summary Table):

$$SS_{bn} = \Sigma \left(\frac{(\text{sum of scores in each cell})^2}{n \text{ of scores in the cell}} \right) - \text{Step 3}$$
$$SS_{bn} = \left(\frac{(24)^2}{3} + \frac{(33)^2}{3} + \frac{(50)^2}{3} + \frac{(12)^2}{3} + \frac{(36)^2}{3} + \frac{(18)^2}{3} \right) - 1662.72$$
$$SS_{bn} = 313.61$$

Step 9   Compute the sum of squares for the A × B interaction:

$$SS_{A \times B} = SS_{bn} - SS_A - SS_B = \text{Step 8} - \text{Step 6} - \text{Step 7}$$
$$SS_{A \times B} = 313.61 - 117.45 - 93.39 = 102.77$$

Step 10   Compute the sum of squares within groups:

$$SS_{wn} = SS_{tot} - SS_{bn} = \text{Step 5} - \text{Step 8}$$
$$SS_{wn} = 412.28 - 313.61 = 98.67$$

Step 11   Compute the degrees of freedom.

a. Factor A: $df_A = k_A - 1$
$$df_A = 3 - 1 = 2$$

b. Factor B: $df_B = k_B - 1$
$$df_B = 2 - 1 = 1$$

c. A × B interaction: $df_{A \times B} = (df_A)(df_B) = $ (Step 9.a)(Step 9.b)

$$df_{A \times B} = (2)(1) = 2$$

d. Within groups: $df_{wn} = N - $ number of cells

$$df_{wn} = 18 - 6 = 12$$

e. Total: $df_{tot} = N - 1$

$$df_{tot} = 18 - 1 = 17$$

Step 12 Compute the mean square for factor A:

$$MS_A = \frac{SS_A}{df_A} = \frac{\text{Step 6}}{\text{Step 11.a}}$$

$$MS_A = \frac{117.45}{2} = 58.73$$

Step 13 Compute the mean square for factor B:

$$MS_B = \frac{SS_B}{df_B} = \frac{\text{Step 7}}{\text{Step 11.b}}$$

$$MS_B = \frac{93.39}{1} = 93.39$$

Step 14 Compute the mean square for $A \times B$ interaction:

$$MS_{A \times B} = \frac{SS_{A \times B}}{df_{A \times B}} = \frac{\text{Step 9}}{\text{Step 10.c}}$$

$$MS_{A \times B} = \frac{102.77}{2} = 51.39$$

Step 15 Compute the mean square within groups:

$$MS_{wn} = \frac{SS_{wn}}{df_{wn}} = \frac{\text{Step 10}}{\text{Step 10.d}}$$

$$MS_{wn} = \frac{98.67}{12} = 8.22$$

Step 16 Compute the F for the main effect of factor A:

$$F_A = \frac{MS_A}{MS_{wn}} = \frac{\text{Step 12}}{\text{Step 15}}$$

$$F_A = \frac{58.73}{8.22} = 7.14$$

Step 17 Find the critical value of F for factor A in Table B.2 of Appendix B, for df_A as the degrees of freedom between groups and df_{wn}. Above, for $\alpha = .05$, $df_A = 2$, and $df_{wn} = 12$, the critical value is 3.89 and the obtained F of 7.14 is significant.

Step 18   Compute the F for the main effect of factor B:

$$F_B = \frac{MS_B}{MS_{wn}} = \frac{\text{Step 13}}{\text{Step 15}}$$

$$F_B = \frac{93.39}{8.22} = 11.36$$

Step 19   Find the critical values of F for factor B in Table B.2 of Appendix B, for df_B as the degrees of freedom between groups and df_{wn}. Above, for $\alpha = .05$, $df_B = 1$, and $df_{wn} = 12$, the critical value is 4.75 and so the obtained F of 11.36 is significant.

Step 20   Compute the F for the A $\times$ B interaction:

$$F_{A \times B} = \frac{MS_{A \times B}}{MS_{wn}} = \frac{\text{Step 14}}{\text{Step 15}}$$

$$F_{A \times B} = \frac{51.39}{8.22} = 6.25$$

Step 21   Find the critical value of F for the interaction in Table B.2 of Appendix B, for $df_{A \times B}$ as the degrees of freedom between groups and df_{wn}. Above, for $\alpha = .05$, $df_{A \times B} = 2$, and $df_{wn} = 12$, the critical value is 3.89, so the obtained F of 6.25 is significant.

Step 22   For each significant F, see section A.7 for *post hoc* procedures, section A.8 for computing effect size, and section A.9 for computing confidence intervals.

A.6.   THE TWO-WAY MIXED-DESIGN ANALYSIS OF VARIANCE

This procedure is discussed in Chapter 8. Table A.9 shows example data from a 2×3 mixed design. Factor A is a between-subjects factor (with 3 subjects per level), and factor B is a within-subjects (repeated-measures) factor.

Step 1   In each cell, compute the sum of the scores (ΣX), the sum of the squared scores (ΣX^2), n, and the mean (the interaction means). Determine k_A, the number of levels of factor A; and, for each row, compute ΣX, n, and the mean (the main effect means of factor A). Then determine k_B, the number of levels of factor B; and, for each column, compute ΣX, n, and the mean (the main effect means of factor B).

Also calculate the sum of the scores obtained by each subject, ΣX_{sub} (the sum of each row).

Step 2   Determine the totals:

$$\Sigma X_{tot} = 36 + 69 + 68 = 173$$
$$\Sigma X_{tot}^2 = 218 + 377 + 838 + 56 + 470 + 116 = 2075$$
$$N = 3 + 3 + 3 + 3 + 3 + 3 = 18$$

TABLE A.9   Data from Two-Way Mixed Design

Factor A is a between-subjects factor, and factor B is a within-subjects factor.

		Factor B		$k_B = 3$
	B_1	B_2	B_3	ΣX_{sub}
Subject 1	4	8	18	30
Subject 2	9	12	17	38
Subject 3	11	13	15	39
A_1	$\overline{X} = 8$	$\overline{X} = 11$	$\overline{X} = 16.7$	$\overline{X} = 11.89$
	$\Sigma X = 24$	$\Sigma X = 33$	$\Sigma X = 50$	$\Sigma X = 107$
	$\Sigma X^2 = 218$	$\Sigma X^2 = 377$	$\Sigma X^2 = 838$	$n = 9$
	$n = 3$	$n = 3$	$n = 3$	
Subject 1	2	9	6	17
Subject 2	6	10	8	24
Subject 3	4	17	4	25
A_2	$\overline{X} = 4$	$\overline{X} = 12$	$\overline{X} = 6$	$\overline{X} = 7.33$
	$\Sigma X = 12$	$\Sigma X = 36$	$\Sigma X = 18$	$\Sigma X = 66$
	$\Sigma X^2 = 56$	$\Sigma X^2 = 470$	$\Sigma X^2 = 116$	$n = 9$
	$n = 3$	$n = 3$	$n = 3$	
	$\Sigma X = 36$	$\Sigma X = 69$	$\Sigma X = 68$	$\Sigma X_{tot} = 173$
	$n = 6$	$n = 6$	$n = 6$	$\Sigma X_{tot}^2 = 2075$
	$\overline{X} = 6$	$\overline{X} = 11.5$	$\overline{X} = 11.33$	$N = 18$

(Factor A, $k_A = 2$, labels the left margin spanning A_1 and A_2 rows.)

Step 3   Compute the correction term:

$$\text{Correction term} = \frac{(\Sigma X_{tot})^2}{N} = \frac{173^2}{18} = 1662.72$$

Step 4   As you perform the following calculations, create the Analysis of Variance Summary Table shown in Table A.10.

Step 5   Compute the total sum of squares:

$$SS_{tot} = \Sigma X_{tot}^2 - \text{Step 3}$$
$$SS_{tot} = 2075 - 1662.72 = 412.28$$

Step 6   Compute the sum of squares for subjects (not reported in summary table):

$$SS_{subs} = \frac{(\Sigma X_{sub1})^2 + (\Sigma X_{sub2})^2 \cdots + (\Sigma X_N)^2}{k_B} - \text{Step 3}$$

$$SS_{subs} = \frac{(30)^2 + (38)^2 + (39)^2 + (17)^2 + (24)^2 + (25)^2}{3} - 1662.72$$

$$SS_{subs} = 122.28$$

TABLE A.10   Summary Table of Two-Way Mixed Design ANOVA

Source	Sum of Squares	df	Mean Square	F
Between Groups				
Factor A	93.39	1	93.39	12.93
Error Between	28.89	4	7.22	
Within Groups				
Factor B	117.45	2	58.73	6.74
A × B interaction	102.77	2	51.39	5.89
Error Within	69.78	8	8.72	
Total	412.28	17		

Step 7   Compute the sum of squares for the between-subjects, row factor A:

$$SS_A = \sum \left(\frac{(\text{sum of scores in each row})^2}{n \text{ of scores in the row}} \right) - \text{Step 3}$$

$$SS_A = \left(\frac{(107)^2}{9} + \frac{(66)^2}{9} \right) - 1662.72 = 93.39$$

Step 8   Compute the sum of squares for the within-subjects, column factor B:

$$SS_B = \sum \left(\frac{(\text{sum of scores in each column})^2}{n \text{ of scores in the column}} \right) - \text{Step 3}$$

$$SS_B = \left(\frac{(36)^2}{6} + \frac{(69)^2}{6} + \frac{(68)^2}{6} \right) - 1662.72 = 117.45$$

Step 9   Compute the sum of squares for error between subjects:

$$SS_{e:bn} = SS_{subs} - SS_A = \text{Step 6} - \text{Step 7}$$
$$SS_{e:bn} = 122.28 - 93.39 = 28.89$$

Step 10   Compute the total sum of squares between groups (not reported in summary table):

$$SS_{bn} = \sum \left(\frac{(\text{sum of scores in each cell})^2}{n \text{ of scores in the cell}} \right) - \text{Step 3}$$

$$SS_{bn} = \left(\frac{(24)^2}{3} + \frac{(33)^2}{3} + \frac{(50)^2}{3} + \frac{(12)^2}{3} + \frac{(36)^2}{3} + \frac{(18)^2}{3} \right) - 1662.72$$

$$SS_{bn} = 313.61$$

Step 11   Compute the sum of squares for the A × B interaction:

$$SS_{A \times B} = SS_{bn} - SS_A - SS_B = \text{Step 10} - \text{Step 7} - \text{Step 8}$$
$$SS_{A \times B} = 313.61 - 93.39 - 117.45 = 102.77$$

Step 12 Compute the sum of squares for error within subjects:

$$SS_{e:wn} = SS_{tot} - SS_{subs} - SS_B - SS_{A \times B}$$
$$SS_{e:wn} = \text{Step 5} - \text{Step 6} - \text{Step 8} - \text{Step 11}$$
$$= 412.28 - 122.28 - 117.45 - 102.77 = 69.78$$

Step 13 Compute the degrees of freedom.

a. Factor A: $df_A = k_A - 1$

$$df_A = 2 - 1 = 1$$

b. Factor B: $df_B = k_B - 1$

$$df_B = 3 - 1 = 2$$

c. A × B interaction: $df_{A \times B} = (df_A)(df_B) = (\text{Step 13.a})(\text{Step 13.b})$

$$df_{A \times B} = (1)(2) = 2$$

d. Error between groups: $df_{e:bn} = (k_A)(n - 1)$

$$df_{e:bn} = (2)(3 - 1) = 4$$

e. Error within subjects: $df_{e:wn} = (k_B - 1)(k_A)(n - 1)$

$$df_{e:wn} = (3 - 1)(2)(3 - 1) = 8$$

f. Total: $df_{tot} = N - 1$

$$df_{tot} = 18 - 1 = 17$$

Step 14 Compute the mean square for factor A:

$$MS_A = \frac{SS_A}{df_A} = \frac{\text{Step 7}}{\text{Step 13.a}}$$
$$MS_A = \frac{93.39}{1} = 93.39$$

Step 15 Compute the mean square for factor B:

$$MS_B = \frac{SS_B}{df_B} = \frac{\text{Step 8}}{\text{Step 13.b}}$$
$$MS_B = \frac{117.45}{2} = 58.73$$

Step 16 Compute the mean square for the A × B interaction:

$$MS_{A \times B} = \frac{SS_{A \times B}}{df_{A \times B}} = \frac{\text{Step 11}}{\text{Step 13.c}}$$
$$MS_{A \times B} = \frac{102.77}{2} = 51.39$$

Step 17   Compute the mean square for error between groups:

$$MS_{e:bn} = \frac{SS_{e:bn}}{df_{e:bn}} = \frac{\text{Step 9}}{\text{Step 13.d}}$$

$$MS_{e:bn} = \frac{28.89}{4} = 7.22$$

Step 18   Compute the mean square for error within subjects:

$$MS_{e:wn} = \frac{SS_{e:wn}}{df_{e:wn}} = \frac{\text{Step 12}}{\text{Step 13.e}}$$

$$MS_{e:wn} = \frac{69.78}{8} = 8.72$$

Step 19   Compute F for the main effect of A:

$$F_A = \frac{MS_A}{MS_{e:bn}} = \frac{\text{Step 14}}{\text{Step 17}}$$

$$F_A = \frac{93.39}{7.22} = 12.93$$

Step 20   Find the critical value of F for factor A in Table B.2 of Appendix B, using df_A as the degrees of freedom between groups and $df_{e:bn}$ as the degrees of freedom within groups. Above, for $\alpha = .05$, $df_A = 1$, and $df_{e:bn} = 4$, the critical value is 7.71.

Step 21   Compute F for the main effect of B:

$$F_B = \frac{MS_B}{MS_{e:wn}} = \frac{\text{Step 15}}{\text{Step 18}}$$

$$F_B = \frac{58.73}{8.72} = 6.74$$

Step 22   Find the critical value of F for factor B in Table B.2 of Appendix B, using df_B as the degrees of freedom between groups and $df_{e:wn}$ as the degrees of freedom within groups. Above, for $\alpha = .05$, $df_B = 2$, and $df_{e:wn} = 8$, the critical value is 4.46.

Step 23   Compute the F for the A × B interaction:

$$F_{A \times B} = \frac{MS_{A \times B}}{MS_{e:wn}} = \frac{\text{Step 16}}{\text{Step 18}}$$

$$F_{A \times B} = \frac{51.39}{8.72} = 5.89$$

Step 24   Find the critical value of F for the interaction in Table B.2 of Appendix B, using $df_{A \times B}$ as the degrees of freedom between groups and $df_{e:wn}$ as the degrees of freedom within groups. Above, for $\alpha = .05$, $df_{A \times B} = 2$, and $df_{e:wn} = 8$, the critical value is 4.46.

Step 25 For each F that is significant, see section A.7 for *post hoc* procedures, section A.8 for computing effect size, and section A.9 for computing confidence intervals.

A.7. TUKEY HSD POST HOC COMPARISONS

Below are two procedures for using the Tukey HSD Multiple Comparisons test, one for *post hoc* comparisons within significant main effects and the other for *post hoc* comparisons within significant interactions.

Post Hoc Comparison for Main Effects

This procedure, which is discussed in Chapters 3, 6, and 8, may be used with either a between-subjects or a within-subjects design in a one-way ANOVA, or to examine main effect means in a multifactor ANOVA. It is appropriate *only* if the ns in all levels of the factor are equal.

Table A.11 presents a summary of the one-way between-subjects ANOVA from section A.4.

Step 1 Find "q_k" in Table B.3 of Appendix B, using k (the number of levels in the factor) and df_{wn} (the df used when calculating the denominator of the obtained F). Below, for $k = 3$, $df_{wn} = 12$; and $\alpha = .05$, $q_k = 3.77$.

TABLE A.11 Data from One-Way Between-Subjects Design

	Factor **A**	
Level A_1	*Level* A_2	*Level* A_3
9	4	1
12	6	3
4	8	4
8	2	5
7	10	2
$n_1 = 5$	$n_2 = 5$	$n_3 = 5$
$\overline{X}_1 = 8$	$\overline{X}_2 = 6$	$\overline{X}_3 = 3$

$k = 3$

$$MS_A = \frac{SS_A}{df_A} = \frac{63.33}{2} = 31.67$$

$$MS_{wn} = \frac{SS_{wn}}{df_{wn}} = \frac{84}{12} = 7.0$$

$$F = \frac{MS_A}{MS_{wn}} = \frac{31.67}{7.0} = 4.52$$

Step 2 Compute HSD:

$$HSD = (q_k)\left(\sqrt{\frac{\text{denominator in } F \text{ ratio}}{n}}\right)$$

where "denominator in F ratio" is the MS used as the denominator when calculating the obtained F, and n is the number of scores that each mean being compared is based upon. Above, $MS_{wn} = 7.0$ and $n = 5$.

$$HSD = (3.77)\left(\sqrt{\frac{7.0}{5}}\right) = 4.46$$

Step 3 Determine the differences between all means, by subtracting each mean from every other mean.

Step 4 Compare the absolute difference between any two means to the HSD value. If the difference is greater than the HSD, then these two means differ significantly. Above, the difference between $\overline{X}_1 = 8$ and $\overline{X}_3 = 3$ is 5, which is greater than 4.46, so these means differ significantly. However, $\overline{X}_2 = 6$ differs from these means by 2 and 3, respectively. Because 2 and 3 are less than 4.46, $\overline{X}_2$ does not differ significantly from the other means.

Post Hoc Comparison for Interaction Effects

This procedure, discussed in Chapter 8, may be used to compare the cell means of an interaction in either a between-subjects or a within-subjects design. It involves a correction developed by Cicchetti (1972) that reduces the probability of making Type II errors, based on adjusting k so that it reflects the actual number of unconfounded comparisons being performed.

Table A.12 presents a summary of the two-way between-subjects ANOVA from section A.5.

Step 1 Determine the "adjusted k" from Table A.13. In the left hand column, locate the type of interaction being examined, regardless of the order of the numbers describing the factors (e.g., a 3 × 2 design is the same as a 2 × 3 design). In the right hand column is the adjusted value of k. In the example the design is a 2 × 3, so the adjusted $k = 5$.

Step 2 Find "q_k" in Table B.3 of Appendix B, using the adjusted value of k and df_{wn} (the df used when calculating the denominator of the obtained F). Above, for $k = 5$, $df_{wn} = 12$, and for $\alpha = .05$, $q_k = 4.51$.

Step 3 Compute HSD:

$$HSD = (q_k)\sqrt{\frac{\text{denominator in } F \text{ ratio}}{n}}$$

TABLE A.12   Data from Two-Way Between-Subjects Design

		Factor A		
		A_1	A_2	A_3
		4 9 11	8 12 13	18 17 15
	B_1	$\overline{X} = 8$ $n = 3$	$\overline{X} = 11$ $n = 3$	$\overline{X} = 16.7$ $n = 3$
		2 6 4	9 10 17	6 8 4
	B_2	$\overline{X} = 4$ $n = 3$	$\overline{X} = 12$ $n = 3$	$\overline{X} = 6$ $n = 3$

(Row labels at left: **Factor B**)

$$MS_{A \times B} = \frac{SS_{A \times B}}{df_{A \times B}} = \frac{102.77}{2} = 51.39$$

$$MS_{wn} = \frac{SS_{wn}}{df_{wn}} = \frac{98.67}{12} = 8.22$$

$$F_{A \times B} = \frac{MS_{A \times B}}{MS_{wn}} = \frac{51.39}{8.22} = 6.25$$

TABLE A.13   Values of Adjusted k

Design of study	Adjusted value of k
2×2	3
2×3	5
2×4	6
3×3	7
3×4	8
4×4	10
4×5	12

where "denominator in F ratio" is the MS used as the denominator when calculating the obtained F, and n is the number of scores that each mean being compared is based upon. Above, $MS_{wn} = 8.22$ and $n = 3$.

$$HSD = (4.51)\left(\sqrt{\frac{8.22}{3}}\right) = 7.47$$

Step 4 Determine the differences between all unconfounded means, by subtracting each mean from every other mean in the same row or in the same column.

Step 5 Compare the absolute difference between any two means to the HSD value. If the difference is greater than the HSD, then these two means differ significantly.

A.8.   MEASURES OF EFFECT SIZE IN t-TESTS AND ANOVA

These procedures are discussed in Chapter 8. As described below, we compute effect size in t-tests by computing r_{pb}^2, and we compute effect size in ANOVA by computing η^2.

Effect Size in *t*-Tests

This procedure may be used to compute r_{pb}^2 in an independent samples (between-subjects) t-test and in a dependent samples (within-subjects) t-test. Calculate r_{pb}^2 using the formula:

$$r_{pb}^2 = \frac{(t)^2}{(t)^2 + df},$$

where $(t)^2$ is the squared value of the obtained t and the degrees of freedom, df, are those calculated in the t-test.

For example, in the independent samples t-test in section A.3, $t = -2.524$ and $df = 18$. Thus:

$$r_{pb}^2 = \frac{(t)^2}{(t)^2 + df} = \frac{2.524^2}{2.524^2 + 8} = .44$$

Note: The square root of r_{pb}^2 equals the correlation coefficient, r_{pb}, between the independent and dependent variables.

Effect Size in ANOVA

Eta squared (η^2) may be calculated for each between-subjects or within-subjects main effect or interaction in an ANOVA, using the formula

$$\eta^2 = \frac{\text{sum of squares of the effect}}{SS_{tot}}$$

where "sum of squares for the effect" is the sum of squares used in calculating the numerator of the obtained F, whether it is SS_A, SS_B, or $SS_{A\times B}$. The SS_{tot} is the total sum of squares in the ANOVA. For example, in the one-way between-subjects ANOVA from section A.4 we produced Table 8.14.

TABLE A.14   Summary Table of One-Way Between-Subjects ANOVA

Source	Sum of Squares	df	Mean Square	F
Factor A	63.33	2	31.67	4.52
Within Groups	84.00	12	7.0	
Total	147.33	14		

Thus, the effect size for factor A is:

$$\eta^2 = \frac{SS_A}{SS_{tot}} = \frac{63.33}{147.33} = .43$$

(The square root of η^2 equals η, the correlation coefficient, η, between the independent and dependent variables.)

A.9.   CONFIDENCE INTERVALS

This procedure is discussed in Chapter 3. Below are the formulas for computing a confidence interval from the results of a t-test and from an ANOVA.

Confidence Intervals in t-Tests

The formula for a confidence interval for a population mean represented by a sample mean is

$$\left(\frac{s_x}{\sqrt{n}}\right)(-t_{crit}) + \overline{X} \le \mu \le \left(\frac{s_x}{\sqrt{n}}\right)(+t_{crit}) + \overline{X}$$

Step 1   Compute s_x from the scores in the group, using the formula for the estimated population standard deviation in section A.2.

Step 2   Determine n, the number of scores in the group.

Step 3   Find t_{crit}, the two-tailed critical value in Table B.1 of Appendix B, for $df = n - 1$, where n is the number of scores in the group. Using $\alpha = .05$ creates a 95% confidence interval and using $\alpha = .01$ creates a 99% confidence interval.

Step 4   Compute $\overline{X}$, the mean of the scores in the group.

As an example, say that a condition in a between-subjects t-test produces the following data: $n = 9$, $s_x = 2.25$, and $\overline{X} = 11.5$. The two-tailed t_{crit} for $df = 8$ and $\alpha = .05$ is ± 2.306. Thus:

$$\left(\frac{s_x}{\sqrt{n}}\right)(-t_{\text{crit}}) + \overline{X} \le \mu \le \left(\frac{s_x}{\sqrt{n}}\right)(+t_{\text{crit}}) + \overline{X}$$

$$\left(\frac{2.25}{\sqrt{9}}\right)(-2.306) + 11.5 \le \mu \le \left(\frac{2.25}{\sqrt{9}}\right)(+2.306) + 11.5$$

$$-1.73 + 11.5 \le \mu \le +1.73 + 11.5$$

$$9.77 \le \mu \le 13.23$$

The 95% confidence interval for the population mean (μ) represented by this sample mean is 9.77 to 13.23.

Confidence Intervals in ANOVA

To compute the confidence interval for the population μ represented by the mean of any level or cell in an ANOVA, use this formula:

$$\left(\sqrt{\frac{MS_{\text{wn}}}{n}}\right)(-t_{\text{crit}}) + \overline{X} \le \mu \le \left(\sqrt{\frac{MS_{\text{wn}}}{n}}\right)(+t_{\text{crit}}) + \overline{X}$$

Step 1   Determine MS_{wn}, the denominator used in computing F.

Step 2   Determine n, the number of scores that the mean is based upon.

Step 3   Find t_{crit}, the two-tailed critical value in Table B.1 of Appendix B, for the df used in computing the denominator of the obtained F. Using $\alpha = .05$ creates a 95% confidence interval and using $\alpha = .01$ creates a 99% confidence interval.

Step 4   Compute $\overline{X}$, the mean of the level or cell being described.

For example, say that a condition in a between-subjects ANOVA produced a $\overline{X} = 8.0$ with $n = 5$, and in computing the main effect F involving that condition, $MS_{\text{wn}} = 7.0$, and $df_{\text{wn}} = 12$. The two-tailed t_{crit} at $df = 12$ and $\alpha = .05$ is ± 2.179. Thus:

$$\left(\sqrt{\frac{7.0}{5}}\right)(-2.179) + 8.0 \le \mu \le \left(\sqrt{\frac{7.0}{5}}\right)(+2.179) + 8.0$$

$$-2.578 + 8.0 \le \mu \le +2.578 + 8.0$$

$$5.42 \le \mu \le 10.58$$

The 95% confidence interval for the population mean (μ) represented by this sample mean is 5.42 to 10.58.

A.10. PEARSON CORRELATION COEFFICIENT, LINEAR REGRESSION, AND STANDARD ERROR OF THE ESTIMATE

Below are procedures for computing the Pearson r, the linear regression equation, and the standard error of the estimate. These procedures are discussed in Chapter 9.

The Pearson Correlation Coefficient

Example data are shown in Table A.15.

Step 1 Calculate ΣX, the sum of the X scores, and $(\Sigma X)^2$, the squared sum of the X scores.

Step 2 Calculate ΣY, the sum of the Y scores, and $(\Sigma Y)^2$, the squared sum of the Y scores.

Step 3 Calculate ΣX^2, the sum of the squared X scores, and ΣY^2, the sum of the squared Y scores.

Step 4 Calculate ΣXY, the sum after multiplying each X score in a pair times its corresponding Y score.

Step 5 Determine N, the number of pairs of scores in the sample.

TABLE A.15   Data for Pearson Correlation Coefficient

Subject	X score	Y score	XY
1	1	2	2
2	1	4	4
3	2	4	8
4	2	6	12
5	2	2	4
6	3	4	12
7	3	7	21
8	3	8	24
9	4	6	24
10	4	8	32
11	4	7	28
$N = 11$	$\Sigma X = 29$	$\Sigma Y = 58$	$\Sigma XY = 171$
	$\Sigma X^2 = 89$	$\Sigma Y^2 = 354$	
	$(\Sigma X)^2 = 841$	$(\Sigma Y)^2 = 3364$	

Step 6 Calculate r:

$$r = \frac{N(\Sigma XY) - (\Sigma X)(\Sigma Y)}{\sqrt{[N(\Sigma X^2) - (\Sigma X)^2][N(\Sigma Y^2) - (\Sigma Y)^2]}}$$

$$r = \frac{11(171) - (29)(58)}{\sqrt{[11(89) - 841][11(354) - 3364]}}$$

$$r = \frac{199}{\sqrt{[138][530]}} = +.736$$

Step 7 Find the critical value of r in Table B.4 of Appendix B, using degrees of freedom (df) equal to $N - 2$, where N is the number of pairs of scores. Above, for $df = 9$ and $\alpha = .05$, the two-tailed critical value is $\pm.602$ (so the obtained r is significant).

The Linear Regression Equation

Step 1 Compute b, the slope of the regression line:

$$b = \frac{N(\Sigma XY) - (\Sigma X)(\Sigma Y)}{N(\Sigma X)^2 - (\Sigma X)^2}$$

In the above Pearson correlation coefficient example (Table A.15), $\Sigma X = 29$, $\Sigma Y = 58$, $\Sigma XY = 171$, $\Sigma X^2 = 89$, $(\Sigma X)^2 = 841$, and $N = 11$.

$$b = \frac{N(\Sigma XY) - (\Sigma X)(\Sigma Y)}{N(\Sigma X)^2 - (\Sigma X)^2} = \frac{11(171) - (29)(58)}{11(89) - 841} = +1.44$$

Step 2 Compute a, the Y-intercept:

$$a = \overline{Y} - (b)(\overline{X})$$

Using the data from above, $\overline{Y} = \frac{58}{11} = 5.27$, $b = 1.44$, and $\overline{X} = \frac{29}{11} = 2.64$.

$$a = \overline{Y} - (b)(\overline{X}) = 5.27 - (+1.44)(2.64) = +1.47$$

Step 3 Complete the linear regression equation:

$$Y' = b(X) + a$$

From above, $b = +1.44$ and $a = +1.47$ so:

$$Y' = +1.44(X) + 1.47$$

Step 4 To compute a subject's predicted score, Y', multiply the subject's X score times the slope and add the Y-intercept. Above, the predicted score for a subject scoring an $X = 2$ is

$$Y' = +1.44(2) + 1.47 = 4.35$$

The Standard Error of the Estimate

The standard error of the estimate, $S_{y'}$, is calculated as:

$$S_{y'} = (S_y)(\sqrt{1 - r^2})$$

Step 1 Use the formula for the sample standard deviation in section A.2 to find S_y, the sample standard deviation of the Y scores.

Step 2 Compute r^2, the squared value of the Pearson correlation coefficient.
For the above linear regression example, $N = 11$, $\Sigma Y = 58$, and $\Sigma Y^2 = 354$, so $S_y = 2.093$ and $r = +.736$:

$$S_{y'} = (S_y)(\sqrt{1 - r^2}) = (2.093)(\sqrt{1 - .736^2}) = 1.42$$

A.11. POINT-BISERIAL AND SPEARMAN CORRELATION COEFFICIENTS

Below are the procedures for computing the point-biserial and Spearman correlation coefficients, as discussed in Chapters 8 and 9.

The Point-Biserial Correlation Coefficient

The point-biserial correlation, r_{pb}, may be calculated directly from the results of a t-test (see section A.8).
For the data shown in Table A.16, a "1" is assigned to each subject in the first group

TABLE A.16 Data for Point-Biserial Correlation Coefficient

Subject	X variable	Y variable	
1	1	35	
2	1	38	$\overline{Y}_1 = 38.50$
3	1	41	$n_1 = 4$
4	1	40	$p = \frac{4}{10} = .4$
5	2	60	
6	2	65	
7	2	65	$\overline{Y}_2 = 65.00$
8	2	68	$n_2 = 6$
9	2	68	$q = \frac{6}{10} = .6$
10	2	64	
$N = 10$		$\Sigma Y = 544$	
		$\Sigma Y = 31344$	
		$S_y = 13.23$	

of the X variable and a "2" is assigned to each subject in the second group of the X variable.

Step 1 Calculate $\overline{Y}_1$, the mean of the scores on the continuous Y variable for one group of the dichotomous variable. Then calculate $\overline{Y}_2$, the mean of the scores on the continuous Y variable for the other group of the dichotomous variable.

Step 2 Calculate S_y, the sample standard deviation of all of the Y scores, found using the formula for the sample standard deviation in section A.2. Above, $S_y = 13.23$.

Step 3 Calculate p, the proportion of all subjects in the sample in one group, and q, the proportion of all subjects in the sample in the other group. Each equals the number of subjects in the group divided by N, the total number of X-Y pairs in the study.

Step 4 Calculate r_{pb}:

$$r_{pb} = \left(\frac{\overline{Y}_2 - \overline{Y}_1}{S_y}\right)(\sqrt{pq})$$

$$r_{pb} = \left(\frac{65.00 - 38.50}{13.23}\right)(\sqrt{(.40)(.60)}) = +.979$$

Step 5 Find the critical value of r_{pb} using those of r in Table B.4 of Appendix B, with degrees of freedom (df) equal to $N - 2$, the number of pairs of scores in the sample minus 2. Above, for $df = 8$ and $\alpha = .05$, the two-tailed critical value is $\pm.632$ (so the obtained r_{pb} is significant).

The Spearman Correlation Coefficient

The following procedure is used when subjects are rank-ordered on each variable and no two subjects receive the same rank within a variable. (Special procedures are needed with "tied ranks"—e.g., if two subjects are ranked 1st on variable X. Consult a statistics text.)

Example data are shown in Table A.17.

Step 1 Compute each D, the difference between a subject's X and Y scores.

Step 2 Compute ΣD^2, the sum of the squared Ds.

Step 3 Determine N, the number of pairs of scores in the sample.

Step 4 Compute r_s.

TABLE A.17 Data for Spearman Correlation Coefficient

Subject	Rank on X variable		Rank on Y variable		D	D^2
1	4	–	3	=	1	1
2	1	–	1	=	0	0
3	9	–	8	=	1	1
4	8	–	6	=	2	4
5	3	–	5	=	-2	4
6	5	–	4	=	1	1
7	6	–	7	=	-1	1
8	2	–	2	=	0	0
9	7	–	9	=	-2	4
$N = 9$						$\Sigma D^2 = 16$

$$r_s = 1 - \frac{6(\Sigma D^2)}{N(N^2 - 1)}$$

$$r_s = 1 - \frac{6(16)}{9(81 - 1)} = 1 - .133 = +.867$$

Step 5 Find the critical value of r_s in Table B.5 of Appendix B, with degrees of freedom, (df) equal to N, the number of pairs of scores. Above, for $df = 9$ and $\alpha = .05$, the two-tailed critical value is $\pm.683$ (so the obtained r_s is significant).

A.12. CHI SQUARE PROCEDURES

Below are the one-way chi square (goodness-of-fit test), the two-way chi square (test of independence), and the procedures for computing effect size (the phi coefficient and C coefficient).

The One-Way Chi Square

This procedure is discussed in Chapter 6. Example data from a one-way design with two categories are shown in Table A.18.

Step 1 Determine the observed frequency, f_o, in each category (i.e., count the number of subjects falling in each category).

Step 2 Determine the expected frequency, f_e, in each category. This is equal to the probability that a subject will fall in that category if the null hypothesis is true, multiplied by the total N in the study. When we are testing for no difference, the expected frequency in each group equals $f_e = \frac{N}{k}$, where k is the number of categories. Thus, above, for each category, $f_e = \frac{60}{2} = 30$.

TABLE A.18   Data from One-Way Chi Square Design

Variable A

Category 1	Category 2	
$f_o = 20$	$f_o = 40$	$k = 2$
$f_e = 30$	$f_e = 30$	$N = 60$

Step 3   Compute χ^2:

$$\chi^2 = \Sigma \left(\frac{(f_o - f_e)^2}{f_e} \right)$$

$$\chi^2 = \frac{(20 - 30)^2}{30} + \frac{(40 - 30)^2}{30} = 3.33 + 3.33 = 6.66$$

Step 4   Find the critical value of χ^2 in Table B.6 of Appendix B, for $df = k - 1$, where k is the number of categories. Above, for $\alpha = .05$ and $df = 1$, the critical value $= 3.84$ (so the obtained χ^2 is significant).

Two-Way Chi Square

This procedure is discussed in Chapter 8. Example data from a two-way design with two categories per variable are shown in Table A.19.

Step 1   Determine the observed frequency, f_o, in each category (i.e., count the number of subjects falling in each category).

TABLE A.19   Data from Two-Way Chi Square Design

		Variable A		
		Category 1	Category 2	
Variable B	Category 1	$f_o = 25$ $f_e = 13.125$ $(35)(30)/80$	$f_o = 10$ $f_e = 21.875$ $(35)(50)/80$	Row total $= 35$
	Category 2	$f_o = 5$ $f_e = 16.875$ $(45)(30)/80$	$f_o = 40$ $f_e = 28.125$ $(45)(50)/80$	Row total $= 45$
		Column total $= 30$	Column total $= 50$	$N = 80$

Step 2 Compute the total of the observed frequencies in each row and in each column. Also determine N, the total number of subjects.

Step 3 Compute the expected frequency, f_e, for each cell:

$$\text{cell } f_e = \frac{(\text{cell's row total } f_o)(\text{cell's column total } f_o)}{N}$$

Thus, for cell $A_1 B_1$ above, $f_e = \frac{(35)(30)}{80} = 13.125$.

Step 4 Compute χ^2:

$$\chi^2 = \Sigma\left(\frac{(f_o - f_e)^2}{f_e}\right)$$

$$\chi^2 = \left(\frac{(25 - 13.125)^2}{13.125}\right) + \left(\frac{(10 - 21.875)^2}{21.875}\right) +$$

$$\left(\frac{(5 - 16.875)^2}{16.875}\right) + \left(\frac{(40 - 28.125)^2}{28.125}\right)$$

$$\chi^2 = 10.74 + 6.45 + 8.36 + 5.01 = 30.56$$

Step 5 Find the critical value of χ^2 in Table B.6 of Appendix B for $df = (\text{number of rows} - 1)(\text{number of columns} - 1)$. Above, for $\alpha = .05$ and $df = (2 - 1)(2 - 1) = 1$, the critical value $= 3.84$. Only if the obtained χ^2 is significant (as above), go to Step 6.

Step 6 Compute the effect size.
In a 2×2 chi square, compute the phi coefficient squared, Φ^2:

$$\Phi^2 = \frac{\chi^2}{N}$$

where χ^2 is the obtained value of chi square and N is the total number of subjects in the study. Above, $\chi^2 = 30.56$ and $N = 80$, so $\Phi^2 = \frac{30.56}{80} = .38$. (The square root of Φ^2 equals Φ, the correlation coefficient between the two variables.)

In a two-way chi square that is not a 2×2 design, compute C^2, the contingency coefficient squared:

$$C^2 = \frac{\chi^2}{\chi^2 + N}$$

where χ^2 is the obtained value of chi square and N is the total number of subjects in the study. (The square root of C^2 equals C, the correlation coefficient between the two variables.)

A.13.   MANN-WHITNEY U AND WILCOXON T TESTS

Below are the procedures for performing the nonparametric versions of *t*-tests.

The Mann-Whitney *U* Test for Independent Samples

The Mann-Whitney test, discussed in Chapter 6, is analogous to the independent samples *t*-test for ranked data. It is appropriate when the *n* in each condition is *less* than 20. Table A.20 shows such data.

Step 1   Compute the sum of the ranks, ΣR, and the *n* for each group.

Step 2   Compute U_1 for group 1, using the formula

$$U_1 = (n_1)(n_2) + \frac{n_1(n_1 + 1)}{2} - \Sigma R_1$$

where n_1 is the *n* of group 1, n_2 is the *n* of group 2, and ΣR_1 is the sum of ranks from group 1. From above,

$$U_1 = (5)(5) + \frac{5(5 + 1)}{2} - 17 = 40 - 17 = 23.0$$

Step 3   Compute U_2 for group 2, using the formula

$$U_2 = (n_1)(n_2) + \frac{n_2(n_2 + 1)}{2} - \Sigma R_2$$

where n_1 is the *n* of group 1, n_2 is the *n* of group 2, and ΣR_2 is the sum of ranks from group 2. From above:

$$U_2 = (5)(5) + \frac{5(5 + 1)}{2} - 38 = 40 - 38 = 2.0$$

TABLE A.20   Ranked Data from Two-Sample Between-Subjects Design

Condition 1	Condition 2
Rank scores	Rank scores
2	7
1	8
5	10
3	4
6	9
$\Sigma R = 17$	$\Sigma R = 38$
$n = 5$	$n = 5$

Step 4 Determine the obtained value of U. In a two-tailed test, the *smaller* value of U_1 or U_2 is the obtained value of U. Above, the obtained U is $U_2 = 2.0$. In a one-tailed test, one group will be predicted to have the higher ranks and thus the larger sum of ranks. The corresponding value of U_1 or U_2 from that group is the obtained value of U.

Step 5 Find the critical value of U in Table B.7 of Appendix B, using n_1 and n_2. Above, for a two-tailed test with $n_1 = 5$ and $n_2 = 5$, the critical value is 2.0. The obtained value of U is significant (and the two groups differ significantly) if U is *equal to or less than* the critical value. Above, the obtained value is significant. (No procedure for directly calculating effect size is available.)

The Wilcoxon *T* Test for Related Samples

The Wilcoxon test, discussed in Chapter 7, is analogous to the dependent samples *t*-test for ranked data. It is used when interval or ratio scores are transformed to ranked scores. Table A.21 shows such data.

Step 1 Determine the difference score, D, in each pair of raw scores. It makes no difference which score is subtracted from which, but subtract the scores the same way in all pairs.

Step 2 Determine N, the number of *nonzero* difference scores. Above, disregard subject 10 because there is no difference, so $N = 9$.

Step 3 Assign ranks to the nonzero difference scores. Ignoring the sign of each difference, assign the rank of "1" to the smallest difference, the rank of "2" to the second smallest difference, and so on.

TABLE A.21 Ranked Data from a Two-Sample Within-Subjects Design

Subject	Condition 1	Condition 2	Difference (D)	Ranked Scores	R−	R+
1	54	76	−22	6	6	
2	58	71	−13	4	4	
3	60	110	−50	9	9	
4	68	88	−20	5	5	
5	43	50	−7	3	3	
6	74	99	−25	7	7	
7	60	105	−45	8	8	
8	69	64	+5	2		2
9	60	59	+1	1		1
10	52	52	0	...		...
			$N = 9$		$\Sigma R = 42$	$\Sigma R = 3$

Step 4 Separate the ranks so that the $R-$ column contains the ranks assigned to negative differences in Step 3. The $R+$ column contains the ranks assigned to positive differences.

Step 5 Compute the sum of ranks, ΣR, for the column labeled $R+$, and compute ΣR for the column labeled $R-$.

Step 6 Determine the obtained value of T. In a two-tailed test, T equals the *smaller* ΣR found in Step 5. Above, the smaller $\Sigma R = 3$, so the obtained $T = 3$. In a one-tailed test, whether most differences are positive or negative will be predicted, and the ΣR that is predicted to be smaller is the obtained value of T.

Step 7 Find the critical value of T in Table B.8 of Appendix B, using N, the number of nonzero difference scores. Above, for $N = 9$ and $\alpha = .05$, the critical value is 5.0. The obtained T is significant (and the two groups differ significantly) when T is *equal to or less than* the critical value, so above, T is significant. (No procedure for computing effect size is available.)

A.14. KRUSKAL-WALLIS H AND FRIEDMAN χ^2 TESTS

Below are the procedures for performing the nonparametric versions of the one-way ANOVA and the corresponding *post hoc* tests.

The Kruskal-Wallis *H* Test

The Kruskal-Wallis H test, discussed in Chapter 6, is analogous to a between-subjects one-way ANOVA for ranks. It requires three or more levels of the factor, with at least five subjects per level. Table A.22 shows such data.

TABLE A.22   Ranked Data from One-Way Between Subjects Design

Factor A		
Level 1	*Level 2*	*Level 3*
2	3	14
6	5	15
4	7	10
8	9	12
1	11	13
$\Sigma R_1 = 21$	$\Sigma R_2 = 35$	$\Sigma R_3 = 64$ $k = 3$
$n_1 = 5$	$n_2 = 5$	$n_3 = 5$ $N = 15$

Step 1 Compute the sum of the ranks, ΣR, in each condition (i.e., each column). Also note the n in each condition, as well as k, the number of levels.

Step 2 Compute the sum of squares between groups:

$$SS_{bn} = \Sigma\left(\frac{(\Sigma R)^2}{n}\right)$$

where $(\Sigma R)^2$ is the squared sum of ranks for each level and n is the n of the level.

$$SS_{bn} = \left(\frac{(21)^2}{5} + \frac{(35)^2}{5} + \frac{(64)^2}{5}\right) = 88.2 + 245 + 819.2 = 1152.4$$

Step 3 Compute H:

$$H = \left(\frac{12}{N(N+1)}\right)(SS_{bn}) - 3(N+1)$$

where N is the total N of the study, and SS_{bn} is from Step 2.

$$H = \left(\frac{12}{15(15+1)}\right)(1152.4) - 3(15+1) = (.05)(1152.4) - 48 = 9.62$$

Step 4 The critical values of H are χ^2 values; find these in Table B.6 of Appendix B, using $df = k - 1$, where k is the number of levels in the factor. Above, for $df = 2$ and $\alpha = .05$, the critical value is 5.99. If the obtained value of H is *larger* than the critical value of χ^2, then the H is significant (and there is at least one significant difference between the groups). When H is significant, go to Step 5.

Step 5 Perform *post hoc* comparisons by comparing each pair of conditions using the Mann-Whitney procedure in section A.13. Treat each pair of conditions as if they constituted the entire study, and re-rank the scores. Then compute the obtained U and determine whether it is significant.

Step 6 Compute η^2, the effect size:

$$\eta^2 = \frac{H}{N-1}$$

where H is the value computed in the Kruskal-Wallis test (Step 3), and N is the total number of subjects.

The Friedman χ^2 Test

The Friedman χ^2 test, discussed in Chapter 7, is analogous to a repeated-measures one-way ANOVA for ranks. It requires three or more levels of the factor. If there are only three levels of the factor, there must be at least 10 subjects in the study. If there are only four levels of the factor, there must be at least five subjects. Table A.23 shows such data.

TABLE A.23   Ranked Scores from One-Way Repeated Measures Design

	Condition 1	*Condition 2*	*Condition 3*	
		Factor **A**		
Subject 1	1	2	3	
Subject 2	1	3	2	
Subject 3	1	2	3	
Subject 4	1	3	2	
Subject 5	2	1	3	
Subject 6	1	3	2	
Subject 7	1	2	3	
Subject 8	1	3	2	
Subject 9	1	3	2	
Subject 10	2	1	3	
	$\Sigma R_1 = 12$	$\Sigma R_2 = 23$	$\Sigma R_3 = 25$	$N = 10$
	$\overline{X} = 1.2$	$\overline{X} = 2.3$	$\overline{X} = 2.5$	

Step 1   Rank-order the scores within each subject. That is, assign "1" to the lowest score received by subject 1, "2" to the second lowest score received by subject 1, and so on. Repeat the process for each subject.

Step 2   Compute the sum of the ranks, ΣR, in each condition (i.e., each column).

Step 3   Compute the mean rank in each condition, by dividing the sum of ranks (ΣR) by the number of subjects.

Step 4   Compute the sum of squares between groups:

$$SS_{bn} = (\Sigma R_1)^2 + (\Sigma R_2)^2 + \ldots (\Sigma R_k)^2$$
$$SS_{bn} = (12)^2 + (23)^2 + (25)^2 = 1298$$

Step 5   Compute the Friedman χ^2:

$$\chi^2 = \left(\frac{12}{(k)(N)(k+1)}\right)(SS_{bn}) - 3(N)(k+1)$$

where N is the total number of subjects and k is the number of levels of the factor, and SS_{bn} is from Step 4.

$$\chi^2 = \left(\frac{12}{(3)(10)(3+1)}\right)(1298) - 3(10)(3+1) = (.10)(1298) - 120 = 9.80.$$

Step 6   Find the critical value of χ^2 in Table B.6 of Appendix B, for $df = k - 1$, where k is the number of levels in the factor. Above, for $df = 2$ and $\alpha = .05$, the critical value is 5.99. Above, χ^2 is larger than the critical value, so the results are significant (and there is at least one significant difference between the levels). When χ^2 is significant, perform Steps 7 and 8.

Step 7 Perform *post hoc* comparisons using Nemenyi's procedure.[2]
  a. Compute the critical difference:

$$\text{Critical difference} = \sqrt{\left(\frac{k(k+1)}{6(N)}\right)(\text{critical value of } \chi^2)}$$

where k is the number of levels of the factor, N is the total number of subjects, and the critical value of χ^2 is the critical value used to test the Friedman χ^2 (Step 6).

$$\text{Critical difference} = \sqrt{\left(\frac{3(3+1)}{6(10)}\right)(5.99)} = \sqrt{(.2)(5.99)} = \sqrt{1.198} = 1.09$$

  b. Subtract each mean rank from the other mean ranks. Any absolute difference between two means that is greater than the critical difference is a significant difference. In Table A.23, the differences between the mean rank of 1.2 in condition 1 and the other mean ranks are 1.10 and 1.30, respectively, so they are significant differences. The difference between the means of conditions 2 and 3 is .20, which is not a significant difference.

Step 8 Compute η^2, the effect size:

$$\eta^2 = \frac{\chi^2}{(N)(k) - 1}$$

where χ^2 was computed in the Friedman χ^2 test (Step 6), N is the number of subjects, and k is the number of levels of the factor. Thus:

$$\eta^2 = \frac{\chi^2}{(N)(k) - 1} = \frac{9.80}{(10)(3) - 1} = \frac{9.80}{30 - 1} = .34$$

---

[2] As reported in Linton & Gallo, 1975.

B
Appendix: Statistical Tables

TABLE B.1 Critical Values of *t*

| | Two-Tailed Test | | | One-Tailed Test | |
| | *Level of significance* | | | *Level of significance* | |
df	α = .05	α = .01	*df*	α = .05	α = .01
1	12.706	63.657	1	6.314	31.821
2	4.303	9.925	2	2.920	6.965
3	3.182	5.841	3	2.353	4.541
4	2.776	4.604	4	2.132	3.747
5	2.571	4.032	5	2.015	3.365
6	2.447	3.707	6	1.943	3.143
7	2.365	3.499	7	1.895	2.998
8	2.306	3.355	8	1.860	2.896
9	2.262	3.250	9	1.833	2.821
10	2.228	3.169	10	1.812	2.764
11	2.201	3.106	11	1.796	2.718
12	2.179	3.055	12	1.782	2.681
13	2.160	3.012	13	1.771	2.650
14	2.145	2.977	14	1.761	2.624
15	2.131	2.947	15	1.753	2.602
16	2.120	2.921	16	1.746	2.583
17	2.110	2.898	17	1.740	2.567
18	2.101	2.878	18	1.734	2.552
19	2.093	2.861	19	1.729	2.539
20	2.086	2.845	20	1.725	2.528
21	2.080	2.831	21	1.721	2.518
22	2.074	2.819	22	1.717	2.508
23	2.069	2.807	23	1.714	2.500
24	2.064	2.797	24	1.711	2.492
25	2.060	2.787	25	1.708	2.485
26	2.056	2.779	26	1.706	2.479
27	2.052	2.771	27	1.703	2.473
28	2.048	2.763	28	1.701	2.467
29	2.045	2.756	29	1.699	2.462
30	2.042	2.750	30	1.697	2.457
40	2.021	2.704	40	1.684	2.423
60	2.000	2.660	60	1.671	2.390
120	1.980	2.617	120	1.658	2.358
∞	1.960	2.576	∞	1.645	2.326

From Table 12 of E. Pearson and H. Hartley, *Biometrika Tables for Statisticians*, Vol 1, 3rd ed. Cambridge University Press, 1966. Reprinted with permission of the Biometrika trustees.

TABLE B.2   Critical Values of *F*

Critical values for α = .05 are in light numbers.
Critical values for α = .01 are in **dark numbers.**

Degrees of freedom within groups (degrees of freedom in denominator of F ratio)	α	\multicolumn{10}{c}{Degrees of freedom between groups (degrees of freedom in numerator of F ratio)}
		1	*2*	*3*	*4*	*5*	*6*	*7*	*8*	*9*	*10*
1	.05	161	200	216	225	230	234	237	239	241	242
	.01	**4,052**	**4,999**	**5,403**	**5,625**	**5,764**	**5,859**	**5,928**	**5,981**	**6,022**	**6,056**
2	.05	18.51	19.00	19.16	19.25	19.30	19.33	19.36	19.37	19.38	19.39
	.01	**98.49**	**99.00**	**99.17**	**99.25**	**99.30**	**99.33**	**99.34**	**99.36**	**99.38**	**99.40**
3	.05	10.13	9.55	9.28	9.12	9.01	8.94	8.88	8.84	8.81	8.78
	.01	**34.12**	**30.82**	**29.46**	**28.71**	**28.24**	**27.91**	**27.67**	**27.49**	**27.34**	**27.23**
4	.05	7.71	6.94	6.59	6.39	6.26	6.16	6.09	6.04	6.00	5.96
	.01	**21.20**	**18.00**	**16.69**	**15.98**	**15.52**	**15.21**	**14.98**	**14.80**	**14.66**	**14.54**
5	.05	6.61	5.79	5.41	5.19	5.05	4.95	4.88	4.82	4.78	4.74
	.01	**16.26**	**13.27**	**12.06**	**11.39**	**10.97**	**10.67**	**10.45**	**10.27**	**10.15**	**10.05**
6	.05	5.99	5.14	4.76	4.53	4.39	4.28	4.21	4.15	4.10	4.06
	.01	**13.74**	**10.92**	**9.78**	**9.15**	**8.75**	**8.47**	**8.26**	**8.10**	**7.98**	**7.87**
7	.05	5.59	4.47	4.35	4.12	3.97	3.87	3.79	3.73	3.68	3.63
	.01	**12.25**	**9.55**	**8.45**	**7.85**	**7.46**	**7.19**	**7.00**	**6.84**	**6.71**	**6.62**
8	.05	5.32	4.46	4.07	3.84	3.69	3.58	3.50	3.44	3.39	3.34
	.01	**11.26**	**8.65**	**7.59**	**7.01**	**6.63**	**6.37**	**6.19**	**6.03**	**5.91**	**5.82**
9	.05	5.12	4.26	3.86	3.63	3.48	3.37	3.29	3.23	3.18	3.13
	.01	**10.56**	**8.02**	**6.99**	**6.42**	**6.06**	**5.80**	**5.62**	**5.47**	**5.35**	**5.26**
10	.05	4.96	4.10	3.71	3.48	3.33	3.22	3.14	3.07	3.02	2.97
	.01	**10.04**	**7.56**	**6.55**	**5.99**	**5.64**	**5.39**	**5.21**	**5.06**	**4.95**	**4.85**
11	.05	4.84	3.98	3.59	3.36	3.20	3.09	3.01	2.95	2.90	2.86
	.01	**9.65**	**7.20**	**6.22**	**5.67**	**5.32**	**5.07**	**4.88**	**4.74**	**4.63**	**4.54**
12	.05	4.75	3.88	3.49	3.26	3.11	3.00	2.92	2.85	2.80	2.76
	.01	**9.33**	**6.93**	**5.95**	**5.41**	**5.06**	**4.82**	**4.65**	**4.50**	**4.39**	**4.30**
13	.05	4.67	3.80	3.41	3.18	3.02	2.92	2.84	2.77	2.72	2.67
	.01	**9.07**	**6.70**	**5.74**	**5.20**	**4.86**	**4.62**	**4.44**	**4.30**	**4.19**	**4.10**

Degrees of freedom between groups
(degrees of freedom in numerator of F ratio)

11	12	14	16	20	24	30	40	50	75	100	200	500	∞
243	244	245	246	248	249	250	251	252	253	253	254	254	254
6,082	**6,106**	**6,142**	**6,169**	**6,208**	**6,234**	**6,258**	**6,286**	**6,302**	**6,323**	**6,334**	**6,352**	**6,361**	**6,366**
19.40	19.41	19.42	19.43	19.44	19.45	19.46	19.47	19.47	19.48	19.49	19.49	19.50	19.50
99.41	**99.42**	**99.43**	**99.44**	**99.45**	**99.46**	**99.47**	**99.48**	**99.48**	**99.49**	**99.49**	**99.49**	**99.50**	**99.50**
8.76	8.74	8.71	8.69	8.66	8.64	8.62	8.60	8.58	8.57	8.56	8.54	8.54	8.53
27.13	**27.05**	**26.92**	**26.83**	**26.69**	**26.60**	**26.50**	**26.41**	**26.35**	**26.27**	**26.23**	**26.18**	**26.14**	**26.12**
5.93	5.91	5.87	5.84	5.80	5.77	5.74	5.71	5.70	5.68	5.66	5.65	5.64	5.63
14.45	**14.37**	**14.24**	**14.15**	**14.02**	**13.93**	**13.83**	**13.74**	**13.69**	**13.61**	**13.57**	**13.52**	**13.48**	**13.46**
4.70	4.68	4.64	4.60	4.56	4.53	4.50	4.46	4.44	4.42	4.40	4.38	4.37	4.36
9.96	**9.89**	**9.77**	**9.68**	**9.55**	**9.47**	**9.38**	**9.29**	**9.24**	**9.17**	**9.13**	**9.07**	**9.04**	**9.02**
4.03	4.00	3.96	3.92	3.87	3.84	3.81	3.77	3.75	3.72	3.71	3.69	3.68	3.67
7.79	**7.72**	**7.60**	**7.52**	**7.39**	**7.31**	**7.23**	**7.14**	**7.09**	**7.02**	**6.99**	**6.94**	**6.90**	**6.88**
3.60	3.57	3.52	3.49	3.44	3.41	3.38	3.34	3.32	3.29	3.28	3.25	3.24	3.23
6.54	**6.47**	**6.35**	**6.27**	**6.15**	**6.07**	**5.98**	**5.90**	**5.85**	**5.78**	**5.75**	**5.70**	**5.67**	**5.65**
3.31	3.28	3.23	3.20	3.15	3.12	3.08	3.05	3.03	3.00	2.98	2.96	2.94	2.93
5.74	**5.67**	**5.56**	**5.48**	**5.36**	**5.28**	**5.20**	**5.11**	**5.06**	**5.00**	**4.96**	**4.91**	**4.88**	**4.86**
3.10	3.07	3.02	2.98	2.93	2.90	2.86	2.82	2.80	2.77	2.76	2.73	2.72	2.71
5.18	**5.11**	**5.00**	**4.92**	**4.80**	**4.73**	**4.64**	**4.56**	**4.51**	**4.45**	**4.41**	**4.36**	**4.33**	**4.31**
2.94	2.91	2.86	2.82	2.77	2.74	2.70	2.67	2.64	2.61	2.59	2.56	2.55	2.54
4.78	**4.71**	**4.60**	**4.52**	**4.41**	**4.33**	**4.25**	**4.17**	**4.12**	**4.05**	**4.01**	**3.96**	**3.93**	**3.91**
2.82	2.79	2.74	2.70	2.65	2.61	2.57	2.53	2.50	2.47	2.45	2.42	2.41	2.40
4.46	**4.40**	**4.29**	**4.21**	**4.10**	**4.02**	**3.94**	**3.86**	**3.80**	**3.74**	**3.70**	**3.66**	**3.62**	**3.60**
2.72	2.69	2.64	2.60	2.54	2.50	2.46	2.42	2.40	2.36	2.35	2.32	2.31	2.30
4.22	**4.16**	**4.05**	**3.98**	**3.86**	**3.78**	**3.70**	**3.61**	**3.56**	**3.49**	**3.46**	**3.41**	**3.38**	**3.36**
2.63	2.60	2.55	2.51	2.46	2.42	2.38	2.34	2.32	2.28	2.26	2.24	2.22	2.21
4.02	**3.96**	**3.85**	**3.78**	**3.67**	**3.59**	**3.51**	**3.42**	**3.37**	**3.30**	**3.27**	**3.21**	**3.18**	**3.16**

TABLE B.2   (cont.) Critical Values of *F*

Degrees of freedom within groups (degrees of freedom in denominator of F ratio)	α	Degrees of freedom between groups (degrees of freedom in numerator of F ratio)									
		1	*2*	*3*	*4*	*5*	*6*	*7*	*8*	*9*	*10*
14	.05	4.60	3.74	3.34	3.11	2.96	2.85	2.77	2.70	2.65	2.60
	.01	8.86	6.51	5.56	5.03	4.69	4.46	4.28	4.14	4.03	3.94
15	.05	4.54	3.68	3.29	3.06	2.90	2.79	2.70	2.64	2.59	2.55
	.01	8.68	6.36	5.42	4.89	4.56	4.32	4.14	4.00	3.89	3.80
16	.05	4.49	3.63	3.24	3.01	2.85	2.74	2.66	2.59	2.54	2.49
	.01	8.53	6.23	5.29	4.77	4.44	4.20	4.03	3.89	3.78	3.69
17	.05	4.45	3.59	3.20	2.96	2.81	2.70	2.62	2.55	2.50	2.45
	.01	8.40	6.11	5.18	4.67	4.34	4.10	3.93	3.79	3.68	3.59
18	.05	4.41	3.55	3.16	2.93	2.77	2.66	2.58	2.51	2.46	2.41
	.01	8.28	6.01	5.09	4.58	4.25	4.01	3.85	3.71	3.60	3.51
19	.05	4.38	3.52	3.13	2.90	2.74	2.63	2.55	2.48	2.43	2.38
	.01	8.18	5.93	5.01	4.50	4.17	3.94	3.77	3.63	3.52	3.43
20	.05	4.35	3.49	3.10	2.87	2.71	2.60	2.52	2.45	2.40	2.35
	.01	8.10	5.85	4.94	4.43	4.10	3.87	3.71	3.56	3.45	3.37
21	.05	4.32	3.47	3.07	2.84	2.68	2.57	2.49	2.42	2.37	2.32
	.01	8.02	5.78	4.87	4.37	4.04	3.81	3.65	3.51	3.40	3.31
22	.05	4.30	3.44	3.05	2.82	2.66	2.55	2.47	2.40	2.35	2.30
	.01	7.94	5.72	4.82	4.31	3.99	3.76	3.59	3.45	3.35	3.26
23	.05	4.28	3.42	3.03	2.80	2.64	2.53	2.45	2.38	2.32	2.28
	.01	7.88	5.66	4.76	4.26	3.94	3.71	3.54	3.41	3.30	3.21
24	.05	4.26	3.40	3.01	2.78	2.62	2.51	2.43	2.36	2.30	2.26
	.01	7.82	5.61	4.72	4.22	3.90	3.67	3.50	3.36	3.25	3.17
25	.05	4.24	3.38	2.99	2.76	2.60	2.49	2.41	2.34	2.28	2.24
	.01	7.77	5.57	4.68	4.18	3.86	3.63	3.46	3.32	3.21	3.13
26	.05	4.22	3.37	2.98	2.74	2.59	2.47	2.39	2.32	2.27	2.22
	.01	7.72	5.53	4.64	4.14	3.82	3.59	3.42	3.29	3.17	3.09
27	.05	4.21	3.35	2.96	2.73	2.57	2.46	2.37	2.30	2.25	2.20
	.01	7.68	5.49	4.60	4.11	3.79	3.56	3.39	3.26	3.14	3.06
28	.05	4.20	3.34	2.95	2.71	2.56	2.44	2.36	2.29	2.24	2.19
	.01	7.64	5.45	4.57	4.07	3.76	3.53	3.36	3.23	3.11	3.03
29	.05	4.18	3.33	2.93	2.70	2.54	2.43	2.35	2.28	2.22	2.18
	.01	7.60	5.42	4.54	4.04	3.73	3.50	3.33	3.20	3.08	3.00

Degrees of freedom between groups
(degrees of freedom in numerator of F ratio)

11	12	14	16	20	24	30	40	50	75	100	200	500	∞
2.56	2.53	2.48	2.44	2.39	2.35	2.31	2.27	2.24	2.21	2.19	2.16	2.14	2.13
3.86	**3.80**	**3.70**	**3.62**	**3.51**	**3.43**	**3.34**	**3.26**	**3.21**	**3.14**	**3.11**	**3.06**	**3.02**	**3.00**
2.51	2.48	2.43	2.39	2.33	2.29	2.25	2.21	2.18	2.15	2.12	2.10	2.08	2.07
3.73	**3.67**	**3.56**	**3.48**	**3.36**	**3.29**	**3.20**	**3.12**	**3.07**	**3.00**	**2.97**	**2.92**	**2.89**	**2.87**
2.45	2.42	2.37	2.33	2.28	2.24	2.20	2.16	2.13	2.09	2.97	2.04	2.02	2.01
3.61	**3.55**	**3.45**	**3.37**	**3.25**	**3.18**	**3.10**	**3.01**	**2.96**	**2.89**	**2.86**	**2.80**	**2.77**	**2.75**
2.41	2.38	2.33	2.29	2.23	2.19	2.15	2.11	2.08	2.04	2.02	1.99	1.97	1.96
3.52	**3.45**	**3.35**	**3.27**	**3.16**	**3.08**	**3.00**	**2.92**	**2.86**	**2.79**	**2.76**	**2.70**	**2.67**	**2.65**
2.37	2.34	2.29	2.25	2.19	2.15	2.11	2.07	2.04	2.00	1.98	1.95	1.93	1.92
3.44	**3.37**	**3.27**	**3.19**	**3.07**	**3.00**	**2.91**	**2.83**	**2.78**	**2.71**	**2.68**	**2.62**	**2.59**	**2.57**
2.34	2.31	2.26	2.21	2.15	2.11	2.07	2.02	2.00	1.96	1.94	1.91	1.90	1.88
3.36	**3.30**	**3.19**	**3.12**	**3.00**	**2.92**	**2.84**	**2.76**	**2.70**	**2.63**	**2.60**	**2.54**	**2.51**	**2.49**
2.31	2.28	2.23	2.18	2.12	2.08	2.04	1.99	1.96	1.92	1.90	1.87	1.85	1.84
3.30	**3.23**	**3.13**	**3.05**	**2.94**	**2.86**	**2.77**	**2.69**	**2.63**	**2.56**	**2.53**	**2.47**	**2.44**	**2.42**
2.28	2.25	2.20	2.15	2.09	2.05	2.00	1.96	1.93	1.89	1.87	1.84	1.82	1.81
3.24	**3.17**	**3.07**	**2.99**	**2.88**	**2.80**	**2.72**	**2.63**	**2.58**	**2.51**	**2.47**	**2.42**	**2.38**	**2.36**
2.26	2.23	2.18	2.13	2.07	2.03	1.98	1.93	1.91	1.87	1.84	1.81	1.80	1.78
3.18	**3.12**	**3.02**	**2.94**	**2.83**	**2.75**	**2.67**	**2.58**	**2.53**	**2.46**	**2.42**	**2.37**	**2.33**	**2.31**
2.24	2.20	2.14	2.10	2.04	2.00	1.96	1.91	1.88	1.84	1.82	1.79	1.77	1.76
3.14	**3.07**	**2.97**	**2.89**	**2.78**	**2.70**	**2.62**	**2.53**	**2.48**	**2.41**	**2.37**	**2.32**	**2.28**	**2.26**
2.22	2.18	2.13	2.09	2.02	1.98	1.94	1.89	1.86	1.82	1.80	1.76	1.74	1.73
3.09	**3.03**	**2.93**	**2.85**	**2.74**	**2.66**	**2.58**	**2.49**	**2.44**	**2.36**	**2.33**	**2.27**	**2.23**	**2.21**
2.20	2.16	2.11	2.06	2.00	1.96	1.92	1.87	1.84	1.80	1.77	1.74	1.72	1.71
3.05	**2.99**	**2.89**	**2.81**	**2.70**	**2.62**	**2.54**	**2.45**	**2.40**	**2.32**	**2.29**	**2.23**	**2.19**	**2.17**
2.18	2.15	2.10	2.05	1.99	1.95	1.90	1.85	1.82	1.78	1.76	1.72	1.70	1.69
3.02	**2.96**	**2.86**	**2.77**	**2.66**	**2.58**	**2.50**	**2.41**	**2.36**	**2.28**	**2.25**	**2.19**	**2.15**	**2.13**
2.16	2.13	2.08	2.03	1.97	1.93	1.88	1.84	1.80	1.76	1.74	1.71	1.68	1.67
2.98	**2.93**	**2.83**	**2.74**	**2.63**	**2.55**	**2.47**	**2.38**	**2.33**	**2.25**	**2.21**	**2.16**	**2.12**	**2.10**
2.15	2.12	2.06	2.02	1.96	1.91	1.87	1.81	1.78	1.75	1.72	1.69	1.67	1.65
2.95	**2.90**	**2.80**	**2.71**	**2.60**	**2.52**	**2.44**	**2.35**	**2.30**	**2.22**	**2.18**	**2.13**	**2.09**	**2.06**
2.14	2.10	2.05	2.00	1.94	1.90	1.85	1.80	1.77	1.73	1.71	1.68	1.65	1.64
2.92	**2.87**	**2.77**	**2.68**	**2.57**	**2.49**	**2.41**	**2.32**	**2.27**	**2.19**	**2.15**	**2.10**	**2.06**	**2.03**

TABLE B.2   (cont.) Critical Values of *F*

Degrees of freedom within groups (degrees of freedom in denominator of F ratio)	α	Degrees of freedom between groups (degrees of freedom in numerator of F ratio)									
		1	*2*	*3*	*4*	*5*	*6*	*7*	*8*	*9*	*10*
30	.05	4.17	3.32	2.92	2.69	2.53	2.42	2.34	2.27	2.21	2.16
	.01	7.56	5.39	4.51	4.02	3.70	3.47	3.30	3.17	3.06	2.98
32	.05	4.15	3.30	2.90	2.67	2.51	2.40	2.32	2.25	2.19	2.14
	.01	7.50	5.34	4.46	3.97	3.66	3.42	3.25	3.12	3.01	2.94
34	.05	4.13	3.28	2.88	2.65	2.49	2.38	2.30	2.23	2.17	2.12
	.01	7.44	5.29	4.42	3.93	3.61	3.38	3.21	3.08	2.97	2.89
36	.05	4.11	3.26	2.86	2.63	2.48	2.36	2.28	2.21	2.15	2.10
	.01	7.39	5.25	4.38	3.89	3.58	3.35	3.18	3.04	2.94	2.86
38	.05	4.10	3.25	2.85	2.62	2.46	2.35	2.26	2.19	2.14	2.09
	.01	7.35	5.21	4.34	3.86	3.54	3.32	3.15	3.02	2.91	2.82
40	.05	4.08	3.23	2.84	2.61	2.45	2.34	2.25	2.18	2.12	2.07
	.01	7.31	5.18	4.31	3.83	3.51	3.29	3.12	2.99	2.88	2.80
42	.05	4.07	3.22	2.83	2.59	2.44	2.32	2.24	2.17	2.11	2.06
	.01	7.27	5.15	4.29	3.80	3.49	3.26	3.10	2.96	2.86	2.77
44	.05	4.06	3.21	2.82	2.58	2.43	2.31	2.23	2.16	2.10	2.05
	.01	7.24	5.12	4.26	3.78	3.46	3.24	3.07	2.94	2.84	2.75
46	.05	4.05	3.20	2.81	2.57	2.42	2.30	2.22	2.14	2.09	2.04
	.01	7.21	5.10	4.24	3.76	3.44	3.22	3.05	2.92	2.82	2.73
48	.05	4.04	3.19	2.80	2.56	2.41	2.30	2.21	2.14	2.08	2.03
	.01	7.19	5.08	4.22	3.74	3.42	3.20	3.04	2.90	2.80	2.71
50	.05	4.03	3.18	2.79	2.56	2.40	2.29	2.20	2.13	2.07	2.02
	.01	7.17	5.06	4.20	3.72	3.41	3.18	3.02	2.88	2.78	2.70
55	.05	4.02	3.17	2.78	2.54	2.38	2.27	2.18	2.11	2.05	2.00
	.01	7.12	5.01	4.16	3.68	3.37	3.15	2.98	2.85	2.75	2.66
60	.05	4.00	3.15	2.76	2.52	2.37	2.25	2.17	2.10	2.04	1.99
	.01	7.08	4.98	4.13	3.65	3.34	3.12	2.95	2.82	2.72	2.63
65	.05	3.99	3.14	2.75	2.51	2.36	2.24	2.15	2.08	2.02	1.98
	.01	7.04	4.95	4.10	3.62	3.31	3.09	2.93	2.79	2.70	2.61
70	.05	3.98	3.13	2.74	2.50	2.35	2.23	2.14	2.07	2.01	1.97
	.01	7.01	4.92	4.08	3.60	3.29	3.07	2.91	2.77	2.67	2.59
80	.05	3.96	3.11	2.72	2.48	2.33	2.21	2.12	2.05	1.99	1.95
	.01	6.96	4.88	4.04	3.56	3.25	3.04	2.87	2.74	2.64	2.55

Degrees of freedom between groups
(degrees of freedom in numerator of F ratio)

11	12	14	16	20	24	30	40	50	75	100	200	500	∞
2.12	2.09	2.04	1.99	1.93	1.89	1.84	1.79	1.76	1.72	1.69	1.66	1.64	1.62
2.90	**2.84**	**2.74**	**2.66**	**2.55**	**2.47**	**2.38**	**2.29**	**2.24**	**2.16**	**2.13**	**2.07**	**2.03**	**2.01**
2.10	2.07	2.02	1.97	1.91	1.86	1.82	1.76	1.74	1.69	1.67	1.64	1.61	1.59
2.86	**2.80**	**2.70**	**2.62**	**2.51**	**2.42**	**2.34**	**2.25**	**2.20**	**2.12**	**2.08**	**2.02**	**1.98**	**1.96**
2.08	2.05	2.00	1.95	1.89	1.84	1.80	1.74	1.71	1.67	1.64	1.61	1.59	1.57
2.82	**2.76**	**2.66**	**2.58**	**2.47**	**2.38**	**2.30**	**2.21**	**2.15**	**2.08**	**2.04**	**1.98**	**1.94**	**1.91**
2.06	2.03	1.98	1.93	1.87	1.82	1.78	1.72	1.69	1.65	1.62	1.59	1.56	1.55
2.78	**2.72**	**2.62**	**2.54**	**2.43**	**2.35**	**2.26**	**2.17**	**2.12**	**2.04**	**2.00**	**1.94**	**1.90**	**1.87**
2.05	2.02	1.96	1.92	1.85	1.80	1.76	1.71	1.67	1.63	1.60	1.57	1.54	1.53
2.75	**2.69**	**2.59**	**2.51**	**2.40**	**2.32**	**2.22**	**2.14**	**2.08**	**2.00**	**1.97**	**1.90**	**1.86**	**1.84**
2.04	2.00	1.95	1.90	1.84	1.79	1.74	1.69	1.66	1.61	1.59	1.55	1.53	1.51
2.73	**2.66**	**2.56**	**2.49**	**2.37**	**2.29**	**2.20**	**2.11**	**2.05**	**1.97**	**1.94**	**1.88**	**1.84**	**1.81**
2.02	1.99	1.94	1.89	1.82	1.78	1.73	1.68	1.64	1.60	1.57	1.54	1.51	1.49
2.70	**2.64**	**2.54**	**2.46**	**2.35**	**2.26**	**2.17**	**2.08**	**2.02**	**1.94**	**1.91**	**1.85**	**1.80**	**1.78**
2.01	1.98	1.92	1.88	1.81	1.76	1.72	1.66	1.63	1.58	1.56	1.52	1.50	1.48
2.68	**2.62**	**2.52**	**2.44**	**2.32**	**2.24**	**2.15**	**2.06**	**2.00**	**1.92**	**1.88**	**1.82**	**1.78**	**1.75**
2.00	1.97	1.91	1.87	1.80	1.75	1.71	1.65	1.62	1.57	1.54	1.51	1.48	1.46
2.66	**2.60**	**2.50**	**2.42**	**2.30**	**2.22**	**2.13**	**2.04**	**1.98**	**1.90**	**1.86**	**1.80**	**1.76**	**1.72**
1.99	1.96	1.90	1.86	1.79	1.74	1.70	1.64	1.61	1.56	1.53	1.50	1.47	1.45
2.64	**2.58**	**2.48**	**2.40**	**2.28**	**2.20**	**2.11**	**2.02**	**1.96**	**1.88**	**1.84**	**1.78**	**1.73**	**1.70**
1.98	1.95	1.90	1.85	1.78	1.74	1.69	1.63	1.60	1.55	1.52	1.48	1.46	1.44
2.62	**2.56**	**2.46**	**2.39**	**2.26**	**2.18**	**2.10**	**2.00**	**1.94**	**1.86**	**1.82**	**1.76**	**1.71**	**1.68**
1.97	1.93	1.88	1.83	1.76	1.72	1.67	1.61	1.58	1.52	1.50	1.46	1.43	1.41
2.59	**2.53**	**2.43**	**2.35**	**2.23**	**2.15**	**2.06**	**1.96**	**1.90**	**1.82**	**1.78**	**1.71**	**1.66**	**1.64**
1.95	1.92	1.86	1.81	1.75	1.70	1.65	1.59	1.56	1.50	1.48	1.44	1.41	1.39
2.56	**2.50**	**2.40**	**2.32**	**2.20**	**2.12**	**2.03**	**1.93**	**1.87**	**1.79**	**1.74**	**1.68**	**1.63**	**1.60**
1.94	1.90	1.85	1.80	1.73	1.68	1.63	1.57	1.54	1.49	1.46	1.42	1.39	1.37
2.54	**2.47**	**2.37**	**2.30**	**2.18**	**2.09**	**2.00**	**1.90**	**1.84**	**1.76**	**1.71**	**1.64**	**1.60**	**1.56**
1.93	1.89	1.84	1.79	1.72	1.67	1.62	1.56	1.53	1.47	1.45	1.40	1.37	1.35
2.51	**2.45**	**2.35**	**2.28**	**2.15**	**2.07**	**1.98**	**1.88**	**1.82**	**1.74**	**1.69**	**1.62**	**1.56**	**1.53**
1.91	1.88	1.82	1.77	1.70	1.65	1.60	1.54	1.51	1.45	1.42	1.38	1.35	1.32
2.48	**2.41**	**2.32**	**2.24**	**2.11**	**2.03**	**1.94**	**1.84**	**1.78**	**1.70**	**1.65**	**1.57**	**1.52**	**1.49**

TABLE B.2   (cont.) Critical Values of F

Degrees of freedom within groups (degrees of freedom in denominator of F ratio)	α	Degrees of freedom between groups (degrees of freedom in numerator of F ratio)									
		1	2	3	4	5	6	7	8	9	10
100	.05	3.94	3.09	2.70	2.46	2.30	2.19	2.10	2.03	1.97	1.92
	.01	6.90	4.82	3.98	3.51	3.20	2.99	2.82	2.69	2.59	2.51
125	.05	3.92	3.07	2.68	2.44	2.29	2.17	2.08	2.01	1.95	1.90
	.01	6.84	4.78	3.94	3.47	3.17	2.95	2.79	2.65	2.56	2.47
150	.05	3.91	3.06	2.67	2.43	2.27	2.16	2.07	2.00	1.94	1.89
	.01	6.81	4.75	3.91	3.44	3.14	2.92	2.76	2.62	2.53	2.44
200	.05	3.89	3.04	2.65	2.41	2.26	2.14	2.05	1.98	1.92	1.87
	.01	6.76	4.71	3.88	3.41	3.11	2.90	2.73	2.60	2.50	2.41
400	.05	3.86	3.02	2.62	2.39	2.23	2.12	2.03	1.96	1.90	1.85
	.01	6.70	4.66	3.83	3.36	3.06	2.85	2.69	2.55	2.46	2.37
1000	.05	3.85	3.00	2.61	2.38	2.22	2.10	2.02	1.95	1.89	1.84
	.01	6.66	4.62	3.80	3.34	3.04	2.82	2.66	2.53	2.43	2.34
∞	.05	3.84	2.99	2.60	2.37	2.21	2.09	2.01	1.94	1.88	1.83
	.01	6.64	4.60	3.78	3.32	3.02	2.80	2.64	2.51	2.41	2.32

						Degrees of freedom between groups (degrees of freedom in numerator of F ratio)							
11	*12*	*14*	*16*	*20*	*24*	*30*	*40*	*50*	*75*	*100*	*200*	*500*	*∞*
1.88	1.85	1.79	1.75	1.68	1.63	1.57	1.51	1.48	1.42	1.39	1.34	1.30	1.28
2.43	**2.36**	**2.26**	**2.19**	**2.06**	**1.98**	**1.89**	**1.79**	**1.73**	**1.64**	**1.59**	**1.51**	**1.46**	**1.43**
1.86	1.83	1.77	1.72	1.65	1.60	1.55	1.49	1.45	1.39	1.36	1.31	1.27	1.25
2.40	**2.33**	**2.23**	**2.15**	**2.03**	**1.94**	**1.85**	**1.75**	**1.68**	**1.59**	**1.54**	**1.46**	**1.40**	**1.37**
1.85	1.82	1.76	1.71	1.64	1.59	1.54	1.47	1.44	1.37	1.34	1.29	1.25	1.22
2.37	**2.30**	**2.20**	**2.12**	**2.00**	**1.91**	**1.83**	**1.72**	**1.66**	**1.56**	**1.51**	**1.43**	**1.37**	**1.33**
1.83	1.80	1.74	1.69	1.62	1.57	1.52	1.45	1.42	1.35	1.32	1.26	1.22	1.19
2.34	**2.28**	**2.17**	**2.09**	**1.97**	**1.88**	**1.79**	**1.69**	**1.62**	**1.53**	**1.48**	**1.39**	**1.33**	**1.28**
1.81	1.78	1.72	1.67	1.60	1.54	1.49	1.42	1.38	1.32	1.28	1.22	1.16	1.13
2.29	**2.23**	**2.12**	**2.04**	**1.92**	**1.84**	**1.74**	**1.64**	**1.57**	**1.47**	**1.42**	**1.32**	**1.24**	**1.19**
1.80	1.76	1.70	1.65	1.58	1.53	1.47	1.41	1.36	1.30	1.26	1.19	1.13	1.08
2.26	**2.20**	**2.09**	**2.01**	**1.89**	**1.81**	**1.71**	**1.61**	**1.54**	**1.44**	**1.38**	**1.28**	**1.19**	**1.11**
1.79	1.75	1.69	1.64	1.57	1.52	1.46	1.40	1.35	1.38	1.24	1.17	1.11	1.00
2.24	**2.18**	**2.07**	**1.99**	**1.87**	**1.79**	**1.69**	**1.59**	**1.52**	**1.41**	**1.36**	**1.25**	**1.15**	**1.00**

Reprinted by permission from *Statistical Methods,* by George W. Snedecor and William G. Cochran, Eighth Edition, Copyright © 1989 by The Iowa State University Press. Used with permission.

TABLE B.3   Values of the Studentized Range Statistic, q_k

Values of q_k for $\alpha = .05$ are light numbers and for $\alpha = .01$ are **dark numbers**

Degrees of freedom within groups (degrees of freedom in denominator of F ratio)	α	2	3	4	5	6	7	8	9	10	11	12
						k = number of means being compared						
1	.05	18.0	27.0	32.8	37.1	40.4	43.1	45.4	47.4	49.1	50.6	52.0
	.01	**90.0**	**135**	**164**	**186**	**202**	**216**	**227**	**237**	**246**	**253**	**260**
2	.05	6.09	8.3	9.8	10.9	11.7	12.4	13.0	13.5	14.0	14.4	14.7
	.01	**14.0**	**19.0**	**22.3**	**24.7**	**26.6**	**28.2**	**29.5**	**30.7**	**31.7**	**32.6**	**33.4**
3	.05	4.50	5.91	6.82	7.50	8.04	8.48	8.85	9.18	9.46	9.72	9.95
	.01	**8.26**	**10.6**	**12.2**	**13.3**	**14.2**	**15.0**	**15.6**	**16.2**	**16.7**	**17.1**	**17.5**
4	.05	3.93	5.04	5.76	6.29	6.71	7.05	7.35	7.60	7.83	8.03	8.21
	.01	**6.51**	**8.12**	**9.17**	**9.96**	**10.6**	**11.1**	**11.5**	**11.9**	**12.3**	**12.6**	**12.8**
5	.05	3.64	4.60	5.22	5.67	6.03	6.33	6.58	6.80	6.99	7.17	7.32
	.01	**5.70**	**6.97**	**7.80**	**8.42**	**8.91**	**9.32**	**9.67**	**9.97**	**10.2**	**10.5**	**10.7**
6	.05	3.46	4.34	4.90	5.31	5.63	5.89	6.12	6.32	6.49	6.65	6.79
	.01	**5.24**	**6.33**	**7.03**	**7.56**	**7.97**	**8.32**	**8.61**	**8.87**	**9.10**	**9.30**	**9.49**
7	.05	3.34	4.16	4.69	5.06	5.36	5.61	5.82	6.00	6.16	6.30	6.43
	.01	**4.95**	**5.92**	**6.54**	**7.01**	**7.37**	**7.68**	**7.94**	**8.17**	**8.37**	**8.55**	**8.71**
8	.05	3.26	4.04	4.53	4.89	5.17	5.40	5.60	5.77	5.92	6.05	6.18
	.01	**4.74**	**5.63**	**6.20**	**6.63**	**6.96**	**7.24**	**7.47**	**7.68**	**7.87**	**8.03**	**8.18**
9	.05	3.20	3.95	4.42	4.76	5.02	5.24	5.43	5.60	5.74	5.87	5.98
	.01	**4.60**	**5.43**	**5.96**	**6.35**	**6.66**	**6.91**	**7.13**	**7.32**	**7.49**	**7.65**	**7.78**
10	.05	3.15	3.88	4.33	4.65	4.91	5.12	5.30	5.46	5.60	5.72	5.83
	.01	**4.48**	**5.27**	**5.77**	**6.14**	**6.43**	**6.67**	**6.87**	**7.05**	**7.21**	**7.36**	**7.48**
11	.05	3.11	3.82	4.26	4.57	4.82	5.03	5.20	5.35	5.49	5.61	5.71
	.01	**4.39**	**5.14**	**5.62**	**5.97**	**6.25**	**6.48**	**6.67**	**6.84**	**6.99**	**7.13**	**7.26**
12	.05	3.08	3.77	4.20	4.51	4.75	4.95	5.12	5.27	5.40	5.51	5.62
	.01	**4.32**	**5.04**	**5.50**	**5.84**	**6.10**	**6.32**	**6.51**	**6.67**	**6.81**	**6.94**	**7.06**
13	.05	3.06	3.73	4.15	4.45	4.69	4.88	5.05	5.19	5.32	5.43	5.53
	.01	**4.26**	**4.96**	**5.40**	**5.73**	**5.98**	**6.19**	**6.37**	**6.53**	**6.67**	**6.79**	**6.90**
14	.05	3.03	3.70	4.11	4.41	4.64	4.83	4.99	5.13	5.25	5.36	5.46
	.01	**4.21**	**4.89**	**5.32**	**5.63**	**5.88**	**6.08**	**6.26**	**6.41**	**6.54**	**6.66**	**6.77**
16	.05	3.00	3.65	4.05	4.33	4.56	4.74	4.90	5.03	5.15	5.26	5.35
	.01	**4.13**	**4.78**	**5.19**	**5.49**	**5.72**	**5.92**	**6.08**	**6.22**	**6.35**	**6.46**	**6.56**
18	.05	2.97	3.61	4.00	4.28	4.49	4.67	4.82	4.96	5.07	5.17	5.27
	.01	**4.07**	**4.70**	**5.09**	**5.38**	**5.60**	**5.79**	**5.94**	**6.08**	**6.20**	**6.31**	**6.41**

TABLE B.3　Values of the Studentized Range Statistic, q_k

Values of q_k for $\alpha = .05$ are light numbers and for $\alpha = .01$ are **dark numbers.**

Degrees of freedom within groups (degrees of freedom in denominator of F ratio)	α	2	3	4	5	6	7	8	9	10	11	12
					k = *number of means being compared*							
20	.05	2.95	3.58	3.96	4.23	4.45	4.62	4.77	4.90	5.01	5.11	5.20
	.01	**4.02**	**4.64**	**5.02**	**5.29**	**5.51**	**5.69**	**5.84**	**5.97**	**6.09**	**6.19**	**6.29**
24	.05	2.92	3.53	3.90	4.17	4.37	4.54	4.68	4.81	4.92	5.01	5.10
	.01	**3.96**	**4.54**	**4.91**	**5.17**	**5.37**	**5.54**	**5.69**	**5.81**	**5.92**	**6.02**	**6.11**
30	.05	2.89	3.49	3.84	4.10	4.30	4.46	4.60	4.72	4.83	4.92	5.00
	.01	**3.89**	**4.45**	**4.80**	**5.05**	**5.24**	**5.40**	**5.54**	**5.56**	**5.76**	**5.85**	**5.93**
40	.05	2.86	3.44	3.79	4.04	4.23	4.39	4.52	4.63	4.74	4.82	4.91
	.01	**3.82**	**4.37**	**4.70**	**4.93**	**5.11**	**5.27**	**5.39**	**5.50**	**5.60**	**5.69**	**5.77**
60	.05	2.83	3.40	3.74	3.98	4.16	4.31	4.44	4.55	4.65	4.73	4.81
	.01	**3.76**	**4.28**	**4.60**	**4.82**	**4.99**	**5.13**	**5.25**	**5.36**	**5.45**	**5.53**	**5.60**
120	.05	2.80	3.36	3.69	3.92	4.10	4.24	4.36	4.48	4.56	4.64	4.72
	.01	**3.70**	**4.20**	**4.50**	**4.71**	**4.87**	**5.01**	**5.12**	**5.21**	**5.30**	**5.38**	**5.44**
∞	.05	2.77	3.31	3.63	3.86	4.03	4.17	4.29	4.39	4.47	4.55	4.62
	.01	**3.64**	**4.12**	**4.40**	**4.60**	**4.76**	**4.88**	**4.99**	**5.08**	**5.16**	**5.23**	**5.29**

From B. J. Winer, *Statistical Principles in Experimental Design,* McGraw-Hill, 1962; abridged from H. L. Harter, D. S. Clemm, and E. H. Guthrie, The probability integrals of the range and of the studentized range, WADC Tech. Rep. 58–484, Vol. 2, 1959, Wright Air Development Center, Table II.2, pp. 243–281. Reproduced with permission of McGraw-Hill, Inc.

TABLE B.4   Critical Values of the Pearson Correlation Coefficient, *r*

Two-Tailed Test			One-Tailed Test		
	Level of significance			*Level of significance*	
df (no. of pairs − 2)	α = .05	α = .01	df (no. of pairs − 2)	α = .05	α = .01
1	.997	.9999	1	.988	.9995
2	.950	.990	2	.900	.980
3	.878	.959	3	.805	.934
4	.811	.917	4	.729	.882
5	.754	.874	5	.669	.833
6	.707	.834	6	.622	.789
7	.666	.798	7	.582	.750
8	.632	.765	8	.549	.716
9	.602	.735	9	.521	.685
10	.576	.708	10	.497	.658
11	.553	.684	11	.476	.634
12	.532	.661	12	.458	.612
13	.514	.641	13	.441	.592
14	.497	.623	14	.426	.574
15	.482	.606	15	.412	.558
16	.468	.590	16	.400	.542
17	.456	.575	17	.389	.528
18	.444	.561	18	.378	.516
19	.433	.549	19	.369	.503
20	.423	.537	20	.360	.492
21	.413	.526	21	.352	.482
22	.404	.515	22	.344	.472
23	.396	.505	23	.337	.462
24	.388	.496	24	.330	.453
25	.381	.487	25	.323	.445
26	.374	.479	26	.317	.437
27	.367	.471	27	.311	.430
28	.361	.463	28	.306	.423
29	.355	.456	29	.301	.416
30	.349	.449	30	.296	.409
35	.325	.418	35	.275	.381
40	.304	.393	40	.257	.358
45	.288	.372	45	.243	.338
50	.273	.354	50	.231	.322
60	.250	.325	60	.211	.295
70	.232	.302	70	.195	.274
80	.217	.283	80	.183	.256
90	.205	.267	90	.173	.242
100	.195	.254	100	.164	.230

From Table VI of R. A. Fisher and F. Yates, *Statistical for Biological, Agricultural and Medical Research,* 6th ed. London: Longman Group Ltd., 1974 (previously published by Oliver and Boyd Ltd., Edinburgh).

TABLE B.5   Critical Values of the Spearman Correlation Coefficient, r_s

Note: To interpolate the critical value for an N not given, find the critical values for the N above and below your N, add them together, and then divide the sum by 2.

| | Two-Tailed Test | | | One-Tailed Test | |
| | Level of significance | | | Level of significance | |
N (no. of pairs)	$\alpha = .05$	$\alpha = .01$	N (no. of pairs)	$\alpha = .05$	$\alpha = .01$
5	1.000	—	5	.900	1.000
6	.886	1.000	6	.829	.943
7	.786	.929	7	.714	.893
8	.738	.881	8	.643	.833
9	.683	.833	9	.600	.783
10	.648	.794	10	.564	.746
12	.591	.777	12	.506	.712
14	.544	.715	14	.456	.645
16	.506	.665	16	.425	.601
18	.475	.625	18	.399	.564
20	.450	.591	20	.377	.534
22	.428	.562	22	.359	.508
24	.409	.537	24	.343	.485
26	.392	.515	26	.329	.465
28	.377	.496	28	.317	.448
30	.364	.478	30	.306	.432

From E. G. Olds (1949), The 5 Percent Significance Levels of Sums of Squares of Rank Differences and a Correction, *Ann. Math. Statist.,* **20,** 117–118, and E. G. Olds (1938), Distribution of Sums of Squares of Rank Differences for Small Numbers of Individuals, *Ann. Math. Statist.,* **9,** 133–148. Reprinted with permission of the Institute of Mathematical Statistics.

TABLE B.6   Critical Values of Chi Square, χ^2

Level of significance

df	$\alpha = .05$	$\alpha = .01$
1	3.84	6.64
2	5.99	9.21
3	7.81	11.34
4	9.49	13.28
5	11.07	15.09
6	12.59	16.81
7	14.07	18.48
8	15.51	20.09
9	16.92	21.67
10	18.31	23.21
11	19.68	24.72
12	21.03	26.22
13	22.36	27.69
14	23.68	29.14
15	25.00	30.58
16	26.30	32.00
17	27.59	33.41
18	28.87	34.80
19	30.14	36.19
20	31.41	37.57
21	32.67	38.93
22	33.92	40.29
23	35.17	41.64
24	36.42	42.98
25	37.65	44.31
26	38.88	45.64
27	40.11	46.96
28	41.34	48.28
29	42.56	49.59
30	43.77	50.89
40	55.76	63.69
50	67.50	76.15
60	79.08	88.38
70	90.53	100.42

From Table IV of R. A. Fisher and F. Yates, *Statistical Tables for Biological, Agricultural and Medical Research,* 6th ed. London: Longman Group Ltd., 1974 (previously published by Oliver and Boyd, Edinburgh).

TABLE B.7 Critical Values of the Mann-Whitney U

To be significant, the U must be equal to or be *less than* the critical value. (Dashes in the table indicate that no decision is possible.) Critical values for $\alpha = .05$ are light numbers and for $\alpha = .01$ are **dark numbers.**

Two-Tailed Test

n_2 (no. of scores in Group 2)	α	1	2	3	4	5	6	7	8	9
					n_1 (no. of scores in Group 1)					
1	.05	—	—	—	—	—	—	—	—	—
	.01	**—**	**—**	**—**	**—**	**—**	**—**	**—**	**—**	**—**
2	.05	—	—	—	—	—	—	—	0	0
	.01	**—**	**—**	**—**	**—**	**—**	**—**	**—**	**—**	**—**
3	.05	—	—	—	—	0	1	1	2	2
	.01	**—**	**—**	**—**	**—**	**—**	**—**	**—**	**—**	**0**
4	.05	—	—	—	0	1	2	3	4	4
	.01	**—**	**—**	**—**	**—**	**—**	**0**	**0**	**1**	**1**
5	.05	—	—	0	1	2	3	5	6	7
	.01	**—**	**—**	**—**	**—**	**0**	**1**	**1**	**2**	**3**
6	.05	—	—	1	2	3	5	6	8	10
	.01	**—**	**—**	**—**	**0**	**1**	**2**	**3**	**4**	**5**
7	.05	—	—	1	3	5	6	8	10	12
	.01	**—**	**—**	**—**	**0**	**1**	**3**	**4**	**6**	**7**
8	.05	—	0	2	4	6	8	10	13	15
	.01	**—**	**—**	**—**	**1**	**2**	**4**	**6**	**7**	**9**
9	.05	—	0	2	4	7	10	12	15	17
	.01	**—**	**—**	**0**	**1**	**3**	**5**	**7**	**9**	**11**
10	.05	—	0	3	5	8	11	14	17	20
	.01	**—**	**—**	**0**	**2**	**4**	**6**	**9**	**11**	**13**
11	.05	—	0	3	6	9	13	16	19	23
	.01	**—**	**—**	**0**	**2**	**5**	**7**	**10**	**13**	**16**
12	.05	—	1	4	7	11	14	18	22	26
	.01	**—**	**—**	**1**	**3**	**6**	**9**	**12**	**15**	**18**
13	.05	—	1	4	8	12	16	20	24	28
	.01	**—**	**—**	**1**	**3**	**7**	**10**	**13**	**17**	**20**
14	.05	—	1	5	9	13	17	22	26	31
	.01	**—**	**—**	**1**	**4**	**7**	**11**	**15**	**18**	**22**
15	.05	—	1	5	10	14	19	24	29	34
	.01	**—**	**—**	**2**	**5**	**8**	**12**	**16**	**20**	**24**
16	.05	—	1	6	11	15	21	26	31	37
	.01	**—**	**—**	**2**	**5**	**9**	**13**	**18**	**22**	**27**
17	.05	—	2	6	11	17	22	28	34	39
	.01	**—**	**—**	**2**	**6**	**10**	**15**	**19**	**24**	**29**
18	.05	—	2	7	12	18	24	30	36	42
	.01	**—**	**—**	**2**	**6**	**11**	**16**	**21**	**26**	**31**
19	.05	—	2	7	13	19	25	32	38	45
	.01	**—**	**0**	**3**	**7**	**12**	**17**	**22**	**28**	**33**
20	.05	—	2	8	13	20	27	34	41	48
	.01	**—**	**0**	**3**	**8**	**13**	**18**	**24**	**30**	**36**

TABLE B.7   (cont.) Critical Values of the Mann-Whitney U

			n_1 (no. of scores in Group 1)							
10	11	12	13	14	15	16	17	18	19	20
—	—	—	—	—	—	—	—	—	—	—
—	—	—	—	—	—	—	—	—	—	—
0	0	1	1	1	1	1	2	2	2	2
—	—	—	—	—	—	—	—	—	**0**	**0**
3	3	4	4	5	5	6	6	7	7	8
0	**0**	**1**	**1**	**1**	**2**	**2**	**2**	**2**	**3**	**3**
5	6	7	8	9	10	11	11	12	13	13
2	**2**	**3**	**3**	**4**	**5**	**5**	**6**	**6**	**7**	**8**
8	9	11	12	13	14	15	17	18	19	20
4	**5**	**6**	**7**	**7**	**8**	**9**	**10**	**11**	**12**	**13**
11	13	14	16	17	19	21	22	24	25	27
6	**7**	**9**	**10**	**11**	**12**	**13**	**15**	**16**	**17**	**18**
14	16	18	20	22	24	26	28	30	32	34
9	**10**	**12**	**13**	**15**	**16**	**18**	**19**	**21**	**22**	**24**
17	19	22	24	26	29	31	34	36	38	41
11	**13**	**15**	**17**	**18**	**20**	**22**	**24**	**26**	**28**	**30**
20	23	26	28	31	34	37	39	42	45	48
13	**16**	**18**	**20**	**22**	**24**	**27**	**29**	**31**	**33**	**36**
23	26	29	33	36	39	42	45	48	52	55
16	**18**	**21**	**24**	**26**	**29**	**31**	**34**	**37**	**39**	**42**
26	30	33	37	40	44	47	51	55	58	62
18	**21**	**24**	**27**	**30**	**33**	**36**	**39**	**42**	**45**	**48**
29	33	37	41	45	49	53	57	61	65	69
21	**24**	**27**	**31**	**34**	**37**	**41**	**44**	**47**	**51**	**54**
33	37	41	45	50	54	59	63	67	72	76
24	**27**	**31**	**34**	**38**	**42**	**45**	**49**	**53**	**56**	**60**
36	40	45	50	55	59	64	67	74	78	83
26	**30**	**34**	**38**	**42**	**46**	**50**	**54**	**58**	**63**	**67**
39	44	49	54	59	64	70	75	80	85	90
29	**33**	**37**	**42**	**46**	**51**	**55**	**60**	**64**	**69**	**73**
42	47	53	59	64	70	75	81	86	92	98
31	**36**	**41**	**45**	**50**	**55**	**60**	**65**	**70**	**74**	**79**
45	51	57	63	67	75	81	87	93	99	105
34	**39**	**44**	**49**	**54**	**60**	**65**	**70**	**75**	**81**	**86**
48	55	61	67	74	80	86	93	99	106	112
37	**42**	**47**	**53**	**58**	**64**	**70**	**75**	**81**	**87**	**92**
52	58	65	72	78	85	92	99	106	113	119
39	**45**	**51**	**56**	**63**	**69**	**74**	**81**	**87**	**93**	**99**
55	62	69	76	83	90	98	105	112	119	127
42	**48**	**54**	**60**	**67**	**73**	**79**	**86**	**92**	**99**	**105**

One-Tailed Test

n_2 (no. of scores in Group 2)	α	n_1 (no. of scores in Group 1)								
		1	2	3	4	5	6	7	8	9
1	.05	—	—	—	—	—	—	—	—	—
	.01	—	—	—	—	—	—	—	—	—
2	.05	—	—	—	—	0	0	0	1	1
	.01	—	—	—	—	—	—	—	—	—
3	.05	—	—	0	0	1	2	2	3	3
	.01	—	—	—	—	—	—	0	0	1
4	.05	—	—	0	1	2	3	4	5	6
	.01	—	—	—	—	0	1	1	2	3
5	.05	—	0	1	2	4	5	6	8	9
	.01	—	—	—	0	1	2	3	4	5
6	.05	—	0	2	3	5	7	8	10	12
	.01	—	—	—	1	2	3	4	6	7
7	.05	—	0	2	4	6	8	11	13	15
	.01	—	—	0	1	3	4	6	7	9
8	.05	—	1	3	5	8	10	13	15	18
	.01	—	—	0	2	4	6	7	9	11
9	.05	—	1	3	6	9	12	15	18	21
	.01	—	—	1	3	5	7	9	11	14
10	.05	—	1	4	7	11	14	17	20	24
	.01	—	—	1	3	6	8	11	13	16
11	.05	—	1	5	8	12	16	19	23	27
	.01	—	—	1	4	7	9	12	15	18
12	.05	—	2	5	9	13	17	21	26	30
	.01	—	—	2	5	8	11	14	17	21
13	.05	—	2	6	10	15	19	24	28	33
	.01	—	0	2	5	9	12	16	20	23
14	.05	—	2	7	11	16	21	26	31	36
	.01	—	0	2	6	10	13	17	22	26
15	.05	—	3	7	12	18	23	28	33	39
	.01	—	0	3	7	11	15	19	24	28
16	.05	—	3	8	14	19	25	30	36	42
	.01	—	0	3	7	12	16	21	26	31
17	.05	—	3	9	15	20	26	33	39	45
	.01	—	0	4	8	13	18	23	28	33
18	.05	—	4	9	16	22	28	35	41	48
	.01	—	0	4	9	14	19	24	30	36
19	.05	0	4	10	17	23	30	37	44	51
	.01	—	1	4	9	15	20	26	32	38
20	.05	0	4	11	18	25	32	39	47	54
	.01	—	1	5	10	16	22	28	34	40

TABLE B.7 (cont.) Critical Values of the Mann-Whitney U

				n_1 (no. of scores in Group 1)							
10	11	12	13	14	15	16	17	18	19	20
—	—	—	—	—	—	—	—	—	0	0
—	—	—	—	—	—	—	—	—	—	—
1	1	2	2	2	3	3	3	4	4	4
—	—	—	0	0	0	0	0	0	1	1
4	5	5	6	7	7	8	9	9	10	11
1	1	2	2	2	3	3	4	4	4	5
7	8	9	10	11	12	14	15	16	17	18
3	4	5	5	6	7	7	8	9	9	10
11	12	13	15	16	18	19	20	22	23	25
6	7	8	9	10	11	12	13	14	15	16
14	16	17	19	21	23	25	26	28	30	32
8	9	11	12	13	15	16	18	19	20	22
17	19	21	24	26	28	30	33	35	37	39
11	12	14	16	17	19	21	23	24	26	28
20	23	26	28	31	33	36	39	41	44	47
13	15	17	20	22	24	26	28	30	32	34
24	27	30	33	36	39	42	45	48	51	54
16	18	21	23	26	28	31	33	36	38	40
27	31	34	37	41	44	48	51	55	58	62
19	22	24	27	30	33	36	38	41	44	47
31	34	38	42	46	50	54	57	61	65	69
22	25	28	31	34	37	41	44	47	50	53
34	38	42	47	51	55	60	64	68	72	77
24	28	31	35	38	42	46	49	53	56	60
37	42	47	51	56	61	65	70	75	80	84
27	31	35	39	43	47	51	55	59	63	67
41	46	51	56	61	66	71	77	82	87	92
30	34	38	43	47	51	56	60	65	69	73
44	50	55	61	66	72	77	83	88	94	100
33	37	42	47	51	56	61	66	70	75	80
48	54	60	65	71	77	83	89	95	101	107
36	41	46	51	56	61	66	71	76	82	87
51	57	64	70	77	83	89	96	102	109	115
38	44	49	55	60	66	71	77	82	88	93
55	61	68	75	82	88	95	102	109	116	123
41	47	53	59	65	70	76	82	88	94	100
58	65	72	80	87	94	101	109	116	123	130
44	50	56	63	69	75	82	88	94	101	107
62	69	77	84	92	100	107	115	123	130	138
47	53	60	67	73	80	87	93	100	107	114

From the *Bulletin of the Institute of Educational Research*, 1, No. 2, Indiana University, with permission of the publishers.

TABLE B.8 Critical Values of the Wilcoxon *T*
Two-Tailed Test

N	α = .05	α = .01	N	α = .05	α = .01
5	—	—	28	116	91
6	0	—	29	126	100
7	2	—	30	137	109
8	3	0	31	147	118
9	5	1	32	159	128
10	8	3	33	170	138
11	10	5	34	182	148
12	13	7	35	195	159
13	17	9	36	208	171
14	21	12	37	221	182
15	25	15	38	235	194
16	29	19	39	249	207
17	34	23	40	264	220
18	40	27	41	279	233
19	46	32	42	294	247
20	52	37	43	310	261
21	58	42	44	327	276
22	65	48	45	343	291
23	73	54	46	361	307
24	81	61	47	378	322
25	89	68	48	396	339
26	98	75	49	415	355
27	107	83	50	434	373

TABLE B.8   (cont.) Critical Values of the Wilcoxon *T*
One-Tailed Test

N	$\alpha = .05$	$\alpha = .01$	N	$\alpha = .05$	$\alpha = .01$
5	0	—	28	130	101
6	2	—	29	140	110
7	3	0	30	151	120
8	5	1	31	163	130
9	8	3	32	175	140
10	10	5	33	187	151
11	13	7	34	200	162
12	17	9	35	213	173
13	21	12	36	227	185
14	25	15	37	241	198
15	30	19	38	256	211
16	35	23	39	271	224
17	41	27	40	286	238
18	47	32	41	302	252
19	53	37	42	319	266
20	60	43	43	336	281
21	67	49	44	353	296
22	75	55	45	371	312
23	83	62	46	389	328
24	91	69	47	407	345
25	100	76	48	426	362
26	110	84	49	446	379
27	119	92	50	466	397

From F. Wilcoxon and R. A. Wilcox, *Some Rapid Approximate Statistical Procedures.* New York: Lederle Laboratories, 1964. Reproduced with the permission of the American Cyanamid Company.

C Appendix: Sample APA-Style Research Report

Running head: EFFECT OF HUMOROUS INTERPRETATIONS ON RECALL

Effect of Humorous Interpretations on

Immediate Recall of Nonsense Figures

Gary W. Heiman

Podunk University

Abstract

The effect of humor on the immediate recall of simple visual
stimuli was investigated. Eighty college students (20 men and 20
women per condition) viewed 28 nonsensical line drawings that
were each accompanied by either a humorous or nonhumorous verbal
interpretation. Although the interpretations were comparable in
the meaningfulness they conveyed, those participants presented
with humorous interpretations correctly recalled significantly
more drawings than those presented nonhumorous interpretations.
The results suggest that a meaningful and humorous context
provides additional retrieval cues beyond those cues provided by
a meaningful yet nonhumorous context. The effect of the cues
produced by humor is interpreted as creating a more distinctive
and thus more accessible memory trace.

Effect of Humorous Interpretations

on Immediate Recall of Nonsense Figures

Researchers have consistently demonstrated that retention
of to-be-learned material improves when the material is
presented in a context that leads to meaningful processing
(Lockhart & Craik, 1990). In particular, Bower, Karlin, and
Dueck (1975) presented college students with a series of
"droodles," which are each a meaningless line drawing that can
be made meaningful by presentation of an accompanying verbal
interpretation. Those individuals who were provided the
interpretations correctly recalled (sketched) significantly more
of the droodles immediately following their presentation than
did those individuals given no interpretations. However, each
interpretation in Bower et al. (1975) defined a droodle in a
humorous fashion, using unexpected and incongruent actors and
actions. Thus, differences in the meaningfulness attributed to
the droodles may have been confounded by differences in the
humor associated with the droodles. The purpose of the present
study was to investigate the effect of humorous interpretations
when the meaningfulness of the droodles is kept constant.

Few studies can be found that directly examine how the
humor associated with a stimulus influences recall of the
stimulus. However, it is reasonable to speculate that the
relevant dimension of humor may be that it is simply one type of
context that makes a stimulus meaningful. Desrochers and Begg
(1987) defined the meaningfulness of a stimulus as the extent to

which the components of the stimulus are organized and
integrated. Therefore, meaningfulness provides retrieval cues
that enhance recall of the components of the stimulus, once the
stimulus has been accessed in memory. From this perspective,
either a humorous or a nonhumorous context should produce
equivalent recall of stimuli, as long as both contexts provide
an equivalent level of meaningful organization.

On the other hand, humor may play a different role than
that of only providing a meaningful context. Because it provides
an unusual and unexpected interpretation, humor may make a
stimulus more distinctive in memory. The distinctiveness of a
stimulus is defined as the number of novel attributes that it
can be assigned (Schmidt, 1985). Research has shown that greater
distinctiveness does improve retrieval (Hunt & Elliott, 1980).
Desrochers and Begg (1987) and Einstein, McDaniel, and Lackey
(1989) suggest that distinctiveness is created by unique cues
that are associated with the particular context in which the
stimulus was encountered. Therefore, distinctiveness enhances
access to the overall memory trace for a stimulus. From this
perspective, a humorous context should facilitate recall of a
stimulus to a greater extent than a nonhumorous context,
because, in addition to organizing the components of a stimulus
through its meaning, humor provides additional retrieval cues
that make the memory trace for the stimulus more distinctive and
thus more accessible.

In this study, I tested the above proposals by determining

Effect of Humorous   5

whether droodles accompanied by humorous interpretations are
better retained than when they are accompanied by nonhumorous
interpretations. For each of the humorous interpretations of
Bower et al. (1975), I produced a non-humorous version that
would provide an equally meaningful interpretation of the
droodle. If humor adds retrieval cues over and above those
produced by meaningful processing, then droodles accompanied by
humorous interpretations should be more frequently recalled
than those accompanied by nonhumorous interpretations.

Method

Participants

Forty female and 40 male undergraduate students from an
introductory psychology course at Podunk University each
received $3.00 for their voluntary participation. All were
between 20 and 22 years of age (mean age = 20.7 years), were
born in the United States, were raised in English speaking
families, and had normal or corrected eyesight and hearing.
Participants were randomly assigned to either the humorous or
nonhumorous condition, with 20 males and 20 females in each
condition.

Materials

The 28 droodles from Bower et al. (1975) were reproduced,
each consisting of a black-ink line drawing involving two
interconnected geometric shapes. Droodles were copied to film
slides for presentation by a standard Kodak carousel projector
(model 28-b).

For each humorous interpretation in Bower et al. (1975), a non-humorous version was created. Each interpretation consisted of a 10 to 14 word sentence, beginning with the phrase "This shows a. . . ." A humorous interpretation referred to an unusual action by unexpected people or animals using incongruent objects. A nonhumorous interpretation was derived by changing the humorous interpretation so that it described common actions by predictable actors using congruent objects. The meaning of each droodle was altered as little as possible, with only the humorous components being replaced with comparable, nonhumorous components. For example, one droodle consisted of a rectangle with a loop attached to the lower right side. The humorous interpretation was "This shows a midget playing a trombone in a telephone booth." The nonhumorous interpretation was "This shows a telephone booth with a repairman inside fixing the broken door handle."

Response forms for recalling the droodles consisted of a grid of 3 by 3 in. (7.62 cm by 7.62 cm) squares printed on standard sheets of paper.

Procedure

Participants were tested individually and viewed all 28 droodles accompanied by either the humorous or nonhumorous interpretations. Participants were instructed to study each droodle during its presentation for later recall and were told that the accompanying interpretation would be helpful in remembering it. A timer in the slide projector presented each slide containing a droodle for 10 s, with approximately 2 s between slides. As each slide was presented, I recited the appropriate interpretation. The recall task began immediately after the final droodle was presented. Participants were instructed to recall the droodles in any order, sketching each droodle within one grid on the response sheet.

Results

Two assistants who were unaware of the purposes of the study scored the participants' sketches. A sketch was considered to indicate correct recall if both scorers agreed that it depicted a droodle. (On only 2% of the responses did the scorers disagree.) Each participant's score was then the total number of correctly recalled droodles.

The mean number of droodles correctly recalled was 20.50 in the humorous interpretation condition ($\underline{SD}$ = 3.25) and 15.20 in the nonhumorous interpretation condition ($\underline{SD}$ = 4.19). With an alpha level of .05, a one-tailed independent samples $\underline{t}$-test indicated a significant difference between the conditions, $\underline{t}(78) = 6.32$, $\underline{p} < .05$. The relationship between amount of humor and recall scores can be seen in Figure 1. Although a positive relationship was obtained, the slope of this curve indicates that the rate of change in recall scores as a function of increased humor was not large.

Discussion

The results of the present study indicate that humorous interpretations lead to greater retention of droodles than do nonhumorous interpretations. Because the meaningfulness of the droodles provided by the interpretations was presumably constant in both conditions, it appears that humor provides an additional source of retrieval cues. This conclusion is consistent with the proposal that humor increases the distinctiveness of a stimulus, thereby facilitating recall by increasing the accessibility of the stimulus in memory.

The improvement in recall produced by humor, however, was relatively small. This result may be due to the fact that all droodles were made meaningful, although sometimes by a nonhumorous interpretation. As in other research (Lockhart & Craik, 1990), the meaningful processing produced by a nonhumorous interpretation may have provided relatively effective retrieval cues. Then the additional retrieval cues produced by the distinctiveness of a humorous interpretation would only moderately improve the retrievability of the droodles. In addition, these results may have occurred because a nonhumorous interpretation given to such a simple visual stimulus produced a reasonably distinctive trace. Additional unique cues provided by a humorous interpretation would then only moderately increase a droodle's distinctiveness, resulting in only a moderate improvement in recall.

It is possible, of course, that humor added to the meaningfulness of a droodle, instead of to its distinctiveness. Desrochers and Begg (1987) suggested that increased meaningfulness results in increased organization of a stimulus

in memory. Humor may have added to the meaningfulness of a
droodle by providing additional ways to organize it, so that its
components were better retrieved. Further research is needed to
determine whether humor produces a more distinctive or a more
meaningful stimulus, especially when the stimulus is more
complex than a simple droodle.

Effect of Humorous   10

References

Bower, G. H., Karlin, M. B., & Dueck, A. (1975). Comprehension and memory for pictures. Memory and Cognition, 3, 216-220.

Desrochers, A., & Begg, I. (1987). A theoretical account of encoding and retrieval processes in the use of imagery-based mnemonic techniques: The special case of the keyword method. In M. A. McDaniel & M. Pressley (Eds.), Imagery and related mnemonic processes: Theories, individual differences, and applications (pp. 56-77). New York: Springer-Verlag.

Einstein, G. O., McDaniel, M. A., & Lackey, S. (1989). Bizarre imagery, interference, and distinctiveness. Journal of Experimental Psychology: Learning, Memory, and Cognition, 15, 137-146.

Hunt, R. R., & Elliott, J. M. (1980). The role of nonsemantic information in memory: Orthographic distinctiveness effects on retention. Journal of Experimental Psychology: General, 109, 49-74.

Lockhart, R. S., & Craik, F. I. M. (1990). Levels of processing: A retrospective commentary on framework for memory research. Canadian Journal of Psychology, 44, 87-112.

Schmidt, S. R. (1985). Encoding and retrieval processes in the memory for conceptually distinctive events. Journal of Experimental Psychology: Learning, Memory, and Cognition, 11, 565-578.

Figure Caption

<u>Figure 1</u>. Mean number of droodles correctly recalled as a function of nonhumorous and humorous interpretations.

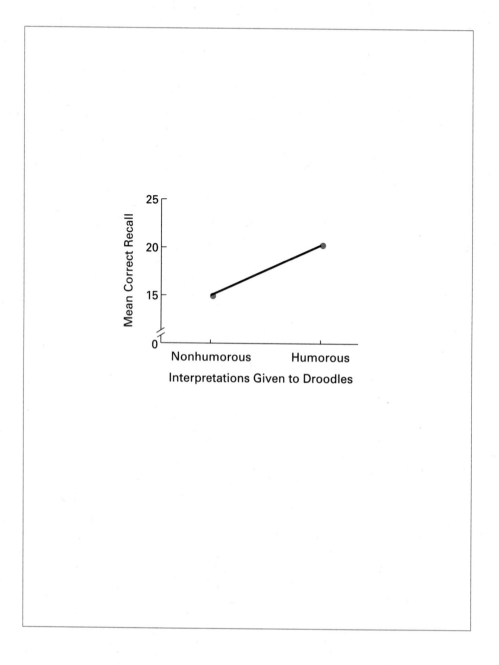

GLOSSARY

Alternative hypothesis   The statistical hypothesis describing the population parameters that the sample data represent if the predicted relationship does exist

Analysis of variance   The parametric procedure for determining whether significant differences exist in an experiment involving two or more sample means

ANOVA   See *Analysis of variance*

Archival research   Research for which written records constitute the source of data on one or more variables

Bar graph   A graph in which a free-standing vertical bar is centered over each score on the X axis; used when the independent variable implies discrete categories that follow no set order

Baseline   The level of performance on the dependent variable when the independent variable is not present, used as a comparison to the level of performance when the independent variable is present

Between-subjects design   A research design in which subjects are randomly assigned to each condition without regard to the subjects in other conditions, and each subject serves in only one condition

Carry-over effects   The influence that a subject's experience of a trial has on his or her performance of subsequent trials

Case study   An in-depth description of one subject, organization, or event

Causal hypothesis   A hypothesis that tentatively explains a particular influence on, or cause of, a behavior

Ceiling effects   A restriction of range problem that occurs when a task is too easy, causing most or all scores to approximate the highest possible score

Chi square procedure   The nonparametric inferential procedure for testing whether the frequencies of category membership in the sample represent the predicted frequencies in the population; used with nominal data

Closed-end question   In a questionnaire or interview, a question accompanied by several alternative answers from which the subject must select

Cluster sampling   A sampling technique in which certain groups are randomly selected and all subjects in each group are observed

Cohort design   A factorial design consisting of a longitudinal study of several groups, each from a different generation

471

Cohort effects   A situation that occurs when age differences are confounded by differences in subject history

Complete factorial design   A research design in which all levels of one factor are combined with all levels of the other factor

Conceptual replication   The repeated test or confirmation of a hypothesis using a design different from that of the original study

Concurrent validity   The extent to which a procedure correlates with the present behavior of subjects

Confederates   People enlisted by a researcher to act as other subjects or "accidental" passers-by, thus creating a social situation to which "real" subjects can then respond

Confidence interval   A statistically defined range of values of the population parameter, any one of which the sample statistic is likely to represent

Confounded variables   See *Confounding*

Confounding   A situation that occurs when an extraneous variable systematically changes along with the variable we hypothesize is a causal variable

Construct validity   The extent to which a measurement reflects the hypothetical construct of interest

Content analysis   A scoring procedure for open-end questions in which the researcher counts specific words or themes in a subject's responses

Content validity   The extent to which a measurement reflects the variable or behavior of interest

Contingency coefficient   The statistic that describes the strength of the relationship in a two-way chi square when there are more than two categories for either variable; symbolized as C

Control   The elimination of unintended, extraneous factors that might influence the behavior being studied

Control group   A group of subjects who are measured on the dependent variable but receive zero amount of the independent variable (i.e., do not experience the treatment), thus providing a baseline for determining the effect of the latter on the experimental group

Convenience sampling   A sampling approach in which the researcher studies the subjects who are conveniently available

Convergent validity   The extent to which the scores obtained from one procedure are positively correlated with the scores obtained from another procedure that is already accepted as valid

Converging operations   Two or more procedures that together eliminate rival hypotheses and bolster our conclusions about a particular behavior

Correlational design A research design in which we measure subjects' scores on two or more variables to determine whether the scores form the predicted relationship

Correlation coefficient See *Pearson correlation coefficient; Point-biserial correlation coefficient; Spearman correlation coefficient*

Counterbalancing The process of systematically changing the order of trials for different subjects in a balanced way, so as to counter the biasing influence of any one order

Criterion validity The extent to which the scores obtained from a procedure correlate with an observable behavior, such that the procedure is capable of distinguishing between subjects on the basis of that behavior

Cross-sectional design A quasi-experimental between-subjects design in which subjects are observed at different ages or at different points in a temporal sequence

Debriefing The procedure by which researchers inform subjects about all aspects of a study after they have participated in it, in order to remove any negative consequences of the procedure

Demand characteristics Cues within the research context that guide or bias a subject's behavior

Dependent samples *t*-test The statistical procedure that is appropriate when the scores meet the requirements of a parametric test, the research design involves matched groups or repeated measures, and there are only two conditions of the independent variable

Dependent variable In an experiment, the variable that is measured under each condition of the independent variable

Descriptive design A research design in which we do not manipulate or change the variables of interest

Descriptive hypothesis A hypothesis that tentatively describes a behavior in terms of its characteristics or the situation in which it occurs

Descriptive methods The research methods used to test descriptive hypotheses

Descriptive statistics Mathematical procedures for summarizing and describing the important characteristics of a sample of data

Design The specific manner in which a research study will be conducted

Diffusion of treatment A threat to internal validity that arises when subjects in one condition are aware of the treatment given in other conditions

Discriminant analysis A procedure by which subjects are categorized along a qualitative Y variable using several quantitative predictor (X) variables

Discriminant validity The extent to which the scores obtained from one procedure are not correlated with the scores obtained from another procedure that measures other variables or constructs

Double-blind procedure   A research procedure in which both the researcher who interacts with the subjects and the subjects themselves are unaware of the treatment being presented

Ecological validity   The extent to which an experimental situation can be generalized to natural settings and behaviors

Effect size   An indication of how dramatically an independent variable influences a dependent variable

Error variance   The variability in Y scores at each X score

Eta squared   The proportion of variance in the dependent variable that is accounted for by changing the levels of a factor, thus describing the measurement of effect size in a sample; symbolized as η^2

Experimental group(s)   Those subjects who receive a nonzero amount of the independent variable (i.e., who experience the treatment) and are then measured on the dependent variable

Experimental methods   The research methods used to test causal hypotheses

Experimental realism   The extent to which the experimental task engages subjects psychologically, such that they become less concerned with demand characteristics

Experimenter expectancies   Subtle cues provided by the experimenter about the responses that subjects should give in a particular condition

***Ex post facto* research**   Research conducted after a phenomenon has occurred

External validity   The extent to which our results generalize to other subjects and other situations

Extraneous variables   Variables that may potentially influence the results of a study but are not the variables of interest (e.g., subject, researcher, environmental, or measurement variables)

Face validity   The extent to which a measurement procedure appears to measure what it is intended to measure

Factor   See *Independent variable*

Factor analysis   A procedure in which intercorrelations between responses to questionnaire or interview questions are used to discover some common underlying factor

Factorial   design. See *Complete factorial design*

Field experiment   An experiment conducted in a natural setting

Field survey   A procedure in which subjects complete a questionnaire or interview in a natural setting

Floor effects A restriction of range problem that occurs when a task is too difficult, causing most or all scores to approximate the lowest possible score

Friedman test The one-way within-subjects ANOVA for ordinal scores, performed when there are more than two levels of one factor

Habituation The process by which subjects are familiarized with a procedure before actual data collection is commenced, in order to reduce reactivity

Hawthorne effect A bias in subjects' behavior–usually an improvement in performance–that results from the special treatment and interest shown by a researcher

Human Subjects Review Committee A committee at colleges and research institutions charged with the responsibility of reviewing all prospective research procedures to ensure the ethical and safe treatment of subjects

Hypothesis A formally stated expectation about a behavior that defines the purpose and goals of a research study

Hypothetical construct An abstract concept used in a particular theoretical manner to relate different behaviors according to their underlying features or causes

Independent samples t-test The statistical procedure that is appropriate when the scores meet the requirements of a parametric test, the research design involves a between-subjects design, and there are only two conditions of the independent variable

Independent variable In an experiment, the variable that is systematically changed or manipulated by the researcher; also called a factor

Individual differences The characteristics that make individuals different from one another and that produce different responses to the same situation

Inferential statistics Mathematical procedures for deciding whether a sample relationship represents a relationship that actually exists in the population

Informed consent The procedure by which researchers inform subjects about a laboratory experiment prior to their participation in it, out of respect for subjects' rights to control what happens to them

Instrumentation effects Changes in measurement procedures that occur through use of equipment over time, making the measurements less reliable

Interaction effect The influence that the combination of levels from the factors has on dependent scores

Internal validity The extent to which the observed relationship reflects the relationship between the variables in a study

Inter-rater reliability The extent to which raters agree on the scores they assign to a subject's behavior

Interrupted time-series design A quasi-experimental repeated-measures design in which observations are made at several spaced times before and then after a treatment

Interval scores   Data on a measurement scale in which each score indicates an actual amount, an equal unit of measurement separates consecutive scores, zero is simply another point on the scale (i.e., not a true zero), and negative scores are possible

Intervening variable   An internal subject characteristic that is influenced by the independent variable and, in turn, influences the dependent variable

Kruskal-Wallis test   The nonparametric version of the one-way between-subjects ANOVA for ranked scores

Linear regression   The procedure for predicting subjects' scores on one variable based on the linear relationship with subjects' scores on another variable

Linear regression equation   The equation that defines the straight line summarizing a linear relationship by describing the value of Y' at each X

Linear regression line   The straight line that summarizes the scatterplot of a linear relationship by, on average, passing through the center of all Y scores

Linear relationship   A relationship between the X and Y scores in a set of data in which the Y scores tend to change in only one direction as the X scores increase, forming a slanted straight regression line on a scatterplot

Line graph   A graph on which adjacent data points are connected with straight lines; used when the independent variable implies a continuous, ordered amount

Literal replication   The precise duplication of the specific design and results of a previous study

Longitudinal design   A quasi-experimental design in which a researcher repeatedly measures a group of subjects in order to observe the effect of the passage of time

Main effect   In a multifactor ANOVA, the influence on the dependent scores of changing the levels of one factor, ignoring all other factors in the study

Mann-Whitney test   The nonparametric version of the independent samples t-test for ranked scores

Margin of error   The confidence interval that is computed when estimating the population's responses to a field survey

Matched-groups design   A research design in which each subject in one condition is matched with a subject in every other condition along an extraneous subject variable

Mean   The average of a group of scores, interpreted as the score around which the scores in a distribution tend to be clustered

Measure of central tendency   A score that summarizes the location of a distribution on a variable by indicating where the center of the distribution tends to be located

Measures of variability   Numbers that summarize the extent to which the scores in a distribution differ from one another

Median   The score located at the 50th percentile

Meta-analysis   Statistical procedures for combining, testing, and describing the results from different studies

Mode   The most frequently occurring score in a set of data

Model   A generalized, hypothetical description that, by analogy, explains the process underlying a set of common behaviors

Multifactor experiment   An experiment in which the researcher examines several independent variables and their interactions

Multiple-baseline design   A research design in which a baseline is established for one behavior from several subjects, for several behaviors from one subject, or for one behavior from one subject in several situations

Multiple correlation and regression   Statistical procedures performed when multiple predictor (X) variables are being used to predict one criterion (Y) variable

Multiple time-series design   A quasi-experimental repeated-measures design in which an experimental group and a nonequivalent control group are observed at several spaced times before and then after a treatment

Multivariate statistics   The inferential statistical procedures used when a study involves multiple dependent variables

Naturalistic observation   The unobtrusive observation of a wide variety of subjects' behaviors in an unstructured fashion

Negative linear relationship   A linear relationship in which the Y scores tend to decrease as the X scores increase

Nominal scores   Data that do not indicate actual amounts but, rather, identify particular qualities or categories

Nonequivalent control group   In a quasi-experiment, a control group whose subject characteristics and experiences are different from those of the experimental group

Nonexperimental methods   See *Descriptive methods*

Nonlinear relationship   A relationship between the X and Y scores in a set of data in which the Y scores change their direction of change as the X scores change

Nonparametric statistics   Inferential procedures employed to analyze interval or ratio scores that are not normally distributed, or to analyze nominal or ordinal scores

Nonprobability sampling   Collectively, the sampling techniques in which every potential subject in the population does not have an equal likelihood of being selected for participation in a study

Normal distribution   A frequency distribution for a set of data, usually represented by a bell-shaped curve that is symmetrical about the mean

Null hypothesis   The statistical hypothesis describing the population parameters that the sample data represent if the predicted relationship does not exist

One-group pretest-posttest design   A quasi-experimental pretest-posttest design for which there is no control group

One-way design   A research design involving the manipulation of just one independent variable

Open-end question   In a questionnaire or interview, a question for which the subject determines both the alternatives to choose from and the response

Operational definition   The definition of a construct or variable in terms of the operations used to measure it

Order effects   The influence on a particular trial that arises from its position in a sequence of trials

Parameters   Numbers that describe the characteristics of a population of scores

Parametric statistics   Inferential procedures employed to analyze normally distributed interval or ratio scores

Partial correlation   A procedure in which the correlation between two variables is determined while keeping the influence of other variables constant

Participant observation   The unobtrusive observation of a group in which the researcher is an active member

Pearson correlation coefficient   The correlation coefficient that describes the strength and type of a linear relationship; symbolized as r

Phi coefficient   The statistic that describes the strength of the relationship in a two-way chi square when there are only two categories for each variable; symbolized as Φ

Placebo   An inactive substance that provides the demand characteristics of a manipulation while presenting zero amount of the independent variable, thus serving as a control in an experiment

Planned comparisons   In ANOVA, statistical procedures for comparing only some conditions in an experiment

Point-biserial correlation coefficient   A statistic that describes the strength of the relationship between two conditions of the independent variable and an interval or ratio dependent variable; symbolized as r_{pb}

Population   The infinitely large group of all possible individuals of interest in a specific, defined situation

Population parameters   See *Parameters*

Positive linear relationship   A linear relationship in which the Y scores tend to increase as the X scores increase

Post hoc **comparisons**   In ANOVA, statistical procedures for comparing all possible pairs of conditions, to determine which ones differ significantly from each other

Power   The probability that a statistical test will detect a true relationship and allow the rejection of a false null hypothesis

Practice effects   The influence on performance that arises from practicing a task

Prediction   A specific statement as to how we will see a behavior manifested in a research situation, describing the specific results that we expect will be found

Predictive validity   The extent to which a procedure allows for accurate predictions about a subject's future behavior

Pretest-posttest design   A research design in which subjects are measured before and after a treatment

Probability sampling   Collectively, the sampling techniques in which every potential subject in the population has an equal likelihood of being selected for participation in a study

Program evaluation   The procedures undertaken to evaluate the goals, activities, and outcomes of social programs

Projective test   A psychological test in which subjects are asked to create a description or interpretation of an ambiguous stimulus, onto which they project their hidden feelings or attributes

Proportion of variance accounted for   The proportion of the error in predicting scores that is eliminated when, instead of using the mean of Y, we use the relationship with the X variable to predict Y scores; the proportional improvement in predicting Y scores thus achieved

Pseudo-explanation   A circular statement that explains an event simply by renaming it

Psychological Abstracts   A monthly publication that describes studies recently published in psychology journals

Publication Manual of the American Psychological Association   The definitive reference source for answering any question regarding the organization, content, and style of a research manuscript

Quasi-experiment   A study in which subjects cannot be randomly assigned to any condition but, instead, are assigned to a particular condition on the basis of some inherent characteristic

Quasi-independent variable   The independent variable in a quasi-experiment

Quota sampling   A sampling technique in which, using convenience sampling, the sample has the same percentage of each subgroup as that found in the population

Random assignment   A method of selecting a sample for an experiment such that the condition each subject experiences is determined in a random and unbiased manner

Randomization   The creation of different random orders of trials under which different subjects are tested

Random sampling   See *Simple random sampling; Systematic random sampling*

Range   The difference between the highest and lowest scores in a set of data

Ratio scores   Data on a measurement scale in which each score indicates an actual amount, an equal unit of measurement separates consecutive scores, zero truly means zero amount, and negative scores are not possible

Reactivity   The bias in responses that occurs when subjects know they are being observed

Regression toward the mean   A change in extreme scores toward less extreme scores that occurs because random influences are not consistently present

Relationship   A pattern in which a change in one variable is accompanied by a consistent change in the other

Reliability   The extent to which a measurement is consistent, can be reproduced, and avoids error

Repeated-measures design   A research design in which each subject is measured under all conditions of an independent variable

Replication   The process of repeatedly conducting studies that test and confirm a hypothesis so that confidence in its truth can be developed

Representative sample   A sample whose characteristics and behaviors accurately reflect those of the population from which it is drawn

Response scale   The number and type of choices provided for each question in a questionnaire or interview

Response set   A bias toward responding in a particular way because of previous responses made

Restriction of range   Improper limitation of the range of scores obtained on one or both variables, leading to an underestimation of the strength of the relationship between the variables

Reversal design   A research design in which the researcher alternates between the baseline condition and the treatment condition

Sample   A relatively small subset of a population that is selected to represent or stand in for the population

Sample standard deviation   The square root of the sample variance

Sample variance   The average of the squared deviations of the scores around the mean

Scientific method The totality of assumptions, attitudes, goals, and procedures for creating and answering questions about nature in a scientific manner

Simple main effect The effect of one factor at one level of a second factor

Simple random sampling A sampling technique in which subjects are randomly selected from a list of the members of the population

Single-blind procedure A research procedure in which subjects are unaware of the treatment they are receiving

Single-subject design A repeated-measures experiment conducted on one subject

Snowball sampling A sampling technique in which the researcher contacts potential subjects who have been identified by previously tested subjects

Social desirability The demand characteristic that causes subjects to provide what they consider to be the socially acceptable response

Social Science Citation Index A reference source that identifies a given research article by authors and date, and then lists subsequent articles that have cited it

Spearman correlation coefficient The correlation coefficient that describes the linear relationship between pairs of ranked scores; symbolized as r_s

Split-half reliability The consistency with which subjects' scores on some trials match their scores on other trials

Squared correlation coefficient The proportion of total variance in Y scores that is systematically associated with changing X scores; symbolized as r^2

Standard deviation See *Sample standard deviation*

Standard error of the estimate A standard deviation indicating the amount that the actual Y scores in a sample differ from, or are spread out around, their corresponding Y' scores; symbolized as $S_{Y'}$

State characteristic A temporary, changeable attribute that is influenced by situational factors

Stratified random sampling A sampling technique involving the identification of important subgroups in the population, followed by the proportionate random selection of subjects from each subgroup

Strong manipulation Manipulation of the independent variable in such a way that subjects' behavior is greatly differentiated, thus producing large differences in dependent scores between the conditions

Structured interview An interview in which subjects are asked a specific set of predetermined questions in a controlled manner

Subject mortality effects The biasing effects that arise when volunteer subjects fail to show up for a study or discontinue their participation before the study is completed

Subject sophistication   The bias in our results that arises when subjects are knowledgeable about research, such that their responses are not generalizable to the population

Subject variables   Inherent, personal characteristics that distinguish one subject from another

Systematic naturalistic observation   The unobtrusive observation of a particular behavior or situation in a structured fashion

Systematic random sampling   A sampling technique in which every nth subject is selected from a list of the members of the population

Systematic variance   The differences in Y scores that occur with, or are associated with, changes in the X variable

Temporal validity   The extent to which our experimental results can be generalized to other time frames

Test-retest reliability   The consistency with which subjects obtain the same overall score when tested at different times

Theory   A logically organized set of proposals that defines, explains, organizes, and interrelates our knowledge about many behaviors

Three-way design   A research design involving three main effects, three two-way interactions, and one three-way interaction

Three-way interaction   The interaction of three factors such that the two-way interaction between two factors changes as the levels of the third factor change

Time-series design   A quasi-experimental repeated-measures design in which subjects' behavior is sampled before and then after the occurrence of an event

Trait characteristic   An attribute that is stable over time and not easily influenced by situational factors

Trial   A single complete instance of testing in an experimental series

True experiment   A study in which the researcher actively changes or manipulates a variable that subjects are exposed to by the researcher

***t*-test**   See *Dependent samples t-test; Independent samples t-test*

Two-way between-subjects design   A research design in which a different group of subjects is tested under each condition of two independent variables

Two-way chi square procedure   The chi square procedure performed in testing whether, in the population, frequency of category membership on one variable is independent of frequency of category membership on the other variable

Two-way design   A research design involving the manipulation of two independent variables

Two-way interaction   The interaction of two factors such that the relationship between one factor and the dependent scores is different for and depends on each level of the other factor

Two-way mixed design   A research design involving one within-subjects factor and one between-subjects factor

Two-way within-subjects design   A research design in which matched groups or the same repeatedly measured subjects are tested in all conditions of two independent variables

Type I error   A statistical decision-making error in which the null hypothesis is rejected even though it is true

Type II error   A statistical decision-making error in which the null hypothesis is retained even though it is false

Unconfounded comparisons   Comparisons of cell means that differ along only one factor

Unobtrusive measures   Procedures by which subjects' behavior is measured without their being aware that measurements are being made

Unstructured interview   An interview in which the questions are not rigidly predetermined, thus allowing for substantial discussion and interaction between subject and interviewer

Validity   The extent to which a procedure measures what it is intended to measure

Variable   Any measurable aspect of a behavior or influence on behavior that may change

Variance   See *Sample variance; Error variance; systematic variance*

Volunteer bias   The bias that arises from the fact that a given sample contains only those subjects who are willing to participate in the study

Wilcoxon test   The nonparametric version of the dependent samples *t*-test for ranked scores

Within-subjects design   A research design in which the same subjects are repeatedly measured in different conditions, or each subject in one condition is matched with each subject in another condition

Y prime   The value of Y that falls on the regression line above any *X*; symbolized as Y'

REFERENCES

Able, K. P., & Able, M. A. (1990). Ontogeny of migratory orientation in the savannah sparrow, *Passerculus sandwhichenis:* Calibration of the magnetic compass. *Animal Behavior, 39,* 905–913.

Adair, J. G. (1973). *The human subject: The social psychology of the psychological experiment.* Boston: Little, Brown.

Albas, D. C., & Albas, C. A. (1989). Meaning in context: The impact of eye contact and perception of threat on proximity. *The Journal of Social Psychology, 129,* 525–531.

Allen, J. B., Kendrick, D. T., Linder, D. E., and McCall, M. A. (1989). Arousal and attraction: A response-facilitation alternative to misattribution and negative-reinforcement models. *Journal of Personality and Social Psychology*, 57, 261–270.

American Psychological Association. (1983). *Publication manual of the American Psychological Association* (3rd ed.). Washington, DC: Author.

American Psychological Association. (1992). Ethical principles of psychologists and code of conduct. *American Psychologist, 47,* 1597–1611.

Anderson, C. A., & Anderson, D. C. (1984). Ambient temperature and violent crime: Tests of the linear and curvilinear hypotheses. *Journal of Personality and Social Psychology, 46,* 91–97.

Anderson, P. (1983). Decision making by objection and the Cuban missile crisis. *Administrative Science Quarterly, 28,* 201–222.

Asch, S. E. (1951). Effects of group pressure upon the modification and distortion of judgement. In H. Guetzknow (Ed.), *Groups, leadership, & men.* Pittsburgh: Carnegie.

Atkinson, J. W., & Litwin, G. H. (1960). Achievement motive and test anxiety conceived as a motive to approach success and to avoid failure. *Journal of Abnormal and Social Psychology, 60,* 52–63.

Atkinson, R. C., & Shiffrin, R. (1968). Human memory: A proposed system and its control processes. In K. Spence & J. Spence (Eds.), *The psychology of learning and motivation* (Vol. 2). New York: Academic Press.

Bandura, A., Ross, D., & Ross, S. A. (1961). Transmission of aggression through imitation of aggressive models. *Journal of Abnormal and Social Psychology, 63,* 575–582.

Barefoot, J. C., Hoople, H., & McClay, D. (1972). Avoidance of an act which would violate personal space. *Psychonomic Science, 28,* 205–206.

Barlow, D. H., & Hernsen, M. (1984). *Single case experimental designs: Strategies for studying behavior change* (2nd ed.). New York: Pergamon Press.

Baumeister, R. F. (1984). Choking under pressure: Self-consciousness and paradoxical effects of incentives on skillful performance. *Journal of Personality and Social Psychology*, 46, 610–620.

Bell, P. A. (1980). Effects of heat, noise, and provocation on retaliatory evaluative behavior. *Journal of Social Psychology, 110,* 97–100.

Bell, P. A., & Baron, R. A. (1976). Aggression and heat: The mediating role of negative affect. *Journal of Applied Social Psychology, 6,* 18–30.

Bergin, A. (1966). Some implications of psychotherapy research for therapeutic practice. *Journal of Abnormal Psychology, 71,* 235–246.

Berkowitz, L. (1987). Mood, Self-awareness, and willingness to help. *Journal of Personality and Social Psychology, 52,* 721–729.

Blakemore, J. E., LaRue, A. A., & Olejnik, A. B. (1979). Sex-appropriate toy preference and the ability to conceptualize toys as sex-role related. *Developmental Psychology, 15,* 339–340.

Block, R. A. (1978). Remembered duration: Effect of event and sequence complexity. *Memory and Cognition, 6,* 320–376.

Boesch–Acherman, H., & Boesch, C. (1993). Tool use in wild chimpanzees: New light from dark forests. *Current Directions in Psychological Science, 2,* 18–21.

Bower, G. H. (1981). Mood and memory. *American Psychologist, 36*(2), 129–148.

Bower, G. H., Karlin, M. B., & Dueck, A. (1975). Comprehension and memory for pictures. *Memory and Cognition, 3*(2), 216–220.

Bower, G. H., & Hilgard, E. R. (1981). *Theories of learning.* Englewood Cliffs, NJ: Prentice Hall.

Brandsford, J. D., and Johnson, J. (1972). Contextual prerequisites for understanding: Some investigations of comprehension and recall. *Journal of Verbal Learning and Verbal Behavior,* 11, 717–726.

Brandsford, J. D., & Franks, J. J. (1971). The abstraction of linguistic ideas: A review. *Cognitive Psychology, 2,* 331–350.

Brennen, T., Bagley, T., Bright, J., & Bruce, V. (1990). Resolving semantically induced tip-of-the-tongue states for proper nouns. *Memory and Cognition, 18,* 339–347.

Brown, S. W. (1985). Time perception and attention: The effect of prospective versus retrospective paradigms and task demands on perceived duration. *Perception and Psychophysics, 38,* 115–124.

Burk, D. M., Mackay, D. G., Worthley, J. S., & Wade, E. (1991). On the tip of the tongue: What causes word finding failures in young and older adults. *Journal of Memory and Language, 30,* 542–579.

Burke, B. F., Chrisler, J. C., & Devlin, A. S. (1989). The creative thinking, environmental frustration, and self-concept of left- and right-handers. *Creativity Research Journal, 2*(4), 279–285.

Cahoon, D., and Edmonds, E. M. (1980). The watched pot still won't boil: Expectancy as a variable in estimating the passage of time. *Bulletin of the Psychonomic Society, 16,* 115–116.

Campbell, D. E., & Herren, K. A. (1978). Interior arrangement of the faculty office. *Psychological Reports, 43,* 234.

Campbell, D. T. (1969). Reforms as experiments. *American Psychologist, 24,* 409–429.

Campbell, D. T., & Stanley, J. C. (1963). *Experimental and quasi-experimental designs for research.* Boston: Houghton Mifflin.

Cann, D. R., & Donderi, D. C. (1986). Jungian personality typology and the recall of everyday and archetypal dreams. *Journal of Personality and Social Psychology, 50,* 1021–1030.

Carlson, M., Marcus-Newhall, A., and Miller, N. (1990). Effects of situational aggression cues: A quantitative review. *Journal of Personality and Social Psychology, 58,* 622–633.

Cattell, R. (1965). *The scientific analysis of personality.* Baltimore: Penguin Books.

Cherry, F., and Deaux, K. (1978). Fear of success versus fear of gender-inappropriate behavior. *Sex Roles, 4,* 97–100.

Christensen, L. (1988). Deception in psychological research: When is it justified? *Personality and Social Psychology Bulletin, 14,* 664–675.

Cicchetti, D. V. (1972). Extension of multiple range tests to interaction tables in the analysis of variance. *Psychological Bulletin, 77,* 405–408.

Cohen, B., Waugh, G., and Place, K. (1989). At the movies: An unobtrusive study of arousal-attraction. *The Journal of Social Psychology, 129,* 691–693.

Cohen, J. (1988). *Statistical power analysis for the behavioral sciences.* Hillsdale, NJ: Lawrence Erlbaum Associates.

Conlon, D. E. (1993). Some tests of the self-interest and group-value models of procedural justice: Evidence from an organizational appeal procedure. *Academy of Management Journal, 36,* 1109–1124.

Connors, J. G., & Alpher, V. S. (1989). Alcohol themes within country-western songs. *International Journal of the Addictions, 24,* 445–451.

Cook, T. D., & Campbell, D. T. (1979). *Quasi-experimentation: Design and analysis issues for field settings.* Chicago: Rand McNally.

Council, J. R. (1993). Context effects in personality research. *Current Directions in Psychological Science, 2*(2), 31–34.

Craik, F. I. M., and Tulving, E. (1975). Depth of processing and the retention of words in episodic memory. *Journal of Experimental Psychology, 104,* 268–294.

Craik, F. I. M., & Lockhart, R. S. (1972). Levels of processing: A framework for memory research. *Journal of Verbal Learning and Verbal Behavior, 11,* 671–684.

Crowder, R. G. (1982). A common basis for auditory sensory storage in perception and immediate memory. *Perception & Psychophysics, 31,* 477–483.

Crusco, A. H., & Wetzel, C. G. (1984). The Midas touch: The effect of interpersonal touch on restaurant tipping. *Personality and Social Psychology Bulletin, 10,* 512–517.

Cunningham, M. R. (1989). Reactions to heterosexual opening gambits: Female selectivity and male responsiveness. *Personality and Social Psychology Bulletin, 15,* 27–41.

Cunningham, M. R., Shaffer, D. R., Barbee, A. P., Wolf, P. L., & Kelley, D. J. (1990). Separate processes in the relation of elation and depression to helping: Social versus personal concerns. *Journal of Experimental Social Psychology, 26,* 13–33.

Cunningham, M. R., Shaffer, D. R., Barbee, A. P., Wolff, P. L., & Kelley, D. J. (1990). Separate processes in the relation of elation and depression to helping: Social versus personal concerns. *Journal of Abnormal and Social Psychology, 26,* 13–33.

Darley, J. M., & Latané, B. (1968). Bystander intervention in emergencies: Diffusion of responsibility. *Journal of Personality and Social Psychology, 8,* 377–383.

Desrochers, A., & Begg, I. (1987). A theoretical account of encoding and retrieval processes in the use of imagery-based mnemonic techniques: The special case of the keyword method. In M. A. McDaniel & M. Pressley (Eds.), *Imagery and related mnemonic processes: Theories, individual differences, and applications* (pp. 56–77). New York: Springer Verlag.

Deutsch, M., & Krauss, R. M. (1960). The effects of threat on interpersonal bargaining. *Journal of Abnormal and Social Psychology, 61,* 181–189.

Dixon, P. N., Willingham, W., Strano, D. A., & Chandler, C. K. (1989). Sense of humor as a mediator during incidental learning of humor-related material. *Psychological Reports, 64,* 851–855.

Dorfman, D. D. (1978). The Cyril Burt question: New findings. *Science, 201,* 1177–1186.

Driscall, R., Davis, K., and Lipetz, J. (1972). Parental interference and romantic love: The Romeo and Juliet effect. *Journal of Personality and Social Psychology, 25,* 1–10.

Duclos, S. E., Laird, J. D., Schneider, E., Sexter, M., Stern, L., & Van Lighten, O. (1989). Emotion-specific effects of facial expressions and postures on emotional experience. *Journal of Personality and Social Psychology, 57,* 100–108.

Dutton, D. G., and Aron, A. P. (1974). Some evidence for heightened sexual attraction under conditions of high anxiety. *Journal of Personality and Social Psychology, 30,* 510–517

Eagly, A. H., Ashmore, R. D., MaKijani, M. G., & Longo, L. C. (1991). What is beautiful is good but ...: A meta-analytic review of research on the physical attractiveness stereotype. *Psychological Bulletin, 110,* 109–128.

Ebert, P. D., & Hyde, J. S. (1976). Selection of agonistic behavior in wild female *Mus musculus*. *Behavior Genetics, 6,* 291–304.

Einstein, G. O., McDaniel, M. A., & Lackey, S. (1989). Bizarre imagery, interference, and distinctiveness. *Journal of Experimental Psychology: Learning, Memory, and Cognition, 15,* 137–146.

Ekman, P., & O'Sullivan, M. (1991). Who can catch a liar? *American Psychologist, 46,* 913–920.

Ellsworth, P. C., Carlsmith, J. M., & Henson, A. (1972). The stare as stimulus to flight in human subjects: A series of field experiments. *Journal of Personality and Social Psychology, 21,* 302–311.

Erdley, C. A., & D'Agostino, P. R. (1988). Cognitive and affective components of automatic priming effects. *Journal of Personality and Social Psychology, 54,* 741–747.

Ericsson, K. A., & Polson, P. G. (1988). An experimental analysis of the mechanisms of a memory skill. *Journal of Experimental Psychology: Learning, Memory, and Cognition, 74,* 476–484.

Exner, J. E. (1974). *The Rorschach: A comprehensive system* (Vol. 1). New York: Wiley.

Eysenck, H. J. (1952). The effects of psychotherapy: An evaluation. *Journal of Consulting Psychology, 16,* 319–324.

Faustman, W., & White, P. (1989). Diagnostic and psychopharmacological treatment characteristics of 536 inpatients with posttraumatic stress disorder. *The Journal of Nervous and Mental Disease, 177,* 154–159.

Felipe, N. J., and Sommer, R. (1966). Invasions of personal space. *Social Problems, 14,* 206–214.

Firth, H., & Britton, P. (1989). "Burnout," absence and turnover amongst British nursing staff. *Journal of Occupational Psychology, 62,* 55–59.

Fisher, J. L., & Harris, M. B. (1973). Effect of note taking and review on recall. *Journal of Educational Psychology, 65,* 321–325.

Flowers, J. H., Warner, J. L., & Polansky, M. L. (1979). Response and encoding factors in "ignoring" irrelevant information. *Memory and Cognition, 7,* 86–94.

Fornell, C. (1992). A national customer satisfaction barometer: The Swedish experience. *Journal of Marketing, 56,* 6–21.

Forsythe, S. M. (1990). Effect of applicant's clothing on interviewer's decision to hire. *Journal of Applied Social Psychology, 20,* 1579–1595.

Frank, M. G., & Gilovich, T. (1988). The dark side of self- and social perception: Black uniforms and aggression in professional sports. *Journal of Personality and Social Psychology, 54,* 74–85.

Fridell, L. (1989). Justifiable use of measures in research on deadly force. *Journal of Criminal Justice, 17,* 157–165.

Fromkin, V. A. (1980). *Errors in linguistic performance.* New York: Academic Press.

Gallup, G. G., Jr., & Suarez, S. D. (1985). Alternatives to the use of animals in psychological research. *American Psychologist, 40,* 1104–1111.

Gathercole, S. E., Willis, C. S., Emslie, H., & Baddeley, A. D. (1992). Phonological memory and vocabulary development during the early school years: A longitudinal study. *Developmental Psychology, 28,* 887–898.

Gazzaniga, M. S. (1983). Right-hemisphere language following brain bisection. *American Psychologist, 38,* 525–537.

Gazzaniga, M. S. (1985). *The social brain: Discovering the networks of the mind.* New York: Basic Books.

George, J. M., Reed, T. F., Ballard, K. A., Colin, J., & Fielding, J. (1993). Contact with AIDS patients as a source of work-related distress: Effects of organizational and social support. *Academy of Management Journal, 36,* 157–171.

Gisner, R., & Schusterman, R. J. (1992). Sequence, syntax, and semantics: Responses of a language-trained sea lion (*Zalophus californianus*) to novel sign combinations. *Journal of Comparative Psychology, 106,* 78–91.

Gladue, B. A., & Delaney, H. J. (1990). Gender differences in perception of attractiveness of men and women in bars. *Personality and Social Psychology Bulletin, 16,* 378–391.

Glick, P., Gottesman, D., and Jolton, J. (1989). The fault is not in the stars: Susceptibility of skeptics and believers in astrology to the Barnum effect. *Personality and Social Psychology Bulletin, 15,* 572–583.

Goodall, J. (1986). *The chimpanzees of Gombe: Patterns of behavior.* Cambridge, MA: Belknap Press.

Goodall, J. (1990). *Through a window: My thirty years with the chimpanzees of Gombe.* Boston: Houghton Mifflin.

Gray, J. A., & Wedderburn, A. A. I. (1960). Grouping strategies with simultaneous stimuli. *Quarterly Journal of Experimental Psychology, 12,* 180–184.

Green, R. G. (1978). Some effects of observing violence upon the behavior of the observer. In B. A. Maher (Ed.), *Progress in experimental personality research* (Vol. 8). New York: Academic Press.

Greenspoon, J. (1955). The reinforcing effect of two spoken sounds on the frequency of two responses. *American Journal of Psychology, 68,* 409–416.

Hamid, P. N., and Newport, A. G. (1989). Effect of colour on physical strength and mood in children. *Perceptual and Motor Skills, 69,* 179–185.

Haney, C., Banks, W. C., & Zimbardo, P. G. (1973). Interpersonal dynamics in a simulated prison. *International Journal of Criminology and Penology, 1,* 69–97.

Hanssel, C. E. M. (1980). *ESP and parapsychology: A critical reevaluation.* Buffalo, NY: Prometheus Books.

Harlow, H. F., & Harlow, M. K. (1962). Social deprivation in monkeys. *Scientific American, 207,* 136–146.

Harris, S., & Sutton, R. (1986). Functions of parting ceremonies in dying organizations. *Academy of Management Journal, 29,* 5–30.

Harrison, L., & Gfroerer, J. (1992). The intersection of drug use and criminal behavior: Results from the national household survey on drug abuse. *Crime and Delinquency, 38,* 422–443.

Harry, J. (1990). A probability sample of gay males. *Journal of Homosexuality, 19,* 89–104.

Hayduk, L. A. (1983). Personal space: Where we now stand. *Psychological Bulletin, 94,* 293–335.

Hearnshaw, L. S. (1979). *Cyril Burt: Psychologist.* London: Hodder & Stoughton.

Heaton, A. W., and Sigall, H. (1991). Self-consciousness, self-presentation, and performance under pressure: Who chokes and when. *Journal of Applied Social Psychology, 21,* 175–188.

Heslin, R., & Boss, D. (1980). Nonverbal intimacy in airport arrival and departure. *Personality and Social Psychology Bulletin, 6,* 248–252.

Hicks, R. E., Miller, G. W., and Kinsbourne, M. (1976). Prospective and retrospective judgements of time as a function of amount of information processed. *American Journal of Psychology, 89,* 719–730.

Hilakivi–Clarke, L. A., & Lister, R. G. (1992). Are there preexisting behavioral characteristics that predict the dominant status of male NIH Swiss mice (*Mus musculus*)? *Journal of Comparative Psychology, 106,* 184–189.

Hillmann, R. B., Brooks, C. I., & O'Brien, J. P. (1991). Differences in self-esteem of college freshman as a function of classroom seating-row preference. *The Psychological Record, 41,* 315–320.

Hinkle, P. E., Wiersma, W., & Jurs, S. G. (1988). *Applied statistics for the behavioral sciences* (2nd ed.). Boston: Houghton Mifflin.

Hockey, G. R. F. (1970). Effect of loud noise on attentional selectivity. *Quarterly Journal of Experimental Psychology, 22,* 28–36.

Holsti, O. (1969). *Content analysis for the social sciences and humanities.* Reading, MA: Addison-Wesley.

Horne, J. A. (1978). A review of the biological effects of total sleep deprivation in man. *Biological Psychology, 7,* 55–102.

Horner, M. S. (1972). Toward an understanding of achievement-related conflicts in women. *Journal of Social Issues, 28,* 157–175.

Hunt, R. R., & Elliott, J. M. (1980). The role of nonsemantic information in memory: Orthographic distinctiveness effects on retention. *Journal of Experimental Psychology: General 109,* 49–74.

Intons–Peterson, M. J. (1983). Imagery paradigms: How vulnerable are they to experimenter's expectations? *Journal of Experimental Psychology: Human Perception and Performance, 9,* 394–412.

Isen, A. M., Daubman, K. A., and Nowicki, G. P. (1987). Positive affect facilitates creative problem solving. *Journal of Personality and Social Psychology, 52,* 1122–1131.

Isen, A. M., Johnson, M. M. S., Metz, E., & Robinson, G. F. (1985). The influence of positive affect on the unusualness of word associations. *Journal of Personality and Social Psychology, 48,* 1–14.

Isen, A. M., & Levin, P. F. (1972). Effect of feeling good on helping: Cookies and kindness. *Journal of Personality and Social Psychology, 21,* 384–388.

Janowsky, J. S., Shimamura, A. P., Kritchevsky, M., & Squire, L. R. (1989). Cognitive impairment following frontal lobe damage and its relevance to human amnesia. *Behavioral Neuroscience, 103,* 548–560.

Jenson, A. R. (1993). Why is reaction time correlated with psychometric *g*? *Current Directions in Psychological Science, 2*(2), 53–56.

Joffee, J. M., Rawson, R. A., & Mulick, J. A. (1973). Control of their environment reduces emotionality in rats. *Science, 180,* 1383–1384.

Kanuk, L., & Berenson, C. (1975). Mail surveys and response rates: A literature review. *Journal of Marketing Research, 12,* 440–453.

Kendrick, D. T., Cialdini, R., and Linder, D. (1979). Misattribution under fear-producing circumstances: Four failures to replicate. *Personality and Social Psychology Bulletin, 5,* 329–334.

Kiesler, C. A. (1993). Mental health policy and mental hospitalization. *Current Directions in Psychological Science, 2,* 93–95.

Klein, G. S. (1964). Semantic power measured through the interference of words with color-naming. *American Journal of Psychology, 77,* 576–588.

Kleinke, C. L., & Singer, D. A. (1979). Influence of gaze on compliance demanding and conciliatory requests in a field setting. *Personality and Social Psychology Bulletin, 5,* 386–390.

Koocher, G. P. (1977). Bathroom behavior and human dignity. *Journal of Personality and Social Psychology, 35,* 120–121.

Kosten, T. R., Silverman, D. G., Fleming, J., and Kosten, T. A., Gawin, F. H., Compton, M., Jatlow, P., and Byck, R. (1992). Intravenous cocaine challenges during naltrexone maintenance: A preliminary study. *Biological Psychiatry, 32,* 543–548.

Kowal, K. H. (1987). Apparent duration and numerosity as a function of melodic familiarity. *Perception and Psychophysics, 42,* 122–131.

Krippendorf, K. (1980). *Content analysis: An introduction to its methodology.* Beverly Hills, CA: Sage.

Kwallek, N., Lewis, C. M., and Robbins, A. S. (1988). Effects of office interior color on workers' mood and productivity. *Perceptual and Motor Skills, 66,* 123–128.

Latané, B., Williams, K., & Harkins, S. (1979). Many hands make light the work: The causes and consequences of social loafing. *Journal of Personality and Social Psychology, 37,* 827–832.

Lavender, A. (1987). The effects of nurses changing from uniforms to everyday clothes on a psychiatric rehabilitation ward. *British Journal of Medical Psychology, 60* (2), 189–199.

Lavrakas, P. J. (1993). *Telephone survey methods* (2nd ed.). Thousand Oaks, CA: Sage.

Leenaars, A. A. (1991). Suicide notes and their implication for intervention. *Crisis, 12,* 1–20.

Linton, M., & Gallo, P. S. (1975). *The practical statistician: Simplified handbook of statistics.* Monterey, CA: Brooks/Cole.

Lipsitt, L. P., Kaye, H., & Bosack, T. N. (1966). Enhancement of neonatal sucking through reinforcement. *Journal of Experimental Child Psychology, 4,* 163–168.

Lockhart, R. S., & Craik, F. I. M. (1990). Levels of processing: A retrospective commentary on the framework for memory research. *Canadian Journal of Psychology, 44,* 87–112.

Loftus, E. F. (1975). Leading questions and the eyewitness report. *Cognitive Psychology, 7,* 560–572.

Lynn, M., and Shurgot, B. A. (1984). Responses to lonely hearts advertisements: Effects of reported physical attractiveness, physique, and coloration. *Personality and Social Psychology Bulletin, 10,* 349–357.

Martin, R., & Wall, T. D. (1989). Attentional demand and cost responsibility as a stressor in shopfloor jobs. *Academy of Management Journal, 32,* 69–86.

Martinez, R., & Dukes, R. L. (1987). Race, gender, and self-esteem among youth. *Hispanic Journal of Behavioral Science, 9,* 427–443.

Martorano, J. (1991). Case study: The use of the CEEG in treating premenstrual syndrome: An opportunity for treatment innovation. *Integrative Psychiatry, 7,* 63–64.

Mastrofski, S., & Parks, R. B. (1990). Improving observational studies of police. *Criminology, 28,* 475–496.

Mathews, K. E., Jr., & Cannon, L. K. (1975). Environmental noise level as a determinant of helping behavior. *Journal of Personality and Social Psychology, 32,* 571–577.

May, J. L., & Hamilton, P. A. (1980). Effects of musically evoked affect on women's interpersonal attraction toward and perceptual judgments of physical attractiveness in men. *Motivation and Emotion, 4*(3), 217–228.

McAninch, C. B., Austin, J. L., & Derks, P. L. (1992). Effect of caption meaning on memory for nonsense figures. *Current Psychology: Research and Reviews, 11,* 315–323.

McCarty, D., Diamond, W., and Kaye, M. (1982). Alcohol, sexual arousal, and the transfer of excitation. *Journal of Personality and Social Psychology, 42,* 977–988.

McClelland, D. C. (1961). *The achieving society.* New York: Free Press.

McConnell, J. V., Cutler, R. L., & McNeil, E. B. (1958). Subliminal stimulation: An overview. *American Psychologist, 13,* 229–242.

McCusker, J., Stoddard, A. M., Zapka, J. G., Morrison, C. S., Zorn, M., & Lewis, B. F. (1992). AIDS education for drug abusers: Evaluation of short-term effectiveness. *American Journal of Public Health, 82,* 533–540.

McKey, R., Cordelli, L., Ganson, H., Barrett, B., McCorkey, C., & Plantz, M. (1985). *The impact of Head Start on children, families, and communities: Final report of the Head Start evaluation, synthesis, and utilization project* (No. OHDS 85-31193). Washington, DC: U.S. Government Printing Office.

McNair, D. M., Loor, M., & Droppleman, L. (1984). Profile of mood states. In D. J. Keyser & R. C. Sweetland (Eds.), *Test critiques.* Kansas City: Test Corporation of America.

Mendrick, M. T., Mendrick, S. A., and Mendrick, E. V. (1964). Incubation of creative performance and specific associative priming. *Journal of Abnormal and Social Psychology, 69,* 84–88.

Meyer, D. E., & Schvanveldt, R. W. (1971). Facilitation in recognizing pairs of words: Evidence of a dependence between retrieval operations. *Journal of Experimental Psychology, 90,* 227–234.

Middlemist, R. D., Knowles, E. S., & Matter, C. F. (1976). Personal space invasions in the lavatory: Suggestive evidence for arousal. *Journal of Personality and Social Psychology, 33,* 541–546.

Middlemist, R. D., Knowles, E. S., & Matter, C. F. (1977). What to do and what to report: A reply to Koocher. *Journal of Personality and Social Psychology, 35,* 122–124.

Milgram, S. (1963). Behavioral study of obedience. *Journal of Abnormal and Social Psychology, 67,* 371–378.

Monahan, L., Kuhn, D., and Shaver, P. (1974). Intrapsychic versus cultural explanations of the "fear of success" motive. *Journal of Personality and Social Psychology, 29,* 60–64.

Mudd, S., Conway, C. G., & Schindler, D. E. (1990). The eye as music critic: Pupil response and verbal preferences. *Studia Psychologica, 32,* 23–30.

Mulligan, R. M., and Schiffman, H. R. (1979). Temporal experience as a function of organization in memory. *Bulletin of the Psychonomic Society, 14,* 417–420.

Neisser, U. (1981). John Dean's memory: A case study. *Cognition, 9,* 1–22.

Nelson, D. L., & Sutton, C. (1990). Chronic work stress and coping: A longitudinal study and suggested new directions. *Academy of Management Journal, 33,* 859–869.

Neri, D. F., Shappell, S. A., & DeJohn, C. A. (1992). Simulated sustained flight operations and performance: I. Effects of fatigue. *Military Psychology, 4*(3), 137–155.

Nolen–Hoeksema, S., & Morrow, J. (1991). A prospective study of depression and posttraumatic stress symptoms after a natural disaster: The 1989 Loma Prieta earthquake. *Journal of Personality and Social Psychology, 61,* 115–121.

Orne, M. T. (1962). On the social psychology of the psychological experiment: With particular reference to demand characteristics and their implications. *American Psychologist, 17,* 776–783.

Ornstein, R. E. (1969). *On the experience of time.* Baltimore: Penguin Books.

Osborn, D. R. (1988). Personality traits expressed: Interior design as behavior-setting plan. *Personality and Social Psychology Bulletin, 14,* 368–373.

Parker, K. A. (1982). Effects of subliminal symbiotic stimulation on academic performance: Further evidence on the adaption-enhancing effects of oneness fantasies. *Journal of Counseling Psychology, 29,* 19–28.

Patterson, F. G. (1978). The gestures of a gorilla: Language acquisition in another pongid. *Brain and Language, 5,* 72–97.

Pellegrini, A. D. (1992). Rough and tumble play and social problem solving flexibility. *Creativity Research Journal, 5,* 13–26.

Pennebaker, J. W., Dyer, M. A., Caulkins, R. S., Litowitz, D. L., Ackreman, P. L., & Anderson, D. B. (1979). Don't the girls get prettier at closing time: A country-western application to psychology. *Personality and Social Psychology Bulletin, 5,* 122–125.

Pfungst, O. (1911). *Clever Hans (the horse of Mr. von Osten): A contribution to experimental animal and human psychology.* New York: Holt, Rinehart & Winston.

Phesterson, G. I., Kiesler, S. B., & Goldberg, P. A. (1971). Evaluation of the performance of women as a function of their sex, achievement, and personal history. *Journal of Personality and Social Psychology, 19,* 114–118.

Posavac, E. J., & Carey, R. G. (1989). *Program evaluation* (3rd ed.). Englewood Cliffs, NJ: Prentice Hall.

Pritchard, R. D., Dunnette, M. D., & Jorgenson, D. O. (1972). Effect of perceptions of equity and inequity on worker performance and satisfaction [Monograph]. *Journal of Applied Psychology, 56,* 75–94.

Pritchatt, D. (1968). An investigation into some of the underlying associative verbal processes of the Stroop colour effect. *Quarterly Journal of Experimental Psychology, 20,* 351–359.

Rafaeli, A., & Sutton, R. I. (1991). Emotional contrast strategies as means of social influence: Lessons from criminal interrogators and bill collectors. *Academy of Management Journal, 34,* 749–755.

Ring, K. (1984). *Heading toward Omega: In search of the meaning of the near death experience.* New York: William Morrow.

Robinson, J. P., Shaver, P. R., & Wrightsman, L. S. (1991). *Measures of personality and social psychological attitudes* (Vol. 1). San Diego, CA: Academic Press.

Roethlisberger, F. J., & Dickson, W. J. (1939). *Management and the worker.* Cambridge, MA: Harvard University Press.

Roper Organization. (1992). *Unusual personal experiences: An analysis of the data from three national surveys.* Las Vegas, NV: Bigelow Holding.

Rosenfeld, O., Tenenbaum, G., Ruskin, H., & Halfron, S. T. (1989). The effect of physical training on objective and subjective measures of productivity and efficiency in industry. *Ergonomics, 32,* 1019–1028.

Rosenhan, D. L. (1973). On being sane in insane places. *Science, 179,* 250–258.

Rosenthal, N. E., Carpenter, C. J., James, S. P., Parry, B. L., Rogers, S. L. B., & Wehr, T. A. (1986). Seasonal affective disorder in children and adolescents. *American Journal of Psychiatry, 143,* 356–358.

Rosenthal, R. (1976). *Experimenter effects in behavioral research.* New York: Ervington.

Rosenthal, R., & Rosnow, R. L. (1975). *The volunteer subject.* New York: Wiley.

Rosenthal, R., & Jacobson, L. (1966). Teachers' expectancies: Determinates of pupils' I.Q. gains. *Psychological Reports, 19,* 115–118.

Runco, M. A., & Albert, R. S. (1986). The threshold theory regarding creativity and intelligence: An empirical test with gifted and nongifted children. *The Creative Child and Adult Quarterly, 11,* 212–218.

Russel, M. J. (1976). Human olfactory communication. *Nature, 260,* 250–252.

Sacks, O. (1985). *The man who mistook his wife for a hat and other clinical tales.* New York: Simon & Schuster.

Schachter, S. (1971). Some extraordinary facts about obese humans and rats. *American Psychologist, 26,* 129–144.

Schachter, S., and Singer, J. (1962). Cognitive, social, and physiological determinants of emotional states. *Psychological Review, 69,* 379–399.

Schackman, S. (1983). A shortened version of the profile of mood states. *Journal of Personality Assessment, 47,* 305–306.

Schacter, S. (1968). Obesity and eating. *Science, 161,* 751–756.

Schacter, S., Goldman, R., & Gordon, A. (1968). Effects of fear, food deprivation and obesity on eating. *Journal of Personality and Social Psychology, 10,* 91–97.

Schiffman, H. R. (1990). *Sensation and perception: An integrated approach* (3rd ed.). New York: John Wiley.

Schiffman, M. R., and Bobko, D. J. (1977). The role of numbers and familiarity of stimuli in the perception of brief temporal intervals. *American Journal of Psychology, 90,* 85–93.

Schmidt, S. R. (1985). Encoding and retrieval processes in the memory for conceptually distinctive events. *Journal of Experimental Psychology: Learning, Memory, and Cognition, 11,* 565–578.

Schwarz, N., & Clore, G. L. (1983). Mood, misattribution, and judgments of well-being: Informative and directive functions of affective states. *Journal of Personality and Social Psychology, 45,* 513–523.

Shaffer, D. R., R. M., Rogel, M., & Hendrick, C. (1975). Intervention in the library: The effect of increased responsibility on bystander willingness to prevent theft. *Journal of Personality and Social Psychology, 5,* 303–319.

Shah, I. (1970). *Tales of the Dervishes.* New York: Dutton.

Shepard, J. A., and Strathman, A. J. (1989). Attractiveness and height: The role of stature in dating preference, frequency of dating, and perceptions of attractiveness. *Personality and Social Psychology Bulletin, 15,* 617–627.

Sherman, S. J., & Gorkin, L. (1980). Attitude bolstering when behavior is inconsistent with central attitudes. *Journal of Experimental Social Psychology, 16,* 388–403.

Sidman, M. (1960). *Tactics of scientific research.* New York: Basic Books.

Silverman, L. H., Ross, D. L., Adler, J. M., and Lustig, D. A. (1978). Simple research paradigm for demonstrating subliminal psychodynamic activation: Effects of Oedipal stimuli on dart-throwing accuracy in college males. *Journal of Abnormal Psychology, 87,* 341–357.

Silverman, L. H., & Weinberger, J. (1985). Mommy and I are one: Implications for psychotherapy. *American Psychologist, 40,* 1296–1308.

Skinner, B. F. (1938). *The behavior of organisms: An experimental analysis.* New York: Appleton-Century-Crofts.

Smith, P. C., Kendall, L. M., & Hulin, C. L. (1969). *The measurement of satisfaction in work and retirement.* Chicago: Rand McNally.

Stagray, J. R., & Truitt, L. (1992). Monaural listening therapy for auditory disorders: Opinions and a case study. *Canadian Journal of Rehabilitation, 6,* 45–49.

Sternberg, S. (1969). Memory scanning: Mental processes revealed by reaction time experiments. *American Scientist, 57,* 421–457.

Stevens, S. S. (1975). *Psychophysics: Introduction to its perceptual, neural, and social prospects.* New York: John Wiley & Sons.

Strack, F., Martin, L. L., & Stepper, S. (1988). Inhibiting and facilitating conditions of the human smile: A nonobtrusive test of the facial feedback hypothesis. *Journal of Personality and Social Psychology, 5,* 768–777.

Stroop, J. R. (1935). Studies of interference in serial verbal reactions. *Journal of Experimental Psychology, 18,* 643–662.

Stuart, G. W., & Day, R. H. (1991). The Fraser illusion: Complex figures. *Perception and Psychophysics, 49,* 456–468.

Suedfield, P., Ballard, E. J., Baker-Brown, G., & Borrie, R. A. (1986). Flow of consciousness in restricted environmental stimulation. *Imagination, Cognition, and Personality, 5,* 219–230.

Taylor, S. P., & Leonard, K. F. (1983). Alcohol and human physical aggression. *Aggression, 2,* 77–101.

Tellegen, A., Lykken, D. T., Bouchard, T. J., Wilcox, K. J., Segal, N. L., & Rich, S. (1988). Personality similarity in twins reared apart and together. *Journal of Personality and Social Psychology, 54,* 1031–1039.

Tokunaga, K., Fukushima, M., Kemnitz, J., & Bray, G. (1986). Comparison of ventromedial and paraventricular lesions in rats that become obese. *American Journal of Physiology, 251,* R1221–R1227.

Torrey, E. F. (1992). *Freudian Fraud: The malignant effect of Freud's theory on American thought and culture*. New York: HarperCollins.

Tronick, E. Z.(1989). Emotions and emotional communication in infants. *American Psychologist, 44,* 112–119.

Turner, M. L., LaPointe, L. B., Cantor, J., Reeves, C. H., Griffeth, R. H., and Engle, R. W. (1987). Recency and suffix effects found with auditory presentation and with mouthed visual presentation: They're not the same thing. *Journal of Memory and Language, 26,* 138–164.

Wade, C., & Tavris, C. (1993). *Psychology* (3rd ed.). New York: HarperCollins.

Wason, P. C. (1968). Reasoning about a rule. *Quarterly Journal of Experimental Psychology, 20,* 273–281.

Weldon, E., & Mustari, E. L. (1988). Felt dispensibility in groups of co–actors: The effects of shared responsibility and explicit anonymity on cognitive effort. Organization. *Organizational, Behavior, and Human Decision Processes, 41,* 330–351.

Werch, C. E., Meers, B. W., & Hallan, J. B. (1992). An analytic review of 73 college-based drug abuse prevention programs. *Health Values, 16*(5), 38–45.

White, G. L., and Knight, T. D. (1984). Misattribution of arousal and attraction: Effects of salience of explanations for arousal. *Journal of Experimental Social Psychology, 20,* 55–64.

Whitley, B. E., Jr., & Frieze, I. H. (1985). Children's causal attributions for success and failure in achievement settings: A meta analysis. *Journal of Educational Psychology, 77,* 608–616.

Zimbardo, P. G., Cohen, A. R., Weisenberg, M., Dworskin, L., & Firestone, I. (1966). Control of pain motivation by cognitive dissonance. *Science, 151,* 217–219.

NAME INDEX

SUBJECT INDEX

TABLE 2.1   A Researcher's Terminology for Questioning the Types of Inferences Made in a Study

Inference Made	Research Term
Do the scores reflect error?	Reliability
Do the scores reflect the variable?	Content validity
Do the scores reflect the hypothetical construct?	Construct validity
Do the results reflect the variables in our study?	Internal validity
Do the results generalize beyond our study?	External validity

TABLE 9.2   Summary of Methods for Ascertaining Reliability and Validity

Reliability

Test-retest:	Each subject's test and retest scores are correlated positively.
Split-half:	Subjects' scores from half of the trials positively correlate with their scores from the other half of the trials.

Validity

Face:	Procedure appears valid.
Convergent:	Procedure correlates with other accepted measures.
Discriminant:	Procedure does not correlate with other unintended measures.
Criterion	
Concurrent:	procedure correlates with a present behavior.
Predictive:	procedure correlates with a future behavior.